T0215528

Cisco ACI: Zero to Hero

A Comprehensive Guide to Cisco ACI Design, Implementation, Operation, and Troubleshooting

Jan Janovic

Apress®

Cisco ACI: Zero to Hero: A Comprehensive Guide to Cisco ACI Design, Implementation, Operation, and Troubleshooting

Jan Janovic
Prague, Czech Republic

ISBN-13 (pbk): 978-1-4842-8837-5
https://doi.org/10.1007/978-1-4842-8838-2

ISBN-13 (electronic): 978-1-4842-8838-2

Managing Director, Apress Media LLC: Welmoed Spahr
Acquisitions Editor: Aditee Mirashi
Development Editor: James Markham
Coordinating Editor: Aditee Mirashi
Copy Editor: Mary Behr

Cover designed by eStudioCalamar

Cover image designed by Freepik (www.freepik.com)

Distributed to the book trade worldwide by Springer Science+Business Media New York, 1 New York Plaza, Suite 4600, New York, NY 10004-1562, USA. Phone 1-800-SPRINGER, fax (201) 348-4505, e-mail orders-ny@springer-sbm.com, or visit www.springeronline.com. Apress Media, LLC is a California LLC and the sole member (owner) is Springer Science + Business Media Finance Inc (SSBM Finance Inc). SSBM Finance Inc is a **Delaware** corporation.

For information on translations, please e-mail booktranslations@springernature.com; for reprint, paperback, or audio rights, please e-mail bookpermissions@springernature.com.

Apress titles may be purchased in bulk for academic, corporate, or promotional use. eBook versions and licenses are also available for most titles. For more information, reference our Print and eBook Bulk Sales web page at www.apress.com/bulk-sales.

Any source code or other supplementary material referenced by the author in this book is available to readers on GitHub via the book's product page, located at www.apress.com. For more detailed information, please visit https://github.com/Apress/Cisco-ACI-Zero-to-Hero.

Printed on acid-free paper

I want to dedicate this book to my beloved wife, Simona, and daughter, Nela, both of whom are a huge source of energy and inspiration in my life. I wouldn't have been able to finish this work without your incredible love, support, and encouragement.

—Jan Janovic

Table of Contents

About the Author

 **Jan Janovic,** 2x CCIE #5585 (R&S|DC) and CCSI #35493, is an IT enthusiast with 10+ years of experience with network design, implementation, and support for customers from a wide variety of industry sectors. Over the past few years, he has focused on datacenter networking with solutions based on mainly, but not limited to, Cisco Nexus platforms-traditional vPC architectures, VXLAN BGP EVPN network fabrics, and Cisco ACI software-defined networking. All have an emphasis on mutual technology integration, automation, and analytic tools. Another significant part of his job is the delivery of professional training for customers all around Europe.

He holds a master's degree in Applied Network Engineering – Network Infrastructure from the Faculty of Management Science and Informatics, University of Zilina, Slovakia. During his university studies, he led a group of students in successfully developing the world's first open-source EIGRP implementation for the Quagga Linux package (development currently continued under the name FRRouting). He also contributed to OSPF features there. His technical focus additionally expands to system administration of Windows and Linux stations plus public cloud topics related to the design and deployment of AWS solutions.

He mantains the following certifications: Cisco Certified Internetworking Expert in Routing and Switching, Cisco Certified Internetworking Expert in Datacenter, Cisco Certified Professional in DevNet, Cisco Certified Systems Instructor, AWS Certified Solution Architect – Associate, AWS Certified Developer – Associate, and AWS Certified SysOps Administrator – Associate, ITILv4.

About the Technical Reviewer

 **David Samuel Peñaloza Seijas** works as a Principal
Engineer at Verizon Enterprise Solutions in the Czech
Republic, focusing on Cisco SD-WAN, ACI, OpenStack,
and NFV. Previously, he worked as a Data Center Network
Support Specialist in the IBM Client Innovation Center in
the Czech Republic. As an expert networker, David has a
wide diapason of interests; his favorite topics include data
centers, enterprise networks, and network design, including
software-defined networking (SDN).

Acknowledgments

First and foremost, I would like to again express my deep and sincere gratitude to my family and friends, who are one the most important pillars to achieving anything in life, even writing a book like this. Thank you, my darlings **Simona** and **Nela**. You were the best support in this challenging feat, throughout all those endless days and nights when writing on the road, in the hospital, or even during a rock concert. Thank you, my parents, **Vladimír** and **Libuša,** and brother, **Vladimir**, for giving me the best possible upbringing, supporting my higher education, being my positive idols, and always encouraging me to follow my dreams.

Sometimes there are moments in life that completely change its direction and become a foundation for a lifelong positive experience. For me, this happened when I first enrolled in **Peter Paluch**'s networking classes during my university studies in 2011. Thank you, Peter, for sparking a huge networking enthusiasm in me and for being my mentor and closest friend ever since. You gave me unprecedent knowledge and wisdom to become professionally as well as personally who I am now.

I cannot be more grateful to the **Apress** team, especially **Aditee Mirashi,** for giving me the opportunity of a lifetime to put my knowledge and practical skills gained over the years into this book and for guiding me through the whole publishing process.

It was an honor to cooperate with my friend **David Samuel Peñaloza Seijas**, who as a technical reviewer always provided spot-on comments and helped me bring the content of this book to the highest possible level. Additionally, thanks a lot **Luca Berton** for your help with automation content and language enhancements.

Big appreciation goes to my employer **ALEF NULA, a. s.** and my coworkers for their constant support and for providing me with all the necessary equipment and significant opportunities to grow personally as well as professionally and gain the knowledge and skills which ended up in this book.

I cannot forget to express my gratitude to my alma mater and its pedagogical collective, **Faculty of Management Science and Informatics, University of Zilina, Slovakia**, for giving me rock-solid knowledge and a lot of practical skills, thus thoroughly preparing me for my professional career.

ACKNOWLEDGMENTS

In conclusion, if I could list everything and everybody to whom I am grateful, you would be bored after the first 100 pages, so to everybody I missed in this section, sorry, but THANK YOU.

—Jan Janovic

Introduction

Dear reader, whether you are network architect, engineer, administrator, developer, student, or any other IT enthusiast interested in modern datacenter technologies and architectures, you are in the right place. Welcome!

In this book, you will explore the ongoing datacenter network evolution driven by modern application requirements, leading to the next-generation networking solution called **Cisco Application Centric Infrastructure (ACI)**. It doesn't matter if you are completely new to ACI or you already have some experience with the technology, my goal in this book is to guide you through the whole implementation lifecycle. I will show you how to simplify the deployment, operation, and troubleshooting of your multi-datacenter networking environment using ACI, how to integrate it effectively with L4-L7 devices, virtualization and containerization platforms, and how to provide unprecedented visibility and security, all with an emphasis on programmability and automation.

You will start "from zero" and discover the story behind ACI. You will build the strong fundamental knowledge about its main components and explore the advantages of the hardware-based Leaf-Spine architecture composed of Nexus 9000 switches. During the first chapters, I describe all of ACI's design options with their specifics, followed by a detailed guide of how to deploy and initially configure the whole solution according to best practices. You will then assemble all the necessary "access policies" for connecting end hosts to ACI and utilize its multi-tenancy capabilities to create logical application models and communication rules on top of the common physical network. You will learn about control-plane and dataplane mechanisms running under the hood, resulting in correct forwarding decisions, and I will help you with troubleshooting any potential problems with end host connectivity in ACI. I will also describe both Layer 2 and Layer 3 external connectivity features to expose datacenter applications and services to the outside world. I will cover integration capabilities with L4-L7 security devices or loadbalancers as well as virtualization solutions. At the end, you will learn how to effectively use ACI's REST API to further automate the whole solution using the most common tools: Postman, Python, Ansible, or Terraform.

Many times throughout the book I provide my own recommendations and views based on knowledge and experience gained from real-world implementations, combined with best practices recommended directly by Cisco. I constantly try as much as possible to support each topic with practical examples, GUI/CLI verification tools, and troubleshooting tips to ultimately build in you the strong confidence to handle any ACI-related task.

Although this book is not directly related to any Cisco certification, I hope it will become a valuable resource for you if you are preparing for the CCNP or CCIE Datacenter exams and that you will use it as a reference later for your own ACI projects.

Let's now dive into the first chapter, which is related to network evolution from legacy architecture to Cisco ACI.

CHAPTER 1

Introduction: Datacenter Network Evolution

What is a datacenter (or "data center," which will be used interchangeably throughout the book)? It's a fairly simple question at first blush to many IT professionals, but let's start with proper definition of this term.

From a physical perspective, a datacenter is a facility used by various organizations to host their mission-critical data. Companies can invest in their own hardware and software resources, which will stay completely under their control, maintenance, and operation, or consume services from public clouds in the form of XaaS (Infrastructure/Platform/Software as a Service).

Internally, we can divide a datacenter into a complex multi-layered architecture of compute, storage, and networking equipment, interconnected to provide fast and reliable access to shared application resources (see Figure 1-1). The networking layer of each datacenter is especially important for the whole system to work correctly. Keep in mind that you can have the most powerful blade server chassis with petabytes of storage space, but without robust, reliable, and secure networking, you won't change the world. Some IT architects often underestimate the importance of this "datacenter undercarriage." My goal in this publication is to give you all the necessary knowledge and skills needed to design, configure, and operate one of the industry-leading data center SDN networking solutions, **Cisco Application Centric Infrastructure (ACI)**.

© Jan Janovic 2023
J. Janovic, *Cisco ACI: Zero to Hero*, https://doi.org/10.1007/978-1-4842-8838-2_1

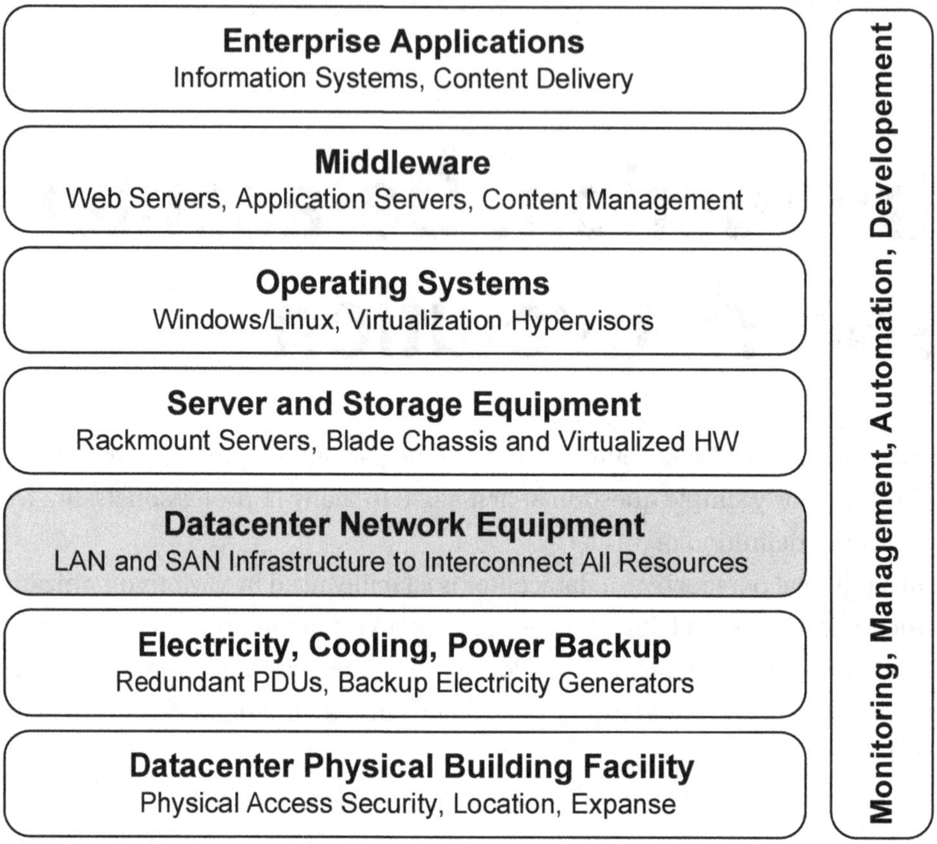

Enterprise Applications Information Systems, Content Delivery	
Middleware Web Servers, Application Servers, Content Management	**Monitoring, Management, Automation, Developement**
Operating Systems Windows/Linux, Virtualization Hypervisors	
Server and Storage Equipment Rackmount Servers, Blade Chassis and Virtualized HW	
Datacenter Network Equipment LAN and SAN Infrastructure to Interconnect All Resources	
Electricity, Cooling, Power Backup Redundant PDUs, Backup Electricity Generators	
Datacenter Physical Building Facility Physical Access Security, Location, Expanse	

Figure 1-1. *Datacenter architecture*

From Traditional to Software-Defined Networking

Before we dive deeper into ACI technology itself, let's explore how the datacenter network has evolved over the past years, what different approaches are available when building datacenter networking, and why software-defined solutions in the form of Cisco ACI are becoming industry standards for modern datacenters.

Traditional Three-Tier Network Architecture

Our journey towards ACI starts in the early 1990s, looking at the most traditional and well known two- or three-layer network architecture, as shown in Figure 1-2. This

Core/Aggregation/Access design was commonly used and recommended for campus enterprise networks and was widely adopted in the datacenter domain as well. At that time, it offered enough quality for typical client-server types of applications.

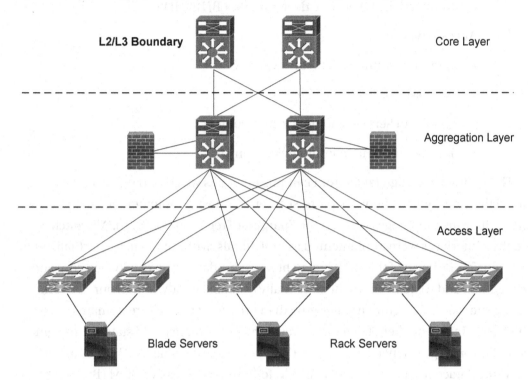

Figure 1-2. *Hierarchical campus LAN design*

In a datacenter, each part of such a network design had its specific purpose:

- **Core layer**

    - Highly powerful backbone for interconnecting multiple aggregation layers, sometimes whole datacenters, enhancing network modularity

    - High speed interfaces

    - Termination of Layer 3 interfaces

    - External routing peering (often implemented also as part of the aggregation layer to prevent the core from being affected by any failures caused by the peering neighbor)

- **Aggregation layer**

  - Aggregation of multiple access segments

  - Connectivity for service devices (FW, LB, IPS, IDS)

- **Access layer**

  - Endpoint connectivity, ToR switches

  - Admission control

  - Quality of Service and policy enforcement

  - Port security (not commonly used in DC)

The traditional design taken from campus networks was based on Layer 2 connectivity between all network parts, segmentation was implemented using VLANs, and the loop-free topology relied on the Spanning Tree Protocol (STP). All switches and their interfaces were implemented as individuals, without the use of virtualization technologies. Because of this, STP had to block redundant uplinks between core and aggregation, and we lost part of the potentially available bandwidth in our network. Scaling such an architecture implies growth of broadcast and failure domains as well, which is definitely not beneficial for the resulting performance and stability. Imagine each STP Topology Change Notification (TCN) message causing MAC tables aging in the whole datacenter for a particular VLAN, followed by excessive BUM (Broadcast, Unknown Unicast, Multicast) traffic flooding, until all MACs are relearned. The impact of any change or disruption could be unacceptable in such a network. I've seen multiple times how a simple flapping interface in a DC provider L2 network caused constant traffic disruptions. Additionally, the 12-bit VLAN ID field in an 802.1Q header limits the number of possible isolated network segments for datacenter customers to 4,096 (often even less due to internal switch reserved VLANs).

One of the solutions recommended and implemented for the mentioned STP problems in the past was to move the L3 boundary from the core layer to aggregation and divide one continuous switched domain into multiple smaller segments. As shown in Figure 1-3, by eliminating STP you can use ECMP load balancing between aggregation and core devices.

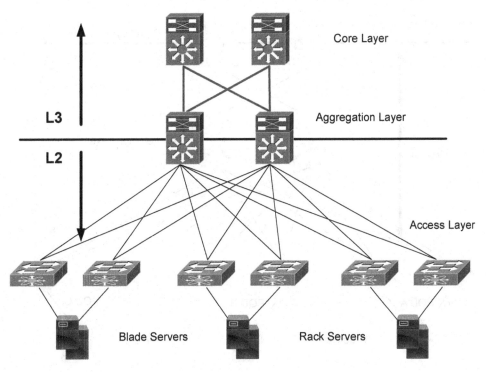

Figure 1-3. *Layer 3 core/aggregation architecture*

Let's Go Virtual

In 1999, VMware introduced the first x86 virtualization hypervisors, and the network requirements changed. Instead of connecting many individual servers, we started to aggregate multiple applications/operating systems on common physical hardware. Access layer switches had to provide faster interfaces and their uplinks had to scale accordingly. For new features like vMotion, which allows live migration of virtual machines between hosts, the network had to support L2 connectivity between all physical servers and we ended up back at the beginning again (see Figure 1-4).

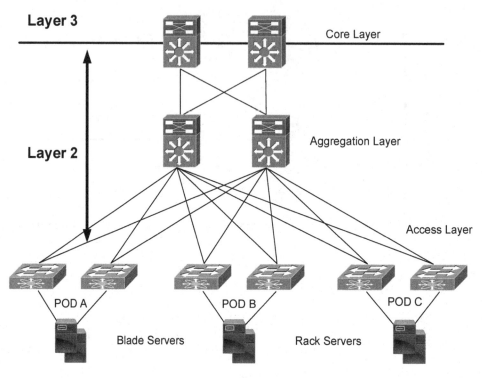

Figure 1-4. *Datacenter network support for server virtualization*

To overcome the already-mentioned STP drawbacks and to keep support for server virtualization, we started to virtualize network infrastructure too. As you can see in Figure 1-5, switches can be joined together into switch stacks, VSS, or vPC architectures. Multiple physical interfaces can be aggregated into logical port channels, virtual port channels, or multi-chassis link aggregation groups (MLAG). From the STP point of view, such an aggregated interface is considered to be an individual, therefore not causing any L2 loop. In a virtualized network, STP does not block any interface but runs in the background as a failsafe mechanism.

Virtualization is deployed on higher networking levels as well. Let's consider virtual routing and forwarding instances (VRFs): they are commonly used to address network multi-tenancy needs by separating the L3 address spaces of network consumers (tenants). Their IP ranges can then be overlapping without any problems

These various types of virtualizations are still implemented in many traditional datacenters, and they serve well for smaller, not-so-demanding customers.

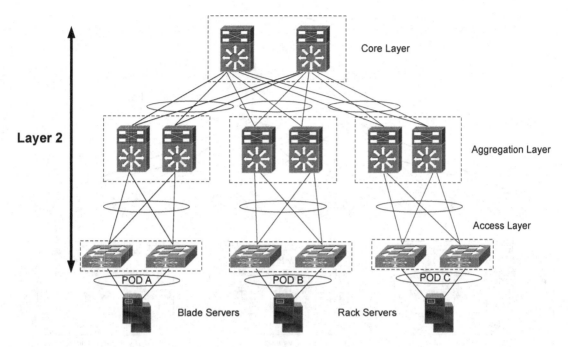

Figure 1-5. *Datacenter network virtualization*

Server virtualization also introduced a new layer of virtual network switches inside the hypervisor (see Figure 1-6). This trend increased the overall administrative burden, as it added new devices to configure, secure, and monitor. Their management was often the responsibility of a dedicated virtualization team and any configuration changes needed to be coordinated inside the company. Therefore, the next requirement for a modern datacenter networking platform is to provide tools for consistent operation of both the physical network layer and the virtual one. We should be able to manage encapsulation used inside the virtual hypervisor, implement microsegmentation, or easily localize any connected endpoint.

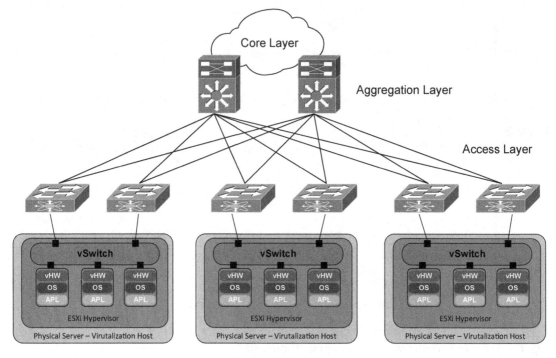

Figure 1-6. *Hypervisor virtual switches*

Along with continuous changes in IT and network infrastructures, we can see another significant trend in datacenter networking: a higher adoption of containerization, microservices, cloud technologies, and deployment of data-intensive applications is causing the transition from a north-south traffic pattern to a majority of east-west traffic. According to Cisco Global Cloud Index, more than 86% of traffic stayed inside datacenters in 2020.

Transition to Leaf-Spine Architecture and VXLAN

The traditional three-layer network design fits well for legacy, more client-server–intensive applications. However, it isn't capable of scaling properly to match the modern loosely coupled applications and resulting customer needs. Therefore, we have to address this growth by implementing a new network architecture that will do the following:

- Simply scale end host interfaces

- Simply scale the overall network bandwidth

- Load-balance the traffic natively

- Eliminate need for a Spanning Tree Protocol in the network

All these desired properties can be provided by two-layer CLOS (leaf-spine) architecture, as shown in Figure 1-7. Invented early in 1938 by Edson Erwin, later formalized in 1952 by Charles Clos, and originally used in circuit-switched telephone networks, it now finds application inside all modern datacenters. The leaf layer generally consists of access switches used to connect any type of end stations (servers, L4-L7 service devices, external switches and routers, etc.). Spines are used as a core layer, interconnecting all leaves into a consistent and symmetric mesh network, often called a "fabric" due to similarities with actual textile fabric.

Devices on the same level don't need to be connected to each other. If some control-plane protocol synchronization is needed between leaf switches, it will be simply handled via spines. From a cost perspective, this is the most optimal network design and requires the least amount of cabling, but with the most bandwidth available for each switch. And notice how easy it is to scale this architecture. If you need to increase the overall amount of access interfaces, you just add new leaf switches without affecting the rest of the existing infrastructure. If you need to increase available uplink bandwidth for each leaf switch, you simply add another spine switch. The same applies when it comes to upgrading; it's easy to define upgrade groups (even/odd switches) without affecting the rest of the infrastructure.

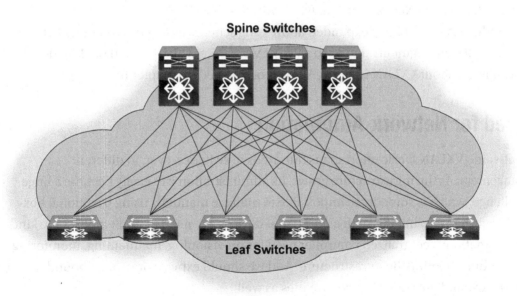

Figure 1-7. *Leaf-spine network architecture*

In order to use all the available bandwidth between leaves and spines, their interconnection needs to be based on Layer 3 interfaces. This eliminates the STP need and provides support for ECMP load-balancing. However, to support virtualization or various other applications features, we still need to ensure Layer 2 connectivity somehow. The solution here is to simply encapsulate any (Layer 2 or Layer 3) traffic at the edge of the network into a new, common protocol called **Virtual eXtensible Local Area Network (VXLAN)**. See Figure 1-8.

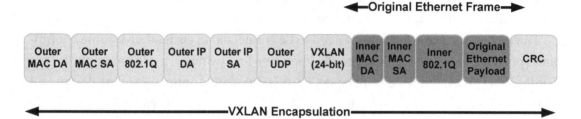

Figure 1-8. *VXLAN encapsulation*

VXLAN is a standardized (RFC 7348) MAC-in-UDP overlay encapsulation addressing all the requirements mentioned above on top of the common Layer 3 routed underlay network. Forwarding of VXLAN encapsulated packets is based on Virtual Tunnel Endpoint (VTEP) IP addresses between the network devices, which are in VXLAN terminology called Network Virtual Edge switches (NVE).

Additionally, VXLAN's expanded addressing scheme allows the creation of 16 million different segments thanks to a 24-bit Virtual Network ID (VNID). More detailed information about VXLAN usage in ACI will be covered in Chapter 6.

Need for Network Automation

Leaf-spine VXLAN fabric often spans hundreds of switches, even in different datacenters. As the infrastructure grows, its administration can easily become a huge challenge, which is sometimes impossible to manage manually using traditional box-by-box fashion. To handle such a number of devices, we need to implement some kind of automation: a centralized controller used for provisioning, maintaining, monitoring, and troubleshooting the infrastructure. And we should expect some northbound API to further expand the controller possibilities as well.

As you can see at this point, we've assembled a significant number of requirements for the modern network infrastructure. Let me briefly summarize which challenges need to be addressed in order to design a future-proof datacenter networking:

- **Spanning tree elimination**: Increasing the overall scalability and stability

- **Traffic pattern change**: Scaling accordingly for east-west application traffic, which is the majority these days

- **L2/L3 services**: Supporting L2/L3 on top of the same infrastructure and with segments stretchable without limitation

- **Server virtualization**: Providing higher access speeds for virtualization hosts and managing a virtual switching layer consistently with the physical network

- **Multitenancy**: Supporting administrative and network separation between tenants (users) of the infrastructure

- **Security**: Applying the least privilege principle on all layers of a network and its management tools

- **Containerization**: Handling individual containers in the same manner as any other physical or virtual endpoint

- **Multi-cloud**: Applying consistent network policies across various cloud environments

- **Automation**: Eliminating manual box-by-box configuration and management of network devices

- **Visibility**: Using various telemetry data gathered from the network to provide advanced insights and analytics

So why are we even discussing Cisco ACI in this book? All of the previously described requirements can be solved by implementing this centrally managed, software-defined networking in your datacenter.

Cisco Application Centric Infrastructure (ACI)

Adopted currently by hundreds of customers, ACI provides the most flexible solution, based on well-known network protocols, creating a highly scalable and resilient datacenter network architecture.

ACI's Application Policy Model describes exactly what applications need to be deployed in the underlying network to ensure low latency and reliable connectivity for all the application components. ACI covers on-prem, hybrid, and multi-cloud use cases with emphasis on deployment simplicity and security from day zero. New containerized applications cause no trouble for ACI either.

It additionally offers multiple AI-driven analytic tools based on hardware telemetry for two-day operation tasks and a completely open Managed Information Model (MIM) accessible through a REST API for further automation and orchestration.

From the high-level view, Cisco ACI consists of following main components:

1. **Cisco Nexus 9000-based underlay**: Routed leaf/spine network architecture used to interconnect all the endpoint devices. They can include servers, external WAN routers and legacy switches, L4-L7 service equipment, and a datacenter interconnect network (DCI).

2. **Application Policy Infrastructure Controller (APIC)**: Cluster of physical appliances used to completely operate the ACI infrastructure. From the initial provisioning, policy configuration, and lifecycle management to monitoring and statistics collection.

3. **Application policy model**: The logical definition of network segmentation based on application communications needs and consisting of multiple mutually related objects: tenants, virtual routing and forwarding (VRF) instances, bridge domains, end point groups, and contracts.

Summary

In subsequent chapters, I will cover each ACI component in detail and you will learn how to design and implement this solution while following best practices and many of my personal practical recommendations, collected during multiple ACI deployments for various customers. They won't always necessarily match according to the situation they are considered in, but the goal is the same: to provide you with a comprehensive toolset to become confident with various ACI-related tasks.

## CHAPTER 2

ACI Fundamentals: Underlay Infrastructure

In this chapter, you will focus on establishing a proper understanding of the main ACI components: the underlay network infrastructure and APIC controllers with their architectural deployment options. In ACI, hardware-based underlay switching offers a significant advantage over various software-only solutions due to specialized forwarding chips. Thanks to Cisco's own ASIC development, ACI brings many advanced features including security policy enforcement, microsegmentation, dynamic policy-based redirect (to insert external L4-L7 service devices into the data path) or detailed flow analytics—besides the huge performance and flexibility.

Cisco Nexus 9000 and CloudScale ASICs

To build the ACI underlay, you need to exclusively use the Nexus 9000 family of switches. You can choose from modular Nexus 9500 switches or fixed 1U to 2U Nexus 9300 models. There are specific models and line cards dedicated for the spine function in ACI fabric, others can be used as leaves, and some of them for both purposes. You can combine various leaf switches inside one fabric without any limitation. Later in this chapter, I will discuss individual models in more detail.

For Nexus 9000 switches to be used as an ACI spine or leaf, they need to be equipped with powerful **Cisco CloudScale ASICs**, manufactured using 16-nm technology, which in general brings following advantages to the whole platform:

- **Ultra-high port densities**
  - For easy device consolidation with less equipment footprint

J. Janovic, *Cisco ACI: Zero to Hero*, https://doi.org/10.1007/978-1-4842-8838-2_2

- **Multi-speed 100M/1/10/25/40/50/100G/400G**

  - Enables you to future-proof your infrastructure and choose from flexible types of interfaces (RJ-45, SFP+, QSPF+, QSFP-DD)

- **Rich forwarding feature set**

  - Basic L2/L3 features, single-pass VXLAN bridging/routing, segment routing support, all ACI features, native FiberChannel and FCoE (-FX models)

- **Flexible forwarding scale**

  - You can apply different forwarding templates on your switches, which define TCAM memory allocation. As shown in Figure 2-1, this enables you to optimally utilize ACI switches according to your needs. Sometimes you can make use of more LPM routes; other times more security policies are needed. If you don't need IPv6, for example, you can completely free up its TCAM space to store more IPv4 and MAC information. Each change of this profile requires a switch reboot, though.

node-101 (N9K-C93240YC-FX2) Scalability Options

▲ Type of Scale	VRF	BD	EPG	ESG	MAC EPs	IPv4 EPs	IPv6 EPs	Multicas	Policy CAM	VLAN	LPM	/32 Routes	/128 Routes
Dual Stack	800	3500	3960	4000	24576	24576	12288	8192	65536	3960	20480	49152	12288
High Dual Stack	800	3500	3960	4000	65536	65536	24576	512	8192	3960	38912	65536	24576
High LPM	800	3500	3960	4000	24576	24576	12288	8192	8192	3960	131072	32768	12288
High Policy	800	3500	3960	4000	16384	16384	8192	8192	102400	3960	8192	24576	8192
IPv4 Scale	800	3500	3960	4000	49152	49152	0	8192	65536	3960	38912	57344	0

Figure 2-1. *Nexus 9000 flexible TCAM allocation profiles in ACI*

- **Intelligent buffering**

  - It's not always about having a huge interface buffer available on your switch, but rather about its intelligent and optimal utilization. In NX-OS standalone mode, Nexus supports three buffer-oriented features: Dynamic Buffer Protection (DBP), Approximate Fair Drop (AFD) and Dynamic Packet Prioritization (DPP).

- DBP controls buffer allocation for congested queues in shared-memory architecture. It prevents any output queue from consuming more than its fair share of buffers.

- AFD maintains throughput while minimizing buffer consumption by elephant flows. It aims to distinguish high bandwidth "elephant" flows from other "mice" flows, and for elephants it sets higher drop probability.

- DPP prioritizes the initial set of 1,023 packets from a new/short-lived flow. They go to a strictly prioritized queue. All others are put in the default queue.

- In Cisco ACI, you can implement various commonly used QoS settings as well, from classification into six different traffic classes through marking, buffering, queuing to ingress/egress policing.

- **Encryption technologies**

  - CloudScale ASICs support wire-rate Media Access Control Security (MACsec) EEE 802.1AE with MACsec Key Agreement (MKA) protocol and AES_256_CMAC encryption algorithm. Additionally, in ACI you can ensure datacenter interconnect (DCI) encryption as well by implementing CloudSec. It's a multi-hop MACsec between two VXLAN tunnel endpoints (spine switches) over a generic L3 network. The currently supported CloudSec encryption algorithm is GCM-AES-256-XPN.

- **Built-in analytics and telemetry**

  - As all the datacenter solutions become more and more complex these days and mutually integrated, it's crucial to achieve a high level of visibility and maintainability. All Nexus devices are equipped with SW/HW telemetry generators and so-called flow tables.

  - In both ACI and stand-alone NX-OS mode, flow tables offer HW offloaded collections of full flow information together with additional metadata. They include

- Five-tuple flow info (src/dst MAC address or src/dst IP, src/dst L4 port and protocol)

- Interface/queue info

- Flow start/stop timestamp

- Flow latency

- Along with flows, you can also gather the current state of the whole switch, utilization of its interface buffers, CPU, memory, various sensor data, security status, and more.

- Telemetry data generation is just the beginning of the whole workflow, though. You have to gather them to some big data collector, process them, and then provide intelligent analysis, recommendations, or speed up the troubleshooting process. For such tasks for the ACI operation phase, Cisco offers a dedicated tool named **Nexus Dashboard**.

CloudScale ASIC Architecture

Each CloudScale ASIC consists of one or more "slices." A slice is basically an internal packet processing unit responsible for managing a subset of interfaces connected to the ASIC. The slice is further divided into ingress and egress parts, each providing different functions for the transiting traffic. Each slice ingress section connects to all other egress sections (including its own) via a common slice interconnect (as shown in Figure 2-2), thus creating full mesh any-to-any connectivity between any two switch interfaces. This architecture is non-blocking and provides full line-rate speeds for all interfaces and for all packet sizes.

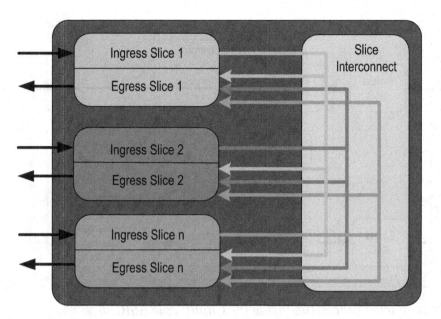

Figure 2-2. *CloudScale ASIC slices*

Let's dig deeper and look at the packet processing workflow inside the individual CloudScale slice, as shown in Figure 2-3. On the ingress part of a slice, we receive the incoming frame through the front switch interface using the Ingress MAC module. It's forwarded into the Ingress Forwarding Controller, where the Packet Parser identifies what kind of packet is inside it. It can be IPv4 unicast, IPv6 unicast, multicast, VXLAN packet, and so on. Based on its type, just the necessary header fields needed for the forwarding decision are sent in the form of a lookup key to the lookup pipeline. The switch doesn't need to process all of the payload inside the packet. However, it will still add some metadata to the lookup process (e.g., source interface, VLAN, queue information).

Once we have a forwarding result, ASIC sends the information together with the packet payload via the slice interconnect to the egress part. There, if needed, the packet is replicated, buffered in some specific queue according to the Quality of Service configuration, and we can apply a defined security policy in case of ACI. After that, ASIC rewrites the fields and puts the frame on the wire.

Each result of this complex forwarding decision for a packet can be analyzed in detail using advanced troubleshooting tools like the Embedded Logic Analyzer Module (ELAM). By using it, you can easily monitor if the packet even arrived in the interface, and if so, what happened inside the ASIC while doing these forwarding actions. You will find more about ELAM in Chapter 6.

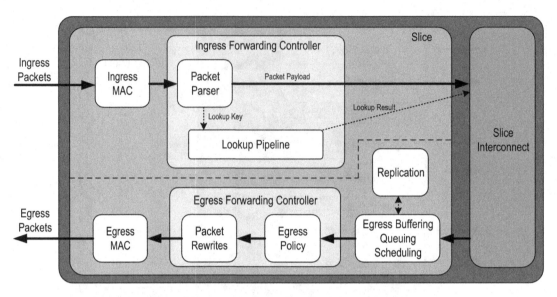

Figure 2-3. *Packet processing inside the CloudScale ASIC slice*

CloudScale ASIC Buffering

Other switches (e.g., Nexus 7000) that use ingress buffering can suffer from a performance-limiting phenomenon called **head-of-line blocking**. It happens when a congested egress interface causes backpressure on a particular ingress (even faster) interface, while preventing traffic delivery to other, non-congested egress interfaces. A solution for this behavior is to implement virtual output queuing (VOQ) or to use some credit system, but it adds another layer of unnecessary complexity to the whole system. This all is eliminated by changing the buffering architecture when speaking about ACI underlay switches. The Nexus 9000 platform exclusively uses **egress** buffering. The main motive for doing so is to simplify packet manipulation, Quality of Service implementation, and completely avoid head-of-line blocking.

Each CloudScale ASIC (and its slice) in general comes with dedicated egress buffer, which is shared for all ports managed by this slice. Interfaces from slice 0 cannot use any buffer available in slice 1. We buffer individually unicast and multicast traffic, so thanks to that, we can apply different Quality of Service setting for both traffic classes.

Different ASIC types with their buffers are shown in Figure 2-4.

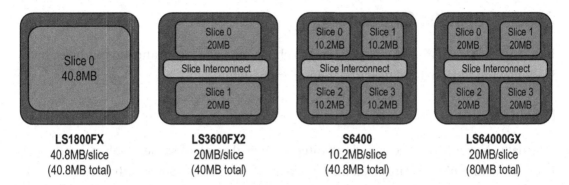

Figure 2-4. *CloudScale ASIC buffering*

Now, let's have a look at the wide palette of device options when choosing from the Nexus 9000 family of switches to build the ACI underlay fabric.

Nexus 9500: Modular Chassis Switches

Nexus 9500s are known for their reliability, high internal throughput, significant interface density, and power and cooling efficiency (chassis doesn't have any solid backplane or midplane, therefore optimal airflow is achieved). An interesting fact is their architectural versatility. By combining various line cards and fabric modules, you can decide if the chassis becomes a modular CloudScale platform and will be used for a standalone VXLAN EVPN leaf/spine switch or an ACI leaf/spine managed by the APIC. Additionally, with Nexus 9500, there are multiple options to use cheaper Broadcom's ASICs (Jericho and Jericho+) to support specific use cases. For example, R series line cards and fabric modules are suitable for applications requiring deep buffering (bringing 4GB to 24GB interface packet buffers). In that case, Nexus 9500 can serve as a "more traditional" L2/L3 vPC device. For the purpose of this ACI-focused book, I will further describe only a CloudScale-based architecture and its components.

In the Nexus 9500 family branch, we can choose from three main chassis options, based on the amount of line card slots needed:

- Nexus 9504 (4 line cards slots)

- Nexus 9508 (8 line cards slots)

- Nexus 9516 (16 line cards slots)

Each chassis consists of multiple components, and while some of them are common for all chassis models, others are device-specific.

Chassis-Specific Components

Based on the size of the chassis, you have to choose specific fabric and fan modules. In the following section, I will describe them in more detail.

Fabric Module

Internally, Nexus 9500 is designed (architecture-wise) as a leaf-spine topology itself. Each fabric module (FM) inserted from the rear of the chassis comes with one or multiple CloudScale ASICs and creates a spine layer for the internal fabric. On the other hand, line cards with their set of ASICs act as leaf layer connected with all fabric modules. Together they provide non-blocking any-to-any fabric and all traffic between line cards is load balanced across fabric modules, providing optimal bandwidth distribution within the chassis (see Figure 2-5). If a fabric module is lost during the switch operation, all others continue to forward the traffic; they just provide less total bandwidth for the line cards. There are five slots for fabric modules in total. If you combine different line cards inside the same chassis, the fifth fabric module is automatically disabled and unusable. This is due to the lack of a physical connector for the fifth module on all line cards (at the time of writing) except for X9736C-FX, which supports all five of them. Generally, you can always use four fabric modules to achieve maximal redundancy and overall throughput.

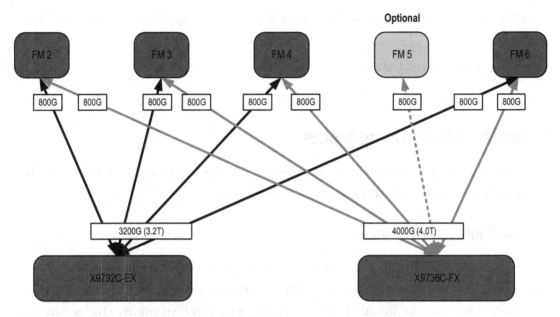

Figure 2-5. *Nexus 9500 internal architecture*

The following fabric modules are available for Nexus 9500s:

- **FM-G** for 4-slot and 8-slot chassis with LS6400GX ASIC that provides up to 1.6 Tbps capacity per line card slot.

- **FM-E2** for 8-slot and 16-slot chassis with S6400 ASIC that provides up to 800 Gbps capacity per line card slot.

- **FM-E** for 4-slot, 8-slot, and 16-slot chassis with older ALE2 ASIC that provides up to 800 Gbps capacity per line card slot.

Note   All fabric modules installed in the chassis should be of the same type.

Fan Module

The Nexus 9500 chassis uses three fan modules to ensure proper front-to-back airflow. Their speed is dynamically driven by temperature sensors inside the chassis. If you remove one of the fan trays, all others will speed up 100% to compensate for the loss of cooling power.

There are two types of fan modules available that are compatible with specific fabric modules:

- **FAN** for FM-E, FM-E2

- **FAN2** for FM-G

Common Chassis Components

The following components can be used in any chassis size and provide the main control plane and management functions for the whole system.

Switch Supervisor Engine

Supervisor modules come in a pair, and they manage all the switch control plane operations. They are deployed in active-standby fashion to dedicated physical slots (they don't take up space for other linecards). In case of any disruption to the active supervisor (or manual failover initiation), they have the ability to do a stateful switchover (SSO) to standby one, without losing any information or need for the control plane protocol data refresh.

As you can see in Table 2-1, there are currently four supervisor models to choose from and your choice depends on the expected control plane utilization. More powerful supervisor can handle larger datasets, do the faster reload/upgrade, or provide more resources for the potential containers running on top of the NX-OS system.

Table 2-1. *Nexus 9500 Supervisors*

	N9K-SUP-A	N9K-SUP-A+	N9K-SUP-B	N9K-SUP-B+
Processor	4 core, 4 thread 1.8GHz x86	4 core, 8 thread 1.8GHz x86	6 core, 12 thread 2.2GHz x86	6 core, 12 thread 1.9GHz X86
DRAM	16GB	16GB	24GB	32GB
SSD	64GB	64GB	256GB	256GB
MTBF Hours	312,070	414,240	292,110	421,040

System Controller

As you already know, the supervisor is responsible for handling all control plane protocols and operations with them. A redundant pair of systems controllers further helps to increase the overall system resiliency and scale by offloading the internal non-datapath switching and device management functions from the main CPU in supervisor engines. The system controllers act as multiple internal switches, providing three main communication paths:

- **Ethernet Out of Band Channel (EOBC)**: 1 Gbps switch for intra node control plane communication. It provides a switching path via its own switch chipset, which interconnects all HW modules, including supervisor engines, fabric modules, and line cards.

- **Ethernet Protocol Channel (EPC)**: 1 Gbps switch for intra node data protocol communication. Compared to EOBC, EPC only connects fabric modules to the supervisor engines. If any protocol packets need to be sent to the supervisor, line card ASICs utilize the internal data path to transfer the packets to fabric modules. They then redirect the packet through EPC to the supervisor.

- **System Management Bus (SMB)**: A redundant communication path for management of power supply units and fan trays

Power Supply Unit

The Nexus 9500 chassis can use 4 to 10 power supplies, based on the chassis size. All of them are hot-swappable and support either AC or DC, besides one universal high voltage AC/DC model. The combination of line cards and fabric modules used inside the chassis then determines the ability to support configurable power supply redundancy modes:

- **Combined (nonredundant)**: This setting doesn't provide any power redundancy. The maximum usable power is the total power capacity of all power supplies.

- **insrc-redundant (grid redundancy)**: If you want to use grid redundancy, you have to correctly connect each half of the power supplies to different grid slots. The total power available will be the amount of power from one grid.

- **ps-redundant (N+1 redundancy)**: One of the available power supplies is considered an extra and can fail to still fully fulfill the power needs of the chassis.

Line Cards

Several line card options are available and universally compatible with any chassis size. For the purpose of this book, I will list only models related to the Cisco ACI architecture. As I've already described, they need to be based on CloudScale ASICs and you can deploy them only as ACI spine switches. The choice depends on the number of interfaces, their speeds, or, for example, CloudSec DCI encryption support needed in your final design. Internal TCAM scalability for the purpose of ACI is consistent across all models and allows you to handle 365,000 database entries. TCAM entry is used for saving information about MAC, IPv4, or IPv6 address of endpoints visible in the fabric for any host connected to ACI. See Table 2-2.

Table 2-2. *Nexus 9500 ACI Spine Line Cards*

Line Card	Interfaces	Performance	Usable Fabric Modules	CloudSec
X9716D-GX	16x 10/25/40/50/100/400G QSFP-DD	12.8 Tbps	4	Yes
X9736C-FX	36x 10/25/40/50/100G QSFP28	7.2 Tbps	5*	Yes (28-36 ports)
X9732C-EX	32x 10/25/40/50/100G QSFP28	6.4 Tbps	4	No

Note   *Inside one chassis you can combine different line cards, but in such a case, the fifth fabric module will be disabled and you won't get maximum throughput for X9736C-FX.

Nexus 9300: Fixed Switches

All currently available fixed Nexus 9300 models are exclusively based on already discussed CloudScale ASICs and they support both standalone NX-OS and ACI operation modes. The decision of which to choose is based on interface types, their speeds, telemetry support, FibreChannel support, or scalability for various ACI tasks. In general, -FX and -GX models have greater TCAM memory available for control plane operations, supporting up to 256,000 MAC or host IP entries. See Table 2-3.

Table 2-3. *Nexus 9300 ACI Switches*

Switch Model	Interfaces	Maximal Throughput	ACI Leaf/ Spine	MACSec Support
9316D-GX	16x 10/25/40/50/100/200/400G QSFP-DD	6.4 Tbps	Both	No
93600CD-GX	28 x 100/40G QSFP28 and 8 x 400/100G QSFP-DD	6.0 Tbps	Both	No
9332D-GX2B	32x 10/25/40/50/100/200/400G QSFP-DD	12.8 Tbps	Both	No
9364C-GX	64 x 100/40G QSFP28	12.8 Tbps	Both	No
9348D-GX2A	48x 10/25/40/50/100/200/400G QSFP-DD	19.2 Tbps	Both	No
9364D-GX2A	64x 10/25/40/50/100/200/400G QSFP-DD	25.6 Tbps	Both	No
9332C	32x 40/100G QSFP28 and 2x 1/10G SFP+	6.4 Tbps	Spine only	Yes
9364C	64x 40/100G QSFP28 and 2x 1/10G SFP+	12.84 Tbps	Spine only	Yes
9336C-FX2	36x 40/100G QSFP28	7.2 Tbps	Leaf only	Yes
9336C-FX2-E	36x 40/100G QSFP28	7.2 Tbps	Leaf only	Yes
93180YC-FX	48x 1/10/25G SFP28 and 6 x 40/100G QSFP28	3.6 Tbps	Leaf only	Yes
93240YC-FX2	48x 1/10/25G SFP28 and 12x 40/100G QSFP28	4.8 Tbps	Leaf only	Yes

(continued)

Table 2-3. (*continued*)

Switch Model	Interfaces	Maximal Throughput	ACI Leaf/ Spine	MACSec Support
93360YC-FX2	96x 1/10/25G SFP28 and 12x 40/100G QSFP28	7.2 Tbps	Leaf only	Yes
93180YC-FX3	48x 1/10/25G SFP28 and 6x 40/100G QSFP28	3.6 Tbps	Leaf only	Yes
93108TC-FX	48x 100M/1/10GBASE-T and 6x 40/100G QSFP28	2.16 Tbps	Leaf only	Yes
9348GC-FXP	48x 100M/1G BASE-T, 4x 1/10/25G SFP28 and 2x 40/100G QSFP28	969 Gbps	Leaf only	Yes
93108TC-FX3P	48x 100M/1/2.5/5/10G BASE-T and 6x 40/100G QSFP28	2.16 Tbps	Leaf only	Yes

Now with all this knowledge about the Nexus 9000 hardware platform, let's have a closer look how it's used for ACI.

ACI Underlay Networking

In the following sections, you will get an overview of ACI's underlay network, control plane and data plane operations, and supported multi-dc architectures.

ACI Leaf-Spine Fabric Topology

As shown in Figure 2-6, ACI uses a very simple and deterministic two-layer leaf-spine topology interconnected into a fabric. Each leaf switch is connected to all spines using at least one physical interface, while switches on the same level don't require mutual interconnection (resulting in cabling optimization compared to traditional NX-OS vPC designs).

The leaf-spine topology offers simple scalability. The overall bandwidth capacity of the whole ACI fabric is based on amount of spine switches used. Each spine adds another and concurrent path for traffic to be sent between any leaf switch. For production ACI fabric, the general recommendation is to use at least two spines. This preserves the necessary redundancy in case of failure and allows you to upgrade them one by one without affecting the production traffic. Adding a new spine switch is just matter of connecting it correctly to the fabric; after registration in APIC, it will automatically become a fabric member without disrupting already deployed devices.

On the other hand, if you need to scale your access interfaces, all you need to do is deploy a new leaf switch (or pair), similar to the previous case. Each new leaf will become part of the fabric and the control plane will converge automatically, all without affecting already running devices.

This simplicity applies analogically when removing any device from ACI. To make sure you won't cause any service disruption in your production network, ACI offers **maintenance mode** (commonly known also as the **graceful insertion and removal** feature). If enabled on some ACI switch, this switch is not considered part of the underlay network anymore and all control plane protocols are gracefully brought down. Additionally, all host interfaces are shut down.

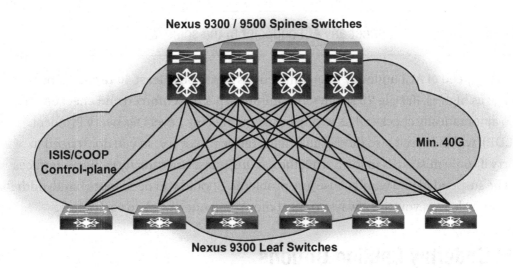

Figure 2-6. *ACI leaf-spine fabric*

To summarize each layer's purpose for ACI, leaf switches provide the following:

- End host connectivity (bare metal servers, virtualization hosts)

- APICs connectivity (from version 5.2.(1), APICs can be connected to ACI also using a generic L3 network. You will find more information about this option in Chapter 3.)

- External L3 connectivity (legacy L3 network, WAN, Internet)

- External L2 connectivity (legacy switched network, indirectly connected endpoints)

- Security policies enforcement and policy-based redirect

- VXLAN encapsulation and decapsulation

Spine switches provide

- A powerful forwarding backbone

- A complete endpoint database

- Secure DCI Connectivity when using ACI Multi-Pod or Multi-Site architectures

---

Note   You cannot connect any ACI endpoint to the spine layer.

The speed of ACI underlay interconnections has to be at least **40 Gigabits**, but it can go as high as 400 Gig these days. A minimum speed is enforced and checked. ACI also automatically checks all its wiring based on the Link Level Discovery Protocol (LLDP), which is used also during automatic fabric discovery, so you don't need to worry if some mistake is made during the cabling phase. Incorrectly cabled interfaces will be suspended and won't cause any problems. Should you need more bandwidth for individual leaves, you can always connect more than one uplink to each spine.

ACI Underlay Cabling Options

Speaking about ACI fabric wiring, it's good to be aware of your options when designing the physical layer of the underlay network. First of all, to ensure dynamic discovery of all fabric devices, you should connect leaves to spines using default fabric interfaces.

In general, these are the last six high-speed QSPF interfaces of the individual leaf switches. Besides them, if the leaf is already registered to the fabric and managed by the APIC, you can convert its downlinks (end-host interfaces) to fabric ports as well. And the same applies the opposite way: if needed, you can covert the default fabric interface to a downlink, except for the last two interfaces of each leaf. All these interface manipulations require a switch reload before the change can take effect.

For the interconnection itself, you can use two main cable types:

1. **Direct attach cables (DAC)**: Already pre-manufactured and ready to use cable with fixed QSFP transceivers on both sides. There are passive copper models and active optical direct attach cables (AOCs). 40/100/400G passive DAC cables can reach up to 5m and AOC up to 30m. If such lengths are sufficient for your planned cable runs between DC racks and you are able to install additional horizontal cabling, using DACs can bring significant benefits:

   a. **Cost**: Up to 50-80% lower price compared with two individual QSPF modules plus fiber.

   b. **Power consumption**: One 100G QSPF consumes around 3.5 to 4 W and 12W in case of 400G, compared with 1.5W for passive DAC or 3.5W (100G) and 12W (400G) of active optical cables.

2. **QSFP transceivers plus an optic patch cord**: If your datacenter facility comes with horizontal cabling already in place with patch panels in your racks, or the distance between some devices exceeds 30m, you can reach for individual 40/100/400G QSFP transceivers and optical patch cables. Here you need to differentiate between fiber types, connectors, and link lengths needed:

   a. **Multimode fiber**: Multimode allows you to use either MPO-12 (12 fibers) or LC-LC (2 fibers) connectors, both with a maximum reach of 100m when connected with OM4 cable standard.

   b. **Singlemode fiber**: Longer distances can be reached using singlemode fibers and LC-LC connectors. The maximum length for 100G transceivers without any DWDM technology in between is 40km.

ACI Control Plane and Data Plane Overview

All leaf-spine underlay interfaces are purely L3 point-to-point. They use the IP unnumbered feature, so you won't find any IP addresses configured for them on the switches. There is no Spanning Tree Protocol running inside the fabric. Forwarding between leaves relies on unique VXLAN Tunnel Endpoint (VTEP) IP addresses, represented by loopbacks and assigned automatically by APIC to each switch during the initial registration to the fabric. APICs themselves have their own VTEP address as well. Each VTEP IP address is then advertised to the rest of the switches by the Intermediate System-to-Intermediate System (IS-IS) protocol, utilizing Level 1 adjacencies. Don't worry; there is no need to have any deeper IS-IS knowledge to deploy and operate ACI. The protocol runs by default without user intervention. Although I don't recommend it, you still have configuration options to tweak some IS-IS properties. They include MTU used, protocol metrics, or internal shortest path first (SPF) timers.

When the leaf switch needs to send a packet from locally connected endpoint whose destination is behind some other remote leaf, it will encapsulate the data into a VXLAN header and put a source/destination VTEP IP address in the outer IP header fields (as shown in Figure 2-7). If the destination isn't known yet, the leaf can forward a packet to one of the spine switches (chosen by ECMP hash) and try destination resolution there using a distributed endpoint database.

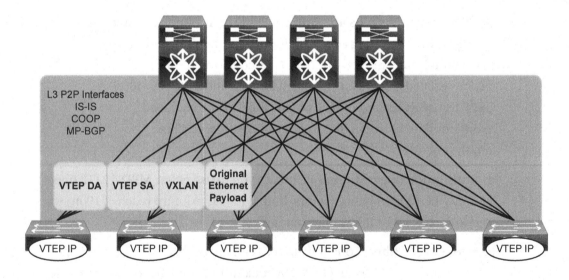

Figure 2-7. *Internal ACI fabric forwarding*

Spine switches act in ACI as the endpoint knowledge base. As soon as any leaf identifies a new locally connected endpoint, it will update a spine endpoint database with this information using Council of Oracles Protocol (COOP). COOP is the second part of ACI's main control plane together with IS-IS. As a result, spines in ACI always know the entire endpoint information and they always synchronize any changes between them via COOP. If neither leaf nor spine is aware about particular endpoint, you won't be able to communicate with it. In some cases, covered later in this book, a spine can still proactively try to resolve unknown endpoint addresses using the so-called ARP gleaning process, but if it still won't help, the communication is dropped.

Then we have the third important control plane operation: external information management. External prefixes and endpoint information from outside the particular fabric are distributed between leaves and spines using Multi-Protocol Border Gateway Protocol (MP-BGP). Prefixes are mutually redistributed on border leaves between MP-BGP and static information or dynamic routing protocols based on configured application policies. MP-BGP uses the concept of redundant route reflectors (RRs) represented by spines to optimize number of BGP peerings needed inside the fabric. You will look deeper at control/data plane operations and forwarding inside the fabric during Chapter 6.

ACI Architecture

Even though some ACI implementations start small, by deploying just one fabric, organizations sooner or later want to expand their datacenter infrastructure. It always makes sense to have geo-redundant datacenter facilities, with flexible networking available for each site. But how to get there? Ideally as quickly and simply as possible, without affecting already deployed resources or compromising already created security policies. You have wide variety of options when deploying multi-datacenter ACI fabric or expanding the already existing implementation. The following sections will describe all of them in detail.

Multi-Tier ACI Fabric

Starting with ACI software version 4.1(1), you can create a multi-tier fabric topology that allows you to connect uplinks of second layer leaves to first layer leaves instead of spines (see Figure 2-8). This can come in handy when longer cable runs are needed between distant datacenter rooms or floors and you cannot reach the spines directly, or when there is not enough horizontal cabling available in the datacenter to connect more distant leaves with all spines.

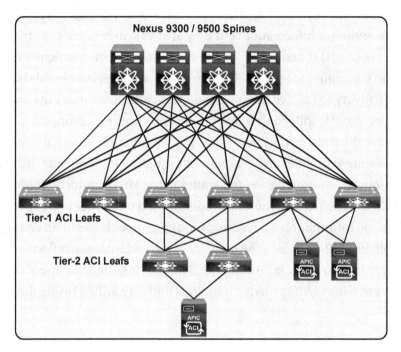

Figure 2-8. *Multi-tier ACI underlay fabric*

I used Tier-2 leaves several times for implementing server management layer utilizing "low speed" copper RJ-45 switches (Nexus 9348GC-FXP), while server data interfaces were connected to the main and "fast" Tier-1 leaves. When there is no dedicated out-of-band infrastructure available for servers in the DC, this design brings a reliable and quite redundant way to access your servers and all are centrally managed using APICs, without increasing the administration load.

Another physical deployment use case for multi-tier ACI is positioning spines to dedicated network racks in the datacenter room. Then the Tier-1 leaves are installed as end-of-row (EoR) "aggregation" for each compute rack row and the Tier-2 leaves serve as a top-of-rack (ToR) switches. This way you can shorten cable runs inside the DC room and optimize your use of horizontal cabling (many times including patch panels in each rack). See Figure 2-9.

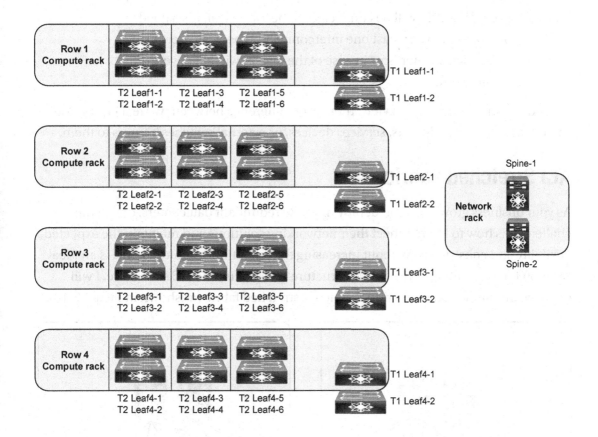

Figure 2-9. *Multi-tier ACI rack design*

Each Tier-2 leaf can be easily connected with more than two Tier-1 leaves (an advantage compared to vPC). The limiting factor here is just the ECMP load balancing, currently supporting 18 links.

Configuration-wise you have to use fabric interfaces for the interconnection. In ACI, each Nexus 9K has some default fabric interfaces (usually high-speed uplinks, or the last four-six interfaces) and you can in addition reconfigure any host port to a fabric uplink, after the switch gets registered with APIC. Here is the recommendation when deploying a Tier-2 architecture:

- If you plan to connect APICs to the Tier-2 leaf, at least one default fabric interface of the Tier-2 leaf has to be connected with the default fabric interface of Tier-1 leaf. Otherwise, APIC won't be able to discover and provision the Tier-1.

- Even if no APIC will be connected to the Tier-2 leaf, it's a good
  practice to have at least one interconnection between tiers using
  default fabric interfaces in case of the Tier-2 switch recovery after
  factory reset.

From a functional point of view, there is no difference between two leaf layers. You
can connect APICs, endpoints, services devices, or external switches/routers to them.

ACI Stretched Fabric

As your business grows and you deploy multiple redundant datacenters, one of the
challenges is how to interconnect their networking solutions and maintain the expected
flexibility and consistency, without increasing the operation complexity. ACI is an ideal
solution for automating network infrastructure across multiple DC sites. Here, I will
describe the simplest design option, which is stretched fabric (as shown in Figure 2-10).

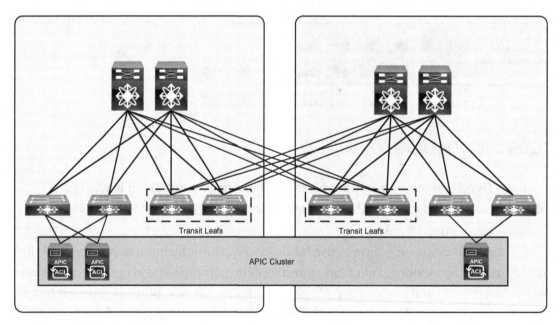

Figure 2-10. *ACI stretched fabric*

The stretched fabric is still a single ACI fabric. All datacenters are part of the
common administration domain and one availability zone. They are configured and
monitored by a single APIC cluster as the one entity, preserving all the fabric capabilities
across the different locations. A maximum of three sites can be part of this stretched
fabric design.

In each fabric, choose at least one, but optimally two, transit leaves, which will be interconnected with all spine switches at a remote site. 40G interface speed is required and enforced for these links, similar to standard ACI fabric.

From a redundancy point of view, it's recommended to provision at least a three-node APIC cluster with two nodes deployed at the main site and one node in the other site. The main site can be considered the one with the majority of switches, the active site, or the main from other operational perspectives. Every change in the ACI configuration is automatically replicated to all APIC cluster nodes in the stretched fabric. This synchronous replication of APIC databases brings us to the important latency factor for a proper cluster performance. You have to ensure maximal 50ms round-trip time (RTT) between APIC nodes.

Maybe you are asking yourself, what happens when the interconnection between these stretched sites is lost? Can I possibly lose the configuration or any data? The answer is no. In such a case, both fabrics continue to work independently and traffic forwarding inside them is not affected. Information about new endpoints is distributed using Council-of-Oracles Protocol (COOP) only to local spines, but as soon as the interconnection is restored, they will merge their databases. What will be affected during the outage, though, is configurability of the fabric. An APIC cluster needs a quorum in order to be configurable; the majority of cluster nodes have to be available, or the configuration becomes read-only. Therefore, if we lose an interconnect, only the first site with two APIC nodes will be configurable; the second one can be monitored by the local APIC, but without permission to do any changes. After the link is restored, their databases will be synchronized as well. A more serious situation is if the first datacenter is lost completely due to some natural disaster, for example. Then we end up with read-only second fabric only. We can avoid this condition by deploying a fourth standby APIC node in the second site and, in case of need, add it to the cluster to regain the quorum. For more information about APIC clustering, refer to a later section of this chapter.

From a configuration point of view, stretched fabric has no specific requirements; the control plane is provisioned automatically. You just need to cable the devices accordingly.

Even though the stretched fabric offers a quite simple architecture, it's not always feasible to implement it and there are drawbacks. Many times, you don't have enough available fiber cables between the datacenter rooms. Sometimes the sites aren't even connected directly but by using intermediate service provider, offering just L3 services. Or there is more scalable architecture needed than three locations. With the release of newer software versions for ACI, the drawbacks of stretched fabric were addressed by introducing new design options. Now we have capabilities to extend the DC infrastructure in a simpler yet powerful way (feature-wise). Therefore, in the next sections, you will look at Multi-Pod and Multi-Site ACI architectures, which are from a practical point of view more optimal, they support a broader set of features, and their scalability is increased to 14 sites, each consisting of 25 Pods (at the time of writing this book). During the design phase of a Multi-DC ACI deployment, I definitely recommend going for one of the following options rather than stretched fabric if possible.

ACI Multi-Pod Architecture

Since ACI version 2.0, Multi-Pod architecture has been the natural evolution of previously described stretched fabric, aiming to connect geo-redundant ACI fabrics without increasing the operational requirements and complexity. Multi-Pod is still managed by single APIC cluster and configured as one entity, but compared with the stretched fabric, it brings several enhancements to isolate as much as possible failure domains between fabrics.

As you can see in Figure 2-11, Multi-Pod separates the control plane protocols between Pods. IS-IS, COOP, and MP-BGP peerings run locally inside each Pod, therefore any potential issue with one fabric is not propagated or affecting all others. For interconnection between different Pods, we use spine switches either connected to generic L3 network called an Inter-Pod Network (IPN), or you can interconnect them directly back to back (from ACI version 5.2(3)). However, the back-to-back option limits the architecture to two Pods only, without further expansion support (remote leaves or multi-site).

All created ACI policies for workloads are made available between each Pod, so you have freedom and total flexibility for connecting your endpoints anywhere needed. Workload migrations, connectivity failover, or insertion of various L4-L7 service devices are easy as well. In general, there are no feature limitations compared to single ACI fabric.

Multi-Pod is convenient also from an APIC cluster perspective. You can simply spread the cluster nodes between Pods, making their operation more reliable and fault tolerant. When the interconnection between Pods is lost, the ACI behaves the same as in the stretched fabric case. The part of the fabric with the APIC quorum (more than a half of available nodes) will be configurable; the other one stays in read-only mode. But in any case, the whole network will continue to work as expected and without any issues.

Note   There is no need to have APIC in each and every Pod. Even without any controller, but with working IPN connectivity, the Pod is manageable and fully configurable.

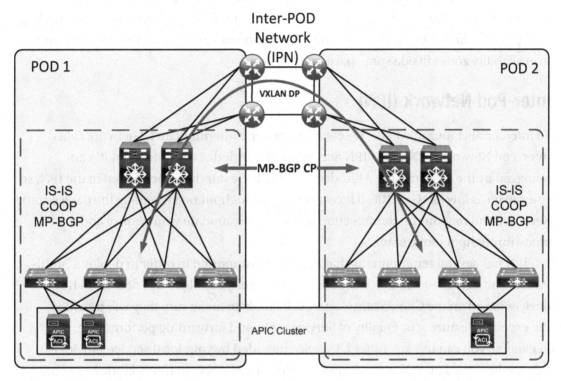

Figure 2-11. *ACI Multi-Pod architecture*

To ensure proper Inter-Pod forwarding, the ACI control plane utilizes a new set of MP-BGP peerings between the spines of Pods, exchanging the routing, endpoint and multicast group information (in the form of BGP VPNv4/VPNv6 and L2VPN EVPN NLRIs). When deploying Multi-Pod, you can either choose to use full mesh BGP peerings or route reflector servers (RR). The general recommendation from Cisco is to use the first option whenever possible: full mesh peerings and with only two spines acting as BGP peers in each Pod, independently from the overall number of spines across all the Pods. Changes to the BGP database are internally distributed to non-BGP spines using COOP.

A multi-Pod data plane uses VXLAN encapsulation for packet forwarding between Pods to achieve seamless L2 and L3 services across the common infrastructure. The VXLAN header carries the same, unaltered information end to end. For detailed information about control and the data plane operation in a Multi-Pod design, see Chapter 6.

Currently, you can deploy as many as 25 Pods, which makes this architecture perfect for scaling further from single datacenter deployments. Multi-Pod commonly finds its usage in various campus datacenters or colocation facilities consisting of multiple buildings that comprise a single logical datacenter. A disaster recovery datacenter is another use case, and you gain easier and faster recovery times by avoiding configuration inconsistencies. In public cloud terminology, the ACI Multi-Pod is similar to availability zones inside some particular region.

Inter-Pod Network (IPN)

To interconnect multiple Pods, we can use a generic intermediate L3 network called Inter-Pod Network (IPN). This IPN acts as an ACI underlay extension, but it's not managed by the APIC cluster. APIC doesn't check the interface speed used in the IPN, so you can go as low as 1G or 10G if it covers your throughput needs among the datacenters. Keep in mind that this interconnection should accommodate your control and data plane throughput requirements.

IPN has several requirements that need to be supported in order to deploy a Multi-Pod ACI infrastructure. It's recommended whenever possible to use dedicated IPN devices based on the CloudScale Nexus 9000 family to make sure they will provide the expected feature sets, Quality of Service tools, and forwarding performance, but in general, you can use any other L3 service provided by your local service provider. I've implemented an IPN in the form of universal VXLAN BGP EVPN fabric based on standalone Nexus 9000s in NX-OS mode (resulting in VXLAN in VXLAN encapsulation but working perfectly fine for ACI).

The following IPN features need to be considered prior to making a design decision for Multi-Pod, and if some of them are not available, you can still implement other variants:

- **P2P L3 subinterfaces**: Spine switches use point-to-point routed subinterfaces when connecting to IPN, with all frames tagged using VLAN 4. This specific is not configurable, so it's important to choose IPN devices capable of creating multiple VLAN 4 subinterfaces on different physical interfaces at the same time.

- **OSPF/BGP protocol**: IPN has to support dynamic routing in order to exchange external VTEP addresses between spine switches used for VXLAN encapsulation and loopback addresses on MP-BGP control plane peerings. OSPF was initially the only option, but from ACI version 5.2(3), BGP support was added. Alternatively, static routing can be used, but you have to consider more difficult maintainability and human-error susceptibility when (re)configuring static routing.

- **Higher MTU**: As we already know, ACI Multi-Pod uses end-to-end VXLAN encapsulation for data transport. We need to count with that in IPN network as well by increasing the available Maximum Transport Unit (MTU), and thus avoid any fragmentation. VXLAN adds 50B to the original header, so the minimal IPN MTU would be 1550 (or even higher if other encapsulation is used on the transport). If possible, it's a best practice to configure your IPN network to support the highest JumboMTU (9216) and prevent any problems caused by this requirement. The maximum MTU used for end host interfaces in ACI is 9000 so you would ensure significant reserve even for the biggest packet possible.

- **DHCP relay**: In a multi-Pod environment, you use one particular "seed" Pod from which the fabric discovery process is initiated (for more information, refer to Chapter 3). All other remote switches use DHCP to discover messages to reach the seed APICs and get their VTEP IP address to be used subsequently for provisioning. In general, the DHCP discover packet is sent as broadcast, so in order to transport it over IPN from the remote Pod, you need to configure the DHCP relay agent. It will take the broadcast discovers and forward them as unicasts to the IP addresses of APICs. Note that in the Multi-Pod environment, you don't need to necessarily have APICs in each deployed Pod.

- **PIM Bidir multicasts**: Each Layer-2 segment in ACI (called bridge domains and explained later) is assigned with an IP multicast group address from a predefined IP pool. When sending multi-destination BUM traffic (broadcasts, unknown unicasts, and multicasts), ACI uses multicast delivery both internally and over the IPN network. To support this transport, PIM Bidir with a phantom rendezvous point (RP) configuration is needed. If you are not familiar with multicast routing, I recommend looking up the general multicast concepts beforehand. I will cover PIM-Bidir with a practical configuration example for IPN in Chapter 3.

- **Quality of Service (QoS)**: ACI allows you to classify and apply QoS policies to six user-defined traffic levels plus four internal control plane levels. It's important when deploying ACI Multi-Pod to consider both APIC and a IPN QoS configuration to ensure proper end-to-end prioritization of important traffic, especially the control plane. Although QoS configuration is not mandatory for Multi-Pod to work, it's highly recommended.

Sometimes all these features may seem overwhelming at first sight, and you may think they add too much complexity to the architecture, but at the end of the day, when we go through the whole IPN configuration later, you will realize how nicely they cooperate together to provide robust, flexible, and optimal forwarding between the distant datacenters.

ACI Multi-Site Architecture

Even though ACI Multi-Pod has many advantages and brings operational simplicity to managing a multi-datacenter network infrastructure, sometimes there is a need for complete isolation across different networks and tenants around the globe without any RTT restrictions. ACI Multi-Site is the next evolution step in this architectural palette, introduced in version 3.0.(1).

As shown in Figure 2-12, ACI Multi-Site enables you to interconnect independent ACI fabrics with their own APIC clusters to achieve flexible L2 or L3 services and apply consistent policies in different distant regions.

Multi-Site architecture shares multiple common functional specifics with Multi-Pod. The control plane is based on MP-BGP, which signals prefixes and endpoint information between the sites. The data plane again uses VXLANs to provide Layer 2 as well as Layer 3 services on top of the common underlay network. Although each fabric is independent this time, you still have a possibility to insert L4-L7 service devices into the datapath between endpoints, or to achieve automatic external connectivity failover between multiple sites in case of potential outage. Furthermore, this fabric independence can become handy when you want to deploy new applications, test a new feature, or upgrade to a new ACI version, but without worries that all your datacenters will be affected by such a change. I've worked for several bank clients that ended up with a Multi-Site ACI design due to regular disaster recovery tests in their datacenters. If you as a bank shut down the entire datacenter (while you have only two of them), that is exactly the moment when you want to have 100% confidence that the other is working as expected on its own.

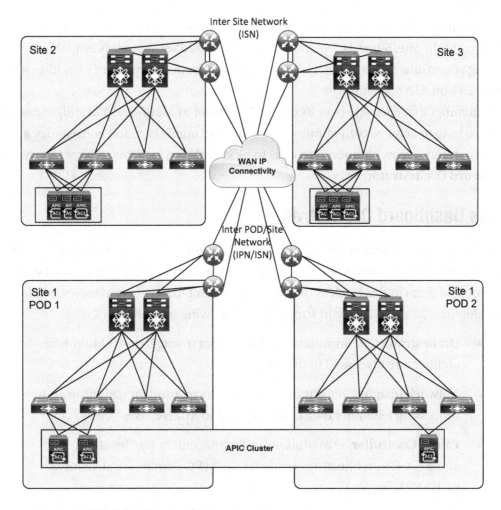

Figure 2-12. *ACI Multi-Site architecture*

In order to achieve connectivity between spines of different sites, this time we use a generic inter-site network (ISN). Compared with an IPN, an ISN doesn't need any multicast or DHCP relay support. Although the multi-destination BUM traffic within each site is still delivered using multicasts, when a multicast packet needs to be sent to any remote site, spines perform so called head-end replication. Each multicast packet is replicated to multiple unicast packets, and they are sent to destination ACI sites via the ISN. What we still have to count with, though, is increased MTU due to additional VXLAN headers and dynamic routing over a statically defined VLAN 4 between the spine and ISN switch. Back-to-back spine connection is supported as well, but between two sites only.

A significant emphasis is put on security in transit among the datacenters when deploying Multi-Site. Since ACI version 4.0(1), the **CloudSec** feature is available, allowing you to line-rate encrypt multi-hop L3 traffic between spine VTEP addresses using a 256-bit AES algorithm.

Remember that each site uses its own APIC cluster in Multi-Site. But still, in case of need, we have to achieve configuration, security, and administration consistency among them. Therefore, a new component needs to be introduced into the architecture: **Nexus Dashboard Orchestrator.**

Nexus Dashboard Orchestrator

Nexus Dashboard is a unified modular software platform built on containers, running independently of APIC nodes, and integrating several additional applications. I won't cover most of them in this book as they are not relevant to our current topics, but for your reference, Nexus Dashboard supports the following modules:

- **Orchestrator**: An important application for managing ACI Multi-Site architecture discussed in this section

- **Network Insights**: Big data analytics platform, used for gathering and processing telemetry data from NX-OS and ACI Nexuses 9000

- **Fabric Controller**: Provisioning and management tool for stand-alone NX-OS architectures (simple L2/L3 vPC domains and VXLAN BGP EVPN fabrics)

- **Nexus Data Broker**: Centralized management for TAP/SPAN data replication around the network infrastructure based on Nexus 9000

Now let's get back to ACI Multi-Site. The **Nexus Dashboard Orchestrator (NDO)** component acts as the ACI inter-site policy manager and centralized management layer to provision, monitor, and handle the full lifecycle of networking policies within the connected sites (as shown in Figure 2-13). Additionally, it ensures policy consistency.

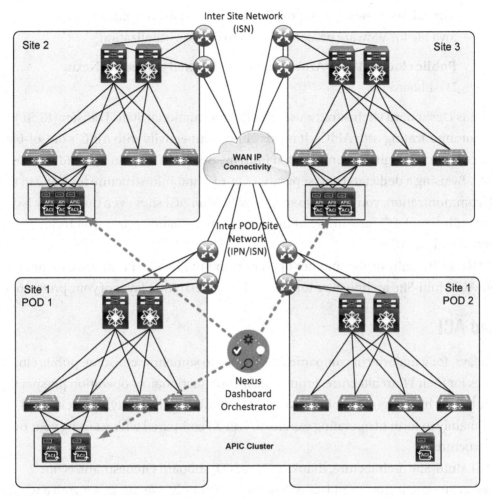

Figure 2-13. *Nexus Dashboard Orchestrator multi-site management plane*

It's the Orchestrator that automatically configures spines for ISN features and runs the MP-BGP peering between each other. You just establish a connection with the management interfaces of the APIC clusters, and from then on, part of the ACI configuration will happen in NDO instead of individual APICs. Based on your needs, you can choose to which sites the configuration will be pushed.

There are three deployments options available for the Nexus Dashboard platform:

- **Physical appliance cluster**: Three (expandable to six) dedicated physical servers, formerly known as the Cisco Application Service Engine, orderable directly from Cisco

- **Virtual machines**: Cluster of up to six VMs, delivered either as an .ova file for VMware or .qcow2 for Linux KVM virtualization

- **Public cloud**: AWS or Azure can be used as well to host the Nexus Dashboard

Nexus Dashboard Orchestrator uses the Representational State Transfer (REST) API when communicating with APICs. It needs either connectivity with APIC's out-of-band interface (which is highly recommended from my point of view), an in-band interface, or both. By using a dedicated and separated out-of-band infrastructure for NDO to the APIC communication, you ensure manageability of all ACI sites even during any issues/outages of internal ACI forwarding or problems with in-band access, which can be caused outside of ACI.

NDO additionally brings another open northbound REST API, so you can include the whole ACI Multi-Site architecture further in the orchestration layer of your preference.

Cloud ACI

Nowadays, for a majority of companies it's a must to somehow consume public cloud services for their IT architecture. From a business, functional, or operation perspective, public clouds bring significant improvement in reliability, flexibility, elasticity, and costs (mainly in form of operating expenses, OPEX) compared with running your own infrastructure.

ACI Multi-Site architecture, thanks to Nexus Dashboard Orchestrator, is not limited to automating on-premises ACI deployments only. We can move with a whole networking infrastructure to the cloud as well (as shown in Figure 2-14). As of ACI version 5.2(3), Amazon Web Services and Microsoft Azure are supported, with other cloud vendors on the roadmap.

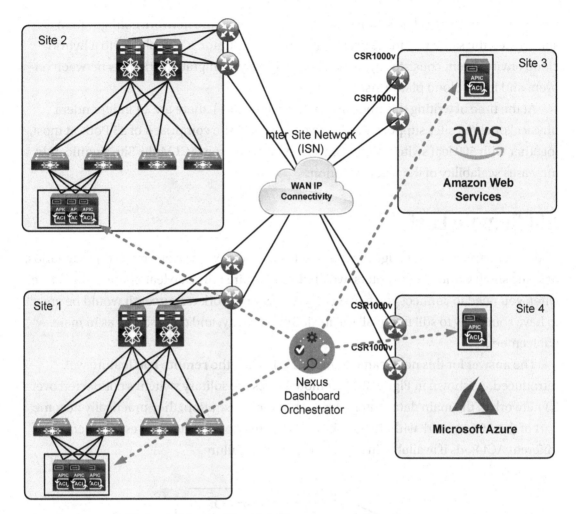

Figure 2-14. *ACI Anywhere – Cloud ACI*

With Cloud ACI deployment, we reuse all the concepts discussed before in the Multi-Site architecture. On-premises leaf-spine ACI fabric is via a generic L3 ISN connected with virtual CSR1000v routers running in the cloud environment. Their lifecycle is completely managed from creation through maintenance and upgrades to termination by Nexus Dashboard Orchestrator. NDO is used to set up the control and data plane protocols (OSPF, MP-BGP, and VXLAN) as well as IPsec encryption between environments.

In the public cloud, there's a new component called the **Cloud APIC (cAPIC)** appliance. cAPIC is an adapted version of standard APIC but for managing the most important cloud network resources. It acts as an abstraction layer to translate ACI application policies to cloud-native objects. Even though the network configuration is still created the same way in Nexus Dashboard Orchestrator, it's deployed to a hybrid cloud environment consistently, making it really easy to migrate workloads between on-prem and multi-cloud platforms.

At the time of writing this book and ACI version 6.0(1), there are 14 independent physical or cloud sites supported, while each physical site comprised of 25 Pods at most, together with 500 leaf switches for each site. As you can see, ACI Multi-Site significantly increases scalability of the whole solution.

ACI Remote Leaf

And now imagine smaller edge locations, telco co-locations, various migration scenarios, or some small witness datacenters, which don't require full scale leaf-spine architecture. Often you need to connect just few servers or other network resources. It would be great to have some way to still retain all the flexibility, security, and consistency as in main datacenters.

The answer for this need came in ACI 4.1(2), when the **remote leaf** feature was introduced. As shown in Figure 2-15, remote leaves are solitary switches connected over L3 network to the main datacenter fabric. After the registration, they practically become part of the ACI network with the special ability to reassociate themselves between different ACI Pods if available in case of connectivity failure.

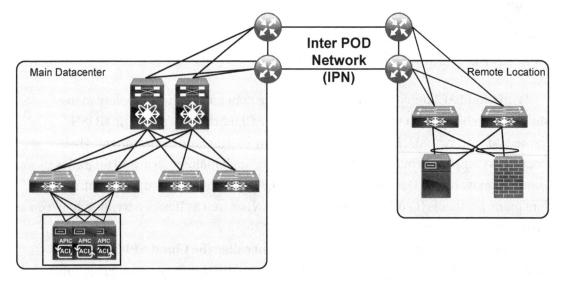

Figure 2-15. *ACI remote leaves*

An intermediate L3 network connects remote leaves with the main datacenter and shares similar requirements with the InterPOD network already discussed:

- **P2P L3 interfaces**: A remote leaf needs dedicated L3 point-to-point routed uplinks in a statically defined VLAN 4

- **Increased MTU**: All packets sent between remote leaves and ACI spines are encapsulated in VXLAN, so count an additional 50B in transport.

- **Dynamic routing**: OSPF or BGP are the protocols to distribute VTEP addresses for VXLAN tunneling.

- **DHCP Relay Agent**: For dynamic discovery, registration, provisioning, and monitoring of remote leaves by APICs

BiDir PIM multicast support is not required for remote leaves. Maximum RTT can go up to 300ms and minimum uplink speed is as low as 10Mbit per second.

Application Policy Infrastructure Controller

We have already covered all the main underlay networking aspects of Cisco ACI and various multi-datacenter deployment options when building the ACI fabric. In the following sections, I will further describe the second main architectural component: a centralized cluster of controllers responsible for all the management tasks named **Cisco Application Policy Infrastructure Controllers (APIC)**.

Even though switches in ACI still have their own NX-OS like command-line interface (CLI) and we can access them using Secure Shell (SSH), it's only for verifying their status or to troubleshoot them. From a configuration perspective, we cannot apply the "legacy" one-by-one provisioning via CLI. All management actions are implemented exclusively using the common data object model pushed to the underlying fabric from an APIC cluster. It becomes single pane of glass (in Multi-Site together with Nexus Dashboard Orchestrator) for provisioning, configuration changes, and fabric operation.

The main features of APIC include

- ACI switch registration and fabric control plane setup

- Fabric inventory management

- Application-centric policies repository based on a defined application object model

- Firmware management with image repository, automated upgrade process of switches, and controllers

- Built-in fabric monitoring and troubleshooting tools

- Fault, event, audit log, and performance management

- Third-party integrations with virtualization hypervisors, container orchestrators, or L4-L7 devices

- A distributed and scalable database system as part of the APIC cluster

- Fully open and documented northbound REST API for additional automation and your own scripts

To communicate with fabric switches, APIC uses an encrypted Layer 3 channel built over an infrastructure VLAN (user configurable during the APIC initialization) and based on assigned VTEP IP addresses. Transmitted instructions for switches are formatted into the standardized **Opflex protocol**. An Opflex is responsible for translating your intents (described by the application model) to the fabric and to declaratively instruct involved switches on how they should configure themselves. Remember that APIC is just a management plane. It's not directly involved in the control plane operation anyhow (as opposed to OpenFlow). Switches have their own "brain" and they run an Opflex agent under the hood. This agent takes the model description from APIC's southbound API and implements it in a form of well-known networking constructs: interface (and protocol) configuration, VLANs, IP interfaces, routing protocols, VXLAN configuration, security policies, and such. In fact, the majority of ACI's configuration is in the end translated to the standard networking protocols.

From my own path to becoming an ACI "hero," I found the most difficult part to grasp was the Application Policy model concepts and mapping them mentally to already known networking principles from the legacy infrastructure. As soon as you reach that state and find your way around how each building block fits together, ACI will become piece of cake for you. And hopefully we are walking towards such a level together in this book.

Hardware Equipment

So far, there were three generations of APIC appliances available, each of them based on a Cisco UCS C220 rack mount server running on CentOS with specialized software on top of it. Currently, only the third generation is fully supported and orderable; others are past their End of Sale (EoS) dates already.

- First generation: Cisco UCS C220 M3 based server – APIC M/L1 (EoS 04/2016)

- Second generation: Cisco UCS C220 M4 based server – APIC M/L2 (EoS 06/2019)

- **Third generation: Cisco UCS C220 M5 based server – APIC M/L3**

According to your needs, you can choose from medium (M) or large (L) versions. As described in Table 2-4, the difference lies in the hardware components used inside the chassis and the amount of end host interfaces supported in ACI. If you plan to scale above the 1,200 access interfaces, you should go for the large APIC. Otherwise, choose the medium one and it will fulfill all the ACI requirements just fine.

Table 2-4. *Third Generation APIC Appliances*

	APIC-M3	APIC-L3
Processor	2x 1.7 GHz Xeon Scalable 3106/85W 8C/11MB Cache/DDR4 2133M	2x 2.1 GHz Xeon Scalable 4110/85W 8C/11MB Cache/DDR4 2400MHz
Memory	6x 16GB DDR4-2666-MHz RDIMM/ PC4-21300/single rank/x4/1.2v	12x 16GB DDR4-2666-MHz RDIMM/ PC4-21300/single rank/x4/1.2v
Hard Drive	2x 1 TB 12G SAS 7.2K RPM SFF HDD	2x 2.4 TB 12G SAS 10K RPM SFF HDD (4K)
PCI Express (PCIe) slots	Cisco UCS VIC 1455 Quad Port 10/25G SFP28 CNA PCIE or Intel X710 Quad-port 10GBase-T NIC – RJ-45	Cisco UCS VIC 1455 Quad Port 10/25G SFP28 CNA PCIE or Intel X710 Quad-port 10GBase-T NIC - RJ-45

You can also encounter an XS APIC cluster, consisting of 1x M3 appliance and 2x virtual APICs, but this is orderable only as part of "ACI Mini," which is intended for lab purposes or testing. Scalability of ACI Mini is incomparable with a standard deployment.

Connecting APIC Nodes to the Network

APIC comes with multiple interfaces and it's good to know how to optimally use them. When preparing an ACI implementation and cabling plan, consider these three interface types:

1. **Cisco Integrated Management Controller (CIMC) interface**: HTTP(S) hardware management access, similar to IPMI or iDRAC used by other server vendors. Allows you to reconfigure (although not recommended) and monitor the HW resources of APIC. Additionally, CIMC comes with a Serial-over-LAN feature (SOL), which enables you to access the KVM console of APIC over HTTP(S). This interface should be connected to the dedicated out-of-band infrastructure, not related to ACI fabric. In general, it's a good practice to dedicate a particular IP subnet and VLAN for server HW management. In case of any problems, the main ACI's management connectivity outage, or a factory reset, this could be your last resort to fix the issues.

2. **APIC Management interfaces**: Two dedicated management interfaces in active-standby configuration for main access to the APIC HTTP(S) graphical user interface (GUI) and SSH CLI. Again, they should be ideally connected to two different out-of-band switches, not related with ACI fabric. The best practice is to separate this management interface to its own VLAN and IP subnet from HW management, but technically nothing prevents you from putting them together on the same network segment.

3. **APIC Data interfaces**: Each APIC node comes with either a Cisco UCS VIC card consisting of 4x SFP28 interfaces and supporting 10/25G speeds, or 4x 10GBase-T, RJ-45 Intel NIC. For redundancy, you have to connect two APIC's data ports into different leaves, specifically to their end host interfaces. By default, all leaf host interfaces are up and even without configuration, ready to connect the controller.

By default, in the third generation of APICs, their four physical data interfaces are grouped together in CIMC to form two logical uplinks of eth2-1 and eth2-2 (as shown in Figure 2-16). Uplinks are further bundled into a single active/standby bond0 interface from the OS perspective and used to manage the ACI. In order to achieve correct LLDP adjacency with leaf switches, you have to connect one interface from both uplink pairs (e.g., ETH2-1 and ETH2-3, or ETH2-2 and ETH2-4); otherwise, the APICs won't form a cluster. Another option I like to use during ACI implementations is to turn off the default hardware port-channel in CIMC. After logging into the CIMC GUI, click-left the menu button and navigate to **Networking -> Adapter Card 1 -> General Tab -> Adapter Card Properties**. Here, uncheck the Port Channel option and click Save Changes. Now you can use any two physical interfaces of your choice.

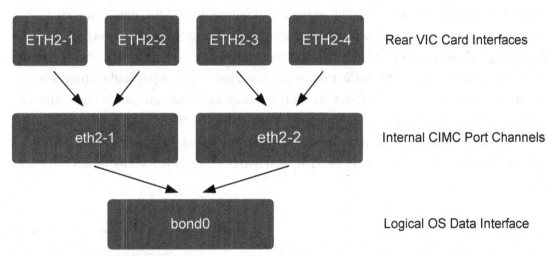

Figure 2-16. *APIC data interfaces*

APIC High Availability

For a production environment, you have to deploy a minimum of three redundant APIC nodes, but you can seamlessly expand the cluster up to seven nodes. In a lab, you can manage ACI fabric even with one node without a problem, if configured so. The amount of APIC nodes is directly proportional to the number of managed switches, resulting in expected transaction-rate performance between them. According to general scalability limits from Cisco, you should follow these recommendations:

- Three-node cluster, up to 80 leaf switches

- Four-node cluster, up to 200 leaf switches

- Five- or six-node cluster, up to 400 leaf switches

- Seven-node cluster, 400-500 leaf switches

- If higher number of switches is required, consider deploying Multi-Site architecture with multiple APIC clusters.

APIC discovery and clustering is an automated process based on initial consistent configuration and LLDP information (details of dynamic ACI fabric buildup will be described in the next chapter).

As you can see in Figure 2-17, an APIC cluster for performance optimization uses horizontal database scaling technique called **sharding**. A shard is basically a data unit, database subset, or group of database rows spread across the cluster nodes to allow parallel processing and data protection in case of failure. Each APIC database shard has always exactly three replicas, and their distribution among the cluster is based on defined shard layouts for each cluster size. Data itself is placed into the shards as a result of a hash function. One APIC is the master (or shard leader) for a particular shard and has read-write rights to edit it; the two others are used as a read replicas. When a master goes down, the remaining APICs negotiate which of them will become the new master. Now you see where the APIC quorum came from. Only shards with at least one backup replica are writable; that's why we need at least two of three APICs available to configure the ACI fabric.

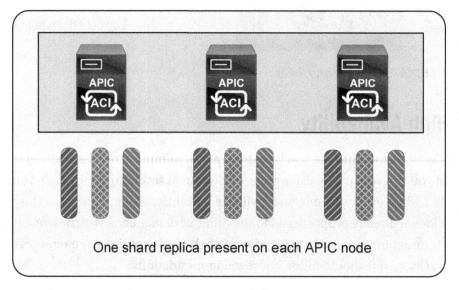

Figure 2-17. *APIC sharding*

But be aware. If you increase a number of APIC cluster nodes to more than three, you will still have three replicas of each shard. Therefore, **more nodes ≠ more reliability and redundancy**. Each additional APIC just means increased scalability and ability to manage more fabric switches.

Let's consider a larger, five-node APIC cluster during a failure scenario. If we lose two nodes, formally we will still have a quorum, but have a look at Figure 2-18. With such a shard layout, some shards will end up in read-only state and others will be still writable. It's highly recommended not to do any changes in this situation and restore the cluster as soon as possible. If more than two nodes are lost, there is actually a high probability that some information will be irreversibly lost.

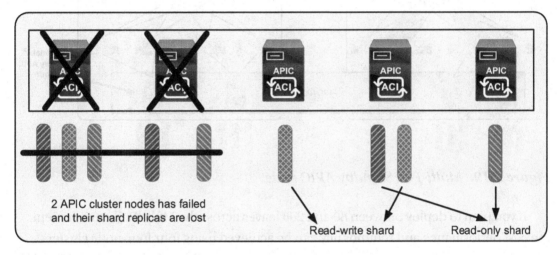

Figure 2-18. *APIC Three+ node cluster failure*

Your goal should be to always to distribute APICs around the ACI fabric in a way that ensures their protection against failure of more than two nodes at the time. Of course, within the single fabric you don't have too much maneuvering space. In that case, try to spread APIC nodes to different racks (or rows), and connect each to independent power outlets.

In Multi-Pod architecture, it's recommended to connect two APICs in Pod 1 and the third APIC in one of the other Pods. In a worst-case scenario, there is a potential for losing two nodes. In such a case, you would end up without a quorum and with read-only ACI fabric. To overcome this problem, there is an option to prepare and deploy a **standby APIC** in advance (as shown in Figure 2-19). This is the same hardware appliance with the specific initial configuration, instructing APIC not to form a cluster with others, but rather it stays in a "background" for the failure situation. In the standby state, APIC does not replicate any data or participate in any ACI operation. However, the main cluster is aware of the standby APIC presence and allows you to replace any failed node with it in case of need. The active APIC will then replicate its database to standby one and form again read-write cluster to fulfill the quorum.

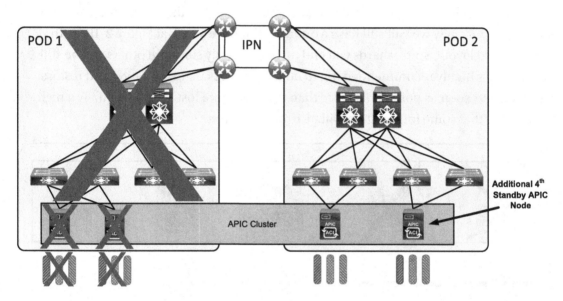

Figure 2-19. *Multi-Pod Standby APIC node*

If you plan to deploy between 80 and 200 leaves across the Multi-Pod environment, the best performance and redundancy can be achieved using four four-node clusters spread as much as possible around Pods. In a two-Pods-only design, put an additional standby APIC in each Pod.

For a five-node cluster in MultiPOD, see the recommended distribution shown in Table 2-5.

Table 2-5. *Five-Node APIC Cluster in ACI Multi-Pod*

	POD1	POD2	POD3	POD4	POD5	POD6
Two Pods *	3	2+1stb	-	-	-	-
Three Pods	2	2	1	-	-	-
Four Pods	2	1	1	1	-	-
Five Pods	1	1	1	1	1	-
Six+ Pods	1	1	1	1	1	-

* Note: *When you completely lose some shards during POD1 outage, there is still a chance for data recovery using a procedure called ID Recovery. It uses configuration snapshots and has to be executed by Cisco Business Unit or Technical Support.*

For a highly scaled ACI deployment consisting of more than 400 switches, a seven-node APIC cluster distribution should be implemented as shown in Table 2-6. Personally, I wouldn't implement this number of switches and APICs in two Pods only. You would end up with four nodes in the first Pod, and in case of failure, there is no guarantee that configuration will be recoverable. A safe minimum for me would be going for at least four Pods.

Table 2-6. *Seven-Node APIC Cluster in ACI Multi-Pod*

	POD1	POD2	POD3	POD4	POD5	POD6
Two Pods	-	-	-	-	-	-
Three Pods *	3	2	2	-	-	-
Four Pods	2	2	2	1	-	-
Five Pods	2	2	1	1	1	-
Six+ Pods	2	1	1	1	1	1

* Note: *The same ID Recovery procedure is applicable here as well.*

ACI Licensing

As with many other network solutions, Cisco ACI is not only about hardware to ensure genuine vendor support of the whole architecture in case of need. Even though ACI uses so called "honor-based" licensing (meaning that all its features are available and working right from the box), to receive any technical assistance from Cisco Customer Experience (CX) centers later, you need to buy the correct software licenses.

Both standalone Cisco NX-OS and ACI switch modes consume tier-based subscription licenses. Simply said, you must have a Cisco Smart Account (centralized license repository in Cisco's cloud) and allow your infrastructure to talk with this licensing service to consume a license. It can be managed via a direct internet connection, a company proxy server, or using a Smart Software Manager (SSM) Satellite server. Only SSM then needs internet connectivity and all your devices can license themselves "offline" using this proxy component.

The advantage of the Smart Licensing architecture is license portability and flexibility. They are not directly tied with any specific hardware anymore; you can upgrade the licensing tiers anytime during the subscription duration and you always have access to all of the newest features or security patches. Consider it as a pool of generic licenses that are consumed over time with your hardware infrastructure.

At the time of writing this book, subscription licenses are offered in three-, five-, and seven-year terms and come in these predefined tiers, based on features needed:

1. **Data Center Networking Essentials Subscription**: Includes all the main ACI features, ACI Multi-Pod support, PTP, and Streaming Telemetry

2. **Data Center Networking Advantage Subscription**: Includes all previous Essentials features plus support for multi datacenter on-prem or cloud sites and ACI Multi-Site features with Nexus Dashboard Orchestrator. Additionally, this license tier includes remote leaves.

3. **Data Center Networking Premier Subscription**: All Advantage tier features plus Cisco Day-2 Operations Suite. It consists of Nexus Dashboard Insights and Network Assurance Engine. Both are big data analytics tools based on ACI telemetry, focused on proactive fabric monitoring, datacenter flow analysis, change modeling, anomaly detection, or drastically shortening the troubleshooting time.

4. **Day-2 Operations Add-On Subscription**: Meant for customers already owning an Essentials or Advantage subscription who would like to increase the ACI value by implementing the additional telemetry analytic tool, Nexus Dashboard Network Insights.

In ACI, spine switches don't require any licenses at all; you have to buy them just for each leaf switch. The minimum for running ACI is always Essentials. If you want to use ACI Multi-Pod with remote leaves functionality, only remote leaves need Advantage; the rest of the fabric can stay on Essentials. In case of Multi-Site or additional analytic tools, all the leaf switches have to consume the Advantage + 2-Day Ops or Premier license.

High-Level ACI Design

Since you now know the ACI components and their architectural options, let's briefly discuss a practical approach to ACI design. In the early high-level design (HLD) phases of a new ACI implementation, I used to spend quite a lot of time putting together the right solution for a particular customer. Each is different, with various needs, so ask yourself (or them) the following questions:

- How many datacenters are you currently running, or planning to operate in the future with ACI?

  - Think of available 25 Pods per potential 14 ACI sites.

- Are they in a similar geographical region, or spread across the continent/world?

  - If under 50ms round-trip time (RTT) is fulfilled, you can reach for a Multi-Pod architecture; otherwise go for Multi-Site.

- Would you like to include multiple datacenter networks into a single administrative domain, or due to different reasons would you prefer their complete fault isolation?

  - The first intention leads to Multi-Pod, the second to Multi-Site.

- What about the datacenter interconnect (DCI)?

- Make sure you fulfill all the necessary functional requirements described in this chapter between your datacenters to implement either IPN or ISN networks. You can use some already present L3 services between the datacenters provided by ISPs, or maybe there will be point-to-point L2 lambda circuits available. Or you can implement your own DWDM solution on top of dark-fiber interconnect.

- I always, if possible, recommend building your own dedicated IPN/ISN network on top of L2 services based on Nexus 9000. Then you won't be limited by the supported/unsupported features and you will have assured bandwidth.

- Many times, I see multicast support as a decision maker between Multi-Pod and Multi-Site. Consider it properly before choosing one or another.

- How many racks with DC resources will you need to cover with networking infrastructure?

  - Count at least two redundant leaf switches for each rack, or alternatively for a pair of racks (if you won't require such a port density).

- What resources will you need to connect?

  - Create a list of all types of interfaces needed, including the ACI fabric itself, plus their speed, form factor, optical SFPs vs. copper RJ-45 modules, and their lengths. Often you can optimize costs using twinax or AOC Direct Attached Cables (DAC).

  - Properly scale leaf-spine uplinks as well. 2x100G wouldn't be enough for leaf switch with 32x 100G connected interfaces.

- Do you plan to dynamically insert L4-L7 services using ACI Policy Based Redirect (PBR)?

  - There are several recommendations for Multi-Site when using dynamic PBR as part of ACI service graphs. For example, you have to use an independent HA pair of devices for each site and can't stretch Active/Standby nodes between sites. In

Multi-Pod, there are no limitations. Then, to achieve symmetric traffic forwarding and especially ingress flow in Multi-Site, you have to enable host route propagation based on endpoint location.

- APIC cluster considerations

  - Based on the expected number of switches, match the optimal APIC cluster size and spread the nodes across potential Pods according to the recommendations from this chapter.

  - Choose the right size according to expected sum of managed interfaces: M3 size up to 1200, L3 for more.

  - Where suitable, deploy standby APICs to help with fabric management in case of failure.

A great way to make sure everything is in a place for ACI, and you haven't forgot something, is to draw a high-level networking schema. I prefer to use MS Visio, but there are many other (and free) tools. In the design drawing, I describe the datacenters' layout, their interconnection, the number and type of leaf-spine switches, APICs, and of course all the interfaces used between the whole infrastructure. Mark their speeds, types, used QSA adapters (QSFP to SFP) where applicable, and such. From my experience, when you see the network design schema in a front of you, you will usually realize things and connections otherwise easily missed.

At the end, when I'm satisfied with the design, I create a Bill of Materials (BoM), which is a list of all hardware and software components, licenses, and supports. Again, it's great to use an already created network schema and go device by device and interface by interface to make sure you included everything needed in the BoM.

Summary

In this chapter, you had the opportunity to explore ACI's main underlay components: a leaf-spine network based on Nexus 9000 switches and their CloudScale ASICs. You saw various ACI architectures covering multi datacenter environments, remote locations, and public cloud services and you explored ACI's centralized management plane, APIC.

In the following chapter, you will take all this theoretical knowledge gained so far and start applying it practically. You will look at how to initialize the whole fabric, register all physical switches, configure various management protocols, and prepare IPNs/ISNs to support multi datacenter communications.

## CHAPTER 3

Fabric Initialization and Management

After two mainly theoretical chapters about ACI concepts and components, you will finally get to practice this new knowledge. My goal for this chapter is to help you deploy the ACI fabric with a best practice configuration and optimize it for maximal durability, all with an emphasis on troubleshooting tools and verification commands available for effective issue resolution. You will start with a switch conversion to ACI mode, the APIC cluster initialization for either single or multi fabric deployment, followed by a dynamic fabric discovery and control plane spin up. Then, you will configure out-of-band and/or in-band management access for your infrastructure and prepare basic fabric policies (NTP, DNS, MP-BGP, Syslog, SNMP, or NetFlow). Last but not least, I will show you how to correctly configure an Inter-Pod network consisting of Nexus 9000 devices in standalone NX-OS mode.

For the next sections, let's assume you have already done the entire hardware racking and cabling, your switches and APICs are properly connected to the management network(s) mentioned in the previous chapter, and you have physical access to all equipment. Now you are ready to start the ACI configuration itself.

Nexus 9000 in ACI Switch Mode

If the switch should run in a centrally managed ACI mode, it has to boot a special image. Devices ordered initially for an ACI use case are directly shipped from a factory with the correct image. However, many times you need to convert a previously standalone NX-OS switch to ACI manually, either during a migration phase or as a result of troubleshooting. Often a failure to discover switches by APIC is caused just because the incorrect image is running in them.

© Jan Janovic 2023
J. Janovic, *Cisco ACI: Zero to Hero*, https://doi.org/10.1007/978-1-4842-8838-2_3

To make it simple, Cisco provides exactly the same ACI file for each Nexus 9000 model and you can directly obtain it from the Cisco Software Download page together with APIC firmware: `https://software.cisco.com/`. It requires an account linked with a service contract. The file naming convention has the structure shown in Figure 3-1.

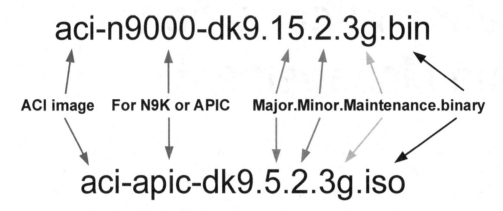

Figure 3-1. *ACI images naming convention.*

The APIC version should ideally be the same or newer than the switches in your fabric. A major version is released around once per year and there are significant features introduced, such as various user interface improvements or new hardware generation support. Then there are several minor updates per year, also enabling new features and hardware support, fixing a bigger number of issues, and so on. Maintenance releases are published one to two times per month and they fix mainly open bugs and identified security vulnerabilities.

At the time of writing this book, we have two long-lived recommended version trains with assured vendor support for the upcoming period. If you don't have any reason to use other version, make sure to implement one of these:

- ACI 4.2

- ACI 5.2

When you hover your mouse over a particular file on the download page, in the Details popup you will find the MD5 or SHA512 hash. By comparing one of these hashes with the uploaded file in the Nexus switch, you can avoid issues with image integrity resulting in problems with booting itself.

Conversion From NX-OS to ACI Mode

Let's now upload the ACI image to a Nexus switch. From my point of view, if you have physical access to the device, the easiest way is to use a USB stick formatted as FAT16 or FAT32 and a console cable to access the command-line interface (CLI).

- Plug the USB stick in switch and verify its content using `dir usb1:` or `dir usb2:`.

- Copy the image from the USB stick to the switch with `copy usb1:<aci-image-name>.bin bootflash:`.

- Disable booting NX-OS with `switch(config)# no boot nxos`.

- Enable ACI boot: `switch(config)# boot aci bootflash:<aci-image-name>.bin`.

- Save the configuration with `copy running-config startup-config`.

- Reload with `switch# reload`.

After Nexus wakes up in ACI mode for the first time, there is one more and often neglected step: setting boot variables to ensure that even after the reload it is still in ACI mode. An unregistered ACI switch allows you to log in using the admin user without a password.

```
User Access Verification
(none) login: admin
*************************************************************************
*
    Fabric discovery in progress, show commands are not fully functional
    Logout and Login after discovery to continue to use show commands.
*************************************************************************
*
```

1. After logging in, issue `setup-bootvars <aci-image>.bin`.

Alternatively, you can use some transfer protocol (e.g., SCP or SFTP) to upload the ACI image remotely. The prerequisite is to have already working IP connectivity to the switch management interface.

2. Enable the SCP server feature on the Nexus switch with `switch (config)# feature scp-server`.

3. Install a SCP client of your choice to your working machine if not already present. On Windows, I prefer Putty SCP (PSCP).

4. Open a command line in the working directory and `pscp.exe -scp <aci-image-name>.bin <username>@<IP>:<destination_ filename>.bin`

5. Continue with Step 2 of the previous instructions.

Note   After this NX-OS conversion, ACI can sometimes notify you about degraded switch health due to a mismatch of BIOS and FPGA firmware versions compared with the main ACI image. This is not an issue from the short-term perspective. It will be fixed during the next standard upgrade administered by APIC. You can avoid this by converting a switch to version N-1 vs. currently running on APIC and upgrade it right away after the registration to fabric.

APIC Cluster Initialization

After making sure every switch in your infrastructure has a correct ACI image running, you can move to APIC initialization. As you already know, APIC is basically a Cisco UCS server with a Cisco Integrated Management Controller (CIMC) configuration interface. CIMC represents both graphical (HTTP/S) and command-line (SSH) server management and diagnostic tools and is always available (if at least one server's power supply is connected to the grid) through a dedicated physical server interface. I recommend connecting the CIMC interface to a separate out-of-band infrastructure to ensure APIC manageability even in case of any failure related to standard APIC management interfaces. For such a purpose, CIMC offers server console access over HTTP/S (called vKVM), which you can use over a LAN, without the need for a physical keyboard and monitor connected to the server. Because of these obvious advantages, the first step of APIC provisioning is the configuration of CIMC IP network parameters.

Start with connecting a keyboard to USB and a monitor to the VGA interface of an APIC. Turn on the server, and during its bootup, keep pressing F8 to enter the CIMC configuration utility (shown in Figure 3-2).

```
Cisco IMC Configuration Utility Version 2.0  Cisco Systems, Inc.
*****************************************************************************
NIC Properties
 NIC mode                              NIC redundancy
  Dedicated:        [X]                 None:               [X]
  Shared LOM:       [ ]                 Active-standby:     [ ]
  Cisco Card:                           Active-active:      [ ]
   Riser1:          [ ]                VLAN (Advanced)
   Riser2:          [ ]                 VLAN enabled:       [ ]
   MLom:            [ ]                 VLAN ID:            1
  Shared LOM Ext:   [ ]                 Priority:           0
IP (Basic)
  IPV4:             [X]       IPV6:   [ ]
  DHCP enabled      [ ]
  CIMC IP:          10.17.89.147
  Prefix/Subnet:    255.255.255.0
  Gateway:          10.17.89.1
  Pref DNS Server:  0.0.0.0


*****************************************************************************
<Up/Down>Selection   <F10>Save   <Space>Enable/Disable   <F5>Refresh   <ESC>Exit
<F1>Additional settings
```

Figure 3-2. *CIMC configuration utility*

Make sure that *NIC Mode* is set to *Dedicated, NIC Redundancy* to *None*, configure the IPv4 properties, and optionally VLAN if used. Press F10 to save the configuration and exit the CIMC utility with ESC.

After the APIC reboot, you can either continue using the keyboard and monitor or connect to the CIMC IP configured recently and enter the Virtual KVM console (see Figure 3-3).

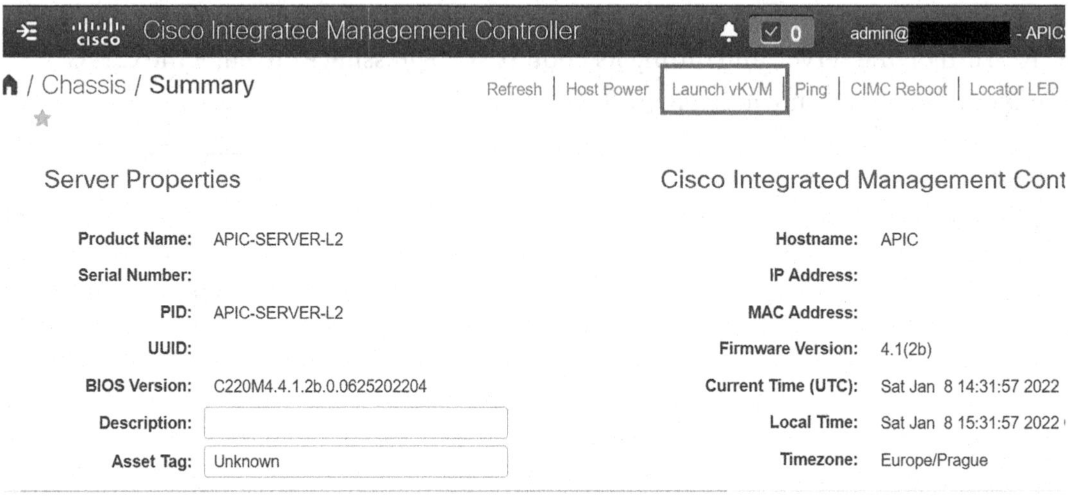

Figure 3-3. *CIMC vKVM console APIC access*

Whichever way you choose, APIC without any initial configuration in the factory default state will offer you a **configuration wizard**. Filling in its fields is a key step to configure APIC for single or Multi-Pod operation.

In the following section, I'll explain each configuration parameter in more detail (with default values in brackets):

Fabric name (ACI Fabric1)

Common name for the ACI fabric and APIC cluster. Has to be configured consistently for all nodes of a single cluster.

Fabric ID (1)

Consistent ID across all APICs of a particular fabric. Cannot be changed unless you perform a factory reset.

Number of active controllers (3)

Initial expected APIC cluster size. Production fabric should have at least three nodes due to database sharding and data replication. However, you can later change its size both ways: up and down. In a lab, it's perfectly fine to use only one APIC node. If you are increasing the size of a cluster, add the next available controller ID. On the other hand, when removing a cluster member, remove the highest one.

Pod ID (1)

This field will become significant when deploying ACI Multi-Pod. Set it according to the Pod where this APIC will be connected.

Standby controller (NO)

If this is a standby controller, set this field to YES.

Standby controller ID (20)

Unique ID for each standby APIC (this option is present only after declaring this APIC standby). This is only a temporary controller ID and later it will be changed to the node ID of APIC, which is replaced by this standby node.

Controller ID (1)

Standard ID for each APIC node. Make sure it's unique among the cluster.

Standalone APIC Cluster (NO)

Since version 5.2(1), you can connect an APIC cluster not only to leaf switches directly, but also to a Multi-Pod IPN network. If this is your case, set YES here. A combination of both options is not supported, though. I will cover this topic later in the chapter.

Controller name (apic1)

Hostname of this APIC

TEP Pool (10.0.0.0/16, minimal /23)

A pool of IP addresses used for dynamic VTEP assignments for each APIC node, leaf-spine switches, vPC domain, or external entities like remote leaves and integrated ACI CNI plugin in Kubernetes nodes.

If you are wondering how large this pool should be, take into consideration the way APIC assigns VTEP addresses. APIC splits the VTEP pool into multiple /27 subnets (32 IPs in each) and if some VTEP IP is needed for any use case, APIC will use one IP from a particular randomly chosen /27 subnet. Another address is assigned from the next random /27 subnet. Therefore, with /16 subnet, you get 2^{27-16} subnets so 2048 x /27 pools, 2048 of addressable entities. This is more than enough for any supported ACI deployment.

In an ACI Multi-Pod environment, you need the a unique TEP pool for each Pod. However, when initially configuring APICs in Multi-Pod, use the same TEP pool belonging to the initial "seed" Pod 1 on all of them. You will set the correct TEP pool for remote Pods later in the GUI. When it comes to APIC servers themselves, they always get the first IP addresses from the Pod 1 TEP pool, regardless of the actual Pod where they are connected. I will describe Multi-Pod configuration and the discovery process later in this chapter.

Make sure not to overlap the VTEP pool with any other subnet used in your production network. Not from a functional point of view, but you won't be able to access APIC OOB management from IPs inside such a subnet. Although APIC receives the incoming packets on its management interface, the reply is routed back to the fabric due to the installed TEP pool static route.

Finally, avoid configuring 172.17.0.0/16 as the TEP pool. This one is already used by default for internal Docker networking between APIC nodes to run additional installable APIC apps.

Infrastructure VLAN (4093)

Dedicated VLAN used between APIC and leaf switches (or IPN since 5.2(1)). There are integration use cases (e.g., Kubernetes) when this VLAN is extended further from ACI to servers or blade chassis, so make sure it's not overlapping with any already existing VLANs in your network. Infra VLAN cannot be changed later unless a factory reset is performed.

IP pool for bridge domain multicast address (GIPo) (225.0.0.0/15)

Each created bridge domain (L2 segment in ACI) will be assigned with one multicast group address from this pool to ensure delivery of multi-destination traffic across ACI fabric. Different Pods must have this pool consistently set. A valid range for GIPo addresses is 225.0.0.0/15 to 231.254.0.0/15 and mask /15 is mandatory.

Out-of-band configuration (-)

Fill in the IP address, mask, default gateway, and speed/duplex configuration of APIC management interfaces. APIC's main GUI will be reachable via this IP. Each APIC node has to have unique management IP address, of course.

Strong password (Y)

Enforce stronger username passwords.

Administrator password

Initial admin password, can be changed later using the GUI or CLI.

Note   If your APIC was for any reason already preconfigured, or the person configuring it made a mistake and you would like to return the server to the factory default state and initiate again the configuration wizard, issue the following commands after logging into the APIC console:

```
apic# acidiag touch clean

This command will wipe out this device. Proceed? [y/N] y

apic# acidiag touch setup

This command will reset the device configuration,
Proceed? [y/N] y

apic# acidiag reboot
```

Congratulations! After entering all the initial configuration parameters on all your APIC nodes, they are ready to discover a fabric, register the switches, and form a cluster. If your out-of-band connectivity is already up and working, try opening the management IP address configured in a previous step in a web browser (Chrome and Firefox are fully supported). You should get the initial APIC login screen shown in Figure 3-4. By entering the initial admin credentials, you can enter the main ACI dashboard.

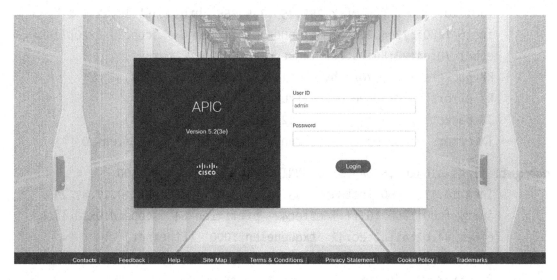

Figure 3-4. *APIC login screen*

Tip   To simply show and review all the configured values from the initial script, issue following command:

```
apic# cat /data/data_admin/sam_exported.config
```

At the same time, you can use Secure Shell (SSH) to access APIC's CLI on a management IP. Log in there and verify its network configuration by issuing the ifconfig command. See Listing 3-1.

Listing 3-1. APIC CLI Network Verification

```
apic1# ifconfig
bond0: flags=5187<UP,BROADCAST,RUNNING,MASTER,MULTICAST>  mtu 1500
        inet6 fe80::72e4:22ff:fe86:3a0d  prefixlen 64  scopeid 0x20<link>
        ether 70:e4:22:86:3a:0d  txqueuelen 1000  (Ethernet)
        RX packets 346486101  bytes 121947233810 (113.5 GiB)
        RX errors 0  dropped 0  overruns 0  frame 0
        TX packets 325970996  bytes 131644580111 (122.6 GiB)
        TX errors 0  dropped 0 overruns 0  carrier 0  collisions 0

bond0.3967: flags=4163<UP,BROADCAST,RUNNING,MULTICAST>  mtu 1496
        inet 10.11.0.1  netmask 255.255.255.255  broadcast 10.11.0.1
        inet6 fe80::72e4:22ff:fe86:3a0d  prefixlen 64  scopeid 0x20<link>
        ether 70:e4:22:86:3a:0d  txqueuelen 1000  (Ethernet)
        RX packets 302179702  bytes 112540443339 (104.8 GiB)
        RX errors 0  dropped 0  overruns 0  frame 0
        TX packets 273578739  bytes 126011698192 (117.3 GiB)
        TX errors 0  dropped 0 overruns 0  carrier 0  collisions 0

oobmgmt: flags=4163<UP,BROADCAST,RUNNING,MULTICAST>  mtu 1500
        inet 10.17.87.60  netmask 255.255.255.0  broadcast 10.17.87.255
        inet6 fe80::86b2:61ff:fec2:ec42  prefixlen 64  scopeid 0x20<link>
        ether 84:b2:61:c2:ec:42  txqueuelen 1000  (Ethernet)
        RX packets 1420543  bytes 386781638 (368.8 MiB)
        RX errors 0  dropped 0  overruns 0  frame 0
        TX packets 977860  bytes 674575237 (643.3 MiB)
        TX errors 0  dropped 0 overruns 0  carrier 0  collisions 0
```

The **oobmgmt** interface is used for the current SSH session as well as GUI and API services. The subinterface configured on top of the **Bond0** interface always represents the main data channel between APIC and leaf switches for management plane traffic (LLDP, DHCP, Opflex, etc.). It uses VTEP IP addresses from the initially specified pool and Infra VLAN dot1q encapsulation.

Graphical User Interface Overview

After logging into the APIC GUI, on the main dashboard you can see the overall system health score, a table on the right side summarizes problems with the ACI platform represented by faults, or you can check the status of your APIC controller cluster in the bottom part.

As you can see in Figure 3-5, APIC has two main horizontal navigation menus in the upper part of the GUI used for configuration and monitoring of the whole platform.

Figure 3-5. *APIC dashboard*

Individual menu items are summarized in the following section, and you will learn about most of them gradually through the book.

1. **System**: Global configuration and overview of a whole platform

   • **Quickstart**: First-time setup wizard with links to the most important documentation whitepapers

   • **Dashboard**: Default page after logging into APIC, providing an overview of the system health

   • **Controllers**: Detailed information about individual APICs, their current state, and configuration policies related to their monitoring, tech support collecting, and local log retention

- **System Settings**: Global ACI configuration settings related to various aspects of fabric operation. I will touch on the most important ones during initial fabric configuration in this chapter.

- **Smart Licensing**: Configuration of Smart Software Licensing for the ACI

- **Faults**: Overall list of currently visible problems in your ACI fabric

- **History**: Local log database consisting of Faults, Events, Audit Logs, Session Logs, and Health Logs

- **Config Zones**: Feature allowing you to divide ACI switches into smaller configuration zones to avoid pushing a particular configuration change to the whole fabric at the same time. Not so commonly used from my experience, though.

- **Active Sessions**: List of currently connected users to all APICs in your cluster

- **Security**: Overview of applied ACI security policies and contracts

2. **Tenants**: ACI configuration of logical policies, abstracted from physical network such as tenants, VRFs, bridge domains, application policies, EPGs, contracts, external connectivity (L2/L3OUT), and more

   - **ALL**: List of all available and visible ACI tenants for the currently logged user. Clicking a particular tenant opens its configuration.

   - **Add Tenant**: Used for creating a new ACI tenant

   - **Tenant Search**: Full-text tenant name search

3. **Fabric**: Discovery, configuration, and monitoring of ACI underlay physical leaf-spine fabric

   - **Inventory**: Here you can verify the status of the whole ACI network for all Pods, create new Pods, or register new switches into ACI fabric.

   - **Fabric Policies**: This settings affecting the whole ACI fabric, global switch policies, and leaf-spine uplink configuration options.

- **Access Policies**: All the settings related to the host-facing leaf interfaces. These policies are crucial in ACI to enable end-host connectivity of any type through the fabric. I dedicate Chapter 4 to this topic.

4. **Virtual Networking**: Section for Virtual Machine Managers (VMM) integrations

   - **Kubernetes**, **Rancher RKE, Openshift, OpenStack, Microsoft, Red Hat, VMware, VMware SDN**: Besides the main ACI leaf/spine fabric, APIC is able to configure and monitor networking in these virtualization platforms as well. In Chapter 9, I cover VMware and Kubernetes integrations.

5. **Admin**: Various system administration tasks and configuration

   - **AAA**: Policies related to local and remote user authentication, authorization, and accounting as well as role-based access control (RBAC) settings

   - **Schedulers**: Backup or upgrade scheduling for ACI fabric

   - **Firmware**: Firmware repository and upgrade management of ACI controllers and switches

   - **External Data Collectors**: Remote server configuration for Callhome, SNMP, Syslog, and TACACS protocols

   - **Config Rollbacks**: Local backup and rollback features

   - **Import/Export**: Configuration export and import policies, tech support, and core file export

6. **Operations**: Section with tools simplifying troubleshooting and providing visibility info for the utilization of ACI

   - **Visibility and Troubleshooting**: This utility takes source and destination information about endpoints in the ACI fabric (MACs, IPs, or VM names) and analyzes their mutual communication such as endpoint locations, forwarding decisions, applied security policies (contracts), interface drops, traceroute, SPAN, and more.

- **Capacity Dashboard**: Overview of actual TCAM utilization of ACI switches with regards to the whole fabric scalability as well

- **EP Tracker**: Simple tool to locate any learned endpoint in the ACI fabric providing information about its source leaf interface, encapsulation, VRF, and EPG, with historic state transitions entries

- **Visualization**: Configuration of atomic counters allowing you to analyze the number of packets, drops, and latencies between all the switches in the ACI fabric

7. **Apps**: Additional applications expanding the capabilities of APIC, downloadable from Cisco's official DC Appstore. All of them run containerized on the Docker platform inside the APIC cluster.

   - **Installed Apps**: Currently installed and running additional applications

   - **Faults**: List of problems (if any) with installed applications

   - **Downloads**: Online file repository accessible through the APIC URL

8. **Integrations**: Additional APIC integration capabilities with Cisco UCS Manager and VMware vRealize

Along with these main menu items, you will find many configuration objects and policies in the left blue panel arranged in a tree hierarchy (as shown in Figure 3-6). Individual policies usually have their default object present and used by ACI in case you haven't created any of your own. To add a new object, just right-click the parent folder where the object should belong and fill in the related object form.

Figure 3-6. *APIC configuration objects*

Fabric Discovery and Registration

After entering the ACI GUI and checking that your APIC is in the *Fully Fit* state on the dashboard, you should get to the **Fabric-Inventory -> Fabric Membership-Nodes Pending Registration** tab.

If ACI switches and APICs are correctly cabled, you will see the first leaf switch here with its serial number. Right-click the entry and register it to the fabric (as shown in Figure 3-7). Fill in the mandatory Pod ID, Node ID, and Node Name (hostname). The switch will subsequently get its VTEP IP from a chosen Pod's TEP pool.

Figure 3-7. *ACI switch discovery and registration*

Pay close attention to the Node ID field. The Node ID can go from 101 to 4000, and it represents a unique ACI switch identifier used as a reference to this device in various ACI policies all around the system. If you want to configure an interface, some switch feature, routing, or create a static mapping for an endpoint behind this switch, you will always refer to its Node ID, not its hostname or a serial number. Additionally, be aware that you cannot change it later without returning the switch to the factory default state and rediscovering it once again. Therefore, it is crucial to prepare a "naming" (or better, numbering) convention for the whole ACI fabric beforehand.

If the amount of leaf switches per Pod won't exceed 80, you can use following convention:

- Leaf Switch: 101-190 (POD1), 201-290 (POD2), 301-390 (POD3), etc.

- Spine Switch:> 191-199 (POD1), 291-299(POD2), 391-399 (POD3), etc.

For larger deployments (let's assume 200 leaves per Pod) it can go like this:

- Leaf Switch: 200-399 (POD1), 400-599 (POD2), 600-799 (POD3), etc.

- Spine Switch: 110-119 (POD1), 121-129(POD2), 131-139 (POD3), etc.

After all, these numbering and naming decisions are completely up to you and your preference. Just try to make them simple. It will ease ACI troubleshooting and operation later.

After a successful registration, the switch should be automatically moved to the **Registered Nodes** tab and be provisioned by APIC. There you can check that it has received its VTEP IP address and the switch status is **Active** (see Figure 3-8).

Fabric Membership

| Registered Nodes | Nodes Pending Registration | Unreachable Nodes | Unmanaged Fabric Nodes | Auto Firmware Update |

| 4 Leafs | ● 0 Decommissioned ● 0 Maintenance ● 4 Active ● 0 Inactive | 0 Virtual Leafs | ● 0 Decommissioned ● 0 Maintenance ● 0 Active ● 0 Inactive | 2 Spines | ● 0 Decommissioned ● 0 Maintenance ● 2 Active ● 0 Inactive | 0 Virtual Spines | ● 0 Decommissioned ● 0 Maintenance ● 0 Active ● 0 Inactive |

Serial Number	Model	Pod ID	Node ID	Name	Node Type	▾ IP	Maintenance Mode	Status
FDO25...	N9K-C9332C	2	299	Spine-299	Spine	10.22.184.64/32	No	Active
FDO22...	N9K-C93240YC...	2	201	Leaf-201	Leaf	10.22.0.64/32	No	Active
FDO22...	N9K-C93240YC...	1	102	Leaf-102	Leaf	10.11.96.66/32	No	Active
FDO25...	N9K-C9332C	1	199	Spine-199	Spine	10.11.96.65/32	No	Active
FDO22...	N9K-C93240YC...	1	101	Leaf-101	Leaf	10.11.72.64/32	No	Active

Figure 3-8. *Registered nodes in the ACI fabric*

In case of need, you can even **pre-provision** a currently non-existing switch in the ACI fabric. Here at the **Registered Nodes** tab, just click the ✕▾ symbol and choose *Create Fabric Member Node*. After filling in the Pod ID, serial number, node ID, and hostname, this switch will pop up in Nodes Pending Registration, but without the need for a manual registration later. You can further refer to its NodeID in all the policies around ACI as for an already available switch. After its discovery, it will be automatically configured according to the existing policies and added to the fabric without your intervention.

ACI Switch Discovery

Let's have a look at what is happening behind the scenes during the discovery. The following steps are taken for each discovered ACI switch:

1. At the beginning, the discovery process relies on the Link Level Discovery Protocol (LLDP). LLDP is sent over the APIC fabric interfaces with specific type-length-value (TLVs) fields, containing information about InfraVLAN and the role being set to "APIC."

2. The ACI switch will, according to the LLDP information, program InfraVLAN on all interfaces behind which it sees APICs.

3. The switch starts sending DHCP Discover messages over InfraVLAN to APIC. At this moment, you will automatically see its presence in the ACI GUI, as described in the previous section.

4. The ACI administrator proceeds with a switch registration and, according to the chosen Pod, APIC will reply with the DHCP offer and finish the DHCP process by assigning a new VTEP IP to the discovered switch.

5. In the Fabric Membership section, you can create an Auto Firmware Update Policy for new devices. Using DHCP Bootfile-name Option (67), APIC will instruct the ACI switch from where to download a boot script. Inside, a switch will find an instruction on how to download firmware and proceed with an automatic upgrade/downgrade of the desired version.

6. Finally, using the Intra Fabric Messaging (IFM) software layer, the whole configuration policy is downloaded to the switch and its control plane is configured accordingly. IFM is the main method to deliver any system messages between software components internally within APIC as well as between APIC and leaf switches.

The first leaf switch discovery process is shown in Figure 3-9. Analogically it applies to others, not directly to connected switches with APIC; just the broadcast DHCP messages are relayed to APIC using unicast packets.

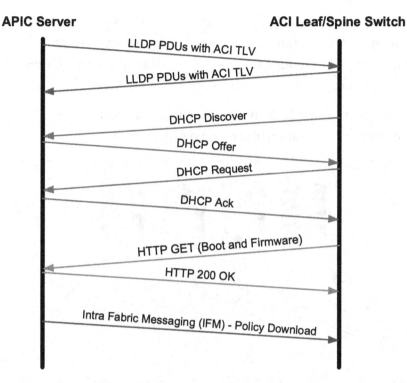

Figure 3-9. *Discovery process between APIC and ACI leaf/spine switch*

Now, since you have discovered and provisioned the first leaf switch, the discovery process continues similarly with the rest of the fabric within a particular Pod (see Figure 3-10):

1. First switch discovery, as described in the previous section

2. The discovery process continues between the first leaf and all spine switches. LLDP runs on their fabric interfaces and the first leaf automatically relays spine DHCP Discover messages to APIC. After the spine nodes registration, APIC ensures their VTEP address assignment and provisioning.

3. Then the rest of leaves in a particular Pod can be discovered, registered, and provisioned.

4. As soon as you identify the other APIC cluster members via LLDP behind the leaf interfaces, the leaf will install a static host /32 route in the IS-IS routing table pointing to the APIC VTEP address and therefore the first member can cluster with them.

5. If configured properly, APICs form a consistent cluster with synchronous replication of the whole ACI database.

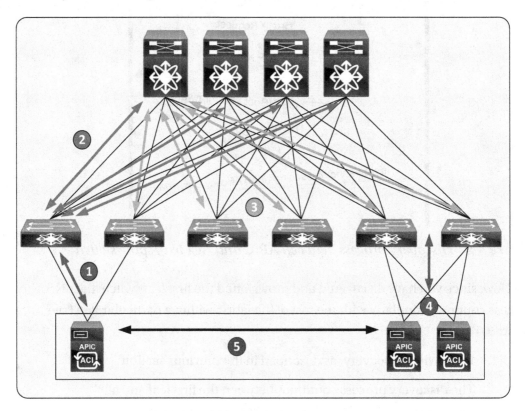

Figure 3-10. *ACI single-fabric discovery*

Multi-Pod Fabric Discovery

What about a fabric discovery in Multi-Pod ACI? All of your APICs should be initialized with consistent information except for the Pod ID, which is set according to the real APIC placement. For the next section, let's assume you already have an Inter-Pod Network (IPN) configured correctly and working.

For Multi-Pod discovery, you choose a "seed" Pod, the initial Pod that is completely discovered first and from which the discovery of all others is made. The TEP pool in initial APIC scripts should always be set to this seed Pod. Even when some APIC is connected to a non-seed Pod, it will still have a seed Pod VTEP IP address. The overall Multi-Pod discovery process then follows these steps (as depicted in Figure 3-11):

1. The first leaf switch is discovered and provisioned in the seed Pod.

2. The rest of the fabric in the seed Pod is discovered and the spine switches configure their IPN-facing interfaces and activate forwarding with an appropriate routing protocol in place over the VLAN 4 subinterface. The prefix of a seed Pod TEP pool is propagated to IPN, and PIM Bidir adjacencies are created.

3. Even though they aren't forwarding any data yet, spine switches from other Pods are sending at least DHCP Discover messages on their IPN-facing subinterfaces in VLAN 4. IPN routers, thanks to the configured DHCP relay, proxy these messages to APIC in the first Pod (using unicast), and the remote spines are discovered.

4. After their registration, the Multi-Pod control plane is provisioned (MP-BGP peerings between spines) and the rest of the remote Pod switches are discovered following the same process as for the seed Pod.

5. When the remote APIC is detected by LLDP behind remote Pod leaves, the switch installs, as usual, a static host route (/32) to APIC's VTEP address (bond0.xxxx). This prefix is automatically propagated to spines via IS-IS, redistributed to MP-BGP, and sent to all other Pods including the seed one.

6. Based on this routing information, seed APICs can open TCP sessions to remote APICs and create a consistent cluster with them. However, keep in mind the 50ms round-trip time (RTT) limitation for this to work reliably.

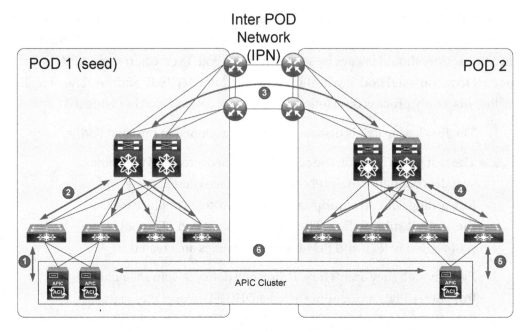

Figure 3-11. *Multi-Pod ACI fabric discovery*

For more detailed information about how the IPN should be configured to provide all the necessary functions for ACI Multi-Pod and to ensure dynamic discovery, please refer to the last section in this chapter.

ACI Switch Discovery Troubleshooting

ACI fabric discovery and provisioning is a highly automated process (except for the manual registration step), so what if something goes wrong? How can we identify the problem if the switch isn't being discovered and visible in the *Nodes Pending Registration* screen?

Fortunately, ACI features a diverse set of useful troubleshooting tools for all its operational aspects. In case of failing switch discovery, you will have to obtain console access to the affected device. Either physically connect the serial cable to the console port of the N9K or implement some sort of remotely accessible terminal server (which I highly recommend when deploying ACI for the production environment).

When logging into the console of an unregistered switch running the ACI image, you can use the **admin** user without any password. Then, to identify the problem with discovery, issue the following command: show discoveryissues. It will provide you with a comprehensive output including a set of 16 checks (in ACI version 5.2.3), precisely analyzing every step related to the ongoing discovery. Not all checks have to be necessarily passed in order for the whole process to succeed (as you can see in Listing 3-2).

Listing 3-2. Show discoveryissues From a Sucessfully Registered ACI Switch

```
leaf-101# show discoveryissues
==============================================================================
Check 1 Platform Type
==============================================================================
Test01 Retrieving Node
Role                                                                    PASSED
      [Info] Current node role: LEAF
      [Info] Please check CH09 DHCP status section for configured node role
==============================================================================
Check 2 FPGA/BIOS in sync test
==============================================================================
Test01 FPGA version check                                              PASSED
      [Info] No issues found for FPGA versions
Test02 BIOS version check                                              FAILED
      [Error] Error occurred while parsing through firmwareCompRunning MOs
==============================================================================
Check 3 HW Modules Check
==============================================================================
Test01 Fans status check                                              PASSED
      [Info] All fans status is ok
Test02 Power Supply status check                                      FAILED
      [Warn] Operational state of sys/ch/psuslot-1/psu is: shut
      [Info] Ignore this if it is a redundant power supply
Test03 Fan Tray status check                                          PASSED
      [Info] All FanTrays status is ok
Test04 Line Card status check                                         PASSED
      [Info] All LineCard status is ok
==============================================================================
```

Check 4 Node Version

```
=============================================================================
```

Test01 Check Current
Version   PASSED
    [Info] Node current running version is : n9000-15.2(3e)

```
=============================================================================
```

Check 5 System State

```
=============================================================================
```

Test01 Check System State   PASSED
    [Info] TopSystem State is : in-service

```
=============================================================================
```

Check 6 Updated LLDP Adjacencies

```
=============================================================================
```

Port: eth1/60
  Test02 Wiring Issues Check   PASSED
      [Info] No Wiring Issues detected
  Test03 Port Types Check   PASSED
      [Info] No issues with port type, type is:fab
  Test04 Port Mode Check   PASSED
      [Info] No issues with port mode, type is:routed
  Test02 Adjacency Check   PASSED
      [Info] Adjacency detected with spine
Port: eth1/1
  Test02 Wiring Issues Check   PASSED
      [Info] No Wiring Issues detected
  Test03 Port Types Check   PASSED
      [Info] No issues with port type, type is:leaf
  Test04 Port Mode Check   PASSED
      [Info] No issues with port mode, type is:trunk
  Test02 Adjacency Check   PASSED
      [Info] Adjacency detected with APIC
Port: eth1/2
  Test02 Wiring Issues Check   PASSED
      [Info] No Wiring Issues detected
  Test03 Port Types Check   PASSED

```
                [Info] No issues with port type, type is:leaf
      Test04 Port Mode Check                                       PASSED
                [Info] No issues with port mode, type is:trunk
      Test02 Adjacency Check                                       PASSED
                [Info] Adjacency detected with APIC
===============================================================================
Check 7 BootStrap Status
===============================================================================
Test01 Check Bootstrap/L3Out config download                      FAILED
      [Warn] BootStrap/L3OutConfig URL not found
      [Info] Ignore this if this node is not an IPN attached device
===============================================================================
Check 8 Infra VLAN Check
===============================================================================
Test01 Check if infra VLAN is received                            PASSED
      [Info] Infra VLAN received is : 3967
Test02 Check if infra VLAN is deployed                            PASSED
      [Info] Infra VLAN deployed successfully
===============================================================================
Check 9 DHCP Status
===============================================================================
Test01 Check Node Id                                              PASSED
      [Info] Node Id received is : 101
Test02 Check Node Name                                            PASSED
      [Info] Node name received is : leaf-101
Test03 Check TEP IP                                               PASSED
      [Info] TEP IP received is : 10.11.72.64
Test04 Check Configured Node Role                                 PASSED
      [Info] Configured Node Role received is : LEAF
===============================================================================
Check 10 IS-IS Adj Info
===============================================================================
Test01 check IS-IS adjacencies                                    PASSED
      [Info] IS-IS adjacencies found on interfaces:
      [Info] eth1/60.13
```

```
================================================================================
Check 11 Reachability to APIC
================================================================================
Test01 Ping check to APIC                                              PASSED
     [Info] Ping to APIC IP 10.11.0.2 from 10.11.72.64 successful
================================================================================
Check 12 BootScript Status
================================================================================
Test01 Check BootScript download                                      PASSED
     [Info] BootScript successfully downloaded at
2022-03-10T10:29:17.418+01:00 from URL http://10.11.0.2:7777/fwrepo/boot/
node-FD022160HJ7
================================================================================
Check 13 SSL Check
================================================================================
Test01 Check SSL certificate validity                                 PASSED
     [Info] SSL certificate validation successful
================================================================================
Check 14 AV Details
================================================================================
Test01 Check AV details                                               PASSED
     [Info] AppId: 1  address: 10.11.0.1  registered: YES
     [Info] AppId: 2  address: 10.11.0.2  registered: YES
     [Info] AppId: 3  address: 10.11.0.3  registered: YES
================================================================================
Check 15 Policy Download
================================================================================
Test01 Policy download status                                         PASSED
     [Info] Registration to all shards complete
     [Info] Policy download is complete
     [Info] PconsBootStrap MO in complete state
```

```
================================================================================
Check 16 Version Check
================================================================================
Test01 Check Switch and APIC Version                                    PASSED
     [Info] Switch running version is : n9000-15.2(3e)
     [Info] APIC running version is : 5.2(3e)
```

When you hit any issues during the discovery phase, focus your attention on these main areas:

- LLDP adjacencies

- Infra VLAN installation

- DHCP for VTEP IP provisioning

- SSL certificate validity

- Switch node bootstrapping

- Firmware versions

For LLDP, you can use the simple show command and compare the output with the cabling matrix used during the hardware installation phase. So far, all problems I've seen related to LLDP are from in misconnected ACI underlay cabling. See Listing 3-3.

Listing 3-3. LLDP Verification

```
(none)# show lldp neighbors
Capability codes:
(R) Router, (B) Bridge, (T) Telephone, (C) DOCSIS Cable Device
(W) WLAN Access Point, (P) Repeater, (S) Station, (O) Other
Device ID        Local Intf    Hold-time    Capability    Port ID
apic1            Eth1/1        120                        eth2-1
apic2            Eth1/2        120                        eth2-1
switch           Eth1/59       120          BR            Eth1/31
switch           Eth1/60       120          BR            Eth1/31
Total entries displayed: 4
```

If this is the first leaf to be discovered, and it's not appearing in APIC GUI or you don't see any APIC in its LLDP neighbors, you can check the protocol from the APIC point of view as well using the acidiag run lldptool out eth2-1 and acidiag run lldptool in eth2-1 commands. These outputs will provide you with detailed information about the entire sent and received LLDP TLVs.

After getting LLDP running, Infra VLAN should be announced to the switches, installed in their VLAN database, and configured on interfaces facing APICs. To check that it happened, use the commands shown in Listing 3-4.

Listing 3-4. Infra VLAN Installation

```
(none)# moquery -c lldpInst
Total Objects shown: 1
# lldp.Inst
adminSt : enabled
childAction :
ctrl :
dn : sys/lldp/inst
holdTime : 120
infraVlan : 3967

(none)# show vlan encap-id 3967
VLAN Name                             Status    Ports
---- -------------------------------- --------- -------------------
8    infra:default                    active    Eth1/1
```

In case of any problem with an Infra VLAN or wiring in general, try also verifying the useful output shown in Listing 3-5.

Listing 3-5. LLDP Wiring Issues

```
(none)# moquery -c lldpIf -f 'lldp.If.wiringIssues!=""'
Total Objects shown: 1
# lldp.If id : eth1/1
adminRxSt : enabled
adminSt : enabled
adminTxSt : enabled
```

```
childAction :
descr :
dn : sys/lldp/inst/if-[eth1/1]
lcOwn : local
mac : 70:0F:6A:B2:99:CF
modTs : 2022-03-10T10:27:04.254+01:00
monPolDn : uni/fabric/monfab-default
rn : if-[eth1/1]
status :
sysDesc :
wiringIssues : infra-vlan-mismatch
```

Next, should the switch indicate an inability to receive an IP from APIC, check if the DHCP process is running by using the well-known tcpdump Linux utility. Interface kpm_inb stands for a switch's CPU in-band channel for all control plane traffic. This approach can be useful in general when troubleshooting any control plane protocols (such as LACP, dynamic routing, COOP, and monitoring protocols). See Listing 3-6.

Listing 3-6. DHCP Troubleshooting

```
(none)# tcpdump -ni kpm_inb port 67 or 68
tcpdump: verbose output suppressed, use -v or -vv for full protocol decode
listening on kpm_inb, link-type EN10MB (Ethernet), capture size 65535 bytes
16:40:11.041148 IP 0.0.0.0.68 > 255.255.255.255.67: BOOTP/DHCP, Request
from a0:36:9f:c7:a1:0c, length 300
^C
1 packets captured
1 packets received by filter
0 packets dropped by kernel
```

To ensure security for all control plane traffic between ACI nodes, it uses SSL encryption. The certificate for this purpose is generated based on a device serial number during the manufacturing and it's burned into a specialized hardware chip. The commands shown in Listing 3-7 let you review the content of a certificate subject, and with the -date flag, they allow you to verify its time validity. Any issue with SSL can be resolved only in cooperation with a technical assistance engineer directly from Cisco.

Listing 3-7. SSL Certificate Verification – Correct Subject Format

```
(none)# cd /securedata/ssl && openssl x509 -noout -subject -in server.crt
subject= /serialNumber=PID:N9K-C93180YC-FX SN:FDOxxxxxxxx/CN=FDOxxxxxxxx
```

Note Previous commands will work only on undiscovered and unregistered nodes.

After the switch obtains IP connectivity with APIC, it should download its policies and acknowledge that this process is successfully completed. The actual state of bootstrapping can be verified by querying the following object, shown in Listing 3-8.

Listing 3-8. ACI Switch Node Policy Bootstrap

```
leaf-101# moquery -c pconsBootStrap
Total Objects shown: 1

# pcons.BootStrap
allLeaderAcked         : yes
allPortsInService      : yes
allResponsesFromLeader : yes
canBringPortInService  : yes
childAction            :
completedPolRes        : yes
dn                     : rescont/bootstrap
lcOwn                  : local
modTs                  : 2022-03-10T10:31:02.929+01:00
policySyncNodeBringup  : yes
rn                     : bootstrap
state                  : completed
status                 :
timerTicks             : 360
try                    : 0
worstCaseTaskTry       : 0
```

Any potential problems with the reachability between the switch and APIC, resulting in the inability to download bootstrap policies, can be identified using the iping utility, as in Listing 3-9.

Listing 3-9. APIC to Leaf IP Connectivity

```
leaf-101# iping -V overlay-1 10.11.0.1
PING 10.11.0.1 (10.11.0.1) from 10.11.0.30: 56 data bytes
64 bytes from 10.11.0.1: icmp_seq=0 ttl=64 time=0.57 ms
64 bytes from 10.11.0.1: icmp_seq=1 ttl=64 time=0.819 ms
64 bytes from 10.11.0.1: icmp_seq=2 ttl=64 time=0.362 ms
64 bytes from 10.11.0.1: icmp_seq=3 ttl=64 time=0.564 ms
64 bytes from 10.11.0.1: icmp_seq=4 ttl=64 time=0.543 ms

--- 10.11.0.1 ping statistics ---
5 packets transmitted, 5 packets received, 0.00% packet loss
round-trip min/avg/max = 0.362/0.571/0.819 ms
```

Note   Remember to always include the correct VRF in troubleshooting commands (overlay-1 in this example to verify the underlay routing).

Finally, if you encounter some problems with a discovery, compare the version of your image running on APICs vs. the version on the switches using the show version command. **The APIC version must be same or newer than the one used in the ACI fabric**. Otherwise, you won't be able to register these switches.

To wrap up this topic, from my experience, when the fabric is correctly cabled, don't expect many issues with this first step in its lifecycle. The discovery process is very reliable. I've encountered few problems related to the wrong versions or images running on Nexus. One time I saw malformed SSL certificates on APIC delivered from the factory (but we were notified about this fact via a Field Notice), and even in a case of some bug hit, a reload always helped to resolve an issue.

ACI Management Access

I hope you were able to successfully register all ACI switches to the fabric at this point, and we can smoothly move to ACI's initial configuration section: management access.

Fabric Out-of-Band Configuration

Even though you cannot configure ACI other than from APIC, each Nexus 9000 still encompasses a physical management (mgmt0) interface and it's highly recommended to connect it to the dedicated out-of-band infrastructure (if available). By default, ACI prefers OOB when configuring connectivity with external servers for protocols like DNS, NTP, SNMP, AAA, Syslog, or for configuration backups. Furthermore, this management interface will come very handy for troubleshooting using show commands on a full-featured Nexus CLI. Network engineers who previously used NX-OS will get comfortable with it very easily.

Therefore, usually one of the first configuration tasks in a fresh clean ACI with registered switches are their out-of-band interfaces. All ACI policies responsible for L3 management access to your fabric devices are located inside a system tenant named **mgmt**. We will get slightly ahead here with the tenant configuration related to OOB and in-band, but don't worry, all used tenant objects will be covered in detail as part of Chapter 5. If something isn't completely clear now, you can refer back to this section later.

To configure OOB IP addresses for ACI switches, navigate to **Tenants -> mgmt -> Node Management Addresses -> Static Node Management Addresses**. Here either right-click the currently highlighted folder in the left menu or click the symbol ✂▾ in the upper right grey bar and choose *Create Static Node Management Addresses.* In the opened form (see Figure 3-12), the node range refers to one or more of the ACI Node IDs associated with switches during their registration. Check the out-of-band addresses and fill the IP information. If you chose a single node, this form expects an individual single static OOB IP address. Otherwise, with multiple devices specified, you can enter a range of addresses and APIC will choose individual OOB IPs on your behalf.

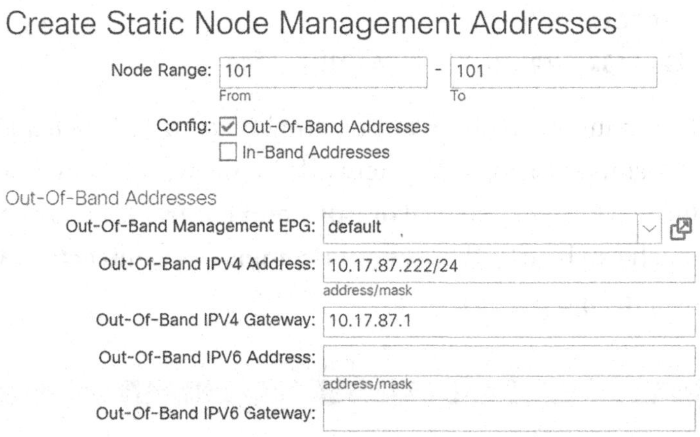

Create Static Node Management Addresses

Node Range: 101 - 101
From   To

Config: ☑ Out-Of-Band Addresses
☐ In-Band Addresses

Out-Of-Band Addresses

Out-Of-Band Management EPG: default

Out-Of-Band IPV4 Address: 10.17.87.222/24
address/mask

Out-Of-Band IPV4 Gateway: 10.17.87.1

Out-Of-Band IPV6 Address:
address/mask

Out-Of-Band IPV6 Gateway:

Figure 3-12. *Out-of-band IP configuration*

As long as your OOB infrastructure is configured correctly, you should be able to connect right away to the switch's CLI using SSH and optionally verify the OOB interface; see Listing 3-10.

Listing 3-10. ACI Node OOB Configuration Verification

```
leaf-101# show vrf
VRF-Name                        VRF-ID State    Reason
black-hole                           3 Up       --
management                           2 Up       --
overlay-1                            4 Up       --

leaf-101# show ip interface vrf management
IP Interface Status for VRF "management"
mgmt0, Interface status: protocol-up/link-up/admin-up, iod: 2, mode: external
  IP address: 10.17.87.222, IP subnet: 10.17.87.0/24
  IP broadcast address: 255.255.255.255
  IP primary address route-preference: 0, tag: 0

leaf-101# show ip route vrf management
IP Route Table for VRF "management"
'*' denotes best ucast next-hop
'**' denotes best mcast next-hop
'[x/y]' denotes [preference/metric]
'%<string>' in via output denotes VRF <string>
```

```
0.0.0.0/0, ubest/mbest: 1/0
    *via 10.17.87.1/32, mgmt0, [0], 4d01h, local
```

By default, all communication from any external IP to an ACI OOB addresses is permitted. However, similar to the legacy network, in ACI we can apply a kind of ACLs to this "line vty" traffic in a form of a special **out-of-band contract**. Create your own or edit the default one, which can be found in **Tenants -> mgmt -> Contracts -> Out-Of-Band Contracts** (as shown in Figure 3-13).

Figure 3-13. *Out-of-band contract*

In the contract object, create at least one subject and add a set of filters defining all allowed protocols on OOB interfaces. It's like creating legacy ACL entries. Then the OOB contract has to be associated with two entities, as displayed in Figure 3-14.

1. Default Out-Of-Band EPG found under **Tenant -> mgmt -> Node Management EPGs**. Here, click the + symbol in the Provided Out-Of-Band Contracts field and associate the chosen contract. This OOB EPG represents all mgmt0 and Eth2-1/Eth2-2 interfaces in the ACI fabric.

2. In the mgmt tenant, create a new External Management Network Instance Profile object. This will represent all clients external to ACI, accessing the management interfaces. Attach the same OOB contract from step 1 here in the Consumer Out-of-Band Contracts field. The Subnets list allows you to specify from which IP addresses/networks the management traffic is permitted.

I won't go into more details of contract or tenant configuration here since I will cover them completely in Chapter 5.

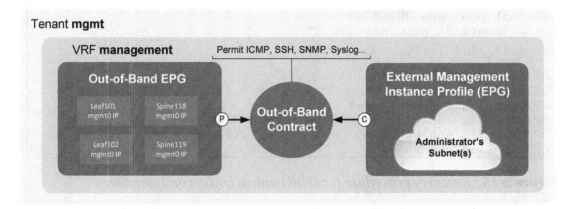

Figure 3-14. *Tenant policies for out-of-band management access*

Warning!   Be aware when applying an OOB contract for the first time, because this is the moment when you can lose the management connectivity of all ACI devices, including the APIC GUI (due to incorrect contract filters or external subnet definition).

If you experience any management connectivity problems after OOB contract configuration, there is a recovery procedure available:

1. Connect to the CIMC interface of any APIC node from the cluster and open the virtual KVM console over HTTP/S.

2. Log into the APIC CLI and follow the configuration steps described in Figure 3-15.

```
APIC# sh run tenant mgmt oob-mgmt epg OOB-MGMT
# Command: show running-config tenant mgmt oob-mgmt epg OOB-MGMT
# Time: Wed Feb 10 22:00:07 2021
  tenant mgmt
    oob-mgmt epg OOB-MGMT
      contract provider OOB_CT
      exit
    exit
APIC#
APIC# conf t
APIC(config)# tenant mgmt
APIC(config-tenant)# oob-mgmt epg OOB-MGMT
APIC(config-oob-epg)# no contract provider OOB_CT
APIC(config-oob-epg)#
```

Figure 3-15. *Recovery procedure for OOB contract miss-configuration*

Fabric In-Band Configuration

The out-of-band infrastructure is not always available in the customer datacenters where ACI is being deployed. Or it is not optimal for some specific applications, such as a bandwidth-hungry telemetry data collection by the Nexus Dashboard platform. In such cases, you can configure, along with OOB, in-band connectivity for all devices. Or just in-band alone. These IP addresses are reachable exclusively through the internal fabric interconnections.

Configuration-wise, in-band management is significantly more complex and encompasses many additional tenant and access policies compared to OOB. Again, I won't go deeper into the theory behind them here as the detailed explanation is part of the following chapters. For better understanding, make sure to review this section if needed after reading through the next chapters.

In-band implementation can start the same way as before, by statically defining IP addresses for all ACI switches and APICs (in **Tenants -> mgmt -> Node Management Addresses -> Static Node Management Addresses**). This time, however, the default gateway address specified for in-band IPs is not external to ACI. As depicted in Figure 3-16, it has to be configured as a gateway subnet in the already existing **inb** bridge domain (**Tenants -> mgmt -> Networking -> Bridge Domains -> inb -> Subnets**).

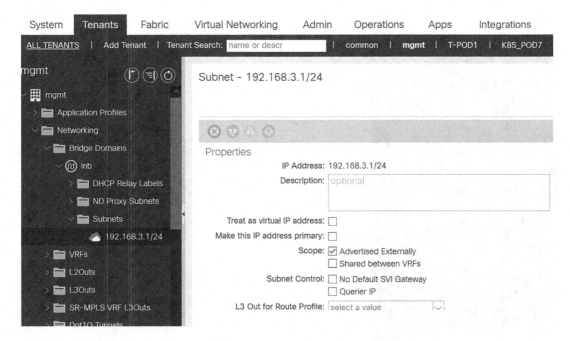

Figure 3-16. *Default gateway for in-band under bridge domain*

Next, you have to create a new in-band EPG under the Node Management EPGs folder, associate it with the **inb** bridge domain, and specify an in-band VLAN (see Figure 3-17). This VLAN will become significant especially for APIC in-band connectivity soon.

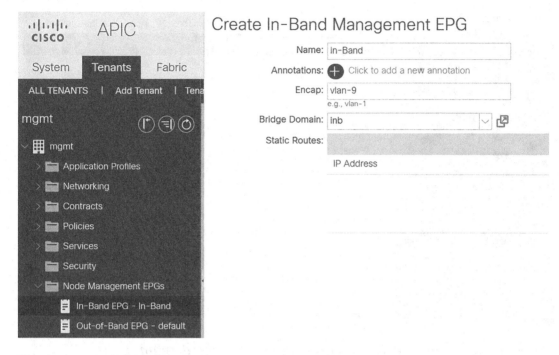

Figure 3-17.   In-band EPG

After the previous configuration steps, you should see a new in-band VRF present on each ACI switch with one VLAN SVI interface. Its primary address has to match the default gateway IP and the secondary address is the actual in-band IP of that switch. In other words, each switch acts as a default gateway for itself. APIC also receives a new subinterface in the corresponding in-band VLAN on top of the bond0 interface. See Listing 3-11.

Listing 3-11. In-Band Configuration Verification

```
leaf-101# show vrf
VRF-Name                        VRF-ID State     Reason
 black-hole                          3 Up        --
 management                          2 Up        --
 mgmt:inb                            9 Up        --
 overlay-1                           4 Up        --

leaf-101# show ip interface vrf mgmt:inb
IP Interface Status for VRF "mgmt:inb"
vlan17, Interface status: protocol-up/link-up/admin-up, iod: 93, mode:
pervasive
```

IP address: 192.168.3.2, IP subnet: 192.168.3.0/24

IP address: 192.168.3.1, IP subnet: 192.168.3.0/24 secondary

IP broadcast address: 255.255.255.255

IP primary address route-preference: 0, tag: 0

apic1# **ifconfig**

bond0.9: flags=4163<UP,BROADCAST,RUNNING,MULTICAST> mtu 1496

      inet 192.168.3.252 netmask 255.255.255.0 broadcast 192.168.3.255

      inet6 fe80::72e4:22ff:fe86:3a0d prefixlen 64 scopeid 0x20<link>

      ether 70:e4:22:86:3a:0d txqueuelen 1000 (Ethernet)

      RX packets 5841 bytes 275040 (268.5 KiB)

      RX errors 0 dropped 0 overruns 0 frame 0

      TX packets 9009 bytes 1382618 (1.3 MiB)

      TX errors 0 dropped 0 overruns 0 carrier 0 collisions 0

When ACI needs to connect any endpoint to its fabric in a particular VLAN, you have to create complete set of access policies: objects defining the exact leaf or spine interface configuration with their available encapsulation resources. In this special and only occasion, each APIC node needs access policies as well for enabling the connectivity over the in-band VLAN. In Figure 3-18, you can see an example of access policies for APIC connected behind the leaf 101 and 102 interface Eth1/1. Each object will be discussed in detail in Chapter 4.

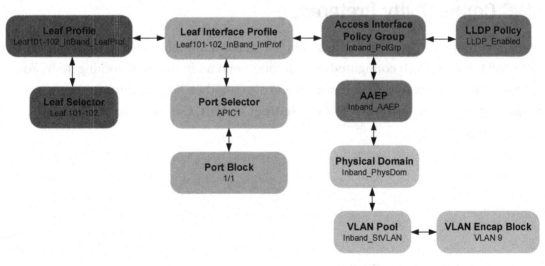

Figure 3-18. *Access policies for APIC allowing in-band VLAN connectivity*

Finally, you have to allow the connectivity to the in-band IP addresses by applying a contract between in-band EPG and any other internal or external EPG configured in the ACI (see Figure 3-19). If you want to reach the in-band subnet from the external network, it will require properly configured routing between ACI and the external network using a L3OUT object. I will cover these features in Chapter 7.

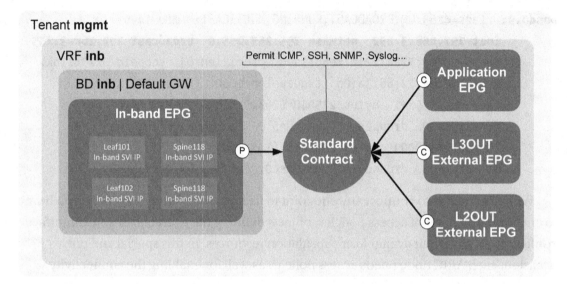

Figure 3-19. *Tenant policies for in-band management access*

APIC Connectivity Preference

If you have both out-of-band and in-band management implemented, APIC doesn't use VRFs and therefore both configured default routes end up in the same routing table. You need to somehow ensure a preference for one over another. For this purpose, there is a configuration knob in **System -> System Settings -> APIC Connectivity Preference** (as shown in Figure 3-20).

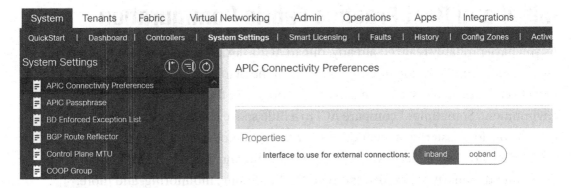

Figure 3-20. *APIC Connecitivity Preferences settings*

In the default settings, APIC prefers the in-band interface as outgoing for all packets sourced from its own IP address, and under the hood, this switch alters the configuration of the default routes metrics. See Listing 3-12.

Listing 3-12. In-Band Connectivity Preference on APIC

```
apic1# bash
admin@apic1:~> ip route
default via 192.168.3.1 dev bond0.9 metric 8
default via 10.17.87.1 dev oobmgmt metric 16
```

When you switch the preference to **ooband**, Listing 3-13 shows the routing table output.

Listing 3-13. Out-of-Band Connectivity Preference on APIC

```
apic1# bash
admin@apic1:~> ip route
default via 10.17.87.1 dev oobmgmt metric 16
default via 192.168.3.1 dev bond0.9 metric 32
```

The previous setting applies exclusively for the connections initiated from APIC to the remote, not directly connected destinations. In the opposite direction, if some packet enters the particular APIC interface from the outside, APIC will reply using the same interface, regardless of this setting. Hence, even if you prefer in-band connectivity, you can still reach the APIC GUI and CLI using an OOB IP address without any problem.

Initial and Best Practice Fabric Configuration

As you have probably realized already, due to ACI's flexibility and versatility, there are countless configuration options available in the platform. Tons of little knobs and checkboxes. At a first sight, it can be challenging to find the best setting for your environment. Sometimes I compare ACI to a little space shuttle with an administrator responsible for mastering its maneuvering and flight modes.

In the following sections, you will explore further the initial configuration, recommendations, best practice settings, ACI hardening, monitoring, and more.

Network Time Protocol

After ensuring the management access to your environment, one of the first protocols to configure for ACI should be NTP (network time protocol). Its importance is significant for synchronizing clocks around the fabric, correlation of ACI events in case of any trouble, and APIC database synchronization.

NTP configuration consists of multiple connected objects. In **System -> System Settings -> Date and Time,** you can configure the time offset and time zone globally for all ACI devices. However, this configuration is not deployed anywhere yet. First, you have to go to **Fabric -> Fabric Policies -> Policies -> Pod -> Date and Time** and either edit the default object or create your own. Here you can add multiple NTP servers with optional authentication, define which management interface will be used to communicate with servers (OOB vs. in-band), or allow ACI to act as a NTP master itself. These individual policies represent universal configuration building blocks, subsequently applicable to a particular Pod (or switch, module, or interface, depending on the policy type).

The next step in the workflow is to create an object called a policy group in **Fabric -> Fabric Policies -> Pods -> Policy Groups** (again, default or your own) and choose the previously configured Date Time Policy. As you can see in Figure 3-21, policy groups in general serve as a configuration definition for particular part of the network. They are aggregating individual protocol policies. Further details about policy groups will be covered in Chapter 4.

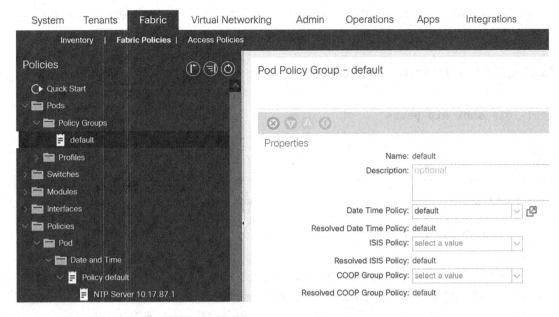

Figure 3-21. *Date Time Policy configuration in the Pod policy group*

The final step is to apply a policy group to a profile, selecting the exact switch resources where the defined configuration should be deployed. In your case, open **Fabric -> Fabric Policies -> Pods -> Profiles** and update the Policy Group field in the Pod Selector (refer to Figure 3-22). Here you can choose exactly which Pod the configuration specified in the policy group will be applied to (based on individual Pod IDs or ALL). By Pod, ACI means all switches within it.

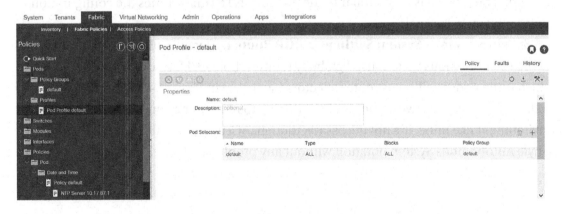

Figure 3-22. *Pod policy group association with a Pod profile*

Eventually APIC instructs all the switches in selected Pods to configure the defined NTP servers and you can verify it using the show ntp commands shown in Listing 3-14.

Listing 3-14. NTP Server Verification

```
leaf-101# show ntp peers
-------------------------------------------------------------------------------
  Peer IP Address                      Serv/Peer Prefer KeyId   Vrf
-------------------------------------------------------------------------------
  10.17.87.1                           Server    yes    None    management
leaf-101# show ntp peer-status
Total peers : 1
* - selected for sync, + - peer mode(active),
- - peer mode(passive), = - polled in client mode
    remote                  local           st poll reach delay vrf
-------------------------------------------------------------------------------
*10.17.87.1                 0.0.0.0          4  64   377   0.000  management
```

Internal ACI MP-BGP

The next essential protocol to configure for ACI is MP-BGP because it provides the ability to exchange and distribute routing information between the fabric and external L3 network. The process is very similar to the previous NTP (many times the configuration philosophy in ACI is analogous).

Start in **System -> System Settings -> BGP Route Reflector Policy**. Here, configure the BGP Autonomous System used globally for the whole ACI fabric and choose which spine nodes will act as route reflectors (as shown in Figure 3-23). From each Pod, configure at least two spines for BGP RR due to redundancy purposes. In a lab environment like mine, it's not necessary, though. ACI accepts both 16-bit (2-byte) and 4-byte Autonomous System notation without any problems.

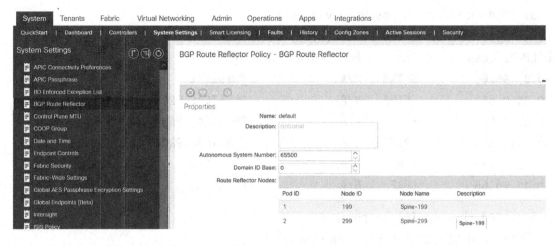

Figure 3-23. *MP-BGP global configuration*

As before, this configuration needs to be deployed to the fabric using fabric policies.
Go to **Fabric -> Fabric Policies -> Pods -> Profiles** and make sure you have some Pod
policy group with default BGP Route Reflector Policy applied to all your Pods. If you
configured NTP consistently for the whole fabric in the previous step, the same policy by
default ensures MP-BGP is running there as well.

To verify MP-BGP sessions between leaf and spine switches, you can use the well-
known BGP show commands directly in the CLI. Look at address-families VPNv4 or
VPNv6 as the one MP-BGP session transports information about all prefixes for all VRFs
available in ACI (similarly to MPLS). See Listing 3-15.

Listing 3-15. MP-BGP Session Verification

```
leaf-101# show bgp vpnv4 unicast summary vrf overlay-1
BGP summary information for VRF overlay-1, address family VPNv4 Unicast
BGP router identifier 10.11.72.64, local AS number 65500
BGP table version is 26156142, VPNv4 Unicast config peers 1,
capable peers 1
1300 network entries and 1930 paths using 269504 bytes of memory
BGP attribute entries [86/15136], BGP AS path entries [0/0]
BGP community entries [0/0], BGP clusterlist entries [1/4]

Neighbor     V    AS MsgRcvd MsgSent   TblVer   InQ OutQ Up/
Down   State/PfxRc
10.11.96.65  4 65500 3522202 6121260 26156142    0    0    6d01h 638
```

```
leaf-101# show isis dteps vrf overlay-1
IS-IS Dynamic Tunnel End Point (DTEP) database:
DTEP-Address        Role    Encapsulation    Type
10.11.96.65         SPINE   N/A              PHYSICAL
10.11.0.65          SPINE   N/A              PHYSICAL,PROXY-ACAST-MAC
10.11.0.64          SPINE   N/A              PHYSICAL,PROXY-ACAST-V4
10.11.0.66          SPINE   N/A              PHYSICAL,PROXY-ACAST-V6
10.11.88.76         LEAF    N/A              PHYSICAL
10.11.96.66         LEAF    N/A              PHYSICAL

soine-199# show ip int loopback 0
IP Interface Status for VRF "overlay-1"
lo0, Interface status: protocol-up/link-up/admin-up, iod: 4, mode: ptep
  IP address: 10.11.96.65, IP subnet: 10.11.96.65/32
  IP broadcast address: 255.255.255.255
  IP primary address route-preference: 0, tag: 0
```

Domain Name System

DNS (domain name system) configuration in ACI comes in handy when you prefer using a hostname instead of a static IP address for referring to external services (typically monitoring servers, AAA, vCenter).

As illustrated in Figure 3-24, configuration again primarily happens in **Fabric -> Fabric Policies -> Policies -> Global -> DNS Profiles**. Here, choose the management interface used for reaching the DNS providers (OOB vs. in-band) and define the provider IPs themselves. Optionally, you can add the local DNS domain name.

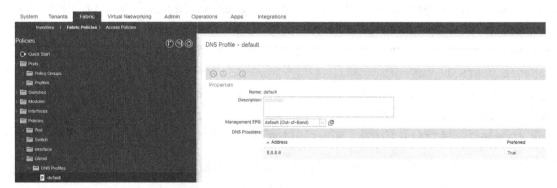

Figure 3-24. *DNS Profile configuration*

This time, it's not necessary to include the DNS Profile in any policy group. Instead, go to **Tenants -> mgmt -> Networking -> VRFs -> oob** and click the **Policy** tab in right upper menu. Scroll down in the form and set the "default" DNS label as shown in Figure 3-25.

Figure 3-25. *Default DNS label configuration*

This label association relates to the name of the DNS Profile from fabric policies. APIC will apply the configuration to all switches where this particular VRF is present. That's why it is beneficial to use the mgmt tenant and the out-of-band management VRF, which is pervasive across the whole fabric.

Note   The DNS configuration will be applied to APIC only if you use the default DNS Profile object, not your own.

To check the results of the DNS configuration, view the contents of the /etc/resolv. conf files on APIC or switches. See Listing 3-16.

Listing 3-16. DNS Configuration Verification

```
apic1# cat /etc/resolv.conf
# Generated by IFC
search apic.local

nameserver 10.11.0.1
nameserver 8.8.8.8

leaf-101# cat /etc/resolv.conf
nameserver 8.8.8.8

leaf-101# nslookup vrf management google.com
In progress
In progress
Done
Context from environment = 0
Server:         8.8.8.8
Address:        8.8.8.8#53

Non-authoritative answer:
Name:   google.com
Address: 142.251.36.78
```

Securing Fabric Management Access

As you already know from previous chapters, to access APIC for configuration and monitoring, you can use either the GUI over HTTP(S), the CLI with SSH, or direct REST API calls. Various security aspects of this management access can be configured using the common policy located in **Fabric -> Fabric Policies -> Policies -> Pod -> Management Access** (shown in Figure 3-26). It's strongly recommended to leave unencrypted protocols like Telnet and HTTP disabled. In case of HTTP, enable redirection to 443 and make sure to choose a custom and valid signed SSL certificate here. The certificate itself can be uploaded to APIC through **Admin -> AAA -> Security -> Public Key Management Tab -> Key Rings Tab**.

As usual, you can edit the default Management Access Policy object or create your own. This policy is applied in the Fabric Pod policy group and subsequently to the Pod profile.

If you have edited the default one and you already have a Pod policy group associated with a profile from a previous protocol configuration, any change will be immediately effective. Just a small note: usually after submitting this form, the APIC web server needs to be restarted, so it will suddenly disconnect you from the GUI. Don't be surprised.

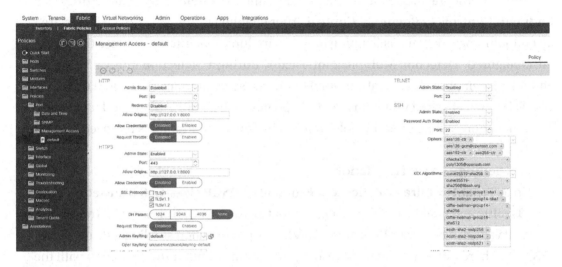

Figure 3-26. *Management access configuration*

Fabric-Wide Best Practice Configuration

In following paragraphs, I will cover additional global settings recommended by Cisco for ACI fabric that lead to higher security, robustness, and risk mitigation. Make sure to configure them right away during the initial deployment.

Enforce Subnet Check

The configuration option is located in **System -> System Settings -> Fabric-Wide Settings.** Enable it to avoid unnecessary learning of endpoints (both local and remote) with an IP not belonging to any of existing gateway subnets configured in a particular ACI VRF.

Endpoint IP Aging

Setting configurable in **System -> System Settings -> Endpoint Controls -> IP Aging Tab.** In the default state, all endpoints have a single aging timer associated with them, the endpoint retention timer. For locally learned endpoints, it is set to 900 seconds; for remote ones, it is 300 seconds. Suboptimal resource utilization occurs in this default setting when you have one MAC address associated with multiple IP addresses and some of them stop communicating. Then all the IP entries still remain learned in the switch's

TCAM memory. By enabling IP aging, IP entries get their own independent timers. At 75% of retention timer, ACI sends an ARP/ND request three times; if no reply is received, the IP entry is removed from the endpoint database.

Rogue Endpoint Control

Another best practice recommendation is found in **System -> System Settings -> Endpoint Controls -> Rogue EP Control**. After enabling this feature, ACI will declare an endpoint rogue when it is flapping between multiple leaf interfaces more times than the configured "Detection Multiplication Factor" during a "detection interval." A rogue endpoint is temporarily statically pinned to the last seen interface for a "hold time" interval so we can avoid rapid, unsolicited updates to the control plane and make the ACI much more stable. After the hold time expiration, the endpoint is removed from the database.

QoS Setting – DSCP Translation

Go to **Tenant -> infra -> Policies -> Protocol -> DSCP class-CoS translation policy for L3 traffic** and enable it. This will ensure that all the ACI QoS classes will translate to DSCP values in the outer IP header of a VXLAN packet when sending it through the IPN/ISN. There, you can ensure the priority forwarding or other manipulation with the specific ACI traffic class. Generally, it's recommended to use the DSCP values currently free and not classified already for other purposes in IPN/ISN. And make sure to prefer the Control-Plane Traffic class between your Pods, which ensures stable and reliable MP-BGP and APIC communication.

Fabric Port Tracking

This feature enables monitoring of a leaf's fabric interfaces (uplinks). If the number of active ones falls below the configured threshold, the leaf will disable all its host-facing interfaces. We expect that this will force the end host switchover to the healthy and active leaf. A best practice recommendation is to set the mentioned threshold to 0 active fabric interfaces. You can find this knob in **System -> System Settings -> Port Tracking.**

Global AES Encryption

From both a security and operational point of view, it's highly recommended to globally enable encryption of sensitive data in ACI (e.g., passwords or credentials for ACI integration). Without this option, when you create an ACI backup, the configuration is exported without any passwords. Therefore, after the potential import, you could break multiple ACI functionalities. Encryption can be enabled in **System -> System Settings -> Global AES Passphrase Encryption Settings**. Set a minimum 16-character passphrase and you are ready to go.

Enforce EPG VLAN Validation

If you don't expect usage of overlapping VLANs in ACI, it's recommended to enable this check to prevent unintended association of multiple physical domains with overlapping VLAN pools with the same EPG. I will cover these objects in Chapter 4, so you can refer back to this setting. Configuration happens in **System -> System Settings -> Fabric Wide Setting.**

IS-IS Redistributed Metric (applicable only for an ACI Multi-Pod architecture).

In **System -> System Settings -> ISIS Policy -> ISIS metric for redistributed routes** you can configure a metric for internal TEP routes, which are redistributed on spines between IPN OSPF/BGP and IS-IS. By setting the default metric value of 63 to 62 or lower, you can enhance the convergence time and eliminate potential connectivity issues after the spine switch is reloaded in a Multi-Pod environment. Principally, when you reboot a spine, even before it downloads a policy from APIC, it starts to advertise IS-IS routes to the IPN with the maximum metric (63) called the overload mode. When you decrease the IS-IS metric for valid and stable spines, routing will prefer them over the rebooted one.

COOP Group

Go to **System -> System Settings -> COOP Group** and set this knob to **Strict**. This will enable MD5 authentication between all COOP nodes in your fabric, which enhances security and avoids unintentional information compromise.

ACI Fabric Monitoring and Backup

By implementing previous settings, you have finalized the initial hardening and optimization of your ACI fabric. Before you start connecting any resources to ACI and configuring application policies, it's highly beneficial to start monitoring the whole infrastructure and ensure continuous backing up of the APIC configuration. The following sections get you started with SNMP, Syslog, NetFlow, and configuration export/import.

Simple Network Management Protocol

Even though I see a clear trend of moving from traditional ways of network infrastructure monitoring using SNMP (Simple Network Management Protocol, a pull model) to utilizing real-time telemetry data (a push model), SNMP is still the first choice when it comes to monitoring for the majority of our customers.

ACI supports SNMPv1, v2, and v3 with the wide selection of both standardized SNMP MIBs and Cisco-specific MIBs that can be all found in the following ACI MIB Support List: www.cisco.com/c/dam/en/us/td/docs/Website/datacenter/aci/mib/ mib-support.html.

ACI doesn't allow you to configure anything using SNMP, so the only supported operations are

- SNMP read queries (Get, Next, Bulk, Walk)

- SNMP traps (v1, v2c, v3) for a maximum of 10 receivers

Note   If you have implemented out-of-band contracts from the previous section, don't forget to add the filters allowing UDP ports 161 (SNMP agents) and 162 (SNMP servers); otherwise, you won't be able to connect to the ACI switches and APICs using SNMP or receive SNMP traps from them.

The SNMP configuration in ACI consists of a fairly simple three-step process. For SNMP traps, you need to configure receiver and data sources; for SNMP read, you will create and apply one more SNMP fabric policy.

First, go to **Admin -> External Data Collectors -> Monitoring Destinations -> SNMP Tab** and click ✂▾ to create a SNMP monitoring destination group. Here you will define one or more SNMP trap receiver servers, their UDP port, version, community, and management EPG preference (as shown in Figure 3-27).

Figure 3-27. *SNMP trap destination group*

Now you need to associate SNMP trap destinations with several data sources. By doing so, you basically define which objects you want to receive events about on your collector. And due to ACI's differentiation between access interfaces, fabric uplinks, and logical tenant configuration, SNMP trap sources can be configured independently in three different locations, based on type of expected monitored objects:

- **Tenants -> <tenant_name> -> Policies -> Monitoring -> default (has to be created) -> Callhome/Smart Callhome/SNMP/Syslog -> SNMP Tab**

- **Fabric -> Fabric Policies -> Policies -> Monitoring -> default (or common or you own) -> Callhome/Smart Callhome/SNMP/ Syslog -> SNMP Tab**

- **Fabric -> Access Policies -> Policies -> Monitoring -> default (or your own) -> Callhome/Smart Callhome/SNMP/Syslog -> SNMP Tab**

The general recommendation is to configure the monitoring for all objects in each category. You don't want to miss any important information, after all. For simplicity, the SNMP trap source configuration form is always identical. ACI allows you to granularly apply different policies for each individual object if you click the little ✏ symbol, or you can leave the same setting for ALL (as shown in Figure 3-28).

Figure 3-28. *SNMP trap source definition*

To deploy these policies to the infrastructure, in Tenants, click the main tenant object (its name) and open the Policy tab. There you will find the Monitoring Policy field with the ability to associate a created policy. APIC will automatically configure SNMP traps on all switches where its logical constructs (application policies) are instantiated.

In both fabric sections you can put individual monitoring policies into an Interface Policy Group, which is then associated with the Interface Profile and Switch Profile (see Figure 3-29). Detailed theory behind these objects will follow in Chapter 4. For now, consider it as a configuration for individual leaf/spine physical interfaces.

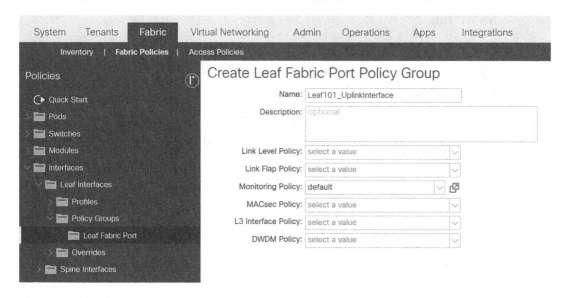

Figure 3-29. *SNMP trap monitoring policy deployment*

A legitimate complaint is that this approach can over time become harder to maintain. Three different places and a monitoring policy for each Interface Policy Group in Fabric and Access Policies; why can't you use one common policy for the whole ACI, for the entire set of objects? In fact, you can! If you noticed, there is a **common monitoring policy** in **Fabric -> Fabric Policies -> Policies -> Monitoring**. If you apply any configuration here, it will have instantly global impact to all ACI objects. Even without any additional association. Common is policy resolved as a last resort, when ACI cannot find any other more specific default or your own monitoring policy objects.

Last but not least, you must configure the standard read access using SNMP. There is only one additional policy needed, located in **Fabric -> Fabric Policies -> Policies -> Pod -> SNMP -> default** (or create your own). Have the Admin state set to Enabled. In client group policies you have to specify the source IPs allowed to communicate with your devices using SNMP (consider it kind of SNMP ACL), and finally set a SNMP community or SNMPv3 user in the respective fields. This object is, like before, applied to **Fabric -> Fabric Policies -> Pod -> Policy Groups** and subsequently to the Pod profile.

If you use default objects and have them already associated from previous configuration tasks, you don't need to do anything more here.

Now you should be able to access all your ACI switches and APIC via SNMP. The configuration can be verified using the commands shown in Listing 3-17.

Listing 3-17. SNMP Verification

```
leaf-101# show snmp summary
Admin State : enabled, running (pid:17907)
Local SNMP engineID: [Hex] 8000000903700F6AB299DF
                     [Dec] 128:000:000:009:003:112:015:106:178:153:223
```

Community	Context	Status
snmpcom		ok

User	Authentication	Privacy	Status

Context	VRF	Status

Client	VRF	Status
10.17.84.48	**management**	**ok**

Host	Port	Ver	Level	SecName	VRF
10.10.1.1	**162**	**v2c**	**noauth**	**snmpcom**	**management**

```
apic1# show snmp summary
```

```
Active Policy: default, Admin State: enabled
```

```
Local SNMP EngineID: 0x800000098088a3297ceab4666100000000
Local SNMP EngineBoots: 6
Local SNMP EngineTime: 3102549


-----------------------------------------
Community            Description
-----------------------------------------

snmpcom


-------------------------------------------------------------
User                 Authentication       Privacy
-------------------------------------------------------------


-------------------------------------------------------------
Client-Group         Mgmt-Epg                  Clients
-------------------------------------------------------------
Zabbix               default (Out-Of-Band)     10.17.84.48


-------------------------------------------------------------
Host                 Port  Version  Level     SecName
-------------------------------------------------------------
10.10.1.1            162   v2c      noauth    snmpcom
```

Logging in ACI Syslog

APIC by default collects and saves into its internal database various useful monitoring information about the whole ACI: faults, events, audit logs, and session logs. In the following sections, I will describe them in a more detail and show you how to easily export all of them using a standardized Syslog format to the external collector for further analysis and backup.

Faults

Faults are objects describing any kind of problems with the system. Each fault is a child object of the main affected object, with its unique fault code, severity, description, and lifecycle, transiting between the following states:

- **Soaking:** First occurrence of a particular problem. During a soaking timer (120sec) ACI monitors if the problem is still present or already resolved.

- **Soaking – Clearing:** When the problem is gone, there is another 120sec timer during which ACI monitors it for a potential reappearance.

- **Raised:** If the problem is not resolved during a soaking interval, it moves to a raised state, telling the administrator that this issue consistently persists.

- **Raised – Clearing:** After resolving the longer lasting problem, ACI starts another 120sec timer for reappearance monitoring.

- **Retaining:** The resolved fault is left in the retaining state for 3600 seconds by default and then it is moved to a history database.

To find currently present faults in ACI, you can navigate to their central list in **System -> Faults**. Besides this, each object has its own Fault tab in the upper right corner of the configuration form. In Figure 3-30, you can see the properties of each fault object. When the description isn't clear enough, look in Troubleshooting tab for more information about the recommended procedure.

Fault Properties

General   Troubleshooting

Fault Code:	F1451
Severity:	minor
Last Transition:	2022-02-10T15:47:30.808+01:00
Lifecycle:	Raised
Affected Object:	**topology/pod-1/node-199/sys/ch/psuslot-1/psu**
Description:	Power supply shutdown. (serial number POG2439ZEB2)
Type:	Environmental
Cause:	equipment-psu-down
Change Set:	almReg:0, cap:91.669998, descr:PSU, drawnCurr:0.000000, fanOpSt:unknown, hwVer:0.0, id:1, mfgTm:not-applicable, model:NXA-PAC-1100W-PE2, operSt:shut, rev:A0, ser:POG2439ZEB2, tc:0, vld:V03, vSrc:220v, vendor:Cisco Systems Inc, volt:12.000000
Created:	2022-02-10T15:45:28.253+01:00
Code:	F1451
Number of Occurrences:	1
Original Severity:	minor
Previous Severity:	minor
Highest Severity:	minor

Figure 3-30. *ACI fault object*

Events

An event represents the more traditional type of object, similar to a log message. It describes a condition that occurred in a specific point in time, without the necessity for user attention. It doesn't have any lifecycle, so once created, it is never changed. You can find a list of all events either in **System -> History -> Events**, or selectively in the History tab of a specific object. The content of an event object is shown in Figure 3-31.

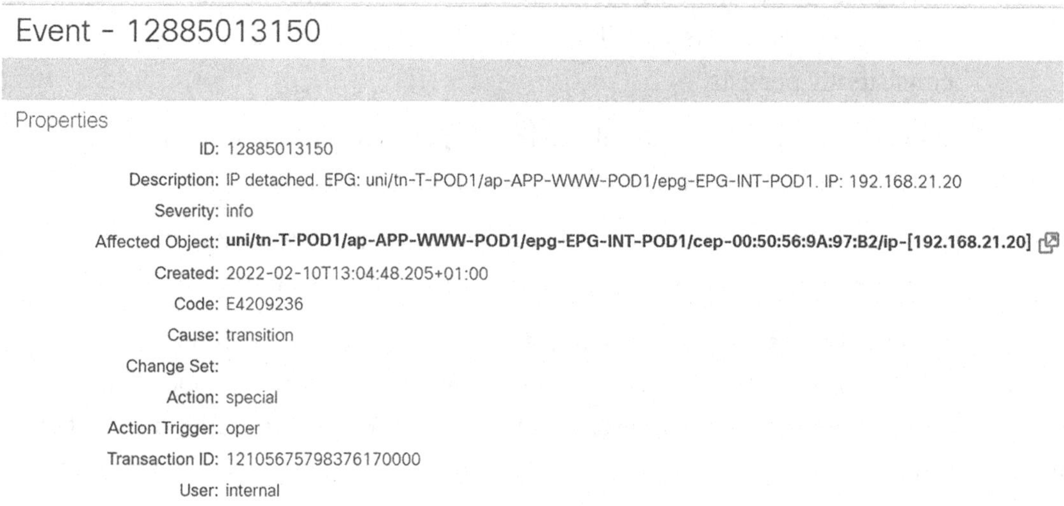

Event - 12885013150

Properties

ID: 12885013150
Description: IP detached. EPG: uni/tn-T-POD1/ap-APP-WWW-POD1/epg-EPG-INT-POD1. IP: 192.168.21.20
Severity: info
Affected Object: **uni/tn-T-POD1/ap-APP-WWW-POD1/epg-EPG-INT-POD1/cep-00:50:56:9A:97:B2/ip-[192.168.21.20]**
Created: 2022-02-10T13:04:48.205+01:00
Code: E4209236
Cause: transition
Change Set:
Action: special
Action Trigger: oper
Transaction ID: 12105675798376170000
User: internal

Figure 3-31. *ACI event object*

Audit Logs

Accounting entries describe which ACI user did what action in APIC, such as creation, modification, or deletion of any object (as shown in Figure 3-32). The complete list of these logs are in the traditional place of **System -> History -> Audit Logs** or in the History tab of a particular object.

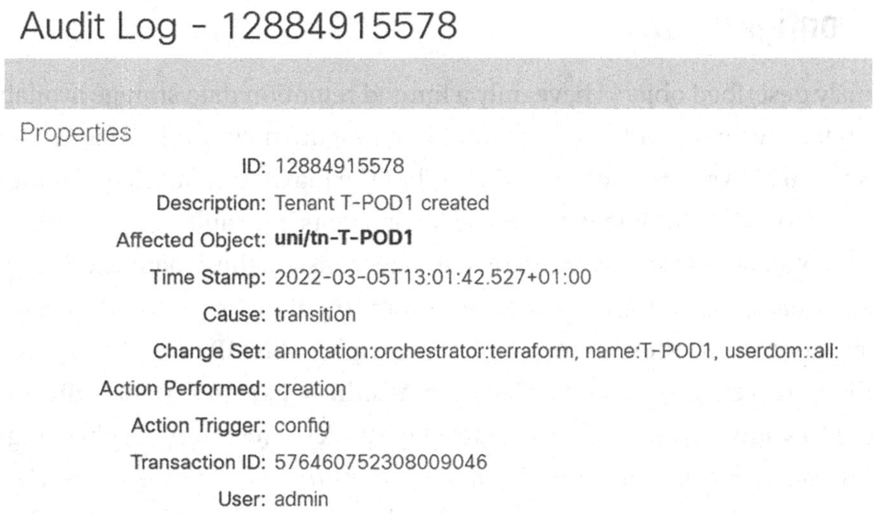

Audit Log – 12884915578

Properties

ID:	12884915578
Description:	Tenant T-POD1 created
Affected Object:	**uni/tn-T-POD1**
Time Stamp:	2022-03-05T13:01:42.527+01:00
Cause:	transition
Change Set:	annotation:orchestrator:terraform, name:T-POD1, userdom::all:
Action Performed:	creation
Action Trigger:	config
Transaction ID:	576460752308009046
User:	admin

Figure 3-32. *ACI audit log*

Session Logs

As you can see in Figure 3-33, the last type of logging entries are session logs. They basically inform an administrator about both successful and failed authentication to the ACI devices using SSH or the REST API (they include standard GUI logins as well). They can be found only in one place in ACI: **System -> History -> Session Logs.**

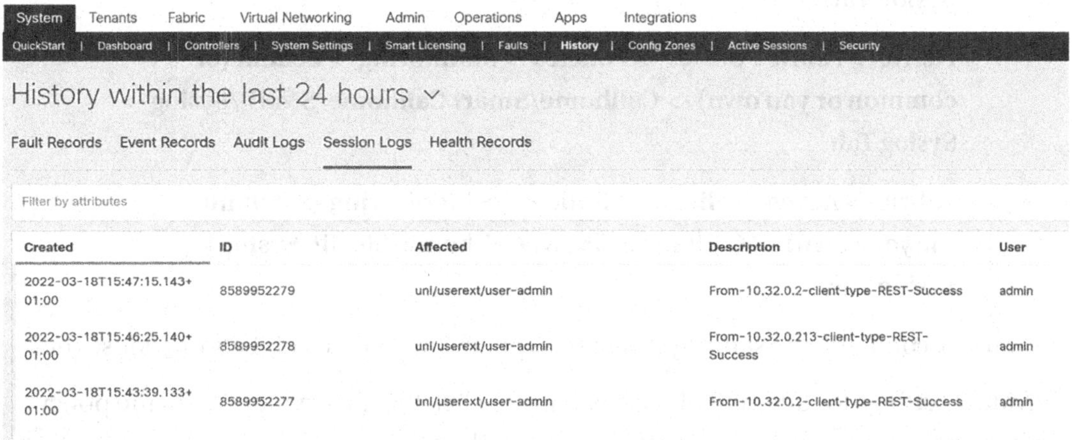

Figure 3-33. *ACI session logs*

Syslog Configuration

All previously described objects have only a limited retention data storage available when saved locally on the APIC cluster. You can configure these properties in **System -> Controllers -> Retention Policies**, but the maximum numbers for log objects are 1 million entries for audit logs and 500,000 for events and faults.

A much better and definitely best practice is to translate these native ACI monitoring objects to standardized Syslog messages and export them to the external collector. The configuration itself follows a very similar principle to SNMP traps. You start with the definition of an external Syslog collector in **Admin -> External Data Collectors -> Monitoring Destinations -> Syslog.** Create a new policy. I recommend checking both *Show Milliseconds in Timestamp* and *Show Time Zone in Timestamp* options. Here you can also enable logging to the console and a local file for defined log severity. On the next page, fill the information about the syslog server: IP address, minimal exported log severity, transport protocol, port, or preferred management EPG to reach the server.

The second part of the configuration consists of defining data sources for Syslog messages. Similar to SNMP traps, you have to configure it either three times in three different places, or use single common policy in **Fabric -> Fabric Policies**:

- **Tenants -> <tenant_name> -> Policies -> Monitoring -> default (has to be created) -> Callhome/Smart Callhome/SNMP/Syslog -> Syslog Tab**

- **Fabric -> Fabric Policies -> Policies -> Monitoring -> default (or common or you own) -> Callhome/Smart Callhome/SNMP/Syslog -> Syslog Tab**

- **Fabric -> Access Policies -> Policies -> Monitoring -> default (or your own) -> Callhome/Smart Callhome/SNMP/Syslog -> Syslog Tab**

You can configure the same Syslog source policy for ALL ACI objects or choose the individual settings for different objects when you click the little symbol ✎ in the policy configuration window. Finally, don't forget to apply the created monitoring policies to the respective objects (tenant policies or interface policy groups and profiles).

Verification of the Syslog configuration can be performed by looking to the Syslog collector or listening for Syslog messages on the eth0 (the physical mgmt0) interface using the tcpdump utility (if you chose OOB EPG during the configuration). See Listing 3-18.

Listing 3-18. Syslog Messages Seen on a Leaf mgmt0 Interface

```
leaf-101# tcpdump -ni eth0 port 514
tcpdump: verbose output suppressed, use -v or -vv for full protocol decode
listening on eth0, link-type EN10MB (Ethernet), capture size 262144 bytes
16:40:26.346279 IP 10.17.87.222.40400 > 10.17.89.22.514: SYSLOG local7.
critical, length: 264
16:40:35.540159 IP 10.17.87.222.40400 > 10.17.89.22.514: SYSLOG local7.
error, length: 227
16:40:35.874568 IP 10.17.87.222.40400 > 10.17.89.22.514: SYSLOG local7.
critical, length: 275
16:40:35.889693 IP 10.17.87.222.40400 > 10.17.89.22.514: SYSLOG local7.
critical, length: 2760 packets dropped by kernel
```

You can also generate a test Syslog message with the severity of your choice directly from APIC, as shown in Listing 3-19.

Listing 3-19. Artifical Syslog Message Generated on APIC

```
apic1# logit severity critical dest-grp Syslog_Server server 10.17.89.22
"TEST SYSLOG MESSAGE"
```

NetFlow

The last, but not less important, monitoring protocol I will describe is NetFlow. From previous chapter, you know that Nexus 9000s contain a hardware-based flow table, collecting metering information about the entire traffic seen in the data plane, such as source and destination MAC/IP addresses, TCP/UDP ports, VLANs, Ethertype, IP protocol, source interfaces, number of packets transferred, and more. In ACI mode, with the assistance of the CPU, you can transform this flow table data into a standardized NetFlow (v1, v5, or v9) entry and continuously it to the collector for further analysis and processing. NetFlow information can be used, for example, for network monitoring and planning, usage billing, anomaly detection, or general traffic accounting.

In ACI, you can gather the NetFlow data only on ingress of individual leaf host interfaces. However, the flows are collected for all packets even before any security policy is applied to them. Therefore, you are also able to see in your NetFlow collector information about the flows that were actually denied by the switch due to applied or missing contract and thus not forwarded further through the fabric.

A prerequisite for enabling NetFlow in ACI is to reconfigure the default **Fabric Node Control** policy located in **Fabric -> Fabric Policies -> Policies -> Monitoring -> Fabric Node Controls -> default.** This setting by default instructs Nexus 9000 HW TCAMs to prefer and install the Cisco Tetration Analytics sensor, which is mutually exclusive with the hardware NetFlow collection. Prior to deploying NetFlow, configure this policy to *NetFlow Priority* (see Figure 3-34).

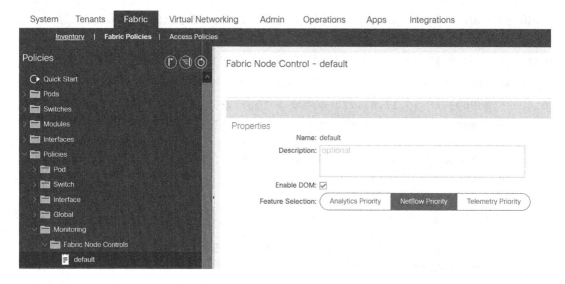

Figure 3-34. *Fabric node controls to NetFlow priority*

The NetFlow configuration follows the Flexible NetFlow structure used in Cisco IOS devices, so you will need to create Record, Monitor, and Exporter policies and apply the results either to the leaf host interface or the bridge domain (logical L2 segment). All three NetFlow configuration objects are located in **Tenants -> <tenant_name> -> Policies -> NetFlow** or **Fabric -> Access Policies -> Policies -> Interface -> NetFlow.**

NetFlow Exporter

The first component to configure is NetFlow Exporter. In this policy, you define how to reach the external data collector, which can be connected in any internal application EPG or behind the external L3 network (in ACI represented by L3OUT and external EPG). Most of the fields are self-explanatory, as you can see in Figure 3-35. In the *Source Type* and *Source IP Address* you can define what IP address the leaf will use when sending the flow information to the collector to identify itself (TEP, OOB, in-band, or custom). In case of a custom Src IP, make sure to use a subnet with a /20 mask or larger. ACI switches will use the last 12 bits of a defined subnet to code their NodeID into the source address.

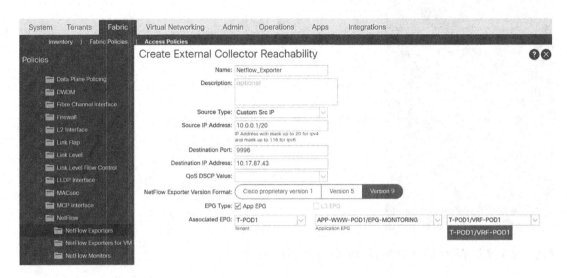

Figure 3-35. *NetFlow exporter configuration*

NetFlow Record

Next, you configure NetFlow Record, where you specify which flow information and statistics you will match and collect (see Figure 3-36). Match parameters must be set with respect to the IPv4, IPv6, or Ethernet address families. You can use these combinations or their subsets:

- Source IPv4, Destination IPv4, Source Port, Destination Port, IP Protocol, VLAN, IP TOS

- Source IPv6, Destination IPv6, Source Port, Destination Port, IP Protocol, VLAN, IP TOS

- Ethertype, Source MAC, Destination MAC, VLAN

- Source IPv4/6, Destination IPv4/6, Source Port, Destination Port, IP Protocol, VLAN, IP TOS

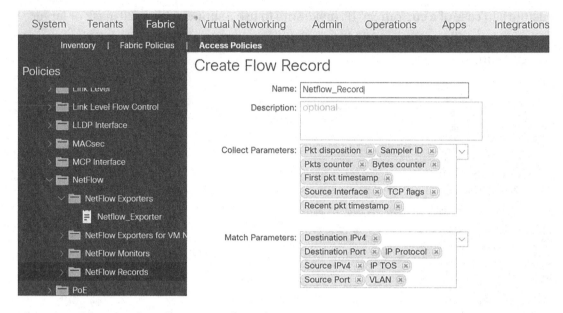

Figure 3-36. *NetFlow flow record configuration*

NetFlow Monitor

In the final object, NetFlow Monitor, you join together the flow record with the flow exporters (as shown in Figure 3-37). Simultaneously only **two active** flow exporters are supported on a particular leaf switch.

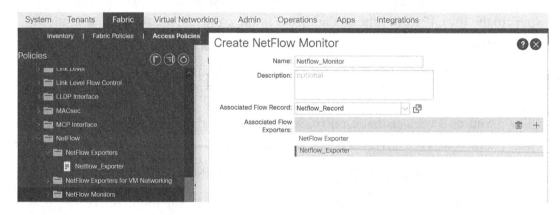

Figure 3-37. *NetFlow Monitor record configuration*

The finished NetFlow monitor is then applied to the individual **Interface Policy Group** in **Fabric -> Access Policies,** or **Tenants -> <tenant_name> -> Networking -> Bridge Domain -> <BD_name> -> Policy tab -> Advanced/Troulbeshooting Tab** (as shown in Figure 3-38). If you applied a NetFlow policy to the bridge domain, APIC will automate the configuration on all leaf interfaces belonging to it and filter the information about incoming traffic to related BD subnets.

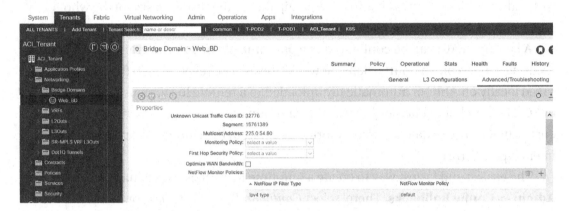

Figure 3-38. *NetFlow monitor association with bridge domain*

To verify the state of your flow cache, you can issue the command on the leaf switch shown in Listing 3-20.

Listing 3-20. NetFlow Flow Cache Verification

```
Leaf-102# show flow cache ipv4
IPV4 Entries
SIP             DIP            BD ID   S-Port   D-Port   Protocol   Byte Count     Packet Count     TCP FLAGS   if_id        flowStart             flowEnd
192.168.21.10   8.8.8.8        516     60643    53       17         210            5                0x0         0x16000005   2534388034  2534396061
192.168.31.10   10.32.0.206    515     3389     62970    17         5304           122              0x0         0x16000005   2534388023  2534430070
192.168.21.20   8.8.8.8        516     58562    53       17         42             1                0x0         0x16000005   2534389042  2534389042
10.32.0.206     192.168.31.10  4720    59303    3389     6          0              41               0x10        0x16000002   2534388027  2534430072
```

ACI Fabric Backup

One of the most important aspects when dealing with any IT technology operation is its backup. I prefer configuring the APIC cluster backup as soon as possible during the ACI implementation, ideally before creating hundreds or even thousands of access policy and tenant objects, just to make sure I won't lose any progress accidentally.

One of ACI's significant advantages lies in its automation capabilities. You can apply a configuration to hundreds of switches around multiple datacenters from the one, centralized place. And in the same way, you can very easily back up the whole configuration of your datacenter networking. Thanks to the object information model used in ACI, all configuration components can be represented and described in a text form (JSON or XML) and therefore easily exported into one single text file. APIC additionally compress it into a tar/gz .zip file, so the resulting size of the whole configuration has usually single units of MBs at most.

A backup in ACI can be configured as a one-time job or you can granularly schedule recuring exports on an hourly, daily, or weekly basis. The resulting .zip file is either saved locally on APIC or automatically uploaded to a remote location using FTP, SFTP, or SCP. Remember to enable global AES encryption, described in a previous section, to ensure that sensitive data are also exported as a part of the configuration file (of course in encrypted form).

The easiest and fastest way to create a one-time local backup is to navigate to **Admin -> Config Rollbacks**. There, select *Config Rollback for Fabric*, optionally add a description, and click *Create a snapshot now* (as shown in Figure 3-39).

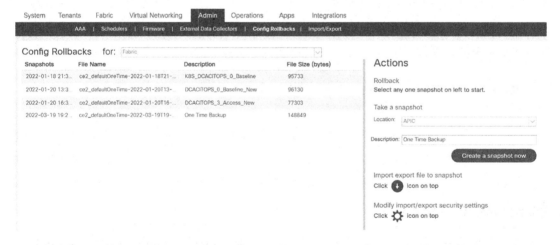

Figure 3-39. *APIC local configuration snapshots*

When you select a specific snapshot, returning to this previous state of ACI configuration is matter of one click on the *Rollback to this configuration* button. Optionally, you can further compare this selected snapshot with others and see the changes. I highly recommend creating this snapshot before implementing any significant change. When something goes wrong or a change causes an outage, you don't want to spend too much time troubleshooting. The best solution in such a case is fast rollback.

Let's now create a remote export location in **Admin -> Import/Export -> Remote Locations** (as shown in Figure 3-40). Fill in the IP address of a remote server, protocol, path, credentials, and, as usual, the preferred management EPG to reach it.

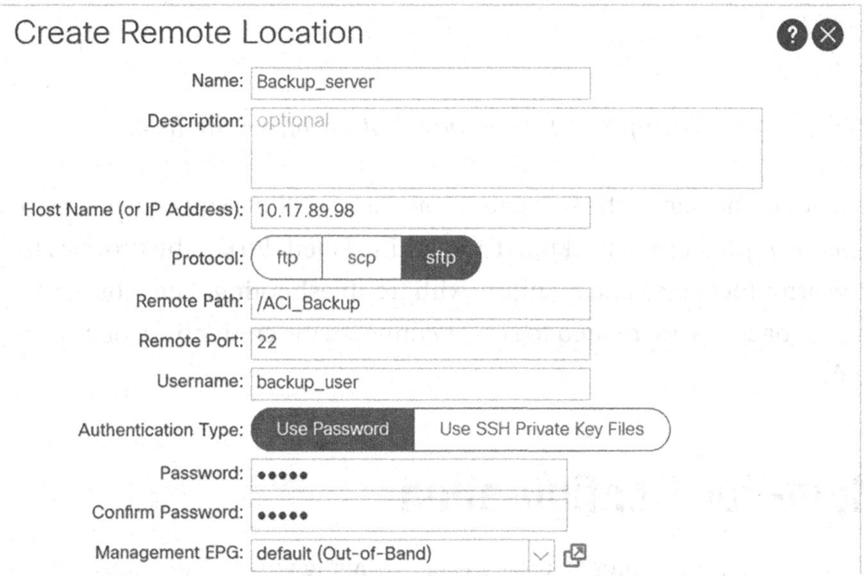

Figure 3-40. *Remote APIC configuration backup*

The remote location can then be used in a configuration export object in **Admin -> Import/Export -> Export Policies -> Configuration.** As depicted in Figure 3-41, choose the export format, start time, and associate export destination and create a new Scheduler object according to your needs and preferences. I recommend performing at least one daily backup, but feel free to increase the recurrence.

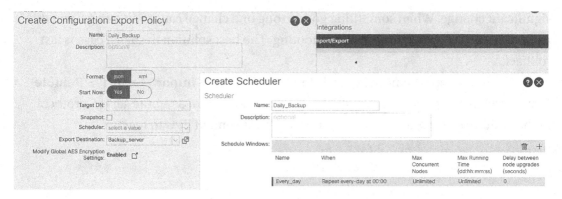

Figure 3-41. *Remote Configuration Export Policy with Scheduler*

In the Operational tab of the Configuration Export Policy, you can check the outcome of the implemented backup. If something failed during the process, there you will find the error messages and continue with troubleshooting. The most common problems with backups are related to server connectivity, credentials, or a wrong remote path specified.

ACI Multi-Pod Configuration

The final section in this chapter is dedicated to showing you all the necessary configuration steps to correctly prepare the Inter-Pod Network and ensure underlay forwarding between ACI Pods including their own configuration in APIC. If ACI Multi-Pod isn't currently a thing for you, feel free to skip this part and continue to the next chapter.

For next paragraphs, let's assume the simple IPN topology shown in Figure 3-42. In production, you can use more interconnections between all devices to increase the available throughput and redundancy.

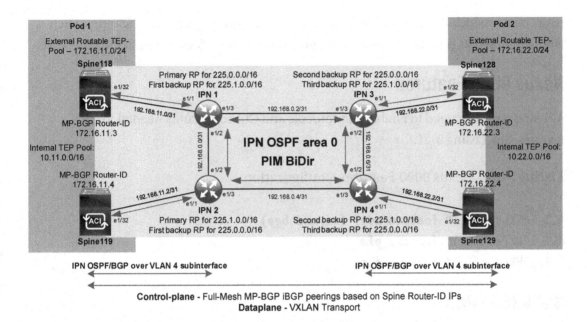

Figure 3-42. ACI IPN architecture and configuration

Before the ACI Multi-Pod deployment itself, prepare the following IP information:

- **Internal TEP Pool** (/16 - /23): One per Pod (first "seed" Pod should be already addressed)

- **External Routable TEP Pool** (/24 - /29): One per Pod, used for control plane and data plane forwarding between Pods. For each spine, a MP-BGP Router ID will be chosen from this pool during the configuration and APIC reserves three more IP addresses: Anycast-mac External TEP, Anycast-v4 External TEP, and Anycast-v6 External TEP. These are for Multi-POD VXLAN bridging and routing purposes.

- **Underlay IPN Routing Subnets** (/XX – /31)**:** Based on the number of L3 interconnections between spines and the IPN (and the IPN itself)

Inter-POD Network Configuration

With your IP plan ready, you can start configuring individual IPN devices. For this example, I will use a Nexus 9000-based IPN, but I'm sure the configuration can be simply adapted to all other platforms or even vendors. Since the IPN is not managed by APIC, it doesn't really matter which devices you use as long as they support the necessary features. Each configuration part is meant to be implemented on all IPN devices unless stated otherwise.

Nexus 9000 Features

As a first step, you need to enable all protocols and CLI commands needed for IPN features. See Listing 3-21.

Listing 3-21. Nexus 9000 Features Configuration

```
ACI-IPNX(config)# feature ospf (or/and bgp)
ACI-IPNX(config)# feature pim
ACI-IPNX(config)# feature dhcp
```

IPN VRF Instance

When you use IPN routers as a single purpose device, this step is not so important. In all other cases, though, I highly recommend that you separate ACI IPN routing information to its own Virtual Routing and Forwarding (VRF) instance. See Listing 3-22.

Listing 3-22. IPN VRF Instance Configuration

```
ACI-IPNX(config)# vrf context IPN
```

OSPF/eBGP Process

Since ACI version 5.2(3), both OSPF and eBGP underlay routing protocols are supported for IPN routing so choose based on your preference or other operational aspects. If you've created an IPN VRF, these protocols need to run as part of it. See Listing 3-23.

Listing 3-23. IPN OSPF Underlay Routing Configuration on IPN1

```
feature ospf
router ospf IPN
  vrf IPN
    router-id 1.1.1.1
    log-adjacency-changes
    passive-interface default
```

At the time of writing, eBGP peerings only are supported between the IPN and spines, so make sure to specify correct neighbor IP addresses and the autonomous system. On the ACI side, BGP AS is configured during internal MP-BGP provisioning. See Listing 3-24.

Listing 3-24. IPN eBGP Underlay Routing Configuration on IPN1

```
ACI-IPN1(config)# feature bgp

router bgp 65534
  vrf IPN
    address-family ipv4 unicast
    neighbor 192.168.11.0
      description Spine118
      remote-as 65500
      log-neighbor-changes
    neighbor 192.168.1.3
      description iBGP Loopback of ACI-IPN3
      remote-as 65534
      log-neighbor-changes
      update-source loopback0
          address-family ipv4 unicast
          next-hop-self
    neighbor 192.168.1.2
      description iBGP Loopback of ACI-IPN2
      remote-as 65534
      log-neighbor-changes
      update-source loopback0
          address-family ipv4 unicast
          next-hop-self
```

L3 IPN Interfaces Facing ACI Spines

ACI uses hardcoded VLAN 4 when communicating with IPN, so the simplest way is to configure L3 point-to-point subinterfaces on the IPN side. Between IPNs, configure whatever is feasible: plain P2P L3 interfaces if no VRFs are used or subinterfaces/SVIs when per VRF L3 connections are needed.

Then it's important to set a MTU to the value at least 50 bytes higher than the maximum size used on your ACI host-facing interfaces or control plane MTU setting, whichever is higher. The default MTU in ACI for the control plane and endpoints is 9000. See Listing 3-25.

Listing 3-25. L3 Interface Configuration for IPN1

```
interface Ethernet1/1
  mtu 9216
  no shutdown

interface Ethernet1/1.4
  description Spine118
  mtu 9216
  encapsulation dot1q 4
  vrf member IPN
  ip address 192.168.11.1/31
  no shutdown

interface Ethernet1/2
  description IPN2
  mtu 9216
  vrf member IPN
  ip address 192.168.0.0/31
  no shutdown

interface Ethernet1/3
  description IPN3
  mtu 9216
  vrf member IPN
  ip address 192.168.0.2/31
  no shutdown
```

PIM Bidir Multicast Configuration

For Multi-Pod purposes, only the PIM Bidir protocol is supported and IPN devices have to support configuring up to /15 multicast IP ranges.

This PIM variant creates common bidirectional shared trees for multicast traffic distribution from the rendezvous point (RP) to receivers and from the sources to the rendezvous point. Both sources and receivers are represented by ACI spines when sending any broadcast, unknown unicast, or multicast (BUM) traffic between Pods. It is optimally scalable without the need for thousands of (S, G) entries in multicast routing tables of IPN devices. Only (*, G) entries are present instead. Furthermore, multicast trees in IPN are created thanks to IGMP as soon as the new bridge domain is activated in ACI, so you don't need to wait for the first multicast packet.

PIM Bidir cannot use standard Anycast RP, AutoRP, or BSR mechanisms for dynamic RP announcements and redundancy. Instead, you will use the concept of statically configured **phantom RPs**. Only one particular IPN device acts as the RP for the whole ACI /15 multicast pool, or for the specific subset of multicast IP addresses, and in case of failure, another IPN will take over. The RP placement and failover completely relies on the basic longest prefix match routing to the RP IP address, which in fact isn't configured anywhere. From an addressing point of view, it just belongs to the loopback subnet with variable masks configured around IPN devices. The one with the most specific mask (longest prefix match) on its loopback interface will act as a current RP. That's the reason for calling it "phantom." If not already, it will become clearer when you go through the configuration example below.

Additionally, in your sample architecture with four IPN devices, assuming the default GIPo multicast pool was used during APIC initialization, you can quite easily even load-balance the multicast traffic with ensured redundancy. Just split the previous /15 pool into two /16s and implement the RP configuration like this:

- IPN1 is the primary RP for multicast range 225.0.0.0/16 and the first backup RP for 225.1.0.0/16

- IPN2 is the primary RP for multicast range 225.1.0.0/16 and the first backup RP for 225.0.0.0/16

- IPN3 is the second backup for multicast range 225.0.0.0/16 and the third backup RP for 225.1.0.0/16

- IPN3 is the second backup for multicast range 225.1.0.0/16 and the third backup RP for 225.0.0.0/16

But why have second and third backups with just two ACI Pods? If you lose both IPN 1 and 2, backups won't be used for anything actually. But imagine having these four IPN devices interconnecting three+ ACI Pods. Then, even after losing the two main IPN devices, you want to ensure that multicast is working and additional backups will take over. I used to implement the phantom RP this way for our customers in production. See Listings 3-26 through 3-28.

Listing 3-26. Phantom RP Loopback Configuration

IPN1	IPN2
interface loopback1	interface loopback1
description BIDIR Phantom RP 1	description BIDIR Phantom RP 1
vrf member IPN	vrf member IPN
ip address 192.168.254.1/**30**	ip address 192.168.255.1/**29**
ip ospf network point-to-point	ip ospf network point-to-point
ip router ospf IPN area 0.0.0.0	ip router ospf IPN area 0.0.0.0
ip pim sparse-mode	ip pim sparse-mode
interface loopback2	interface loopback2
description BIDIR Phantom RP 2	description BIDIR Phantom RP 2
vrf member IPN	vrf member IPN
ip address 192.168.255.1/**29**	ip address 192.168.255.1/**30**
ip ospf network point-to-point	ip ospf network point-to-point
ip router ospf IPN area 0.0.0.0	ip router ospf IPN area 0.0.0.0
ip pim sparse-mode	ip pim sparse-mode

IPN3	IPN4
interface loopback1	interface loopback1
description BIDIR Phantom RP	description BIDIR Phantom RP
1 vrf member IPN ip address	1vrf member IPNip address
192.168.254.1/**28** ip ospf network	192.168.255.1/**27**ip ospf network
point-to-point ip router ospf	point-to-pointip router ospf
IPN area 0.0.0.0 ip pim sparse-	IPN area 0.0.0.0ip pim sparse-
modeinterface loopback2 description	modeinterface loopback2description
BIDIR Phantom RP 2 vrf member IPN	BIDIR Phantom RP 2vrf member IPNip
ip address 192.168.255.1/**27** ip ospf	address 192.168.255.1/**28**ip ospf
network point-to-point ip router ospf	network point-to-pointip router ospf
IPN area 0.0.0.0 ip pim sparse-mode	IPN area 0.0.0.0ip pim sparse-mode

Listing 3-27. Phantom RP Multicast Groups, All IPNs

```
vrf context IPN
 ip pim rp-address 192.168.254.2 group-list 225.0.0.0/16 bidir
 ip pim rp-address 192.168.255.2 group-list 225.1.0.0/16 bidir
  ip pim rp-address 192.168.254.2 group-list 239.255.255.240/28 bidir
```

Listing 3-28. Multicast L3 Interface Configuration

```
interface Ethernet1/1.4
  ip pim sparse-mode
  no shutdown

interface Ethernet1/2
  ip pim sparse-mode
  no shutdown

interface Ethernet1/3
  ip pim sparse-mode
  no shutdown
```

DHCP Relay Agent Configuration

An important feature to enable automated Multi-Pod discovery is the DHCP relay. It takes a broadcast DHCP Discover message and proxies it to the APIC as a unicast packet. Configure all IPN interface-facing spines with a relay to all used APIC VTEP addresses (their bond0.xxxx interface). See Listing 3-29.

Listing 3-29. DHCP Relay Configuration Example

```
ACI-IPNX(config)# service dhcp
ACI-IPNX(config)# ip dhcp relay

interface Ethernet 1/1
  ip dhcp relay address 10.11.0.1
  ip dhcp relay address 10.11.0.2
  ip dhcp relay address 10.11.0.3
```

Quality of Service for ACI Control-Plane in IPN

Quality of Service (QoS) is for some network engineers kind of abstract "magic" (true story 😊). If configured, usually they just hope it will do its job somehow in case of network congestion. In Multi-Pod ACI, where the APIC cluster can be stretched between distinct locations and spines are exchanging a lot of control plane information along the production data, it's even more important to ensure prioritization for the control plane traffic. Let me show you how. It's actually not so difficult to tune the IPN performance for ACI from a QoS perspective to support its operation in any circumstances.

The first prerequisite to use QoS in IPN was already recommended in the "Fabric-Wide Best Practices" section in this chapter: enable the DSCP class to CoS translation for L3 traffic between ACI Pods or sites, as shown in Figure 3-43 (**Tenant -> infra -> Policies -> Protocol -> DSCP class-CoS translation policy for L3 traffic**). By enabling this feature, configured ACI QoS classes will translate into DSCP values in the outer IP header of a VXLAN packet when sending it through the IPN/ISN.

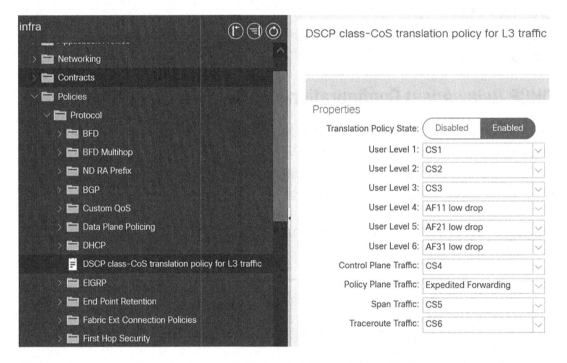

Figure 3-43. *Quality of Service DSCP to CoS Translation Policy*

For your purposes, the most important traffic classes are Control Plane Traffic with CS4 (DSCP value 32) and Policy Plane Traffic with Expedited Forwarding (DSCP value 46). You will match these two and use them in the Nexus 9000 QoS CLI. If you have deployed some other networking devices as IPNs, just map the configuration in their CLI.

At first, create a QoS class map matching the control plane DSCP values and a policy map classifying the traffic into an internal N9K QoS group 7. The policy map will be then applied on all IPN ingress interfaces where the spines are connected. See Listing 3-30.

Listing 3-30. QoS Classification of ACI Control Plane Traffic in IPN

```
class-map type qos match-all ACI_Control_Plane
  match dscp 32,46

policy-map type qos ACI_QoS_Classification
  class ACI_Control_Plane
    set qos-group 7

interface Eth1/1.4
  description Spine291
  service-policy type qos input ACI_QoS_Classification

interface Eth1/2.4
  description Spine292
  service-policy type qos input ACI_QoS_Classification
```

Next, you need to prepare the queuing configuration, defining that matched control plane traffic will get priority in case of any interface congestion. Class names in the following example are predefined on Nexus 9000 and they match internal QoS classes. So, if you classify ACI control plane traffic into the qos-group 7, in the following queuing policy map, it will be part of class c-out-8q-q7. Any control plane traffic in this class will be put into the priority queue. See Listing 3-31.

Listing 3-31. Queuing Configuration for ACI Traffic

```
policy-map type queuing ACI-8q-out-policy
  class type queuing c-out-8q-q7
    priority level 1
  class type queuing c-out-8q-q6
    bandwidth remaining percent 0
  class type queuing c-out-8q-q5
    bandwidth remaining percent 0
  class type queuing c-out-8q-q4
    bandwidth remaining percent 0
  class type queuing c-out-8q-q3
    bandwidth remaining percent 0
  class type queuing c-out-8q-q2
    bandwidth remaining percent 0
  class type queuing c-out-8q-q1
    bandwidth remaining percent 0
  class type queuing c-out-8q-q-default
    bandwidth remaining percent 100
```

Note   As you can see, Nexus 9000s support eight different traffic classes for queuing. In the same way as you configured priority for the control plane, you can reserve bandwidth for any other ACI traffic class defined in APIC. Just match different DSCP values, put the traffic in the respective qos-group, and define the amount of bandwidth available for a particular queue in the previous queuing policy map.

The completed queuing policy map now needs to be globally assigned on the switch using the commands shown in Listing 3-32.

Listing 3-32. Custom ACI Queuing Policy Map Application

```
system qos
  service-policy type queuing output ACI-8q-out-policy
```

To verify QoS operation, first have a look at ingress interfaces to see if there are matched control plane packets, defined in your class map. See Listing 3-33.

Listing 3-33. ACI Control-Plane QoS Classification Verification in IPN

```
ipn-1# show policy-map interface e1/1.4 input
Global statistics status :    enabled

Ethernet1/1.4
  Service-policy (qos) input:   ACI_QoS_Classification
    SNMP Policy Index:  285213859

    Class-map (qos):   ACI_Control_Plane (match-all)

      Slot 1
        156729 packets
      Aggregate forwarded :
        156729 packets
       Match: dscp 32,46
       set qos-group 7
```

Second, check the output IPN interface-facing IP network between Pods from a queuing perspective, as shown in Listing 3-34.

Listing 3-34. IPN Custom Queuing Verification for ACI Control-Plane Traffic

```
ipn-1# show queuing interface eth1/5 | b "GROUP 7"
|                          QOS GROUP 7                           |
+---------------------------------------------------------------+
|                       | Unicast        |Multicast      |
+---------------------------------------------------------------+
|               Tx Pkts |           72215|              0|
|               Tx Byts |        17213375|              0|
```

```
| WRED/AFD & Tail Drop Pkts |                     0|                     0|
| WRED/AFD & Tail Drop Byts |                     0|                     0|
|             Q Depth Byts  |                     0|                     0|
|        WD & Tail Drop Pkts |                    0|                     0|
+-------------------------------------------------------------------+
```

Now, with all the previous IPN configuration in place, you are ready to create additional necessary objects in ACI and enable Multi-Pod features.

APIC Multi-Pod Wizard

Since ACI version 4.2(1), adding a new Pod to your ACI infrastructure is literally matter of few clicks thanks to the highly recommended configuration wizard. It creates the entire set of ACI objects needed for Multi-Pod on your behalf and ensures you don't miss anything. To use it, navigate to **Fabric -> Inventory** and on the QuickStart page choose Add Pod. **The Multi-Pod configuration using the wizard must start with the first "seed" Pod and then repeat the process for all other Pods.**

When started, the wizard presents you with following steps (pages):

- **Page 1 "Overview:"** A theoretical overview about Multi-Pod concepts and needs, for your reference

- **Page 2 "Pod Fabric:"** Allows you to configure the Pod ID, TEP pool, and L3 interfaces used between spines and the IPN

- **Page 3 "Routing Protocol:"** Focused on OSPF/BGP underlay routing. In the OSPF Interface Policy, make sure to match the parameters of the IPN protocol configuration (OSPF is especially prone to MTU, timer, or a network type mismatch).

- **Page 4 "External TEP:"** Lets you configure the external routable TEP pool. After entering the pool subnet, APIC will automatically fill the data plane TEP IP and Router-ID for MP-BGP peering, so no need to change anything here.

- **Page 5 "Confirmation:"** APIC will inform you here about all the objects created for Multi-Pod purposes and optionally you can change their names.

After submitting the whole form, repeat the process for all other Pods present in your ACI infrastructure.

ACI Multi-Pod Verification and Troubleshooting

To verify the correct operation of Multi-Pod architecture, you can start by checking the IPN OSPF. Make sure you have FULL adjacencies between all devices and that you see ACI TEP prefixes announced from spines to the IPN. See Listing 3-35.

Listing 3-35. IPN OSPF Verification

```
ACI-IPN1# show ip ospf neighbors vrf IPN
 OSPF Process ID IPN VRF IPN
 Total number of neighbors: 3
 Neighbor ID      Pri State        Up Time   Address         Interface
 2.2.2.2           1 FULL/ -        3w2d      192.168.0.1     Eth1/2
 3.3.3.3           1 FULL/ -        3w2d      192.168.0.3     Eth1/3
 172.16.11.3       1 FULL/ -        3w2d      192.168.11.0    Eth1/1.4

ACI-IPN1# show ip route ospf-IPN vrf IPN
 IP Route Table for VRF "IPN"
 '*' denotes best ucast next-hop
 '**' denotes best mcast next-hop
 '[x/y]' denotes [preference/metric]
 '%<string>' in via output denotes VRF <string>

10.11.0.0/16, ubest/mbest: 1/0
    *via 192.168.11.0, Eth1/1.4, [110/20], 3w2d, ospf-IPN, type-2
10.11.0.1/32, ubest/mbest: 1/0
    *via 192.168.11.0, Eth1/1.4, [110/20], 1w4d, ospf-IPN, type-2
10.11.0.2/32, ubest/mbest: 1/0
    *via 192.168.11.0, Eth1/1.4, [110/20], 1w4d, ospf-IPN, type-2
10.11.0.3/32, ubest/mbest: 2/0
    *via 192.168.0.3, Eth1/3, [110/20], 2w0d, ospf-IPN, type-2
10.22.0.0/16, ubest/mbest: 2/0
    *via 192.168.0.3, Eth1/3, [110/20], 3w2d, ospf-IPN, type-2
...output omitted...
```

Check that each IPN-facing spine switch has the following IP interfaces configured for Multi-Pod operation (loopback numbers may vary):

- Loopback 5: Data plane VXLAN anycast TEP for MAC bridging

- Loopback 6: Data plane VXLAN anycast TEP for IPv4 routing

- Loopback 7: Data plane VXLAN anycast TEP for IPv6 routing

- Loopback 8: Anycast external TEP address used as a next hop for EVPN (MAC and IP endpoint entries) in BGP

- Loopback 15: Router ID for MP-BGP protocol peering (EVPN control plane)

- Now see Listing 3-36.

Listing 3-36. Spine Multi-Pod L3 Interfaces

```
soine-118# show ip interface vrf overlay-1
IP Interface Status for VRF "overlay-1"
lo5, Interface status: protocol-up/link-up/admin-up, iod: 83, mode:
anycast-mac,external
  IP address: 10.11.0.33, IP subnet: 10.11.0.33/32
  IP broadcast address: 255.255.255.255
  IP primary address route-preference: 0, tag: 0
lo6, Interface status: protocol-up/link-up/admin-up, iod: 84, mode:
anycast-v4,external
  IP address: 10.11.0.34, IP subnet: 10.11.0.34/32
  IP broadcast address: 255.255.255.255
  IP primary address route-preference: 0, tag: 0
lo7, Interface status: protocol-up/link-up/admin-up, iod: 85, mode:
anycast-v6,external
  IP address: 10.11.0.35, IP subnet: 10.11.0.35/32
  IP broadcast address: 255.255.255.255
  IP primary address route-preference: 0, tag: 0
lo8, Interface status: protocol-up/link-up/admin-up, iod: 86, mode: etep
  IP address: 172.16.11.1, IP subnet: 172.16.11.1/32
  IP broadcast address: 255.255.255.255
```

```
  IP primary address route-preference: 0, tag: 0
lo15, Interface status: protocol-up/link-up/admin-up, iod: 97,
mode: cp-etep
  IP address: 172.16.11.3, IP subnet: 172.16.11.3/32
  IP broadcast address: 255.255.255.255
  IP primary address route-preference: 0, tag: 0
... output omitted ...
```

Next, you should find the MP-BGP peerings in VRF overlay-1 on spines for address families VPNv4, VPNv6, and L2VPN EVPN. See Listing 3-37.

Listing 3-37. MP-BGP peerings verification

```
soine-118# show bgp l2vpn evpn summary vrf overlay-1
BGP summary information for VRF overlay-1, address family L2VPN EVPN
BGP router identifier 172.16.11.3, local AS number 65534
BGP table version is 66324, L2VPN EVPN config peers 1, capable peers 1
444 network entries and 460 paths using 75888 bytes of memory
BGP attribute entries [13/2288], BGP AS path entries [0/0]
BGP community entries [0/0], BGP clusterlist entries [0/0]

Neighbor        V   AS MsgRcvd MsgSent    TblVer  InQ OutQ Up/Down
State/PfxRcd
172.16.22.3     4 65532   71387 22706209   66324   0    0   3w2d
163
172.16.22.4     4 65532   71385 22706210   66324   0    0   3w2d
163
```

For endpoint connectivity to work between ACI Pods, both local and remote endpoint entries should be visible in the MP-BGP database (see Figure 3-44). The EVPN information is quite complex, but I will cover it later in detail as part of Chapter 6.

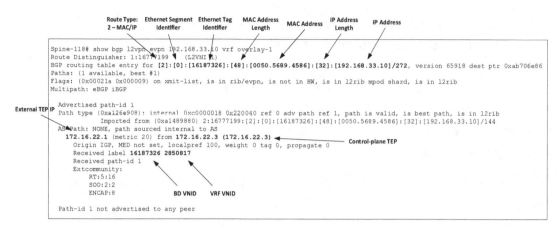

Figure 3-44. *MP-BGP endpoint database entry*

And finally, you should see the same information redistributed from MP-BGP to the local COOP database, which can be checked by issuing the command shown in Listing 3-38.

Listing 3-38. COOP Database Verification

```
soine-118# show coop internal info ip-db key 2850817 192.168.33.10

IP address : 192.168.33.10
Vrf : 2850817
Flags : 0x2
EP bd vnid : 16187326
EP mac :  00:50:56:89:45:86
Publisher Id : 172.16.22.1
Record timestamp : 01 01 1970 00:00:00 0
Publish timestamp : 01 01 1970 00:00:00 0
Seq No: 0
Remote publish timestamp: 03 19 2022 17:16:03 301209130
URIB Tunnel Info
Num tunnels : 1
        Tunnel address : 10.22.0.34
        Tunnel ref count : 1
```

Summary

By the end of this chapter, you should have gained the necessary knowledge and practical skills to initialize ACI for both single-fabric and Multi-Pod architectures. You've gone through the automated switch discovery process, out-of-band and in-band management access, best practice recommendations for the initial fabric configuration, and protocols related to the fabric management, operation, and monitoring. You also learned how to correctly configure an Inter-Pod Network to support all the necessary features for ACI.

Since the fabric is currently up and running, you can start connecting endpoints to it. The next chapter will focus on ACI access policies representing configuration options for the physical underlay leaf host interfaces.

CHAPTER 4

ACI Fundamentals: Access Policies

ACI, due to its application-centric philosophy and multi-tenancy, differentiates between the common physical underlay network consisting of leaf/spine switches and the logical network model describing tenant application policies and the logical network configuration (VRFs, BDs, EPGs, etc.). In this chapter, you will look closer at underlay access policies, the first and very important configuration aspect to ensure end host connectivity.

Access policies are a group of universal configuration objects associated between each other to completely describe settings for individual end host-facing interfaces on leaf or spine switches. This implies that all end hosts without a difference need them. It doesn't matter if you plan to connect a bare-metal server, virtualization hypervisor, external router, legacy switch, firewall, load balancer, or IPN/ISN device. All of them must have an entire set of access policies in place to communicate through ACI.

Additionally, they describe encapsulation resources (VLAN IDs or VXLAN VNIDs) usable on specified interfaces. The important term is **usable**. In access policies you **don't define actually used encapsulation** or how it will be specifically configured on particular interface (e.g., mode access or trunk). You just grant a usage permission for encapsulation IDs and the mapping itself will happen later in the tenant policies.

Access policies are global and usually configured by the global ACI administrator. This especially applies to datacenter service providers. On the other hand, tenants can be maintained by completely different subjects without admin rights to the whole ACI configuration. By the proper design of access policies, the global admin can easily ensure separation of hardware and encapsulation resources between ACI tenants, preconfigure the underlay networking for them, and simply expose all the settings using the single object mapping I will describe in the following sections.

© Jan Janovic 2023
J. Janovic, *Cisco ACI: Zero to Hero*, https://doi.org/10.1007/978-1-4842-8838-2_4

In Figure 4-1, you can view the complete set of access policies and their relation to tenant policies. I will gradually focus on each object and describe its significance for the whole.

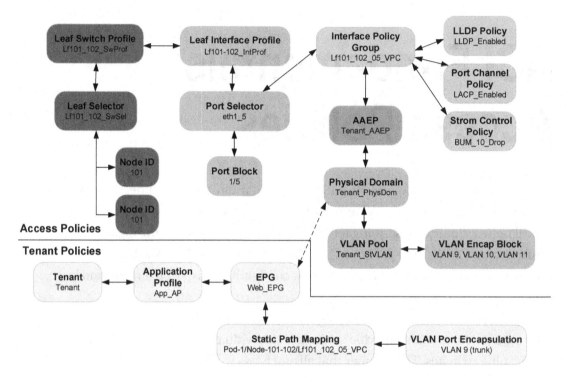

Figure 4-1. *Overview of ACI access policies with relation to tenant EPGs*

The philosophy of access policy configuration is the same as with fabric policies in the previous chapter. First, you need to create individual policy objects where each policy is related to a specific protocol or functionality, but without an exact affiliation to a concrete switch or interface. Consider them to be universal building blocks. Then you create lists of individual policies (kind of a policy template) called policy groups. Finally, the policy group is applied to a switch or interface profile. In general, it doesn't matter in which order you create individual access policy objects, just make sure to have all of them at the end.

Switch Policies

You will start the configuration by creating switch policies. These objects define global switch settings related to access connectivity and vPC domain parameters. Most importantly, they allow you to specify switch node IDs on which you will later configure individual access interfaces.

Switch Protocol Policies and vPC

When you navigate to **Fabric -> Access Policies -> Policies -> Switch**, you will find individual policies for various switch-wide functions: Dot1x, bidirectional forwarding detection parameters, control plane policing, fiber channel, forwarding scale profiles, and many more. As usual in ACI, each of them has a precreated default object, which is resolved in case no custom object is used. If there is a need to change some property, the best practice is to create a new policy instead of changing the default one. By doing so you avoid an unintentional configuration change on all switches in the default state. Another recommendation is to name the object according to its actual purpose and settings inside.

- **Optimal names:** IPv4_BFD_Enable, High_LPM_ScaleProfile, CoPP_Permissive

- **Ambiguous names:** BFD_Policy, NetFlow, PTP_Profile

Mostly I don't customize default individual switch policies if not explicitly required, but there is one exception almost always. As compared to legacy NX-OS mode, when you plan to create vPC port channels, a pair of switches has to be bundled into a vPC domain. For this purpose, in switch policies, navigate to the **Virtual Port Channel default** object. Here you can create so-called explicit VPC protection groups (as shown in Figure 4-2). The logical pair ID corresponds to the vPC domain ID.

Figure 4-2. *Explicit VPC protection groups*

Notice that each pair of leaves in the vPC receives another common "Virtual IP" from a respective POD VTEP pool. This IP represents their anycast VTEP address since at that moment, all traffic originated from or destined to a vPC port-channel will be routed inside the fabric to this virtual anycast VTEP address instead of individual switch-specific addresses.

vPC policy doesn't need to be applied anywhere; it's sufficient to create a protection group, and the configuration is immediately pushed to the fabric. On ACI leaves, the vPC domain is implemented in a very similar manner compared to NX-OS, just without need for a physical vPC peer-link and peer-keepalive between leaves. The vPC control plane is established via spine switches instead. To verify the configuration deployment, you can use well-known show commands from NX-OS, as shown in Listing 4-1.

Listing 4-1. vPC Verification

```
Leaf-101# show ip int lo1
IP Interface Status for VRF "overlay-1"
lo1, Interface status: protocol-up/link-up/admin-up, iod: 86, mode: vpc
   IP address: 10.11.88.76, IP subnet: 10.11.88.76/32  <- Anycast VTEP IP
   IP broadcast address: 255.255.255.255
   IP primary address route-preference: 0, tag: 0

Leaf-101# show vpc brief
Legend:
                (*) - local vPC is down, forwarding via vPC peer-link

vPC domain id                     : 1
Peer status                       : peer adjacency formed ok
vPC keep-alive status             : Disabled
Configuration consistency status  : success
Per-vlan consistency status       : success
Type-2 consistency status         : success
vPC role                          : primary
Number of vPCs configured         : 4
Peer Gateway                      : Disabled
Dual-active excluded VLANs        : -
Graceful Consistency Check        : Enabled
Auto-recovery status              : Enabled (timeout = 200 seconds)
Delay-restore status              : Enabled (timeout = 120 seconds)
Delay-restore SVI status          : Enabled (timeout = 0 seconds)
Operational Layer3 Peer           : Disabled
```

```
vPC Peer-link status
-------------------------------------------------------------------------
id   Port   Status Active vlans
--   ----   ------ --------------------------------------------------------
1           up     -

Leaf-101# show vpc role

vPC Role status
-----------------------------------------------------
vPC role                     : primary
Dual Active Detection Status : 0
vPC system-mac               : 00:23:04:ee:be:01
vPC system-priority          : 32667
vPC local system-mac         : 70:0f:6a:b2:99:e5
vPC local role-priority      : 101
```

Switch Policy Group

Individual customized switch policies have to be put inside a switch policy group, creating a template for a switch configuration. This object can be created in **Fabric -> Access Policies -> Switches -> Leaf Switches -> Switch Policy Group** (see Figure 4-3).

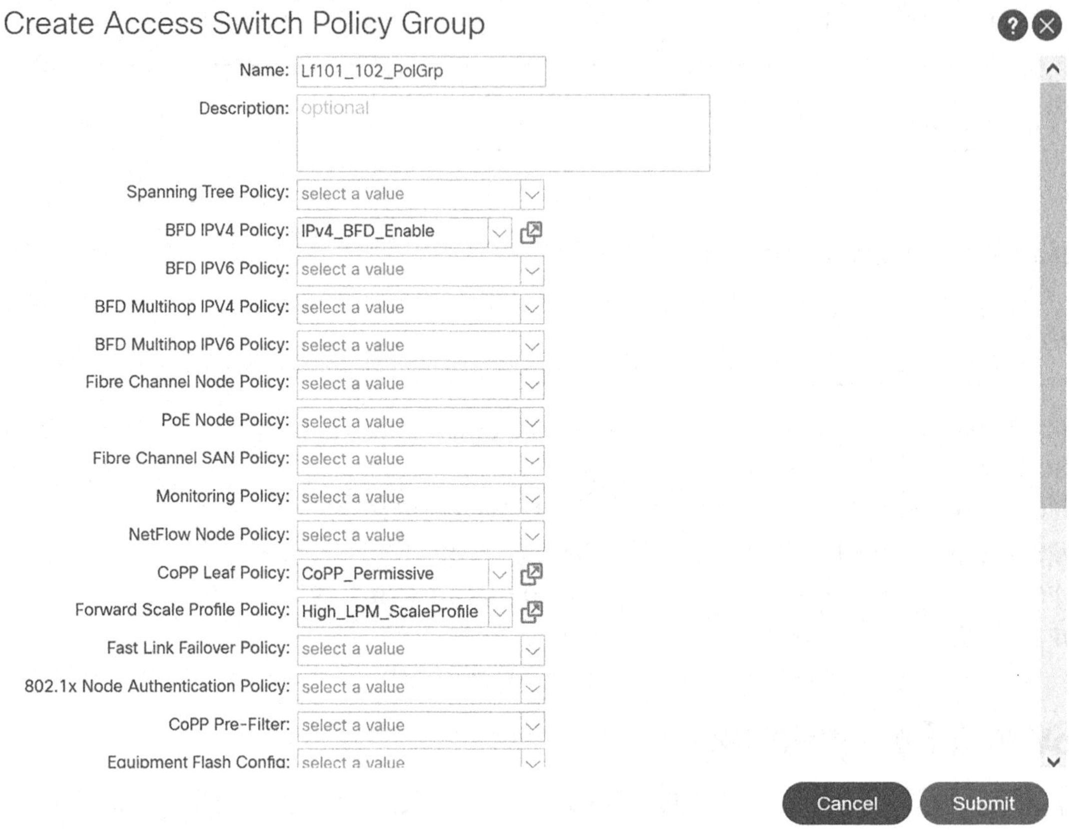

Create Access Switch Policy Group

Name:	Lf101_102_PolGrp
Description:	optional
Spanning Tree Policy:	select a value
BFD IPV4 Policy:	IPv4_BFD_Enable
BFD IPV6 Policy:	select a value
BFD Multihop IPV4 Policy:	select a value
BFD Multihop IPV6 Policy:	select a value
Fibre Channel Node Policy:	select a value
PoE Node Policy:	select a value
Fibre Channel SAN Policy:	select a value
Monitoring Policy:	select a value
NetFlow Node Policy:	select a value
CoPP Leaf Policy:	CoPP_Permissive
Forward Scale Profile Policy:	High_LPM_ScaleProfile
Fast Link Failover Policy:	select a value
802.1x Node Authentication Policy:	select a value
CoPP Pre-Filter:	select a value
Equipment Flash Config:	select a value

Cancel   Submit

Figure 4-3. *Switch policy group*

Note   All fields without a custom policy result in the default one.

Switch Profile

In **Fabric -> Access Policies -> Switches -> Leaf Switches -> Switch Profiles,** you can create the most important object of switch policies: the switch profile. It allows you to map switch policy groups to concrete leaf or spine switches based on their Node IDs and at the same time it defines on which switches you will configure interfaces when the switch profile is associated to the interface profile (as shown in Figure 4-4).

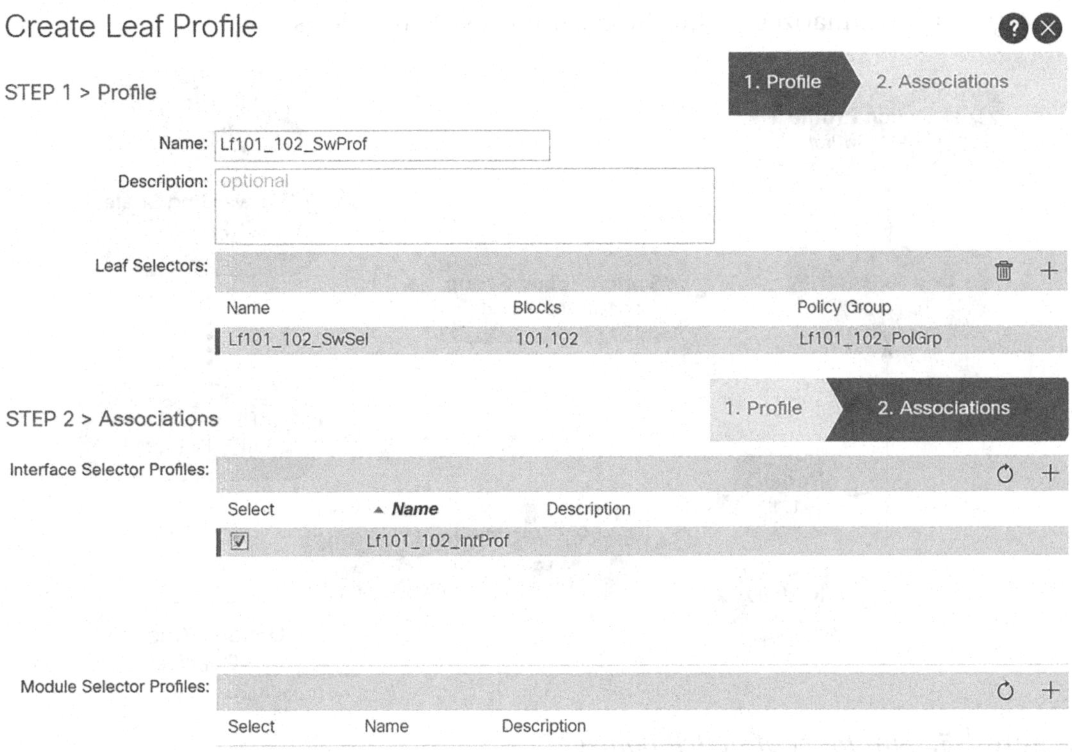

Create Leaf Profile

STEP 1 > Profile

| 1. Profile | 2. Associations |

Name: Lf101_102_SwProf

Description: optional

Leaf Selectors:

Name	Blocks	Policy Group
Lf101_102_SwSel	101,102	Lf101_102_PolGrp

STEP 2 > Associations

| 1. Profile | 2. Associations |

Interface Selector Profiles:

Select	▲ Name	Description
☑	Lf101_102_IntProf	

Module Selector Profiles:

Select	Name	Description

Figure 4-4. *Switch profile*

There are multiple ways to design switch profiles:

1. **All switches in one profile**: Useful for applying common switch settings using a single switch policy group to a profile association

2. **Two switches in one profile**: Useful in a vPC pair to keep the consistent configuration between the two

3. **One switch per profile**: Good practice when you want to configure each switch and its interfaces independently

4. **Combination of above**: It's not a problem to combine the previous approaches and create one profile per switch used for individual interface configurations and then add additional profiles for vPC pairs and finally create one universal profile covering the entire fabric for a switch policy group association.

One switch can be part of multiple profiles; you just can't overlap the interfaces configured in them. ACI displays an error message in such a case.

Figure 4-5 summarizes all the objects forming switch policies.

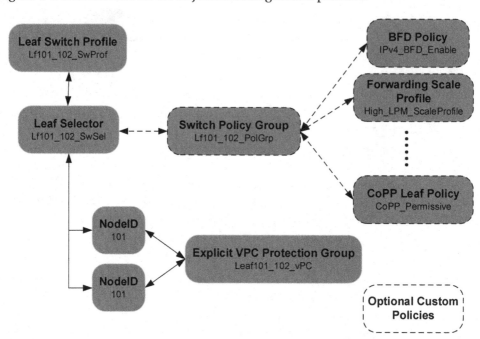

Figure 4-5. *Summary of switch policies*

Interface Policies

Switch policies universally describe ACI leaves or spines and their global access settings, but not how their interfaces should be configured. For this purpose, you will use interface policies, another set of stand-alone ACI objects. Only after associating interface profiles with switch profiles will you achieve the resulting access interface configuration.

Interface Protocol Policy

On the legacy switch, you can apply various commands or create interface templates for each interface. ACI uses a modular object-oriented approach instead of that. The first step is to create individual interface protocol policies.

In **Fabric -> Access Policies -> Policies -> Interface**, you can update the default or create your own objects defining independent protocols settings for your access interfaces. At this point, they are not related to any specific interface; they just describe the setting. The protocol policy can go from a simple enable/disable knob (e.g., for CDP or LLDP protocols) to more complex types such as a port channel or data plane policing, involving various configurable fields, values, and thresholds. Similar to switch policies, make sure to use descriptive object names here as well. It will ease your life later during policy group definition.

If you are wondering what the most important individual policies for access interfaces are, I created this basic set of objects during the initial ACI provisioning for customers:

- **CDP**: CDP_Enable, CDP_Disable

- **LLDP**: LLDP_RxTx_Enable, LLDP_RxTx_Disable

- **Port Channel**: LACP_Active, LACP_Passive, LACP_Active_ NoSuspend, Static_PCH

- **Port Channel Member**: LACP_Rate_Fast

- **Spanning Tree Interface**: BPDU_Guard, BPDU_Guard_Filter, BPDU_Filter

- **MisCabling Protocol (MCP) Interface**: MCP_Enable, MCP_Disable (MCP needs to be globally enabled before use in **Fabric -> Access Policies -> Policies -> Global -> MCP Instance Policy default**)

- **L2 Interface**: VLAN_Port_Local_Scope

- **Netflow Monitor**: Netflow_Monitor

- **Storm Control**: BUM_10percent

All these objects must be created only once at the beginning of ACI provisioning and then you just keep reusing them in interface policy groups.

Interface Policy Group

You can now put individual protocol policies into the interface policy group in **Fabric -> Access Policies -> Interfaces -> Leaf Interfaces -> Policy Groups.** As you can see in Figure 4-6, policy groups are lists of objects universally describing the interface configuration. However, at this moment, they are still without an exact relationship with a specific switch interface. Consider the interfaces policy group as a universal configuration template.

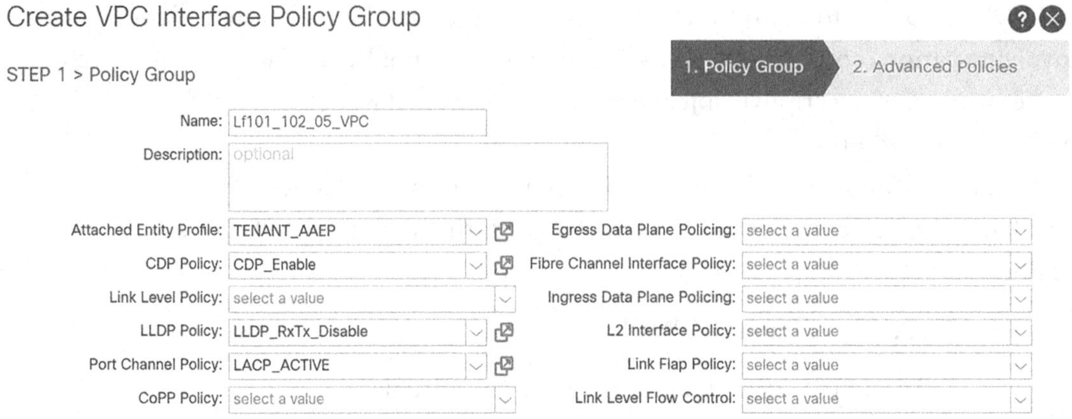

Create VPC Interface Policy Group

STEP 1 > Policy Group

1. Policy Group   2. Advanced Policies

Name:	Lf101_102_05_VPC
Description:	optional

Attached Entity Profile:	TENANT_AAEP	Egress Data Plane Policing:	select a value
CDP Policy:	CDP_Enable	Fibre Channel Interface Policy:	select a value
Link Level Policy:	select a value	Ingress Data Plane Policing:	select a value
LLDP Policy:	LLDP_RxTx_Disable	L2 Interface Policy:	select a value
Port Channel Policy:	LACP_ACTIVE	Link Flap Policy:	select a value
CoPP Policy:	select a value	Link Level Flow Control:	select a value

Figure 4-6. *Interface policy groups*

Another significance of interface policy groups lies in their types. In most cases, you will choose from these three main options:

- **Leaf Access Port**: Representing the configuration of an individual interface, without any kind of port channel. Don't interchange it with legacy L2 "access" (untagged) interface. This object has nothing to do with VLAN usage on the interface. The single-access interface policy group is greatly reusable between multiple interfaces with the same configuration needs.

- **PC Interface**: The interface associated with this interface policy group will become a member port of a standard port channel. It represents a logical group of physical interfaces between a single ACI switch and the connected device. Each port channel interface needs its own interface policy group object because a unique port channel ID is generated based on it.

- **VPC Interface:** The interface associated with this interface policy group will become a member port of a virtual port channel (vPC). Similar to a standard port channel, each vPC interface needs its own interface policy group. This time, the port channel and the vPC IDs are generated based on this access policy object.

Tip   Pay special attention to the **name** of the PC and VPC interface policy group. ACI will display it in most of the show commands or GUI outputs related to port channels instead of the actual physical interface name or port channel ID. Therefore, it's my good practice to code into the interface policy group name at least the Node ID and corresponding physical interface on that switch. Example: Lf101_102_05_VPC, where 101 and 102 stand for the Node IDs of the vPC pair and 05 is a physical vPC member port on both of them.

With interface policy groups you can also configure interface breakout (to split, for example, a 100G interface into 4x25G) or SAN interfaces such as a fiber channel individual or port channel. These are minor options, and they are not used often.

Interface Profile

The ACI access configuration philosophy leads us to interface profiles, located in **Fabric -> Access Policies -> Interfaces -> Leaf Interfaces -> Profiles.** As shown in Figure 4-7, now you create object mapping between interface policy groups and concrete interface identifiers (e.g., Ethernet 1/5). However, it is another universal object, so you don't specify on which switch these interfaces are configured yet.

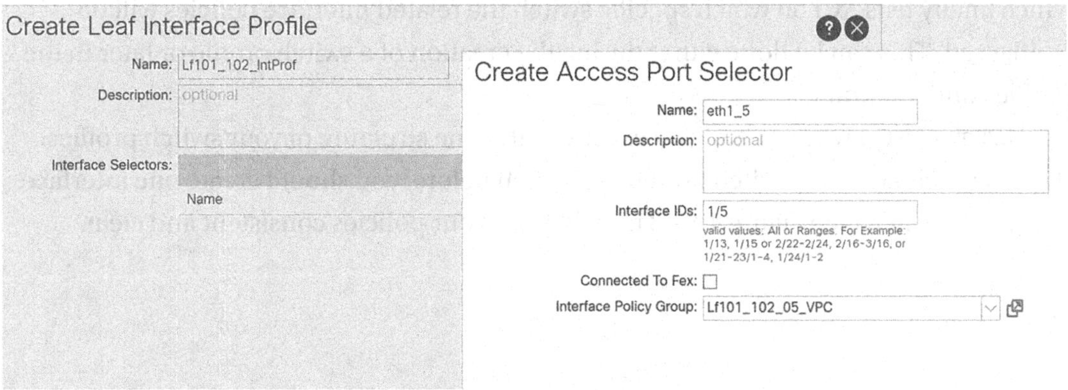

Figure 4-7.   Interface profile and interface selector

Each interface profile contains multiple interface selectors, which can further contain either a single interface entry or a range of multiple interfaces. I always put only one interface per one selector, though. The main reason is to preserve an ability to change the configuration of any individual interface in the future. Otherwise, if you're using interface ranges and a sudden single interface change requirement arises, you will need to delete the whole interface selector range and create multiple entries instead, resulting in a potential undesirable network disruption.

In Figure 4-8, you can see the summary of all interface-related access policies.

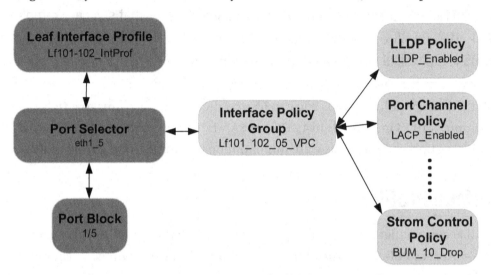

Figure 4-8. *Interface policy group and profile summary*

The completed interface profile now needs to be associated with the switch profile, which finally tells ACI on which specific switch the related interface policies will be configured. This can be done either during the creation of a switch profile or later in the profile configuration.

Design-wise, I recommend you exactly match the structure of your switch profiles. If you have created one switch profile per switch before, you should create one interface profile per switch (see Figure 4-9). This will keep your policies consistent and clear.

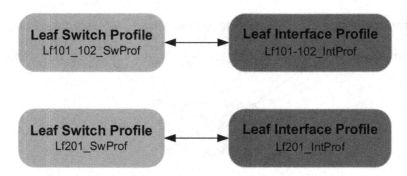

Figure 4-9. Interface and switch profile mutual association

Attachable Access Entity Profile

At this point, you have all access interfaces prepared from a protocol configuration and port channels point of view. But as I mentioned at the beginning of this chapter, you also need to grant encapsulation resources to them. Before doing so, ACI requires an Attachable Access Entity Profile (AAEP) object, found in **Fabric -> Access Policies -> Policies -> Global -> Attachable Access Entity Profile.** Often called "glue," it groups together a set of interfaces (represented by interface policy groups) with similar infrastructure policies (or encapsulation requirements) and interconnects them with physical domains and VLAN pools discussed in the following sections (as depicted in Figure 4-10). At the same time, it allows the administrator to easily map tenant EPGs to all interfaces associated with AAEP in one step, avoiding the need for hundreds of static mappings in tenant policies.

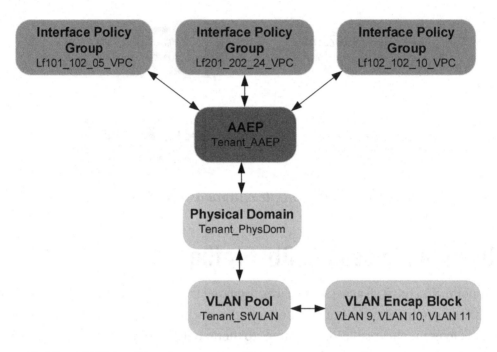

Figure 4-10. *AAEP position in access policies*

How many AAEP objects do you need for ACI? It depends. You need at least one per fabric to effectively provide access to physical resources for your tenants. Sometimes it makes sense to create more of them for a single tenant, especially when a tenant uses consistently configured clusters of virtualization servers with the same encapsulation requirements. Instead of constructing tons of individual VLAN mappings to all EPGs and all interfaces, you can do it in AAEP with a single entry (as shown in the EPG Deployment section of Figure 4-11). An analogy to a legacy network is the need to add a particular VLAN on a range of a trunk or access interfaces using single configuration command. I will discuss this topic in Chapter 5.

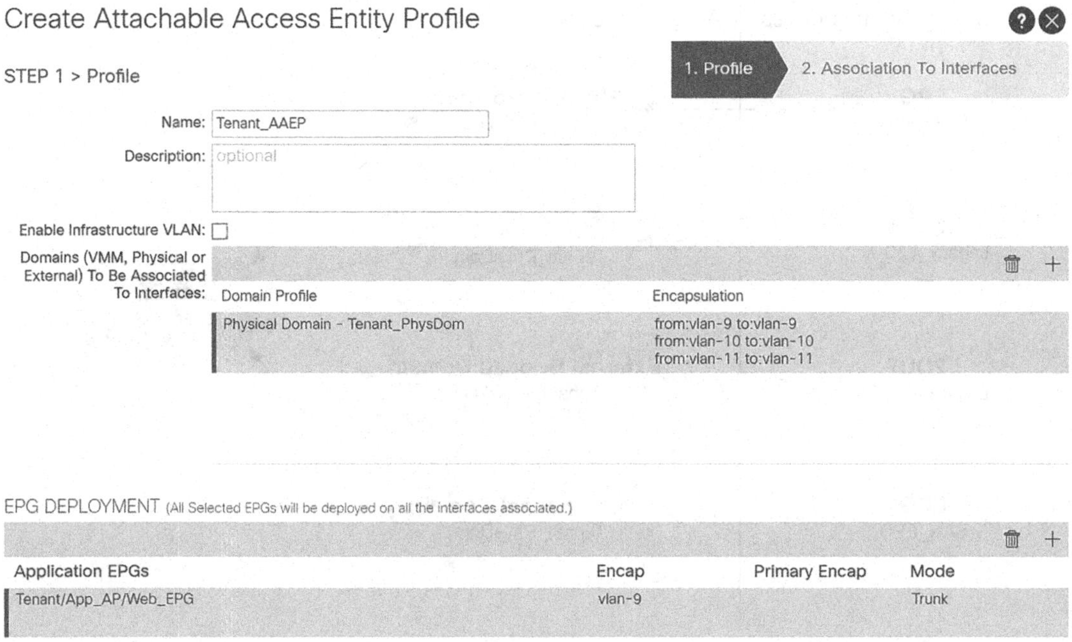

Create Attachable Access Entity Profile

STEP 1 > Profile

| 1. Profile | 2. Association To Interfaces |

Name: Tenant_AAEP

Description: optional

Enable Infrastructure VLAN: ☐

Domains (VMM, Physical or External) To Be Associated To Interfaces:

Domain Profile	Encapsulation
Physical Domain - Tenant_PhysDom	from:vlan-9 to:vlan-9 from:vlan-10 to:vlan-10 from:vlan-11 to:vlan-11

EPG DEPLOYMENT (All Selected EPGs will be deployed on all the interfaces associated.)

Application EPGs	Encap	Primary Encap	Mode
Tenant/App_AP/Web_EPG	vlan-9		Trunk

Figure 4-11. *Attachable Access Entity Profile*

When troubleshooting physical connectivity to ACI, always make sure that all your interfaces policy groups have the correct AAEP associated. When you refer back to Figure 4-7, it's the first associated object in the list.

Physical and External Domains

From AAEP we continue to the next object in the access policy hierarchy: the physical or external domain (**Fabric -> Access Policies -> Physical and External Domains**). Its purpose is to interconnect physical interfaces included in AAEP with the encapsulation resources described in the VLAN pool and grant access to all of them from the tenant policies (see Figure 4-12).

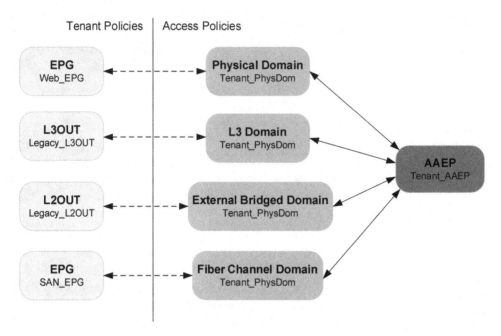

Figure 4-12. *Physical and external domains*

Domains provide the only existing relation between the otherwise abstracted tenant and access policies. For different use cases in tenant policies, you must differentiate between four types of domains:

- **Physical domain**: The most common one, used to provide connectivity for all standard end stations attached to ACI switches, including L4-L7 service devices. Physical domains can be associated only with standard application EPG or L4-L7 device objects.

- **L3 domain**: Type of external domain granting access to ACI physical resources for external L3 connectivity, configured inside an L3OUT tenant object

- **External bridge domain**: Another external domain, but this time used for dedicated external L2 connectivity, L2OUT tenant object

- **Fiber channel domain**: Domain related to storage network VSAN resources, enabling interfaces to be configured as F or NP ports. Associable again with standard application EPGs.

Each ACI tenant has to have at least one physical domain to attach internal endpoints and one L3 domain to ensure external connectivity if applicable.

VLAN I VXLAN I VSAN Pools

In **Fabric -> Access Policies -> Pools**, you can find the last piece of the access policy puzzle: the encapsulation resource pools. Each pool simply defines which VLAN, VXLAN, or VSAN IDs are usable for interfaces associated to a particular physical domain. By specifying a pool, you grant encapsulation resources permissions for the EPGs that are associated with the physical domain using this pool.

Inside pools are encapsulation blocks that allow you to configure a single or a range of encapsulation IDs. It's similar to interface profiles and their interface selectors. I recommend always implementing rather individual encapsulation blocks for longer ranges. In case of need, you will still have an option to change a single entry without affecting all others and avoid an outage.

In Figure 4-13, you can see the relationship between the VLAN pool and the physical domain. The same structure applies to all other domain types as well.

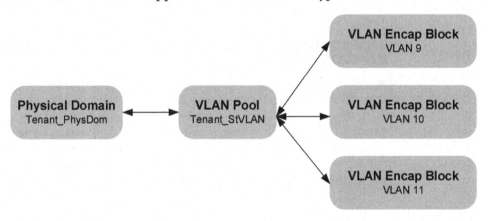

Figure 4-13. *Physical domain and VLAN pool relationship*

VLAN pools additionally differentiate between two allocation modes:

- **Static:** The most common type, used for all standard situations when static VLAN mapping is needed for EPG, L3OUT, or L2OUT. If you don't deal with ACI integration with some virtualization platform (VMM), static pools are all you need to work with.

- **Dynamic:** In case of VMM integration, instead of manual static VLAN mappings, APIC is responsible for choosing the VLAN ID on your behalf and dynamically configures it for a particular EPG on related interfaces and a virtual distributed switch. The range of assigned VLAN IDs is taken from a dynamic VLAN pool.

Each encapsulation block inside a pool has its own allocation mode as well. By default, it inherits the mode from a parent pool, but sometimes there is a need to explicitly change it to something other than that. For VMM integration (discussed in Chapter 9), there is still an option to use static VLAN allocation and mappings for EPGs instead of dynamic. In such a case, you create a dynamic main VLAN pool object, but the range of VLANs used for static mapping is explicitly set to static. If needed, you can even combine both approaches, as shown in Figure 4-14.

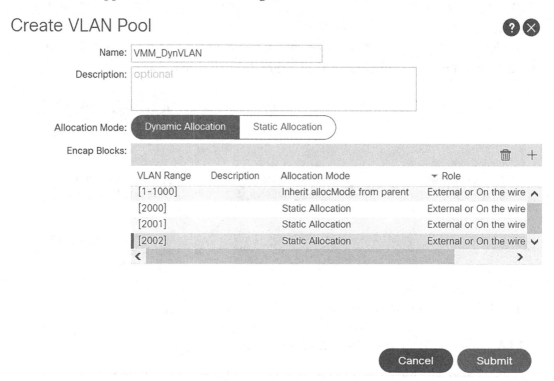

Figure 4-14. *VLAN pool and allocation modes*

The most common issues during an ACI operation with access policies actually relates to incomplete or misconfigured VLAN pools. Always remember when configuring any VLAN mapping in tenant policies, especially when adding a new VLAN or creating new L3 external connectivity over SVI interfaces, to add these VLANs to the VLAN pool first. And with the correct allocation mode (mostly static).

Practical Example for Access Policies

ACI access policies introduce a lot of configuration objects, as you can see. This object-oriented philosophy is significantly different compared to any legacy system you are probably used to working with. For my students, this part is usually the most difficult to grasp when getting into ACI.

For me, the best learning tool, of course, is a practical experience. So, let's now imagine you recently connected and registered a new pair of leaf switches 201 and 202 for a freshly onboarded ACI TenantX and you are tasked to ensure the connectivity for the bare metal server with following properties (see Figure 4-15):

- The server is connected behind interfaces e1/25 of both Leaf 201 and Leaf 202.

- Both switches are part of a new vPC domain.

- The vPC port channel is expected with LACP protocol enabled.

- **Protocol policies:** LACP rate fast, LLDP, CDP, and MCP are enabled and storm control shouldn't allow more than 10% of interface bandwidth for BUM traffic.

- The tenant expects static VLANs mapping for this server with IDs 9-11.

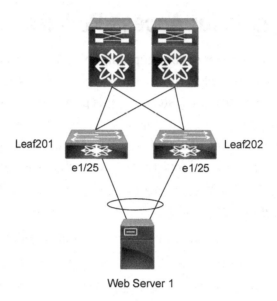

Figure 4-15. *The server is connected using a vPC port-channel to ACI.*

You will now go through a step-by-step process of creating all the necessary access policies and ensuring their deployment on the leaf switches.

1. As the new pair of switches expects vPC connected endpoints, first you must include it in the vPC Explicit Protection Group and create a vPC domain in **Fabric -> Access Policies -> Policies -> Switch -> Virtual Port Channel default.**

2. You know that all of the following access policies are intended for a new tenant, so let's create separate objects where applicable. For VLANs 9-11, you have to prepare a new VLAN pool in **Fabric -> Access Policies -> Pools -> VLAN**. Set its mode to static and create individual encapsulation blocks for each VLAN.

3. Assign the VLAN pool to a new physical domain in **Fabric -> Access Policies -> Physical and External Domains -> Physical Domain.**

4. The physical domain object associates with a new AAEP created in **Fabric -> Access Policies -> Policies -> Global -> Attachable Access Entity Profile.**

5. Now go to **Fabric -> Access Policies -> Policies -> Interface** and create all the necessary partial protocol policies (if not already present):

    a. Port channel policy enabling LACP active mode

    b. Port channel member policy activating LACP rate fast

    c. LLDP, CDP, and MCP policy enabling the respective protocols

    d. And finally, a storm control policy specifying 10% of interface bandwidth for BUM traffic types with drop as a storm control action

6. Create a vPC interface policy group in **Fabric -> Access Policies -> Interfaces -> Leaf Interfaces -> Policy Groups -> VPC Interface** and list all previously created protocol policies together with AAEP association in it. The port channel member policy goes to the override access policy group section in the advanced tab.

7. For both switches, create an independent interface profile in **Fabric -> Access Policies -> Interfaces -> Leaf Interfaces -> Profiles**. Each interface profile should contain one interface selector specifying eth1/25 with the recently created interface policy group.

8. Then create two independent switch profiles in **Fabric -> Access Policies -> Switches -> Leaf Switches -> Profiles** and associate the respective interface profiles.

After the configuration, you should end up with the structure of access policies objects shown in Figure 4-16.

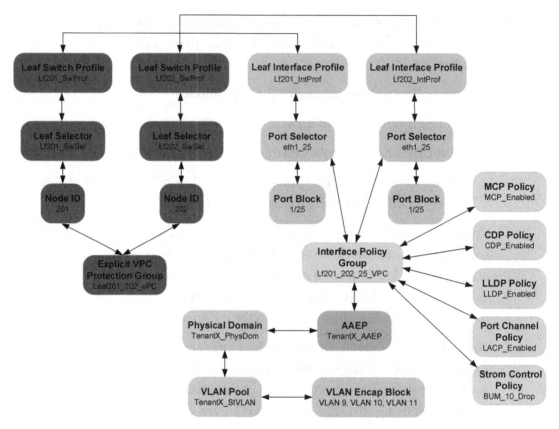

Figure 4-16. *Access policies structure*

Note   The configuration steps shown in previous section don't need to be implemented in the exact order, but at the end you need to have all objects in place and with appropriate associations between them.

A good practice is also to check for any new faults related to these objects after their configuration and verify the deployment of individual policies using the CLI on leaf switches. See Listing 4-2.

Listing 4-2. Access Policies Verification

```
Leaf-201# show port-channel extended
Flags:  D - Down        P - Up in port-channel (members)
        I - Individual  H - Hot-standby (LACP only)
```

```
        s - Suspended    r - Module-removed
        b - BFD Session Wait
        S - Switched     R - Routed
        U - Up (port-channel)
        M - Not in use. Min-links not met
        F - Configuration failed
--------------------------------------------------------------------------
Group Port-Channel        BundleGrp               Protocol  Member Ports
--------------------------------------------------------------------------
3     Po3(SU)             Lf201_202_25_VPC        LACP      Eth1/25(P)
```

Leaf-201# **show lacp interface ethernet 1/25 | egrep "Local|LACP"**
Local Port: Eth1/25   MAC Address= 70-0f-6a-d7-27-3a
  LACP_Activity=active
  LACP_Timeout=Short Timeout (1s)

Leaf-201# **show vpc brief**
Legend:
                (*) - local vPC is down, forwarding via vPC peer-link

```
vPC domain id                 : 2
Peer status                   : peer adjacency formed ok
vPC keep-alive status         : Disabled
Configuration consistency status  : success
Per-vlan consistency status   : success
Type-2 consistency status     : success
vPC role                      : primary, operational secondary
Number of vPCs configured     : 3
Peer Gateway                  : Disabled
Dual-active excluded VLANs    : -
Graceful Consistency Check    : Enabled
Auto-recovery status          : Enabled (timeout = 200 seconds)
Delay-restore status          : Enabled (timeout = 120 seconds)
Delay-restore SVI status      : Enabled (timeout = 0 seconds)
Operational Layer3 Peer       : Disabled
```

```
vPC Peer-link status
------------------------------------------------------------------------
id   Port   Status Active vlans
--   ----   ------ ------------------------------------------------------
1           up     -

vPC status
------------------------------------------------------------------------
id   Port   Status Consistency Reason                   Active vlans
--   ----   ------ ----------- ------                   ------------
684  Po3    up     success     success                  9-11
```

Leaf-201# **show cdp interface e1/25**
Ethernet1/25 is
    CDP enabled on interface
    Refresh time is 60 seconds
    Hold time is 180 seconds

Leaf-201# **show lldp interface e1/25**
Interface Information:
Enable (tx/rx/dcbx): Y/Y/N   Port Mac address: 70:0f:6a:d7:27:0b

Leaf-201# **show mcp internal info interface e1/25**

Interface: Ethernet1/25
        Native PI VLAN: 0
     Native Encap VLAN: 0
            BPDU Guard: disabled
           BPDU Filter: disabled
            Port State: up
           Layer3 Port: false
       Switching State: enabled
           Mac Address: 70:f:6a:d7:27:b
 Interface MCP enabled: true

Leaf-201# **show interface e1/25 | egrep storm**
    0 jumbo packets **0 storm suppression bytes**

```
```

Access Policies Naming Convention

Object names in ACI are generally highly important due to the inability to change them after their creation. Mostly, the only way is to delete an object and create it once again, resulting in a network disturbance. Therefore, it's crucial to prepare a thorough implementation plan beforehand with a proper naming convention for all types of ACI objects. In Table 4-1, I provide my own blueprint for access policy object names. Feel free to use it as it is or to inspire you when creating your own.

Table 4-1. *ACI Access Policies Naming Convention*

Access Policies Object	Name Structure	Examples
VLAN pool	[Tenant]_[Type]VLAN	TenantX_StVLAN TenantY_DynVLAN
Physical domains	[Tenant / Usage]_PhysDom [Tenant / Usage]_L3Dom	TenantX_PhysDom TenantY_ESXi_PhysDom TenantZ_WAN_L3Dom
Attachable Access Entity Profile (AAEP)	[Tenant]_[Usage]_AAEP	TenantX_General_AAEP TenantY_ESXi_AAEP
Interface protocol policy	[ProtocolName]_State (Enable | Disable, Active | Off | On)	CDP_Enable LLDP_Disable LACP_Active
Access interface policy group	[DeviceType]_APG	Firewall_APG Server_APG
Port channel interface policy group	Lf[NodeID] _ [InterfaceID] _ PCH	Lf201_5_PCH InterfaceID is the ID of the lowest physical interface from a port-channel.
vPC interface policy group	Lf[Lower NodeID] _ [Higher NodeID] _ [InterfaceID] _VPC	Lf101_102_10_VPC InterfaceID is the ID of the lowest physical interface from a port-channel.
Interface profile	Lf[NodeID]_IfProf	Lf102_IfProf, Lf201_IfProf
Access port selector	eth1_[interface ID]	eth1_1, eth1_50
Switch profile	Lf[NodeID]_SwProf All_SwProf	Lf101_SwProf All_SwProf
Switch selector	Lf[NodeID]_SwSel All_SwSel	Lf101_SwSel All_SwSel
Virtual port channel policy group	Lf[NodeID1]_[NodeID]_VPCGrp	Lf101_102_VPCGrp Lf201_202_VPCGrp

Summary

In this chapter, you had the opportunity to explore all the necessary objects related to ACI access policies, which are (as the name suggests) used for an individual end host interface configuration as well as switch global access-related settings. They bring a new, object-oriented philosophy to the underlay network configuration and together with physical domains and encapsulation pools define the exact hardware consumable resources for ACI tenants. Access policies are mandatory prerequisites for any type of endpoint connected to the fabric.

My goal for the next chapter is to follow up this underlay configuration and actually consume it in tenant policies. You are going to create a logical, segmented application and network policies on top of the shared physical resources and ensure the proper L2 switching as well as L3 routing over ACI for the connected endpoints.

## CHAPTER 5

ACI Fundamentals: Application Policy Model

After the previous chapter, you should have a good idea about how to prepare the physical underlay network for ACI to connect your endpoints to the fabric. Each of them needs to have the entire set of access policies in place to define both access interface settings and encapsulation resources. This alone won't provide any mutual IP (or FC) connectivity between endpoints yet.

You have certainly noticed that you haven't any access or trunk interface types, you haven't specified actually used VLANs on them, IP configurations, default gateways for end hosts, and such. In order to do that, you need to define *application* (many times referred to as *tenant*) *policies*. Remember, ACI uses an allowlisting model, so what is not defined or explicitly allowed will be denied by default.

ACI uses this differentiation between physical access and logical application policies to abstract the application needs from the underlying network. In fact, from the application policies perspective, it's absolutely insignificant what hardware running behind the scenes and the configuration of the physical switches. ACI tenants transparently build on top of that their logical policies, and APIC is responsible for translating the application needs into various configuration objects to make the connectivity happen.

Application Policy Model Overview

First of all, before diving deeper into application policies, let's have a look at the application policy model shown in Figure 5-1. The whole ACI solution is object oriented, based on the underlying information model, and application policies are no exception.

© Jan Janovic 2023
J. Janovic, *Cisco ACI: Zero to Hero*, https://doi.org/10.1007/978-1-4842-8838-2_5

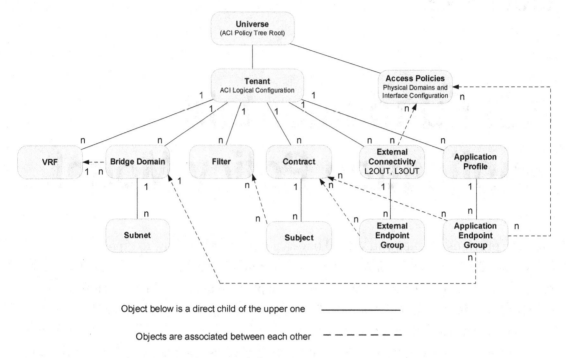

Object below is a direct child of the upper one ————————————

Objects are associated between each other — — — — — — —

Figure 5-1. *Application policy model overview*

ACI's object model is organized into a tree structure with a common tree root called Universe. From Universe, it expands to all areas related to ACI configuration and operations. We have already gone through one of the tree branches, access policies (the physical configuration), which "grows" right from the root. Similarly, we will now explore another tree branch, application policies (the logical configuration).

Application policies start with the definition of tenants, which is the logical administrative domains belonging to a particular ACI consumer. For each tenant, we further create Virtual Routing and Forwarding instances (VRFs) to differentiate between their separated L3 routing tables, bridge domains (BDs) to define L2 broadcast domains, segment our endpoint resources into endpoint groups (EPGs), connect them to the external networks, and enable the communication between them using contracts. For EPGs and external connectivity, we have to create a reference to access policies in order to consume some of the ACI's physical fabric resources, but besides that these two worlds are significantly independent and not directly related.

Many objects, as you can see in a model tree, have parent-child relationships (the solid line), where parents can have multiple children of the same type, but the child object can have only exactly one parent. In addition, we will often create "n to n" associations (or references) between them (the dashed line).

The ultimate goal of ACI's application policies is to universally describe the required network structure and the application communication needs, emphasizing the reusability, security, and automation of their deployment. APIC acts as a central repository for these policies and translates them to the actual networking constructs on leaf and spine switches. It also constantly verifies their state and makes sure they meet the administrator's intention.

Although the configuration philosophy in ACI is quite different from the traditional network, sometimes objectively more complex and suitable for further automation, the end result is often similar to what we already know and are used to. During the following sections and chapters, I will provide you with a mental map to easily imagine the actual network impact with a particular policy definition. From my experience, it will help you to remember important information, effectively troubleshoot, and know precisely where to look for potential problems.

ACI Tenants

Your first object to focus on, the tenant, represents the separated logical container for all other application policies created inside it. ACI, as you know already, builds its operation around a multi-tenancy concept to differentiate between potential datacenter network consumers. Tenants can be managed by a single administrator entity together with all other ACI policies or theoretically they can be completely unrelated to the main ACI administrator. As you can see in Figure 5-2, the most common tenant designs isolate distinct companies, internal departments, or various environments (e.g., test, prod, dev). Alternatively, you can always implement a combination of the above.

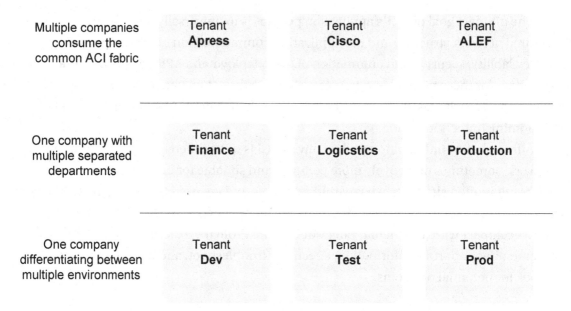

Multiple companies consume the common ACI fabric	Tenant **Apress**	Tenant **Cisco**	Tenant **ALEF**
One company with multiple separated departments	Tenant **Finance**	Tenant **Logicstics**	Tenant **Production**
One company differentiating between multiple environments	Tenant **Dev**	Tenant **Test**	Tenant **Prod**

Figure 5-2. *Possible tenant object designs*

Tenant Security and Access Control

The tenant itself doesn't have any networking construct deployed on switches when created, but due to the separation of endpoints into different VRFs and eventually EPGs, by default no connected resources can communicate between tenants. However, all configuration objects and policies are by default mutually visible for users with admin, read-all, tenant-admin, or tenant-ext-admin privileges. The best practice when creating new tenants is to restrict access to its objects by using *security domains*.

In the **Admin -> AAA -> Security -> Security Domains** tab, you can create a specialized security label granting visibility only to objects associated with it. Each security domain has a *Restricted Domain* knob in the configuration, which has to be set to "yes" in order to enforce the object separation. Now when you create a local user in **Admin -> AAA -> Users**, in the second step of its configuration you can associate it to one or more currently existing security domains. The same option is available when authenticating remote users by returning a predefined AV pair in the format shell:domains=**<security_domain_name>**/<write_role>/<read_role. The final step is to associate the chosen security domain(s) with a tenant when creating its object. From that moment, your user won't see any other tenants or their child policies. Figure 5-3

describes combinations of security domains with tenants that effectively secure user access. The same concept can be applied to physical domains or fabric leaf switches as well.

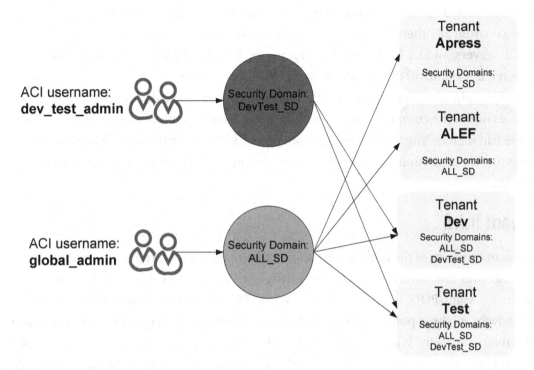

Figure 5-3. *Restricting tenant access using security domains*

System Tenants

In the default ACI state, without any user application policies, there are three preconfigured system tenants in the *Tenants* main menu section. You cannot delete them; you can only make use of them.

Tenant common

As mentioned, all tenants in ACI are entirely separated and their endpoints cannot communicate with each other in the default state without unique contract interfaces, which I will discuss later. The common tenant, however, is an exception to this rule. The entire set of its objects is fully visible and available for all other tenants. Using standard contracts, even communication between resources in common and other tenants is allowed (I will cover contracts later in this chapter). The common tenant also serves as a default policy repository for APIC to resolve if no other more specific user-created policies are available in the user tenant.

The common tenant is thus perfect for managing shared endpoint resources accessed from all others such as central network services like NTP servers, DNS servers, DHCP servers, and L4-L7 devices used for policy-based redirect in service graphs (covered in Chapter 8) or shared external L2/L3 connectivity.

With endpoints there comes another frequent use case: creating shared application policies under the common tenant and inheriting them in standard user-created tenants. These can include any object ranging from networking constructs like VRFs, BDs, and EPGs to contract definitions, contract filters, various L3OUT settings, or monitoring policies.

Tenant infra

The main purpose of the infra tenant is to configure policies related to the enablement of datacenter interconnect (DCI) connectivity over VRF overlay-1 between distinct ACI fabrics for Multi-POD, Multi-Site, or Remote Leaf architectures. In most cases, but not exclusively, all these policies are created automatically, and you don't need to intervene with them manually. When deploying Multi-POD and Remote Leaf, infra tenant policies will be configured by the APIC wizard and in the Multi-Site case from Nexus Dashboard Orchestrator.

For corner case scenarios, if you're using virtual L4-L7 devices (in ACI 5.X ASAv and Palo Alto FWs are supported) for policy-based redirect together with virtualization (VMM) integration, the infra tenant encompasses special policies allowing APIC to dynamically spin up new VM instances according to the PBR needs.

Tenant mgmt

You have already met the mgmt tenant in Chapter 3 during the ACI fabric initialization. As the name suggests, it is primarily used to configure out-of-band or in-band access to fabric switches and APICs. By default, it already includes and manages VRF *management* (oob) and *mgmt:inb*. Only inside the mgmt tenant can you configure the individual management IP addresses, enhance the management access security, and provide access to in-band resources from an external network if needed. For more information about these ACI configuration aspects, refer to Chapter 3.

User Tenants

Along with first three already created tenants, you can add up to 3,000 (with five- or seven-node APIC clusters) user tenants for arbitrary use. To create a new tenant, navigate to the **Tenant -> Add Tenant** menu option. There is not much to configure yet, as you can see in Figure 5-4. Just set its name and you can add a security domain to restrict later ACI user access to only objects of this particular tenant.

Figure 5-4. ACI tenant creation

After the creation, you will directly enter its configuration with following menu options in the left pane:

- **Application Profiles**: Application profile objects with associated endpoint groups (EPGs), microEPGs, and endpoint security groups (ESGs)

- **Networking**: VRFs, BDs, and L2/L3 OUTs with optional segment routing hand-off capabilities and QinQ tunneling configuration

- **Contracts**: Communication policies between EPGs and ESGs

- **Policies**: Various partial policies for unicast and multicast routing protocols, Quality of Service, NetFlow, first hop security, policy-based redirect, route maps, or monitoring and troubleshooting tools

- **Services**: Primarily used for L4-L7 service graphs definitions and deployments with few more beta features related to DNS and identity servers

- **Security**: New addition to the ACI GUI in 5.X gives you an overview of your EPGs and their contract associations with actual hit count for each contract

Tenant Monitoring

As discussed in Chapter 3, for each tenant I highly recommend that you create a monitoring policy in **Tenants -> Tenant_name -> Policies -> Monitoring** (or alternatively use the common one from tenant common). There you can enable SNMP traps, create Syslog data sources for tenant objects, configure Callhome, statistic collection, or, for example, alter the fault and event severities. The monitoring policy then has to be applied in the main tenant object Policy tab.

The collection of this data is especially important from the long-term visibility point of view, to have a historical information in hand when you have troubleshooting needs.

Virtual Routing and Forwarding

For each tenant in ACI, you need to create at least one or more VRF instances (current scalability goes to 3,000 VRFs with a five+ APIC node cluster). The purpose of this object is exactly the same as in traditional networking: to separate L3 IP spaces from each other. VRFs represent independent routing tables, enabling network tenants to use overlapping IP subnets and dedicated external connectivity settings without worrying about potential duplicate addresses and other IP plan collisions.

As you can see in Figure 5-5, by default, no endpoints inside one VRF can communicate with other VRFs due to complete separation of routing tables and missing prefix information. However, thanks to its flexibility, ACI can deploy automatic prefix leaking between VRFs based on your contract policies applied to EPGs. This traffic engineering is usually related to MPLS networks in the traditional world. I will cover inter-VRF communication later in this chapter.

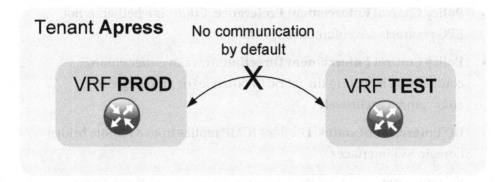

Figure 5-5. *Virtual routing and forwarding instances*

To create a new VRF, navigate to **Tenant -> Tenant_name -> Networking -> VRFs** and right-click **Create VRF**. In the form (shown in Figure 5-6), there is no need to change anything from the default state. Just uncheck the *Create a Bridge Domain* option (I will cover bridge domain objects later in detail).

Create VRF

STEP 1 > VRF   1. VRF

Name:	PROD
Alias:	
Description:	optional

Annotations: ➕ Click to add a new annotation

Policy Control Enforcement Preference: Enforced / Unenforced

Policy Control Enforcement Direction: Egress / Ingress

BD Enforcement Status: ☐

Endpoint Retention Policy: select a value
This policy only applies to remote L3 entries

Monitoring Policy: select a value

DNS Labels:
enter names separated by comma

Transit Route Tag Policy: select a value

IP Data-plane Learning: Disabled / Enabled

Create A Bridge Domain: ☐
Configure BGP Policies: ☐
Configure OSPF Policies: ☐
Configure EIGRP Policies: ☐

Figure 5-6. *Creating a VRF*

VRF's various configuration knobs mostly relate to other ACI features and their behavior inside a VRF, so I will return to them in more detail during the respective sections. Here you can find at least a brief overview:

- **Policy Control Enforcement Preference**: Controls whether or not EPG contracts are enforced in a VRF

- **Policy Control Enforcement Direction**: You can either enforce contracts on ingress to the fabric (if possible) or prefer egress enforcement exclusively

- **BD Enforcement status**: Disables ICMP replies from a remote bridge domain SVI interfaces

- **Endpoint Retention Policy**: Aging timer for remote IP endpoints

- **Monitoring Policy**: Selectively configurable monitoring settings for this VRF object only, instead of generic tenant monitoring policy

- **DNS Labels**: Usually sets only in the mgmt tenant to configure DNS settings for fabric switches (refer to the DNS section in Chapter 3)

- **Transit Route Tag Policy**: L3 loop prevention mechanism based on route tags, to avoid relearning the same prefixes via an external network that was already propagated using L3OUT from this VRF

- **IP Data-Plane Learning**: Can disable learning of local and remote IP addresses from data plane packets. Control plane learning from ARP, GARP, and ND learning still occurs.

- **BGP, OSPF and EIGRP Policies**: Specific configuration of address families for dynamic routing protocol in this VRF

At the moment of creation, VRF isn't instantiated anywhere in the fabric yet because you don't have any interfaces or endpoints associated with it. APIC dynamically creates VRFs only where needed to optimize switch resource utilization. Later, when deployed, you can check its presence on respective leaf switches using the commands in Listing 5-1.

Listing 5-1. VRF Deployment Verification

```
Leaf-101# show vrf
VRF-Name                        VRF-ID State    Reason
Apress:PROD                          5 Up       --
black-hole                           3 Up       --
management                           2 Up       --
overlay-1                            4 Up       --
```

```
Leaf-101# show vrf Apress:PROD detail
VRF-Name: Apress:PROD, VRF-ID: 5, State: Up
    VPNID: unknown
    RD: 101:3080193
    Max Routes: 0  Mid-Threshold: 0
    Table-ID: 0x80000005, AF: IPv6, Fwd-ID: 0x80000005, State: Up
    Table-ID: 0x00000005, AF: IPv4, Fwd-ID: 0x00000005, State: Up
```

VRFs instances on fabric switches always use the name format **Tenant:VRF** (in this case Apress:PROD). All names are case-sensitive, and you should pay attention to their length when designing the tenant object structure. Long names can become opaque and create an unnecessary administrative burden when you have to work with them repeatedly in the switch CLI during verification or troubleshooting tasks. The VRF route distinguisher (RD) on each switch consists of **NodeID:L3VNI**. I will cover this in more detail in Chapter 6, which describes ACI fabric forwarding.

Note   The fact that all L3 endpoint information or configuration in ACI is enclosed in some VRF other than the default one implies the requirement to use the *vrf* suffix in all show commands where applicable, for instance show ip route vrf Apress:PROD, show ip int brief vrf Apress:PROD, show bgp ipv4 unicast summary vrf Apress:PROD.

Bridge Domains

Even though in a particular tenant you can have multiple VRFs, let's stay for a while inside a single VRF only.

In traditional networking, to implement network segmentation and enhance the security, we use VLANs primarily. However, VLAN encapsulation wasn't originally meant to be tied with a single IP prefix and associated communication rules (ACLs, FW rules, etc.). Its main intention was just to split up large broadcast domains on a single device or cable. The ACI logical model returns to this concept but with bridge domains.

A bridge domain represents a separate Layer 2 broadcast domain inside a VRF that can span multiple switches or even distinct ACI fabrics, but without a direct relation to traditional VLANs. Each BD receives its own VXLAN L2 VNID, which ensures transparent forwarding of any unicast, multicast, or broadcast frames over the fabric. Endpoints are put into a specific BD by associating EPGs with the BD, and VLAN affiliation happens at EPG-to-leaf interface mappings. As a result, traditional VLANs became just a local encapsulation identifier between the connected endpoint and ACI leaf switch. All main forwarding decisions in ACI are instead related to bridge domains, VRFs and EPGs.

A bridge domain offers two types of network services based on an enabled or disabled unicast routing configuration option:

- **Layer 2 bridging**: Considers the ACI fabric as a single, distributed switch with forwarding exclusively based on MAC addresses. ACI won't even learn IP addresses in the endpoint table. Default gateways are then expected to be situated outside the ACI fabric (in a legacy network, a connected firewall, or a router)

- **Layer 3 routing**: ACI implements distributed default gateways for endpoints on all leaf switches where applicable and ensures L3 routing between them inside the associated VRF

In Figure 5-7, you can see the bridge domain configuration without unicast routing enabled. Each bridge domain has to have its own L3 default gateway connected somewhere in the fabric and ACI provides just L2 bridging between the endpoints.

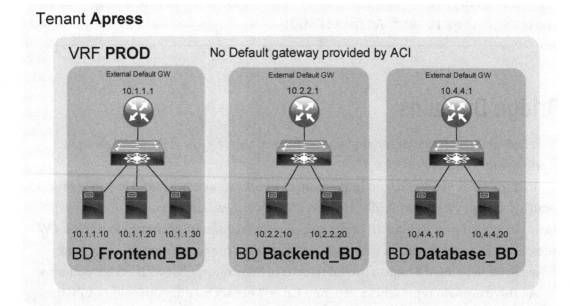

Figure 5-7. *ACI bridge domains without unicast routing enabled*

On the other hand, with routing enabled for a bridge domain, the ACI fabric becomes a distributed router logically, allowing you to configure one or even multiple default gateways for each Layer 2 segment (as shown in Figure 5-8). The default gateway is created directly on leaf switches in the form of an SVI interface.

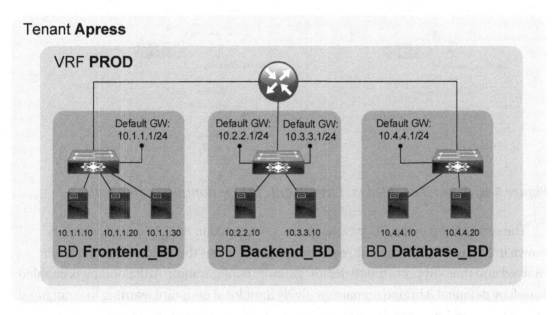

Figure 5-8. *ACI bridge domains with unicast routing enabled*

In order to configure a bridge domain, navigate to **Tenants -> Tenant_name -> Networking -> Bridge Domains** and right-click the BD folder to create a new bridge domain. During the first step shown in Figure 5-9, primarily choose the associated VRF (even if not L3 BD yet) and the rest of configuration depends on the BD type:

- **For a Layer 3 bridge domain**: Leave the default configuration of each field as is. Optionally, you can set specific policies for endpoint retention or IGMP/MLD snooping.

- **For a Layer 2 bridge domain**: It's highly recommended and a best practice to change *Forwarding settings* to *Custom* and set *L2 Unknown unicast* to *Flood*. This will ensure the correct forwarding of traffic to unknown, silent hosts connected in the fabric. In the L2 bridge domain, it is also convenient to flood ARP packets, and this option is enabled by default in ACI 5.X versions.

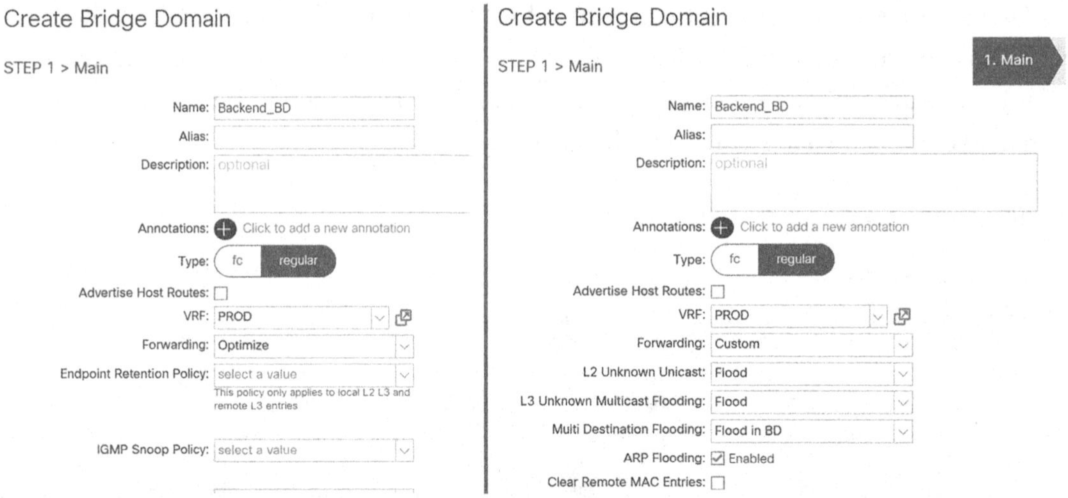

Create Bridge Domain

STEP 1 > Main

Name: Backend_BD

Alias:

Description: optional

Annotations: ⊕ Click to add a new annotation

Type: (fc   regular)

Advertise Host Routes: ☐

VRF: PROD

Forwarding: Optimize

Endpoint Retention Policy: select a value

This policy only applies to local L2 L3 and
remote L3 entries

IGMP Snoop Policy: select a value

Create Bridge Domain

STEP 1 > Main   1. Main

Name: Backend_BD

Alias:

Description: optional

Annotations: ⊕ Click to add a new annotation

Type: (fc   regular)

Advertise Host Routes: ☐

VRF: PROD

Forwarding: Custom

L2 Unknown Unicast: Flood

L3 Unknown Multicast Flooding: Flood

Multi Destination Flooding: Flood in BD

ARP Flooding: ☑ Enabled

Clear Remote MAC Entries: ☐

Figure 5-9. *Layer 3 enabled vs. Layer 2 only bridge domain configuration*

The second step in the BD creation process is related to the L3 configuration (as shown in Figure 5-10). By default, each bridge domain has the Unicast Routing knob enabled and thus supports the IP default gateway configuration. ARP flooding is enabled as well by default. L3 bridge domains natively limit local endpoint learning to configured subnets (this option is visible at the bottom and will be covered shortly).

To make the bridge domain Layer 2 only, uncheck the *Unicast Routing* option. Other configuration settings on this page related to IPv6 or external connectivity using L3OUTs are not important for you at this point, and you can leave them in the default state.

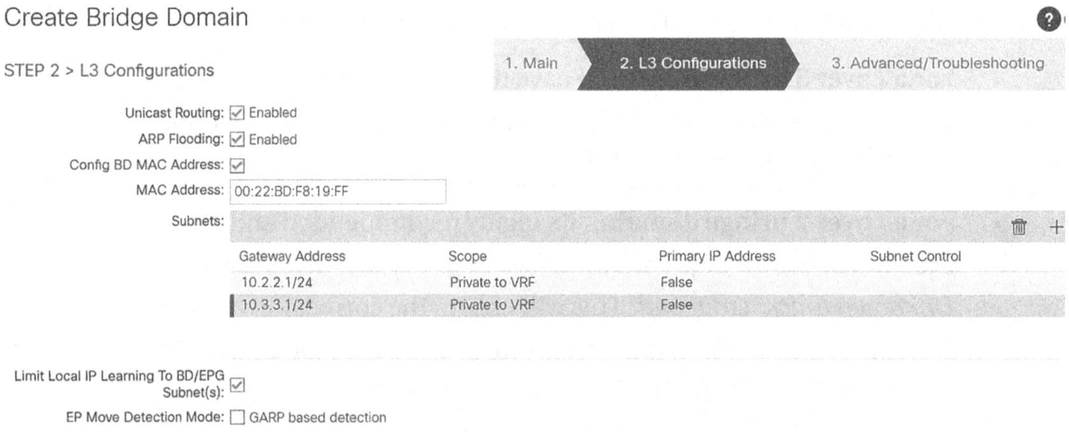

Create Bridge Domain   ❓

STEP 2 > L3 Configurations   1. Main   2. L3 Configurations   3. Advanced/Troubleshooting

Unicast Routing: ☑ Enabled

ARP Flooding: ☑ Enabled

Config BD MAC Address: ☑

MAC Address: 00:22:BD:F8:19:FF

Subnets: 🗑 +

Gateway Address	Scope	Primary IP Address	Subnet Control
10.2.2.1/24	Private to VRF	False	
10.3.3.1/24	Private to VRF	False	

Limit Local IP Learning To BD/EPG
Subnet(s): ☑

EP Move Detection Mode: ☐ GARP based detection

Figure 5-10. *Bridge domain L3 configuration*

The third advanced/troubleshooting step of the BD configuration form includes the monitoring policy, first hop security, or NetFlow monitor associations. Mainly no change is needed there, depending on your intentions of course. At last, you can finally click Finish to complete the BD creation.

Bridge Domain Subnets

Subnets refer to default GW address definitions available for endpoints inside the bridge domain. Suppose unicast routing is enabled and some EPG mappings exist for the bridge domain. In that case, APIC will instruct related leaf switches to create an SVI interface in a random internal VLAN for each subnet. The same gateway address is then installed on every leaf switch with some potential endpoints connected, so each of them will have a gateway on the closest switch, creating a pervasive anycast gateway.

Internal VLANs used for default gateways are always different for each leaf switch, so don't try to find any pattern there. Always check them locally on a particular leaf and work with the local information. See Listing 5-2.

Listing 5-2. ACI Default GW Deployment

```
Leaf-101# show ip int brief vrf Apress:PROD
IP Interface Status for VRF "Apress:PROD"(5)
Interface            Address              Interface Status
vlan15               10.2.2.1/24          protocol-up/link-up/admin-up
vlan17               10.1.1.1/24          protocol-up/link-up/admin-up
vlan19               10.4.4.1/24          protocol-up/link-up/admin-up

Leaf-101# show vlan extended

 VLAN Name                            Encap             Ports
 ---- -------------------------------- ---------------- -----------
 ---------
  14  infra:default                   vxlan-16777209,   Eth1/1
                                      vlan-3967

  15  Apress:Backend_BD               vxlan-16318374    Eth1/20, Po1
  17  Apress:Frontend_BD              vxlan-16089026    Eth1/20, Po1
  19  Apress:Database_BD              vxlan-16449430    Eth1/20, Po1
```

```
Leaf-101# show ip interface vlan15
IP Interface Status for VRF "Apress:PROD"
vlan15, Interface status: protocol-up/link-up/admin-up, iod: 89, mode:
pervasive
  IP address: 10.3.3.1, IP subnet: 10.3.3.0/24 secondary
  IP address: 10.2.2.1, IP subnet: 10.2.2.0/24
  IP broadcast address: 255.255.255.255
  IP primary address route-preference: 0, tag: 0
```

Notice that if you define multiple subnets for a single bridge domain, APIC will create just one SVI interface and all additional IP addresses are included as a part of it in the form of secondary IPs.

ARP Handling

Correctly delivered ARP between hosts is a crucial part of network communication in IPv4. In ACI version 5.X, ARP is by default always flooded within a BD (regardless of unicast routing configuration). Therefore, its delivery is ensured in every situation, even if you have silent hosts connected to ACI, whose endpoint information is not yet learned by the control plane in the COOP database. The best practice recommendation for a L2 bridge domain is never to turn off ARP flooding.

With unicast routing enabled, on the other hand, you can optimize ARP delivery by unchecking the ARP flooding configuration option. Then, instead of sending ARP broadcasts to all interfaces mapped to a particular bridge domain, ARP requests are routed directly and only to the individual connected host based on the information in the leaf local and spine COOP endpoint database. If some silent host is present in the ACI fabric and the switches don't have its endpoint information yet, the spines will drop the original ARP packet and generate a so-called *ARP Glean* message instead. Glean is sent to all leaves with the appropriate bridge domain deployed, instructing them to create and locally flood the artificial ARP request destined to the original host and sourced from BD's SVI interface. ACI expects that this should "wake up" the silent host, which will subsequently respond to ARP. The leaf switch will learn its location and update the spine COOP database. All following ARPs will be delivered between the end hosts directly.

For internal forwarding, ACI doesn't build and maintain a traditional ARP table. It relies on the endpoint database filled by information learned from data plane traffic to obtain a next-hop MAC address for a particular IP.

This approach isn't scalable enough for external endpoints and prefixes learned through L3OUTs, though. Imagine having tens of thousands of /32 IP endpoints behind the same external router MAC address (while current ACI scalability in 5.X version is only 4,096 host IP entries behind one MAC address). For this case only, ACI uses the traditional routing information base (routing table) and ARP table to resolve the external MAC address to IP next-hop relationship.

If there is a potential, some of your hosts (especially VMs) will change the MAC address over time but retain the same IP behind the single interface; in the default state, ACI won't trigger endpoint relearning. You need to wait for the endpoint aging timer to pass. In such a case, you can enable GARP-based *endpoint move detection* in the bridge domain L3 configuration section. As soon as the end host sends a gratuitous ARP with the new MAC information, ACI will instantly update its endpoint databases.

Application Profiles

With bridge domains in place, you can move further to application profiles and EPGs. Application profiles act as a logical container grouping together multiple endpoint groups. To create an application profile, go to **Tenants -> Tenant_name -> Application Profiles**. This object has only a single configuration option available: the selective monitoring policy applicable to all EPGs included inside (as shown in Figure 5-11).

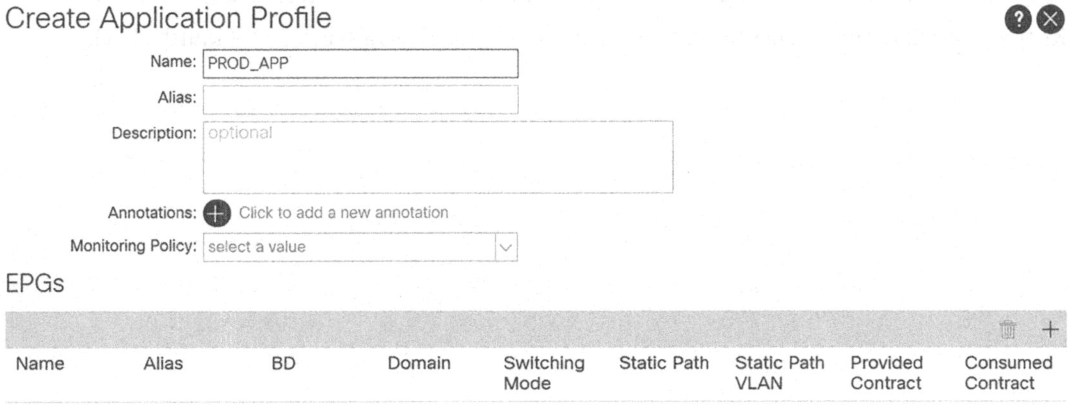

Figure 5-11. *Application profile creation*

Using application profiles, you can differentiate between distinct applications or create other EPG separation schemes based on your preferences. However, application profiles alone do not enforce any segmentation in ACI. It's the contracts and their configurable scope that can alter the behavior. In few sections, I'll show you how to configure a contract to universally allow communications inside the VRF or just inside the EPGs included in a single application profile.

Endpoint Groups

One of the main segmentation tools and concepts in ACI is represented by endpoint groups. The idea behind application profiles and EPGs is to enforce network communication policies between resources connected to the fabric, but without direct dependencies on VLANs, subnets, or a physical network. As the name suggests, EPGs allow the administrator to create separated groups of connected resources in the fabric named endpoints.

An endpoint is simply any host (bare-metal, virtualized, or containerized) with a unique MAC and IP address pair (in L2 bridge domains, ACI learns only MACs). The fabric doesn't differentiate between various types of connected resources, so each packet is delivered uniformly and solely based on endpoint information learned and saved in leaf endpoint tables and the spine COOP database.

As shown in Figure 5-12, the EPG is associated with exactly one bridge domain, which defines its L2 broadcast boundary, and one BD can provide forwarding services for multiple EPGs. Compared to traditional networks, there is no solid relation between endpoints in an EPG and their IP address. You can split one subnet into more EPGs (frontend EPGs) or endpoints from multiple subnets in single EPG (backend EPG).

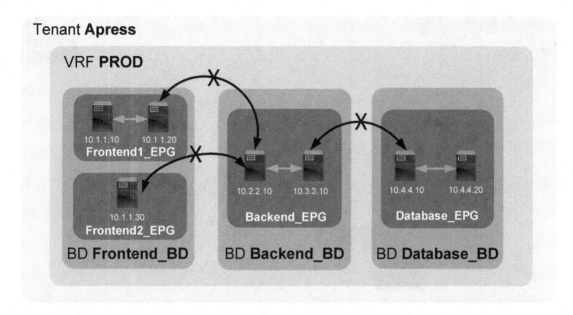

Figure 5-12. *Endpoint groups*

The ACI fabric by default allows the entire communication between endpoints within the same EPG, but without additional contract policies in place, no communication can happen between different EPGs. This allowlist philosophy further enhances datacenter network security from day 0 and makes sure only explicitly permitted traffic will flow through the fabric.

In order to create an EPG, navigate to **Tenant -> Tenant_name -> Application Profiles -> Profile_name -> Application EPGs** and right-click this folder. Within the configuration form shown in Figure 5-13, there are only two mandatory fields: Name and the bridge domain association.

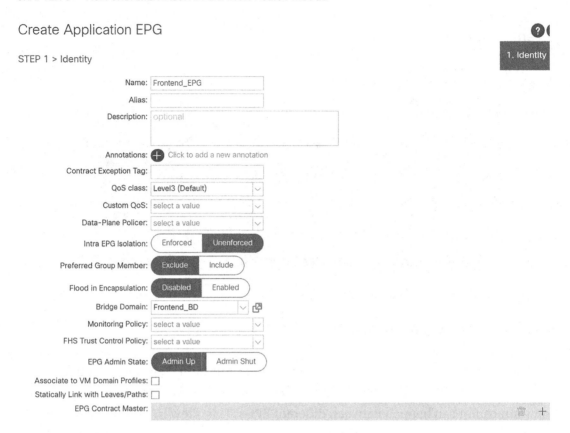

Figure 5-13. *Creating an EPG*

Mostly you don't need to alter the default EPG configuration, but I will briefly describe the configuration knobs available during its creation. I will touch on some of them later during this and the following chapters:

- **Contract Exception Tag**: Allows you to exclude this EPG from particular contract relations. These tags can be matched in a contract configuration later.

- **Qos Class**: Traffic classification of this EPG into one of QoS' six classes (levels)

- **Data-Plane Policer**: QoS tool to limit the traffic rate on all interfaces for this EPG. You can choose from One-Rate Two-Color, or Two-Rate Three-Color policers.

- **Intra EPG Isolation**: ACI is capable of changing the default endpoint communication behavior inside EPG from "permit any" to isolate. With intra-EPG isolation enforced, no endpoint will be able to communicate with its EPG "siblings." However, with this option enabled, you can apply a special intra-EPG contract and explicitly define allowed traffic within EPG.

- **Preferred Group Member**: In each VRF, you can create a set of EPGs called a preferred group, which won't enforce any contracts mutually between them. Contracts will be enforced only to EPGs external to the preferred group.

- **Flood in Encapsulation**: An option limiting BUM traffic propagation only to the endpoints connected over the same encapsulation (VLAN, VXLAN), instead of the whole bridge domain

- **Bridge Domain**: The main and the most important association, inserting an EPG in the chosen Layer 2 domain.

- **Monitoring Policy**: Selective monitoring configuration applicable only to resources in this EPG

- **FHS Trust Control Policy**: First hop security configuration. Endpoints in this EPG are considered trusted for DHCPv4 and v6, ARP, ND, and RA services.

- **EPG Admin State**: Allows the administrator to preconfigure EPGs without actual deployment to the fabric. Shutting down the EPG causes all fabric resources related to it to be released.

- **Associate to VM Domain profile** and **Statically Link with Leaves/ Paths**: Checking these boxes activates additional configuration form pages to immediately map the EPG to physical access policies domains and create mappings to physical interfaces

- **EPG Contract Master**: Allows contract inheritance from another EPGs defined in this list

Mapping EPGs to Interfaces

After creation, EPGs are empty. Therefore, as a next step, you always need to define who will actually be part of them. Such endpoint-to-EPG mapping can be configured in two ways:

1. **Static**: The administrator will statically define the exact VLAN and interface associations to the EPG

2. **Dynamic**: Used as a part of ACI VMM integration

Both options come with pros and cons, so let's have a closer look at them.

Static EPG to Interface Mapping

The most common method for putting endpoints into the EPG is a static description of which interface and VLAN they will use when communicating with ACI leaves, also called a static path. As depicted in Figure 5-14, you must create two EPG associations:

1. Reference to physical domains from ACI access policies

2. Static path definitions themselves with related encapsulation mapping

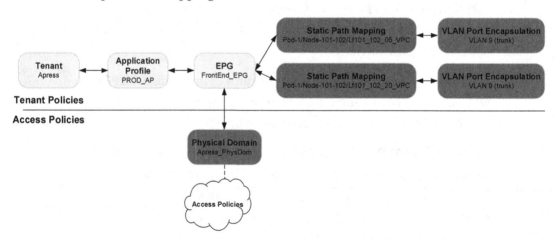

Figure 5-14. *Static endpoint to EPG mapping*

The endpoints are always connected behind some physical leaf interfaces and, as you already know, you must create access policies to enable physical access. All together, they will grant interface and encapsulation resources to a particular tenant.

Now, from the tenant perspective, you will consume the access policies by associating one or more physical domains with EPGs. That's the only existing relationship between the logical application (tenant) policies and the physical access policies. To do so, right-click the EPG and choose *Add Physical Domain Association*. There's nothing much to configure there, as you can see in Figure 5-15. This will just unlock the access to ACI's physical and encapsulation resources. In other words, by creating this association you say, "Endpoints of this EPG can potentially use any interface mapped to the physical domain and they can use any VLAN (VXLAN) defined in VLAN (VXLAN) pool in that physical domain."

Add Physical Domain Association

Physical Domain Profile: Apress_PhysDom

Figure 5-15. Physical domain to EPG association

The second step is to specify the exact static path to the particular interface(s) and VLANs used for this EPG. Right-click the EPG and choose *Deploy Static EPG on PC, VPC, or Interface* to open the configuration form (shown in Figure 5-16).

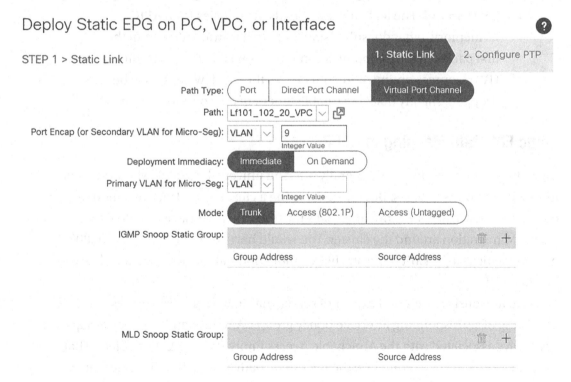

Figure 5-16. EPG static path configuration

Here you need to choose the *Path Type*, the individual interface or (vPC) port channel. Based on your choice, the Path field will allow you to configure either a leaf switch with one particular interface or a reference to the PC/vPC interface policy group. Then fill in the *Port Encap*, which is the actual VLAN on the wire that the endpoints are expected to use when communicating with ACI. For the only one VLAN on each interface, *Mode* can be set to *Access (Untagged)*; this defines either the traditional untagged access interface or the native VLAN on a trunk port. All other VLANs must have the trunk mode configured and ACI will expect dot1q tagged communication. By creating this static mapping, you have exactly defined that all endpoints behind this interface and VLAN will belong to this EPG. And the same concept applies to all other EPGs.

There is one leaf TCAM optimization option called *Deployment Immediacy.* As you can see in Figure 5-16, two settings are available:

- **Immediate**: The leaf installs to its hardware ASIC all the policies (contracts) related to this EPG as soon as the mapping is created and submitted in APIC.

- **On Demand**: The leaf only downloads the policies from APIC to its memory, but it doesn't install them to hardware ASIC until the first packet of the endpoint communication is seen. This results in HW resources optimization but causes the first few packets to be dropped, slightly delaying establishment of the communication.

Static EPG Path Mapping to AAEP

Individual static mappings are generally fine and universally usable when you need to attach endpoints to EPGs. But imagine having a cluster of 100 virtualization hosts connected to ACI, all using the same 100 VLANs on their interfaces due to the need for a live VM migration around the cluster. You would have to create 100*100 = 10,000 of individual mappings. Isn't there any better, more optimal way for situations like this? Yes, there is!

The previously mentioned cluster of servers has to have access policies in place, consisting of corresponding interface policy groups. And remember, policy groups are always associated with the Attachable Access Entity Profile (AAEP) object. That's the place where you can configure the EPG static path as well, but this time using only one mapping per VLAN and EPG for all interfaces that are part of AAEP. To do so, just navigate to **Fabric -> Access Policies -> Policies -> Global -> Attachable Access Entity Profiles -> Policy** (see Figure 5-17).

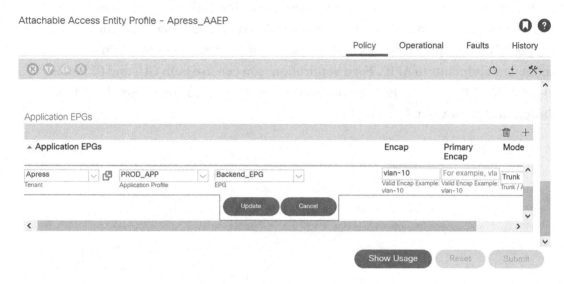

Figure 5-17. *EPG static path defined in AAEP objects*

Dynamic EPG to Interface Mapping

Although for standard, bare-metal endpoints you will always need to use one of the static mapping options, there is a way to avoid it completely: virtual machine manager (VMM) integration. APIC can create a relationship with a virtualization manager (e.g., VMware vCenter or Microsoft SCVMM) and take responsibility for managing its virtual networking layer, usually in the form of the virtual distributed switch. It dynamically takes care of encapsulation management, and for each EPG created in the application profile and associated with a special VMM domain, APIC will create its analogy in the virtualization platform with an automatically chosen VLAN from a specified VLAN pool (in case of VMware, for each EPG there is a vDS port-group created). Additionally, APIC will gain visibility into the VMM inventory and, thanks to neighbor discovery protocols CDP or LLDP, it will learn the exact physical location of your virtualization hypervisors in the ACI fabric. With the mutual correlation of this information, APIC knows exactly which VLANs (VXLANs) should be allowed on which interfaces and how to map them to particular EPGs. I will focus on this concept in detail in Chapter 9.

Endpoint Learning Verification

After creating static or dynamic path mappings to your EPGs and when the connected hosts communicate using the correct encapsulation, the end result you should expect is endpoint learning on leaf switches. They will insert new information to their local endpoints tables, update the COOP database on the spines, and send information about new endpoints to APIC. For a verification, you can use both GUI and CLI tools. In the APIC GUI, open the EPG of your choice and navigate to **Operational -> Client Endpoints** (as shown in Figure 5-18).

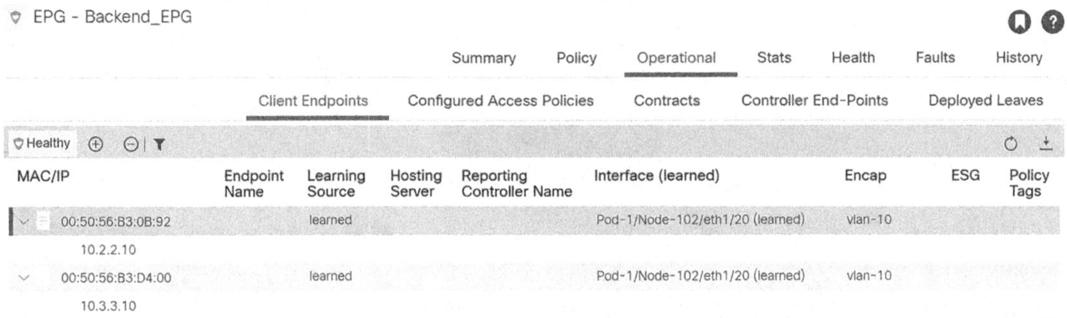

Figure 5-18. *Endpoint learning verification in the GUI*

For CLI verification of endpoint learning on APIC or a leaf switch, you can use the commands shown in Listing 5-3.

Listing 5-3. EPG Endpoint Learning Verification on APIC and the Leaf Switch CLI

```
apic1# show endpoints
Legends:
(P):Primary VLAN
(S):Secondary VLAN

Dynamic Endpoints:
Tenant      : Apress
Application : PROD_APP
AEPg        : Backend_EPG
```

```
 End Point MAC       IP Address      Source        Node
Interface      Encap
 ----------------   ---------------  ------------  -----------
------------ ---------
 00:50:56:B3:0B:92  10.2.2.10        learned       102
eth1/20        vlan-10

 00:50:56:B3:D4:00  10.3.3.10        learned       102
eth1/20        vlan-10


Tenant      : Apress
Application : PROD_APP
AEPg        : Database_EPG

 End Point MAC       IP Address      Source        Node
Interface      Encap
 ----------------   ---------------  ------------  -----------
------------ ---------
 00:50:56:B3:08:50  10.4.4.10        learned       102
eth1/20        vlan-11

Tenant      : Apress
Application : PROD_APP
AEPg        : Frontend_EPG

 End Point MAC       IP Address      Source        Node
Interface      Encap
 ----------------   ---------------  ------------  -----------
------------ ---------
 00:50:56:B3:86:DD  10.1.1.10        learned       102
eth1/20        vlan-9
```

Leaf-102# **show endpoint vrf Apress:PROD**
Legend:
```
 S - static       s - arp          L - local        O - peer-attached
 V - vpc-attached a - local-aged   p - peer-aged    M - span
 B - bounce       H - vtep         R - peer-attached-rl D - bounce-to
                                                        -proxy
```

```
E - shared-service   m - svc-mgr
```

VLAN/ Domain	Encap VLAN	MAC Address IP Address	MAC Info/ IP Info	Interface
28	vlan-10	0050.56b3.0b92	L	eth1/20
Apress:PROD	vlan-10	10.2.2.10	L	eth1/20
28	vlan-10	0050.56b3.d400	L	eth1/20
Apress:PROD	vlan-10	10.3.3.10	L	eth1/20
20	vlan-11	0050.56b3.0850	L	eth1/20
Apress:PROD	vlan-11	10.4.4.10	L	eth1/20
29	vlan-9	0050.56b3.86dd	L	eth1/20
Apress:PROD	vlan-9	10.1.1.10	L	eth1/20

Leaf-102# show system internal epm endpoint vrf Apress:PROD

```
VRF : Apress:PROD ::: Context id : 5 ::: Vnid : 3080193

MAC : 0050.56b3.0850 ::: Num IPs : 1
IP# 0 : 10.4.4.10 ::: IP# 0 flags :  ::: l3-sw-hit: No
Vlan id : 20 ::: Vlan vnid : 8492 ::: VRF name : Apress:PROD
BD vnid : 16449430 ::: VRF vnid : 3080193
Phy If : 0x1a013000 ::: Tunnel If : 0
Interface : Ethernet1/20
Flags : 0x80005c04 ::: sclass : 49157 ::: Ref count : 5
EP Create Timestamp : 05/01/2022 14:51:37.293798
EP Update Timestamp : 05/01/2022 15:47:54.017876
EP Flags : local|IP|MAC|host-tracked|sclass|timer|

::::
output omitted
```

Note   ACI will learn both MAC and IP information if the bridge domain is configured with unicast routing enabled, as in this case. Otherwise, you should see only the MAC address.

If you cannot see any endpoints in EPG after configuring path mappings, check the following:

- **Faults related to EPG**: If present, they will usually tell you exactly what the problem is. In most cases, administrators are missing the EPG to physical domain association or a configured VLAN in the VLAN pool.

- **Correct interface and encapsulation**: Did you specify an appropriate individual interface or interface policy group from the access policies? And if so, is the configured VLAN correct and used by the connected host as well?

- **Host IP configuration**: By default, in a bridge domain with unicast routing enabled, there is also an enabled feature called *Limit Local IP Learning to BD/EPG Subnet(s)* (a configurable checkbox). If the connected endpoint is communicating using an IP address not corresponding to any subnets configured in the BD, the leaf will not learn its information.

- **Silent Host?** ACI will learn about an endpoint as soon as its first packet is seen. If the endpoint is silent, this can result in a missing entry in the database as well.

EPG Design Options

Since you already know how to divide ACI endpoints into multiple endpoint groups, maybe you are wondering what the correct way to do so is. In fact, there is no general guideline because application policies allow you to place any endpoint into any EPG based on your needs and decisions, but there are two main approaches: network-centric and application-centric.

Network Centric

Especially during a migration phase to ACI, it makes sense to "imitate" your current segmentation deployed in a legacy network and create a 1:1 mapping between VLANs and ACI constructs. For each legacy VLAN you configure exactly one bridge domain and one associated EPG (see Figure 5-19). All static or dynamic path mappings also use only one VLAN encapsulation. As a result, endpoints from the legacy network can be physically moved to ACI, while preserving their configuration, IP addressing, and logical placement. Initially, such a bridge domain can stay at Layer 2 only with the default gateway connected externally; later, it can take over with Layer 3 services as well. For my customers, this is the first and preferred step into ACI.

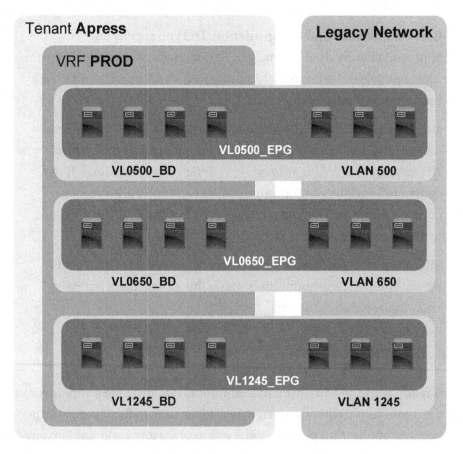

Figure 5-19. *Network-centric EPG design*

Application Centric

If you are implementing a greenfield ACI, or all your endpoints are already migrated into it, you can start thinking about moving to an application-centric EPG design. For this approach, it's expected that you have information about the architecture of your applications and their communication matrix. Then you can fully utilize ACI's tenant policies to exactly describe the individual application tiers and their network requirements without a direct relation to the legacy VLAN segments or IP subnets. As shown in Figure 5-20, each application tier is mapped to its own EPG, and you can differentiate between individual servers based on their encapsulation and the interface used in the static or dynamic path to EPG mappings. VLAN IDs will become just a locally significant EPG identifier between servers and leaf switches instead of broadcast domain boundaries with closely coupled IP subnets. Just make sure not to use the same VLAN identifier for multiple EPGs on the same pair of leaf switches. ACI will raise a fault in that case. By default, without additional configuration, VLAN IDs are global per switch or vPC pair.

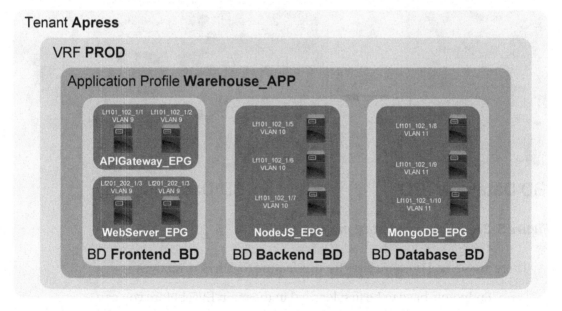

Figure 5-20. Application-centric EPG design

At this moment, there is no communication allowed between defined EPGs. Later in this chapter, you will add contracts for them to enforce the connectivity rules and complete the application profile.

Microsegmentation uEPGs

Standard application EPGs and their endpoint segmentation based on VLANs and interface mappings can support many use cases, but sometimes, especially with an application-centric philosophy, you need to go even further and differentiate between endpoints more granularly. As displayed in Figure 5-21, APIC enables you to configure micro endpoint groups (uEPG), separating individual endpoints based on these specific attributes:

- **IP and MAC addresses**: In case of endpoints connected to ACI using the physical domain (bare-metal hosts)

- **VM attributes**: VM operating system, hypervisor, datacenter, VM identifier, VM name, VM tag, or other custom attributes. All of them can be used if ACI is integrated with a VM manager like VMware vCenter.

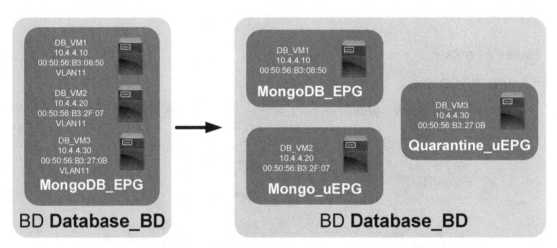

Figure 5-21. *Microsegmentation using uEPGs*

There are several prerequisites for this feature to work correctly:

- Endpoints have to be first learned in the main EPG before you can microsegment them into uEPGs. Then the uEPG mapping happens regardless of the encapsulation/interface.

- A new uEPG needs to be put inside the same bridge domain as the parent EPG.

- The bridge domain must have an IP subnet configured and unicast routing enabled.

- The new uEPG has to be associated with the same physical (or VMM) domain as the parent EPG.

- If the physical domain is used, you need to statically map the leaves to the uEPG.

To demonstrate the functionality, let's assume you have three endpoints (from Figure 5-21) in the main Database_EPG associated with Database_BD. See Listing 5-4.

Listing 5-4. Endpoint Learning Verification

```
apic1# show tenant Apress endpoints
Dynamic Endpoints:

Tenant      : Apress
Application : PROD_APP
AEPg        : Database_EPG

 End Point MAC       IP Address    Source        Node
 Interface   Encap
 ----------------   -----------   ------------   ----------
 ----------- -----------
 00:50:56:B3:08:50  10.4.4.10     learned        102
 eth1/8      vlan-11

 00:50:56:B3:27:0B  10.4.4.30     learned        102
 eth1/9      vlan-11

 00:50:56:B3:2F:07  10.4.4.20     learned        102
 eth1/10     vlan-11
```

They can freely communicate between each other without restrictions, as you can see in Figure 5-22, when pinging from DB_VM1 to DB_VM2 and DB_VM3.

```
[root@DB_VM1 ~]# ping 10.4.4.20
PING 10.4.4.20 (10.4.4.20) 56(84) bytes of data.
64 bytes from 10.4.4.20: icmp_seq=1 ttl=64 time=0.605 ms
64 bytes from 10.4.4.20: icmp_seq=2 ttl=64 time=0.219 ms
64 bytes from 10.4.4.20: icmp_seq=3 ttl=64 time=0.212 ms
64 bytes from 10.4.4.20: icmp_seq=4 ttl=64 time=0.227 ms
^C
--- 10.4.4.20 ping statistics ---
4 packets transmitted, 4 received, 0% packet loss, time 3004ms
rtt min/avg/max/mdev = 0.212/0.315/0.605/0.168 ms
[root@DB_VM1 ~]# ping 10.4.4.30
PING 10.4.4.30 (10.4.4.30) 56(84) bytes of data.
64 bytes from 10.4.4.30: icmp_seq=1 ttl=64 time=0.472 ms
64 bytes from 10.4.4.30: icmp_seq=2 ttl=64 time=0.234 ms
64 bytes from 10.4.4.30: icmp_seq=3 ttl=64 time=0.214 ms
64 bytes from 10.4.4.30: icmp_seq=4 ttl=64 time=0.345 ms
^C
--- 10.4.4.30 ping statistics ---
4 packets transmitted, 4 received, 0% packet loss, time 3003ms
rtt min/avg/max/mdev = 0.214/0.316/0.472/0.103 ms
[root@DB_VM1 ~]#
```

Figure 5-22. *Working connectivity in the main EPG between endpoints*

To create microEPGs, go to **Tenant -> Tenant_name -> Application Profiles -> Profile_name** and right-click the menu folder **uSeg EPGs**. Put them inside the same BD as the original parent EPG and create associations with the same physical (or VMM) domain. Especially for bare-metal uEPGs with a physical domain, there is a need for the static leaf switch mapping (as demonstrated in Figure 5-23). This will ensure a correct reclassification of endpoints in leaf hardware tables.

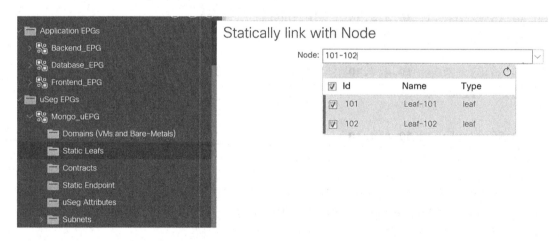

Figure 5-23. *uEPG static leaf mapping*

Finally, set the *uSeg Attributes* in the uEPG configuration, where you can choose from *Match Any (OR)* or *Match All (AND)* logical expressions and the attributes themselves (as shown in Figure 5-24). In the case of the IP attribute, you can specify the single end host IP or a subnet configured under the uEPG.

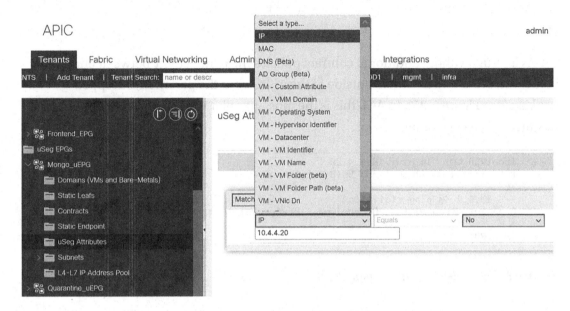

Figure 5-24. *uEPG microsgementation attributes*

After a few moments from submitting the previous configuration, you will see that specified endpoint(s) were learned inside this new microEPG, as shown in Listing 5-5.

Listing 5-5. Endpoint Relearning in microEPG

```
apic1# show tenant Apress endpoints

Dynamic Endpoints:

Tenant       : Apress
Application  : PROD_APP
AEPg         : Mongo_uEPG
```

```
End Point MAC       IP Address      Source         Node
Interface    Encap
---------------     -------------- -------------   ----------
----------   ----------
 00:50:56:B3:2F:07  10.4.4.20       learned         102
eth1/9       vlan-11
```

As a result, without additional contract policies the connectivity between endpoints in the microEPG and all others outside of the uEPG or in the parent EPG stopped working (see Figure 5-25). In ACI, this is the most granular way to separate connected resources from each other.

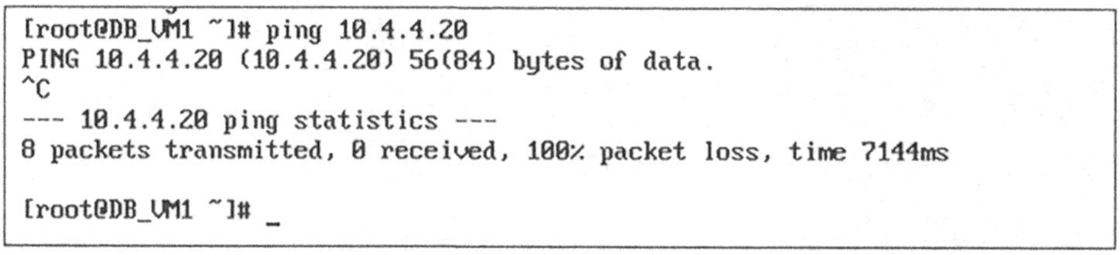

```
[root@DB_VM1 ~]# ping 10.4.4.20
PING 10.4.4.20 (10.4.4.20) 56(84) bytes of data.
^C
--- 10.4.4.20 ping statistics ---
8 packets transmitted, 0 received, 100% packet loss, time 7144ms

[root@DB_VM1 ~]# _
```

Figure 5-25. *uEPG network isolation*

Endpoint Security Groups

Although microEPGs bring significant flexibility to the definitions of your ACI application policies, they still have one drawback: they can contain endpoints from a single bridge domain only.

The newest addition to ACI's segmentation capabilities is endpoint security groups (ESGs), which removed this limitation since version 5.0.(1). An ESG is in many aspects comparable to an EPG or uEPG; it represents an isolated group of endpoints to which you can apply contract policies and allow their communication with surroundings when needed. This time the scope from which you can choose any endpoint for ESG is VRF. You just need to define a ESG selector from these options:

- **Tag Selector**: Available from 5.2(1), it allows you to match endpoints based on policy tags associated with MAC or IP addresses. A policy tag (key-value pair) object is configured in **Tenant -> Tenant_name -> Policies -> Endpoints Tags** and its goal is to match dynamically learned endpoints inside the specified BD or VRF, without any relation to a particular EPG.

- **EPG Selector**: Available from 5.2(1), it matches all endpoints inside a defined EPG. At the same time, it inherits all the contracts from EPG, so this represents the best way to migrate from EPG to ESGs seamlessly.

- **IP Subnet Selector**: Introduced in 5.0.(1), it allows the defining of a single host IP or subnet to match endpoints. In newer versions, this functionality is redundant with tag selector.

- **Service EPG Selector**: From 5.2.(4), it supports matching service EPGs together with application EPGs, allowing you to create a segmentation rule including L4-L7 service graph.

ESGs are configured in **Tenant -> Tenant_name -> Application Profile -> App_ name -> Endpoint Security Groups**. In the first step, you just specify the name and VRF for ESG (Figure 5-26).

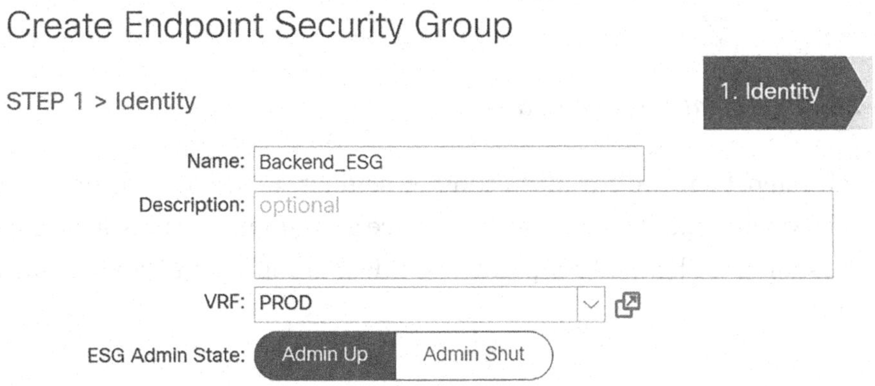

Create Endpoint Security Group

STEP 1 > Identity

1. Identity

Name: Backend_ESG

Description: optional

VRF: PROD

ESG Admin State: Admin Up   Admin Shut

Figure 5-26. ESG creation, step one

During the second step, you need to add a combination of ESG selectors. For the simple demonstration shown in Figure 5-27, I've picked one endpoint from each previously used EPGs and put it inside an IP tag policy (**Tenant -> Policies -> Endpoint Tags**). Each endpoint entry is configured with a key-value tag in the format EPG_ Name: <name>.

Endpoint IP

IP	VRF	Tags	Matching Tag Selector
10.1.1.10	PROD	EPG_Name Frontend	uni/tn-Apress/ap-PROD_APP/esg-Backend_ESG/tagse
10.2.2.10	PROD	EPG_Name Backend	uni/tn-Apress/ap-PROD_APP/esg-Backend_ESG/tagse
10.4.4.10	PROD	EPG_Name Database	uni/tn-Apress/ap-PROD_APP/esg-Backend_ESG/tagse

Figure 5-27. *IP endpoint tag policy*

These policy tags are now used in an ESG configuration for an endpoint classification (see Figure 5-28).

Create Endpoint Security Group

STEP 2 > Selectors   1. Identity   **2. Selectors**   3. Advanced (Optional)

Tag Selectors:

Tag Key	Value Operator	Tag Value	Description
EPG_Name	Equals	Frontend	
EPG_Name	Equals	Backend	
EPG_Name	Equals	Database	

Figure 5-28. *ESG creation, step two*

In the third step, there are advanced contract settings (to be covered later in this chapter), so leave the default configuration in place and submit the finished form. Right after that you should see learned endpoints according to your specification (shown in Figure 5-29).

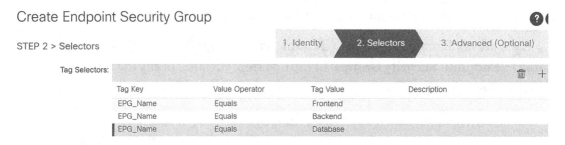

ESG - Backend_ESG

Summary   Policy   Operational   Health   Faults   History

Client Endpoints   Contracts   Deployed Leaves   Tag Selectors

Healthy

MAC/IP	Learning Source	Hosting Server	Reporting Controller Name	Interface (learned)	Encap	Base EPG	Policy Tags
00:50:56:B3:0B:92	learned			Pod-1/Node-102/eth...	vlan-10	Apress:PROD_APP:Backend_EPG	
10.2.2.10						Apress:PROD_APP:Backend_EPG	EPG_Name Backend
00:50:56:B3:08:50	learned			Pod-1/Node-102/eth...	vlan-11	Apress:PROD_APP:Database_EPG	
10.4.4.10						Apress:PROD_APP:Database_EPG	EPG_Name Database
00:50:56:B3:86:DD	learned			Pod-1/Node-102/eth...	vlan-9	Apress:PROD_APP:Frontend_EPG	
10.1.1.10						Apress:PROD_APP:Frontend_EPG	EPG_Name Frontend

Figure 5-29. *ESG endpoint learning*

ACI Contracts

Now, since you have ACI resources in a fabric segmented into EPGs, microEPGs, or ESGs, the last and crucial component of an application policy is the *contracts*, specifying communication needs between them. Contracts represent the implementation of a fundamental security architecture in ACI, using allowlist to permit the required traffic between EPGs explicitly. Contracts are directional, reusable, and universally describe protocols with their L4 ports (where applicable).

For better understanding, consider contracts as non-stateful access lists (ACLs) with dynamic MAC/IP entries based on currently learned endpoints in related EPGs. ACI in this regard acts as a distributed, non-stateful, zone-based firewall.

By default, no communication between EPGs, uEPGs, or ESGs is permitted thanks to the per-VRF configurable option *Policy Control Enforcement Preference* set to *Enforced.* If you set this knob to Unenforced, ACI completely stops using contracts and all traffic between endpoints in a particular VRF will be allowed. This feature can come in handy to quickly troubleshoot non-working communication between existing endpoints in ACI. If it doesn't go against your security policy, disabling the contract enforcement momentarily can immediately show problems in contract definitions or associations if the connectivity starts working.

As described in Figure 5-30, contracts have a pretty granular structure, allowing the administrator to thoroughly design the communication policies between endpoints, consisting of the following:

- **Root Contract Object**: Primarily encompasses the configuration of the contract scope explained in the next section. You can configure QoS classification for the traffic matched by contract policies or change the target DSCP when communicating with external L3OUT.

  - **Contract Subject**: Sublevel with the ability to apply selective L4-L7 service graphs (a traffic redirection). There are further configuration options to automatically permit both directions for specified traffic when the contract is applied between EPGs and reverse filter ports for a reply.

  - **Contract Filters**: One or more filters can be applied on a subject with the ability to specify a permit or deny an action for them, or optionally log the matched traffic

- **Filter Entries**: One or more entries inside a filter finally defines the exact traffic type to match.

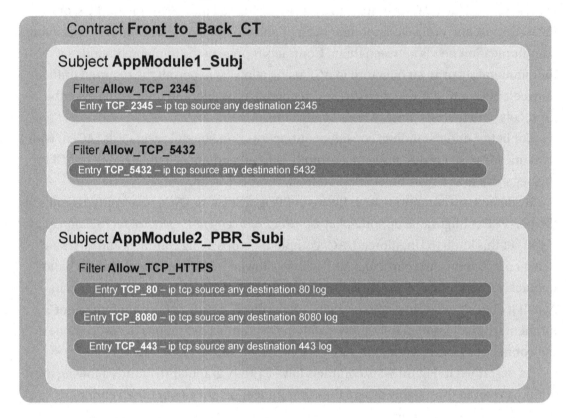

Figure 5-30. *ACI contract structure overview*

Each contract comes with two universal logical connectors: *consumer* and *provider*. In order to work correctly, both of them have to be connected to some of the following entities (I will cover external EPGs in Chapter 7):

- Standard application EPG

- Endpoint security group

- EPG preferred group

- VRF vzAny object

- L3OUT external EPG

- L2OUT external EPG

Caution   At the time of writing, ACI in version 5.2 didn't support the application of a contract between ESG and EPG, just two ESGs mutually.

A contract is, like many other application policy objects, a universal building block so you can attach it to multiple EPG/ESGs and easily allow connectivity to shared resources (as shown in Figure 5-31).

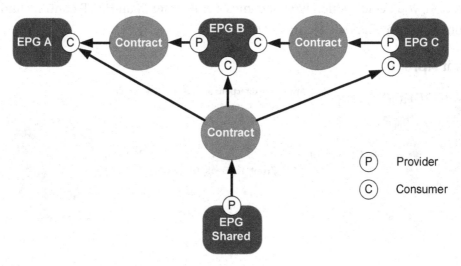

Figure 5-31. *Contract and EPG relationships*

When designing contracts and their relations, I recommend consulting the official scalability guide for your implemented ACI version as their amount is not unlimited (although it is quite high). In ACI version 5.2, there can be a maximum of 100 EPGs attached on each side of a single contract. Another important value is the maximum TCAM space for deployment of contracts to the leaf's hardware ASICs. Based on a given leaf model and currently configured Forwarding Scale Profile, the amount of TCAM memory can go from 64.000 up to 256.000, while the approximate consumption can be calculated using the following formula:

Number of filter entries in a contract **X** Number of consumer EPGs **X** Number of provider EPGs **X 2**

Note   Contracts are enforced on unicast traffic only. Broadcast, unknown unicast, and multicast (BUM) is implicitly permitted between EPGs.

Consumer and Provider EPGs

Let's consider that, for simplicity, there is a need to enable HTTP communication between endpoints in frontend EPG and a backend EPG. For this purpose, you create a contract specifying in its filters TCP traffic with any source port and the destination port 80. As mentioned, contracts are directional, so it always depends who is the initiator of particular traffic and who is the destination on the other side. Based on this specification, you decide which EPG becomes a consumer of an HTTP contract and which one is its provider (see Figure 5-32).

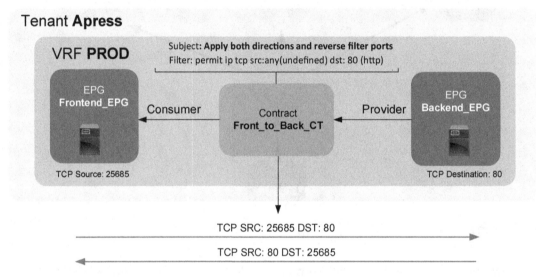

Figure 5-32. *Contract consumer and provider relationships*

The provider EPG is (as the name suggests) the provider of an application service allowed by the contract. That means its endpoints are destinations of a traffic defined in the contract. In your example, you expect that endpoints in provider EPG Backend_EPG have the HTTP service enabled and open on port 80.

The consumer EPG, on the other side, consumes the service allowed by the contract. Endpoints in consumer EPGs are therefore initiators of traffic flow or TCP sessions. In your example, servers from Frontend_EPG initiate communication using a random source TCP port to Backend_EPG endpoints with destination port 80.

A contract generally describes the allowed traffic from consumers to providers, in case of TCP/UDP from a consumer source port to a provider destination port. But what about the replies to such traffic? ACI isn't stateful, so it won't automatically create a session to permit an incoming reply. Fortunately, thanks to default contract subject settings *Apply Both Directions* and *Reverse Filter Ports*, each contract is in fact applied two times, consumer to provider and provider to consumer, but the second time with reversed TCP/UDP ports. If you enable destination port 80 from any source, APIC will also implement a permit for a reply from source port 80 to destination ANY. You don't need to create multiple contracts or associate the one in both directions manually.

Contract Configuration

Configuration-wise, to create a new contract you need to go to **Tenant -> Tenant_name -> Contracts** and right-click the **Standard** folder. As you can see in Figure 5-33, besides the object name, you can set the contract scope and QoS properties and create a list of subjects.

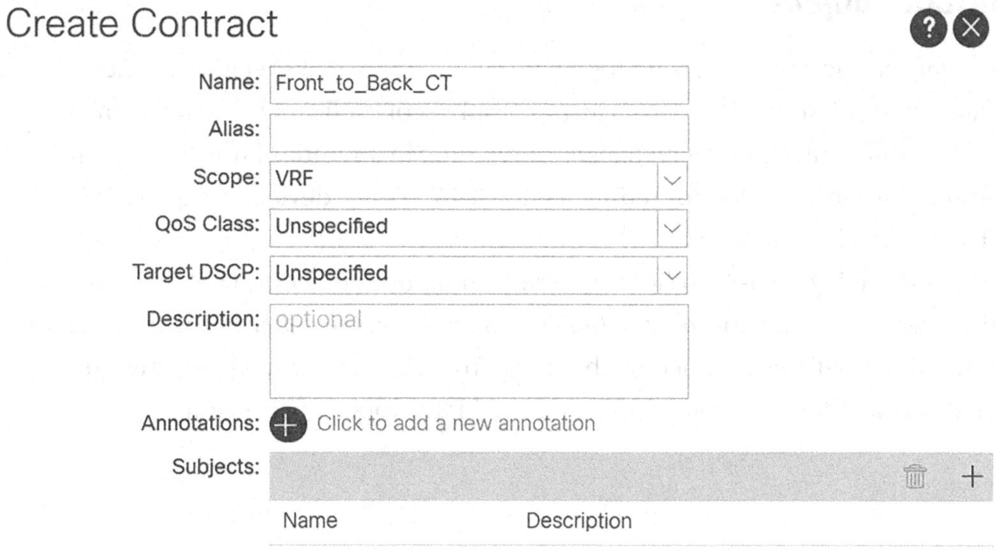

Figure 5-33. *Main contract object creation*

Contract Scope

By default, the contract is applicable and valid between any EPGs inside a single VRF. A contract scope configuration option gives this at the root object level. You can choose from the following values:

- **Application Profile:** Traffic defined by this contract will be permitted only between EPGs that are part of the same application profile, regardless of their VRF affiliation. This can be helpful with the proper application policies design to apply the same contract to many EPGs, but still without cross-talking between different applications.

- **VRF (default)**: When a contract is applied, it permits communication universally between any two EPGs as long as they are part of the same VRF.

- **Tenant**: ACI is capable of automatic route-leaking between VRFs if communication of their EPGs is needed, and one of the prerequisites to do so is a contract with scope tenant between them.

- **Global**: If inter-tenant (and inter-tenant VRFs) communication is viable, a global scoped contract is one part of the solution.

Contract Subject

Individual contract subjects group together traffic rules with a specific treatment. Here you can apply different QoS policies just for a subset of traffic matched by the main contract or differentiate between packets forwarded in a standard way through the ACI fabric and the communications redirected to L4-L7 service devices using ACI's service graphs (covered in Chapter 8).

As shown in Figure 5-34, other important configuration knobs, by default enabled, are the already-mentioned *Apply Both Direction* and *Reverse Filter Ports*. They ensure that the subject will permit not only the traffic from the initiator consumer to the destination provider EPGs, but also the replies in the opposite direction.

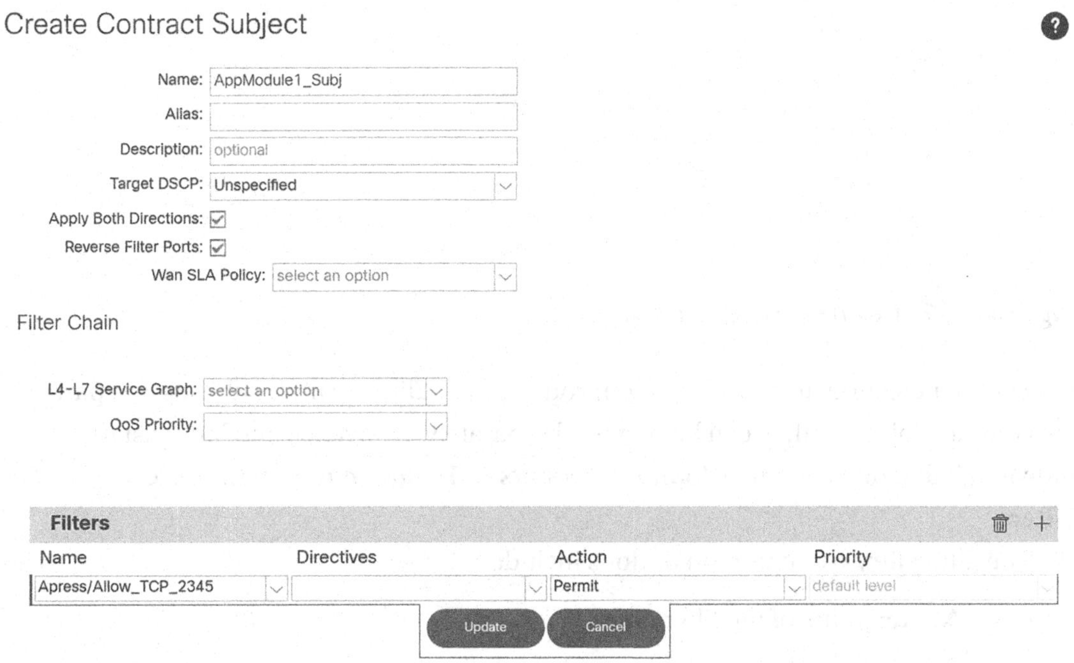

Create Contract Subject

Name: AppModule1_Subj

Alias:

Description: optional

Target DSCP: Unspecified

Apply Both Directions: ☑

Reverse Filter Ports: ☑

Wan SLA Policy: select an option

Filter Chain

L4-L7 Service Graph: select an option

QoS Priority:

Filters   🗑   +

Name	Directives	Action	Priority
Apress/Allow_TCP_2345		Permit	default level

Update   Cancel

Figure 5-34. *Contract subject creation*

When adding multiple filter objects to the subject, you can choose which of them will permit or deny the specified traffic. Optionally, you can enable logging for particular filters using the *Directives* setting or decide to conserve the TCAM memory when you choose the *Enable Policy Compression* directive. In that case, ACI won't save any statistics about matched packets by that rule in exchange for less TCAM consumption.

Contract Filter

The last contract component is filters (see Figure 5-35). Using filter entries, they describe exactly the type of traffic, permitted or denied, based on subject settings when the filter is applied.

Figure 5-35. *Contract subject creation*

For filter creation and configuration, you can get it directly from subjects as a part of the contract object, or they can be prepared separately in advance and later just used. Individual filter objects can be found in **Tenants -> Tenant_name -> Contracts -> Filters.**

The filter entry configuration options include

- **Name**: Name of the filter entry

- **EtherType**: Matched EtherType: IP, IPv4, IPv6, MPLS Unicast, Trill, ARP, FCoE, MACsec, or Unspecified (meaning any)

- **ARP Flag**: If you've chosen ARP as EtherType, this field specifies a further ARP Request or ARP Reply.

- **IP Protocol**: If EtherType is IP, this field further determines its type: TCP, UDP, ICMP, ICMPv6, PIM, EIGRP, OSPF, IGMP, L2TP, or Unspecified (any)

- **ApplyToFrag**: Enables matching only fragmented IP packets with the offset field in the header set to a greater value than 0

- **Stateful**: Enables matching only packets that have a direction provider to consumer TCP ACK flag set

- **SFromPort**: Range of TCP/UDP source ports

- **SToPort**: Range of TCP/UDP source ports

- **DFromPort**: Range of TCP/UDP destination ports

- **DToPort**: Range of TCP/UDP destination ports

Contract Application to EPGs/ESGs

The final step in contract configuration is its association with application endpoint groups or endpoint security groups. When you navigate to the EPG object in **Tenants -> Tenant_name -> Application Profiles -> Profile_name -> Application EPGs,** right-click the *EPG_name* and choose *Add Provided/Consumed Contract.* Then just choose the right contract and submit the form (shown in Figure 5-36).

Add Consumed Contract

Contract:	Front_to_Back_CT
	Type at least 4 characters to select contracts
QoS:	Unspecified
Contract Label:	
Subject Label:	

Figure 5-36. Contract to EPG application

Graphically, the result can be checked when you navigate to the contact object and open the *Topology* tab. It describes just the associations of one contract (see Figure 5-37). Note that the arrows characterize the relationship from a contract perspective: the arrow goes from a provider EPG to a contract and from a contract to a consumer EPG. The actual traffic between endpoints is initiated in the opposite direction.

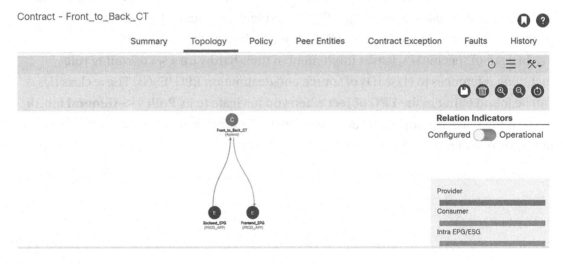

Figure 5-37. Contract to EPG application

Another way to show contract relations graphically is when you open the application profile object and navigate to the *Topology* tab (shown in Figure 5-38). You'll find an overview of the whole application structure.

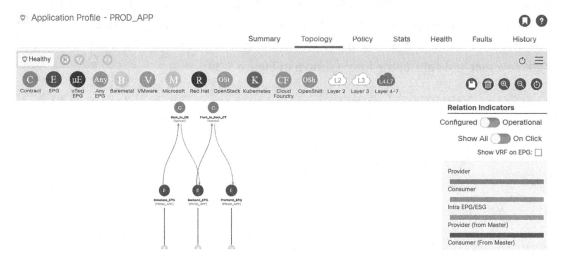

Figure 5-38. *Contract to EPG application*

Contract Zoning Rules on Leaf Switches

Maybe you are wondering how ACI can enforce contracts without any direct relation to an IP address of endpoints, just the traffic specification. As you attach EPGs to both sides of a contract, ACI relies upon unique EPG identifiers called class IDs (also referred to as pcTags or sClasses). MicroEPGs and ESGs have their own class ID as well.

Instead of specific IPs, leaves implement in their hardware a set of zoning rules including references to class IDs of source and destination EPG/ESGs. These class IDs can be found either in the **EPG object** when you navigate to its **Policy -> General** tab, or while at the main **Tenant object** and opening the **Operational -> Resource IDs -> EPGs** tab (shown in Figure 5-39).

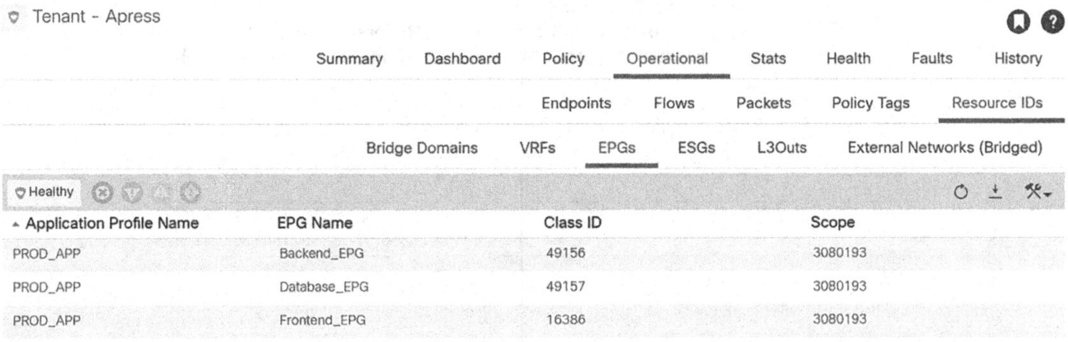

Tenant - Apress

| Summary | Dashboard | Policy | Operational | Stats | Health | Faults | History |

| Endpoints | Flows | Packets | Policy Tags | Resource IDs |

| Bridge Domains | VRFs | EPGs | ESGs | L3Outs | External Networks (Bridged) |

Healthy

▲ Application Profile Name	EPG Name	Class ID	Scope
PROD_APP	Backend_EPG	49156	3080193
PROD_APP	Database_EPG	49157	3080193
PROD_APP	Frontend_EPG	16386	3080193

Figure 5-39. *EPG's class ID (pcTag)*

In your case, Frontend_EPG has class ID 16386 and Backend_EPG has class ID 49156. Common scope 3080193 refers to a VRF instance they are both part of. Now when you apply a simple contract between them, allowing destination TCP port 80 with default subject configuration (apply both directions and reverse filter ports), the outcome is documented in Figure 5-40.

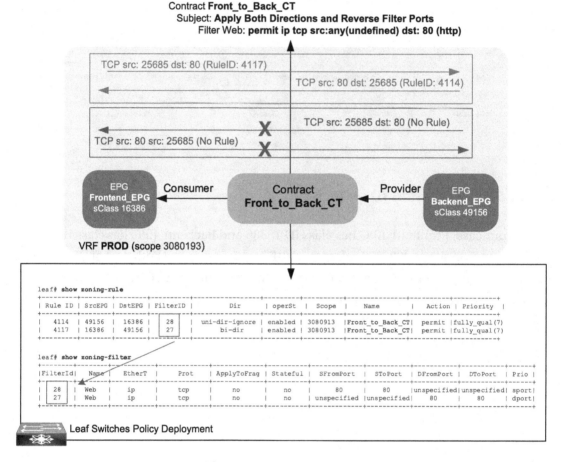

Figure 5-40. *Contract zone rules*

Each contract relationship between two unique EPGs creates by default a number of new entries in zoning tables of all affected leaf switches, where you have some static or dynamic EPG to interface mappings. The number of entries depends on the amount of filter rules included in the contract. These zoning tables are basically the end result and hardware implementation of security policies in ACI. As you can see in Figure 5-34, you can view their current content on a particular leaf switch by issuing `show zoning-rule`. The structure of a zoning table is the following:

- **Rule ID**: Unique zone-rule identifier, switch local value

- **Src/Dst EPG**: Source and destination pcTags (ClassID, sClass) of related EPGs

- **Filter ID**: Reference to another table with filter definitions

- **Dir**: Direction of the rule. With *apply both directions* enabled, there will be always *bidir* rules from the consumer to the provider EPG and *uni-dir-ignore* rules for returning traffic from the provider to the consumer EPG.

- **operSt**: Enabled/Disabled

- **Scope**: Reference to VRF L3 VNI

- **Name**: Contract name

- **Action**: Permit/Deny/Redirect/Log, based on a contract subject configuration

- **Priority:** To some extent a configurable precedence of entries when multiple subjects or contracts are associated between the same EPGs. The lower the number, the higher the priority, with the range between 0 and 22.

In your case with the contract permitting TCP destination port 80 using a single filter, you can see two entries: rule ID 4117 for a consumer to provider direction and 4114 for returning traffic. That's the result of setting *Apply Both Directions* in the contract subject. There are, of course, many other entries in the zoning table, but I've omitted them for clarity. You will always find entries implicitly permitting ARP in each VRF and implicitly denying and logging all other traffic, not matched by any more specific custom contract. Implicitly denied entries have the lowest possible priority of 22 so all your custom contracts will take precedence over it.

Note   Although the rule 4117 (consumer to provider) from the previous example specifies the *bi-dir* direction according to the zoning table, it suggest that you can also permit TCP destination port 80 in the other way, provider to consumer. In fact, ACI enforces this bi-dir entry only in one and the correct direction. Lab tests showed that all TCP SYNs to a destination port 80 from provider to consumer are dropped.

Another important security policy-related database is the zoning filter table, in which content can be checked using show zoning-filter. Each contract zoning rule has a particular filter entry referenced from this table. The filter structure goes as follows (mostly matches the configuration options of the filter object discussed later):

- **Filter ID**: Unique contract filter identifier, switch local value

- **Name**: Name of filter object related to this entry

- **EtherT**: Configured EtherType: IP, IPv4, IPv6, ARP, FCoE, etc.

- **Prot**: IP protocol definition: TCP, UDP, ICMP, PIM, EIGRP, OSPF, IGMP, etc. Set only if previous EtherType field is IP.

- **ApplyToFrag**: Enables matching only fragmented IP packets with the offset field in the header set to a greater value than 0

- **Stateful**: Enables matching only packets that have a direction provider to consumer TCP ACK flag set

- **SFromPort**: Range of TCP/UDP source ports

- **SToPort**: Range of TCP/UDP source ports

- **DFromPort**: Range of TCP/UDP destination ports

- **DToPort**: Range of TCP/UDP destination ports

- **Prio**: Filter can be prioritized based on a specificity. The exact definition of source or destination ports over unspecified.

The *Reverse Filter Ports* option in a contract subject configuration causes that for each filter defined in a contract. You can see two individual entries in a zoning filter table with automatically switched TCP/UDP port definitions. Filter ID 27 from your example defines the TCP any source port connection to destination port 80, while the automatically created Filter ID 28 reverses the definition to TCP source port 80 and any destination port.

Just as a side note, when you consider contracts permitting "ip any any" (all filter fields unspecified), thanks to this zoning rule and zoning filter implementation, it actually doesn't matter which way the contract is applied between two EPGs. It will permit the entire traffic in both directions, regardless of consumer-provider association. Only more specific port definitions have this directional behavior.

Endpoint Classification and Zoning Enforcement

The last piece of the contract enforcement puzzle is endpoint classification and association to its EPG. You already know that if the ACI administrator creates a static or dynamic interface/VLAN to EPG mappings, leaf switches will learn all the endpoint

MAC/IP addresses behind local interfaces and update this information using COOP on spines as well. By default, the same learning process happens for remote endpoints communicating with local ones. For zoning rules enforcement, all these endpoints must be internally associated with pcTags (sClass) of their EPG/ESG/uEPG. This information can be then verified with the commands in Listing 5-6.

Listing 5-6. Endpoint pcTag/sClass Verification

```
apic1# show epg Frontend_EPG detail
Application EPg Data:
Tenant                      : Apress
Application                 : PROD_APP
AEPg                        : Frontend_EPG
BD                          : Frontend_BD
uSeg EPG                    : no
Intra EPG Isolation         : unenforced
Proxy ARP                   : none
Policy Tag                  : 16386
Vlan Domains                : Apress_PhysDom

--output ommited—


Leaf-101# show system internal epm endpoint ip 10.1.1.10

MAC : 0050.56b3.86dd ::: Num IPs : 1
IP# 0 : 10.1.1.10 ::: IP# 0 flags : sclass| ::: l3-sw-hit: No ::: sclass :
17 ::: flags2 : dyn-useg|
Vlan id : 30 ::: Vlan vnid : 8292 ::: VRF name : Apress:PROD
BD vnid : 16089026 ::: VRF vnid : 3080193
Phy If : 0x1a013000 ::: Tunnel If : 0
Interface : Ethernet1/20
Flags : 0x80005c04 ::: sclass : 16386 ::: Ref count : 5
EP Create Timestamp : 05/06/2022 15:42:07.377423
EP Update Timestamp : 05/11/2022 11:24:35.170177
EP Flags : local|IP|MAC|host-tracked|sclass|timer|
```

When a packet arrives from the source endpoint, the leaf will internally associate it with a specific policy tag (pcTag) based on previous endpoint learning. As a next step, the contract enforcement decision is made.

If the leaf switch already knows about a destination endpoint, it can right away search through its zoning rules, looking for matching source and destination pcTag entries there. Based on the result, the packet is either permitted to further processing or denied. This happens thanks to the default setting of *Policy Control Enforcement Direction* to *Ingress* in the VRF policy. That's why leaves prefer to enforce contracts on ingress whenever possible.

If the leaf switch is not currently aware of a destination endpoint and thus it cannot derive its pcTag, such a packet is forwarded through the ACI fabric to the egress leaf switch and zoning rules are applied there instead.

Note   Previously discussed reclassification of endpoints from a parent EPG to micro EPG or ESG is, in fact, about changing their sClass values and therefore instantly applying different contract policies and zoning rules on leaf switches.

EPG/ESG Preferred Groups

Creating new contracts between each pair of EPGs can become quite complicated and harder to maintain over time. ACI offers a couple of options to optimize the contract usage. The first tool I have already described: endpoint security groups themselves. They provide a simple way to group together multiple EPGs and, instead of individual contract relationships, apply the only one for the whole group.

Another option is to use the preferred group feature. As shown in Figure 5-41, in each VRF you can create one group of EPGs or ESGs, without enforced contracts mutually between all members, so they can communicate freely. Only non-members then need to use a standard contract to allow communication with members of a preferred group.

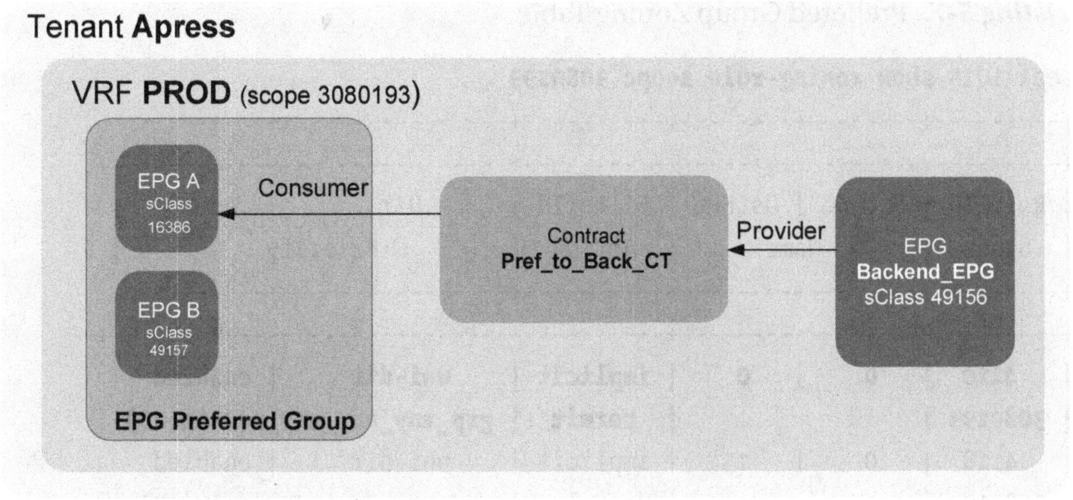

Figure 5-41. *EPG preferred groups*

In order to configure the preferred group feature, you need to do two steps:

- Enable the preferred group in the VRF object policy. There is a configuration knob named *Preferred Group*, which is by default in the Disabled state, found in **Tenants -> Tenant_name -> Networking -> VRF -> Policy.**

- Include the EPG object to the preferred group in its policy configuration at **Tenants -> Tenant_name -> Application Profiles -> App_name -> Application EPGs -> EPG_Name -> Policy**. There is a configuration knob named *Preferred Group Member* with the option *Include.* The same approach works for ESGs as well.

The resulting implementation of zoning rules for a preferred group is shown in Listing 5-7.

Listing 5-7. Preffered Group Zoning Table

```
Leaf-101# show zoning-rule scope 3080193
+---------+--------+--------+----------+----------------+---------
+---------+--------+--------+----------+---------------------------+
| Rule ID | SrcEPG | DstEPG | FilterID |      Dir       | operSt
|  Scope  |         Name    |  Action  |       Priority            |
+---------+--------+--------+----------+----------------+---------
+---------+--------+--------+----------+---------------------------+
|  4110   |   0    |   0    | implicit |    uni-dir     | enabled
| 3080193 |                 |  permit  | grp_any_any_any_permit(20) |
|  4118   |   0    |   15   | implicit |    uni-dir     | enabled
| 3080193 |                 | deny,log | grp_any_dest_any_deny(19)  |
|  4119   | 49156  | 16386  |    25    |    bi-dir      | enabled
| 3080193 | Pref_to_Back_CT |  permit  |      fully_qual(7)         |
|  4148   | 16386  | 49156  |    26    | uni-dir-ignore | enabled
| 3080193 | Pref_to_Back_CT |  permit  |      fully_qual(7)         |
|  4130   |3080193 |   0    | implicit |    uni-dir     | enabled
| 3080193 |                 | deny,log | grp_src_any_any_deny(18)   |
|  4131   | 49156  |   0    | implicit |    uni-dir     | enabled
| 3080193 |                 | deny,log | grp_src_any_any_deny(18)   |
|  4129   |   0    | 49156  | implicit |    uni-dir     | enabled
| 3080193 |                 | deny,log | grp_any_dest_any_deny(19)  |
+---------+--------+--------+----------+----------------+---------
+---------+--------+--------+----------+---------------------------+
```

As you can see in Rule ID 4110, communication within the preferred group is implicitly permitted because there is no more specific entry for the sClasses of group members. All of their packets will hit this implicit rule in their VRF. However, if this was the only additive rule in the zoning table, in fact all other EPGs/ESGs without a specific contract would match it as well, not only the preferred group members. To solve this, ACI adds another two implicit deny entries (Rule IDs 4131 and 4129) per each non preferred group member. Thanks to them, in your case Backend_EPG won't be able to communicate with group members without a more specific contract in place. As these implicit denies have lower priorities of 18 and 19, any standard permit contract will override them if needed. That's the case with Rule IDs 4119 and 4148 and the standard contract between a preferred group member and Backend_EPG.

VRF vzAny Object

Another useful feature to optimize the amount of contract relationships between your EPGs is the vzAny object (sometimes called an EPG collection). Each VRF has one such an item, representing the entire set of current and future EPG/ESGs (as shown in Figure 5-42).

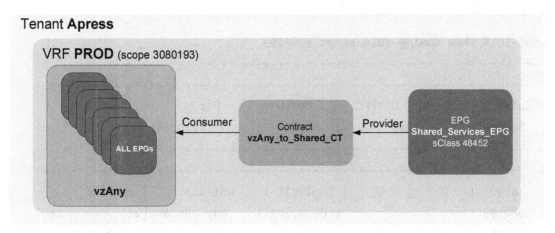

Figure 5-42. *VRF vzAny*

Typical use cases for vzAny are the following:

- Need to permit access from one specific EPG to all others in the same VRF, or vice versa

- Universally permit specific communication between all EPGs mutually

- If the customer doesn't want to enforce a contract security using ACI, but rather would like to use the connected firewall for inspection of all the north-south and/or east-west traffic between EPGs, it's very easy to implement it with a single contract allowing everything (IP any any) attached with both consumer and provider connectors to vzAny. Then you just include the ACI service graph (covered in Chapter 8) in such a contract and the entire traffic between any two EPGs/ESGs will be redirected to the firewall.

Configuration of vzAny is pretty simple. Just go to **Tenants -> Tenant_Name ->
Networking -> VRF -> EPG|ESG Collection for VRF object**. There you can attach the
provided or consumed connectors of the chosen contract.

The vzAny implementation in leaf hardware can be observed in the zoning rules
output in Listing 5-8.

Listing 5-8. vzAny Zoning Table

```
Leaf-101# show zoning-rule scope 3080193
+---------+--------+--------+----------+----------------+---------
+---------+------------------+----------+--------------------------+
| Rule ID | SrcEPG | DstEPG | FilterID |      Dir       | operSt
|  Scope  |        Name       |  Action |      Priority            |
+---------+--------+--------+----------+----------------+---------
+---------+------------------+----------+--------------------------+
|   4130  |   0    |   0    | implicit |    uni-dir     | enabled
| 3080193 |                  | deny,log |  any_any_any(21)          |
|   4138  |   0    |   0    |  imparp  |    uni-dir     | enabled
| 3080193 |                  |  permit  |·  any_any_filter (17)    |
|   4118  |   0    |   15   | implicit |    uni-dir     | enabled
| 3080193 |                  | deny,log |  any_vrf_any_deny(22)     |
|   4139  |   0    | 48452  |    25    |    uni-dir     | enabled      •
| 3080193 |vzAny_to_Shared_CT|  permit  |  any_dest_filter(14)     |
|   4128  | 48452  |   0    |    26    |    uni-dir     | enabled
| 3080193 |vzAny_to_Shared_CT|  permit  |   src_any_filter(13)     |
+---------+--------+--------+----------+----------------+---------
+---------+------------------+----------+--------------------------+
```

Responsible entries for vzAny contract enforcement are Rules 4139 and 4128. The
first one permits communication to be initiated from any EPG (sClass 0) to the provider
EPG (sClass 48452), and the returning traffic is then allowed using the second rule with
reversed filter ports.

Image you have implemented a universal permit for some TCP protocol where vzAny
is both provider and consumer, as shown in Figure 5-43.

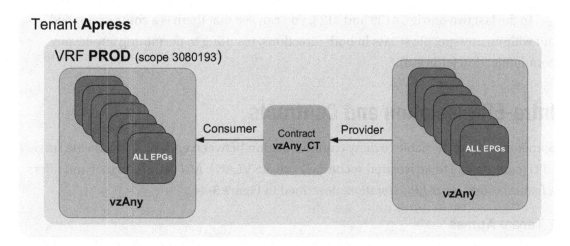

Figure 5-43. *vzAny-to-vzAny contracts*

The subsequent outcome in the leaf hardware tables would look like Listing 5-9.

Listing 5-9. vzAny-to-vzAny Contract

```
Leaf-101# show zoning-rule scope 3080193
```

| Rule ID | SrcEPG | DstEPG | FilterID | Dir | operSt |
Scope		Name	Action	Priority	
4130	0	0	implicit	uni-dir	enabled
3080193			deny,log	any_any_any(21)	
4138	0	0	imparp	uni-dir	enabled
3080193			permit	any_any_filter (17)	
4118	0	15	implicit	uni-dir	enabled
3080193			deny,log	any_vrf_any_deny(22)	
4139	**0**	**0**	**26**	**uni-dir-ignore**	**enabled**
3080193	**vzAny_CT**		**permit**	**any_any_filter(17)**	
4128	**0**	**0**	**25**	**bi-dir**	**enabled**
3080193	**vzAny_CT**		**permit**	**any_any_filter(17)**	

In the last two entries, 4139 and 4128, you can see that there is a contract applied but without any specific sClass in both directions, resulting in permitting any-to-any communication (sClass 0).

Intra-EPG Isolation and Contracts

Sometimes it can be viable to deny communication between endpoints inside the single EPG (comparable to an isolated secondary private VLAN). ACI counts on that and offers a feature called *intra-EPG isolation*, described in Figure 5-44.

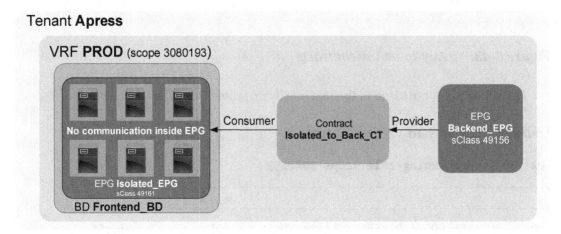

Figure 5-44. *Intra-EPG isolation*

Even though endpoints inside the isolated EPG won't communicate between each other, the EPG is still attachable using standard application contracts with other EPGs. To enable the endpoint isolation, open the EPG object and navigate to **Policy -> General** and switch the *Intra-EPG Isolation* knob to *Enforced*.

After enabling the isolation, in zoning rules you will find one new entry denying all traffic with the source and destination being the same sClass of the isolated EPG (49161). See Listing 5-10.

Listing 5-10. Intra-EPG Isolation Enforcement

```
Leaf-101# show zoning-rule scope 3080193
+---------+--------+--------+---------+---------------+---------
+---------+-----------------------+---------+---------------------+
| Rule ID | SrcEPG | DstEPG | FilterID |      Dir      |  operSt
|  Scope  |                 Name           |  Action  |   Priority          |
+---------+--------+--------+---------+---------------+---------
+---------+-----------------------+---------+---------------------+
|  4142   | 49161  | 49161  | implicit |   uni-dir     | enabled
| 3080193 |                                | deny,log |  class-eq-deny(2)   |
+---------+--------+--------+---------+---------------+---------
+---------+-----------------------+---------+---------------------+
```

If you still need to permit at least some traffic between the otherwise isolated endpoints, ACI allows you to configure the *intra-EPG contract* (depicted in Figure 5-45). It's a standard contract applied using a special configuration option. Right-click the isolated EPG object and choose *Add Intra-EPG Contract*.

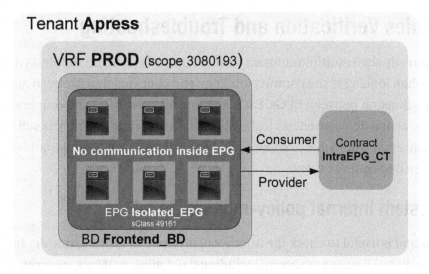

Figure 5-45. *Intra-EPG contracts*

To the previous single zoning rule effectively isolating endpoints two more entries are added now, overriding the deny by higher priority, but only for traffic specified in the filter of this intra-EPG contract. See Listing 5-11.

Listing 5-11. Intra-EPG Isolation Enforcement

Leaf-101# **show zoning-rule scope 3080193**

```
+---------+--------+--------+----------+---------------+---------
+---------+--------------------------+---------+----------------------+
| Rule ID | SrcEPG | DstEPG | FilterID |      Dir      | operSt
|  Scope  |        |        Name       |  Action  |      Priority       |
+---------+--------+--------+----------+---------------+---------
+---------+--------------------------+---------+----------------------+
|   4142  | 49161  | 49161  | implicit |    uni-dir    | enabled
| 3080193 |                           | deny,log |   class-eq-deny(2)   |
|   4142  | 49161  | 49161  |    53    |    bi-dir     | enabled
| 3080193 |        IntraEPG_CT        |  permit  |  class-eq-filter(1)  |
|   4142  | 49161  | 49161  |    52    | uni-dir-ignore | enabled
| 3080193 |        IntraEPG_CT        |  permit  |  class-eq-filter(1)  |
+---------+--------+--------+----------+---------------+---------
+---------+--------------------------+---------+----------------------+
```

Zone Rules Verification and Troubleshooting

You have already seen multiple contract verification tools from the simplest GUI methods, when looking at the contract topology and checking that it's been applied in a correct direction between EPGs/ESGs, to more advanced CLI show commands, verifying the actual deployment on leaf switches in zoning tables. There is still more to offer, though, and I would like to show you some additional and useful troubleshooting options related to contract rules.

show system internal policy-mgr stats

This command is useful to check the number of hits for each zoning rule deployed on a given leaf switch. All rules are shown, including the denies, so if you are unsure whether you are hitting your own, more specific rule (with higher priority) or just an implicit deny, this could be one way to find out. See Listing 5-12.

Listing 5-12. Contract Zone Rules Hit Logging

Leaf-101# **show system internal policy-mgr stats**
Requested Rule Statistics
Rule (4096) DN (sys/actrl/scope-16777200/rule-16777200-s-any-d-any-f-
implicit) Ingress: 0, Egress: 0, Pkts: 0
Rule (4097) DN (sys/actrl/scope-16777200/rule-16777200-s-any-d-any-f-
implarp) Ingress: 0, Egress: 0, Pkts: 0
Rule (4098) DN (sys/actrl/scope-2981888/rule-2981888-s-any-d-any-f-
implicit) Ingress: 0, Egress: 0, Pkts: 0
Rule (4099) DN (sys/actrl/scope-2981888/rule-2981888-s-any-d-any-f-implarp)
Ingress: 0, Egress: 0, Pkts: 0
Rule (4100) DN (sys/actrl/scope-2981888/rule-2981888-s-any-d-15-f-implicit)
Ingress: 0, Egress: 0, Pkts: 0
Rule (4101) DN (sys/actrl/scope-3080193/rule-3080193-s-any-d-49155-f-
implicit) Ingress: 0, Egress: 0, **Pkts: 47**
Rule (4102) DN (sys/actrl/scope-3080193/rule-3080193-s-any-d-any-f-
implicit) Ingress: 0, Egress: 0, Pkts: 0
Rule (4103) DN (sys/actrl/scope-3080193/rule-3080193-s-any-d-any-f-implarp)
Ingress: 0, Egress: 0, Pkts: 0
Rule (4104) DN (sys/actrl/scope-3080193/rule-3080193-s-any-d-15-f-implicit)
Ingress: 0, Egress: 0, Pkts: 0
Rule (4105) DN (sys/actrl/scope-3080193/rule-3080193-s-any-d-49154-f-
implicit) Ingress: 0, Egress: 0, **Pkts: 12**
Rule (4106) DN (sys/actrl/scope-3080193/rule-3080193-s-any-d-32770-f-
implicit) Ingress: 0, Egress: 0, **Pkts: 124**
Rule (4117) DN (sys/actrl/scope-3080193/rule-3080193-s-16386-d-49156-f-27)
Ingress: 0, Egress: 0, Pkts: 0
Rule (4118) DN (sys/actrl/scope-3080193/rule-3080193-s-any-d-any-f-default)
Ingress: 0, Egress: 0, Pkts: 0
Rule (4119) DN (sys/actrl/scope-3080193/rule-3080193-s-16386-d-49156-f-5)
Ingress: 0, Egress: 0, Pkts: 0
Rule (4120) DN (sys/actrl/scope-3080193/rule-3080193-s-49156-d-16386-f-5)
Ingress: 0, Egress: 0, Pkts: 0

```
Rule (4121) DN (sys/actrl/scope-3080193/rule-3080193-s-49156-d-49157-f-5)
Ingress: 0, Egress: 0, Pkts: 0
Rule (4122) DN (sys/actrl/scope-3080193/rule-3080193-s-49157-d-49156-f-5)
Ingress: 0, Egress: 0, Pkts: 0
```

show logging ip access-list internal packet-log deny

Most of the time, when the troubleshooting process starts, it's due to some communication between endpoints either not working at all or suddenly not working. In ACI, this can often be caused by a misconfigured or missing contract. Fortunately, as you saw in the leaf zoning rule table, all implicit deny rules are logged by default. And you can examine them in detail when issuing the show commands in Listing 5-13.

Listing 5-13. Detailed Contract Deny Logs

```
Leaf-101# show logging ip access-list internal packet-log deny
[2022-05-15T16:21:12.168900000+02:00]: CName: Apress:PROD(VXLAN: 3080193),
VlanType: FD_VLAN, Vlan-Id: 30, SMac: 0x005056b386dd, DMac:0x0022bdf819ff,
SIP: 10.1.1.10, DIP: 10.4.4.10, SPort: 47964, DPort: 22, Src Intf:
Ethernet1/20, Proto: 6, PktLen: 74

[2022-05-15T16:21:10.120649000+02:00]: CName: Apress:PROD(VXLAN: 3080193),
VlanType: FD_VLAN, Vlan-Id: 30, SMac: 0x005056b386dd, DMac:0x0022bdf819ff,
SIP: 10.1.1.10, DIP: 10.4.4.10, SPort: 47964, DPort: 22, Src Intf:
Ethernet1/20, Proto: 6, PktLen: 74

[2022-05-15T16:21:09.108067000+02:00]: CName: Apress:PROD(VXLAN: 3080193),
VlanType: FD_VLAN, Vlan-Id: 30, SMac: 0x005056b386dd, DMac:0x0022bdf819ff,
SIP: 10.1.1.10, DIP: 10.4.4.10, SPort: 47964, DPort: 22, Src Intf:
Ethernet1/20, Proto: 6, PktLen: 74
```

In this output you can see the information about denied attempts to establish a SSH connection from 10.1.1.10 (the frontend endpoint in your example) to 10.4.4.10 (the DB endpoint). By filtering the show command using grep based on the source or destination IP address, you can pretty easily and quickly confirm if the packet drops are caused by contracts on this particular leaf switch.

A good practice is to export all of these logs from the entire ACI fabric to some external syslog collector. Before ACI will do so, first you need to edit the fabric syslog

message policy found in **Fabric -> Fabric Policies -> Policies -> Monitoring ->
Common Policy -> Syslog Message Policies -> default** (see Figure 5-46). There the
default Facility Filter has to be set from alerts to *information*.

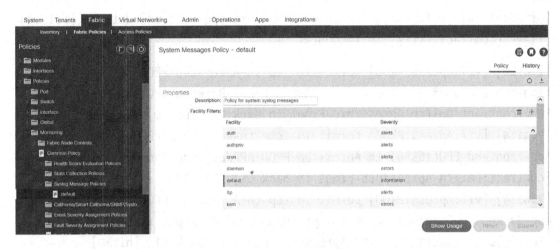

Figure 5-46. *Syslog export about ACI packet denial*

Tip   This kind of logging can be alternatively enabled for permit rules in contracts
as well. Just choose the *Log* directive in the contract subject definition. In the CLI,
then use `show logging ip access-list internal packet-log permit`.

APIC contract_parser.py

Another great utility to help you with contract troubleshooting is a Python script located
natively in each leaf switch called **contract_parser.py**. It takes all the information from
the previous show commands, resolves the actual names of the VRFs and EPGs used in
zoning rules, and presents the consolidated output. See Listing 5-14.

Listing 5-14. Contract Parser Utility

```
Leaf-101# contract_parser.py
Key:
[prio:RuleId] [vrf:{str}] action protocol src-epg [src-l4] dst-epg [dst-l4]
[flags][contract:{str}] [hit=count]

[7:4120] [vrf:Apress:PROD] permit ip tcp tn-Apress/ap-PROD_APP/epg-
Frontend_EPG(16386) tn-Apress/ap-PROD_APP/epg-Backend_EPG(49156) eq
80  [contract:uni/tn-Apress/brc-Front_to_Back_CT] [hit=0]
[7:4114] [vrf:Apress:PROD] permit ip icmp tn-Apress/ap-PROD_APP/
epg-Frontend_EPG(16386) tn-Apress/ap-PROD_APP/epg-Backend_EPG(49156)
[contract:uni/tn-Apress/brc-Front_to_Back_CT] [hit=8]
[7:4119] [vrf:Apress:PROD] permit ip tcp tn-Apress/ap-PROD_APP/
epg-Backend_EPG(49156) eq 80 tn-Apress/ap-PROD_APP/epg-Frontend_
EPG(16386)  [contract:uni/tn-Apress/brc-Front_to_Back_CT] [hit=0]
[7:4117] [vrf:Apress:PROD] permit ip icmp tn-Apress/ap-PROD_APP/
epg-Backend_EPG(49156) tn-Apress/ap-PROD_APP/epg-Frontend_EPG(16386)
[contract:uni/tn-Apress/brc-Front_to_Back_CT] [hit=8]
[7:4121] [vrf:Apress:PROD] permit ip icmp tn-Apress/ap-PROD_APP/
epg-Backend_EPG(49156) tn-Apress/ap-PROD_APP/epg-Database_EPG(49157)
[contract:uni/tn-Apress/brc-Back_to_DB] [hit=0]
[7:4122] [vrf:Apress:PROD] permit ip icmp tn-Apress/ap-PROD_APP/
epg-Database_EPG(49157) tn-Apress/ap-PROD_APP/epg-Backend_EPG(49156)
[contract:uni/tn-Apress/brc-Back_to_DB] [hit=0]
[16:4099] [vrf:management] permit arp epg:any epg:any
[contract:implicit] [hit=0]
[16:4106] [vrf:Apress:PROD] permit any epg:any tn-Apress/bd-Database_
BD(32770) [contract:implicit] [hit=124]
[16:4105] [vrf:Apress:PROD] permit any epg:any tn-Apress/bd-Frontend_
BD(49154) [contract:implicit] [hit=12]
[16:4101] [vrf:Apress:PROD] permit any epg:any tn-Apress/bd-Backend_
BD(49155) [contract:implicit] [hit=47]
[16:4103] [vrf:Apress:PROD] permit arp epg:any epg:any
[contract:implicit] [hit=0]
```

```
[21:4098] [vrf:management] deny,log any epg:any epg:any
[contract:implicit] [hit=0]
[21:4102] [vrf:Apress:PROD] deny,log any epg:any epg:any
[contract:implicit] [hit=202]
[22:4100] [vrf:management] deny,log any epg:any pfx-0.0.0.0/0(15)
[contract:implicit] [hit=0]
[22:4104] [vrf:Apress:PROD] deny,log any epg:any pfx-0.0.0.0/0(15)
[contract:implicit] [hit=0]
```

Contract Policy TCAM Utilization

An important aspect of ACI operation, especially when a higher number of contracts is being deployed to the fabric, is monitoring the HW policy TCAM utilization. There are two ways available: the GUI and the CLI.

In the APIC GUI, when you navigate to **Operations -> Capacity Dashboard -> Leaf Capacity**, you can check the current utilization of leaf HW resources including but not limited to Policy CAM (shown in Figure 5-47). If needed, the TCAM memory can be reallocated per leaf switch to provide more security policy space using forwarding profiles, configurable on the same page.

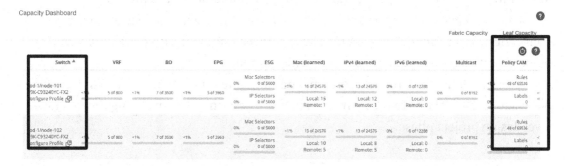

Figure 5-47. *ACI capacity dashboard*

Caution   Any potential change in a leaf forwarding profile always require its reboot.

Using the CLI, you can receive the same information when issuing the show command in Listing 5-15.

Listing 5-15. Leaf Policy TCAM Utilization

```
Leaf-101# vsh_lc -c "show platform internal hal health-stats"
|Sandbox_ID: 0  Asic Bitmap: 0x0
|------------------------------------

--output omitted--
Policy stats:
=============
policy_count                 : 48
max_policy_count             : 65536
policy_otcam_count           : 84
max_policy_otcam_count           : 8192
policy_label_count               : 0
max_policy_label_count           : 0

--output omitted--
```

Naming Convention for ACI Application Policies

Similar to the previous chapter, before starting the implementation process of application policies, it's important to create a good object structure with a naming convention. You cannot change names later without removing and recreating the objects, and this usually causes a network disruption.

Before we finish the chapter, I offer my naming rules and examples, which I use for our customers. Feel free to reuse them as they are or as inspiration during the ACI low-level design project phase.

Table 5-1. *ACI Application Policies Naming Convention*

Access Policies Object	Name Structure	Examples
Tenant	<Tenant_name>	Apress
VRF	<VRF_name>	Apress, PROD, TEST
Bridge domain	Legacy: VL<vlan_id>_BD Application-centric: <Purpose>_BD	VL0900_BD App_BD, DMZ_BD, Web_BD
Bridge domain for firewall PBR	<FW_name>FW_BD	XXXFW_BD
Application profiles	<VRF_name>_APP <Application_name>_APP	PROD_APP TestApp_APP
EPG	Legacy: VL<vlan_id>_EPG Application Centric: <Purpose>_EPG	VL0900_EPG Frontend_EPG, DMZ_EPG, Application_EPG
Contract	<Purpose>_CT Traffic flow direction in name: <Consumer_EPG>_to_<Provider _EPG>_CT	Legacy_Permit_ANY_CT Frontend_to_Backend_CT
Contract with L3OUT on provider side	<App EPG >_to_<L3OUTname> _<External EPG>_CT	Web_to_MPLS_ Default_ExtEPG_CT
Contract with L3OUT on customer side	<L3OUT_Name>_<External EPG>_ to_<App EPG>_CT	MPLS_Default_ ExtEPG_to_Web_CT
Subject	<Purpose>_(PBR)_Subj	ANY_Subj, Web_PBR_Subj
Filter	<Allow|Deny>_<Protocol>_<Port range|Custom ports>	Allow_HTTP_8080 Deny_HTTP Allow_TCP_2459-3000

(continued)

Table 5-1. (*continued*)

Access Policies Object	Name Structure	Examples
L3OUT main object	<External_Device>_L3OUT <VRF>_<Device>_L3OUT	MPLS_PE25_L3OUT PROD_MPLS_PE25_L3OUT
L3OUT external routed network (default)	<Purpose>_ExtEPG	Default_ExtEPG
L4-L7 service graph	<Device>_SG	FW_Internal_SG FW_DMZ_SG
L4-L7 service SLA monitor	<Device>_MON	FW_Internal_MON FW_DMZ_MON
L4-L7 service health group	<Device>_HG	FW_Internal_HG FW_DMZ_HG
Tenant monitoring policy	<Tenant_Name>_Monitoring	Apress_Monitoring

Summary

The application policy model is one of the main ACI components, enabling the network administrator to match the application connectivity requirements with the actual network configuration. Its goal is to provide flexible and universal building blocks to enable network multitenancy, describe application segmentation, or enforce connectivity rules between the ACI endpoints connected behind leaf switches.

During this chapter you learned how to create and manage fundamental application policy objects including tenants, application profiles, endpoint (security) groups, and contracts. Additionally, you explored how to provide Layer 2 connectivity with bridge domains inside a L3 space represented by VRFs for all internal ACI endpoints with correct mapping to their EPGs. This knowledge will become your basis for further expansion to the areas of ACI internal forwarding as well as external connectivity or L4-L7 service insertion.

The next chapter will focus on more details of ACI internal forwarding between the endpoints and the logic behind the scenes. Understanding this is key for effective and successful connectivity troubleshooting.

CHAPTER 6

Fabric Forwarding (and Troubleshooting)

It doesn't matter if you are dealing with a traditional network or software defined ACI. One of the important aspects of network operation is understanding how the control plane mechanisms work and how forwarding decisions are made. Especially when it comes to issues with mutual endpoint connectivity, for an effective and fast troubleshooting process, you should have your toolset ready.

My goal for this chapter is to develop such expertise and confidence in you. I will start by revisiting the data plane operations with an emphasis on VXLAN encapsulation used during the ACI fabric transport, supplemented with a detailed look at the control plane as well. These topics will be followed by a description of multiple intra-fabric forwarding scenarios, expanded by specific differences when forwarding in ACI Multi-Pod and Multi-Site architectures. To complete the picture, at the end, I will cover multiple forwarding troubleshooting tools.

ACI Data Plane - iVXLAN Encapsulation

When you return to the beginning, during ACI initialization you always have to specify the internal TEP pool, the IP space from which APICs allocate VTEP IP addresses for each leaf and spine switch. VTEP IPs are then configured on loopback interfaces and used when forwarding traffic internally between switches.

For a modern datacenter network, there is a requirement to support all kinds of traffic types and both Layer 2 and Layer 3 services on top of the common infrastructure. In any case, the transport should be additionally transparent to the communicating end hosts. To do so, you need to utilize a tunneling mechanism, a standardized *VXLAN encapsulation* (RFC 7348). This MAC-in-UDP transport system solves not only the

© Jan Janovic 2023

J. Janovic, *Cisco ACI: Zero to Hero*, https://doi.org/10.1007/978-1-4842-8838-2_6

transparent Layer-2 frame shipment across the ACI fabric, but also the scalability of available logical segments. While traditional VLAN encapsulation allows you to address only 4,096 segments due to the 12-bit VLAN ID header field, VXLAN offers up to 16M segments thanks to a 24-bit addressing space.

As shown in Figure 6-1, when forwarding any traffic between two endpoints, ACI generally performs so-called *encapsulation normalization*.

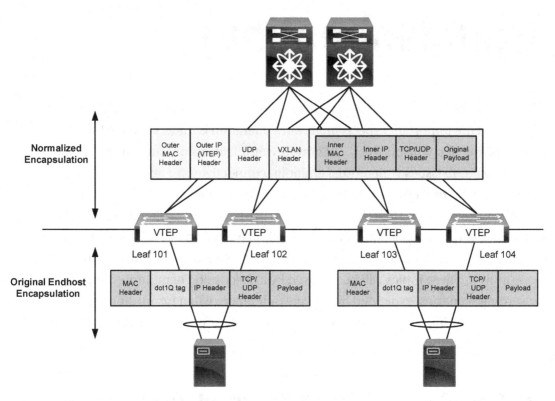

Figure 6-1. *ACI encapsulation normalization*

Regardless of the type or ingress encapsulation ID (dot1Q VLAN ID, VXLAN VNID), when the ACI leaf has to forward the incoming frame to another leaf, it removes the original encapsulation and replaces it with common internal iVXLAN header. Consequently, the entire traffic is forwarded across the fabric in a normalized way, consistently using internal VXLAN VNID segments. When the original frame arrives to an egress leaf, it will strip down the internal iVXLAN header and add the correct egress encapsulation and deliver the frame to the connected end host. Thanks to this concept, the original encapsulation and its ID is just a locally significant value describing how the connected endpoints communicate with their closest leaf switch. Normalization to common VXLAN segments inside the fabric allows ACI to interconnect any endpoints, even those not using same VLAN IDs or not using the same encapsulation type at all. This provides significant flexibility not otherwise available in a traditional network.

Figure 6-2 illustrates the internal iVXLAN header in detail with all field sizes listed.

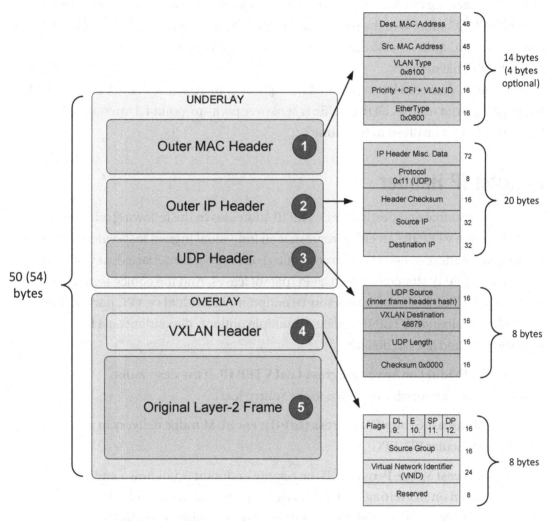

Figure 6-2. *ACI iVXLAN header*

Although the iVXLAN header originates from the RFC standard, ACI expands its capabilities by using many otherwise reserved fields for the forwarding purposes. In next sections, I will go through them and describe their significance.

1) Outer MAC Header

Let's consider the fully encapsulated original frame being forwarded through ACI fabric, as shown in Figure 6-2. The set of its three first outer headers serve for underlay forwarding, starting as usual with Layer-2 MAC headers. Into a source header field ACI inserts the MAC address of the source interface used for forwarding and the destination carries the MAC address of the next-hop IP. These fields are rewritten on a per-hop basis, as in a traditional network.

In general, there can be an optional dot1q header included with the VLAN ID field, but in ACI it's not used as all the traffic is sent over point-to-point L3 interfaces. No VLAN trunking is involved in the fabric.

2) Outer IP Header

ACI specifies source and destination VTEP IP addresses in the following outer IP header.

The source VTEP IP can either represent an individual ingress leaf switch (it acts as its physical IP address, even though configured on loopback interfaces), or you can use an anycast VTEP IP shared between a vPC pair of leaves. And the choice is made based on the type of interface used by the source endpoint: individual vs. vPC port channel.

With a destination VTEP IP you have multiple options, depending on a forwarding scenario (covered later in detail):

- **Individual or Anycast Egress Leaf VTEP IP**: If the destination remote endpoint is known to the source leaf

- **Multicast Group IP Address (GiPO)**: For BUM traffic delivery in a particular BD/EPG

- **Anycast Spine-Proxy IP**: If the remote endpoint is unknown and based on BD settings, the ingress leaf can decide to forward this VXLAN encapsulated frame to spines for an endpoint resolution. The spines then differentiate between three anycast VTEP IPs, each for a different type of traffic: bridged (MAC) or two-routed (IPv4 and IPv6).

3) UDP Header

After the outer IP header is the L4 UDP header, which is still used for the underlay routing process. Maybe you are wondering why you even need it. The reason is pretty simple and clever: *loadbalancing*.

Since the ACI physical fabric is designed as a leaf-spine topology and between any two leaves there are multiple exactly the same L3 paths (with the same cost), you can easily utilize Equal-Cost Multi-Path routing (ECMP). But how, if you are constantly routing between the same VTEP addresses in underlay? That's when UDP comes into play.

The destination UDP port is statically set to a decimal value of 48879 (by the way, try converting it to hexadecimal ☺) and the source UDP port is always a hash of all original, inner L2-L4 headers. For each communicating pair of end hosts you will therefore calculate a unique source port number, and the fabric can natively forward their packets over different links in the underlay (also called source port entropy).

4) VXLAN Header

You're finally getting to the important VXLAN header itself. Using the Virtual Network Identifier (VNID) field you can differentiate between various traffic segments on top of the common underlay network. If the inner traffic is simply bridged through the ACI fabric, the leaf switches will use the bridge domain segment ID as the VNID. Similarly, if the traffic is routed between different BDs, the VRF Segment ID (Scope ID) is used as the VNID. Concrete values for the BD or VRF VNIDs can be found in the GUI, after looking at **Tenants -> Tenant_Name -> Operational -> Resource IDs.**

This alone won't offer everything needed for ACI operation, therefore ACI expands original VXLAN RFC 7348 by utilizing multiple reserved fields along with the main VNID, especially the Flags and Source Group field. By setting the *Don't Learn (DL)* bit to 1, the ingress leaf can force all others not to learn the remote endpoint. This feature was primarily used in earlier ACI versions with first gen N9K switches. The *Exception (E)* bit is set to some flows to avoid looping their packets back to the fabric after being processed. A typical example is a flow already proxied through spine switches. The *Source/Destination Policy (SP/DP) Flags* inform a remote leaf switch if a contract was already applied for this traffic at the ingress node or if the egress leaf is expected to apply it instead. In such a case, the egress node has to have guaranteed information to which EPG (sClass) the source traffic belongs. And that's what the *Source Group* field is used for. The ingress leaf will always put there the sClass (pcTag) identifier of the associated source EPG.

5) Original Layer-2 Frame

All previously described encapsulation headers are internally added on top of the original frame at the ingress leaf switch. Except for the dot1Q tag or the host-based VXLAN encapsulation, which are removed and replaced by iVXLAN, no other original header manipulation is done here. The goal is to ensure transport transparency for all end hosts. For them, ACI is either one big, distributed switch or one routed next-hop on a path to the destination.

Fabric Control Plane Mechanisms Reviewed

Although you have transport mechanism already in place, providing universal forwarding for traffic between any two switch nodes in the fabric, you still need additional control plane protocols to distribute information where the required endpoints are and how to get to them. Figure 6-3 summarizes the control plane operations and components.

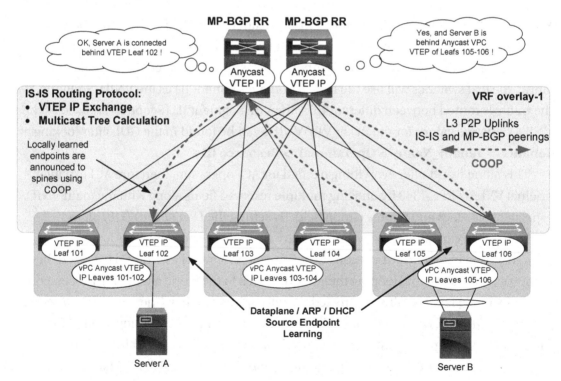

Figure 6-3. *ACI control plane overview*

For all its fabric ACI uses the *point-to-point interfaces IP Unnumbered* feature to conserve IP space and simultaneously provide routing capabilities; this completely eliminates any reliance on the Spanning Tree protocol. Instead of individual IP addresses, all uplinks borrow a single IP from Loopback 0 (VTEP IP). Uplinks are always configured with a subinterface, but internally no VLAN encapsulation is used. See Listing 6-1.

Listing 6-1. Point-to-Point L3 Unnumbered Uplink Interfaces

```
Leaf-101# show int status
--------------------------------------------------------------------------

Port        Name    Status      Vlan      Duplex    Speed    Type
--------------------------------------------------------------------------

Eth1/53     --      connected   routed    full      40G      QSFP-40G-SR-BD
Eth1/53.9   --      connected   routed    full      40G      QSFP-40G-SR-BD
Eth1/54     --      connected   routed    full      40G      QSFP-40G-SR-BD
Eth1/54.7   --      connected   routed    full      40G      QSFP-40G-SR-BD
```

```
Leaf-101# show int Eth1/53.9
Ethernet1/53.9 is up
admin state is up, Dedicated Interface, [parent interface is Ethernet1/53
  Hardware: 1000/10000/100000/40000 Ethernet, address: 0000.0000.0000 (bia
c4f7.d5e3.e5fd)
  MTU 9366 bytes, BW 40000000 Kbit, DLY 1 usec
  reliability 255/255, txload 1/255, rxload 1/255
  Encapsulation ARPA, medium is broadcast <<<- ARPA, not 802.1Q Virtual LAN
```

```
Leaf-101# show ip int Eth1/53.9
IP Interface Status for VRF "overlay-1"
  IP unnumbered interface (lo0)
```

After fabric initialization, leaves and spines establish IS-IS L1 adjacencies between each other over fabric interfaces in transport VRF overlay-1. This routing protocol is primarily used to ensure a distribution of VTEP addresses around the fabric and create multicast distribution trees (which I will describe later in this chapter). See Listing 6-2.

Listing 6-2. IS-IS Routing Protocol Verification

```
Leaf-101# show isis adjacency vrf overlay-1
IS-IS process: isis_infra VRF:overlay-1
IS-IS adjacency database:
System ID        SNPA           Level  State  Hold Time  Interface
4042.ED0A.0000   N/A            1      UP     00:00:51   Ethernet1/54.7
4342.ED0A.0000   N/A            1      UP     00:00:53   Ethernet1/53.9
Leaf-101# show isis dteps vrf overlay-1

IS-IS Dynamic Tunnel End Point (DTEP) database:
DTEP-Address       Role    Encapsulation   Type
10.11.66.70        LEAF    N/A             PHYSICAL
10.11.66.67        SPINE   N/A             PHYSICAL
10.11.66.64        SPINE   N/A             PHYSICAL
10.11.76.194       SPINE   N/A             PHYSICAL,PROXY-ACAST-V4
10.11.76.192       SPINE   N/A             PHYSICAL,PROXY-ACAST-MAC
10.11.76.193       SPINE   N/A             PHYSICAL,PROXY-ACAST-V6
10.11.76.197       LEAF    N/A             PHYSICAL

Leaf-101# show ip route vrf overlay-1
IP Route Table for VRF "overlay-1"
'*' denotes best ucast next-hop
'**' denotes best mcast next-hop
'[x/y]' denotes [preference/metric]
'%<string>' in via output denotes VRF <string>

10.11.66.70/32, ubest/mbest: 2/0
    *via 10.11.66.67, eth1/53.9, [115/3], 1y3w, isis-isis_infra,
isis-l1-int
    *via 10.11.66.64, eth1/54.7, [115/3], 1y3w, isis-isis_infra,
isis-l1-int
10.11.76.197/32, ubest/mbest: 2/0
    *via 10.11.66.64, eth1/54.7, [115/3], 1y2w, isis-isis_infra,
isis-l1-int
    *via 10.11.66.67, eth1/53.9, [115/3], 1y2w, isis-isis_infra,
isis-l1-int
```

Thanks to routing information about remote VTEP addresses, you know *how* to get VXLAN encapsulated traffic to the distant leaf switches or spine proxy, but you still need the information on *who* is behind them. Traditional MAC tables on legacy switches are replaced with an *endpoints database* in ACI. Each leaf switch in the default state learns about locally connected endpoints by observing their source packets, generated ARPs requests, or DHCP messages. MAC addresses (in case of L2 BD) and MAC+IP couples (L3 BD) are put into the local endpoint database, together with additional metadata like encapsulation ID, source interface, or EPG/BD/VRF affiliation (sClass). In the endpoint database, besides local entries, you can find remote MAC or IPs, which are easily identifiable by the tunnel interface instead of local EthX/X. This approach, called *conversational learning,* is in place to optimize a leaf's HW resources by learning only those remote endpoints that are actively communicating with the local ones. The source of information about the remote endpoint can be a standard bridged or routed packet incoming from the fabric, encapsulated to iVXLAN or a flooded ARP (GARP) packet, if ARP flooding is enabled on a BD level.

ACI avoids stale endpoints by attaching *aging timers* to both local and remote entries. They are configurable in **Endpoint Retention Policy** located in **Tenants -> Tenant_ name -> Policies -> Protocol -> Endpoint Retention** and applied per bridge domain in its general policy configuration. Timers are refreshed as soon as a leaf sees any traffic from a particular endpoint. The default value for local endpoints is 900 seconds, while for a remote it's 300 seconds. After the timer expires, the related entry is removed from the endpoint database. If the endpoint is learned in a L3-enabled BD with default GW in ACI, the leaves additionally perform *host tracking.* This feature proactively aims to refresh the endpoint information after crossing 75% of its aging timer without any packet seen during the interval. In case of need, the leaf sends three artificially generated ARP requests destined to the end host IP from its bridge domain SVI interface. If the host is still present, the aging is reset by replying to the ARP requests. See Listing 6-3.

Listing 6-3. ACI Endpoint Database

```
Leaf-101# show endpoint
Legend:
 S - static       s - arp       L - local       O - peer-attached
 V - vpc-attached a - local-aged p - peer-aged   M - span
 B - bounce       H - vtep      R - peer-attached-rl D - bounce-to-proxy
 E - shared-service m - svc-mgr
```

```
+------------+------------+-----------------+-------------+------------+
      VLAN/     Encap         MAC Address        MAC Info/     Interface
      Domain    VLAN          IP Address         IP Info
+------------+------------+-----------------+-------------+------------+
29                vlan-10    0050.56b3.d400 L                    eth1/20
Apress:PROD       vlan-10            10.3.3.10 L  <<-local entry->>  eth1/20
20                vlan-11    0050.56b3.2f07 O                    tunnel3
Apress:PROD       vlan-11            10.4.4.20 O                    tunnel3
Apress:PROD                          10.4.4.10    <<-remote entry->> tunnel19
30                vlan-9     0050.56b3.86dd L                    eth1/20
Apress:PROD       vlan-9             10.1.1.10 L                    eth1/20
```

Leaf-101# **show system internal epm endpoint ip 10.3.3.10**

MAC : 0050.56b3.d400 ::: Num IPs : 1
IP# 0 : 10.3.3.10 ::: IP# 0 flags :   ::: l3-sw-hit: No
Vlan id : 29 ::: Vlan vnid : 8392 ::: VRF name : Apress:PROD
BD vnid : 16318374 ::: **VRF vnid : 3080193**
Phy If : 0x1a013000 ::: Tunnel If : 0
Interface : Ethernet1/20
Flags : 0x80005c04 ::: **sclass : 49156** ::: Ref count : 5
EP Create Timestamp : 05/06/2022 15:42:15.380695
EP Update Timestamp : 05/24/2022 11:46:31.021739
EP Flags : local|IP|MAC|host-tracked|sclass|timer|

Even though leaves are not aware of all endpoints in the ACI fabric, they have to be able to send traffic to unknown ones as well. In such a case and based on the bridge domain setting (described later), they can either flood the iVXLAN encapsulated traffic through the fabric using multicast to all leaves with that the bridge domain configured or send the packet to the spine acting as an *endpoint resolution proxy*. The spine, if possible, resolves the destination endpoint in its distributed database and the iVXLAN packet is forwarded to the egress leaf. The spine endpoint database is filled exclusively using the control plane and that's when the *Council of Oracles Protocol (COOP)* comes into play.

From a COOP terminology point of view, leaves are "citizens" periodically updating the spine "oracle" endpoint repository. Each locally learned endpoint on a leaf is immediately announced using COOP adjacency to the spine as well as any change to it. The spines are therefore expected to have absolute visibility into all known endpoints to a single fabric. When checking the COOP database for a single given endpoint, you have to specify a *key*, a bridge domain VNID (segment ID) for a MAC address endpoint or VRF VNID (segment ID) in case of IP+MAC endpoints. See Listing 6-4.

Listing 6-4. COOP Protocol and Spine Proxy Endpoint Repository

```
Leaf-101# show coop internal info global
System info:
Local Adjacency (Citizen)    <<- Local Leaf Switch
Addr          : 10.11.66.65
Identity      : 0.0.0.0
Name          : overlay-1
-- output ommited --

Oracle Adjacency             <<- Spine Switch
Addr          : 10.11.66.67
Identity      : 0.0.0.0
Name          : Spine-198
HelloIntvl    : 60
-- output ommited -

Spine-198# show coop internal info repo ep key 16318374 00:50:56:B3:D4:00

Spine-198# show coop internal info ip-db key 3080193 10.3.3.10

IP address : 10.3.3.10
Vrf : 3080193
Flags : 0
EP bd vnid : 16318374
EP mac :  00:50:56:B3:D4:00
Publisher Id : 10.11.24.64
Record timestamp : 05 24 2022 15:38:17 482300
Publish timestamp : 05 24 2022 15:38:17 1155657
Seq No: 0
Remote publish timestamp: 01 01 1970 00:00:00 0
URIB Tunnel Info
Num tunnels : 1
        Tunnel address : 10.11.24.64
        Tunnel ref count : 1
```

IS-IS and COOP protocols ensure intra-fabric forwarding information, but you can't forget about external connectivity when discussing control plane operations. All external prefixes or endpoint information between distinct ACI fabrics are distributed around using *Multi-Protocol BGP (MP-BGP)* with spines acting as a route reflectors for all leaf switches. When ACI learns about a prefix via L3OUT, it is redistributed within its VRF on a border leaf switch to the BGP in the address family VPNv4 or VPNv6. For internal BD prefixes being propagated to external routers via L3OUTs, it works vice versa. In Multi-Pod and Multi-Site architectures, spines, besides external prefixes, also exchange endpoint information in the L2VPN EVPN address family. More details about inter-fabric connectivity awaits you later in this chapter, and the next one will be completely dedicated to external connectivity, including L3OUTs. See Listing 6-5.

Listing 6-5. MP-BGP Protocol

```
Spine-198# show bgp vpnv4 unicast summary vrf overlay-1
BGP summary information for VRF overlay-1, address family VPNv4 Unicast
BGP router identifier 192.168.1.130, local AS number 65534
BGP table version is 1306, VPNv4 Unicast config peers 4, capable peers 3
0 network entries and 0 paths using 0 bytes of memory
BGP attribute entries [0/0], BGP AS path entries [0/0]
BGP community entries [0/0], BGP clusterlist entries [0/0]

Neighbor     V    AS MsgRcvd MsgSent    TblVer  InQ OutQ Up/
Down  State/PfxRcd
10.11.66.70 4 65534   37946   37877      1306    0    0  3w5d       48
10.11.66.71 4 65534   37987   37872      1306    0    0  3w5d       48
```

ACI Forwarding Scenarios

After reviewing control plane and data plane operations, let's strengthen this knowledge by multiple subsequent practical scenarios. I will cover step by step and in detail Layer 2 bridging through the ACI fabric, as well as Layer 3 routing, both with particular attention to ARP handling, which is an essential component for endpoint connectivity in IPv4.

Before you begin, have a look at the general high-level forwarding process when sending traffic between two ACI endpoints (as shown in Figure 6-4).

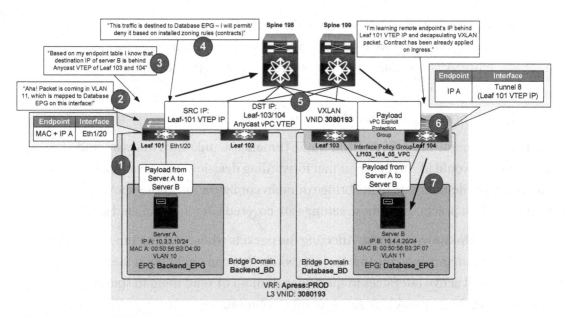

Figure 6-4. *ACI forwarding overview*

1. When the source endpoint generates any traffic, the closest leaf switch will learn and save its MAC address or MAC+IP information to a local endpoint table.

2. The leaf switch will interpret an encapsulation used by the source station on its interface and eventually consider other specified criteria and classify the endpoint into its EPG/uEPG/ESG. This information is saved in the endpoint table as well.

3. Based on destination MAC or IP of the original packet, the source leaf tries to identify where the target endpoint resides. It can be a local interface, remote leaf, or unknown location.

4. If the destination endpoint is known (thus the destination EPG as well), the ingress leaf will apply zoning rules and permit or drop the packet. With an unknown destination endpoint, zoning rules are applied on the egress switch node (in case the fabric is able to deliver the packet there).

5. If locally permitted, the packet is then sent out to a local interface or encapsulated in iVXLAN and sent towards the remote leaf via spines. It will use routing information thanks to IS-IS in VRF overlay-1.

6. The egress leaf will decapsulate the iVXLAN packet and save the source endpoint location behind the source leaf as a remote entry to its endpoint table. If not already, it will apply contract zoning rules.

7. The original packet is delivered to the destination host.

In case of multi-destination BUM traffic (broadcast, unknown unicasts, and multicasts), I would like to pinpoint that forwarding decisions can be altered by modifying the default state of the bridge domain configuration knobs shown in Figure 6-5. Best practices for these settings are covered later in the related sections.

- **L2 Unknown Unicast**: Affecting the packets whose destination is not unknown to the ingress leaf switch. You can either flood them to all active interfaces in the bridge domain or send them to spines (hardware proxy) for an endpoint resolution.

- **L3 Unknown Multicast Flooding**: By default, multicast traffic is flooded within a bridge domain and forwarded to all leaves' front interfaces, as long as there is at least one "router" port on that leaf. Router ports are those with either PIM adjacency or an IGMP Report seen from a multicast receiver. The *Optimized Flooding* setting then forwards traffic exclusively to router ports.

- **IPv6 L3 Unknown Multicast**: The same as in the previous point, just for IPv6 multicast with the use of PIMv6 and MLD protocols

- **Multi Destination Flooding**: This setting covers all other types of multi-destination traffic like broadcasts, L2 multicasts, or Link Layer protocols.

- **ARP Flooding**: ARP has its own dedicated checkbox here, allowing you to optimize the delivery in L3-enabled bridge domains. Instead of flooding, you can start delivering ARP directly to the destination endpoint, based on endpoint table information.

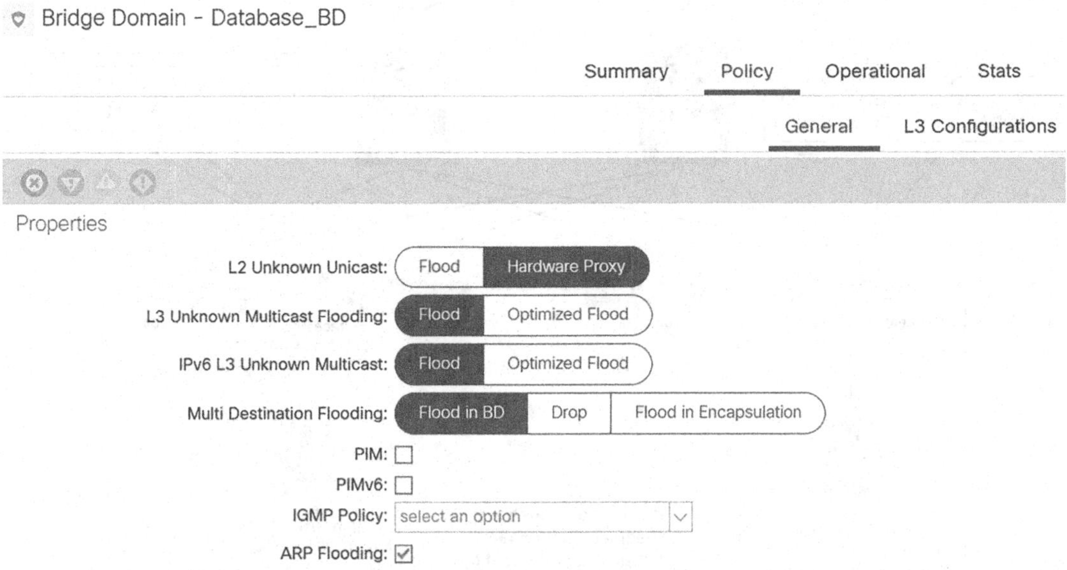

♥ Bridge Domain - Database_BD

Summary   Policy   Operational   Stats

General   L3 Configurations

⊗ ⊗ △ ⓘ

Properties

L2 Unknown Unicast:	Flood · **Hardware Proxy**
L3 Unknown Multicast Flooding:	**Flood** · Optimized Flood
IPv6 L3 Unknown Multicast:	**Flood** · Optimized Flood
Multi Destination Flooding:	**Flood in BD** · Drop · Flood in Encapsulation
PIM:	☐
PIMv6:	☐
IGMP Policy:	select an option ▼
ARP Flooding:	☑

Figure 6-5. Bridge domain BUM forwarding settings

Layer 2 Forwarding

Let's start by a closer look at simple traffic bridging between two ACI endpoints inside one bridge domain (as shown in Figure 6-6). The Bridge domain has unicast routing disabled, so there is no default gateway configured in ACI. Server A is connected behind an individual interface using Access Policy Group, whereas Server B utilizes a VPC port-channel and vPC Interface Policy Group.

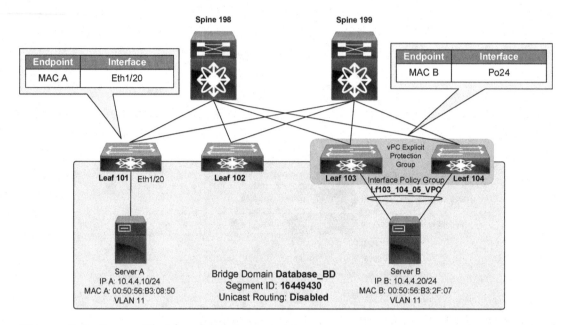

Figure 6-6. *Layer 2 bridge domain scenario*

In the Layer 2 bridge domain, ACI is not learning IP addresses at all. From this perspective, it acts similarly to a traditional switch, just looking at the source MAC addresses from the data plane.

Multi-Destination (ARP) Forwarding in a Layer 2 Bridge Domain

Before the source endpoint generates any traffic, it has to resolve either the MAC address of a destination host in its own subnet or the default gateway's MAC address when routing is needed. ARP packet forwarding is therefore a crucial component of any network communication. But what happens when broadcast packets like an ARP request enter the leaf switch?

In a Layer 2 bridge domain, *ARP is always flooded* within the BD boundaries, regardless of ARP Flooding setting in bridge domain configuration. Additionally, ARPs are implicitly permitted in contract zoning rules.

To be flooded for ACI means that the ingress leaf utilizes one of 13 multicast trees built automatically by IS-IS in the fabric to deliver the multi-destination data. All trees have their roots evenly spread across available spine switches and are identified by a Forwarding Tag ID (FTag). The decision of which to use is based on a hash of the internal packet headers at the ingress leaf switch. Next, in order to deliver the flooded packet to the correct recipients, instead of a unicast outer destination VTEP address, ACI uses a Group IP outer (GiPO) address, dynamically assigned to each bridge domain after creation. Figure 6-7 illustrates this operation.

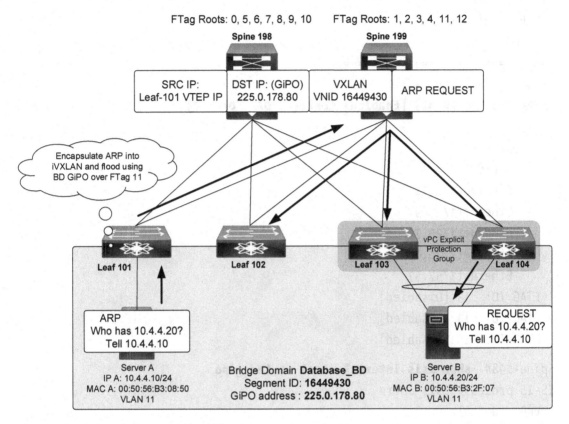

Figure 6-7. *Broadcast ARP delivery*

Note   In fact, ACI supports 16 FTags, but IDs 13, 14, 15 are not used and are implicitly disabled.

The placement of FTag roots can be verified using the spine CLI, together with the configuration for individual GiPO addresses. See Listing 6-6.

Listing 6-6. FTag and GiPO Forwarding Verification

```
Spine-198# show isis internal mcast routes ftag
IS-IS process: isis_infra
  VRF : default
FTAG Routes
=====================================
-- output omitted --
 FTAG ID:  11 [Root] [Enabled] Cost:(   0/   0/   0)
 ----------------------------------
    Root port: -
    OIF List:
      Ethernet1/1.71
      Ethernet1/2.69
      Ethernet1/25.70
      Ethernet1/26.67
      Ethernet1/57.57
  FTAG ID:  13 [Disabled]
  FTAG ID:  14 [Disabled]
  FTAG ID:  15 [Disabled]

Spine-198# show isis internal mcast routes gipo
IS-IS process: isis_infra
  VRF : default

GIPo Routes
=====================================
  System GIPo - Configured: 0.0.0.0
               Operational: 239.255.255.240
=====================================
-- output omitted --
GIPo: 225.0.178.80 [TRANSIT]
    OIF List:
      Ethernet1/1.71
      Ethernet1/2.69
      Ethernet1/25.70
      Ethernet1/26.67
      Ethernet1/57.57(External)
```

Multicast data will be forwarded to all interfaces listed in Output Interface List (OIF). There you should find local downlinks to leaf switches as well as an external interface leading to an IPN if Multi-Pod architecture is deployed.

Known Layer 2 Unicast

After the initial ARP request/reply exchange, the endpoint tables on both ingress and egress leaf switches are populated with endpoint information and further unicast communication is handled according to them. The traffic forwarding overview is shown in Figure 6-8.

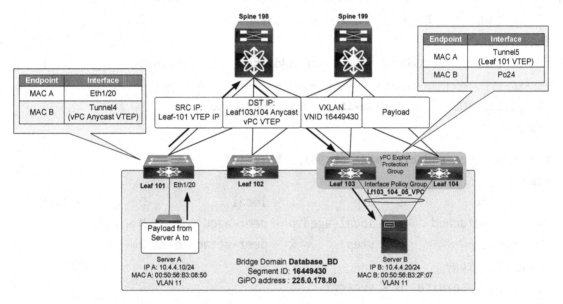

Figure 6-8. *Known L2 unicast delivery*

In this situation, when you view the endpoint table on Leaf 101, you should see information about both endpoints: MAC A with an associated local interface and MAC B behind the TunnelX interface. For the local endpoint, you can see associated on-wire encap VLAN 11, matching the static interface to EPG mapping. Notice there is another VLAN 20 shown for this entry at the beginning of the row. That's the locally significant internal VLAN. The leaf switch always operates with internal VLANs instead of the encap ones due to fact that you can have the same encap VLAN mapped to multiple interfaces and always in a different EPG. Internally, the leaf needs to differentiate between them, and this is how it is done. See Listing 6-7.

Listing 6-7. Ingress Leaf Endpoint Table Verification

```
Leaf-101# show endpoint mac  00:50:56:B3:08:50
Legend:
 S - static          s - arp       L - local           O - peer-attached
 V - vpc-attached    a - local-aged p - peer-aged       M - span
 B - bounce          H - vtep       R - peer-attached-rl D -
bounce-to-proxy
 E - shared-service  m - svc-mgr
+--------------+---------------+-----------------+--------------+-------------+
        VLAN/       Encap             MAC Address       MAC Info/
Interface
        Domain      VLAN              IP Address        IP Info
+--------------+---------------+-----------------+--------------+-------------+
20/Apress:PROD          vlan-11     0050.56b3.0850   L
eth1/20

Leaf-101# show endpoint mac  00:50:56:B3:2F:07
Legend:
 S - static          s - arp       L - local           O - peer-attached
 V - vpc-attached    a - local-aged p - peer-aged       M - span
 B - bounce          H - vtep       R - peer-attached-rl D -
bounce-to-proxy
 E - shared-service  m - svc-mgr
+--------------+---------------+-----------------+--------------+-------------+
        VLAN/       Encap             MAC Address       MAC Info/
Interface
        Domain      VLAN              IP Address        IP Info
+--------------+---------------+-----------------+--------------+-------------+
21/Apress:PROD  vxlan-16449430    0050.56b3.2f07
tunnel4
```

The remote endpoint behind the tunnel interface uses VXLAN encapsulation with a VNID corresponding to the BD Segment ID. The tunnel itself represents a logical non-stateful VXLAN connection between two leaves, specifically their VTEP addresses. They are created automatically on demand as soon as the leaf receives the iVXLAN packet from a new VTEP IP address and closes with the expiration of the last endpoint mapped to them. The tunnel's destination IP address should be routed in the VRF overlay-1 towards all spines, utilizing ECMP loadlbalancing. See Listing 6-8.

Listing 6-8. VXLAN Tunnel Interfaces and Underlay Routing

```
Leaf-101# show interface tunnel4
Tunnel11 is up
    MTU 9000 bytes, BW 0 Kbit
    Transport protocol is in VRF "overlay-1"
    Tunnel protocol/transport is ivxlan
    Tunnel source 10.11.66.65/32 (lo0)  <<-- local VTEP IP
    Tunnel destination 10.11.66.70 <<-- remote VTEP IP
    Last clearing of "show interface" counters never
    Tx
    0 packets output, 1 minute output rate 0 packets/sec
    Rx
    0 packets input, 1 minute input rate 0 packets/sec

Leaf-101# show ip route 10.11.66.70 vrf overlay-1
IP Route Table for VRF "overlay-1"
'*' denotes best ucast next-hop
'**' denotes best mcast next-hop
'[x/y]' denotes [preference/metric]
'%<string>' in via output denotes VRF <string>

10.11.66.70/32, ubest/mbest: 2/0
    *via 10.11.66.67, eth1/53.9, [115/3], 1y4w, isis-isis_infra, isis-l1-int
    *via 10.11.66.64, eth1/54.7, [115/3], 1y4w, isis-isis_infra, isis-l1-int
```

If you are wondering who the owner of tunnel destination IP is, you can easily find its Node ID using the query command in the APIC CLI (Listing 6-9). Two entries mean it's a anycast VTEP IP configured on both vPC leaves.

Listing 6-9. VTEP IP Address Query

```
apic1# moquery -c ipv4Addr -f 'ipv4.Addr.addr=="10.11.66.70"' | grep dn
dn: topology/pod-1/node-103/sys/ipv4/inst/dom-overlay-1/if-[lo2]/addr-
[10.11.66.70/32]
dn: topology/pod-1/node-104/sys/ipv4/inst/dom-overlay-1/if-[lo2]/addr-
[10.11.66.70/32]
```

On destination egress leaves 103-104, the situation is similar, just with reversed information: MAC B is a local one and the MAC A learnt is remote. Notice that internal VLANs are totally different and not related to the ingress leaf. The only common denominator is the logical segment, the bridge domain VNID you are forwarding the Layer 2 traffic in. See Listing 6-10.

Listing 6-10. Egress Leaf Endpoint Table Verification

```
Leaf-103# show endpoint mac  00:50:56:B3:2F:07
Legend:
 S - static          s - arp        L - local        O - peer-attached
 V - vpc-attached    a - local-aged p - peer-aged     M - span
 B - bounce          H - vtep       R - peer-attached-rl D -
bounce-to-proxy
 E - shared-service  m - svc-mgr
+--------------+--------------+----------------+--------------+-------------+
       VLAN/       Encap          MAC Address      MAC Info/
Interface
       Domain      VLAN           IP Address       IP Info
+--------------+--------------+----------------+--------------+-------------+
34/Apress:PROD         vlan-11    0050.56b3.2f07 L
Po24

Leaf-103# show endpoint mac 00:50:56:B3:08:50
Legend:
 S - static          s - arp        L - local        O - peer-attached
 V - vpc-attached    a - local-aged p - peer-aged        M - span
```

```
 B - bounce            H - vtep         R - peer-attached-rl D -
bounce-to-proxy
 E - shared-service  m - svc-mgr
+-------------+-------------+----------------+------------+-------------+
     VLAN/       Encap        MAC Address      MAC Info/      Interface
     Domain      VLAN         IP Address       IP Info
+-------------+-------------+----------------+------------+-------------+
29/Apress:PROD   vxlan-16449430    0050.56b3.0850
tunnel5
```

Unknown Layer 2 Unicast

Remember that remote endpoint entries by default have a shorter aging timer of 300s. Without active communication, the remote destination endpoint can easily expire faster from the leaf endpoint table than the related ARP entry from a source station ARP cache. In such a case, when source sends traffic for leaf, the destination is unknown and the forwarding will behave according to the *L2 Unknown Unicast* configuration knob in bridge domain policy.

Bridge Domain in Flood Mode

For pure Layer 2 bridge domains, it is highly recommended and a best practice to change the default setting to *Flood* for *L2 Unknown Unicast*. This will ensure behavior similar to traditional legacy switches: if the destination endpoint is not present in a leaf's endpoint table, it will encapsulate the original packet into iVXLAN with a multicast (GiPO) destination address and flood it through the fabric via one of 13 FTag trees. The exact mechanism is applied as described earlier for ARP. The packet will be delivered to all leaf switches and interfaces that have some EPG mapping configured inside a given bridge domain.

This setting at the same time addresses situation when you have a *silent host* connected to the Layer 2 bridge domain. Neither the leaves nor the spines know any information about it, so the only way to get some traffic to that station is by flooding. After waking it up like this, however, the endpoint information will be learned, and the subsequent traffic will flow according to the standard forwarding process for known endpoints.

Bridge Domain in Hardware Proxy Mode

On the other hand, there is a default setting for L2 unknown unicast called *hardware proxy*. This will, instead of flooding, try to use the spine COOP database. The expected prerequisite for this forwarding method to work is that spine knows about all endpoints around the fabric. If you have some silent hosts, like mentioned above, hardware proxy forwarding will not be able to deliver any traffic to them until the endpoint information is learned.

When the hardware proxy is enabled and the ingress leaf doesn't know about destination endpoint, it will encapsulate the original packet into iVXLAN and, as the outer destination IP address, the anycast spine VTEP IP is used (as shown in Figure 6-9). This indicates to the spines that they are required to resolve the endpoint information in the COOP database and, in case of a match, rewrite the destination VTEP address of the iVXLAN packet to the correct egress leaf VTEP before sending it there. If the spine cannot find any match in the COOP database, the packet will be dropped without any additional signalization to the source endhost. That's the reason why hardware proxy is not recommended for L2 bridge domains where the potential for silent hosts exists.

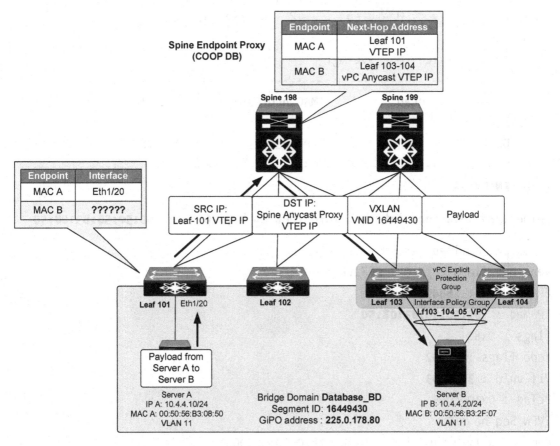

Figure 6-9. *Unknown L2 unicast with HW proxy*

When the destination endpoint is missing in the endpoint table, you won't see any entry when searching on the ingress leaf. What you can check in such a case, though, is the spine COOP database. Use the bridge domain VNID as a key and specify the MAC address of the destination endpoint. If present in the COOP database with the correct tunnel next hop, ACI should be able to deliver traffic to it. See Listing 6-11.

Listing 6-11. Unkwnown Destination Endpoint and COOP Database Verification

```
Leaf-103# show endpoint mac 00:50:56:B3:08:50
Legend:
 S - static       s - arp        L - local       O - peer-attached
 V - vpc-attached a - local-aged p - peer-aged    M - span
```

```
 B - bounce            H - vtep        R - peer-attached-rl D -
bounce-to-proxy
 E - shared-service  m - svc-mgr
+--------------+--------------+----------------+--------------+-------------+
        VLAN/       Encap           MAC Address       MAC Info/
Interface
        Domain      VLAN            IP Address        IP Info
+--------------+--------------+----------------+--------------+-------------+
-- NO ENTRY --
```

Spine-198# **show coop internal info repo ep key 16449430 00:50:56:B3:08:50**

```
-- output ommited --
Repo Hdr flags : IN_OBJ ACTIVE
EP bd vnid : 16449430
EP mac :  00:50:56:B3:08:50
flags : 0x80
repo flags : 0x102
Vrf vnid : 3080193
PcTag : 0x100c005
EVPN Seq no : 0
Remote publish timestamp: 01 01 1970 00:00:00 0
Snapshot timestamp: 05 28 2022 11:48:28 483522044
Tunnel nh : 10.11.66.70
MAC Tunnel  : 10.11.66.70
IPv4 Tunnel : 10.11.66.70
IPv6 Tunnel : 10.11.66.70
ETEP Tunnel : 0.0.0.0
-- output ommited -
```

Layer 2 Forwarding Summary

For your reference, in the Figure 6-10, you can find the overview of Layer 2 bridging in ACI and the related decision process.

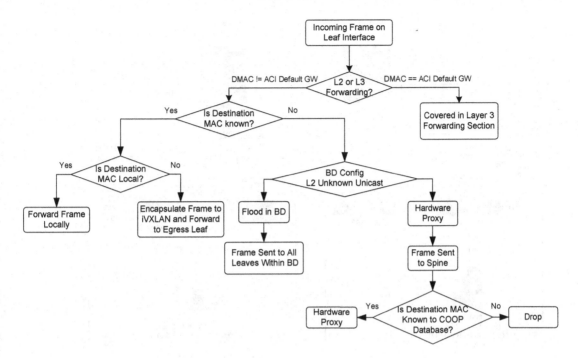

Figure 6-10. *Layer 2 bridging summary*

Layer 3 Forwarding

As soon as you can enable the *Unicast Routing* checkbox and configure subnet IP(s) in bridge domain L3 configurations (**Tenants -> Tenant_name -> Networking -> Bridge Domains -> BD_Name -> Policy -> L3 Configurations**), ACI starts to act as a default gateway for all endpoints in related EPGs. It will deploy SVI interfaces with BD subnet IPs on all leaves (depending on the immediacy setting), where at least one EPG to interface mapping exists. Additionally, leaves will start learning MAC addresses together with endpoint IP information.

Let's now examine the forwarding behavior for two endpoints in different L3 bridge domains as depicted in Figure 6-11.

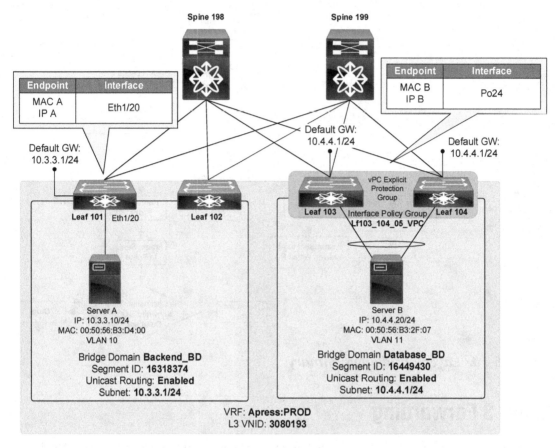

Figure 6-11. *Layer 3 bridge domain scenarios*

To ensure routing outside an endpoint's "home" bridge domain, you can check the pervasive gateways presence on the related leaf switches. See Listing 6-12.

Listing 6-12. L3 Bridge Domain Pervasive Gateways

```
Leaf-101# show ip int vrf Apress:PROD
IP Interface Status for VRF "Apress:PROD"
vlan15, Interface status: protocol-up/link-up/admin-up, iod: 89, mode:
pervasive
  IP address: 10.3.3.1, IP subnet: 10.3.3.0/24
  IP broadcast address: 255.255.255.255
  IP primary address route-preference: 0, tag: 0
```

Leaf-103# **show ip int vrf Apress:PROD**
IP Interface Status for VRF "Apress:PROD"
vlan21, Interface status: protocol-up/link-up/admin-up, iod: 95, mode:
pervasive
   IP address: 10.4.4.1, IP subnet: 10.4.4.0/24
   IP broadcast address: 255.255.255.255
   IP primary address route-preference: 0, tag: 0

Leaf-104# **show ip int vrf Apress:PROD**
IP Interface Status for VRF "Apress:PROD"
vlan21, Interface status: protocol-up/link-up/admin-up, iod: 95, mode:
pervasive
   IP address: 10.4.4.1, IP subnet: 10.4.4.0/24
   IP broadcast address: 255.255.255.255
   IP primary address route-preference: 0, tag: 0

The following step before the communication in IPv4 between endpoints can happen is, as always, the ARP resolution.

ARP Processing in a Layer 3 Bridge Domain

First, let's compare ARP forwarding behavior within the same bridge domain to the Layer 2 bridge domain. With Unicast Routing enabled, you can newly choose from two different forwarding behaviors for ARP packets:

- **ARP Flooding**: By default, each ARP packet will be flooded within its bridge domain exactly as in Layer 2 mode, by using the BD GiPO multicast address as a iVXLAN destination IP and specific FTag Tree for fabric delivery. It's a best practice to enable this setting for all L3 bridge domains with servers, firewalls, or loadbalancers inside. Then ACI will ensure flooding not only for ARPs but also for gratuitous ARPs, which are required for correct failovers or IP movement detection.

- **Directed ARP**: Optimization for ARP flooding is offered in L3 bridge domains by utilizing IP information from endpoint tables. When the *ARP Flooding* checkbox is disabled in the bridge domain policy, the ACI fabric will deliver each ARP packet as unicast directly to the destination following the same rules as described in following sections for all other unicast traffic.

Now, when communication outside your own bridge domain is needed, the endpoint must use ARP to resolve the MAC address of its default gateway (in your case, the ACI pervasive SVI interface). The ARP reply for such a request is always processed and sent from the closest leaf switch; no further forwarding is made. You can verify that it's happening from the ACI point of view by issuing the command in Listing 6-13.

Listing 6-13. ARP Processing Verification

```
Leaf-101# show ip arp internal event-history event | grep 10.3.3.1
    [116] TID 29623:arp_handle_arp_request:6647: TID 29623 : [DBG_ARP_
EVENT]: log_collect_arp_pkt; sip = 10.3.3.10; dip = 10.3.3.1;interface =
Vlan15; phy_inteface = Ethernet1/20; flood = 0; Info = Sent ARP response.
    [116] TID 29623:arp_process_receive_packet_msg:9081: TID 29623 : [DBG_
ARP_EVENT]: log_collect_arp_pkt; sip = 10.3.3.10; dip = 10.3.3.1;interface =
Vlan15; phy_interface = Ethernet1/20;Info = Received arp request
```

In the output you see that the leaf received the ARP request on a physical interface Ethernet 1/20 from the end host with IP 10.3.3.10. The destination (target) IP was 10.3.3.1, which matched ACI's own pervasive gateway of SVI VLAN15. Therefore, the leaf generated the ARP reply, enabling the end station to reach all the subnets outside of its bridge domain.

Another very useful tool in general for control plane operation verification, including the ARP Protocol, is the well-known **tcpdump** utility available on all ACI devices. However, you can only capture and analyze traffic heading to the leaf/spine CPU, not a standard data plane packet. For data plane analysis I will soon provide you with other options. Regarding ARP, with tcpdump you can see in real time whether the endhost is sending ARP requests to the leaf switch with the correct information. Even if you don't have access to it, at least you can confirm the expected behavior or right away identify issues on the endpoint side and possibly involve the related team in troubleshooting. See Listing 6-14.

Listing 6-14. TCP Dump to Capture the ARP Packet

```
Leaf-101# tcpdump -ni kpm_inb -vv | grep ARP
tcpdump: listening on kpm_inb, link-type EN10MB (Ethernet), capture size
262144 bytes
10:11:11.420319 ARP, Ethernet (len 6), IPv4 (len 4), Request who-has
10.3.3.1 (ff:ff:ff:ff:ff:ff) tell 10.3.3.10, length 46
```

Based on ARP packets, leaves will learn the placement of local endpoints and save them to their endpoint table. In a Layer 3-enabled bridge domain you will find both MAC+IP entries. See Listing 6-15.

Listing 6-15. Local L3 Endpoint Entry

```
Leaf-101# show endpoint ip 10.3.3.10
Legend:
 S - static         s - arp        L - local        O - peer-attached
 V - vpc-attached   a - local-aged p - peer-aged     M - span
 B - bounce         H - vtep       R - peer-attached-rl D -
bounce-to-proxy
 E - shared-service m - svc-mgr
+--------------+--------------+-----------------+--------------+-------------+
        VLAN/       Encap           MAC Address      MAC Info/
Interface
        Domain      VLAN            IP Address       IP Info
+--------------+--------------+-----------------+--------------+-------------+
20                  vlan-10    0050.56b3.d400  L
eth1/20
Apress:PROD         vlan-10         10.3.3.10  L
eth1/20
```

To wrap up ARP forwarding in ACI, the schema in Figure 6-12 illustrates the decision process for ARPs in an L3 bridge domain.

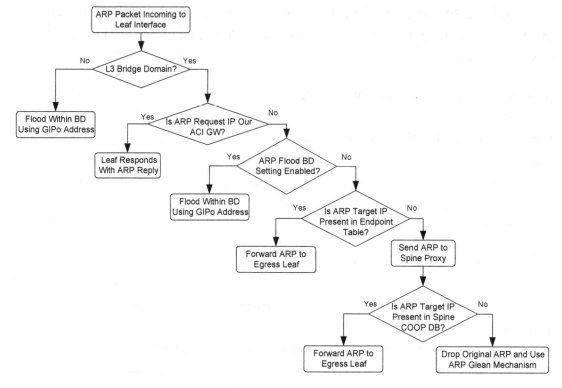

Figure 6-12. *ARP forwarding summary in L3 bridge domain*

Unknown Layer 3 Unicast

So, let's suppose now both communicating stations have the MAC addresses of their gateways correctly resolved using ARP. Related leaves, after learning about their locally connected endpoints, have already updated the spine COOP database with complete endpoint information. You need to use VRF L3 VNI (segment ID) as a key when searching through it. Notice that all entries for an L3-enabled bridge domain in COOP now have MAC+IP information included as well. See Listing 6-16.

Listing 6-16. Spine COOP Database for L3 Entries

Spine-198# **show coop internal info ip-db key 3080193 10.3.3.10**

IP address : **10.3.3.10**
Vrf : **3080193**
Flags : 0
EP bd vnid : **16318374**
EP mac : **00:50:56:B3:D4:00**

```
Publisher Id : 10.11.66.65
Record timestamp : 05 29 2022 08:38:12 213146976
Publish timestamp : 05 29 2022 08:38:12 213833526
Seq No: 0
Remote publish timestamp: 01 01 1970 00:00:00 0
URIB Tunnel Info
Num tunnels : 1
        Tunnel address : 10.11.66.65
        Tunnel ref count : 1

Spine-198# show coop internal info ip-db key 3080193 10.4.4.20

IP address : 10.4.4.20
Vrf : 3080193
Flags : 0
EP bd vnid : 16449430
EP mac :  00:50:56:B3:2F:07
Publisher Id : 10.11.66.70
Record timestamp : 05 29 2022 08:38:09 962932484
Publish timestamp : 05 29 2022 08:38:09 963037266
Seq No: 0
Remote publish timestamp: 01 01 1970 00:00:00 0
URIB Tunnel Info
Num tunnels : 1
        Tunnel address : 10.11.66.70
        Tunnel ref count : 1
```

Even though the spine has all of the endpoint information, there was actually no packet exchange between the endpoints themselves yet, just ARPing of their local gateway so that leaves won't have any remote endpoint entries in their tables. See Listing 6-17.

Listing 6-17. Missing L3 Endpoint Information in the Leaf Endpoint Table

```
Leaf-101# show endpoint ip 10.4.4.20
Legend:
 S - static        s - arp       L - local        O - peer-attached
 V - vpc-attached  a - local-aged p - peer-aged    M - span
 B - bounce        H - vtep      R - peer-attached-rl D -
bounce-to-proxy
 E - shared-service  m - svc-mgr
+--------------+--------------+----------------+--------------+-------------+
      VLAN/       Encap            MAC Address     MAC Info/
Interface
      Domain      VLAN             IP Address      IP Info
+--------------+--------------+----------------+--------------+-------------+
-- NO ENTRY --
```

In the L3 bridge domain, you don't perform any flooding of unknown unicasts. Instead, the leaf will refer to the *Routing Information Base (RIB)*, or simply a routing table, and search for the remote bridge domain subnet prefix, marked as pervasive. Its presence is a mandatory prerequisite to forward the unknown unicast packet. Forwarding itself will be then handled according to the routing next-hop information. See Listing 6-18.

Listing 6-18. Routing Table Entry for Remote BD Prefix

```
Leaf-101# show ip route 10.4.4.20 vrf Apress:PROD
IP Route Table for VRF "Apress:PROD"
'*' denotes best ucast next-hop
'**' denotes best mcast next-hop
'[x/y]' denotes [preference/metric]
'%<string>' in via output denotes VRF <string>
```

10.4.4.0/24, ubest/mbest: 1/0, attached, direct, **pervasive**
   *via **10.11.76.194**%overlay-1, [1/0], 21:20:59, static, tag 4294967294
      recursive next hop: **10.11.76.194**/32%overlay-1

And guess what actually represents this next-hop IP? Yes, it's the anycast spine VTEP address, dedicated for the IPv4 forwarding proxy. See Listing 6-19.

Listing 6-19. Spine Anycast VTEPs

Leaf-101# **show isis dteps vrf overlay-1**

IS-IS Dynamic Tunnel End Point (DTEP) database:

DTEP-Address	Role	Encapsulation	Type
10.11.76.194	**SPINE**	**N/A**	**PHYSICAL,PROXY-ACAST-V4**
10.11.76.192	SPINE	N/A	PHYSICAL,PROXY-ACAST-MAC
10.11.76.193	SPINE	N/A	PHYSICAL,PROXY-ACAST-V6

Based on previous information, the ingress leaf will encapsulate the packet to iVXLAN with the IPv4 anycast proxy destination address and send it to one of the spine switches, indicating a need for endpoint resolution in the COOP database (as shown in Figure 6-13). Notice that in case of L3 routing between bridge domains, ACI will use VRF Segment ID (VNID) inside the corresponding header of the iVXLAN encapsulated packet.

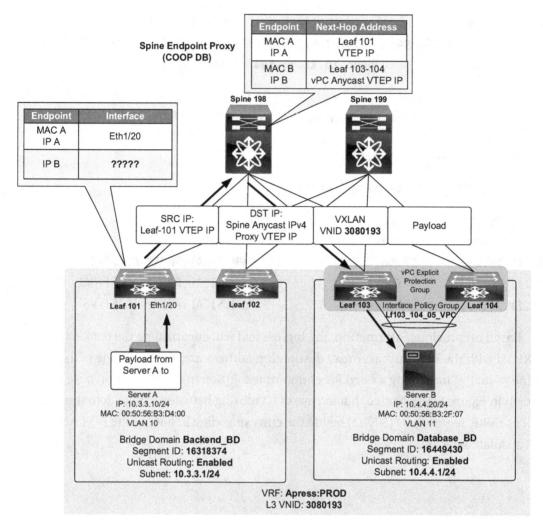

Figure 6-13. *L3 unknown remote endpoint for ingress leaf*

When the spine receives the iVXLAN destined to its own anycast VTEP address, it will proceed with endpoint lookup in the COOP database, and if the match is found, it will rewrite the iVXLAN outer destination IP address to the egress leaf VTEP IP and forward the packet towards its destination.

But what if spine cannot find any endpoint? In a Layer 2 bridge domain, it would drop such traffic. Here with Unicast Routing enabled, the original traffic is dopped as well, but ACI has an additional feature available called *silent host tracking* or *ARP gleaning* (summarized in Figure 6-14).

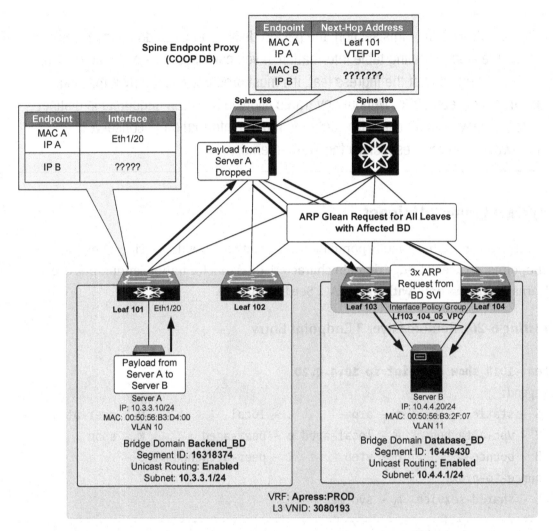

Figure 6-14. *Silent host tracking or ARP gleanning for unknown endpoint*

The spine generates an *ARP glean request* for unknown endpoints and sends it to all leaves where the destination bridge domain resides. Each leaf then creates three artificial ARP requests sourced from its pervasive gateway SVI interface, flooding them to all interfaces in a given bridge domain and asking for the unknown target IP address. The goal is to "nudge" the silent host and make it reply to ARP. This will populate the endpoint table on a local leaf with subsequent updates of the COOP database on spines.

The same ARP gleaning process works within one bridge domain as well, but just for ARP traffic, no other data-plane packets. If you disabled ARP flooding in an L3 bridge domain and the source station is ARPing for an unknown silent host, the spine will generate ARP glean in the same way as discussed above.

281

> **Tip**   As described in this section, the packet delivery in L3 bridge domains is closely related to routing table information. If you can't see the destination prefix in the routing table of the ingress leaf, it's most probably caused by a missing contract between EPGs. Without any traffic allowed between endpoints in distinct BDs, ACI leaves won't even distribute the routing information to conserve the hardware resources, especially the TCAM memory.

Known Layer 3 Unicast

Finally, you are getting to fully populated end point tables with both local and remote endpoints. A Layer 3 bridge domain characteristic is that for remote endpoints, a leaf learns IP address only, without a MAC. See Listing 6-20.

Listing 6-20. Remote Layer 3 Endpoint Entry

```
Leaf-101# show endpoint ip 10.4.4.20
Legend:
 S - static       s - arp       L - local         O - peer-attached
 V - vpc-attached a - local-aged p - peer-aged     M - span
 B - bounce       H - vtep       R - peer-attached-rl D -
bounce-to-proxy
 E - shared-service  m - svc-mgr
+--------------+--------------+----------------+--------------+-------------+
        VLAN/      Encap          MAC Address       MAC Info/
Interface
        Domain     VLAN           IP Address        IP Info
+--------------+--------------+----------------+--------------+-------------+
Apress:PR
OD                             10.4.4.20                       tunnel19
Leaf-101# show system internal epm endpoint ip 10.4.4.20
MAC : 0000.0000.0000 ::: Num IPs : 1 <<-- NO MAC Learned
IP# 0 : 10.4.4.20 ::: IP# 0 flags :  ::: l3-sw-hit: No
```

```
Vlan id : 0 ::: Vlan vnid : 0 ::: VRF name : Apress:PROD
BD vnid : 0 ::: VRF vnid : 3080193
Phy If : 0 ::: Tunnel If : 0x18010013
Interface : Tunnel19
Flags : 0x80004400 ::: sclass : 49157 ::: Ref count : 3
EP Create Timestamp : 05/29/2022 14:34:40.217255
EP Update Timestamp : 05/29/2022 14:39:11.306366
EP Flags : IP|sclass|timer|

::::
```

The rest of forwarding process happens in a standard fashion (as described in Figure 6-15). The ingress leaf looks up the destination endpoint and, based on the tunnel interface destination address, it encapsulates the original packet to iVXLAN headers, sending it via spines directly to the destination VTEP.

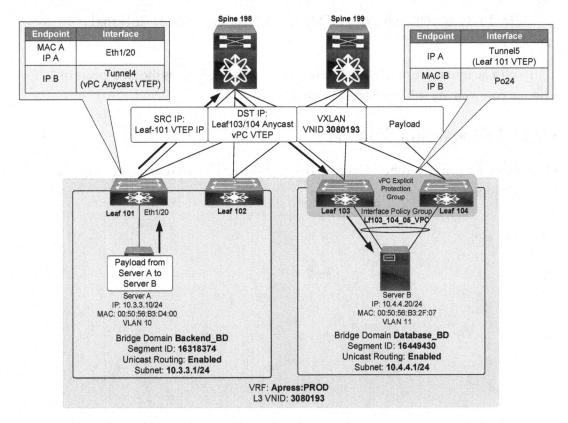

Figure 6-15. *Known Layer3 unicast delivery*

External Forwarding in a Layer 3 Bridge Domain

When dealing with L3 bridge domain forwarding, you need to consider external routing information as well. If the ingress leaf can't find any destination endpoint in its endpoint table, nor the pervasive destination bridge domain subnet, the last option could potentially be the standard IP prefix received from the external router, distributed around the fabric using MP-BGP. In such a case, the leaf will forward the original packet according to the routing table directly to the border leaf. See Listing 6-21.

Listing 6-21. External IP Prefix Learned via MP-BGP

```
Leaf-101# show ip route 10.5.5.10 vrf Apress:PROD
10.5.5.0/24, ubest/mbest: 2/0
    *via 10.11.82.68%overlay-1, [1/0], 40w00d, bgp-65520, internal,
tag 65520
    *via 10.11.82.69%overlay-1, [1/0], 40w00d, bgp-65520, internal,
tag 65520
```

I won't go into more details about external forwarding here as the all aspects of ACI external connectivity will be covered in Chapter 7.

Layer 3 Forwarding Summary

Once again, for your reference, Figure 6-16 describes an overview of forwarding in a Layer 3 bridge domain.

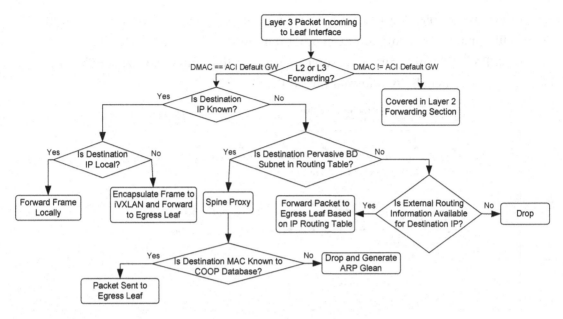

Figure 6-16. *Layer 3 forwarding summary*

Multi-Pod Forwarding

So far, we have discussed various forwarding scenarios inside a single ACI fabric. When Multi-Pod architecture comes into play, in fact, not much will change. Multi-Pod is still considered a single fabric, with multiple availability zones, under a single administration domain and follows the same forwarding principles. In the following sections, you will mainly examine additions to control plane operations with regards to forwarding between ACI Pods.

Multi-Pod Control Plane

One of the main advantages of this architecture is separating Pod control planes from each other to increase the robustness and reliability. Each Pod uses its own VTEP pool for internal forwarding, whose prefix is exchanged through the IPN via underlay OSPF/BGP and redistributed to IS-IS in every fabric. IPN routers likewise distribute special external TEP addresses used for Inter-Pod forwarding between spines. COOP databases as well as routing tables of all switches are then synchronized using Inter-Pod multi-protocol BGP peerings established between spines.

As soon as the spine learns about a new endpoint via the COOP protocol, in Multi-Pod it will signal this information to all other remote spines using MP-BGP in address family L2VPN EVPN. In Figure 6-17, you can examine the format of L2VPN EPVN Network Layer Reachability Information (NLRI).

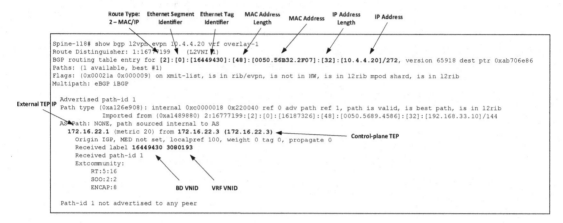

Figure 6-17. *L2VPN EVPN Endpoint Reachability Information in MP-BGP*

A single route type 2 entry can describe both MAC address for L2 BDs or MAC+IP couples in L3 enabled BD. Route Type 5 is then similarly used to exchange routing information between spines in a given VRF (address families VPNv4, VPNv6).

Notice that these external entries carry in a next-hop field already mentioned external TEP address, configured on spines during Multi-Pod initiation. External TEPs are redistributed to the COOP database as a next hop for all external endpoints. As you can see in Figure 6-18, it's the only significant difference from standard internal endpoints.

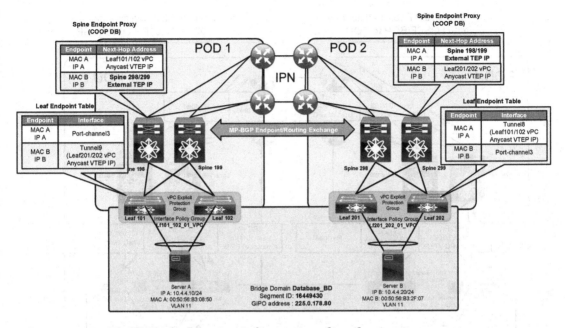

Figure 6-18. *Multi-Pod endpoint information distribution*

Leaf endpoint tables still use tunnel interfaces for remote endpoint reachability and their destination address for Inter-Pod endpoints refers to the actual remote VTEP address of the distant leaf switch.

Multi-Pod Data Plane

Forwarding for known bridged endpoints is pretty straightforward in the Multi-Pod architecture. All Pods mutually exchange their VTEP pool prefixes through underlay fabric IS-IS and IPN routing, so the source leaf just needs to encapsulate the original packet to iVXLAN directly by remote egress leaf VTEP IP in the outer IP header and send it towards the spines. During the whole path, the iVXLAN packet is not manipulated at all. This process is illustrated in Figure 6-19.

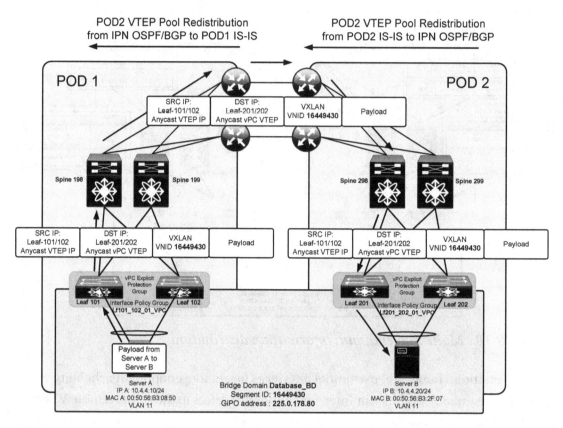

Figure 6-19. *Multi-Pod known endpoint forwarding*

When the local leaf switch doesn't know about destination endpoint and the bridge domain is configured for a hardware proxy for an unknown L2 unicast, the iVXLAN packet is sent to an anycast spine VTEP address. There, if the endpoint information exists in the COOP database learned from MP-BGP peering with a remote Pod, the iVXLAN outer destination IP header is rewritten to an external TEP address and sent over the IPN toward the remote spine switch. The remote spine will finally resolve its local endpoint in COOP, rewrite the outer iVXLAN destination IP to the egress leaf VTEP, and deliver the packet locally in a standard fashion. Hardware proxy forwarding is indicated in Figure 6-20.

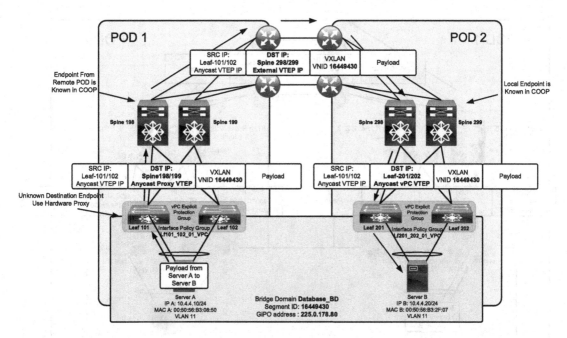

Figure 6-20. *Multi-Pod L2 unkwnown unicast forwarding – hardware proxy*

For Layer 3 routed traffic, there is no special behavior compared to single fabric or previously described data plane operations. Known L3 endpoints are directly routed with the egress VTEP address in the iVXLAN IP header. For unknown L3 endpoints, you need at least their bridge domain pervasive subnet in the routing table, pointing to spines, where the COOP resolution happens. And for entirely silent hosts not known to the COOP database, spines generate ARP glean messages, which are flooded through the whole Multi-Pod environment where the destination bridge domain exists.

Multi-Destination Traffic Delivery

BUM traffic (*L2 Unknown Unicasts* with the BD set to *Flood, Broadcasts and Multicasts*) is forwarded around the Multi-Pod fabric using the bridge domain multicast GiPO address and FTAg trees as described in a previous sections. GiPOs are synchronized across all ACI switches managed by a single APIC cluster, so the bridge domains act as a single broadcast domain even when stretched between Pods. Multi-destination forwarding is illustrated in Figure 6-21.

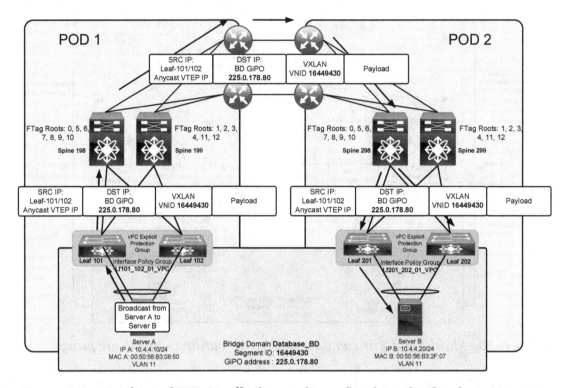

Figure 6-21. *Multi-Pod BUM traffic forwarding – flood in a bridge domain*

In order to deliver multicast traffic through IPN as well, you need to utilize PIM-Bidir multicast routing with phantom RPs as discussed in previous chapters. Spines in each Pod, thanks to IS-IS, internally elect one of them to become the authoritative forwarder of multicast packets towards the IPN for a particular bridge domain. At the same time, they will send the IGMP Report over a single chosen interface facing the IPN, indicating interest in receiving multicast traffic for a given GiPO address. This way, they can simply achieve BUM traffic loadbalancing.

When looking at the IPN multicast routing table, if the connected spine registered an intention to receive a multicast for GiPO address, you will see the interface over which the IGMP was received in the Outgoing Interface List. Alternatively, you can look in the IGMP Snooping table if enabled. See Listing 6-22.

Listing 6-22. IPN Multicast Routing Table and IGMP Snooping

IPN-1# **show ip mroute vrf ACI_IPN**
IP Multicast Routing Table for VRF "ACI_IPN"

(*, 225.0.20.176/32), bidir, uptime: 1w4d, igmp ip pim
  Incoming interface: loopback1, RPF nbr: 192.168.11.50
  Outgoing interface list: (count: 3)
    Vlan2102, uptime: 1w4d, pim
    loopback1, uptime: 1w4d, pim, (RPF)
    Ethernet5/5.4, uptime: 1w4d, igmp

IPN-2# **show ip mroute vrf ACI_IPN**
IP Multicast Routing Table for VRF "ACI_IPN"

(*, 225.1.157.208/32), bidir, uptime: 19w0d, igmp ip pim
  Incoming interface: loopback1, RPF nbr: 192.168.11.33
  Outgoing interface list: (count: 2)
    Vlan2111, uptime: 19w0d, pim,
    loopback1, uptime: 19w0d, pim, (RPF)
    Ethernet6/5.4, uptime: 19w0d, igmp

IPN-1# **show ip igmp groups vrf ACI_IPN**
IGMP Connected Group Membership for VRF "ACI_IPN" - 30 total entries
Type: S - Static, D - Dynamic, L - Local, T - SSM Translated

Group Address	Type	Interface	Uptime	Expires	Last Reporter
225.0.20.176	D	Ethernet1/5.4	1w4d	00:03:42	172.16.12.25
225.0.94.192	D	Ethernet1/6.4	1w4d	00:04:14	172.16.12.17
225.0.129.80	D	Ethernet1/5.4	2w5d	00:03:42	172.16.12.25
225.0.157.208	D	Ethernet1/6.4	33w4d	00:04:14	172.16.12.17
225.0.165.96	D	Ethernet1/5.4	33w3d	00:03:42	172.16.12.25

Figure 6-22 graphically describes the IGMP operation in a Multi-Pod architecture.

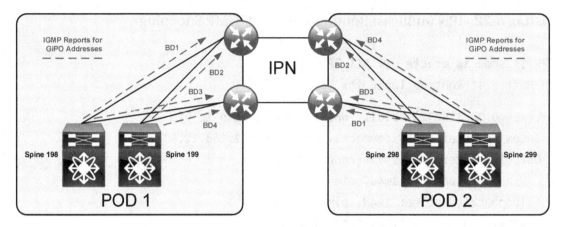

Figure 6-22. *IGMP Reports for bridge domain GiPO addresses*

Multi-Site Forwarding

In ACI Multi-Site architecture, forwarding follows similar concepts to Multi-Pod with few variations and additions. ISN OSPF/BGP routing exchanges overlay VTEP IPs (similar to external TEPs in Multi-Pod) between spines. You now differentiate between Unicast Overlay TEP (O-UTEP) and Multicast Overlay TEP (O-MTEP) IPs used for forwarding respective traffic types. ISN doesn't require any multicast support; the spines will perform the ingress-replication of BUM packets instead. Multiple unicast copies of previously broadcasted/multicasted traffic are sent to O-MTEP IPs of remote spines.

Endpoint information in spine COOP databases (and subsequently leaf endpoint tables) is synchronized thanks to MP-BGP between sites in the L2VPN EVPN address family. If routing is needed, VPNv4 and VPNv6 entries are exchanged. As you can see in Figure 6-23, remote endpoint entries always refer to O-UTEP IP addresses.

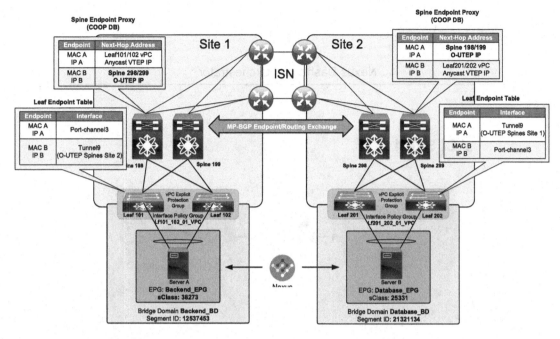

Figure 6-23. *Multi-Site control plane information exchange*

Name-Space Normalization (Translation)

For each internal or external EPG (with its bridge domain and VRF) that requires mutual inter-site connectivity, you need to deal with a slight complication. Due to the fact that you use two otherwise completely independent ACI fabrics, with separated APIC clusters, each fabric has its own sClasses for EPGs and VNIDs for BD and VRFs. To enable communication and correct contract policy enforcement, all inter-site tenant application policies are created in the Nexus Dashboard Orchestrator (NDO) platform instead of local APIC clusters.

NDO then pushes tenant objects consistently to all chosen site-local APIC clusters and synchronizes object's sClass and VNID identifiers. This is done by creating mutual "shadow" objects and special name-space normalization tables on all spines, utilized for ID translation when forwarding iVXLAN packets.

I will describe the multi-site normalization process in following practical example. Imagine you have created a simple application policy in NDO for the tenant Apress consisting of VRF PROD stretched between both sites. Then you define a bridge domain backend with an EPG backend to be created just in Site 1 and a bridge domain database with an EPG database for Site 2 only. Finally, you need to ensure communication between EPGs using a contract (as shown in Figure 6-24).

Nexus Dashboard Orchestrator

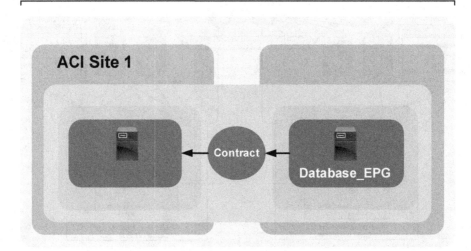

Figure 6-24. *Application policy definition in NDO*

When you push such a policy from NDO to both APIC clusters, the resulting configuration will look like this:

1. **ACI Site 1**

    a. Apress:PROD VRF– VNID (Segment ID) 3047424

    b. Backend BD - VNID 125374532

    c. Backend EPG - sClass 38273

2. **ACI Site 2**

    a. Apress:PROD VRF – VNID (Segment ID) 2097153

    b. Database BD - VNID 21321134

    c. Database EPG - sClass 25331

However, there is a contract applied between EPGs, so NDO needs to synchronize zoning rules somehow to permit the required traffic on both sites. As a first step, it will artificially create mutual *shadow objects* in the Site 1 EPG and BD for Database segment and in the Site 2 EPG and BD for Backend segment:

1. **ACI Site 1 (Shadow Objects)**

   a. Database BD - VNID 28923167 – in fact non-existing BD
      in Site 1

   b. Database EPG - sClass 29834 – in fact non-existing EPG
      in Site 1

2. **ACI Site 2 (Shadow Objects)**

   a. Backend BD - VNID 25538742 – in fact non-existing BD
      in Site 2

   b. Backend EPG - sClass 45793 – in fact non-existing EPG in Site 2

Shadow EPG sClasses are then installed to local zoning rule tables and mapped to local EPGs, ostensibly simulating the local relationship. The output shown in Listing 6-23 would be seen in the zoning rule table of Site 1 leaves. Notice especially the SrcEPG and DstEPG fields.

Listing 6-23. ACI Site 1 Zoning Rules

```
leaf-101# show zoning-rule scope 3047424
+---------+--------+--------+----------+----------------+---------
+---------+------------------------+----------+--------------------+
| Rule ID | SrcEPG | DstEPG | FilterID |      Dir       |  operSt
|  Scope  |         Name          |  Action  |    Priority        |
+---------+--------+--------+----------+----------------+---------
+---------+------------------------+----------+--------------------+
|  4243   | 38273  | 29834  |    25    |     bi-dir     | enabled
| 3047424 |    Inter-Site_CT       |  permit  |   fully_qual(7)    |
|  4244   | 29834  | 38273  |    26    | uni-dir-ignore | enabled
| 3047424 |    Inter-Site_CT       |  permit  |   fully_qual(7)    |
+---------+--------+--------+----------+----------------+---------
+---------+------------------------+----------+--------------------+
```

If you check the leaves of Site 2, you get the output shown in Listing 6-24.

Listing 6-24. ACI Site 2 Zoning Rules

Leaf-201# **show zoning-rule scope 2097153**

```
+---------+--------+--------+----------+----------------+--------+--------
+-----------------+----------+--------------------------+
| Rule ID | SrcEPG | DstEPG | FilterID |      Dir       | operSt | Scope
|      Name       | Action   |        Priority          |
+---------+--------+--------+----------+----------------+--------+--------
+-----------------+----------+--------------------------+
|   4157  | 45793  | 25331  |    25    |    bi-dir      | enabled | 2097153
| Inter-Site_CT   | permit   |      fully_qual(7)       |
|   4156  | 25331  | 45793  |    26    | uni-dir-ignore | enabled |
2097153  | Inter-Site_CT  | permit   |      fully_qual(7)       |
+---------+--------+--------+----------+----------------+--------+--------
+-----------------+----------+--------------------------+
```

The second step is related to data plane traffic normalization. NDO has to create a translation database called the *Name-Space Normalization Table* on all spine switches. Based on it, the spines will rewrite the iVXLAN header fields when the inter-site packet is being forwarded. Figure 6-25 and the following paragraph describe the whole process.

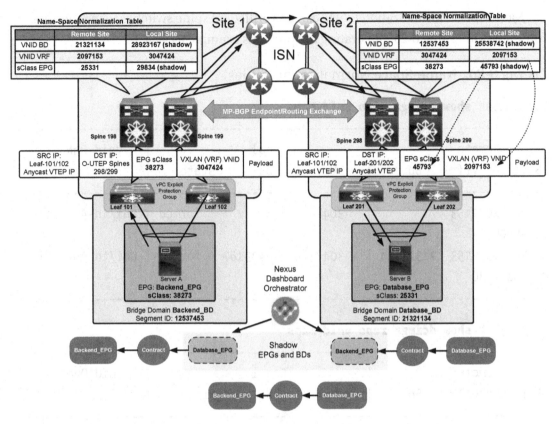

Figure 6-25. *Multi-Site Name-Space Normalization – forwarding from the backend to the database*

In this example, the backend endpoint from Site 1 sends a packet to the database endpoint in Site 2. Ingress leaf 101/102 matches the zoning rules related to the local backend EPG and shadow database EPG. The permitted packet is encapsulated into iVXLAN with headers set to Backend_EPG sClass 38273 and Apress:PROD VRF VNID 3047424. The packet is forwarded to destination O-UTEP of spines 298/299. The Destination spine identifies inter-site traffic, so its headers must be translated for local use and delivery. VRF VNID will be according to the normalization table translated from remote 3047424 to local 2097153 and remote sClass 38273 of the actual backend EPG in Site 1 is translated to artificial shadow sClass 45793 of the backend EPG in local Site 2. The outer destination IP of the iVXLAN header is changes as well to the local egress leaves anycast VTEP. After receiving a packet on the egress leaf, it will see that the contract was already applied in the source site, so it will just deliver the payload to the destination endpoint.

Name-space normalization tables can be verified on spine switches using the show commands in Listing 6-25, illustrating the previous example as well.

Listing 6-25. Name-Space Normalization Tables

Spine-199# **show dcimgr repo vnid-maps**

```
-------------------------------------------------------------------------
        Remote            |      Local            |  Vnid-DnName
   Site    Vrf      Bd    |   Vrf       Bd     State    |
-------------------------------------------------------------------------
    2   2097153           |  3047424           formed | uni/tn-Apress/
ctx-PROD
    2   2097153  21321134 |  3047424  28923167  formed | uni/tn-Apress/BD-
Database_BD
-------------------------------------------------------------------
```

Spine-299# **show dcimgr repo vnid-maps**

```
-------------------------------------------------------------------------
        Remote            |      Local            |  Vnid-DnName
   Site    Vrf      Bd    |   Vrf       Bd     State    |
-------------------------------------------------------------------------
    1   3047424           |  2097153           formed | uni/tn-Apress/
ctx-PROD
    1   3047424  12537453 |  2097153  25538742  formed | uni/tn-Apress/BD-
Backend_BD
------------------------------------------------------------------
```

Spine-199# **show dcimgr repo sclass-maps**

```
------------- --------------------------------------------------------
      Remote          |     Local              |  PcTag-DnName
  site  Vrf      PcTag | Vrf      PcTag  Rel-state |
------------- --------------------------------------------------------
    2   2097153  32770 | 3047424   16386   formed | uni/tn-Apress/ctx-PROD
    2   2097153  25331 | 3047424   29834   formed | .../ap-PROD_APP/epg-
Database_EPG
```

```
Spine-299# show dcimgr repo sclass-maps
--------------------------------------------------------------------------
      Remote            |     Local              |  PcTag-DnName
site  Vrf      PcTag | Vrf       PcTag  Rel-state |
--------------------------------------------------------------------------
  1   3047424  32770 | 2097153   16386     formed | uni/tn-Apress/ctx-PROD
  1   3047424  38273 | 2097153   45793     formed | .../ap-PROD_APP/epg-
Backend_EPG
```

Of course, this normalization works not only to interconnect separated ACI segments between sites, but also in the same way to stretch them. All stretched objects existing on both sites will be just directly mapped between each other without creating an artificial shadow object. In the previous example, VRF is such a case.

Additional Troubleshooting Toolset for Fabric Forwarding

Troubleshooting of inoperative forwarding can be a challenging task in any network environment and ACI is no exception. So far, you have seen many useful CLI commands and outputs in this chapter. Hopefully they've given you an extensive toolset for verification that the control plane and data plane are in a good shape and performing as expected. There is more to it, though. In subsequent sections, I will go through multiple tools I find personally very useful when dealing with some ACI forwarding issues.

Endpoint Tracker

Navigating to **Operations -> EP Tracker** you will find a useful GUI tool to simply and quickly verify if some endpoint is known to the fabric or not (as shown in Figure 6-26). In the search field, you can put either a MAC address, IP address, or when integrated with a VMM domain even a VM name. If an endpoint is learned behind some leaf switch, you will get one or more search results with information on where it is currently connected and to which tenant/application profile/EPG it belongs.

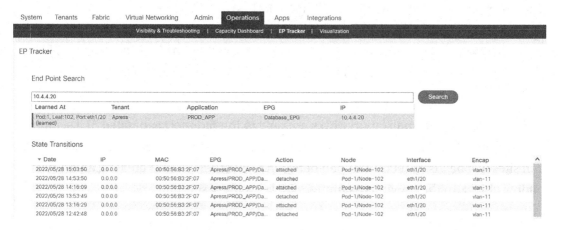

Figure 6-26. *ACI Endpoint Tracker*

Learning an endpoint is an elementary prerequisite for its connectivity to work, so not seeing any in the EP tracker can direct you to some problem between the connected station and the closest ACI leaf: a silent host, misconfigured end station network interface, or access policies on the ACI side, missing static/dynamic EPG mapping, or some problem with ACI control-plane (bug?).

Additionally, EP Tracker can provide comprehensive information about endpoint movements in time, which can potentially help with debugging a flapping or generally unstable endhost.

Embedded Logic Analyzer Module

In this chapter, you have seen that ACI administrators can use the well-known tcpdump utility to capture the traffic incoming to the ACI node CPU. But what about the actual data plane traffic on host interfaces or uplinks? *Embedded Logic Analyzer Module (ELAM)* is a low-level debugging tool looking directly at Nexus switch ASIC. It is able to catch a single packet according to a precise filter definition and then analyze it in comprehensive detail, describing the exact forwarding result for it when going through the ASIC. This can be used to simply confirm that a specific frame has arrived from an endhost/fabric to a particular interface, or you can dig deeper to see its handling. ELAM is very useful to find the outgoing interface(s) of a chosen traffic or even more to identify a drop reason when some communication is not working.

Originally, ELAM was a CLI utility, initiated in a special line card shell (vsh_lc) with a quite complicated filter configuration and output ranging up to thousands of lines full of internal codes and hex values. If you are not Cisco CX (TAC) Engineer, it can be hard to find that one information you currently need. Thankfully, help is provided in the form of the additive *ELAM Assistant app*, which can be download from DC App Center store (`https://dcappcenter.cisco.com/`). The Package needs to be installed in the **Apps -> Installed Apps** section in the ACI GUI and enabled before use (as you can see in Figure 6-27).

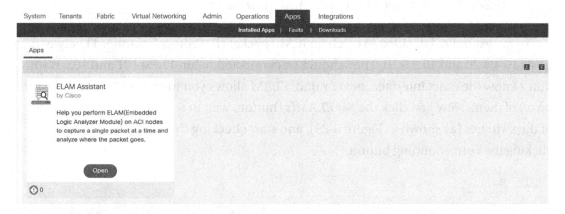

Figure 6-27. *ELAM Assistant*

ELAM Assistant will significantly (really hugely) simplify the ELAM operation, providing a graphical way to configure the utility for catching the correct packet. If the filter rule is triggered on a specified ASIC, ELAM Assistant will further download the resulting detailed output and parse it on your behalf. This will translate the sawdust hex values into a human-readable and useful information.

The fastest procedure to set up ELAM is to open the app, log in with your credentials, choose *Capture (Perform ELAM)* in the left navigation pane, and click on *Quick Add* to choose up to three ACI switches where the traffic filter will be configured and will define a wide variety of packet parameters to match (MAC, IP, CoS, DSCP, IP Protocol Number, L4 source/destination port, ARP sender/target IP, ARP MAC, or its Opcode). If needed, you can even match the iVXLAN packet headers on a fabric interface (as shown in Figure 6-28).

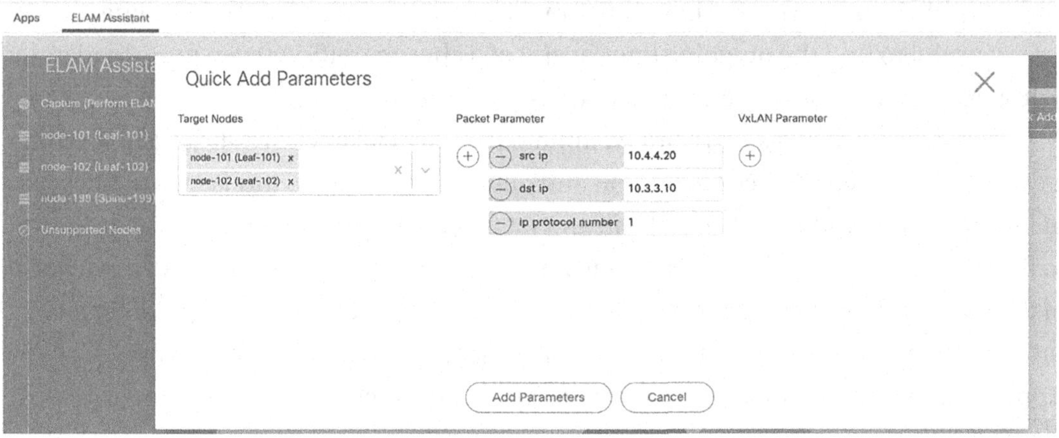

Figure 6-28. *ELAM Assistant's Quick Add parameters*

In my example, I decided to catch an ICMP packet (IP Protocol number 1) between hosts 10.4.4.20 and 10.3.3.10. They should be connected behind Leaf 101 and 102. If you don't know the exact interface, never mind; ELAM allows you to specify "any" and listen on all of them. Now just click the *Set ELAM(s)* button, wait to see the "Set" status on all of the switches (as shown in Figure 6-29), and start checking the trigger by repeatedly clicking the corresponding button.

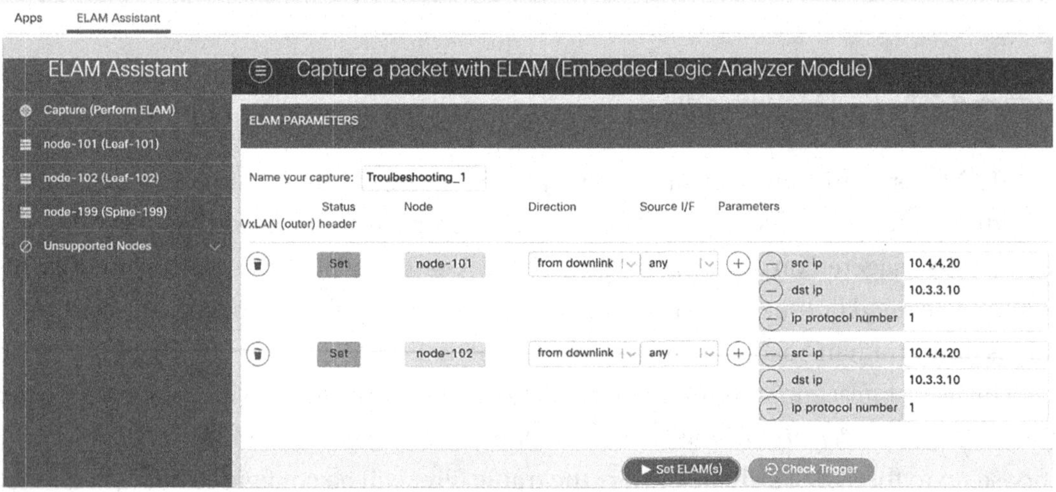

Figure 6-29. *Setting up ELAM Assistant for traffic analysis*

If the defined filter is hit, ELAM Assistant will start by downloading the report file from the ACI switch and parsing it for you. Click the *Report Ready* button in the Status field and view the output. Besides the traffic header analysis at the beginning, the most crucial part is the *Packet Forwarding Information* section (shown in Figure 6-30).

Packet Forwarding Information	
Forward Result	
Destination Type	To another ACI node (LEAF, AVS/AVE etc.)
Destination TEP	10.11.24.64 (Leaf-101)
Destination Physical Port	eth1/60
Contract	
Destination EPG pcTag (dclass)	0xC004 / 49156 (Apress:PROD_APP:Backend_EPG)
Source EPG pcTag (sclass)	0xC005 / 49157 (Apress:PROD_APP:Database_EPG)
Contract was applied	1 (Contract was applied on this node)
Drop	
Drop Code	no drop

Figure 6-30. *ELAM packet forwarding result*

As you can see, ELAM offers confirmation about forwarding decision on this node (e.g., local delivery, unicast forwarding through the fabric to the egress leaf, flood or drop) together with contract hit information and a drop code if applicable.

fTriage

ELAM is a powerful tool for performing a deep packet forwarding analysis, but as you've seen, it's a kind of one-time type and maximally on three concurrent ACI nodes. How great would it be if you could start ELAM on a given ingress node(s), specify the traffic of your interest, and some tool would gather all the outputs from the ELAM report and based on them automatically perform further ELAMs along the whole path around the ACI fabric (even in Multi-Pod/Multi-Site architectures)? All with comprehensive and detailed documentation about the packet manipulation on each hop? That's exactly what APIC's *fTriage* utility (written in Python) is for.

fTriage can analyze the whole forwarding path of a defined communication by entering the initial information about where you expect the traffic to ingress. The command itself has a plethora of flexible options and flags you can explore by issuing `ftriage example` or a specific `-h` flag for bridged or routed variants. Some of the common examples are shown in Listing 6-26.

Listing 6-26. fTriage Usage Examples

```
# Bridged traffic ingressing single Leaf switch
apic1# ftriage -user admin bridge -ii LEAF:Leaf-101 -dmac 02:02:02:02:02:02

# Routed traffic ingressing specific VPC interface
apic1# ftriage -user admin route -ii VPC:vpc20_Leaf1_Leaf3 -sip 101.1.2.53
-dip 101.1.1.53

# Broadcast
apic1# ftriage -user admin bridge -ii LEAF:Leaf-101 -dmac FF:FF:FF:FF:FF:FF

apic1# ftriage route -h
optional arguments:
  -h, --help     show this help message and exit
  -ii intf       ingress if (siteid::(node:if|LEAF:<leaf-name>|VPC:<vpc-
                 name>[:<leaf-name>,..]|PC:<pc-name>[:<leaf-
                 name>,..]|L3OUT:<tnname>:<l3name>)[+vtep])
  -ie encap      ingress encap (VLAN/VNID)
  -iie encap     ingress inner encap (VLAN/VNID)
  -ei intf       egress if (siteid::(node:if|LEAF:<leaf-name>|VPC:<vpc-
                 name>[:<leaf-name>,..]|PC:<pc-name>[:<leaf-
                 name>,..]|L3OUT:<tnname>:<l3name>)[+vtep])
  -ee encap        egress encap (VLAN/VNID)
  -eie encap       egress inner encap (VLAN/VNID)
  -dip addr        destination IP
  -sip addr        source IP
  -l4-type l4type    l4-type (0:TCP 1:UDP 2:IVXLAN 3:VXLAN 4:NVGRE 7:ND)
  -l4-src-port l4srcport      l4-src-port
  -l4-dst-port l4dstport      l4-dst-port
```

Let's start fTriage and analyze the communication between endpoints 10.4.4.20 and 10.3.3.10 in different EPGs behind different leaf switches. Notice especially how detailed information about forwarding decisions along the path fTriage can provide (I removed timestamps and few not useful fields from each line to make the output more readable). See Listing 6-27.

Listing 6-27. fTriaging the Endpoint Communications

apic1# **ftriage -user admin route -ii LEAF:Leaf-102 -sip 10.4.4.20 -dip**
10.3.3.10
Request password info for username: admin
Password:
main:2064 Invoking ftriage with username: admin
fcls:2379 Leaf-102: Valid ELAM for asic:0 slice:1 srcid:106 pktid:1586
main:1295 **L3 packet Seen on Leaf-102 Ingress: Eth1/20 Egress:**
Eth1/60 Vnid: 3080193
main:1337 **Leaf-102: Incoming Packet captured with [SIP:10.4.4.20,**
DIP:10.3.3.10]
main:1364 **Leaf-102: Packet's egress outer [SIP:10.11.24.66,**
DIP:10.11.24.64]
main:1371 **Leaf-102: Outgoing packet's Vnid: 3080193**
main:353   **Computed ingress encap string vlan-11**
main:464   **Ingress BD(s) Apress:Database_BD**
main:476   **Ingress Ctx: Apress:PROD Vnid: 3080193**
main:1566 Ig VRF Vnid: 3080193
main:1610 SIP 10.4.4.20 DIP 10.3.3.10
unicast:1607 Leaf-102: Enter dbg_sub_ig with cn HEA and inst: ig
unicast:1934 Leaf-102: **Dst EP is remote**
unicast:840 Leaf-102: Enter dbg_leaf_remote with cn HEA and inst: ig
misc:891 Leaf-102: caller unicast:976 DMAC(00:22:BD:F8:19:FF) same as
RMAC(00:22:BD:F8:19:FF)
misc:893 Leaf-102: L3 packet caller unicast:985 getting routed/bounced in HEA
misc:891 Leaf-102: caller unicast:996 Dst IP is present in HEA L3 tbl
misc:891 Leaf-102: caller unicast:1054 RwDMAC DIPo(10.11.24.64) is one of
dst TEPs ['10.11.24.64']
main:1770 dbg_sub_ig function returned values on node Leaf-102 done False,
nxt_nifs {Spine-199: ['Eth1/32']}, nxt_dbg_f_n nexthop, nxt_inst ig, eg_ifs
Eth1/60, Vnid: 3080193
main:958 **Found peer-node Spine-199 and IF: Eth1/32 in candidate list**
fcls:2379 Spine-199: Valid ELAM for asic:0 slice:0 srcid:56 pktid:31
main:1295 **L3 packet Seen on Spine-199 Ingress: Eth1/32 Egress:**
Eth1/31 Vnid: 3080193

main:1333 **Spine-199: Incoming Packet captured with Outer [SIP:10.11.24.66, DIP:10.11.24.64] .... Inner [SIP:10.4.4.20, DIP:10.3.3.10]**

main:1371 Spine-199: Outgoing packet's Vnid: 3080193

fib:737   **Spine-199: Transit in spine**

unicast:1957 Spine-199: Enter dbg_sub_nexthop with cn BKY and inst: ig

unicast:1979 Spine-199: Enter dbg_sub_nexthop with Transit inst: ig infra: False glbs.dipo: 10.11.24.64

unicast:2196 **Spine-199: EP is known in COOP (DIPo = 10.11.24.64)**

unicast:2271 **Spine-199: Infra route 10.11.24.64 present in RIB**

main:1770 dbg_sub_nexthop function returned values on node Spine-199 done False, nxt_nifs {Leaf-101: ['Eth1/60']}, nxt_dbg_f_n nexthop, nxt_inst eg, eg_ifs Eth1/31, Vnid: 3080193

main:**958   Found peer-node Leaf-101 and IF: Eth1/60 in candidate list**

fcls:2379 Leaf-101: Valid ELAM for asic:0 slice:0 srcid:64 pktid:997

main:1295 **L3 packet Seen on   Leaf-101 Ingress: Eth1/60 Egress: Eth1/20   Vnid: 10**

main:1333 **Leaf-101: Incoming Packet captured with Outer [SIP:10.11.24.66, DIP:10.11.24.64] .... Inner [SIP:10.4.4.20, DIP:10.3.3.10]**

main:1371 Leaf-101: Outgoing packet's Vnid: 10

main:781   **Computed egress encap string vlan-10**

main:**519   Egress Ctx Apress:PROD**

main:520   **Egress BD(s): Apress:Backend_BD**

unicast:1957 Leaf-101: Enter dbg_sub_nexthop with cn HEA and inst: eg

unicast:1979 Leaf-101: Enter dbg_sub_nexthop with Local inst: eg infra: False glbs.dipo: 10.11.24.64

unicast:1986 Leaf-101: dbg_sub_nexthop invokes dbg_sub_eg for ptep

unicast:2649 Leaf-101: Enter dbg_sub_eg with cn HEA and inst: eg

unicast:2706 Leaf-101: **Dst EP is local**

unicast:372 Leaf-101: Enter dbg_leaf_local with cn HEA and inst: eg

misc:891 Leaf-101: caller unicast:584 EP if(Eth1/20) same as egr if(Eth1/20)

misc:891 Leaf-101: caller unicast:652 Dst IP is present in HEA L3 tbl

misc:891 Leaf-101: caller unicast:734 RW seg_id:10 in HEA same as EP segid:10

main:1770 dbg_sub_nexthop function returned values on node Leaf-101 done True, nxt_nifs None, nxt_dbg_f_n , nxt_inst , eg_ifs Eth1/20, Vnid: 10

Note   Triaging ACI fabric can take up to several minutes, so be patient after running the command. The result will be worth it.

Switch Port Analyzer

For those interested not only in a single packet trace analysis but also visibility to the whole data plane traffic of your choice, ACI offers a well-known traffic mirroring feature called Switch Port Analyzer (SPAN). SPAN will take all the data (headers with payload) from one or a defined set of source interfaces and copy it to a destination interface, without disrupting the original traffic. Mirroring is completely done in hardware, so it has no effect on device performance. A common SPAN destination endpoint for your customers is some monitoring server with Wireshark installed, a security device like an intrusion detection system (IDS) inspecting the traffic, or specialized SPAN/TAP traffic aggregation solutions.

ACI supports two types of SPAN sessions:

- **Local SPAN**: Source and destination interfaces of SPAN traffic are on a single switch.

- **Encapsulated Remote SPAN (ERSPAN)**: Destination of ERSPAN is not an actual interface, but rather an IP address. The source switch will take all the mirrored traffic and encapsulates it into a generic routing encapsulation (GRE) header. This IP-in-IP tunneling technique enables the delivery of SPAN traffic anywhere in the fabric or even outside of it using L3OUTs.

Additionally, you can differentiate between multiple places where to configure SPAN session in ACI, each with its own specifics:

- **Access SPAN**: Configurable in access policies, providing either local mirroring between two interfaces or ERSPAN to remote IP

  - The SPAN source has to be a leaf host interface where ACI endpoints are connected.

  - The SPANed traffic is in case of need filterable by tenant, application profile, or EPG.

- **Fabric SPAN**: Configurable in fabric policies, with support of ERSPAN only

  - The SPAN source has to be a fabric interface on a leaf or spine switch.

  - The traffic is SPANed with iVXLAN headers and, due to this fact, you can filter it based on VRF or BD (their VNIDs).

- **Tenant SPAN**: Configurable in tenant policies, with support of ERSPAN only

  - The SPAN focuses on mirroring EPG traffic, but without a specific leaf switch or interface definition. APIC will automatically configure individual SPAN sessions around the fabric according to the interface to EPG mappings.

  - No other filtering available

SPAN Configuration

Each SPAN type is configured in the same way, just in different places (access policies, fabric policies, tenant policies). The configuration itself has two components: creating a SPAN destination group and mapping it to the SPAN source group.

To create a SPAN destination in access policies, navigate to **Fabric -> Access Policies -> Policies -> Troubleshooting -> SPAN -> SPAN Destination Groups**. Here you will create an object describing either a single destination interface on a particular leaf switch or an ERSPAN destination IP address connected in the chosen EPG (as shown in Figure 6-31).

Create SPAN Destination Group

Name: Apress_SPANDest

Description: optional

Destination Type: **EPG** | Access Interface

Destination EPG: Apress ∨ | ⊡ | PROD_APP ∨ | Backend_EPG ∨
Tenant | Application Profile | EPG

SPAN Version: Version 1 | **Version 2**

Enforce SPAN Version: ☐

Destination IP: 10.2.2.10

Source IP/Prefix: 10.0.0.0/24

Flow ID: 1

TTL: 64

MTU: 1518

DSCP: Unspecified

Figure 6-31. *Access SPAN destination group configuration*

In the Source IP/Prefix field you can choose from which IP address the ERSPAN traffic will arrive at the destination monitoring station. It doesn't need to be real IP available in ACI. If you enter a prefix (e.g., 10.0.0.0/24), ACI will incorporate into a ERSPAN source IP the Node ID of originating leaf (for Leaf-101, 10.0.0.101).

As the second step, you need to create SPAN source group in **Fabric -> Access Policies -> Policies -> Troubleshooting -> SPAN -> SPAN Source Groups.** There you can configure one or more physical interfaces, PC/vPC interface policy groups, or even individual vPC member ports. Filtering is possible on top of the main object, related to all defined traffic sources or individually per defined source (see Figure 6-32).

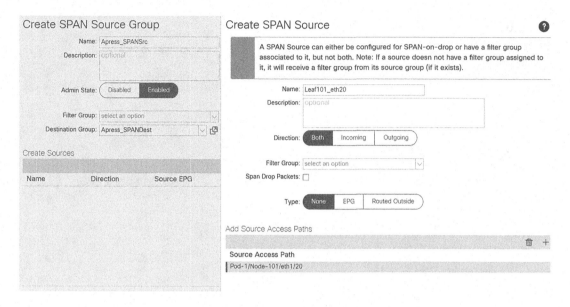

Figure 6-32. *Access SPAN source group configuration*

After submitting the form, SPAN is instantly deployed to the fabric without any additional association needed. In order to verify it happened, you can connect to affected leaf CLI and check the output shown in Listing 6-28.

Listing 6-28. Access ERSPAN Verification

```
Leaf-101# show monitor

Session  State        Reason                          Name
-------  -----------  ----------------------          ----------------------
3        up           active                          Apress_SPANSrc

Leaf-101# show monitor session 3
   session 3
---------------
name            : Apress_SPANSrc
description     : Span session 3
type            : erspan
version         : 2
oper version    : 2
```

```
state                : up (active)
erspan-id            : 1
granularity          :
vrf-name             : Apress:PROD
acl-name             :
ip-ttl               : 64
ip-dscp              : ip-dscp not specified
destination-ip       : 10.2.2.10/32
origin-ip            : 10.0.0.101/24
mode                 : access
Filter Group         : None
source intf          :
    rx               : [Eth1/20]
    tx               : [Eth1/20]
    both             : [Eth1/20]
source VLANs         :
    rx               :
    tx               :
    both             :
filter VLANs         : filter not specified
filter L3Outs        : filter not specified
```

Visibility & Troubleshooting Tool

The last troubleshooting tool I want to mention is the native application **Visibility & Troubleshooting** found under **Operations Tab**. This built-in utility allows an administrator to analyze the flow between two internal or external endpoints. For internal endpoints, the prerequisite is that ACI actually knows about them. They have to be learned somewhere in the fabric (see Figure 6-33).

Figure 6-33. *Visibility & Troubleshooting Tool initiation*

After submitting the form, you will receive a graphical representation of mutual endpoint forwarding with the possibility to analyze traffic statistics, drops, related faults, events, applied contracts, or initiate traceroute between endpoints. All functions are accessible from the left menu (shown in Figure 6-34).

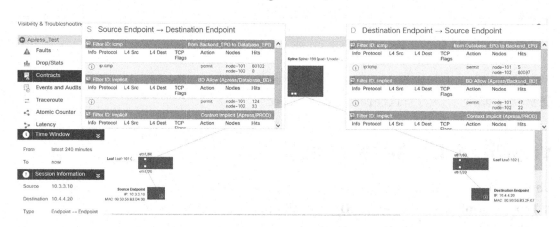

Figure 6-34. *Visibility & Troubleshooting – Forwarding and Contract Analysis*

Interface Drops Analysis

A widespread problem with traffic forwarding is dropped packets, and sometimes it can be quite difficult to troubleshoot the cause of the drops. ACI differentiates between these significant types of drops:

- **Forward Drops**: The counter is increased when the packet is dropped during the initial lookup phase of processing its headers. Multiple reasons can cause forward drops, but especially these:

  - **SECURITY_GROUP_DENY**: There is a missing contract between EPGs for this matched type of traffic.

  - **VLAN_XLATE_MISS**: The incoming frame had invalid VLAN encapsulation. You are either missing some part of an access policy and/or tenant policy causing this interface not to have encapsulation VLAN configured, or the network interface of connected endpoint is not configured properly.

- **Error Drops**: Packets can be discarded due to an invalid or malformed format. They can include frames with invalid FCS or CRC sums.

- **Buffer Drops**: Cisco Nexus 9000 buffers frames exclusively on egress on all interfaces. If there are no buffer credits left for a forwarding, the packet is dropped and the buffer drop counter increases. Buffer drops can be resolved by proper configuration of QoS or they can be caused by incorrect QoS configuration.

To view individual hardware drop counters for Nexus interfaces, you can attach to a special line card shell (vsh_lc) and use the command in Listing 6-29.

Listing 6-29. Nexus 9000 HW Packet Drop Counters

```
Leaf-101# vsh_lc
module-1# show platform internal counters port 20
Stats for port 20
(note: forward drops includes sup redirected packets too)
IF          LPort              Input                     Output
                        Packets      Bytes          Packets      Bytes
eth-1/20    20   Total   53458772   3831638779        946076    125371600
                 Unicast    82427      8736812        944230    125244266
                 Multicast      0            0          1846       127334
                 Flood       5270       366424             0            0
             Total Drops  53371075                          0
```

```
        Storm Drops(bytes)                          0
            Buffer          0                       0
            Error           0                       0
            Forward     53371075
            LB              0
```

Note   These described packet drop reasons can be viewed in ELAM as well for a single packet.

Summary

Understanding forwarding mechanisms with control plane and data plane operations in ACI is a fundamental and highly important aspect of its operation, especially when it comes to troubleshooting of non-working connectivity between distinct endpoints. In this chapter, you had the opportunity to explore all the main forwarding concepts for both bridged and routed unicast traffic, as well as for flooded unknown traffic or ARP operation. You covered intra-fabric forwarding together with Multi-Pod and Multi-Site ACI architectures, all supplemented with wide range of tools and procedures to simplify the forwarding troubleshooting. If you would like to continue further expanding your knowledge in this area, I recommend reading through the Endpoint Learning or Multi-Pod, Multi-Site official Cisco's whitepapers. Each of them is a great study resource.

You probably noticed that this chapter was entirely oriented to the east-west traffic pattern between internal endpoints. In the following chapter, you will start looking at the ways to interact with ACI fabric from external L2 and L3 networks in various scenarios. I will cover a Layer 2 EPG or bridge domain extension for stretching ACI connectivity to a legacy network for a migration purposes, as well as L3OUT objects representing the complete static and dynamic routing configuration of ACI with an external L3 network.

## CHAPTER 7

External Layer 2 and Layer 3 Connectivity

So far, you have learned how to get individual ACI fabrics up and running and how to configure physical underlay as well as overlay policies to understand their forwarding behavior and troubleshooting. All this will ensure east-west communication between internal ACI endpoints. But what about north-south traffic, clients accessing datacenter resources and application services from outside of ACI? You need to provide them with Layer 3 routing with the fabric. Additionally, if ACI is not built on greenfield, you need tools to interconnect the fabric with legacy networking equipment, stretch Layer 2 segments, and progressively migrate all the physical devices, usually followed by L3 default gateways to ACI.

In this chapter, you will have a closer look at the external Layer 2 and Layer 3 ACI connectivity features, coupled with verification, troubleshooting tools, and best practices to avoid potential problems. My goal isn't be to explain the principles or theory behind the discussed L2/L3 protocols, though, but rather to show you how to incorporate them reasonably in ACI.

Layer 2 External Connectivity

Let's start with Layer 2 extension, which is crucial for migration phases of endpoints between a legacy network and ACI. It is often also required for longer coexistence of the ACI fabric and legacy switching infrastructure, considering customer hardware lifecycles. As you can see in Figure 7-1, there are two main approaches:

1. **Extending a bridge domain**: Utilizing the new ACI construct L2OUT and enclosing external endpoints to dedicated external EPG

315

© Jan Janovic 2023
J. Janovic, *Cisco ACI: Zero to Hero*, https://doi.org/10.1007/978-1-4842-8838-2_7

2. **Extending an Endpoint Group**: Mapping external endpoints to the existing EPG together with internal endpoints

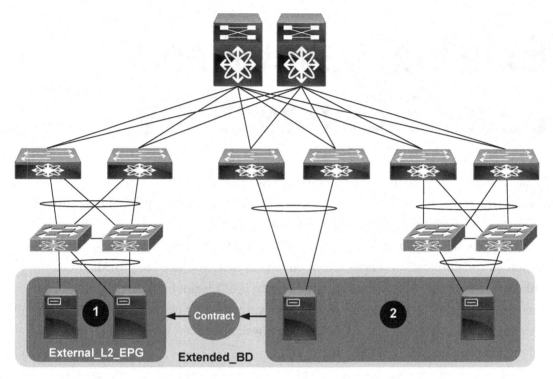

Figure 7-1. *External Layer 2 extension*

Both variants have their pros and cons, but the end goal is ultimately the same: to provide adequate connectivity based on ACI policies for internal as well as external endpoints. In the following sections, I will describe and compare both of them. Configuration of Layer 2 extensions is completely abstracted from the underlay ACI network, so you can use any approach, even combined with later-described external L3 routing over the same physical interfaces.

Bridge Domain Extension

If your intention is to strictly differentiate and separate all external endpoints from other ACI resources, extending a bridge domain can be a potential way to go for you. This feature is based on dedicated tenant object L2OUT, carrying VLAN mappings to individual fabric interfaces. Each L2OUT represents single a VLAN in a legacy network, isolating all resources communicating in it to a new external L2 EPG (as shown in Figure 7-2).

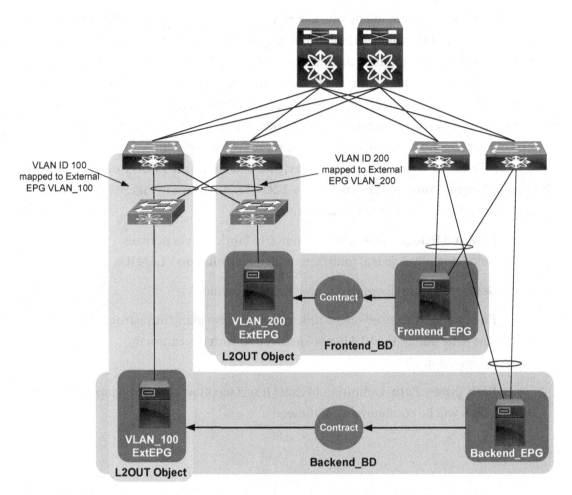

Figure 7-2. *Extending ACI bridge domains using L2OUT objects*

From a tenant policies point of view, this L2 external EPG is no different compared to a standard EPG. It has its own pcTag and all contained endpoints must meet zoning rule definitions from the contract in order to communicate outside of their EPG.

The similarity continues to how the external L2 EPG consumes physical fabric resources. Standard EPGs need to have some physical domain associated with them to gain access to physical interfaces and encapsulation VLAN IDs. For L2OUT you need to create special *external bridged domain* found in the same place as the physical domains in the *fabric access policies* discussed in Chapter 4. The rest of the access policies remains the same; the external bridged domain is mapped to a static VLAN pool and AAEP of your choice, listing the interfaces used for legacy network interconnection.

Finally, for bridge domain extension, navigate and create the L2OUT object in **Tenants -> Tenant_Name -> Networking -> L2OUTs.** As shown in Figure 7-3, besides the name, mandatory information includes:

- **External Bridged Domain**: Reference to fabric access policies, unlocking physical leaf interfaces with encapsulation VLAN IDs

- **Bridge Domain**: Extended tenant bridge domain

- **Encap**: VLAN ID used on a trunk to legacy networking infrastructure. Has to be part of the VLAN pool associated with the external bridged domain.

- **Path Type + Path**: Definition of exact interface(s) where the Encap VLAN will be configured and allowed

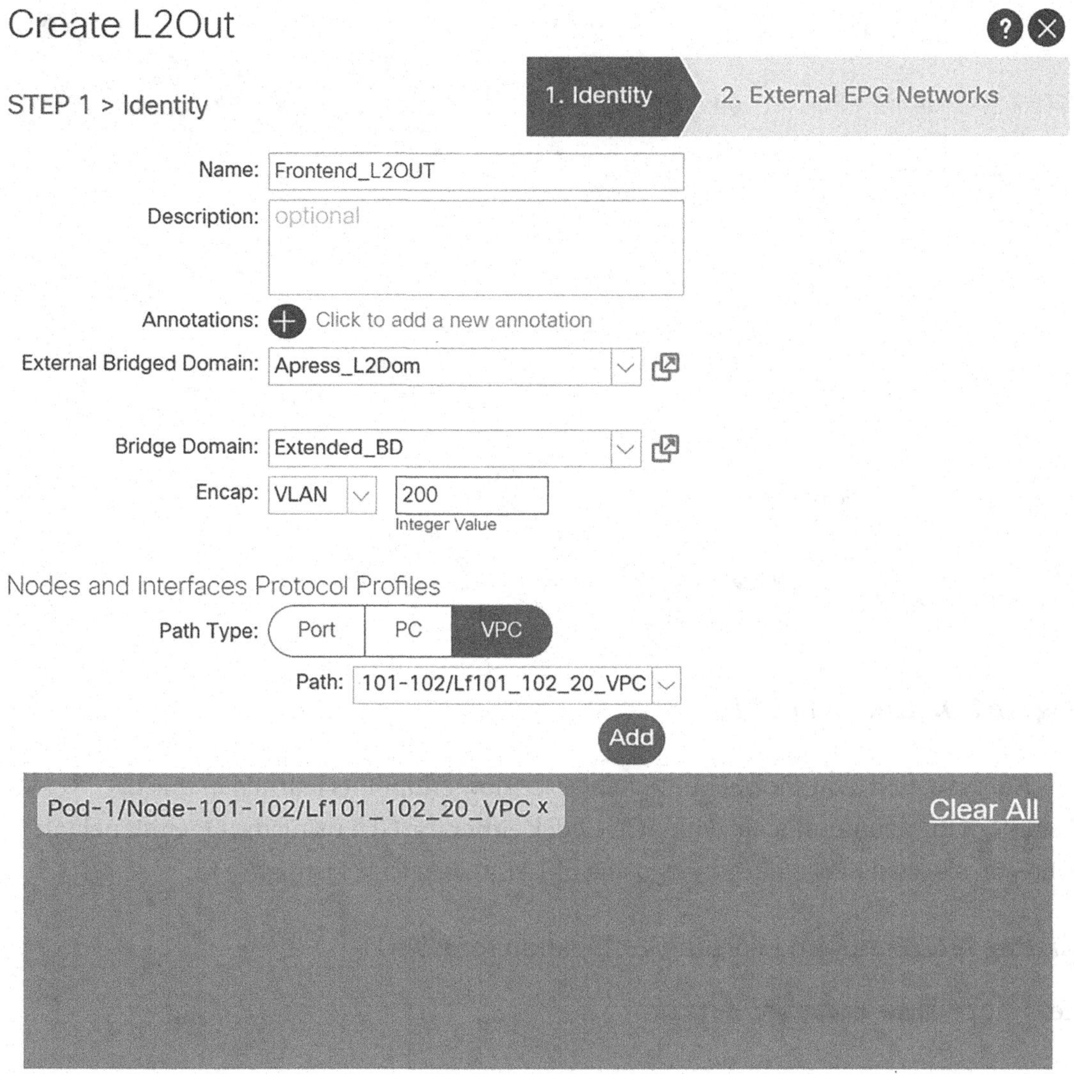

Create L2Out

STEP 1 > Identity

| 1. Identity | 2. External EPG Networks |

Name: Frontend_L2OUT

Description: optional

Annotations: ⊕ Click to add a new annotation

External Bridged Domain: Apress_L2Dom

Bridge Domain: Extended_BD

Encap: VLAN ∨   200
Integer Value

Nodes and Interfaces Protocol Profiles

Path Type: (Port   PC   **VPC**)

Path: 101-102/Lf101_102_20_VPC ∨

Add

Pod-1/Node-101-102/Lf101_102_20_VPC ×   Clear All

Figure 7-3. Creating L2OUT objects

On the second page of the L2OUT configuration form, you must create at least one external EPG with optional settings allowing to change its QoS class or put it to a preferred group in its VRF (see Figure 7-4).

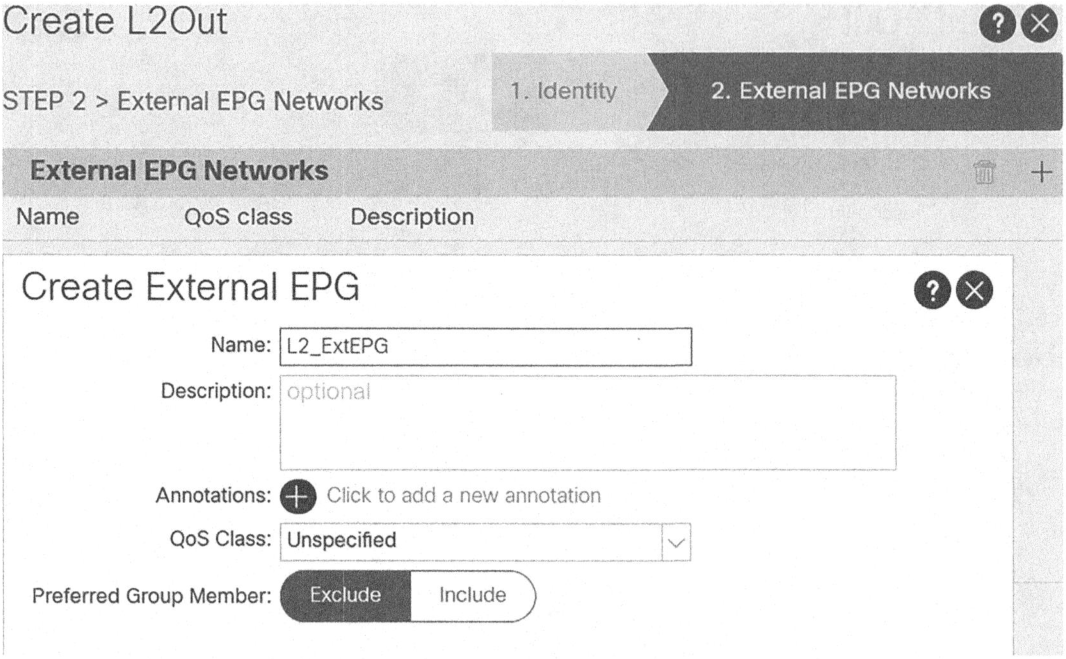

Create L2Out

STEP 2 > External EPG Networks   1. Identity   2. External EPG Networks

External EPG Networks

| Name | QoS class | Description |

Create External EPG

Name: L2_ExtEPG

Description: optional

Annotations: ➕ Click to add a new annotation

QoS Class: Unspecified

Preferred Group Member: **Exclude** | Include

Figure 7-4. External L2 EPG

After creation, you should immediately see new endpoints learned in this **L2_ExtEPG** if they communicate with ACI. Check either the GUI using the Operational tab when on external EPG object, or by using the APIC/leaf CLI (Listing 7-1).

Listing 7-1. Endpoint Learning Verification for L2OUT

Leaf-102# **show endpoint detail**

```
+-----------+---------+-----------------+-----------+-----------+--------+
    VLAN/     Encap     MAC Address       MAC
Info/   Interface    Endpoint Group
   Domain     VLAN      IP Address      IP Info                  Info
+-----------+---------+-----------------+-----------+-----------+--------+
22          vlan-200   0050.56b3.362b L              eth1/20
Apress:Frontend_L2OUT:L2_ExtEPG
Apress:PROD  vlan-200      10.0.200.30 L              eth1/20
```

By default, these external endpoints will have the connectivity only to the ACI BD gateway (if configured and the extended BD has Unicast Routing enabled). Therefore, the final step in the process is to associate a contract with an external EPG and connect it to internal resources, defining application profiles as shown in Figure 7-5.

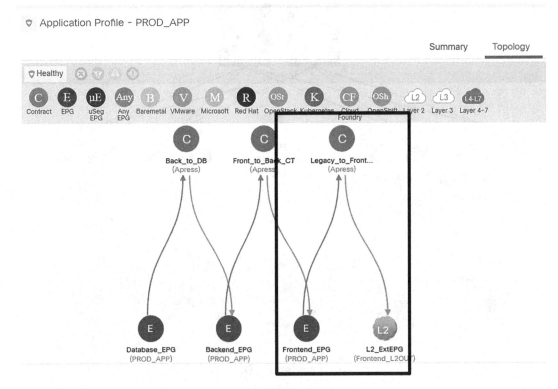

Figure 7-5. *Application profile including L2OUT*

Even though this L2 extension approach is fully supported and functional, due to multiple required configuration steps and unnecessary complexity, it actually hasn't gained so much popularity when connecting ACI to a legacy network. The unambiguous winner is the next option: the EPG extension.

Endpoint Group Extension

In Chapter 5, you learned how to create static interface mappings to EPG for internal endpoints connected to the ACI fabric. Actually, in the same way, you can easily include external endpoints as well. Just this time they won't be connected directly to a leaf switch but rather behind some external legacy switch. By extending EPG, we mean just extending the legacy VLAN to ACI; statically mapping it to EPG (as shown in Figure 7-6). ACI will without any additional configuration apply exactly the same connectivity policies for external endpoints as defined in the application profile for the main EPG.

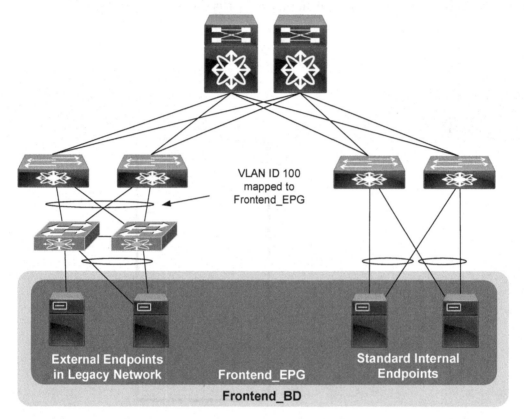

Figure 7-6. *Extending the internal EPG*

External endpoints benefit from this approach especially during brownfield migrations to ACI. You are able to stretch all the legacy VLAN segments to ACI EPGs and then gradually relocate the hardware resources without logically changing their network connectivity. The default gateway can in the first phase still remains in the legacy world (the ACI bridge domain only L2 bridging the traffic), and when the majority of endpoints are migrated to ACI, you shift their gateway as well (by enabling the Unicast Routing on the BD).

Thanks to its simplicity, I highly recommend EPG extension as a primary tool to achieve Layer 2 external connectivity in ACI. It's been repeatedly proven in our customer environments as well.

Spanning Tree Protocol and ACI

With Layer 2 forwarding between switches, there comes the infamous topic of the Spanning Tree Protocol. STP in all its forms (original 802.1d, RSTP 802.1w, or Multiple STP 802.1s) has one goal: mitigation of switching loops and broadcast storms, ultimately avoiding network outages in common Layer 2 broadcast domains. By exchanging bridge protocol data units (BPDUs) and following the given decision process, switches elect "STP Root Bridge" and calculate a loop-free path from it by blocking some of the interfaces that would otherwise create an issue.

STP is a must for all legacy networks, but on the other hand we want to avoid its drawbacks as much as possible in modern architectures, including ACI. So how to make these two worlds to coexist? In following paragraphs, I will cover the main characteristics and best practices when it comes to stretching an STP domain (with each Layer 2 extension) to ACI.

Extending STP Domain to ACI

First of all, it needs to be said: **ACI switches do not** influence nor **participate in Spanning Tree topology** at all. Even though they don't generate any STP BPDUs, **ACI leaves are capable of flooding BPDUs within EPG in the same VLAN** in which they were received. This flooding behavior differs from all other control plane and routing protocols (ARP/GARP, EIGRP, OSPF, BGP, PIM, etc.), which are flooded in BD instead.

ACI basically acts as a hub or directly attached cable between two external switches if their interfaces are mapped to the same EPG in the same VLAN. Flooding of STP BPDUs over the ACI fabric is achieved by dedicating a special VXLAN VNID for each external encapsulation configured on leaf switch interfaces. The calculation of VNID is additionally tied with a common physical domain object and VLAN pool from access policies using the following formula:

`EPG Encap VXLAN VNID = Base + (encap_id - from_encap)`

where `Base` is a unique value chosen for each physical domain and VLAN pool encap block in it, `encap_id` represents actually used VLAN ID on the physical interfaces, and `from_encap` is the lowest VLAN ID of the encap block in the associated VLAN pool. You can check actual values used for calculation by querying `stpAllocEncapBlkDef` objects on each leaf switch. See Listing 7-2.

Listing 7-2. VLAN Pool Encap Blocks Relation to STP

```
Leaf-101# moquery -c stpAllocEncapBlkDef
Total Objects shown: 1

# stp.AllocEncapBlkDef
encapBlk     : uni/infra/vlanns-[Apress_StVLAN]-static/from-[vlan-90]-to-
[vlan-110]
base         : 8292
childAction  :
descr        :
dn           : allocencap-[uni/infra]/encapnsdef-[uni/infra/vlanns-[Apress_
StVLAN]-static]/allocencapblkdef-[uni/infra/vlanns-[Apress_StVLAN]-static/
from-[vlan-90]-to-[vlan-110]]
from         : vlan-90
to           : vlan-110
```

If you, for example, deploy VLAN 100 from above the VLAN pool encap block, the resulting VNID for BPDU flooding would be 8292 + (100 – 90) = **8302**. The CLI command in Listing 7-3 can confirm the VNIDs. Both VNID for BD forwarding as well as EPG flooding in encapsulation are listed there:

Listing 7-3. VXLAN VNIDs Configured on Leaf Switch

```
Leaf-101# show system internal epm vlan all
```

VLAN ID	Type	Access Encap (Type Value)	Fabric Encap	H/W id	BD VLAN	Endpoint Count
14	Infra BD 802.1Q	3967	16777209	25	14	1
21	Tenant BD NONE	0	16744308	32	21	0
22	FD vlan 802.1Q	62	8694	33	21	2
26	**Tenant BD NONE**	**0**	**16023499**	**34**	**26**	**0**
27	**FD vlan 802.1Q**	**100**	**8302**	**35**	**26**	**1**
29	FD vlan 802.1Q	10	8392	27	15	2
30	FD vlan 802.1Q	9	8292	29	17	1

Summed and wrapped, when two leaves (or pairs of leaves) are supposed to flood STP BPDUs, their interfaces have to

- Be part of the same physical domain using the same VLAN pool.

- Use the same on wire encapsulation.

- Be mapped to the same EPG.

The outcome can be seen in Figure 7-7. Flooded BPDUs through ACI between multiple physical interfaces in the same VLAN and EPG causes external switch participating in STP to block its interface(s), effectively mitigating a Layer 2 loop and following the broadcast storm.

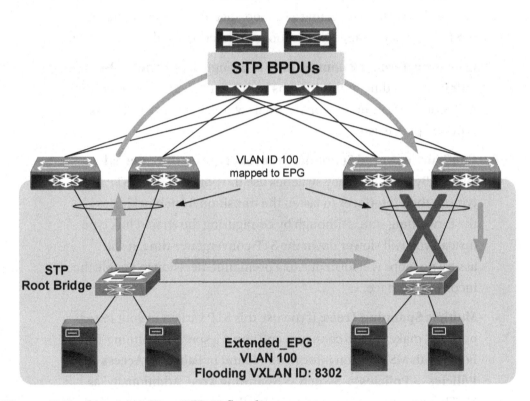

Figure 7-7. *Spanning Tree BPDU flooding*

Interface blocking is always a task for an external switch. ACI will never block its interface due to STP. Therefore, make sure your legacy network devices are configured correctly and optimally to minimize the potential for any unintended switching loop.

Best Practices for STP-Related Configuration

By following a few recommendations offered directly from Cisco or based on ACI user experience, you can significantly harden and stabilize your DC infrastructure during either migration to ACI or longer co-existence with the legacy network:

- **Enable MCP on external L2 interfaces**: The ACI-specific protocol from previous chapters, with the ability to error-disable the interface if its own packet is seen, indicating a L2 loop. Includes also counters related to STP Topology Change Notifications as described in the next section.

- **Connect external L2 domain only to a single leaf switch (vPC pair)**: Try avoiding multiple paths between the legacy network and ACI. Configure interfaces on external switches as PortFast (trunk) if only one path exists.

- **Configure a shared Spanning Tree link type on the external switch**: By default, legacy switches use the point-to-point STP link type on their interfaces to fasten the transition from blocking to the forwarding state. Although by configuring the shared link type instead you will slower down the STP convergence time, it will assure no loops will form due to a premature decision to enable the incorrect interface.

- **Multiple Spanning Trees**: If you use this STP variant in your legacy network, make sure to configure and apply a special Spanning Tree Policy with MST Region information found in **Fabric -> Access Policies -> Policies -> Switch -> Spanning Tree**. Additionally, as MSTP sends BPDUs in native VLAN without any tag, create a "native EPG" for them in order to correctly flood them through the ACI fabric.

- **Keep your Topology Change Notifications low**: Try to minimize number of TCN BPDUs in your network to avoid constant flushing of forwarding information from both legacy and ACI tables. More info is coming in the following section.

Topology Change Notification (TCNs)

Even though not participating in STP, ACI reacts to received *STP Topology Change Notifications (TCNs)*. Comparable to legacy switches, it will flush all endpoints in particular EPG where TCN was received. This can potentially cause intermittent connectivity outages in ACI, negatively affecting the datacenter applications.

The number of TCNs for each encap VLAN can be observed thanks to the MCP protocol (another reason why it is recommended to always enable it on physical access interfaces) using the show commands in Listing 7-4.

Listing 7-4. STP TCN Verification

```
Leaf-101# show mcp internal info vlan
Vlan Table
--------------------------------------------------------------
PI VLAN    Encap VLAN      |  PI VLAN    Encap VLAN
--------------------------------------------------------------
14         3967               27         100
22         62                 30         9
20         11

Leaf-101# show mcp internal info vlan 100
-------------------------------------------------------
             PI VLAN: 27 Up
         Encap VLAN: 100
      PVRSTP TC Count: 4
        RSTP TC Count: 0
Last TC flush at Wed Apr 27 17:03:51 2022
 on port-channel5
```

The interface shown in the above output can either point to a local access port or bridge domain SVI. In the second case, it means the last TCN was flooded within EPG from another leaf switch, and to find its source, you should look further around the fabric.

In general, your goal should be to minimize as much as possible the number of TCNs by implementing the following countermeasures:

- All access interfaces in the legacy network not connected to another switch should have BPDU Guard and PortFast features enabled. A change in their state will not generate a TCN then.

- Use (vPC) port-channeling whenever possible. Instead of generating a TCN for each physical interface state change, the port channel interface remains up even when a single member port fails.

- Permit only really used VLANs on trunk interfaces; map only really used VLANs to EPGs.

- Keep the number of legacy switches connected to ACI to a minimum needed.

Be Aware of Overlapping VLANs!

Due to ACI's multi-tenant nature, you can eventually end up in a situation where either one or multiple of your tenants want to use the same VLAN ranges on access interfaces of the same leaf switches.

Fortunately, ACI, thanks to its flexibility, actually allow you to do so. By default, each VLAN used on a particular leaf switch interface is considered to be global. You cannot use it for multiple EPG associations on one switch. However, there is an Interface Protocol Policy object named *L2 Interface*, found in **Fabric -> Access Policies -> Policies -> Interface -> L2 Interface**, where you can change the VLAN significance from *Global* to *Port Local* (as shown in Figure 7-8).

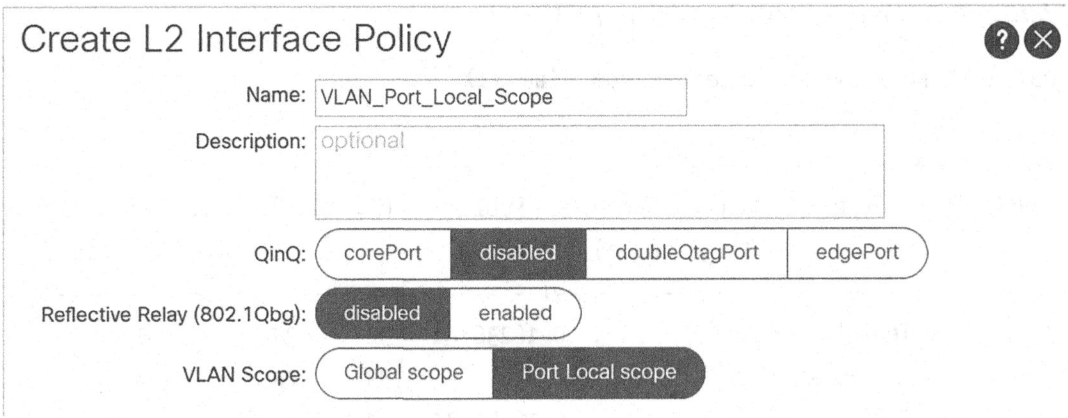

Create L2 Interface Policy

Name: VLAN_Port_Local_Scope

Description: optional

QinQ: (corePort | disabled | doubleQtagPort | edgePort)

Reflective Relay (802.1Qbg): (disabled | enabled)

VLAN Scope: (Global scope | Port Local scope)

Figure 7-8. *Port local VLAN scope*

After applying this policy through the interface policy group, all VLANs mapped to a particular leaf interface can be reused for other interfaces as well. ACI will remap each overlapping VLAN to different internal VLAN in order to differentiate between them. Moreover, for this function to work, you have to separate interfaces into a different physical (or virtual) domain with their dedicated VLAN pools carrying overlapping VLANs. This is no problem and is supported for internal ACI endpoints. The issue can arise when combining overlapping VLANs with external L2 extensions, mainly if they consist of multiple external switches.

Imagine having two pair of vPC leaves, as depicted in Figure 7-9. Just this time, multiple tenants are connected with their own L2 switches to them, both extending VLAN 100. It will result in multiple physical domains configured on the same switches with the same VLAN 100 encap block in associated VLAN pools. After configuring Layer 2 extension for these particular EPGs, you would find consistent VXLAN ID information on all leaf switches. See Listing 7-5.

Listing 7-5. Overlapping VLANs in ACI

```
Leaf-101# show system internal epm vlan all
```

VLAN ID	Type	Access Encap (Type Value)	Fabric Encap	H/W id	BD VLAN	Endpoint Count
24	Tenant BD	NONE	0 16236241	32	24	0
25	FD vlan	802.1Q	100 8302	33	24	2
26	Tenant BD	NONE	0 16991234	34	26	0
27	FD vlan	802.1Q	100 8634	35	26	1

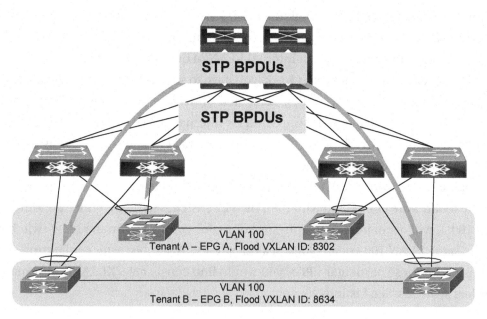

Figure 7-9. *Overlapping VLANs when extending L2*

However, as soon as you upgrade (or wipe) one vPC pair, due to overlapping VLAN pools and different physical domains, ACI can configure different base values for their encap blocks. This results in different VXLAN VNIDs, tearing apart BPDU flooding in EPGs and ultimately causing a bridging loop because external switches won't block their interfaces without receiving BPDUs (see Figure 7-10).

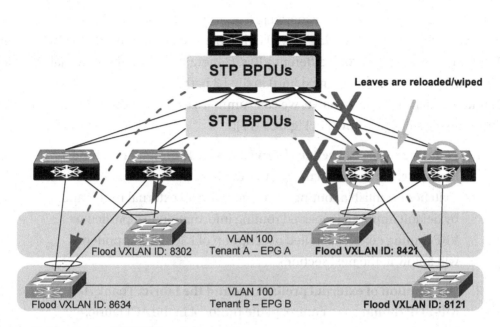

Figure 7-10. *Teared EPG flood domain*

Personally, I recommend completely avoiding the described scenario; if multiple customer use overlapping VLAN pools, dedicate a different pair of leaf switches to each of them.

Layer 3 External Connectivity

Layer 2 VLAN extension plays an important role during migrations or ACI co-existence with legacy networks, but considering the north-south traffic pattern, without external Layer 3 routing to other network modules like WAN or Internet, we wouldn't be able to deliver any datacenter application to our clients. I will dedicate the rest of this chapter to the no-less-important tenant policies object *L3OUT* (and its related topics).

ACI utilizes the VRF-lite approach for external Layer 3 connectivity. Each VRF requires at least one L3OUT object, carrying specific routing protocol configuration, interface level configuration, and external L3 EPG definitions. As an L3 interface you can use a single physical leaf interface, subinterfaces, or SVI VLAN interfaces. It's not a problem to share the same physical interfaces for multiple L3OUTs (VRFs); they just need to be separated on a VLAN level (using SVIs or subinterfaces).

At the beginning, ACI was considered just as a stub network, but long since (version 1.1), we can achieve transit routing as well either between multiple L3OUTs in the same VRF, or by route-leaking among different VRFs. Generally, consider the ACI fabric as a single distributed router (single next hop) in the L3 path.

From the high-level perspective, we can summarize external Layer 3 routing in ACI to the following steps (as shown in Figure 7-11):

1. **Learning external prefixes from L3 devices connected behind leaf switches**: Based on the L3OUT configuration, border leaf switches establish a routing adjacency with an external router and by default import all received routing information to a particular VRF routing table. A detailed description of L3OUT components will follow in the next sections.

2. **Distribution of external prefixes around the fabric**: Thanks to MP-BGP running as a control plane protocol in the ACI fabric, border leaves can redistribute external prefixes to the MP-BGP database and send them via spines (route reflectors) in VPNv4/v6 address families to other internal leaves.

3. **Advertise BD subnets to the external network**: In order to reach internal ACI prefixes represented by bridge domain subnets, leaves need to vice versa advertise them to border leaves where L3OUTs are configured, and they will redistribute the prefix information to external routing protocols.

4. **Create traffic zoning rules using contracts**: Propagation of routing information itself is not enough to provide actual connectivity between endpoints. The L3OUT object defines a new external L3 EPG and, following the already discussed ACI application policy model, contracts will be needed to permit the traffic. Instead of individual /32 endpoints, the affiliation to L3 EPG is defined using the whole IP ranges (subnets).

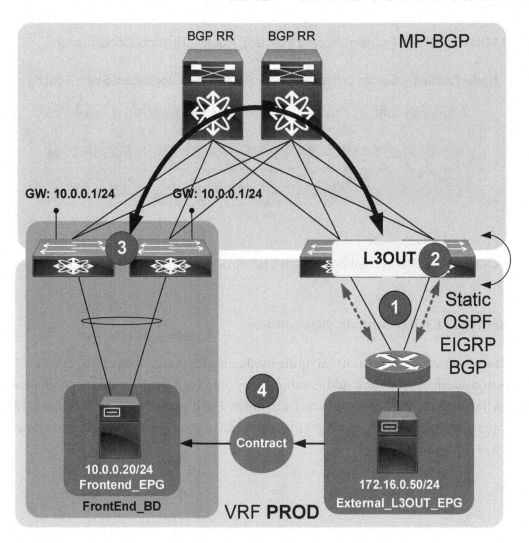

Figure 7-11. *ACI Layer 3 external routing concept*

I will now go through each area in more detail and focus on the configuration and troubleshooting aspects of interaction between ACI and the external L3 world.

Main L3OUT Components

The L3OUT object represents a configuration container for provisioning L3 interfaces, routing protocols and external EPGs on defined border leaf switches. Internally, it has a hierarchical structure consisting of multiple child levels and objects shown in Figure 7-12.

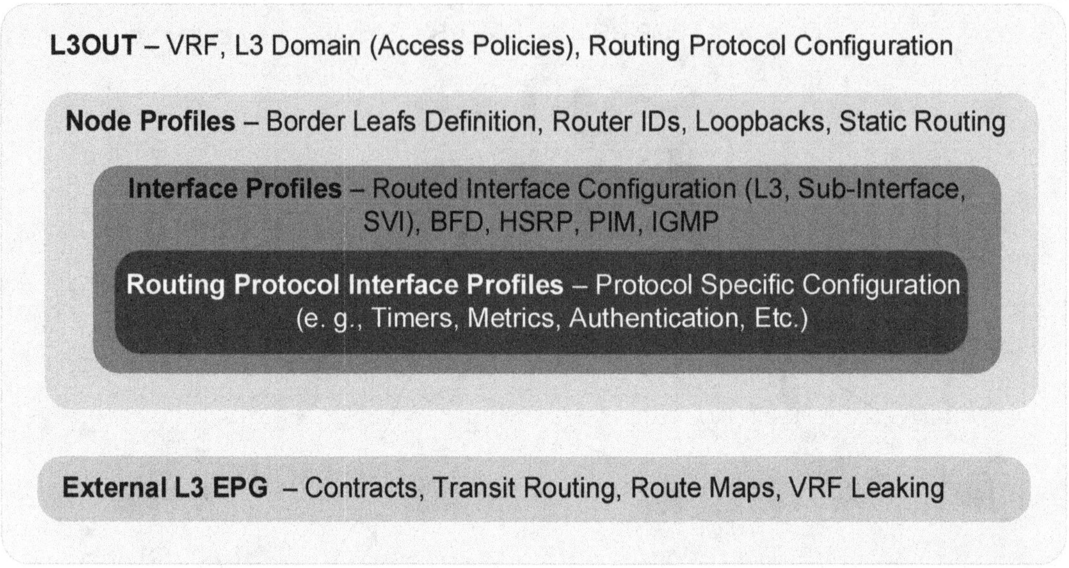

L3OUT – VRF, L3 Domain (Access Policies), Routing Protocol Configuration

Node Profiles – Border Leafs Definition, Router IDs, Loopbacks, Static Routing

Interface Profiles – Routed Interface Configuration (L3, Sub-Interface, SVI), BFD, HSRP, PIM, IGMP

Routing Protocol Interface Profiles – Protocol Specific Configuration (e. g., Timers, Metrics, Authentication, Etc.)

External L3 EPG – Contracts, Transit Routing, Route Maps, VRF Leaking

Figure 7-12. *L3OUT components overview*

The object structure is (as usual) quite modular, with multiple design options I will cover in subsequent sections. Additionally, in my opinion it's convenient to familiarize yourself with the L3OUT object hierarchy in the ACI GUI as well (shown in Figure 7-13). ACI operations often include changes in external L3 routing, so it's important to know your way around.

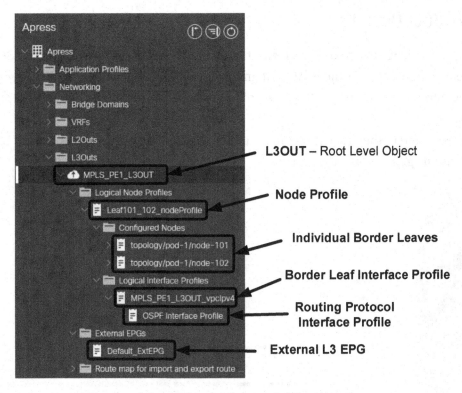

Figure 7-13. *L3OUT components overview in the ACI GUI*

At the end of the day, your ultimate goal with L3OUTs will be to completely describe external L3 connectivity needs for mutual exchange of routing prefixes and ensure the connectivity rules enforcement between external and internal ACI resources. Let's have a closer look at what configuration options L3OUT offers.

L3OUT Related Access Policies

First of all, before connecting any L3 device to ACI, which is meant to peer with leaf switches using L3OUT, you need to prepare access policies for it. Generally, their object structure is almost the same as for any other use case, just instead of the standard physical domain you have to associate a VLAN pool and AAEP to a special L3 domain object (found at **Fabric -> Access Policies -> Physical and External Domain -> L3 Domains**). External L3 connectivity can then be configured using all types of interface policy groups: access (single individual interface), port channel, or VPC.

L3OUT Root Object

With access policies in place, go to **Tenants -> Tenant_name -> Networking -> L3Outs** and create a new L3OUT object. ACI will invoke a configuration wizard assisting you with the initial configuration. All created objects in wizard are editable later (except for their names).

The first step in the process, as illustrated on Figure 7-14, will create the main L3OUT object with its global configuration.

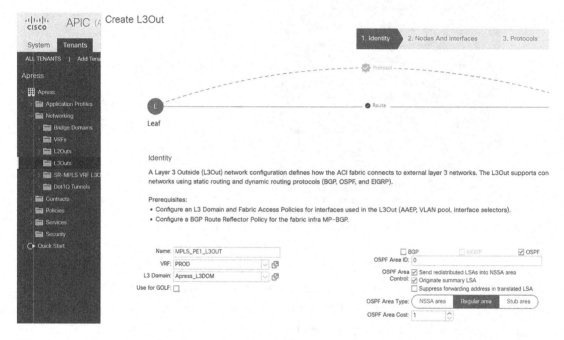

Figure 7-14. *L3OUT configuration wizard – L3OUT root object*

Take into account that this initial wizard actually won't show you all the options available for configuring a particular object, just the most important fields. For the entire configuration, you need to return manually to the L3OUT hierarchy after submitting the wizard form. I will start with an overview of the mandatory and global configuration fields in the wizard for a root L3OUT object:

- **Name:** I find useful to include a name (in some form) of the external L3 device in the L3OUT name. If you have more than one L3OUT per VRF, you can easily differentiate what external connectivity they provide based on their names.

- **VRF**: Related routing context for which this L3OUT will provide external connectivity

- **L3 Domain**: Reference to access policies, providing access to physical leaf interfaces and VLAN encapsulation

- **Routing Protocol**: Dynamic routing protocol to be enabled on specified leaf nodes and their interfaces. Generally, you can use only single protocol per L3OUT (OSPF, EIGRP, BGP), with the exception of the BGP+OSPF combination. OSPF can ensure prefix exchange to reach BGP peering IPs. Each protocol has different global configuration options available at this L3OUT root level and I will describe them later in the respective protocol section.

From the additional options available when navigating to the main L3OUT object after finishing the wizard, these are the most important worth mentioning (shown in Figure 7-15):

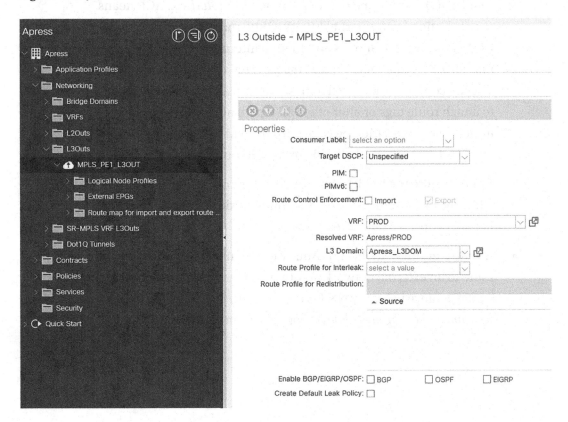

Figure 7-15. *Additional L3OUT object configuration*

- **PIM**: In general, multicast routing with all its components is being configured at the VRF level, where you can also enable it for L3OUTs. That will automatically check this configuration box. Optionally, you can enable/disable it here as well with the same result.

- **Route Control Enforcement**: By default, L3OUT unlimitedly learns all the prefixes from external routers in the inbound direction but won't propagate any internal information outbound without further explicit configuration. This behavior is influenced by this Route Control Enforcement setting. If inbound filtering is needed as well, check the import option here.

- **Route Profile for Interleak**: Later in this chapter I will cover how to create custom route maps (in ACI terminology, route profiles) to manipulate routing information attributes. There are multiple places where they can be attached, and the interleak route profile at root L3OUT level is one of them. By the term *interleak*, ACI means redistribution from external EIGRP/OSPF routing protocols to BGP IPv4/IPv6 address families and then to internal MP-BGP (BGP is not influenced by this route map as the external routing information directly comes to the BGP database). Interleak is especially useful to attach route tags or alter other BGP path attributes during prefix import, which can then be transported via MP-BGP to another leaf and used for outbound filtering or transit routing.

- **Route Profile for Redistribution**: Another route map, this time allowing you to redistribute static routes or directly connected networks on a particular leaf switch

- **Create Default Leak Policy**: Ability to originate and send a default route to an external network pointing at ACI. The same behavior you would achieve in legacy NX-OS (IOS) devices by using the *default-information originate (always)* configuration command.

Logical Node and Interface Profiles

As you proceed to the second step of the L3OUT configuration wizard, it expects a path definition and L3 configuration of leaf interfaces (as shown in Figure 7-16). The main goal is to define the L3 interconnection between external router and ACI leaves.

Figure 7-16. *L3OUT configuration wizard – node and interface profiles*

In the end, the provided information in this step will transform into logical node profiles and related interface profiles. The main configuration options include

- **Name**: With by default checked option "Use Defaults", the name of the node profile will consist of <L3OUT_Name>_NodeProfile. I prefer to uncheck this option and use LeafXXX_XXX_NodeProfile to later instantly identify which leaf this L3OUT is configured to, even before opening the node profile itself.

- **Interface Types**: Here you can choose either an individual interface, subinterface, or SVI from a L3 configuration point of view, in combination with an L2 interface type referring to access policies. The L3 interface can be configured on top of a single physical interface (leaf access policy group), standard port channel (PC interface policy group), or vPC port channel (vPC interface policy group).

- **Address Type:** IPv4, IPv6, or both (dual stack)

- **Path**: Based on the previously chosen interface type, you will have to specify the path to leaf nodes as well as their interfaces. Either exactly by choosing Nodes IDs and Interface IDs, or they will be resolved automatically from selected interface policy group. There is a + sign for both nodes and interfaces, allowing you to configure multiple objects using the same form (with the exception of vPC SVI, where the wizard allows to configure only single pair or vPC switches).

- **Router ID & Loopback Address**: Especially for dynamic routing protocols it's important that each router has unique Router ID to ensure correct information exchange and loop-free path calculation. By specifying the Router ID in ACI, a loopback with corresponding IP will be automatically created as well (it can be used, for example, to establish BGP peerings). The scoopback address is not mandatory, though, so feel free to remove its address if you don't plan to use it. Later on, it will be configurable back.

- **VLAN Encap**: L3 interface VLAN for SVIs and subinterfaces. Has to be included in the VLAN pool associated with the L3 domain for this L3OUT.

- **IP Address**: L3 interface address. Usually it's a single IP; just in case of SVI vPC port channel combination, ACI allows you to configure primary and secondary addresses for both vPC peers. While the primary address is always unique, the secondary one can be shared between vPC leaves and act similar to VIP in HSRP for redundant static routing.

- **MTU**: Even though it may seem insignificant, MTU plays an important role (besides the data plane itself) for correct OSPF adjacency establishment or BGP database exchange. When ACI by default indicates "inherit" MTU in the L3OUT configuration, it means actually the default fabric MTU 9000B. If the external device uses standard 1500B, make sure to specify it here explicitly.

When dealing with node and interface profiles, there are multiple supported design options, all deployed in the same way to the fabric switches (see Figure 7-17). The L3OUT wizard, regardless of the number of leaves specified or interfaces configured for each leaf, will end up creating the first variant shown: a single node profile incorporating all leaves with a single interface profile describing all user interfaces. Alternatively, you could create a single node profile but separate interface profiles (second option), or completely isolate both nodes as well as interfaces to their own profile objects (third option).

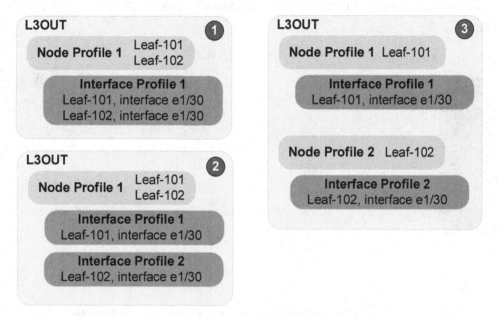

Figure 7-17. *L3OUT node and interface profile design options*

Personally, I prefer a combination of the first and third options. For vPC pairs, I usually create single node and interface profiles, supporting the fact that these two switches are related and so is their configuration. For all other individual L3 interfaces, I go for the third option.

Note   If using dual-stack IPv4 and IPv6 on the same interfaces, both protocols will need separated interface profiles.

Routing Protocol Interface Profile

Moving forward to the third step of the L3OUT wizard, you are able to alter the
configuration of dynamic routing protocols for particular interfaces (if you selected some
routing protocol at the beginning). As shown in Figure 7-18, the interface profile (policy)
object substitutes commands you would otherwise apply to the L3 interface in the
legacy NX-OS world for routing protocols. The set of options varies between individual
protocols, and I will cover them later in detail, but generally these settings relate to
authentication, timers, metric manipulation, network types, or other protocol-specific
functions.

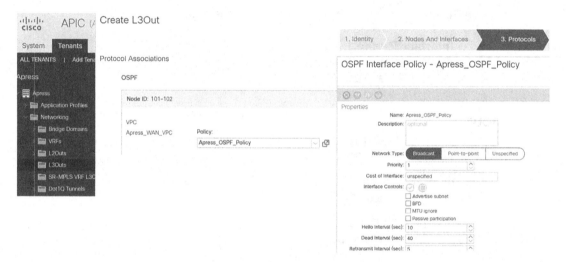

***Figure 7-18.** L3OUT configuration wizard – routing protocol interface profile*

External EPG

The last section in the L3OUT wizard brings us to the crucial object for external
connectivity, the external EPG (see Figure 7-19). For simplicity, the wizard allows you
to create only single EPG, and when you leave the option *Default EPG for all external
networks* checked, any external IP address communicating via this L3OUT will be
considered as a part of this EPG.

Figure 7-19. *L3OUT configuration wizard – external EPG*

Like any other EPG, to permit communication in and out, you have to apply standard
application contracts to it. As shown in Figure 7-20, each external EPG receives its own
pcTag (or sClass); you can enable intra-EPG isolation or include it in a VRF preferred
group. External EPGs are also part of vzAny group in the parent VRF, together with all
standard internal EPGs.

Figure 7-20. *External EPG configuration*

But how can ACI classify the external endpoints to EPG and differentiate between
various external EPGs in the same L3OUT or even between multiple L3OUTs? The
mechanism here is slightly different from a standard application EPG. Instead of
relying on VLAN and interface mappings, you need to define *subnets* (with their
scope set by default to *External Subnets for the External EPG*). Be aware, for endpoint

classification, the term "subnet" doesn't relate to actual prefixes learned via L3OUT. A subnet is perceived more like a range of IP addresses. Even if you receive the default route 0.0.0.0/0 from external router, a subnet can be used in more specific range (e.g., 192.168.0.0/16). All endpoints within a defined subnet are logically a part of a given external EPG with related contracts applied to their communication. If multiple subnets contain the source/destination IP address of the packet being forwarded, Longest Prefix Match (LPM) is used; the external EPG with the most specific subnet will be matched for contract policy enforcement. Subnet scope is VRF (not L3OUT), so you can't have the same subnet defined in multiple L3OUTs within the same VRF.

If you do not intend to differentiate between external endpoints, often for clarity (like in this example), you can create a single subnet entry with 0.0.0.0/0, representing "any" IP address. It can also serve as a last resort if the forwarding process hasn't found any other more specific subnet matching the forwarded packet addresses.

From endpoint learning and forwarding point of view, it wouldn't be feasible or scalable for leaves to learn tens of thousands of external /32 IP endpoints. Therefore, ACI, when forwarding traffic to L3OUT, completely relies on IP prefixes received from an external source and it just learns related next hops and their MAC addresses using ARP. It's the same as in a traditional L3 network. If the destination IP of the forwarded packets is not learned in a leaf's internal endpoint table and it cannot find a pervasive gateway subnet there, the last option can be a standard routing table lookup for external routing information (as shown in the forwarding decision diagrams in Chapter 6).

L3OUT Subnet Scope

Besides the most important external endpoint classification, the L3OUT subnet object in an external EPG has many more purposes. Figure 7-21 illustrates its creation form, where you can notice various Route Control and External EPG Classification checkboxes. I will dedicate following sections to their more detailed description as they can play significant role in achieving expected external connectivity.

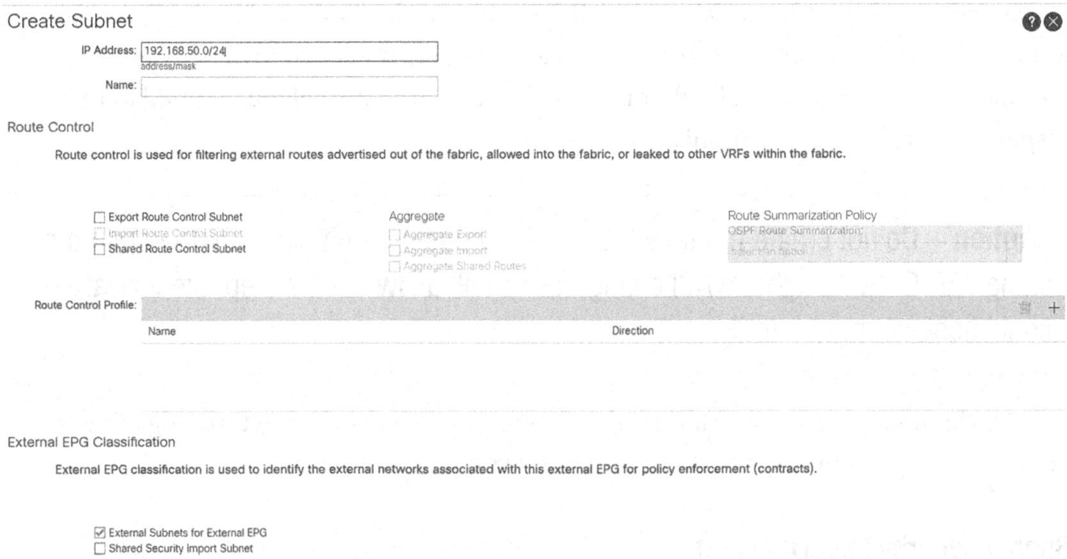

Create Subnet

IP Address: 192.168.50.0/24
address/mask

Name:

Route Control

Route control is used for filtering external routes advertised out of the fabric, allowed into the fabric, or leaked to other VRFs within the fabric.

☐ Export Route Control Subnet   Aggregate   Route Summarization Policy
☐ Import Route Control Subnet   ☐ Aggregate Export   OSPF Route Summarization
☐ Shared Route Control Subnet   ☐ Aggregate Import   Selection Policy
                                       ☐ Aggregate Shared Routes

Route Control Profile: 🗑 +
          Name   Direction

External EPG Classification

External EPG classification is used to identify the external networks associated with this external EPG for policy enforcement (contracts).

☑ External Subnets for External EPG
☐ Shared Security Import Subnet

Figure 7-21. *ExtEPG subnet configuration options*

External Subnets for External EPG (default)

This by default enabled checkbox in the External EPG Classification section represents the already discussed external endpoint mapping to the external EPG. Based on subnets defined with this scope, ACI per VRF creates an internal mapping table on border leaves. IP headers of L3 packets forwarded via L3OUTs are then checked against it, searching for the EPG with the most specific subnet definition (Longest Prefix Match). That EPG's contracts are applied to the traffic.

Deployed mapping tables can be verified directly on leaf switches using the vShell show command in Listing 7-6.

Listing 7-6. Subnet to external EPG mapping

```
Leaf-101# vsh -c "show system internal policy-mgr prefix"
Requested prefix data
```

Vrf-Vni	VRF-Id	Table-Id	Table-State	VRF-Name	Addr	Class
3080193	5	0x5	Up	Apress:PROD	0.0.0.0/0	15
3080193	5	0x5	Up	Apress:PROD	10.0.0.0/8	32773

I created two subnets in ExtEPG: 0.0.0.0/0 and 10.0.0.0/8. While "any" subnet has a special common pcTag (class) of 15, used as a last resort in each VRF, when no more specific subnet is available, all other more specific definitions will be mapped to their respective ExtEPGs (32773 in this case).

Caution   Do not create multiple 0.0.0.0/0 subnets in multiple L3OUTs within the same VRF. Even though the ACI configuration will allow such a step, the forwarding could behave unexpectedly.

Besides creating mapping tables, this subnet scope **doesn't** affect routing tables or actual exchange or prefixes between ACI and external L3 devices.

Shared Security Import Subnet

Similar to the first subnet scope, this is another contract-related option. It ensures the correct propagation of ExtEPG pcTAG information when leaking prefixes between L3OUTs in different VRFs. However, it cannot be used alone and has to cooperate with two other subnet scopes as well.

Imagine having L3OUT A with ExtEPG A in VRF A and you want to leak prefix 192.168.10.0/24 from it to L3OUT B in VRF B. VRF leaking requires an explicit subnet definition in the source L3OUT with following configuration:

1. Subnet 192.168.10.0/24 in ExtEPG A has *External Subnets for External EPG* checked. This ensures that the original L3OUT A in VRF A knows to which pcTag traffic this subnet belongs.

2. Subnet 192.168.10.0/24 in ExtEPG A has *Shared Security Import Subnet* checked. This permits pcTag information leaking between VRF mapping tables, so the target VRF knows to which pcTag the traffic within this prefix belongs.

3. Finally, the same subnet 192.168.10.0/24 in ExtEPG A has *Shared Route Control Subnet* checked to actually leak the prefix between routing tables on leaf switches (will be covered later in this section).

These three options together enable prefix 192.168.10.0/24 to be exchanged together with its security policy information from originating VRF to any other VRF, according to applied contract relations between ExtEPGs (with contract scope tenant or global). Of course, to achieve mutual connectivity, you need to apply the same configuration vice versa to prefixes from other VRFs as well.

Export Route Control Subnet

Next, three route control scopes (export, import, and shared) will actively affect the prefix exchange between ACI switches and other L3 devices. Each subnet created with these scopes will end up being included in the prefix list on the border leaf, thus matching the subnet definition exactly (not Longest Prefix Match, like in previous cases). If you configure subnet 10.0.0.0/8, exactly 10.0.0.0/8 route will be matched and not for example 10.0.0.0/16.

The export route control subnet is the explicit definition of the prefix from the routing table in the same VRF, which can be advertised to the outside via this L3OUT. Mainly this option is used for transit routing (to exchange prefixes between different L3OUTs), but it has the same effect on bridge domain subnets as well.

Let's say you have a bridge domain with Unicast Routing enabled and configured subnet 10.1.1.1/24 (scope advertised externally). By matching this prefix in the L3OUT ExtEPG subnet 10.1.1.0/24 with export route control subnet scope instead of the default one, the bridge domain prefix will be advertised to outside of ACI. The result can be seen on border leaves in their automatically created redistribution route maps and prefix lists, as well as in routing tables of external routers. See Listing 7-7.

Listing 7-7. Export Route Control Subnet Deployment on Leafs

```
Leaf-101# show ip route 10.1.1.0/24 vrf Apress:PROD
IP Route Table for VRF "Apress:PROD"

10.1.1.0/24, ubest/mbest: 1/0, attached, direct, pervasive
    *via 10.11.144.65%overlay-1, [1/0], 08w00d, static, tag 4294967294
        recursive next hop: 10.11.144.65/32%overlay-1

Leaf-101# show ip ospf vrf Apress:PROD
Routing Process default with ID 192.168.1.1 VRF Apress:PROD
 Stateful High Availability enabled
Graceful-restart helper mode is enabled
 Supports only single TOS(TOS0) routes
 Supports opaque LSA
```

```
 Table-map using route-map exp-ctx-3080193-deny-external-tag
 Redistributing External Routes from
   direct route-map exp-ctx-st-3080193
   static route-map exp-ctx-st-3080193
   bgp route-map exp-ctx-proto-3080193
   eigrp route-map exp-ctx-proto-3080193
   coop route-map exp-ctx-st-3080193
<output ommitted>
```

```
Leaf-101# show route-map exp-ctx-st-3080193
<output ommitted>
route-map exp-ctx-st-3080193, permit, sequence 15803
  Match clauses:
    ip address prefix-lists: IPv4-st32773-3080193-exc-ext-inferred-
export-dst
    ipv6 address prefix-lists: IPv6-deny-all
  Set clauses:
    tag 4294967295
```

```
Leaf-101# show ip prefix-list IPv4-st32773-3080193-exc-ext-inferred-
export-dst
ip prefix-list IPv4-st32773-3080193-exc-ext-inferred-export-dst: 1 entries
   seq 1 permit 10.1.1.0/24
```

```
Ext-RTR# show ip route
IP Route Table for VRF "default"
```

```
10.1.1.0/24, ubest/mbest: 2/0
    *via 192.168.50.1, Po1.500, [110/20], 00:00:21, ospf-ACI, type-2,
tag 429496
```

More information about ACI transit routing related to export route control subnets will be discussed later in this chapter.

Import Route Control Subnet

Import scope is related to the L3OUT global setting of *Route Control Enforcement*, described before. In the default state, *Import Route Control Subnet* is disabled (and the checkbox greyed out) because ACI doesn't filter incoming routing information at all. If you intend to start filtering inbound prefixes, do the following:

- Enable the *Import Route Control Enforcement* checkbox at the global L3OUT level.

- Create subnets with the import route control subnet scope in ExtEPGs.

The deployment philosophy is similar to the previous export scope: each import route control subnet will be put precisely as defined into the route map and prefix list. For OSPF, it's table-map filtering inbound information is installed to RIB; in the case of BGP, the route map is applied on a BGP peer. I configured 10.10.10.0/24 as the import route control subnet and the result you can see in Listing 7-8.

Listing 7-8. Import Route Control Subnet Deployment on Leaves

```
Leaf-101# show ip ospf vrf Apress:PROD

 Routing Process default with ID 192.168.1.1 VRF Apress:PROD
 Stateful High Availability enabled
Graceful-restart helper mode is enabled
 Supports only single TOS(TOS0) routes
 Supports opaque LSA
 Table-map using route-map exp-ctx-3080193-deny-external-tag
<output immitted>

Leaf-101# show route-map exp-ctx-3080193-deny-external-tag
<output omitted>
route-map exp-ctx-3080193-deny-external-tag, permit, sequence 15801
  Match clauses:
    ip address prefix-lists: IPv4-ospf-32773-3080193-exc-ext-inferred-
import-dst-rtpfx
    ipv6 address prefix-lists: IPv6-deny-all
    ospf-area: 0
  Set clauses:

Leaf-101# show ip prefix-list IPv4-ospf-32773-3080193-exc-ext-inferred-
import-dst-rtpfx
```

```
ip prefix-list IPv4-ospf-32773-3080193-exc-ext-inferred-import-dst-rtpfx:
1 entries
   seq 1 permit 10.10.10.0/24
```

Shared Route Control Subnet

As already indicated, shared route control subnets enable you to leak defined external prefixes from the current originating VRF to another (based on contracts applied between ExtEPGs). Prefixes will end up again in a prefix list used as a filter for route-target export/import in MP-BGP.

Aggregate Export & Import

Specifying individual prefixes in previous subnet scopes can be a significant administrative burden and hardly manageable from long-term point of view. Thus, ACI offers an alternative in creating aggregate subnets. Currently, both aggregate export and import scopes can be only used for the 0.0.0.0/0 subnet, though.

If aggregate checkboxes are configured alone, they match exactly the default route and nothing else. If you enable them together with the export/import route control subnet scope, ACI will deploy the "permit 0.0.0.0/0 le 32" prefix, matching all prefixes. For import, the result is actually the same as the default behavior without global import route control enforcement enabled.

Aggregate Shared Routes

Aggregate shared routes for route-leaking between VRFs can be used universally together with the shared route control subnet, always creating prefix list X.X.X.X/M **le 32**. If you configure shared aggregation for 172.16.0.0/16, the result will be 172.16.0.0/16 le 32, matching for example 172.16.1.0/24, 172.16.2.0/24, and so on.

Note   Should you need a more granular approach to route filtering, but without individual subnets in ExtEPG, you can create customized route maps with prefix lists called route profiles in ACI. This topic will be covered at the end of this chapter.

External Route Propagation

With an L3OUT object created and properly configured, ACI border leaves should be able to establish external routing protocol adjacency and learn the external prefixes to their routing tables (RIBs). The next component that comes into play to distribute routing information around the fabric is the *MP-BGP protocol*.

To refresh the initial fabric requirements for MP-BGP, you need to configure the following:

- In the global ACI policy found at **System -> System Settings -> BGP Route Reflector**, set the BGP AS number and choose at least two spines acting as MP-BGP route reflectors (RR). All leaves then automatically became RR clients and establish BGP peerings with defined RRs.

- The BGP route reflector policy needs to be specified in **Fabric -> Fabric Policies -> Pods -> Policy Groups** and then applied in **Fabric -> Fabric Policies -> Pods -> Pod Profile**.

Multi-Protocol BGP Operation

Figure 7-22 illustrates in more detail how MP-BGP distributes external routing information learned from L3OUTs to other leaf switches.

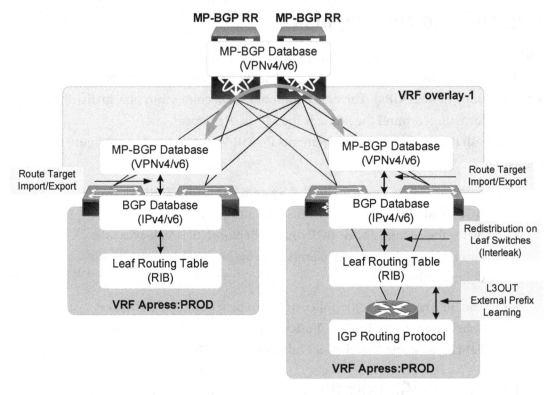

Figure 7-22. *External route information propagation*

We can summarize the external prefix exchange process to the following elements:

- All leaf switches deploy the BGP IPv4/IPv6 address family in user-created VRFs.

- All leaves and route reflector spines deploy the MP-BGP VPNv4/VPNv6 address family (AF) and establish mutual peerings in this AF.

- As soon as L3OUT is configured on a particular border leaf, a redistribution rule is created to enable automatic prefix transfer within the same VRF from the L3OUT IGP routing protocol to the BGP IPv4/IPv6 address family. ACI uses "interleaking" terminology for this redistribution. When BGP is used as an external protocol, no redistribution is needed as the information comes directly from the IPv4/IPv6 address family.

- Each user VRF comes with automatically configured route distinguisher (RD) and route target (RT in a form of <ACI_BGP_

AS>:<VRF_VNID>). Redistributed prefixes are exported from user VRF with their RD and RT to the VPNv4/VPNv6 address family and exchanged via the spine RR between leaf switches in VRF overlay-1.

- Thanks to a consistent route target configuration for each VRF around the fabric, VPNv4/v6 prefixes are then imported on each leaf switch to the correct VRF, without undesirable leaking (if not explicitly configured).

Internal Bridge Domain Subnet Advertisement

Just learning of the external routing information and distributing it across the fabric is not enough to ensure mutual Layer 3 connectivity. Additionally, you need to advertise internal BD subnets to the external world.

There are two main prerequisites for BD subnet advertisement:

1. The BD subnet has its scope set to *Advertised Externally* (which is not the default)

2. The BD subnet prefix is permitted in the prefix list and route map and applied to redistribution from ACI to the L3OUT external routing protocol. This step can be achieved in three different ways:

   a. Association of L3OUT to the bridge domain

   b. L3OUT ExtEPG configuration with export route control subnet scope

   c. Route profile (route map) applied in L3OUT

In the following sections, I'll show you how to configure and verify each aspect of publishing bridge domain IP prefixes.

Subnet Scope - Advertised Externally

By default, all created subnets in ACI are internal to VRF and to the fabric itself. Border leaves won't propagate them over any L3OUT without their scope set to *Advertise Externally*. This serves like a flag to later permit the redistribution.

The configuration is very simple. Just navigate to **Tenants -> Tenant_name -> Networking -> bridge domains -> BD_name -> Subnets** and check the *Advertised Externally* option on a specific subnet object (as shown in Figure 7-23). This setting alone won't affect the leaf configuration or prefix advertisement yet. It always needs to be coupled with one of additional configuration components described in the following sections.

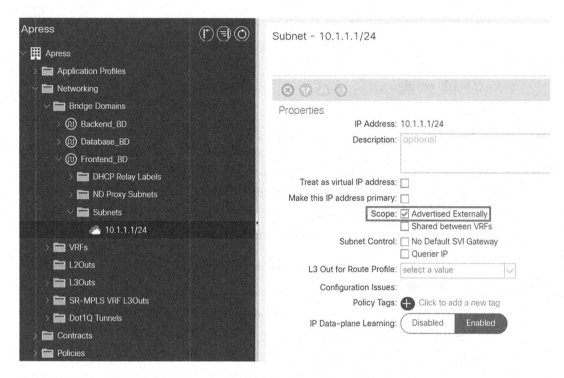

Figure 7-23. *Advertised externally bridge domain subnet scope*

Note   There is another self-explanatory scope for subnet "Shared between VRFs," permitting inter-VRF route leaking.

Association of L3OUT to Bridge Domain

Together with the correct subnet scope, ACI needs to implement internal prefix lists and route maps, controlling the redistribution between routing protocols and route leaking between VRFs if needed.

The first option to do that is the association of the L3OUT object to the bridge domain in its L3 configuration. This setting is found at **Tenants -> Tenant_name -> Networking -> bridge domains -> BD_name -> Policy -> L3 Configurations**, where you can add multiple L3OUTs to the Associated L3 Outs list (as shown in Figure 7-24). In the default state, all BD subnets with the scope of advertised externally will be automatically advertised via the chosen L3OUTs and their routing protocols.

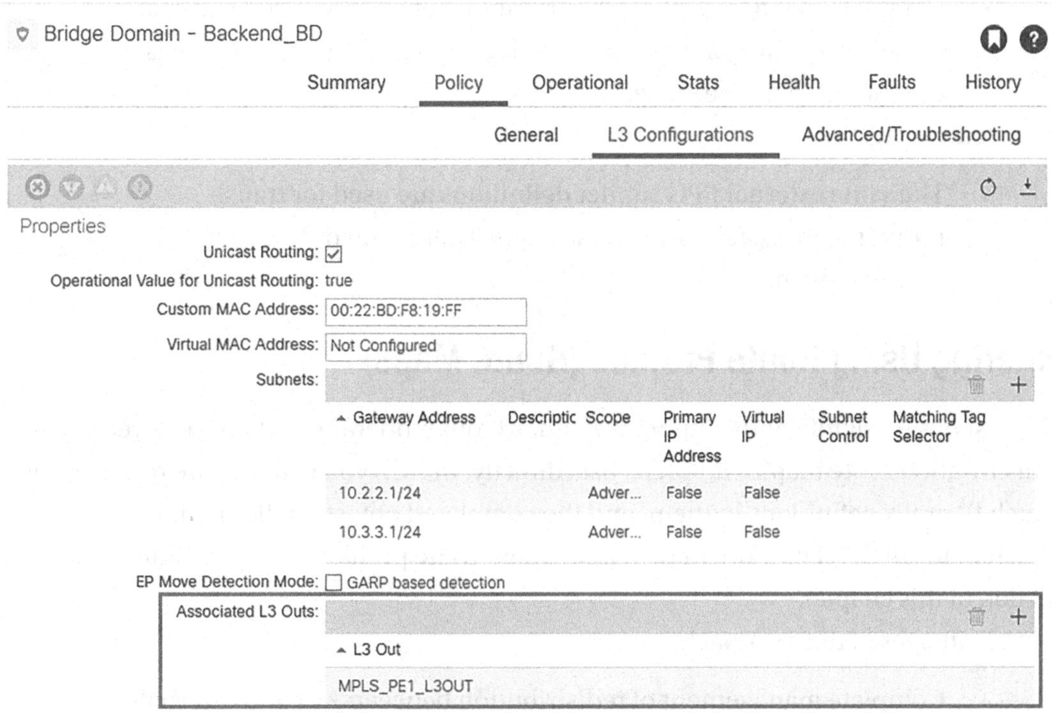

Figure 7-24. L3OUT to bridge domain association

Advantage of this approach:

- Bridge domains are the "single source of truth" about which internal subnets are redistributed to which L3OUTs.

Disadvantage:

- In the L3OUT object you don't see any information about advertised subnets.

L3OUT ExtEPG Configuration

The second way to announce externally advertised subnets via L3OUTs is by using the already described external EPG subnets with the export route control scope. Each such a subnet is directly configured in redistribution prefix lists, so if the bridge domain prefix is present in a border leaf routing table, it's right away advertised to the outside.

Advantage of this approach:

- Complete management of redistribution between ACI and external L3 devices is the domain of the L3OUT object. The configuration is concentrated in one place.

Disadvantage:

- The same external EPG subnet definitions are used for transit routing prefixes as well as BD subnets. There is no differentiation between them.

Filtering Using Route Profiles (Route Maps)

This last option significantly mimics a standard router operation where you create redistribution route maps with prefix lists directly. In ACI, you can prepare route profiles, match IP prefix definitions in them, and the completed object applies in the export direction to L3OUT. For more information about route profiles, please refer to the last section of this chapter.

Advantages of this approach:

- Complete management of redistribution between ACI and external L3 devices is the domain of the L3OUT object.

- Well-known configuration philosophy compared to traditional routers

Disadvantage:

- A more complex object structure is needed due to higher flexibility.

All these three variations result in the same leaf switch configuration, so it's completely up to your preference which to choose. From my experience with customers, we usually ended up using either the first or third option. I definitely recommend not to mix them. If you choose one, stick with it entirely; otherwise the maintenance of external routing can become a pain.

Contract Application to External EPG

Even though we are able at this point to mutually exchange the routing information, ACI, as always, won't allow any traffic flow between internal and external EPGs without contracts. Actually, if border leaves don't have directly connected endpoints in the externally advertised bridge domain, its prefix won't be even present in their routing tables without a contract.

Therefore, this last step and the components illustrated in Figure 7-25 complete the application profile picture for external L3 connectivity.

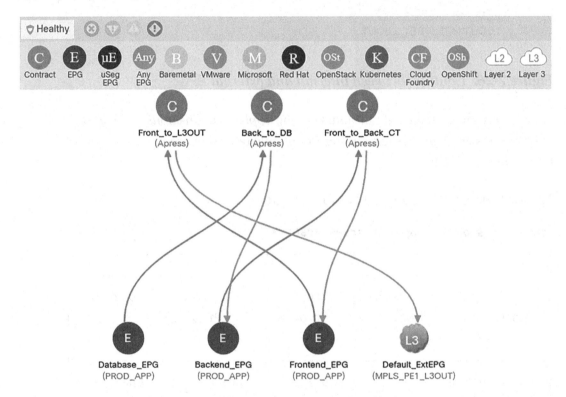

Figure 7-25. *Application profile with contract applied to external L3 EPG*

The configuration philosophy of contracts for L3OUT is no different from the standard internal EPG. Just open the external EPG and navigate to the **Contracts** tab, where after clicking 🔧

symbol you can apply a provided or consumed contract.

To practically demonstrate the L3OUT contract deployment, suppose you have an external EPG with two subnets: generic "any" 0.0.0.0/0 and specific 172.16.0.0/16. Both subnets have the external subnets for external EPG scope set, and a contract is applied on this EPG (as shown in Figure 7-26).

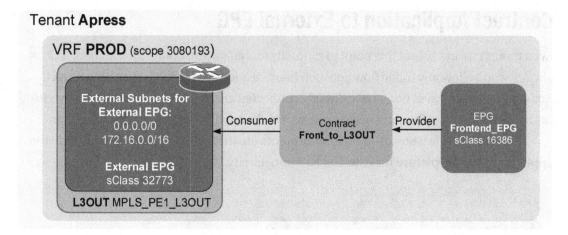

Figure 7-26. *Contract between internal and external EPG*

The contract is in the default state with the *apply both directions* and *reverse filter ports* options enabled, so the resulting zoning rule table on border leaf switch looks as follows in Listing 7-9.

Listing 7-9. L3OUT Contracts Enforcement

```
Leaf-101# show zoning-rule scope 3080193
```

| Rule ID | SrcEPG | DstEPG | FilterID | Dir | operSt |
Scope		Name		Action	Priority	
4110	0	0	implicit	uni-dir	enabled
3080193			permit	grp_any_any_any_permit(20)	
4118	0	15	implicit	uni-dir	enabled
3080193			deny,log	grp_any_dest_any_deny(19)	
4151	**16386**	**32773**	**28**	**uni-dir-ignore**	**enabled**
3080193	**Front_to_L3OUT**		**permit**	**fully_qual(7)**	
4176	**16386**	**15**	**28**	**uni-dir**	**enabled**
3080193	**Front_to_L3OUT**		**permit**	**fully_qual(7)**	

```
|    4159 |   32773  |   16386 |     27    |     bi-dir    | enabled
| 3080193 |  Front_to_L3OUT | permit |       fully_qual(7)        |
|    4127 |   49153  |   16386 |     27    |    uni-dir    | enabled
| 3080193 |  Front_to_L3OUT | permit |       fully_qual(7)        |
+---------+--------+--------+----------+----------------+---------
+---------+----------------+----------+---------------------------+
```

When there is at least one specific subnet in an external EPG, ACI will deploy two standard zoning rules (bi-dir and uni-dir-ignore) between internal and external pcTags (sClasses). In Listing 7-9, see Rule IDs 4151 and 4159.

With the "any" subnet 0.0.0.0/0, ACI follows this generic concept: there are two additional rules in the zoning tables.

- Rule ID 4176: If the External EPG with 0.0.0.0/0 is the destination, ACI uses always the same special *pcTag 15*.

- Rule ID 4127: If the External EPG with 0.0.0.0/0 is the source, ACI uses VRF *pcTag*, in this case *49153*.

Dynamic Routing Protocols in ACI

Dynamic routing is an inevitable part of today's networks and is commonly deployed around each enterprise. ACI offers an extensive set of dynamic routing features for every protocol, in most cases matching the feature sets from the NX-OS and IOS operating systems.

It's not my goal in this section to explain in detail how various routing protocols work, but rather to discuss configuration specifics and possibilities in ACI, eventually limitations, and give you the verification toolset to make sure that intended configuration was deployed to the fabric as expected.

When dealing with dynamic routing, in my practice, I first configure or troubleshoot establishing the protocol adjacency/peering. Without that, the rest of the configuration won't even come to play. Prerequisites for adjacency vary between routing protocols and I will recap them in upcoming sections. Then in the second step, I focus on correct exchange of routing information, applying the route filtering, prefix manipulation, and finally deploying contracts for requested communication.

OSPF

The Open Shortest Path First (RFC 2328) protocol, based on a link state database and Dijkstra's shortest path calculation algorithm, is a widely deployed routing mechanism to exchange IP prefix information within the single autonomous system. The routing domain is split into areas, where area 0 is considered the "backbone" and all other non-zero areas have to be interconnected though it. All routers in the single area share complete topology information (link states) between each other in a form of List State Advertisements (LSAs) and recalculate the best path to each subnet after link state change.

To dynamically discover OSPF neighbors, the protocol uses Hello packets sent to a multicast address (225.0.0.5) over enabled interfaces. But actual full OSPF adjacency is established only after these properties are correctly configured:

- **IP subnet**: The ACI leaf and external L3 device must be on the same subnet with the same network mask.

- **Area**: Both router's interfaces need to belong to the same area. It doesn't necessarily have to be 0.

- **Area Type**: Regular, Stub, Totally Stubby or Not-So-Stubby-Area (NSSA), the type has to match between OSPF routers.

- **Timers**: The Hello (default 10) and Dead (default 40) timers have to match.

- **MTU**: An often and a little bit hidden and forgotten parameter causing trouble with OSPF adjacencies. Additionally, ACI by default puts "inherit" in the MTU field during configuration of OSPF, setting it to 9000B. Make sure to explicitly edit it.

- **Network Type**: OSPF differs between point-to-point interfaces or Ethernet broadcast segments, therefore network type configuration on interfaces has to match as well.

- **Router ID:** Always make sure to have a unique router ID set for your border leaves in a particular VRF. Duplicate router IDs would prevent OSPF routers becoming neighbors, or if not directly connected, they would cause reachability issues in the network due to the inability to exchange routing information correctly.

- **Authentication**: If used, its type and key have to match between L3 neighbors.

When the OSPF protocol is enabled at the root L3OUT object, ACI allows the administrator to configure several policies related to its operation. In Figure 7-27, you can see the global OSPF (per L3OUT) configuration.

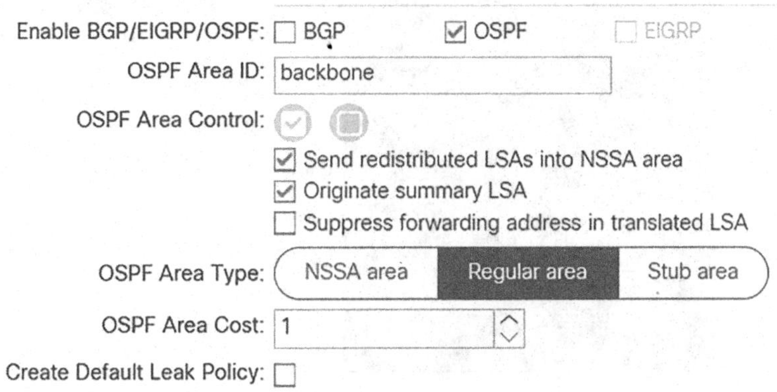

Enable BGP/EIGRP/OSPF: ☐ BGP   ☑ OSPF   ☐ EIGRP

OSPF Area ID: `backbone`

OSPF Area Control: ☑ ⬛

☑ Send redistributed LSAs into NSSA area
☑ Originate summary LSA
☐ Suppress forwarding address in translated LSA

OSPF Area Type: (NSSA area   **Regular area**   Stub area)

OSPF Area Cost: `1` ⌃⌄

Create Default Leak Policy: ☐

Figure 7-27. *L3OUT OSPF configuration*

- **OSPF Area ID**: Area configured on each interface of this L3OUT. By default, ACI sets area 1 here, so make sure to change if using 0 (backbone).

- **OSPF Area Control**: Specific options meant for Stub or NSSA area to filter advertised LSA, making the area Totally Stubby

- **OSPF Area Type**: Regular, Stub, or Not-So-Stubby Area, influencing the LSA propagation between areas

- **OSPF Area Cost**: Cost (metric) for default route if the ACI border leaf generates it in the Stub area

- **Default Leak Policy**: Default route advertisement, comparable to well-known default-information originate (always) command.

Another important configuration object is located in the L3OUT logical interface profile level when OSPF is enabled: the OSPF interface profile. This object is either created automatically during the initial L3OUT wizard, or you need to create it manually later by right-clicking the logical interface profile and choosing *Create OSPF Interface Profile* (as shown in Figure 7-28).

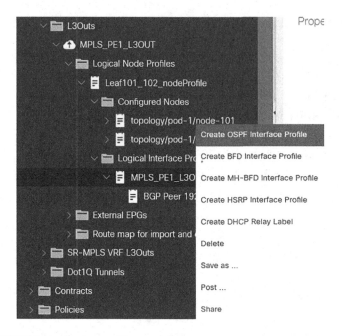

Figure 7-28. OSPF interface profile creation

As illustrated in Figure 7-29, for all L3 interfaces in the particular profile, you can configure the following:

- **Authentication Key**: Pre-shared string, has to match on both sides of OSPF adjacency

- **Authentication Key ID**: Has to match between OSPF neighbors. Key IDs provide a way to reference multiple passwords for MD5 authentication, which is useful, for example, to easily migrate from one passphrase to another.

- **Authentication Type**: No authentication, plain text, or MD5 hash

- **OSPF Interface Policy**: Additional level and set of OSPF configuration parameters

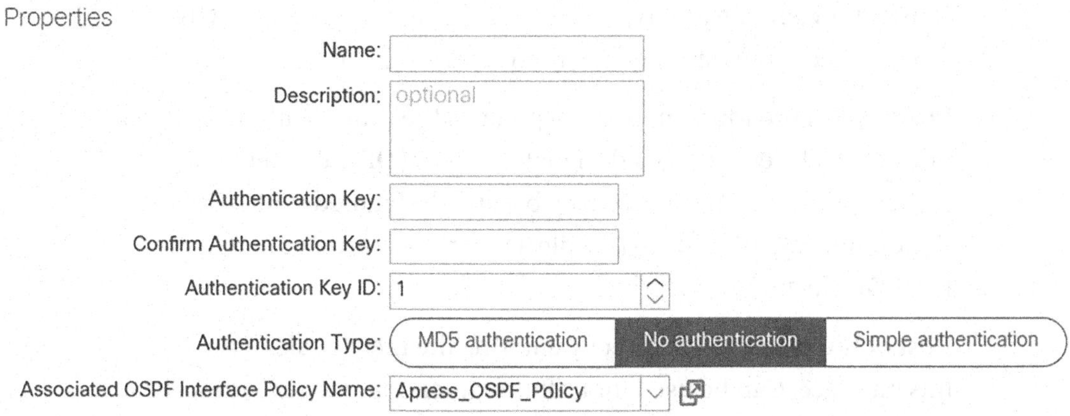

Properties

Name:

Description: optional

Authentication Key:

Confirm Authentication Key:

Authentication Key ID: 1

Authentication Type: (MD5 authentication | No authentication | Simple authentication)

Associated OSPF Interface Policy Name: Apress_OSPF_Policy

Figure 7-29. *OSPF logical interface profile*

The last option in the previous policy, the OSPF interface policy, provides an additional modular object carrying a couple of configuration options you would in a legacy network configure by individual commands on each interface (see Figure 7-30).

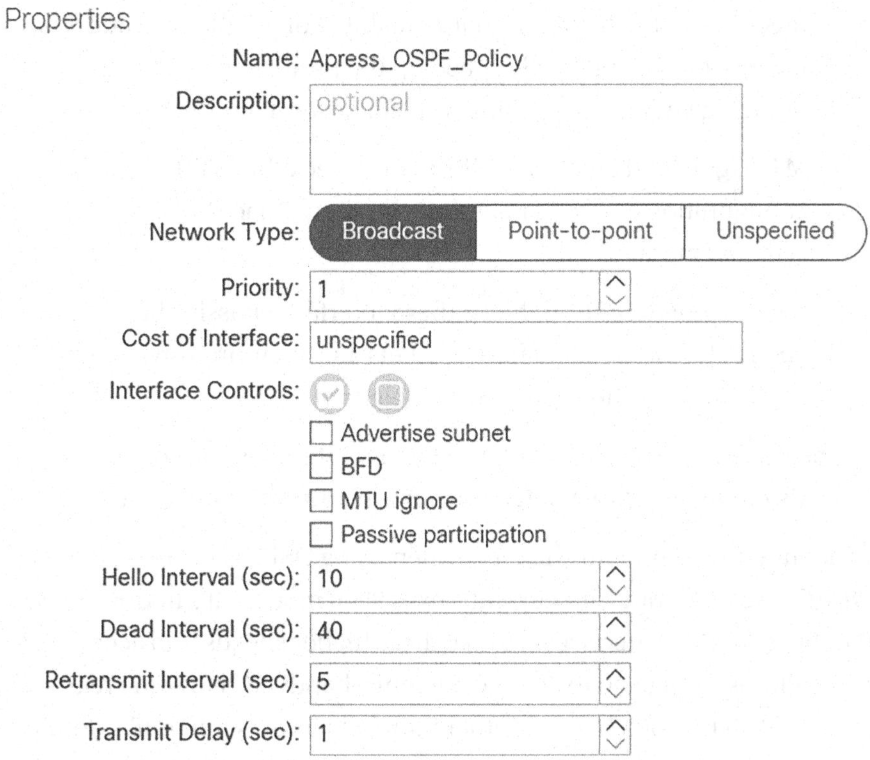

Properties

Name: Apress_OSPF_Policy

Description: optional

Network Type: (Broadcast | Point-to-point | Unspecified)

Priority: 1

Cost of Interface: unspecified

Interface Controls:
☐ Advertise subnet
☐ BFD
☐ MTU ignore
☐ Passive participation

Hello Interval (sec): 10

Dead Interval (sec): 40

Retransmit Interval (sec): 5

Transmit Delay (sec): 1

Figure 7-30. *OSPF protocol interface policy*

- **Network Type**: Network type affects LSA 2 generation and DR/BDR election, therefore has to match both OSPF neighbors

- **Priority**: On broadcast network segments, the router with the highest priority will be elected as a designated router (DR). The second highest priority then becomes the backup designated router (BDR). In ACI, the default value is 1, while 0 means no participation in the DR/BDR election at all.

- **Cost of Interface**: Value directly entering the metric calculation via this interface. Can be used for traffic engineering in OSPF network.

- **Interface Controls**: Knobs to enable specific functions for OSPF, such as

  - **Advertise subnet**: Currently unusable feature to advertise a real loopback IP mask instead of the default /32. ACI so far in version 5.2.X supports only /32 loopbacks.

  - **BFD** (Bidirectional Forwarding Detection) : Fast keepalive mechanism to ensure mutual availability of neighbor IP address, used also to dramatically speed up the protocol converge by reducing fault detection times to sub-second intervals.

  - **MTU Ignore**: If enabled, OSPF won't check the MTU configuration between neighbors for their adjacency establishment.

  - **Passive participation**: Make these interfaces passive in OSPF. They won't send hello packets, but their prefix will be still advertised to other non-passive neighbors.

- **Timers**: Group of timers configurable per interface. Has to be consistent between two neighbors for their adjacency to come up.

What I definitely recommend changing when using OSPF is the default reference bandwidth. ACI uses 40G, but with current Nexus 9000 models, it's nothing special to deploy 100G or even 400G interfaces. To take these higher speeds into account when calculating OSPF cost, you need to change reference bandwidth to some reasonable value, ideally the highest 400G. Together with other more advanced settings like administrative distance, or fine tuning of LSA timers, you can find the policy at the VRF object level of **Tenants -> Tenant_name -> Networking -> VRF -> VRF_name -> OSPF Timer Policy**.

If multiple OSPF areas are required on the same border leaf, they need to be separated to different L3OUTs.

OSPF Protocol Verification

In order to verify the correct OSPF operation, all well-known show commands from IOS, or NX-OS are also available in ACI. Just remember always to add VRF statement at the end.

- `show ip ospf vrf Apress:PROD`

- `show ip ospf database vrf Apress:PROD`

- `show ip ospf neighbors vrf Apress:PROD`

- `show ip ospf interface (brief) vrf Apress:PROD`

- `show ip ospf route vrf Apress:PROD`

- `show ip route ospf vrf Apress:PROD`

If case of problems with protocol packets exchange, it's good to use the tcpdump utility on affected border leaf, as shown in Listing 7-10.

Listing 7-10. OSPF Verification in tcpdump

```
Leaf-101# tcpdump -ni kpm_inb proto 89
tcpdump: verbose output suppressed, use -v or -vv for full protocol decode
listening on kpm_inb, link-type EN10MB (Ethernet), capture size
262144 bytes
15:35:01.427139 IP 192.168.50.2 > 224.0.0.5: OSPFv2, Hello, length 52
15:35:01.427465 IP 192.168.50.3 > 224.0.0.5: OSPFv2, Hello, length 52
15:35:06.427745 IP 192.168.50.3 > 224.0.0.6: OSPFv2, LS-Update, length 76
15:35:06.427769 IP 192.168.50.2 > 224.0.0.5: OSPFv2, LS-Update, length 76
22:50:14.274389 IP 192.168.50.1 > 224.0.0.5: OSPFv2, Hello, length 52
22:50:16.434410 IP 192.168.50.1 > 224.0.0.5: OSPFv2, LS-Ack, length 44
15:35:09.738144 IP 192.168.50.2 > 224.0.0.5: OSPFv2, Hello, length 52
15:35:09.742403 IP 192.168.50.3 > 224.0.0.5: OSPFv2, Hello, length 52
```

EIGRP

Originally Cisco's proprietary but now open and standardized, the Enhanced Interior Gateway Routing Protocol (RFC 7868 with already existing open-source implementation) is an additional option in a dynamic routing rig of ACI. EIGRP belongs with OSPF to the same Interior Gateway Protocol category, exchanging prefix information within the single autonomous system. Still, instead of being a link state, it is an advanced distance vector protocol. EIGRP builds its topology table and calculates the best loop-free paths to all destinations using the DUAL algorithm, based on information from its neighbor's advertisements. The neighbor advertising to the local EIGRP router the best loop-free path to the destination is called the successor. If available and also loop-free, EIGRP can right away calculate the backup path as well, the "feasible successor." Compared to OSPF, when the topology changes, EIGRP calculates new paths only for affected prefixes instead of a recalculation of the whole OSPF link-state database. These specifics make EIGRP incredibly scalable and it often achieves the best converge performance compared to other routing protocols.

EIGRP requires these settings to match between neighbors in order to create an adjacency:

- **IP subnet**: ACI leaf and external L3 device has to be on the same subnet with the same network mask.

- **EIGRP Autonomous System**: Each EIGRP process has its own autonomous system assigned. Peers have to match in this value.

- **K-values**: Metric calculation in EIGRP consists of multiple values (Ks): interface bandwidth, load, delay, and reliability. Using the K-value setting, you can give each component weight in the metric formula or choose if it will be even used. These settings have to match between the EIGRP neighbor; otherwise we would end up with inconsistent metric prone to routing loops.

- **Authentication**: If used, its type and key have to match between L3 neighbors.

EIGRP is not sensitive to timer mismatch, duplicate router IDs, or different IP MTUs. However, as a best practice, I always ensure that these values are set consistently and correctly.

Going back to ACI, you need to enable EIGRP as always at the root L3OUT object level. As you can see in Figure 7-31, there is not much to configure here. Just set the correct autonomous system number to match the external router and optionally configure the default route advertisement. Only single EIGRP L3OUT can be deployed on the same border leaf per VRF due to a single configurable autonomous system per EIGRP process.

Enable BGP/EIGRP/OSPF:	☐ BGP		☐ OSPF	☑ EIGRP
Autonomous System Number:	1			
Create Default Leak Policy:	☐			

Figure 7-31. *EIGRP protocol L3OUT configuration*

Similar to OSPF, EIGRP needs an additional interface policy to enable its operation for given leaf interfaces. If the protocol isn't enabled during the initial L3OUT wizard, you will need to create the policy manually by right-clicking the logical interface profile and choosing *Create EIGRP Interface Profile* (as shown in Figure 7-32).

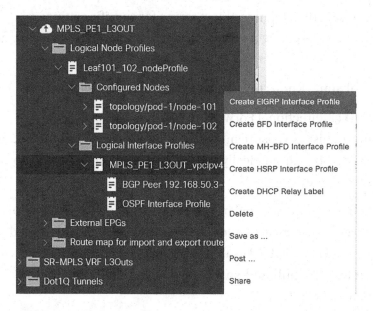

Figure 7-32. *EIGRP interface profile*

As illustrated in Figure 7-33, for authenticating the exchange of EIGRP protocol packets, you can enable this feature in the interface profile and configure the authentication keychain with optional key rotation settings (similar to IOS/NX-OS).

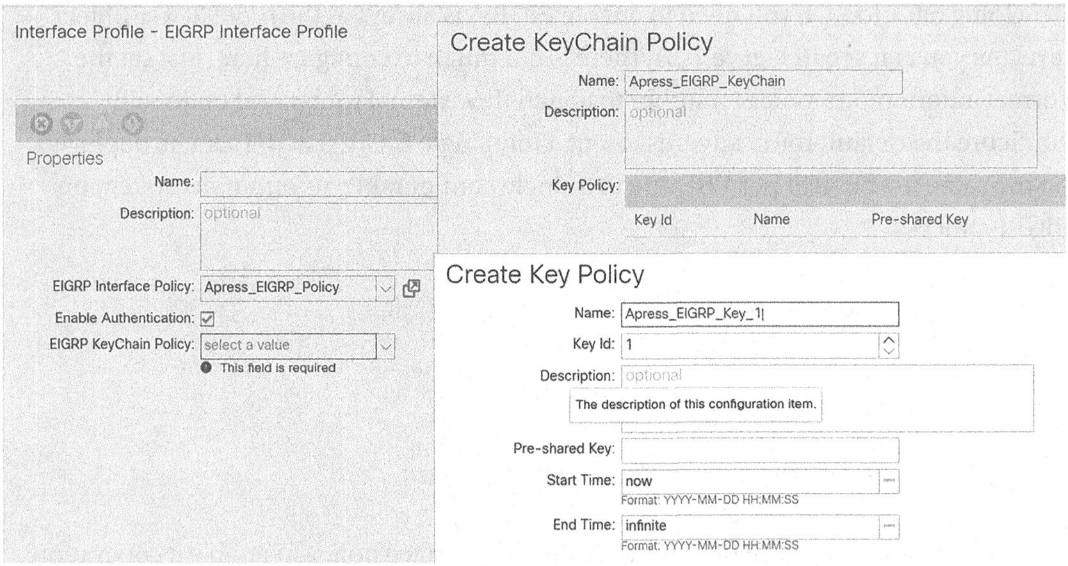

Figure 7-33. *EIGRP authentication in the interface profile*

Another configuration option available in the interface profile is the EIGRP interface policy. Like in the case of OSPF, this object serves for specific settings related to EIGRP that you would otherwise configure using the CLI per interface in a legacy network (see Figure 7-34):

- **Control State**: Knobs to enable EIGRP interface functions like

    - **BFD (**Bidirectional Forwarding Detection): Fast keepalive mechanism to ensure mutual availability of neighbor IP address, used also to dramatically speed up the protocol converge to sub-second intervals.

    - **Self Nexthop**: Enabled by default, instructing the border leaf to set its own local IP address as a next hop for all advertised networks in EIGRP. Disabling this feature is primarily used for DMVPN hub-and-spoke topologies and doesn't find any benefit in ACI.

    - **Passive**: Passive interface for EIGRP not to participate in dynamic routing via this interface. EIGRP won't send Hello packets through it but will still advertise its IP prefix and mask to other neighbors.

- **Split Horizon**: Routing loop prevention mechanism in EIGRP (enabled by default) to avoid sending routing information and queries through the same interface as they were learned.

- **Timers**: Configurable Hello and Hold intervals, not checked between neighbors during the adjacency establishment. The hold timer is actually instructing.

- **Bandwidth**: Value entering the metric calculation for EIGRP. The protocol considers the lowest bandwidth value between routers along the whole path. The bandwidth setting has no impact on the physical interface, speed, or other property.

- **Delay**: Similar to the previous point, the delay is used in EIGRP metric calculation. This time-cumulative value is carried with EIGRP updates. Again, it has actually no impact on the physical interface.

EIGRP Interface Policy - Apress_EIGRP_Policy

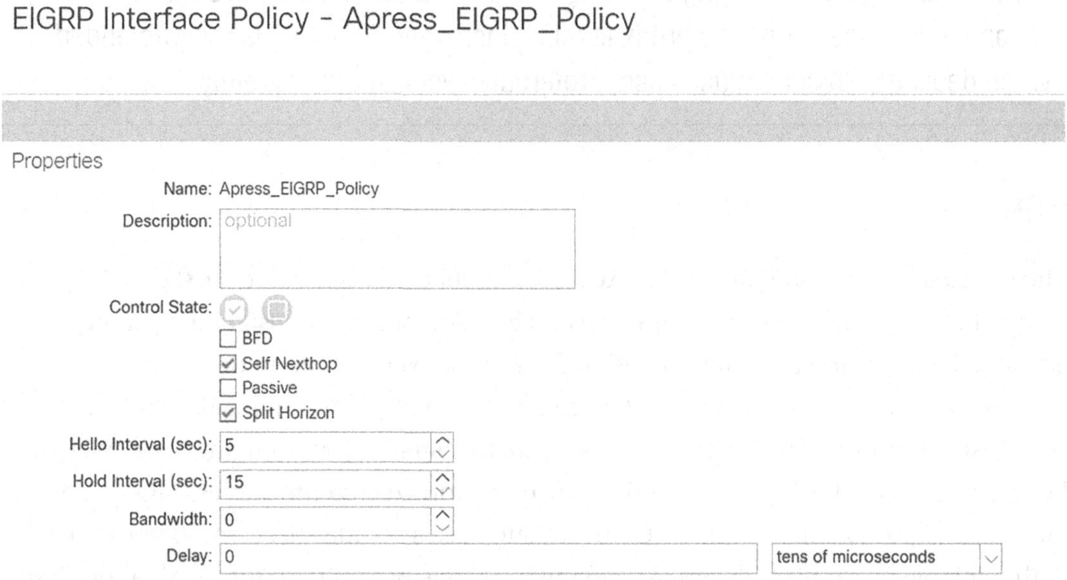

Figure 7-34. *EIGRP interface policy configuration*

More advanced EIGRP settings like administrative distances for internal and redistributed prefixes, narrow/wide metric style, or active intervals can be found at the VRF level when you navigate to **Tenants -> Tenant_name -> Networking -> VRF -> VRF_name -> EIGRP Context Per Address Family** and there apply a custom EIGRP family context policy.

EIGRP Protocol Verification

The concept of the show commands remains the same for EIGRP as well as OSPF. You can get well-known outputs by issuing the following commands:

- `show ip eigrp vrf Apress:PROD`

- `show ip eigrp neighbors vrf Apress:PROD`

- `show ip eigrp interfaces (brief) vrf Apress:PROD`

- `show ip eigrp topology vrf Apress:PROD`

- `show ip route eigrp vrf Apress:PROD`

Note   It's good to know, that when advertising BD subnets or prefixes from other L3OUTs for transit routing, EIGRP and OSPF share the same route map on the same border leaf and VRF. Changing a setting in one protocol can negatively affect the second and cause unwanted prefix leaking. Increased attention is recommended when dealing with such a use case, preferably avoiding it completely.

BGP

The last available routing protocol in ACI, the Border Gateway Protocol (RFC 4271), represents a path-vector, exterior routing mechanism, primarily designed to support advanced routing and path manipulation features between different domains (autonomous systems). Together with prefixes, it exchanges multiple path attributes, some used for routing loop prevention (AS Path), others for traffic engineering (Weight, Local Preference, Multi-Exit Discriminator), or customized communities (tags) for prefix filtering and policy enforcement. BGP by default uses a standardized and deterministic path selection procedure, always identifying the single best path to the destination (but configurable for multi-path routing as well). The protocol is robust and scalable enough to support the whole Internet backbone routing and often becomes popular for internal networks as well due to its benefits.

BGP establishes its peerings reliably thanks to the TCP protocol on well-known port 179. It differentiates between external BGP (eBGP) peerings interconnecting distinct autonomous systems or internal BGP (iBGP) peerings within the same autonomous system. Routers have to consistently configure these properties in order to create an adjacency:

- **BGP Peer Reachability**: In BGP, peers don't have to be necessarily directly connect. But they always have to ensure mutual IP connectivity. Administrator can deploy static routing or OSPF in ACI to meet the condition.

- **Remote AS Number**: Each BGP router has to specify a correct AS of its peer. ACI by default uses the AS number of internal MP-BGP as configured in global policies.

- **Local AS Number** (optional): If custom local AS on a given interface is used, different from the main BGP process AS, you need to count with it when configuring the other peer.

- **BGP Peering Source Address**: BGP expects to be configured with the exact IP address of its peers. Therefore, the source IP address is equally as important when building the adjacency. In ACI, you can use either a leaf switch loopback address (usually matching the Router ID in VRF) or peer based on configured L3OUT interfaces (routed L3, sub-interface, or SVI).

When you enable the BGP protocol in the root L3OUT object, there are actually no configuration options available at this level. The BGP process is already running thanks to MP-BGP policies deployed in the ACI fabric Pod policies.

All main BGP peer configuration options in ACI are grouped to the *BGP Peer Connectivity Profile.* The placement of this object defines which source interfaces will be used for peering itself. There are two alternatives (as you can see in Figure 7-35).

- **Node Profile**: BGP uses loopback IP addresses defined for each leaf node as a source for a peering session.

- **Interface Profile** – BGP uses L3 interfaces defined in the L3OUT interface profile as a source for a peering session.

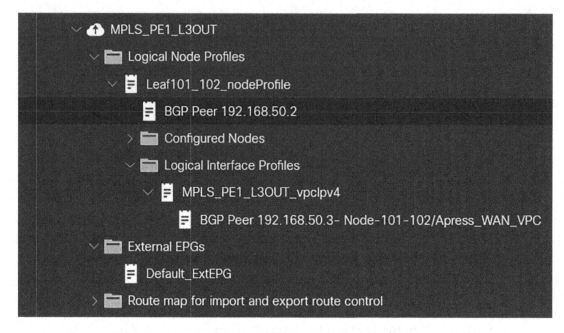

Figure 7-35. *BGP peer connectivity profiles*

To create both types of BGP peer connectivity profiles, simply navigate to **L3OUT ->** **Logical Node Profiles -> Node Profile** and add the required type of profile in BGP Peer Connectivity section (shown in Figure 7-36).

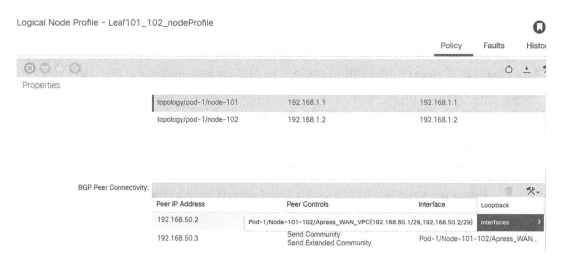

Figure 7-36. *BGP peer connectivity profiles creation*

BGP Peer Configuration Options

The peer connectivity profile brings a wide variety of available options, matching basically the same feature set compared with NX-OS or IOS "router bgp XXX" sections (refer to Figure 7-37):

- **Peer Address**: Remote BGP peer IP used for establishing the adjacency. The remote router has to configure this address as a source IP. ACI can also create dynamic peerings with multiple IPs if you specify a subnet here instead of an individual host IP.

- **Remote AS**: Remote peer's autonomous system. Based on the value, BGP distinguishes between eBGP (different AS from ours) and iBGP (the same AS ours) peerings.

- **Admin State**: Option to individually shut down the BGP peering without affecting others

- **BGP Controls** : Knobs to enable/disable special BGP behavior for each peer

  - **Allow Self AS**: BGP accepts from eBGP peers even routes with its own AS in the AS_PATH attributes. Normally this is denied to prevent routing loops.

  - **AS override**: For eBGP peers, BGP replaces the remote AS number with its own AS number to override AS _PATH loop avoidance. Mainly used when performing transit routing through the local AS.

  - **Disable Peer AS Check**: Allows ACI to advertise a prefix to eBGP even if the most recent AS number in AS_PATH is the same as the remote peer's AS.

  - **Next-hop Self**: By default, BGP route advertisement between iBGP peers doesn't change the original next-hop address. This option changes the behavior and, when getting routes from eBGP and advertising them to iBGP, ACI replaces the original next-hop IP with its own.

- **Send Community**: Enabling transport of 2-byte regular BGP communities. Otherwise, all communities are deleted from the route when traversing the ACI.

- **Send Extended Community**: The same as previous point, just for extended 4-byte communities

- **Send Domain Path**: Additional loop prevention mechanism for BGP, adding a special domain ID of originating VRF to the AS path attributes.

- **Password**: MD5 BGP peering authentication

- **Allowed Self AS Count:** Field enabled when the Allow Self AS option is checked and defines the maximum count for self AS numbers seen in AS_PATH

- **Peer Controls**

  - **BFD:** Bidirectional Forwarding Detection speeds up the detection of issues with mutual IP connectivity.

  - **Disable Connected Check**: In eBGP, the protocol assumes that the peer router is a directly connected neighbor in the same subnet. Therefore, it uses TTL 1 in all its IP packets. eBGP peerings via loopbacks would be therefore denied by default. This option overrides the check for directly connected neighbors.

- **Address Type Controls**: BPG;s modular nature enables it to forward information not only for standard unicast routing tables, but also to support PIM routing and multicast tables. The same option applies to ACI as well.

- **EBGP Multihop TTL**: Similar feature to Disable Connected Check, just this time you can set the exact amount of IP hops allowed between eBGP peers. The value will be then used in the TTL field of the IP header for BGP messages.

- **Weight**: Cisco proprietary, non-transitive BGP path attribute. The higher the value, the more preferred routing information received from this peer.

- **Private AS Control**: Multiple options related to manipulating Private AS used in the AS_PATH attribute. These are applicable only if ACI uses a public BGP AS.

  - **Remote Private AS**: ACI will remote all private AS numbers from AS_PATH as long as it consist only from private ones.

  - **Remove all private AS**: This time ACI remotes all private AS numbers regardless of public AS number presence in AS_PATH.

  - **Replace private AS with local AS**: All private AS numbers are removed from AS_PATH and a local one is inserted instead.

- **BGP Peer Prefix Policy**: Maximum number of prefixes received from the BGP peer. It's a control plane security feature.

- **Site of Origin (SoO)**: ACI 5.2 added support for this BGP transitive extended community attribute, providing another way to avoid routing loops by looking at information where the prefix originated. BGP can automatically deny relearning of such a route in the source site.

- **Local AS Number**: Instead of using the main BGP AS number configured for internal MP-BGP, you can define another to peer with this BGP neighbor.

- **Route Control Profile**: Set of route maps applied to prefixes either learned or advertised to this BGP neighbor.

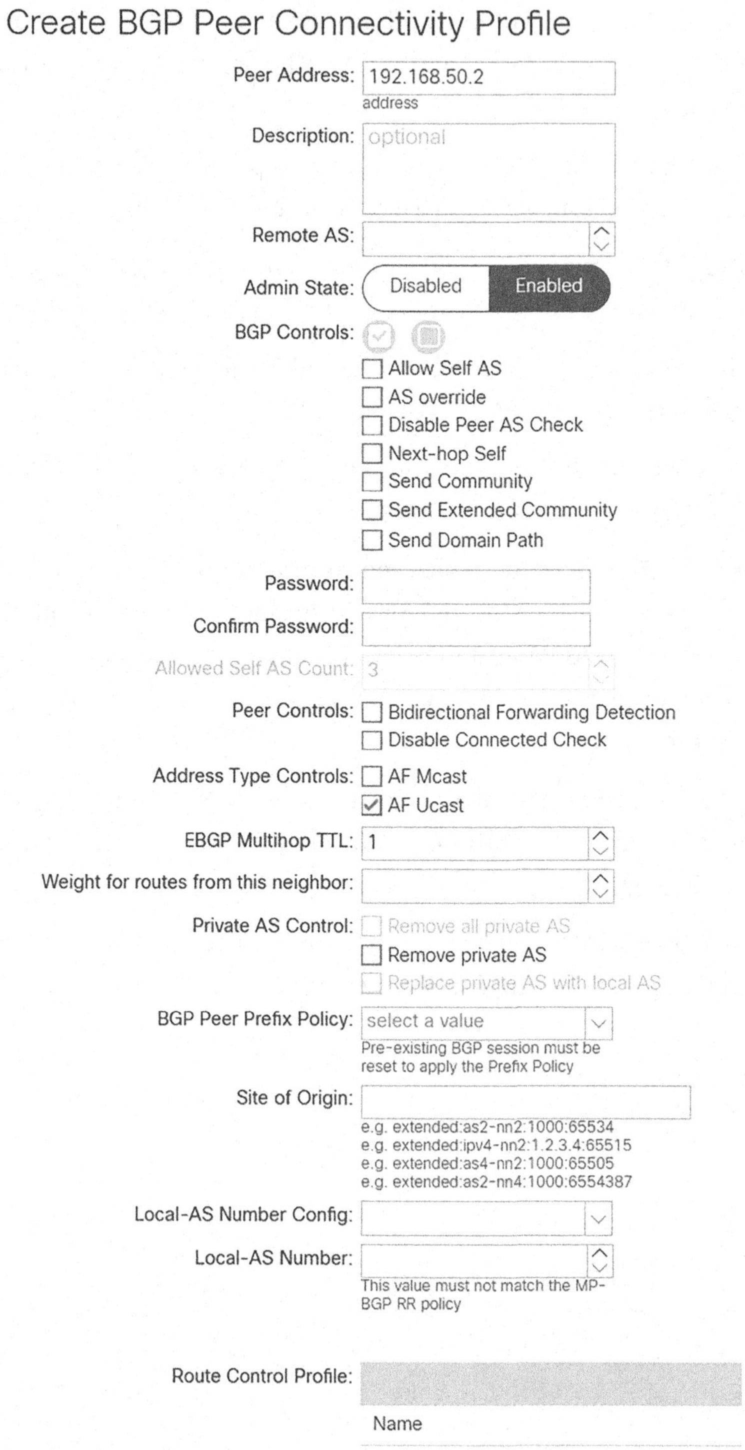

Create BGP Peer Connectivity Profile

Peer Address: 192.168.50.2
address

Description: optional

Remote AS:

Admin State: Disabled | **Enabled**

BGP Controls:
- [ ] Allow Self AS
- [ ] AS override
- [ ] Disable Peer AS Check
- [ ] Next-hop Self
- [ ] Send Community
- [ ] Send Extended Community
- [ ] Send Domain Path

Password:

Confirm Password:

Allowed Self AS Count: 3

Peer Controls:
- [ ] Bidirectional Forwarding Detection
- [ ] Disable Connected Check

Address Type Controls:
- [ ] AF Mcast
- [x] AF Ucast

EBGP Multihop TTL: 1

Weight for routes from this neighbor:

Private AS Control:
- [ ] Remove all private AS
- [ ] Remove private AS
- [ ] Replace private AS with local AS

BGP Peer Prefix Policy: select a value
Pre-existing BGP session must be
reset to apply the Prefix Policy

Site of Origin:
e.g. extended:as2-nn2:1000:65534
e.g. extended:ipv4-nn2:1.2.3.4:65515
e.g. extended:as4-nn2:1000:65505
e.g. extended:as2-nn4:1000:6554387

Local-AS Number Config:

Local-AS Number:
This value must not match the MP-
BGP RR policy

Route Control Profile:

Name

Figure 7-37. *BGP peer connectivity configuration options*

Although you have seen a huge number of options for BGP, the minimal peer configuration consists of the peer IP, remote AS number, and eBGP TTL multihop if necessary.

BGP Protocol Verification

After creating BGP peer policies, you should be able to verify the configuration and presence of BGP neighbors in the show commands outputs, as usual, with the same syntax as for other Cisco routers:

- `show bgp ipv4 unicast summary vrf Apress:PROD`

- `show bgp ipv4 unicast neighbor 192.168.50.2 vrf Apress:PROD`

- `show bgp ipv4 unicast vrf Apress:PROD`

- `show bgp ipv4 unicast 192.168.1.0/24 vrf Apress:PROD`

- `show ip route bgp vrf Apress:PROD`

Static Routing with L3OUTs

Sometimes, dynamic routing protocols are not available on the connected L3 device, or they are just less suitable due to unnecessary complexity. For such cases, static routing is more convenient. In ACI's L3OUTs, static routes are configured individually for each deployed border leaf in its logical node profile.

First, navigate to **L3OUT -> Logical Node Profiles -> Profile_name -> Configured Nodes -> topology/pod-X/-node-XXX**. As illustrated in Figure 7-38, there you can configure the following:

- **Prefix:** Destination IP subnet and mask

- **Fallback Preference**: Administrative distance for this static route.

- **Route control**: BFD to monitor IP next-hop availability

- **Track Policy**: Static route can be installed in routing table conditionally based on a state of IP address reachability defined in this policy

- **Next Hop Addresses**: One or more addresses where to forward the packet for this subnet

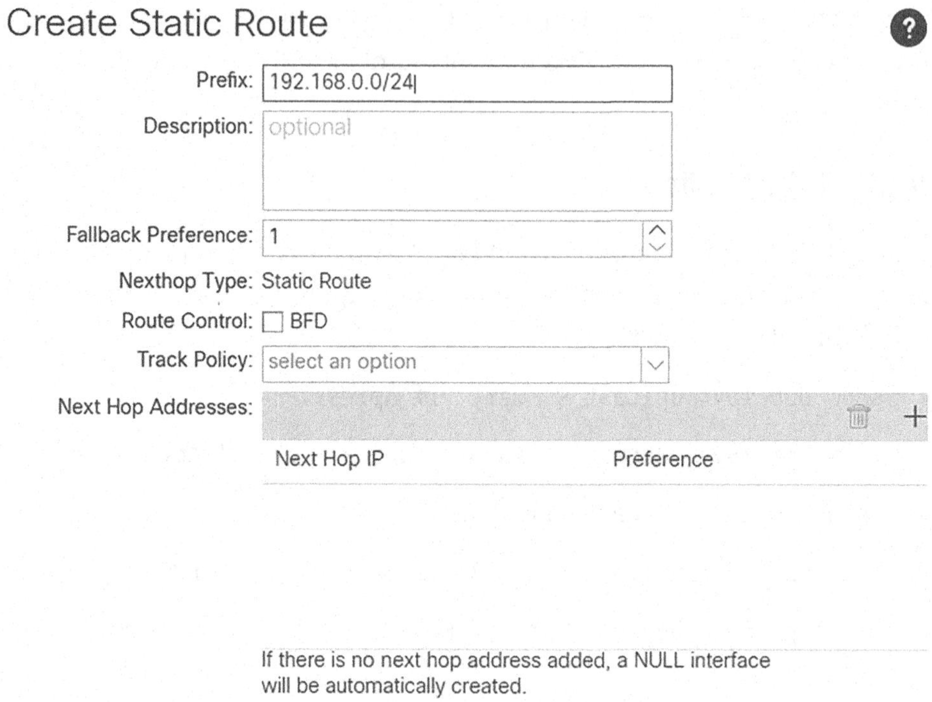

Create Static Route

Prefix: 192.168.0.0/24|

Description: optional

Fallback Preference: 1

Nexthop Type: Static Route

Route Control: ☐ BFD

Track Policy: select an option

Next Hop Addresses: 🗑 +

Next Hop IP   Preference

If there is no next hop address added, a NULL interface
will be automatically created.

Figure 7-38. *Static route configuration*

Next hops are other objects in ACI and their configuration again consists of multiple
options (as shown in Figure 7-39).

- **Next Hop Address:** Self-explanatory

- **Preference:** Acts as administrative distance for next hops

- **Next Hop Type:** If None is chosen, ACI will create a special static
  route pointing to Null0.

- **IP SLA Policy:** Feature to track reachability of the next-hop IP. If
  the tracking object is down, this IP will not be considered usable
  anymore.

- **Track Policy:** Usability of the next hop can depend on some other IP
  or a set of IPs defined in the track policy.

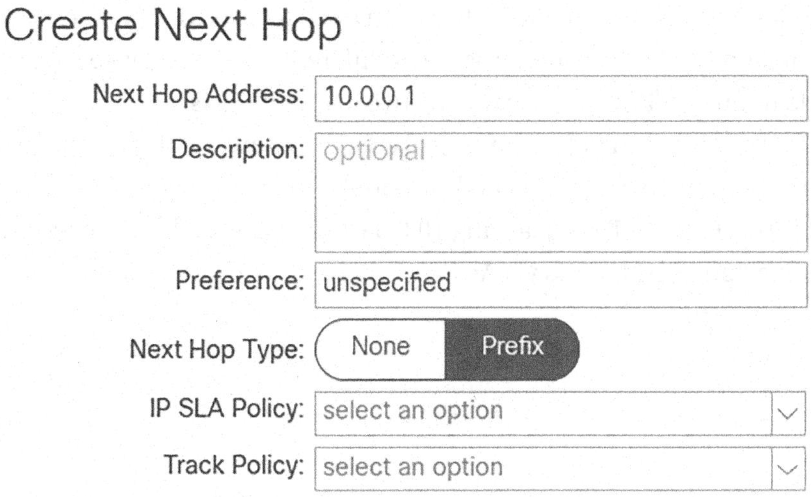

Create Next Hop

Next Hop Address: | 10.0.0.1

Description: | optional

Preference: | unspecified

Next Hop Type: | None | Prefix

IP SLA Policy: | select an option

Track Policy: | select an option

Figure 7-39. *Static route next hop configuration*

To verify the deployment of static routes, just refer to the related border leaf routing table and check their presence there using the code in Listing 7-11.

Listing 7-11. Static Route Verification in Routing Table

```
Leaf-101# show ip route 192.168.0.0/24 vrf Apress:PROD
IP Route Table for VRF "Apress:PROD"
'*' denotes best ucast next-hop
'**' denotes best mcast next-hop
'[x/y]' denotes [preference/metric]
'%<string>' in via output denotes VRF <string>

192.168.0.0/24, ubest/mbest: 1/0
    *via 10.0.0.1, vlan38, [1/0], 00:00:04, static
```

ACI Transit Routing

As already mentioned during this chapter, ACI doesn't necessarily have to be always a stub network. You can simply achieve transit routing where ACI acts as a single distributed router, one next hop in path between external networks. In this section, I will look under the hood with you to see what configuration components are needed to achieve this functionality.

Technically, to transit via the ACI fabric, you need to advertise prefixes learned from one L3OUT to another L3OUT (in the same or different VRF) and make sure that zoning rules include mutual pcTag entries between two external EPGs.

Figure 7-40 describes in detail the typical configuration and deployment principle of transit routing between two L3OUTs and two prefixes for simplicity. L3OUT A is learning prefix 172.16.0.0/16, L3OUT B is learning 10.0.0.0/8 and the goal is to ensure connectivity between their external endpoints via ACI.

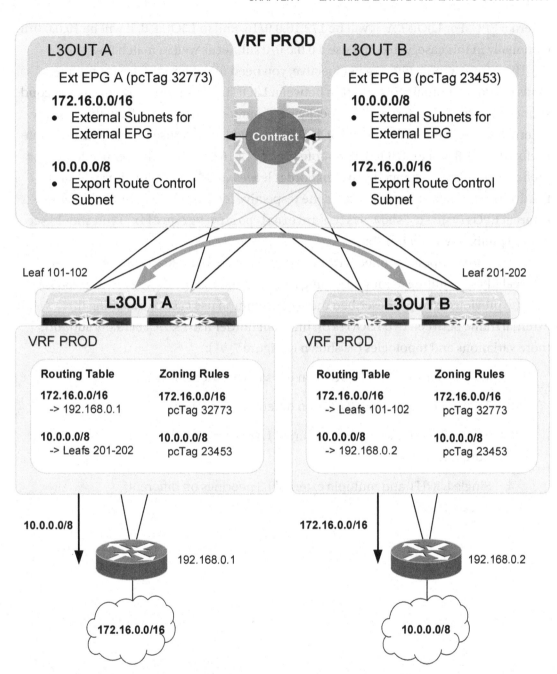

Figure 7-40. *Transit routing overview*

First, you need to accurately classify both local prefixes. In each L3OUT, therefore, create an external EPG and respective subnet with the scope of External Subnets for

External EPG. For L3OUT A, it will be 172.16.0.0/16, and in L3OUT B, it will be 10.0.0.0/8. Optionally in this case, you could use a 0.0.0.0/0 subnet as well to match any prefix.

Then, from a route filtering perspective, you need to deploy prefix lists and route maps to enable mutual redistribution between L3OUTs. This is done by adding a second subnet entry to each external EPG, specifying a remote, transiting prefix with the scope External Route Control Subnet. In L3OUT A, you need to advertise the externally remote prefix 10.0.0.0/8 and for L3OUT B, remote prefix 172.16.0.0/16. At this point, all the prefixes should be exchanged between border leaves via MP-BGP and they will start to advertise them to external peers. In the respective local prefix mapping tables for external EPGs (`vsh -c "show system internal policy-mgr prefix"`) you should see remote prefixes with their pcTags.

Finally, for endpoint connectivity to work, you need to deploy a contract between external EPGs, resulting in mutual zoning rules installation (pcTags 32773 and 23453).

The previous example described the most common use case of transiting the external traffic between two L3OUTs on different border leaves. ACI actually supports more variations and topologies (as shown in Figure 7-41):

1. Transit between two L3OUTs on the same border leaf switch

2. Transit between two L3OUTs on different border leaves

3. Single L3OUT and multiple external L3 peerings on the same border leaf

4. Single L3OUT and multiple external L3 peerings on different border leaves

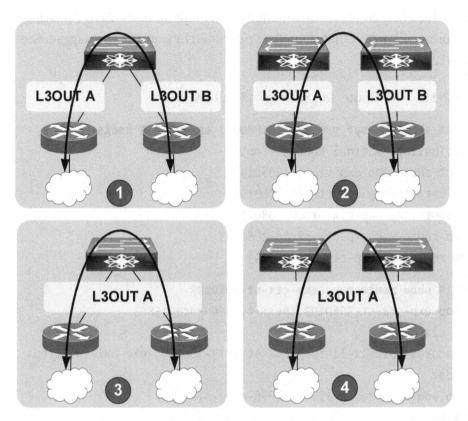

Figure 7-41. *Transit routing supported topologies*

When using multiple OSPF instances on the same border leaves, which are meant to be transitive, one of them needs to be configured in area 0 due to direct inter-area prefix distribution without MP-BGP involvement.

Another side note: the latter two supported topologies listed with a single L3OUT introduce a limitation of using the 0.0.0.0/0 subnet in an external EPG. The "any" subnet cannot match both source and destination prefixes at the same time. You have to split the range at least to 0.0.0.0/1 and 128.0.0.0/1 with a scope of external subnets for the external EPG.

VRF Route Tagging in ACI

Another feature worth mentioning related to transit routing is VRF route tagging. Each VRF in ACI has its own associated route tag, which is by default set to the same value of 4294967295 (0xFFFFFFFF). All prefixes redistributed via L3OUT to OSPF and EIGRP will carry this tag with them, regardless of their origin (internal BD subnet or transit route from another L3OUT). The Main purpose of this tagging, as you may have guessed, is *routing loop mitigation*.

In automatically created redistribution route maps for each L3OUT (if using EGRP or OSPF protocol) notice, that all prefixes permitted by prefix-list are tagged. See Listing 7-12.

Listing 7-12. VRF Route Tag Setting in Route Maps

```
Leaf-101# show ip ospf vrf Apress:PROD | egrep -A 5 Redist
 Redistributing External Routes from
   direct route-map exp-ctx-st-3080193
   static route-map exp-ctx-st-3080193
   bgp route-map exp-ctx-proto-3080193
   eigrp route-map exp-ctx-proto-3080193
   coop route-map exp-ctx-st-3080193

Leaf-101# show route-map  exp-ctx-st-3080193
route-map exp-ctx-st-3080193, permit, sequence 15803
  Match clauses:
    ip address prefix-lists: IPv4-st32773-3080193-exc-ext-inferred-
export-dst
    ipv6 address prefix-lists: IPv6-deny-all
  Set clauses:
    tag 4294967295

Leaf-101# show route-map exp-ctx-proto-3080193
route-map exp-ctx-proto-3080193, permit, sequence 15801
  Match clauses:
    ip address prefix-lists: IPv4-proto32773-3080193-exc-ext-inferred-
export-dst
    ipv6 address prefix-lists: IPv6-deny-all
  Set clauses:
    tag 4294967295
```

Should the same prefix already advertised from ACI return back to ACI in the same VRF, it will be automatically denied, as in Listing 7-13.

Listing 7-13. VRF Route Tag Setting in Route Maps

Leaf-101# **show ip ospf vrf Apress:PROD**

```
Routing Process default with ID 192.168.1.1 VRF Apress:PROD
<output ommited>
```
Table-map using route-map exp-ctx-3080193-deny-external-tag

Leaf-101# **show route-map exp-ctx-3080193-deny-external-tag**
```
route-map exp-ctx-3080193-deny-external-tag, deny, sequence 1
  Match clauses:
    tag: 4294967295
  Set clauses:
```

In VRF object policy configuration (**Tenants -> Tenant_name -> Networking -> VRF -> VRF_name -> Policy**), there is an inconspicuous little option to set your own route tag in case of need (shown in Figure 7-42). Especially when you would like to exchange prefixes between VRFs via external network (often through some core network layer, or firewall performing inter-zone inspection), without a custom and different route tag for each VRF, they would be denied on ingress.

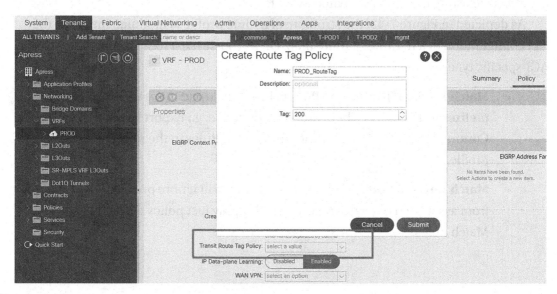

Figure 7-42. *Transit route tag policy*

Route Profiles (Route Maps)

I will wrap up this chapter with a brief description of route profiles, or in other words, a more commonly known construct from traditional networks: route maps. ACI uses many automatically generated route maps internally for L3OUT operations. You have seen them throughout this chapter for prefix filtering, transit routing features, or routing loop prevention.

Route profiles allow administrators to create customized route maps and apply them on multiple different ACI components to support various use cases such as

- BD subnets advertisement via L3OUTs

- Transit routing and redistribution between L3OUTs

- Prefix filtering on ingress from L3OUT

- Interleak prefix manipulation when redistributing to internal BGP

They offer a much more granular and easier-to-maintain prefix manipulation tool compared with subnets in external EPGs or bridge domains to L3OUT associations. Each route profile, more specifically its rules, will be after configuration simply appended to the already existing route maps created by ACI.

As depicted in Figure 7-43, the structure of a route profile is modular, imitating the CLI configuration of a traditional route map. On its root level, a route profile offers two ACI-specific type settings:

- **Match Prefix AND Routing Policy**: Resulting route maps with merge prefixes from objects where they are applied (e. g., Export Route Control Subnets in ExtEPG) and from Match Rules in the route profile.

- **Match Routing Policy Only**: The route map will ignore prefixes from associated objects, and exclusively apply just policy defined in Match Rules.

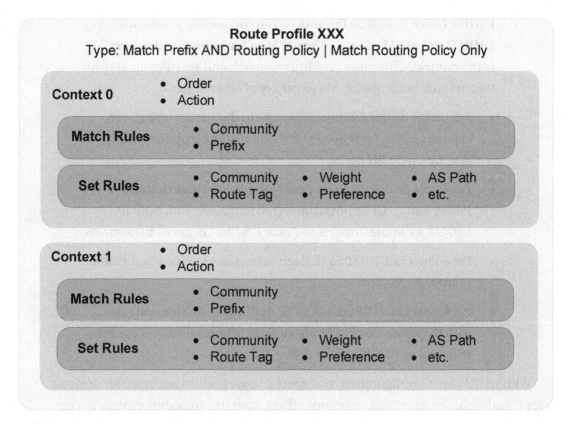

Figure 7-43. *Route profile overview*

Inside the route policy you can configure a set of contexts equivalent to sequence blocks with permit/deny statements in route maps. Each context includes match statements, configurable to match the prefix lists or collection of communities. Then, if the context is permissive, on matched routing information you can apply **a** wide selection of set rules.

Configuration-wise, route profiles can be created at two levels:

- **Tenant Level**: Found in **Tenants -> Tenant_name -> Policies -> Protocol**. Three building blocks are located here: *Match Rules, Set Rules*, and the folder for main objects, *Route Maps for Route Control.* A route profile created here can be used for interleak and redistribution of directly connected or static routes configurable at the root L3OUT level, as well as for BGP peer connectivity Profiles such as ingress/egress prefix or AS path manipulation per BGP peer.

- **L3OUT Level**: Found in **Tenants -> Tenant_name -> Networking -> L3OUTs -> L3OUT_name -> Route Map for import and export route control.** This route profile uses match and set rules created on tenant level, but is applicable to variety of other objects:

  - Per bridge domain subnet: navigate to the subnet object and choose *L3OUT for Route Profile + Route Profile* options. Affects just the single BD prefix.

  - Per whole bridge domain: Configurable in **bridge domain -> Policy Tab -> L3 Configuration** tab and again with options *L3OUT for Route Profile* and *Route Profile.* Affects all BD subnets.

  - Per subnet in L3OUT EPG: Each subnet has a directional *Route Control Profile* option.

  - Per whole L3OUT External EPG: Applied in the **General** tab with the *Route Control Profile* option. Affects all L3OUT prefixes matched by ExtEPG in the defined direction.

With L3OUT level configuration, two special route profiles are available: *default-import* and *default-export.* You can choose them from the drop-down menu during object creation, instead of typing a custom name. These objects automatically affect all the prefixes in chosen direction related to a particular L3OUT. You don't need to apply them anywhere, just have them created. Often, they can be the simplest solution for custom routing manipulation and personally I prefer them whenever possible for our customers.

For a practical demonstration, say you need to filter BGP prefixes advertised from the production network to ACI and set a particular BGP local preference to them when incoming via a specific L3OUT. The BGP peering is already up and import route control enforcement in the global L3OUT configuration is enabled as well. To create the required policy, go to the **Route Map for import and export route control** folder in L3OUT and choose the already mentioned **default-import** route profile name. Add a new context with Order 0 and action Permit (as shown in Figure 7-44).

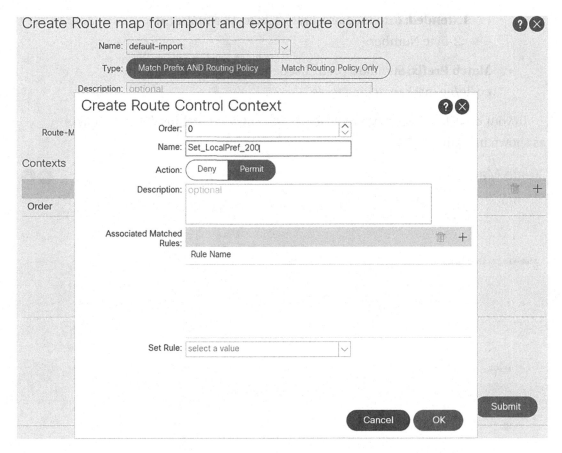

Figure 7-44. *Default-import route profile for BGP manipulation*

When the import route control is enforced for L3OUT, you need to somehow match the incoming prefixes. Add a new match rule to the Associated Matched Rules list, where you will find three main options for prefix classification:

- **Match Regex Community Terms**: BGP community matched by regular expressions. It's a popular way to classify the prefixes based on advanced rules. The same type of community (regular or extended) cannot be matched in both regexp and non-regexp sections, though.

- **Match Community Terms**: Exact BGP community matching. APIC syntax for communities consists of a specific prefix:

  - **Regular**: regular:as2-nn2:<2-byte AS Number >:<2-byte Number>

- **Extended:** extended:as4-nn2:<4-byte AS Number >: <2-byte Number>

- **Match Prefix**: Standard prefix list definition with well-known eq/le/ge mask matching tools

In your case, for simplicity, create few prefix entries matching /24 le 32 masks (as shown in Figure 7-45).

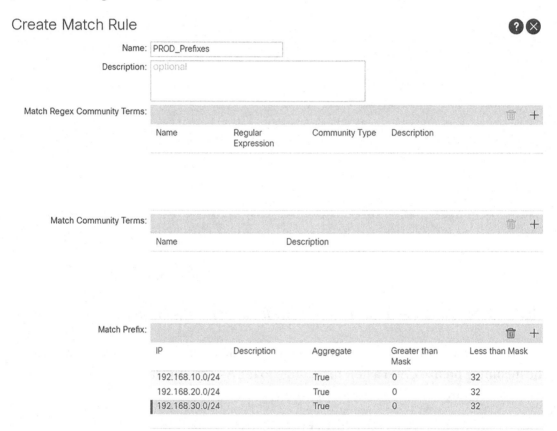

Figure 7-45. Default-import route profile for BGP manipulation

Then for matched prefixes, create a new *Set Rule* with a preference such as 200. As shown in Figure 7-46, there are many different options resembling NX-OS route maps. This step finishes the route profile object configuration.

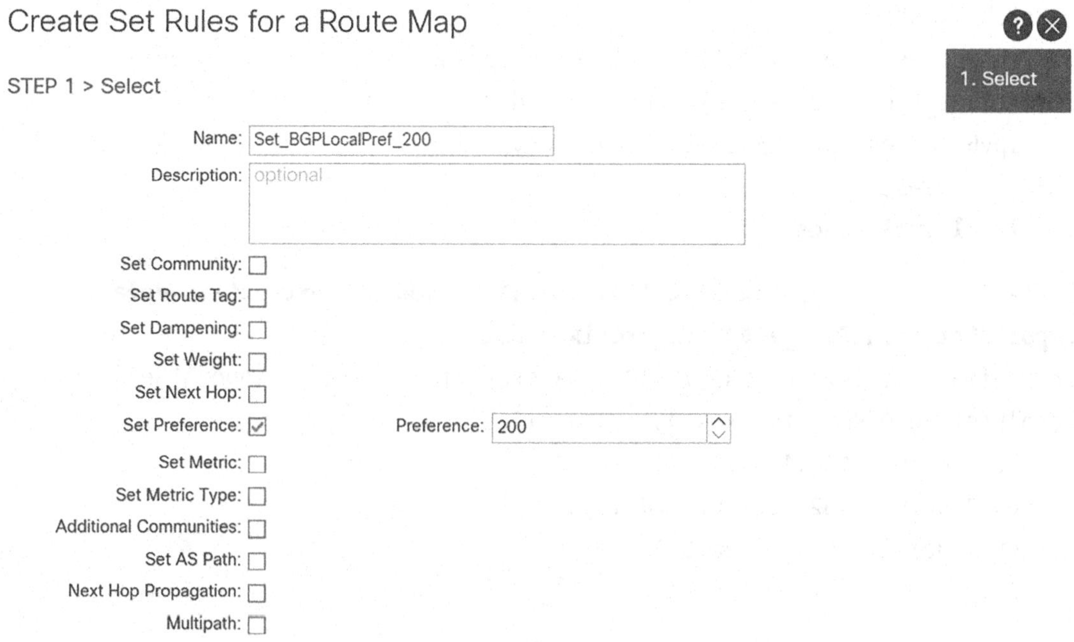

Create Set Rules for a Route Map   ❓ ✖

1. Select

STEP 1 > Select

Name: Set_BGPLocalPref_200

Description: optional

Set Community: ☐
Set Route Tag: ☐
Set Dampening: ☐
Set Weight: ☐
Set Next Hop: ☐
Set Preference: ☑   Preference: 200
Set Metric: ☐
Set Metric Type: ☐
Additional Communities: ☐
Set AS Path: ☐
Next Hop Propagation: ☐
Multipath: ☐

Figure 7-46. *Default-import route profile for BGP manipulation*

Thanks to the default-import route profile, you don't need to explicitly further apply it; ACI will automatically update all the applicable route maps, for example in case of BGP, the inbound neighbor route-map as in Listing 7-14.

Listing 7-14. VRF Route Tag Setting in Route Maps

```
Leaf-101# show bgp ipv4 unicast summary vrf Apress:PROD
Neighbor        V    AS MsgRcvd MsgSent   TblVer   InQ OutQ Up/
Down   State/PfxRcd
192.168.50.3    4 65000      7      13       31    0     0 00:00:47 3

Leaf-101# show bgp ipv4 unicast neighbor 192.168.50.3 vrf Apress:PROD
<output ommitted>
Inbound route-map configured is imp-l3out-MPLS_PE1_L3OUT-peer-3080193,
handle obtained
Outbound route-map configured is exp-l3out-MPLS_PE1_L3OUT-peer-3080193,
handle obtained

Leaf-101# show route-map imp-l3out-MPLS_PE1_L3OUT-peer-3080193
route-map imp-l3out-MPLS_PE1_L3OUT-peer-3080193, permit, sequence 8201
```

```
  Match clauses:
    ip address prefix-lists: IPv4-peer32773-3080193-exc-ext-in-default-
import2Set_LocalPref_2000PROD_Prefixes-dst
    ipv6 address prefix-lists: IPv6-deny-all
  Set clauses:
    local-preference 200

Leaf-101# show ip prefix-list IPv4-peer32773-3080193-exc-ext-in-default-
import2Set_LocalPref_2000PROD_Prefixes-dst
ip prefix-list IPv4-peer32773-3080193-exc-ext-in-default-import2Set_
LocalPref_2000PROD_Prefixes-dst: 3 entries
    seq 1 permit 192.168.10.0/24 le 32
    seq 2 permit 192.168.30.0/24 le 32
    seq 3 permit 192.168.20.0/24 le 32
```

Summary

ACI offers an extensive palette of features related to external connectivity, as you have seen during this chapter. To support migrations or coexistence with a legacy networking infrastructure, you can utilize Layer 2 EPG or bridge domain extensions, ensuring the same communication policies are applied on both internal and external endpoints. For publishing applications and services running inside the ACI, you can then configure a plethora of Layer 3 routing features grouped into L3OUT objects, starting with static routes, going through dynamic interior gateway protocols OSPF and EIGRP, up to the BGP protocol. You learned how ACI can offer for them comparable route filtering and attribute manipulation tools in the form of route profiles than any other Layer 3 router. And you saw that the fabric doesn't necessarily have to be the stub network only. You can also enable transit routing and automated internal VRF-leaking, if needed.

Now with both east-west and north-south traffic patterns in place, let's continue further and include additional L4-L7 devices into the picture to significantly enhance the security and performance of your applications. In the upcoming chapter, I will discuss another very important feature: dynamic *L4-L7 service insertion* between ACI endpoints using service graphs.

CHAPTER 8

Service Chaining with L4-L7 Devices

Cisco ACI includes a significant number of tools to implement and enhance security and segmentation from day 0. I have already discussed tenant objects like EPGs, uEPGs, ESGs, and contracts permitting traffic between them. Even though the ACI fabric is able to deploy zoning rules with filters and act as a distributed firewall itself, the result is more comparable with a stateless set of access lists ACLs. They are perfectly capable of providing coarse security for traffic flowing through the fabric, but its goal is not to replace fully featured and specialized equipment with deep traffic inspection capabilities like application firewalls, intrusion detection (prevention) systems (IDS/IPS), or load balancers often securing the application workloads. These devices still play a significant role in the datacenter design, and ACI offers multiple useful features to easily and dynamically include them in the data path between endpoints, no matter whether the traffic pattern is east-west or north-south.

In this chapter, I will focus on *ACI's service graph and policy-based redirect (PBR)* objects, bringing advanced traffic steering capabilities to universally utilize any L4-L7 device connected in the fabric, even without the need for it to be a default gateway for endpoints or part of a complicated VRF sandwich design and VLAN network stitching. And you won't be limited to a single L4-L7 appliance only; ACI is capable of chaining many of them together, or even loadbalancing between multiple active nodes, all according to your needs. You will get started with a little bit of essential theory and concepts about service insertion, followed by a description of supported design options for both routed Layer 3 and transparent Layer 2 devices. Then you will review the configuration concepts and verification techniques for multiple use cases of PBR service graphs. Although my goal is not to cover every possible option and aspect of ACI service insertion (in fact, this topic is enough for another whole book), I'll definitely offer a strong foundation of knowledge for you to build on later.

© Jan Janovic 2023
J. Janovic, *Cisco ACI: Zero to Hero*, https://doi.org/10.1007/978-1-4842-8838-2_8

To Use or Not to Use Service Insertion

First of all, service graphs in ACI are not mandatory for L4-L7 device insertion into a data path between two endpoints. It's just a suggested and often a quite optimal option. Before you dive deeper into this technology, let me generally summarize how to approach such a task. I see four main design variants (depicted in Figure 8-1):

1. **L4-L7 device is part of consumer/provider EPGs**: Let's suppose your bridge domains (and thus EPGs) are L2 only. In this case, a L4-L7 device can serve as a L3 default gateway for endpoints and "stitch" the communication flows to its interfaces this way. The downside is in low scalability of such solution. The entire traffic between any two endpoints has to go through the connected device, and there must be an L3 interface in each EPG. Additionally, you cannot apply any ACI contracts on such traffic.

2. **L4-L7 device in its own EPG**: In this design, the L3 interfaces of the L4-L7 device are mapped to the dedicated EPG and contracts are needed to permit the traffic from other EPGs. You expect that the service appliance is a destination of traffic, a default gateway for servers, so the design is suitable especially for accessing loadbalancer VIPs or performing NAT on the L4-L7 appliance. However, this approach is suboptimal when you consider the amount of zoning rules needed for each new EPG communicating to the L4-L7 device, requiring constant manual interventions to ACI's application profiles. Such a solution would be unmanageable after a while.

3. **VRF Sandwich**: Represents a very common (traditional, but often preferred by customers) design to encompass the L4-L7 device in the data path. When VRFs at the same time serve as separate security zones, ACI can provide all the intra-VRF routing and filtering using contracts between EPGs. For inter-VRF communication, it then utilizes L3OUTs connected to the L4-L7 device (usually a firewall), which handles the routing and inspection when crossing the security zones. This service insertion is based solely on standard L3 routing between L4-L7 boxes and ACI leaves.

4. **ACI Service Graph**: The last option is our current topic: the utilization of service graphs. They allow you to insert the L4-L7 service device into a forwarding path by specifying a so-called service graph template in an already existing contract between EPGs. There's no need to create new contract relationships or new L4-L7 EPGs. This way you can focus on standard application policies instead of complicated application profile changes to get traffic to the L4-L7 appliance.

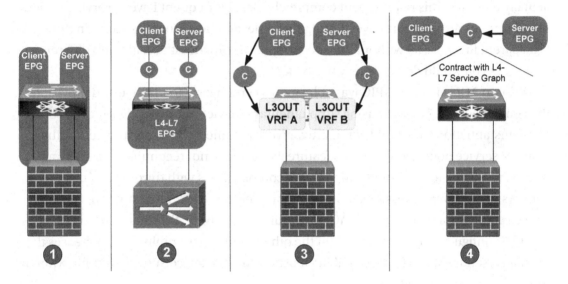

Figure 8-1. *L4-L7 service insertion options*

Usually, multiple factors affect decision-making about the service insertion approach. For brownfield ACI deployments, we always try to preserve the legacy network operation (and forwarding) model, which needs to be migrated to ACI in the first step. It's not common to jump to new service insertion capabilities right away; rather, we move the existing infrastructure as is. Later, when the new application profiles are created in ACI, they may start utilizing service graphs. If ACI is built greenfield, the situation will be easier for you and so will the path to service insertion features.

Let's look closer at what service graphs consist of and how they carry out the data plane traffic forwarding.

Service Graph Overview

I'm sure you already picked up the idea that the main purpose of service graph objects in ACI is a simplified approach to service device insertion. Your goal will be to steer the traffic universally and selectively to any L4-L7 appliance, without almost any special modification applied to the existing application profiles deployed in ACI (and their objects like VRFs, BDs, EPGs, and contracts). Some designs described later in the chapter still count with the L4-L7 device as a default gateway for server endpoints; others actually eliminate this requirement completely. Besides frequent Layer 3 service devices, service graphs also support Layer 2 bridging in the common broadcast domain through transparent firewalls, all without the need to split the broadcast domain into different VLANs, as you would do in a legacy network.

Prior to ACI version 5, APIC was able up to a certain level to manage and provision the connected L4-L7 devices using supplementary "device packages." During the service graph instantiation, you could configure network parameters or security rules for the inserted service node. However, this feature was actually not recommended and was discontinued due to recurring compatibility complications with third-party device vendors; in the current version 5.X it was completely removed. From now on, consider service graphs as a tool to modify ACI forwarding exclusively. External L4-L7 devices must be configured independently. On the other hand, such a philosophy increases the overall versatility of this feature, making it usable for any device and any vendor, without direct relation to Cisco ACI.

In general, service graphs can be considered as an extension of already well-known contracts. They are universal definitions of the logical service chain, applicable to any contract subject and enforced by ACI for all traffic allowed in subject filters. Initially, to describe a service graph, you need to create a *service graph template.* It consists of an ordered chain of *function nodes* theoretically defining the path that allowed traffic should take between the consumer and provider EPGs. Matching the contract philosophy, each function node has two logical connectors, enabling it to be linked either to the internal/external EPG or another function node in the service graph. Internally, each function node carries a single *L4-L7 logical device* object, which represents a container for a detailed description of where and how the actual concrete service devices are connected to the ACI fabric. It's a similar concept to ACI's logical tenant model, abstracting logical configuration and segmentation from the actual placement of physical endpoints in the fabric and their access interface configuration. Logical devices are configured independently of service graphs and, therefore, can be easily reused in multiple service graph templates and interconnected with each other without any change to their definition. You will take a practical look at the configuration of all mentioned objects later in this chapter.

Figure 8-2 illustrates the standard contract between two EPGs with a service graph applied in the subject, defining the chain of three function nodes for the communication path. The sample L4-L7 logical device used in the load balancer function node internally describes a HA cluster of two concrete (physical) load balancers connected behind interfaces Eth1/1-2 of Leaf 101-102, over VLANs 10 and 20.

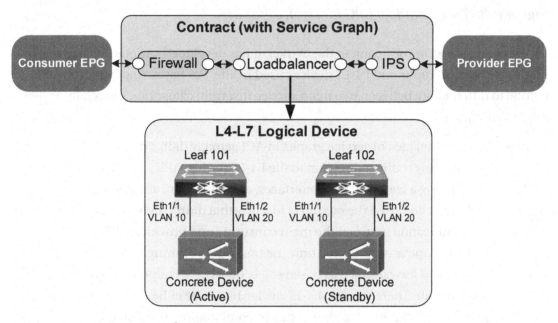

Figure 8-2. *Service graph concept overview*

When such a contract is applied between EPGs, ACI "renders" a service graph instance and implements all the necessary policies, interface configurations, VLANs, and zoning rules on leaf switches to divert the endpoint traffic according to the description. As you can see in Figure 8-3, APIC automatically deploys a new set of shadow EPGs for L4-L7 device interfaces and implements additional contracts allowing communication with them (or instructing leaves to perform the traffic redirect action instead of simple forwarding based on learned endpoint information).

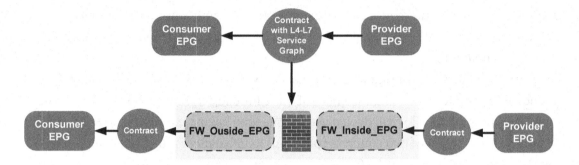

Figure 8-3. *L4-L7 shadow EPG for service graphs*

Since ACI's first introduction to the market, it has developed various deployment modes for service graphs and L4-L7 devices used inside. For better understanding, it's helpful to differentiate between two main service insertion categories, especially as they might look similar:

- The original idea of service graphs in ACI actually didn't directly perform any traffic redirection to the L4-L7 device. APIC, besides configuring a leaf's physical interfaces, encapsulation, and shadow EPGs, just deployed the contracts in a way that didn't allow direct communication between the main consumer and provider EPGs. Instead, contracts permitted only the traffic going through the L4-L7 device, and forwarding was based solely on a leaf's endpoint table information. Therefore, the L4-L7 device had to be either the default gateway for related endpoints (often in combination with L3OUT peerings with external routers) or a transparent node bridging the provider and consumer bridge domains, while the default gateway was provided externally or by ACI. It implies that L4-L7 interfaces were also expected to be part of each related consumer/provider bridge domain.

- A more recent approach (and a much more popular one from my experience with our customers) is utilizing service graphs with policy-based redirect (PBR). It shares some characteristics with the first option: APIC is responsible for the configuration of leaf interfaces, encapsulation, or shadow L4-L7 EPGs together with contract relationships to consumer and provider EPGs. This time, however, L4-L7 interfaces and their shadow EPGs are mapped to dedicated (L2 or L3) service bridge domains. The contracts created between the main EPGs transform into "redirect" zoning rules to the specified PBR node, defined as a MAC or MAC+IP next-hop addresses. The whole traffic matched by the contract's subjects with the PBR service graph is then redirected to the L4-L7 appliance based on this policy instead of being forwarded according to the standard endpoint table.

L4-L7 Device Deployment (Design) Modes

In this section, I'll summarize the available L4-L7 design options belonging to both previously mentioned categories.

Traditional Service Graph Designs

I will start with more conventional service graph designs, automating the contract deployment between main EPGs and shadow ones created for L4-L7 nodes, but without actual traffic redirection.

1. **Go-To Mode** (routed mode): For the routed mode, we assume that the L4-L7 device is always a default gateway for connected servers. There are two bridge domains needed for this design: Client BD, in which the outside interface of the L4-L7 device is connected, and Server BD for the inside L4-L7 interface (always L2 only). Based on the routing solution implemented from the external clients to ACI, we can further divide this design into following subcategories:

   a. **Routed Mode using L2 Outside Bridge Domain**: The outside interface of the L4-L7 device is connected over the L2 bridge domain to the external router, which provides a default gateway for the L4-L7 device and routes in the opposite way the server segments back to it (see Figure 8-4). BDs can be associated to a single VRF, but just to comply with the ACI object model. No routing inside ACI itself is performed.

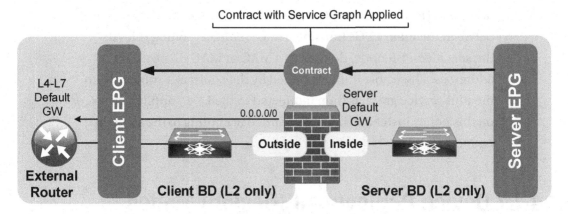

Figure 8-4. *Routed L4-L7 node with L2 BDs only*

    b. ***Routed Mode using NAT and external WAN L3OUT***: A design
       suitable for FW or LB performing NAT translation between
       client and server IP addresses. Outbound connectivity for
       the L4-L7 device is implemented by a static default route
       pointing to the external BD's subnet IP, and external routing
       from ACI is handled using WAN L3OUT (see Figure 8-5).
       The NAT pool of the L4-L7 device should be advertised by
       L3OUT to the external network. A contract with a service
       graph is then applied between the server EPGs and the WAN
       L3OUT ExtEPG.

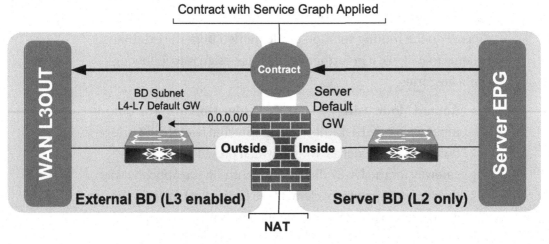

Figure 8-5. *Routed L4-L7 node with WAN L3OUT*

c. ***Routed Mode with L3OUT to L4-L7 device***: This is a variation
    of the previous design, where the outside L4-L7 interface
    is connected via L3OUT to ACI. We need separate VRFs for
    internal (even though not used) and external forwarding
    together with two L3OUTs (see Figure 8-6). One connects
    ACI to the external WAN network, the other the outside
    interface of FW or LB. Mutual external routing from/to such an
    architecture can be implemented statically, using a dynamic
    protocol, or by a combination of both. A contract with a
    service graph is applied between the server EPG and the WAN
    L3OUT ExtEPG.

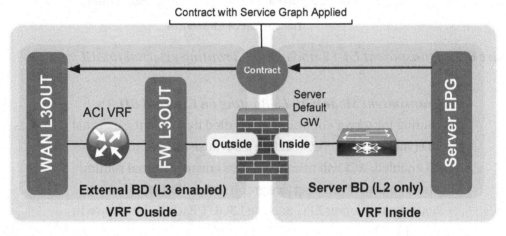

Figure 8-6. *Routed L4-L7 node connected directly to L3OUT*

2. **Go-Through Mode**: The second mode, often referred as a pass-
    through or transparent, is used when you intend to include a
    transparent L4-L7 device in the path. We use two bridge domains,
    one for servers and the other for clients (external connectivity),
    but this time the L4-L7 device doesn't provide a default gateway.
    It just transparently forwards packets between both bridge
    domains. As a default gateway, servers need to utilize either ACI
    SVI interface configured in the external bridge domain or some
    other external router. These options further divide the go-through
    design into following:

a. **Transparent Mode with Layer 2 Bridge Domains**: A default gateway for servers is on a router external to ACI, connected via an external L2 BD (see Figure 8-7).

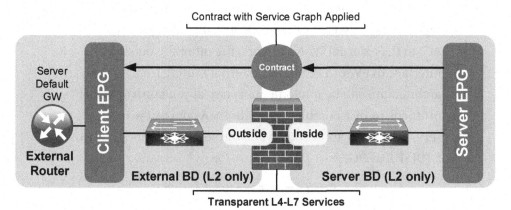

Figure 8-7. *Transparent L4-L7 node with L3 routing external to ACI*

b. *Transparent Mode with L3 Routing on External BD*: The routing for server endpoints is handled by ACI in the external BD (via its subnet SVI interface). Because the external BD is L3 enabled, ACI will need L3OUT to ensure external routing and a contract with a service graph is therefore applied between the server EPG and the L3OUT ExtEPG (as shown in Figure 8-8).

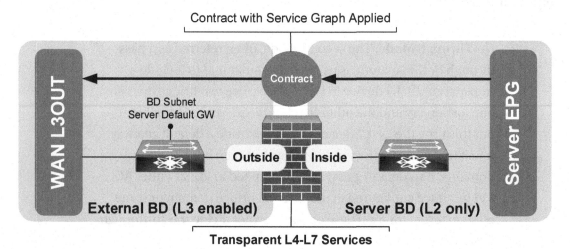

Figure 8-8. *Transparent L4-L7 node with L3 routing in the external ACI BD*

402

Policy-Based Redirect Service Graph Designs

The main difference between the traditional approach and the policy-based redirect lies in dedicated bridge domains created for the interfaces of the L4-L7 device and the contract deployment actively steering matched packets from ingress leaves to the L4-L7 node. Let's first compare from a high-level point of view various design options for PBR service Graphs and then I will describe their operation in much more detail. Having deployed devices through both methods, this newer approach to service insertion in ACI brings more consistency to the network design, simplification, and more optimal utilization of both ACI and L4-L7 device resources.

1. **Go-To Mode (Routed Mode) with PBR**: This model doesn't require (but supports) multiple VRF instances, L3OUTs, or L4-L7 devices performing NAT. In routed PBR mode, there is just a single prerequirement: that all used bridge domains have unicast routing enabled with the configured subnet (thus acting like a default gateway for endpoints or L3 interconnection for the L4-L7 devices). Two main design sub-options exist:

   a. **Policy-Based Redirect with Service Bridge Domains**: The standard PBR model, where L4-L7 device connectors must be part of their own service bridge domain in L3 mode. You can use either a two-arm (as shown in Figure 8-9) or a one-arm connection with just one service BD. The source and destination endpoints can belong to internal as well as external L3OUT EPGs, so this approach is universally suitable for east-west and north-south traffic. Besides a single VRF for all bridge domains, PBR supports inter-VRF connectivity as well, with a design rule that the L4-L7 device and its interfaces have to be part of a consumer or provider VRF (or both). It just cannot be placed in the third, non-related VRF.

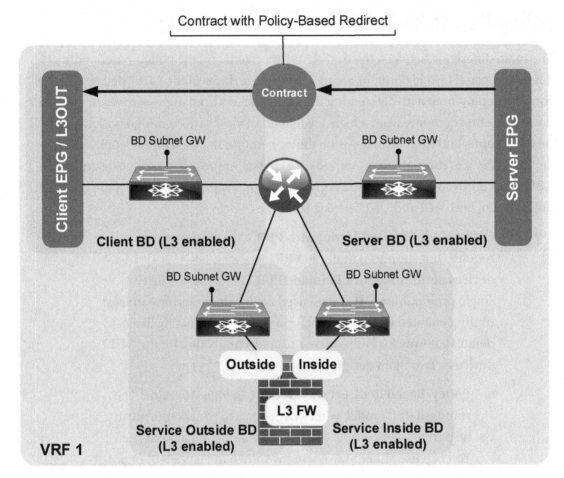

Figure 8-9. *Routed policy-based redirect with bridge domain*

    b.   ***Policy-Based Redirect with L3OUTs***: Since ACI version 5.2
        there is also an option to utilize dynamic routing between ACI
        and the L4-L7 device by configuring two L3OUTs instead of
        standard bridge domains (see Figure 8-10).

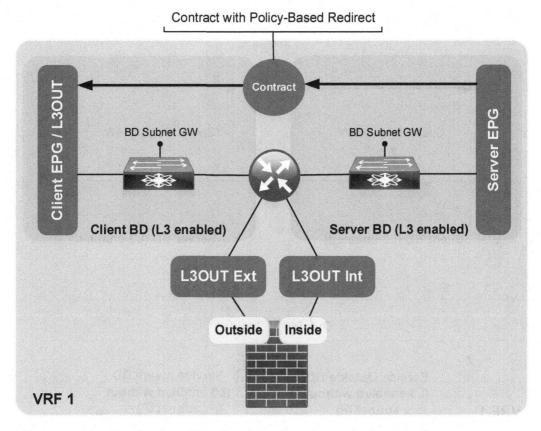

Figure 8-10. *Routed policy-based redirect to two-arm L4-L7 node*

2. ***Go-Through (Transparent Mode) with PBR***: Policy-based
   redirection is supported in a very similar way for transparent
   bridging via an intermediate L4-L7 appliance. Now the
   transparent device can be connected two-arm only using two
   dedicated service bridge domains. Although their unicast routing
   has to be enabled, they are configured without any specific subnet
   IP address (as illustrated in Figure 8-11). The consumer/provider
   bridge domains are L3 enabled and the regularly provided default
   gateway. Also, transparent redirect doesn't require any specific
   changes to the rest of the application profile.

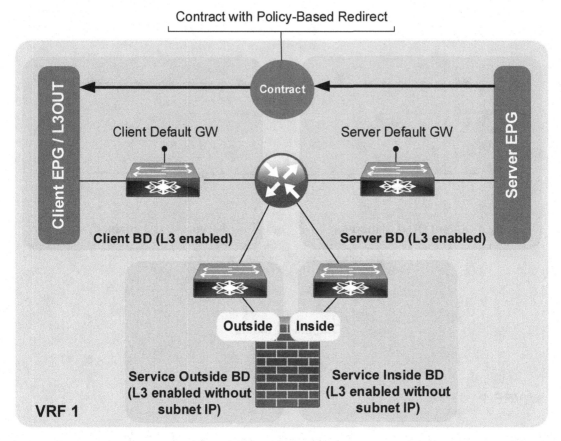

Figure 8-11. *Transparent policy-based redirect to two-arm L4-L7 node*

Note   For all previously described designs, always refer to the official ACI whitepapers before implementing a particular one as various specifics and limits may apply, sometimes related to the currently used ACI version. In the Appendix of this book, you will find links to the most important and useful official resources.

L4-L7 Policy-Based Redirect

As indicated, when it comes to service insertion in ACI, after our discussions with customers, we mostly end up using both traditional routings between VRFs based on L3OUTs (a VRF sandwich) as well as a service graph with a policy-based redirect. PBR offers basically everything you need to simply and effectively create a chain of L4-L7 service devices to which ACI forwards deterministically based on a predefined MAC or MAC+IP next-hop addresses. All that with single (one-arm) or double (two-arm) interfaces on L4-L7 appliances. Even when new contracts or provider/consumer EPGs are configured in ACI's application profile with service insertion, it won't affect the networking settings of the L4-L7 devices. Usually, you just need to add new firewall rules or load balancer policies.

Due to the significant advantages and popularity, I will dedicate the rest of this chapter exclusively to policy-based redirect, which I will analyze in more detail.

VRF Sandwich vs. Policy-Based Redirect

Figure 8-12 illustrates the traditional VRF sandwich design. In ACI, it's implemented using L3OUTs from each VRF to the external L3 device (often a L4-L7 service device). Bridge domain subnets (IPs) shown in Figure 8-12 represent the configuration of the default gateways in ACI for connected end hosts. Both L3OUTs use /29 interconnection subnets due to the need for addressing at least two borders' leaves and the connected L4-L7 device (consuming one or more IP addresses). All inter-VRF traffic is required to pass it and each VRF requires a new L3 interface. It's suitable for securing the whole inter-zone north-south traffic.

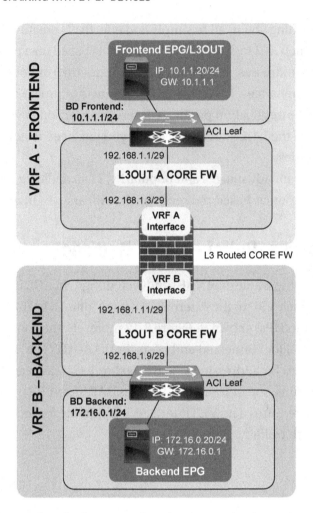

Figure 8-12. *VRF sandwich design without ACI service insertion*

On the other hand, Figure 8-13 shows an example of a service graph with policy-based redirect, which can deviate the traffic selectively and consistently to the same set of interfaces on L4-L7 devices (and BDs) even within the same VRF. New VRFs or communicating EPGs/ESGs don't result in new interfaces on the intermediate service node.

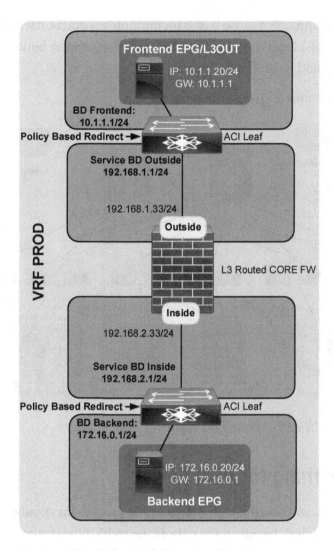

Figure 8-13. *Service graph with policy-based redirect*

Regarding PBR selectiveness, we can differentiate between various traffic patterns in two ways:

1. In a single contract, we can deploy multiple subjects with different filters and PBR is applied only for some of them. The rest of the traffic can flow directly through the fabric without a service device inserted in a path. Using the same concept, subjects can differentiate between multiple L4-L7 devices.

2. Another approach may be based on multiple contracts, each using different L4-L7 devices. A typical use case is separation between east-west and north-south firewalls.

Figure 8-14 illustrates both described options.

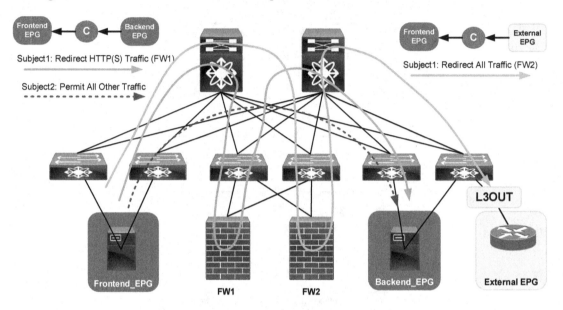

Figure 8-14. *Selective PBR based on contract subject filters*

Endpoint Learning for PBR Device

In previous chapters, you saw the endpoint learning process for standard EPGs and bridge domains. Each leaf, based on the data-plane traffic observation, learns both locally connected stations as well as endpoints behind the remote leaves (VTEPs). This happens thanks to the (by default) enabled option in each bridge domain called *Endpoint Dataplane Learning.* With PBR deployed between EPGs, this standard behavior can potentially cause forwarding problems, though.

Consider the example shown in Figure 8-15. Server A with IP 10.1.1.10 is normally learned by all other leaves in the fabric behind Leaf 101. If we include a PBR service graph for the communication to Server B (10.3.3.20), the packets will be redirected to FW on Leaf 102. However, FW won't change the source or destination Ips; it just routes the traffic. As soon as FW returns the traffic to Leaf 102, the switch will learn the locally connected endpoint 10.1.1.10, it will update the COOP database, and after forwarding traffic to its destination, Leaf 103 will incorrectly learn endpoint 10.1.1.10 being connected behind Leaf 102 as well. In the end, this will disrupt not only the PBR traffic, but likewise all others.

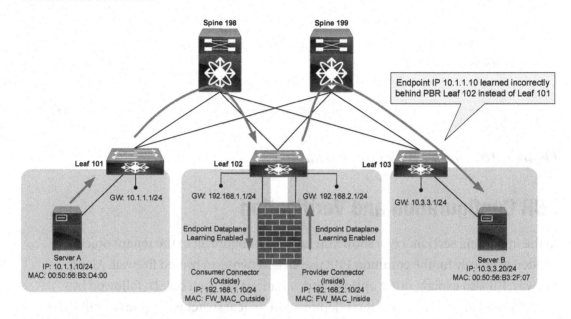

Figure 8-15. *PBR bridge domain dataplane endpoint learning*

It is highly recommended and considered a best practice to disable the Endpoint *Dataplane Learning* setting on all bridge domains where PBR devices are connected. Even though this step is not mandatory since ACI version 3.1 (ACI should automatically disable learning on PBR EPGs during the deployment), I still recommend you do so. Just in case.

This configuration knob can be found in **Tenants -> Tenant_name -> Networking -> Bridge Domains -> BD_name**, under the **Policy -> Advanced/Troubleshooting** tab (shown in Figure 8-16).

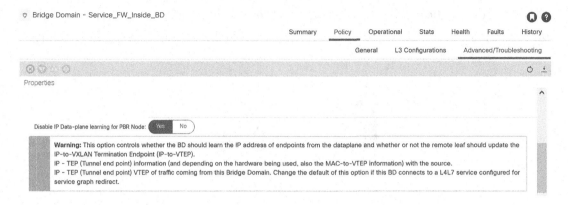

Figure 8-16. *Disable IP dataplane learning*

PBR Configuration and Verification

In the upcoming section, I will show you how to configure all of the tenant objects needed primarily for the common PBR use case: a two-arm routed firewall. Along the way, I'll also explain other options and variations for each object, followed by verification and description of their deployment on leaf switches. Figure 8-17 illustrates the intended design for this example.

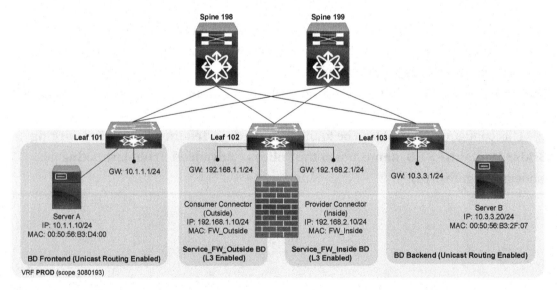

Figure 8-17. *External Layer 2 extension*

The depicted firewall physically consists of two appliances, both connected to Leaf-102 (active/standby), interfaces eth1/10-13.

Note Before starting with the tenant configuration, don't forget to prepare ACI's access policies for the L4-L7 service device. They are required, just like for any other connected endpoint.

Service Bridge Domain(s)

First, you will prepare two dedicated service bridge domains. With PBR, the advantage is that their configuration is independent of the consumer/provider bridge domains and won't affect the endpoints themselves. The service bridge domain should follow these recommended properties (see Figure 8-18):

- **Unicast Routing**: Enabled

- **Subnet (Default GW)**: Created, if the connected L4-L7 device is routed. In case of a transparent one, subnet is not needed (but unicast routing is still yes).

- **EP Move Detection Mode**: GARP Based Detection

- **Dataplane Endpoint Learning**: Disabled

Networking - Bridge Domains

▲ Name	▼	Alias	Type	Segment	VRF	Multicast Address	Custom MAC Address	L2 Unknown Unicast	ARP Flooding	Unicast Routing	Subnet
Backend_BD			regular	16318374	PROD	225.1.189.176	00:22:BD:F8:19:FF	Hardware Proxy	True	True	10.2.2.1/24, 10.3.3.1/24
Database_BD			regular	16449430	PROD	225.0.178.80	00:22:BD:F8:19:FF	Hardware Proxy	True	True	10.4.4.1/24
Frontend_BD			regular	16089026	PROD	225.1.150.240	00:22:BD:F8:19:FF	Hardware Proxy	True	True	10.1.1.1/24
Service_FW_Inside_BD			regular	16056266	PROD	225.0.80.176	00:22:BD:F8:19:FF	Hardware Proxy	True	True	192.168.2.1/24
Service_FW_Outside_BD			regular	15859680	PROD	225.0.212.0	00:22:BD:F8:19:FF	Hardware Proxy	True	True	192.168.1.1/24

Figure 8-18. *L4-L7 service bridge domains*

L4-L7 PBR Policy

Another essential object for PBR to work is the definition of the next-hop addresses where the traffic should be redirected by ACI leaves. The PBR policy can be found in **Tenants -> Tenant_name -> Policies -> Protocol -> L4-L7 Policy-Based Redirect**.

Consider this object as a universal building block usable in multiple service graphs later. If the L4-L7 device is connected in two-arm mode, you will need two separate policies, one for each logical connector–provider interface and consumer interface. In the case of a one-arm device, a single policy is enough. Multiple active devices with different IPs can be configured as destination next-hops and ACI will ensure symmetric load balancing between them.

Figure 8-19 illustrates the configuration form for a FW outside interface in the model topology. Analogically, one is created for the FW inside interface as well.

Figure 8-19. *L4-L7 PBR Policies*

For PBR, the only mandatory field is the destination definition, but as you can see, the L4-L7 policy-based redirect policy offers many other (useful) configuration options, including the following:

- **Destination Type**: Here you can differentiate between the type of connected device, resulting in different next-hop definitions (MAC only or MAC+IP):

- **L1 Device**: Typically, a completely transparent security device, not participating in any VLAN translation or routing. It acts more like simple virtual wire (often referred to as wire or inline mode). The next hop to the L1 PBR device is specified as a MAC address, which will be installed on a leaf in the form of a static MAC endpoint.

- **L2 Device**: Usually performing a VLAN translation on its interfaces, while bridging the traffic between them. Supported by many firewalls and IPSes. The next hop to the L2 device is again specified as a MAC address only.

- **L3 Device**: Default routed mode, where L4-L7 is actively participating in a routing based on the destination IP address lookup. The next-hop definition for the L3 device is IP+MAC.

- **Rewrite Source MAC**: Enables a rewrite of a source MAC address when forwarding packets from a leaf to a service device. By default, ACI preserves the original client MAC address, which can cause forwarding problems if the service device uses some form of "source MAC-based forwarding" instead of IP. With this option, the source MAC is changed to the BD's subnet MAC and proper reverse routing to the service default gateway is ensured.

- **IP SLA Monitoring Policy:** A feature to allow tracking availability of the destination MAC or IP addresses. You can choose from the simple ICMP ping mode, destination TCP port tracking, L2 ping, or HTTP GET to a specified URI, all with granular timers and threshold configurations.

- **Threshold**: After IP SLA is enabled, you can define the minimum and maximum (expressed in percentage) amount of available service devices (next hops). If they go under a certain threshold, the whole L4-L7 object is considered down and one of the configurable actions will be performed:

  - **Permit:** Traffic will be forwarded directly through the fabric without PBR.

- **Bypass**: If the service graph consists of multiple function nodes, this down node is skipped, and traffic will be redirected to the next one.

- **Deny**: Traffic is dropped.

- **Enable POD Aware Redirection**: In a multi-POD environment, you can optimize the forwarding by preferring the local L4-L7 node for local traffic whenever possible. In case of failure, ACI can still utilize the remote PBR node in the distant Pod.

- **Hashing Algorithm**: Alters how the traffic is loadbalanced between multiple active PBR nodes with different interface MAC+IPs, if configured.

- **Anycast Endpoint**: Allows forwarding of traffic to the same Anycast IP+MAC address of multiple PBR nodes, always choosing the closest one.

- **Resilient Hashing Enabled:** By default, when you use multiple active PBR nodes and one fails, ACI will evenly rehash all flows between the rest of available ones. This can temporarily affect even healthy flows. Resilient hashing makes sure only flows from a failed node are redistributed among others.

- **L1/L2/L3 Destinations**: A mandatory list containing the specification of next hops to PBR devices (their interfaces). For IP SLA monitoring or resilient hashing in case of multiple active nodes, all destinations should share the same Redirect Health Group as well (see Figure 8-20).

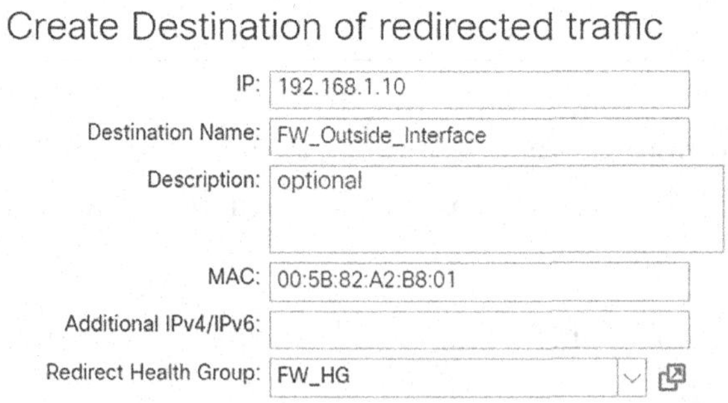

Figure 8-20. *PBR destination configuration*

In the two-arm FW example, you will end up creating two L4-L7 redirect policies: FW_Outside with the outside interface destination IP+MAC (192.168.1.10, 00:58:82:A2:B8:01) and FW_Inside with the inside interface destination IP+MAC (192.168.2.10, 00:58:82:A2:B8:02).

Note   If you enable the IP SLA to track the destination IP address of the L4-L7 node, since ACI version 5.2 you don't need to actually fill in the MAC address in this policy object. Just put all zeros there or leave the field blank. ACI will automatically ARP for it during the IP SLA operation and use the received MAC address.

L4-L7 Device

Thanks to the previous PBR policy object, ACI knows where to redirect the traffic from an addressing point of view. The L4-L7 device object further describes the logical service node, its physical location in the ACI fabric, the encapsulation used on its interfaces, and the definition of multiple physical nodes composing a logical device HA cluster. This object is again a universal building block for later use in service graphs, usable for both traditional and policy-based redirect approaches. You can create it in **Tenants -> Tenant_name -> Services -> L4-L7 -> Devices.**

Figure 8-21 shows the sample configuration of the L4-L7 device for your two-arm firewall, consisting of two physical active-standby nodes connected to Leaf-102 interfaces eth1/10-13.

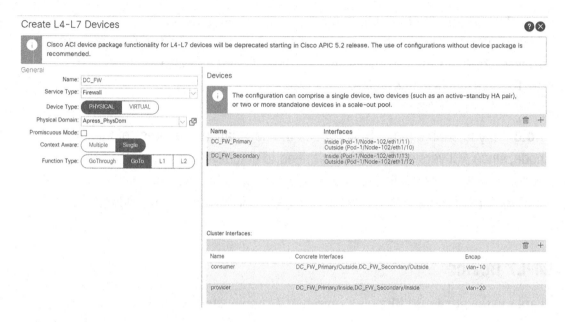

Figure 8-21. *L4-L7 device configuration*

Let's look closer at all the options provided here:

- **Service Type**: Choose from three available options based on the connected device: firewall, application delivery controller (ADC), meaning load balancer, or other. The last one is used for connecting L1/L2 firewalls.

- **Device Type**: You should leave this knob to default *Physical* mode for any physical service appliance, or even an appliance running as a VM, but without VMM integration with ACI (described in the following chapter). If the virtualization platform is integrated with ACI and you intend to use a virtual L4-L7 device, switch to *Virtual* here.

- **Physical Domain**: An important reference to ACI access policies. Service devices require complete access configuration like any other endpoint connected to ACI. So make sure you have the correct VLAN blocks in the VLAN pool used for forwarding to L4-L7 devices.

- **Promiscuous Mode**: Option enabling promiscuous mode for VM L4-L7 devices in case of VMM integration. A typical use case is a virtual IDS system, gaining visibility of all traffic flowing through the virtual switch thanks to this setting.

- **Context Aware**: By default, the L4-L7 device is considered to be used only within the single ACI tenant. If the goal is to share it between multiple users, *Context Awareness* should be set to *Multiple*. This option is ignored for ADC service type devices.

- **Function Type**: Go-Through for transparent devices, Go-To for routed, or L1 for completely inline (virtual wire) nodes. The last L2 option is concurrent with Go-Through. This is just for historical and backward compatibility reasons.

- **Devices**: This list describes so-called "concrete devices." Here you should configure all physical/virtual nodes with their exact interfaces connected to ACI, which forms a logical HA cluster. Single node, active-standby HA pair, or multiple active nodes for symmetric load balancing of flows (scale-out).

- **Cluster Interfaces**: These represent already mentioned logical connectors of a function node in a service graph with the definition of encapsulation used. You always need to have two: for the consumer side and one for the provider side. Therefore, it's best practice to name them likewise.

For your example, consider a physical firewall L4-L7 with a single context and GoTo (routed) mode since you will use L3 PBR. A firewall HA pair is defined in the Devices section by two entries: the primary and secondary nodes. Each has an outside and inside interface definition (two-arm mode). Then two logical connectors for a service graph are created. The consumer (client side) contains the outside interfaces of both FW nodes with encapsulation VLAN 10 and the provider (server side) contains the inside interfaces with VLAN 20. The firewall network configuration should, of course, match the defined VLANs. At the same time, it's a simple way to split a single physical service device into multiple virtual device contexts (VDCs) if supported. Just create multiple L4-L7 device objects with the same configuration except for VLANs, which will differentiate between firewall VDCs on top of the same physical interfaces.

All these settings put together completely describe the firewall cluster and its connectivity with ACI. Now it's time to join the L4-L7 device object with previous L4-L7 redirect policies into a service graph template.

Service Graph Templates

ACI requires you to prepare a service graph template before deploying it to the fabric in a particular contract. The template is like a prescription of how the service insertion should universally work between any two EPGs, to which the contract carrying it will be deployed. You can chain multiple L4-L7 devices or enable policy-based redirection this step.

To configure a service graph template, head to **Tenants -> Tenant_name -> Services -> L4-L7 -> Service Graph Template** (as shown in Figure 8-22).

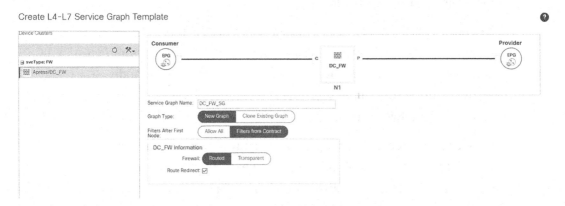

Figure 8-22. *L4-L7 service graph template configuration*

In the left pane, you will find all L4-L7 logical devices created in the previous step, and by dragging-and-dropping them between the generic consumer and provider EPG placeholders shown on the right you define the service graph operation. Multiple devices can be chained here as well if needed. For your example, use the following settings:

- Single PBR node between consumer and provider EPG (L4-L7 Device DC_FW)

- **Graph Type:** New Graph. Optionally you can copy settings from the existing one.

- **Filters After First Node**: This setting applies to filters in the zoning rule that don't have the consumer EPG's Class ID as a source or destination (meaning after the first service node). The default setting of *Allow All* simply permits all traffic, directing it to consecutive service nodes. *Filters from Contract* enables more granular traffic control between multiple nodes if needed.

- **Firewall**: Routed/Transparent, must match the L4-L7 device setting

- **Route Redirect**: **(!!!) It's crucial to enable this knob in order to implement policy-based redirect.** This directly affects if the zoning rules will enforce the traffic redirection.

Applying a Service Graph Template to a Contract

The completed service graph template now needs to be instantiated by deploying in an existing or new contract between two actual EPGs (internal/external) or ESGs. To do so, right-click the service graph template object and choose *Apply L4-L7 Service Graph Template*. A two-step form opens (as you can see in Figure 8-23).

Figure 8-23. *L4-L7 service graph template application – Step 1*

The first configuration step is related to the contract definition. Choose the consumer and provider EPGs or ESGs where the contract with the service graph will be applied (at the time of writing this book, the newest ACI 6.0 does not support mixed EPG/ESG relationships). Then fill in the contract information; either choose an existing contract subject or create a completely new contract. By default, no filter is predefined, meaning that the contract will match all traffic, and all traffic will be redirected to the L4-L7 device. The common option is to specify the matched traffic instead manually.

Proceeding to the second step will bring you to the configuration of the Logical Interface Contexts as part of Devices Selection Policy object (see Figure 8-24). The Devices Selection Policy will be later located in **Tenants -> Tenant_Name -> Services -> L4-L7 -> Devices Selection Policy**. The main purpose of these objects is to set the bridge domain affiliation and map the L4-L7 redirect policies with logical connectors of each functional node in the service graph template. Based on Devices Selection Policy, ACI will also deploy a new shadow service EPG for each interface of the service device.

Apply L4–L7 Service Graph Template to EPG/ESG(s)

STEP 2 > Graph

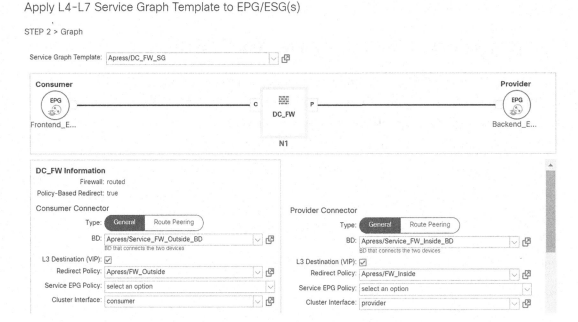

Figure 8-24. *L4-L7 service graph template application – Step 2*

For each L4-L7 logical device (DC_FW in your case), there will be two configuration sections: the consumer and provider connectors. Both offer the following options:

- **Connector Type**: General for interfaces connected via service bridge domains or route peering for service devices behind L3OUTs

- **BD**: Service bridge domain definition for each connector

- **L3 Destination (VIP)**: Flag to differentiate between PBR nodes or non-PBR within the same service graph template. For PBR interfaces, it's always enabled.

- **Redirect Policy**: Previously prepared L4-L7 redirect policy, instructing ACI where to steer the traffic. In case of a two-arm service device, make sure to map the correct policy to the correct connector, usually the outside interface to the consumer side and inside to the provider.

- **Service EPG Policy**: Allows you to include shadow service EPGs to a VRF's preferred group

- **Cluster Interface**: Consumer/Provider, automatically set to match the connector type

After submitting the form, ACI will finally merge and deploy all the previously defined settings and policies resulting in a service graph instantiation.

PBR Service Graph Deployment Verification

You will now closely examine the created service graph objects and rules from both GUI and CLI points of view starting with the service graph instance in **Tenants -> Tenant_ name -> Services -> L4-L7 -> Deployed Graph Instances.** When you click and open the main service graph instance object, ACI will provide you with an information summary about its deployment between two actual EPGs, the configuration of the L3-L4 device and its interfaces, redirect policies, and more (as shown in Figure 8-25). Make sure to check for faults related to this object. If there is some problem with graph "rendering" in the fabric, APIC will let you know here. The most common issues are related to interface encapsulation missing in access policies or an incorrect BD assignment.

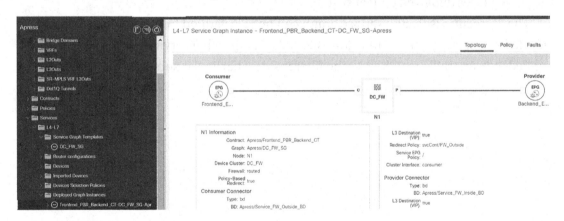

Figure 8-25. *Deployed graph instances – main object*

Next, expand the service graph instance object, where you will find a list of all applied function nodes in general. In your example, you see just one logical FW node named **N1** (default name)**.** After opening the function node object, you'll see an important overview of cluster logical and concrete interfaces, together with function connectors and their configuration (refer to Figure 8-26).

Figure 8-26. *Deployed graph instances – function node*

The cluster interfaces section provides an opportunity to check if the actual physical interfaces of the L4-L7 devices are mapped in a correct VLAN to the correct service graph function node connector. Then, in the function connectors section, notice that each connector finally received a ClassID. These are policy tags (pcTags) of shadow EPGs, ensuring connectivity for firewall interfaces, and you will check them in a while in the zoning rules deployed on leaf switches.

The correctly associated service graph can be also verified from a contract point of view in its subject (as shown in Figure 8-27). Remember that service graphs are always applied only on traffic matched by the filter inside a particular subject.

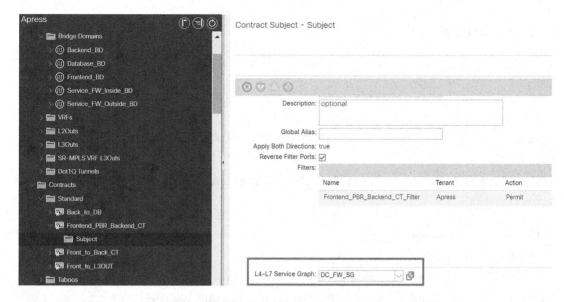

Figure 8-27. *L4-L7 service graph deployed in contract subject*

When you move to the CLI, one of the main verification tools used on the provider and consumer leaves where the policy-based redirect should be enforced is the command and its output shown in Listing 8-1.

Listing 8-1. Policy-Based Redirect Verification

```
Leaf-102# show service redir info

 List of Dest Groups
GrpID Name       destination                               HG-name        operSt
  operStQual  TL   TH
===== ====   ===========                               ============== =======
=========== === ===
3     destgrp-3  dest-[192.168.2.10]-[vxlan-3080193] Apress::FW_HG  enabled
no-oper-grp  50   100
2     destgrp-2  dest-[192.168.1.10]-[vxlan-3080193] Apress::FW_HG  enabled
no-oper-grp  50   100
```

```
 List of destinations
Name                    bdVnid           vMac            vrf          operSt
HG-name
====                    ======           ====            ====         =====
======
dest-[192.168.1.10]    vxlan-15859680   00:5B:82:A2:B8:01 Apress:PROD enabled
Apress::FW_HG
dest-[192.168.2.10]    vxlan-16056266   00:5B:82:A2:B8:02 Apress:PROD enabled
Apress::FW_HG

 List of Health Groups
HG-Name         HG-OperSt  HG-Dest                               HG-Dest-OperSt
=======         =========  =======                               ==============
Apress::FW_HG enabled     dest-[192.168.1.10]-[vxlan-3080193]]  up
                          dest-[192.168.2.10]-[vxlan-3080193]]  up
```

Consistent information should be present on all leaf switches where the provider or consumer EPGs with their bridge domains are deployed. They are primarily performing the policy-based redirect. Look especially for correctly configured destination IPs and MACs, enabled health groups, and an operational state of *Enabled*. If you have IP SLA configured (I highly recommend doing so) and there is some reachability issue with the configured addresses, this output will notify you the about operational status of *Disabled* with a further explanation of *tracked-as-down* in the operStQual column. Destination group IDs shown at the beginning of each group line will play their role in zoning.

PBR Contracts Programming

For PBR verification, it's also useful to be aware how contracts with PBR are programmed into a zoning rule table of leaf switches. Let's start with a simple review of a contract between two internal EPGs without any PBR service graph (as shown in Figure 8-28).

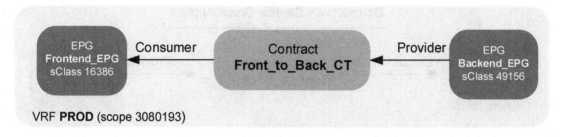

Figure 8-28. *Standard contract between two application EPGs*

This standard contract in its default configuration with both options of *Apply both directions* and *Reverse filter ports* enabled will result in two zoning rules shown in Listing 8-2. Scope 3080193 refers to a VRF SegmentID, SrcEPG, and DstEPG then to EPG's pcTag or sClass.

Listing 8-2. Standard Contract Implementation Without a PBR Service Graph

```
Leaf-101# show zoning-rule scope 3080193
```

| Rule ID | SrcEPG | DstEPG | FilterID | Dir | operSt |
Scope	Name		Action	Priority	
4130	16386	49156	27	bi-dir	enabled
3080193	Front_to_Back_CT		permit	fully_qual(7)	
4131	49156	16386	28	uni-dir-ignore	enabled
3080193	Front_to_Back_CT		permit	fully_qual(7)	

Now consider the previously discussed PBR service graph applied between standard EPGs (shown in Figure 8-29).

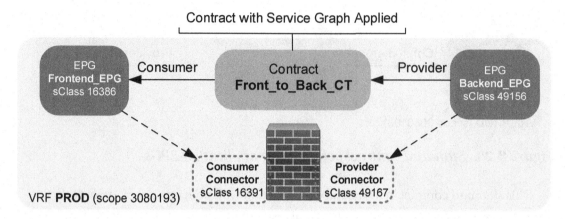

Figure 8-29. *L4-L7 service graph deployed between two application EPGs*

The same source and destination rules for application EPGs are still preserved, just their action is changed from a simple permit to *redir* or *threshold-redir*. Redirect actions further refer to PBR destination groups, which you saw in the show service redir info output. Notice that new zoning rules are added with shadow EPG pcTags as source and destination (RuleID 4230 and 4231 in Listing 8-3). The purpose of these rules is to permit the forwarding from the egress interface of the L4-L7 device to the destination EPG in each direction.

Listing 8-3. PBR Service Graph Zoning Rules

```
Leaf-101# show zoning-rule scope 3080193
+---------+--------+--------+----------+----------------+---------+
---------+----------------------------------------+----------------+
| Rule ID | SrcEPG | DstEPG | FilterID |      Dir       |  operSt
|  Scope  |       Name       |        Action        |    Priority   |
+---------+--------+--------+----------+----------------+---------+
---------+----------------------------------------+----------------+
|   4130  | 16386  | 49156  |    27    |     bi-dir     | enabled |
  3080193 |                  | threshold_redir(destgrp-2) | fully_qual(7) |
|   4230  | 49167  | 49156  |    27    |     uni-dir    | enabled |
  3080193 |                  |        permit        | fully_qual(7) |
```

```
|   4131  | 49156  | 16386  |   28    | uni-dir-ignore | enabled |
 3080193  |                  | threshold_redir(destgrp-3) | fully_qual(7) |
|   4231  | 16391  | 16386  |   28    |     uni-dir    | enabled |
 3080193  |                  |        permit              | fully_qual(7) |
+---------+--------+--------+---------+----------------+--------+
---------+------------------------------------------+---------------+
```

When an endpoint from the consumer EPG (pcTag 16386) initiates a connection to the provider (pcTag 49156), its packets are matched by RuleID 4130, instructing the leaf to perform a redirect to the destination group 2: the outside/consumer connector of the L4-L7 device. The packet is then processed by the service device and returned to the leaf via the inside/provider connector (shadow pcTag 49167). Thanks to the new RuleID 4230, this traffic is permitted and delivered to the destination. The reply from the provider EPG is redirected to destination group 3 based on RuleID 4131 and the returning traffic from the service device via the outside/consumer connector (shadow pcTag 16391) is permitted by RuleID 4231.

Tip   To actually see the redirected traffic, it's convenient to use the already described ELAM tool or to configure SPAN sessions with source interfaces of L4-L7 devices. Alternatively, you can also enable some traffic capture utility directly on the service device if it is equipped with that.

Traffic Flow Between EPGs with PBR

Speaking about policy-based redirect traffic, I want to further strengthen your understanding by extending the previous example to show you how actual traffic flow works in the ACI fabric with a PBR service graph applied. Let's suppose you have two communicating endpoints: consumer Server A with IP 10.1.1.10 and provider Server B with IP 10.3.3.10. They have already resolved their default gateway using ARP (so the endpoints are locally learned, and the spine's COOP database is populated), but this will be their first mutual traffic flow (refer to Figure 8-30).

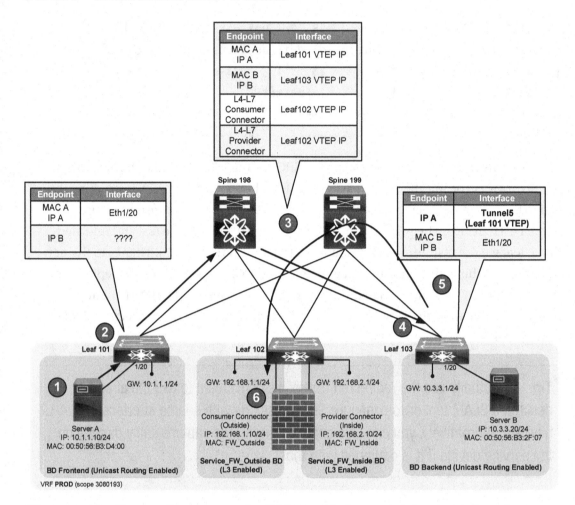

Figure 8-30. *Forwarding process for PBR-enabled communication – Part 1*

The step-by-step traffic forwarding process goes like this:

1. Server A generates a packet with its own source IP address and the destination IP of Server B. The packet is sent to Leaf 101, which acts as a default gateway for the server's bridge domain.

2. Leaf 101 hasn't learned the IP address of the destination server yet. Therefore, it cannot resolve the destination EPG ClassID (pcTag) or apply the zoning rules. As the traffic is being routed and Leaf 101 should have at least a pervasive subnet of Backend BD in the routing table (10.3.3.0/24), the original packet is encapsulated into the VXLAN header with the VRF VNID and sent towards

the spines based on the VRF routing table information (to spine
Anycast VTEP IP). In the VXLAN header, there is the sClass of the
source EPG carried as well.

3. Spines have in their COOP database complete information about
    both communicating endpoints as well as L4-L7 consumer/
    provider interfaces from PBR objects configured in APIC. We
    will get to PBR soon, but at this point the server endpoints are
    important. The spine, based on a destination IP from the inner
    IP header, resolves the Server B MAC+IP entry, which is learned
    behind the leaf 103 VTEP IP address. The destination IP address in
    the outer VXLAN header is rewritten and the packet is forwarded
    to Leaf 103.

4. The incoming VXLAN packet causes Leaf 103 to learn the source
    endpoint with its source VTEP address of Leaf 101 and it will
    create the dynamic VXLAN tunnel interface. Additionally, Leaf 103
    will learn the EPG information of Server A thanks to the VXLAN
    header field carrying the source sClass. Now, Leaf 103 has both
    source and destination EPG information in its endpoint table, and
    it can perform a zoning table lookup and enforce the PBR contract
    applied between EPGs. Just to remind you, ingress Leaf 101
    couldn't enforce any contract due to missing information, so it set
    Source/Destination Policy (SP 0/DP 1) flags in the VXLAN header
    to instruct the destination Leaf to apply for a contract instead.

5. The PBR zoning rule instructs Leaf 103 to redirect traffic from
    the consumer EPG based on a given destination group to the
    consumer connector of the L4-L7 device. To do so, the VXLAN
    VNID is rewritten to the L4-L7 consumer bridge domain VNID,
    and the destination MAC address is rewritten to a L4-L7 consumer
    interface. Leaf 103, however, doesn't know where the destination
    MAC address is located in the fabric. It has to forward the VXLAN
    packet again to the spines for a second resolution. The spines
    will, thanks to COOP data, resolve as a destination Leaf 102 VTEP
    address and forward the packet there.

6. Leaf 102 won't learn Server A's IP address because the endpoint
    data plane learning feature is disabled for service bridge domains.
    The VXLAN packet is now finally decapsulated and delivered to
    the PBR service device.

The first part of the forwarding process ensures the traffic delivery to the consumer
connector (outside interface) of the L4-L7 service device. After the device performs
any configured inspections or data manipulation, it will return the packet via the
provider connector (inside interface) back to the fabric. The next steps are illustrated in
Figure 8-31.

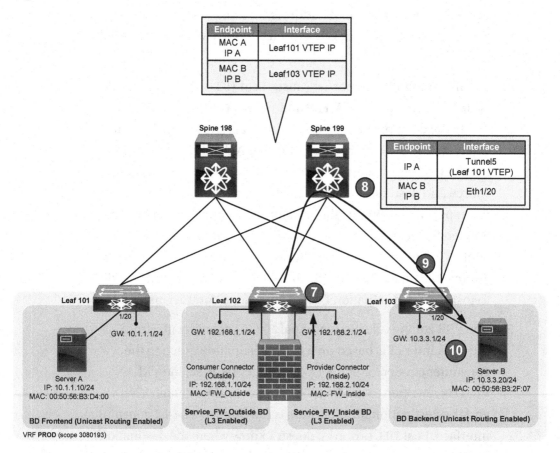

Figure 8-31. *Forwarding process for PBR-enabled communication – Part 2*

The second part of PBR traffic delivery consists of the following steps:

1. The L4-L7 service device returns the packet to the default GW of the inside service bridge domain, represented by SVI on Leaf 102. Leaf 102 is not aware of the destination endpoint, so it needs to send the packet to the spine for a COOP resolution. The packet is encapsulated into VXLAN, with the source sClass of the L4-L7 node shadow provider EPG, VRF VNID, and sent towards the spines (to spine anycast VTEP IP). No zoning rule policies are applied on this node, and again, the Source/Destination Policy (SP 0/DP 1) flags are set in the VXLAN header.

2. The selected spine resolves the destination endpoint in its COOP database, rewrites the outer destination IP, and sends the packet to Leaf 103's VTEP IP.

3. After receiving the VXLAN packet, Leaf 103 will apply the automatically created zoning rule, permitting all traffic from the provider L4-L7 connector to the provider EPG. It will decapsulate the traffic and send it via the local port to the destination endpoint.

4. The destination endpoint receives the original packet.

You have successfully delivered the first packet in a flow between consumer and provider endpoints with policy-based redirect applied. Let's now continue with examining the return traffic, as described in Figure 8-32.

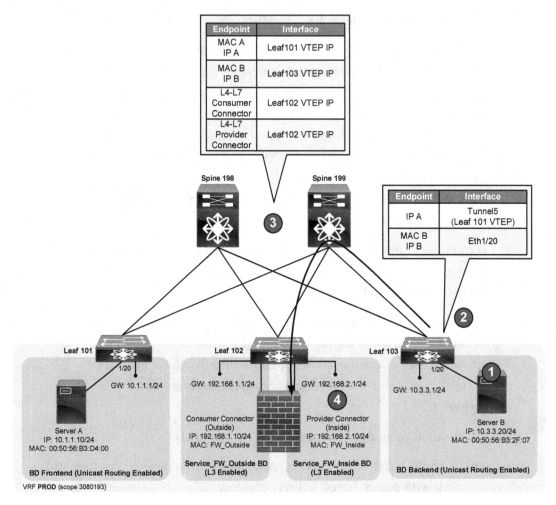

Figure 8-32. *Forwarding process for PBR-enabled communication – Part 3*

Server B sends a reply to Server A and the following actions happen around the ACI fabric:

1. Server B generates a reply packet with its own source IP address and the destination address of Server A. The packet is sent to the default gateway, which is configured as part of a bridge domain on Leaf 103.

2. Leaf 103 knows about both source and destination endpoints and their EPG affiliation, so it will apply a zoning rule instructing them to perform a redirect. Based on a related PBR destination group, it will identify the MAC and IP address of the provider L4-L7

connector. The original packet is then encapsulated into VXLAN
with the L4-L7 provider BD VNID and sent to a spine anycast
VTEP address for a COOP resolution where the L4-L7 MAC
address lives.

3. The spine based on a COOP database rewrites the VXLAN outer
   destination IP to the Leaf 102 VTEP and forwards the packet there.

4. On Leaf 102, the VXLAN packet is decapsulated and forwarded to
   the provider connector interface of the L4-L7 appliance.

Figure 8-33 illustrates the final forwarding part for your traffic.

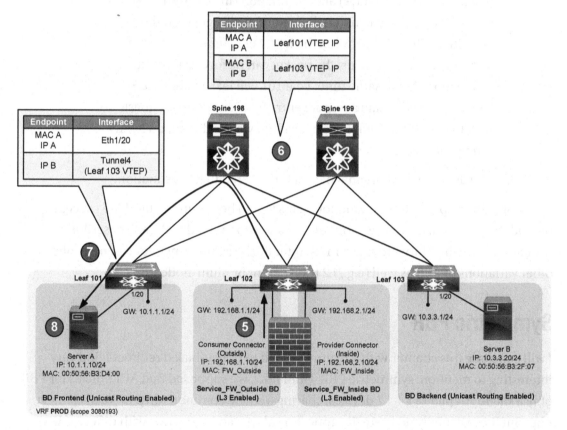

Figure 8-33. *Forwarding process for PBR-enabled communication – Part 4*

5. The L4-L7 device, after performing a stateful traffic inspection,
   returns the packet to the default gateway of the consumer service
   BD on Leaf 102. It doesn't know about the destination endpoint,

so the zoning policies are not applied on this node. The packet is encapsulated into VXLAN with Source/Destination Policy (SP 0/ DP 1) flags set, VRF VNID, and sClass of the shadow consumer connector EPG. The VXLAN packet is then sent to spine anycast VTEP IP for a COOP resolution.

6. The spine has in its COOP entries information about the location of Server A, so the VLXAN destination IP will be rewritten to the Leaf 101 VTEP IP, and the packet will be sent towards it.

7. Leaf 101 is able to apply a zoning rule thanks to known source (from the VXLAN header) and destination (from the endpoint table) sClasses. It will match the automatically generated rule permitting all traffic between the L4-L7 consumer connector and consumer EPG. Thus, the packet can be forwarded to its destination. At the same time, Leaf 101 will learn about the Server B endpoint and create a remote entry in its endpoint database with the Leaf 103 VTEP IP as a next hop via the dynamic VXLAN tunnel interface.

8. The decapsulated original packet is delivered to its destination.

I hope this step-by-step explanation helps you to better understand the process behind the policy-based redirect forwarding and expanded the already described standard intra-fabric forwarding from Chapter 6. The same principles can be applied to other variations of PBR as well (e.g., L2 transparent or multi-node PBR).

Symmetric PBR

I will conclude this chapter with a feature related to policy-based redirect I find very interesting to mention: symmetric PBR. Until now, we supposed that ACI utilizes for PBR only a single HA pair of L4-L7 devices, sharing a single common MAC or MAC+IP next hop. But it can actually do more. It supports multiple active devices with different IPs and MACs and provides symmetric load balancing between them.

This behavior is very simple to configure. All you need to do is add multiple destinations in the L4-L7 policy-based redirect object (located in **Tenants -> Tenant_ name -> Policies -> Protocol -> L4-L7 Policy-Based Redirect**). Even with multiple active devices, from the ACI point of view it's still a single logical L4-L7 device.

When the traffic is redirected to a multi-node logical device, the leaf switch will perform a hash from the IP traffic header and choose one active physical node. By default, the hash is calculated based on the original (inner) source and destination IP addresses together with the IP protocol number. In an L4-L7 policy-based redirect object, you have an option to configure just the source or destination hashing only. In that case, make sure to create two separate policies, for one PBR connector with the source and for the provider PBR connector with a destination hashing to preserve the traffic symmetricity (as shown in Figure 8-34).

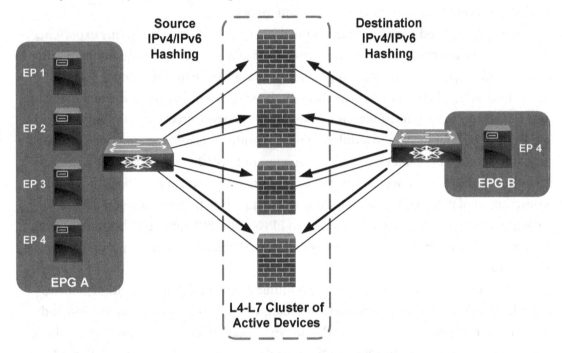

Figure 8-34. *Symmetric policy-based redirect to multiple active devices*

Summary

In this chapter, you have further expanded your knowledge of ACI by learning about its significant feature, service insertion using L4-L7 service graphs and policy-based redirect. ACI itself builds its operation on a security-first philosophy with an allowlist model and zoning rules enforcement based on defining contracts between EPGs/ESGs. It cannot provide stateful and deep inspection using next-gen security devices like specialized firewalls, load balancers, or IPS/IDS devices, though.

You can either manually ensure that the traffic will flow through the mentioned devices using network (VLAN) stitching or thanks to a routing configuration. However, this traditional approach may not be scalable or maintainable with hundreds or thousands of bridge domain segments and EPGs in ACI.

Service insertion tools provide a diverse set of options, allowing you to automatically permit the traffic to the specialized L4-L7 devices without actually changing the already deployed contracts. You can stay focused on standard application profiles instead of worrying how to incorporate an external firewall between your EPGs. ACI will handle additional contracts and service EPG creation for you.

With policy-based redirect, which is the most popular (according to my experience) form of service insertion, leaf switches are even able to directly steer the traffic flow by implementing special redirect zoning rules, all in a selective manner, giving you the ability to choose which traffic will go through the service appliance. At the end of the day, this results in a significant saving of service device resources.

During the chapter, you saw different design options related to the service insertion for Layer 3 routed appliances as well as transparent Layer 2 or wire-like Layer 1 devices. You went through the policy-based redirect configuration and verification, including a description of their deployment in the leaf's zoning rule tables. Then you looked closely at a forwarding process between two EPGs with PBR applied in between. Finally, you explored a symmetric PBR, allowing ACI to load balance between multiple active service nodes.

In the next chapter, you will examine another very useful ACI integration feature, providing additional automation and significant visibility into your virtualization and container environments. Both network and virtualization teams can benefit from these capabilities, resulting in shorter downtimes and troubleshooting sessions, followed by the increased service quality offered to your customers.

CHAPTER 9

Integrating ACI with Virtualization and Container Platforms

You have already gone quite far with all the various ACI configuration, operation, and troubleshooting aspects in previous chapters. You already know how to configure physical interfaces, dedicate encapsulation resources to ACI tenants, create application profiles, provide external access for ACI fabric, and insert L4-L7 devices into a communication data path. However, so far, you have always considered connected endpoints to be simple bare-metal servers/network devices with statically defined EPG affiliation and their encapsulation on the wire of some interface.

Let's push ACI's boundaries further and explore the benefits of its broad integration capabilities. You can significantly simplify network operation for virtualized workloads, utilize ACI fabric resources more optimally and increase visibility into your virtual environments as well. In this chapter, I will describe both virtual (VMware) and container (Kubernetes) integration with their added value to the whole solution.

Virtualization platform Integration

Virtualization platforms like VMware vSphere, Microsoft HyperV, and Linux KVM introduce virtual distributed switches to the data center infrastructure. It's another layer and networking component to manage, which adds an additional administrative burden. Usually, a dedicated virtualization team is responsible for its configuration, and any network-related change needs to be properly arranged with them, increasing the potential for unnecessary human errors. Why not make the life of both sides easier? You can delegate all virtual networking tasks after the integration to APICs and start

439

© Jan Janovic 2023
J. Janovic, *Cisco ACI: Zero to Hero*, https://doi.org/10.1007/978-1-4842-8838-2_9

managing the virtual networking layer in a similar manner as the ACI fabric itself. APIC gets the ability to see the whole virtualization inventory, including hypervisors, their uplink interfaces, virtual switches with associated networks, and virtual machines with their entire properties. In the end, all your ACI application profiles consisting of various EPGs can be dynamically mapped into the virtualization platform without the need for complicated static encapsulation management or specific interface path definitions.

VMware Integration Overview

The main prerequisites for ACI integration in the case of VMware are the availability of distributed switching (the feature comes with a vSphere Enterprise Plus license) and an implemented vCenter manager with all the ESXi hosts under its administration.

For ACI, you then have to create a dedicated user in vCenter (or optionally use the administrator user, if it complies with your security rules) with the following minimum access privileges:

- Alarms

- Distributed Switch

- dvPort Group

- Folder

- Network

- Host

  - Host.Configuration.Advanced settings

  - Host.Local operations. Reconfigure virtual machine

  - Host.Configuration.Network configuration

- Virtual machine (the following VM privileges are needed only for L4-L7 service device VMs if you plan to use them in ACI service graphs after the integration)

  - Virtual machine.Configuration.Modify device settings

  - Virtual machine.Configuration.Settings

After vCenter preparation, Figure 9-1 describes all the steps involved in the integration process itself with the explanation following.

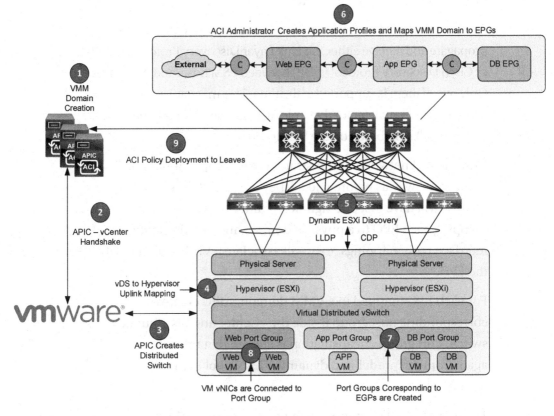

Figure 9-1. *ACI VMM integration overview*

1. The ACI Administrator creates the VMM domain object defining the relation to ESXi access policies (the leaf interfaces behind which the ESXi hosts are or will be connected in the future), vSwitch configuration, and vCenter credentials used for integration.

2. APIC performs the authentication handshake with the vCenter API.

3. Based on information in the VMM domain object, a virtual distributed vSwitch (vDS) is created inside the vCenter. This switch is exclusively managed by APIC.

4. The VMware administrator maps vDS uplinks to vmnics of all managed ESXi hosts (resulting in mapping to physical server interfaces used to connect to ACI).

5. Based on the VMM domain configuration, the vDS switch start to propagate and receive either the Link Layer Discovery Protocol (LLDP) or Cisco Discovery Protocol (CDP) between ESXi hosts and ACI leaves. Only one of them is supported at the time. This mechanism will become important later for dynamic ACI interface configuration and policy installation based on the ESXi location.

6. Now the ACI network administrator creates application policies in the same way as before and as they are already used to. The process will have just one significant difference: instead of mapping each EPG to a physical domain and creating static interface path mappings, they will associate a VMM domain with the EPG.

7. For each EPG mapped to a VMM domain, APIC creates a corresponding port group inside the vCenter and distributed switch. Port group encapsulation is chosen dynamically again from the predefined dynamic VLAN pool in the VMM domain object.

8. The only manual operation from now on for the VMware administrator is to properly connect virtual interfaces of virtual machines to correct the already existing port group created by APIC. Logically, this step will put a VM into the corresponding EPG for that port group will use all ACI policies.

9. Based on the ESXi location discovered by LLDP or CDP and information on which host the particular VM is running from vCenter, ACI will push all the necessary interface configuration and contract policies to the correct leaves. And to only relevant ones, which optimizes the resource utilization.

The integration process itself is not very complicated; however, there are various configuration options along the road for each object, so let's take a closer look at how to proceed to avoid any problems and make the most from this feature.

Access Policies for ESXi Hosts

As always, to connect any ESXi server to ACI, you need to create access policies for it. In the case of VMM integration, the process includes the same already well-known objects: switch profiles, interface profiles, interface policy groups, attachable entity profiles, and the VLAN pool. Their relations are depicted in Figure 9-2.

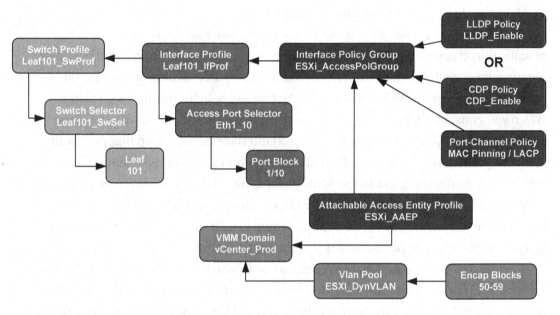

Figure 9-2. *ACI access policies for VMM domain integration*

The main difference between access policies for bare-metal endpoints is the missing physical domain (replaced by VMM domain object) and the fact that you have to use a *dynamic* VLAN pool instead of static (as shown in Figure 9-3).

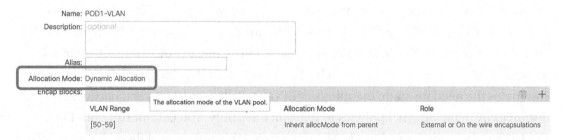

Figure 9-3. *Dynamic VLAN pool for a VMM domain*

VLAN ranges should by default inherit dynamism from the parent pool, and this is due to the way APIC creates port groups in VMware when the VMM domain is associated with EPG. Each port group will automatically get one VLAN ID from this pool. For use cases where you still need a static and manual VLAN to port group mapping, ACI allows you to do that as well. In these situations, you have to include a static VLAN range in a dynamic VLAN pool. Anyway, always make sure to include a reasonable amount of VLAN ranges in your VLAN pool for all the EPGs.

It doesn't matter whether you use access or vPC interface policy groups, LACP, or static port channeling. These settings just have to match later from the vDS switch perspective as well. Actually, from my practical experience, avoiding port channels in this case can significantly simplify your ACI access policies for the ESXi cluster. When you consider that all ESXi interfaces are usually standardized with the same configuration, all you need is a single (access) interface policy group mapped to all interface profiles and consequently to all switch profiles. Server redundancy can still be achieved by configuring vDS to use MAC pinning based on a VM source MAC hash. The only downside of this approach could be the fact, that for each VM (and its MAC), you have a more limited amount of throughput equal to a single leaf interface. You cannot load-balance the traffic per flow on top of the port channel.

Opposed to that, if you decide to create an individual VPC interface policy group for each vPC port channel, it will definitely be supported and working. However, it can become more difficult to manage over time for hundreds of servers. Regardless of the option you choose, at the end of the day, make sure all your access policies are in place for each ESXi server to ensure the correct VMware integration.

To Use LLDP/CDP or Not to Use LLDP/CDP

When ESXi hosts are directly connected to ACI leaves, you can enable either LLDP or CDP in all interface policy groups to allow dynamic application policy deployment for VMM integrated EPGs. Thanks to information from these protocols, ACI is capable of identifying the exact location of each VM (endpoint) and its host, which not only eliminates the need for static mappings in EPGs, but also optimizes leaf hardware resources by deploying ACI policies to relevant ones only. You cannot run both LLDP and CDP at the same time, though. Make sure to enable only one of them. Later on, you will match this configuration from the vDS perspective when the VMM domain object is created.

There is an option not to rely on LLDP/CDP discovery at all, for ESXi hosts connected to ACI via an intermediate switch layer, non-managed from APIC. The most common use case is a blade server chassis with blade switches but without support for transparent LLDP/CDP forwarding (see Figure 9-4).

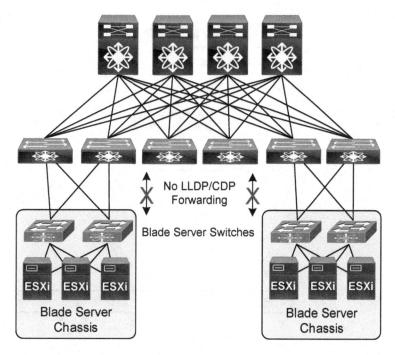

Figure 9-4. *ESXi hosts are connected through intermediate switches*

Without LLDP/CDP information, you can later ensure policy deployment simply to all interfaces and leaf switches that are part of the particular AAEP object, without any relation to the ESXi host presence behind them.

The decision to rely or not to rely on dynamic discovery protocols for particular EPG endpoints happens later, during VMM domain to EPG mapping, and is individually configurable for each EPG and VMM domain. I will cover it in the next sections.

ACI VMM Domain

After you finish the preparation of the ESXi access policies, navigate to the **Virtual Networking** -> **VMware** menu and create a new VMM domain. In the open form, fill the domain name (vDS switch will carry this name), choose Attachable Entity Profile (AEP) connecting the VMM domain with access policies, add a dynamic VLAN pool, and specify vCenter IP/hostname with credentials to be used for integration (as shown in Figure 9-5).

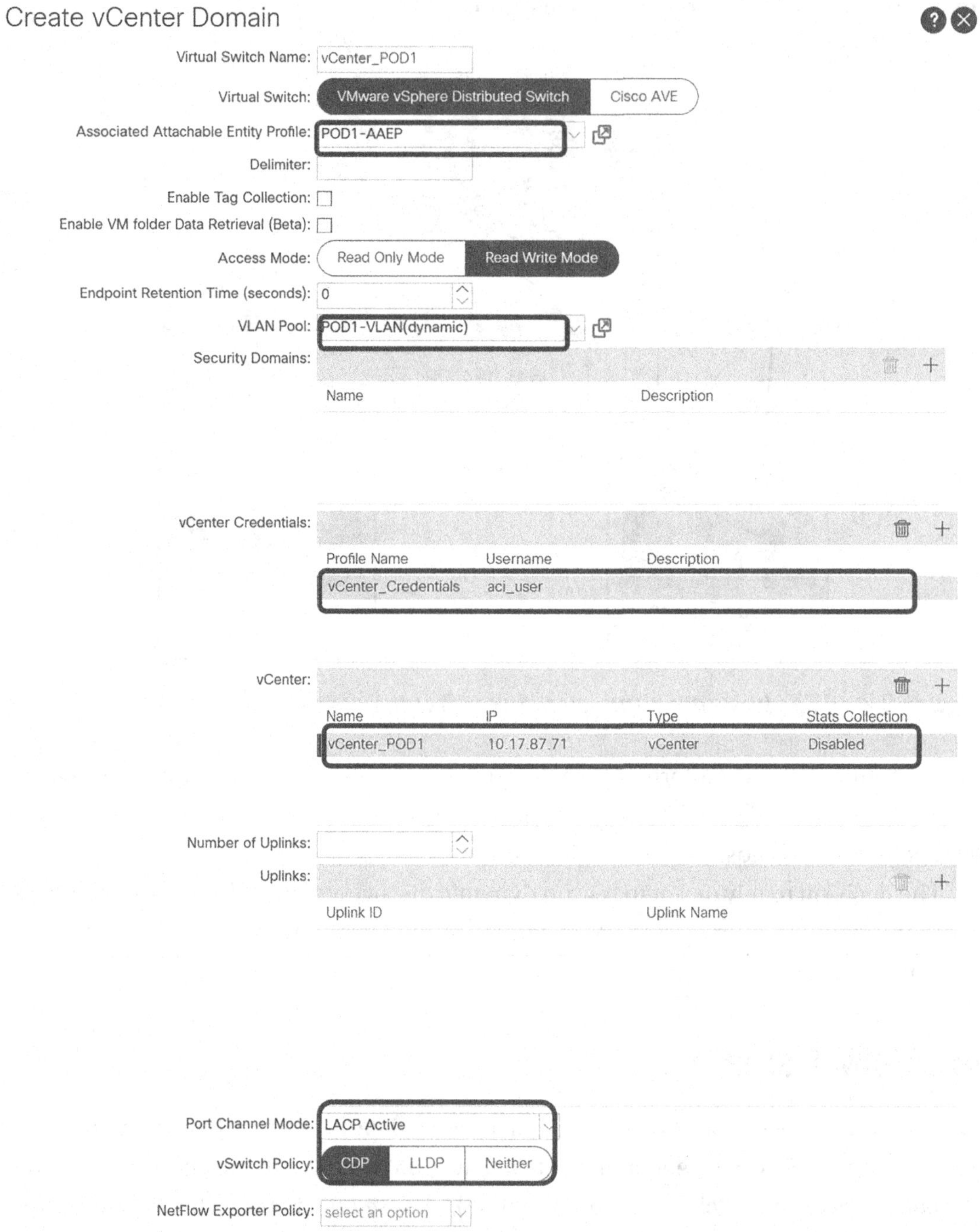

Create vCenter Domain

Virtual Switch Name:	vCenter_POD1
Virtual Switch:	VMware vSphere Distributed Switch / Cisco AVE
Associated Attachable Entity Profile:	POD1-AAEP
Delimiter:	
Enable Tag Collection:	☐
Enable VM folder Data Retrieval (Beta):	☐
Access Mode:	Read Only Mode / Read Write Mode
Endpoint Retention Time (seconds):	0
VLAN Pool:	POD1-VLAN(dynamic)

Security Domains:

Name	Description

vCenter Credentials:

Profile Name	Username	Description
vCenter_Credentials	aci_user	

vCenter:

Name	IP	Type	Stats Collection
vCenter_POD1	10.17.87.71	vCenter	Disabled

Number of Uplinks:

Uplinks:

Uplink ID	Uplink Name

Port Channel Mode:	LACP Active
vSwitch Policy:	CDP / LLDP / Neither
NetFlow Exporter Policy:	select an option

Figure 9-5. *Create vCenter domain form*

446

In the Delimiter field, you can alter the naming convention of the automatically created port groups in VMware. The default delimiter in ACI version 5.X and newer is underscore (_), resulting in following name format: *<TenantName>_<ApplicationProfile Name>_<EPGName>*. Therefore, if your EPG names contain underscores (mine always), it won't allow you to create a port group with a corresponding name. In such a case, change the delimiter, for example, to pipe (|), which was actually the default prior to ACI version 5.

At the bottom, starting with the *Number of Uplink* field you can find the vSwitch policies configuration. All these settings are deployed to newly created virtual distributed switch in vCenter and especially the Port Channel Mode with vSwitch LLDP/CDP policy should exactly reflect your ESXi access policies created in a previous step. Otherwise, you end up with connectivity and VM endpoint learning issues.

When talking about vDS, let's stay a while at the form to define vCenter in the VMM domain shown in Figure 9-6.

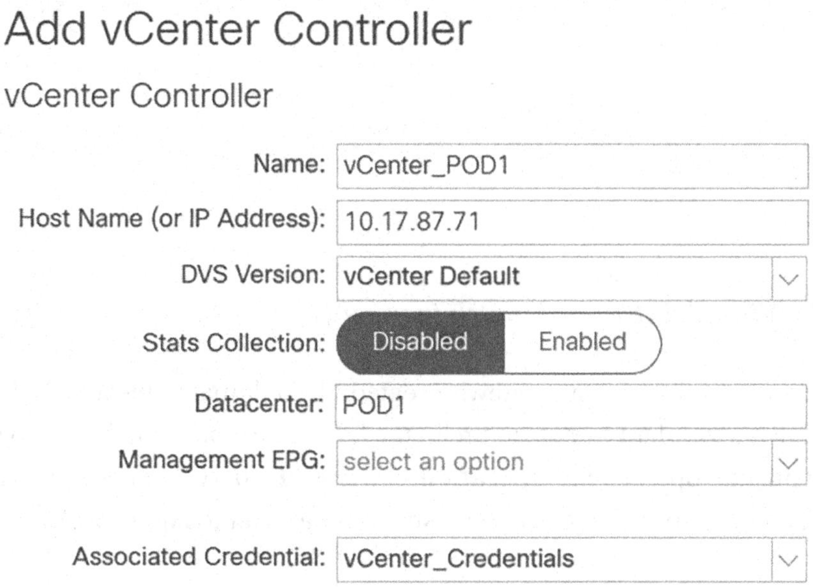

Add vCenter Controller

vCenter Controller

Name:	vCenter_POD1
Host Name (or IP Address):	10.17.87.71
DVS Version:	vCenter Default ⌄
Stats Collection:	**Disabled** Enabled
Datacenter:	POD1
Management EPG:	select an option ⌄
Associated Credential:	vCenter_Credentials ⌄

Figure 9-6. vCenter controller setting inside the VMM domain object

To avoid any issues with the integration, make sure to set the DVS version correctly. The vCenter default means the actual version of your vCenter, which does not necessarily have to be the same version running on your ESXi servers. DVS has to match your ESXi platform, or you will get a compatibility error. Currently, with ACI v5.X+, all vSphere versions from 5.1 to 7.0 are fully supported.

Another important field is *Datacenter,* referring to a name of your datacenter inventory container in vCenter. It has to match the existing object in vCenter in order to create a vSwitch.

Finally, with all the necessary fields set in the main VMM domain object and if your configuration and vCenter credentials are correct, after submitting this form, you should see a new distributed switch in vCenter with the relevant configuration (as shown in Figure 9-7).

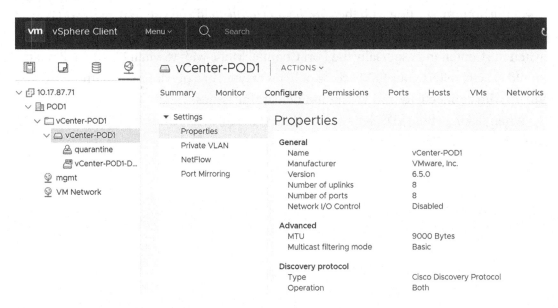

Figure 9-7. *Virtual distributed switch in vCenter*

Also, check for any faults in the newly created VMM domain object in ACI. When you expand ACI's standard tree structure in the left menu, you should see all vCenter inventory, and after opening the **Operation -> General** tab, vCenter has to be in the Online state, with all the managed hypervisors visible (refer to Figure 9-8).

Figure 9-8. *VMM domain in APIC*

The same information is available through the CLI as well if needed for verification or troubleshooting purposes. See Listing 9-1.

Listing 9-1. VMM Domain CLI Verification

```
APIC# show vmware domain name POD1-DVS vcenter 10.17.87.71
Name                   : POD1-vCenter
Type                   : vCenter
Hostname or IP         : 10.17.87.71
Datacenter             : POD1
DVS Version            : 6.5
Status                 : online
Last Inventory Sync    : 2022-02-17 09:05:11
Last Event Seen        : 2022-02-06 18:45:02
Username               : root
Number of ESX Servers  : 1
Number of VMs          : 9
Faults by Severity     : 0, 0, 0, 0
Leader                 : APIC
Managed Hosts:
  ESX            VMs      Adjacency   Interfaces
  ---------------  --------  ----------  -----------------------------
  10.17.87.11    12       Direct      leaf-101-102 eth1/25
```

In case of any problems, first check the APIC <-> vCenter connectivity and verify that the vCenter user specified in the VMM domain has all the necessary privileges described at the beginning of this chapter.

Now, from the moment of integration, the VMware administrator shouldn't manually change any properties of vDS, which were created and managed from APIC. Each change will result in a fault in ACI. The entire list of managed settings is summarized in Table 9-1.

Table 9-1. *VDS Parameters Managed by APIC*

VMware VDS Parameter	Default Value	Configurable from APIC?
Name	VMM domain object name	Yes (matching VMM domain)
Folder Name	VMM domain object name	Yes (matching VMM domain)
Version	vCenter version	Yes
Discovery Protocol	LLDP	Yes
Uplink Ports and Names	8	Yes (since ACI 4.2(1))
Uplink Name Prefix	Uplink	Yes (since ACI 4.2(1))
Maximum MTU	9000	Yes
LACP Policy	Disabled	Yes
Port Mirroring	0 sessions	Yes
NetFlow	No Policy	Yes
Alarms	Two alarms added in vCenter to folder level	No

vDS Uplink to ESXi Mapping

The next step required to enable VM communication through ACI is a manual assignment of vDS uplinks to all your ESXi servers inside the vCenter cluster. Right-click the distributed vSwitch and choose the *Add and Manage Hosts* option. Here, add all your ESXi servers and assign at least two uplink interfaces to their vmnics corresponding with physical interfaces connected to ACI leaves (as you can see in Figure 9-9).

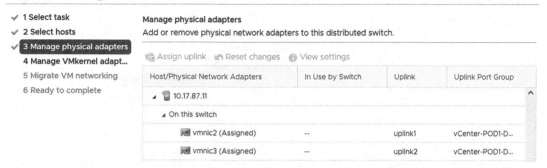

Figure 9-9.   vDS uplinks to ESXi mapping

If you choose to use one of the LLDP or CDP protocols, ACI should now see your ESXi hosts, and no faults will be visible for the VMM domain. In other cases, APIC will notify you which ESXi hosts are not detected on any leaf switch and you can start troubleshooting access policies, which are probably causing this issue.

VMM Domain to EPG Binding

Now, go to your application profile. There you will finally utilize the VMM domain by associating it with EPGs. Right-click a particular EPG and choose *Add VMM Domain Association* (as shown in Figure 9-10).

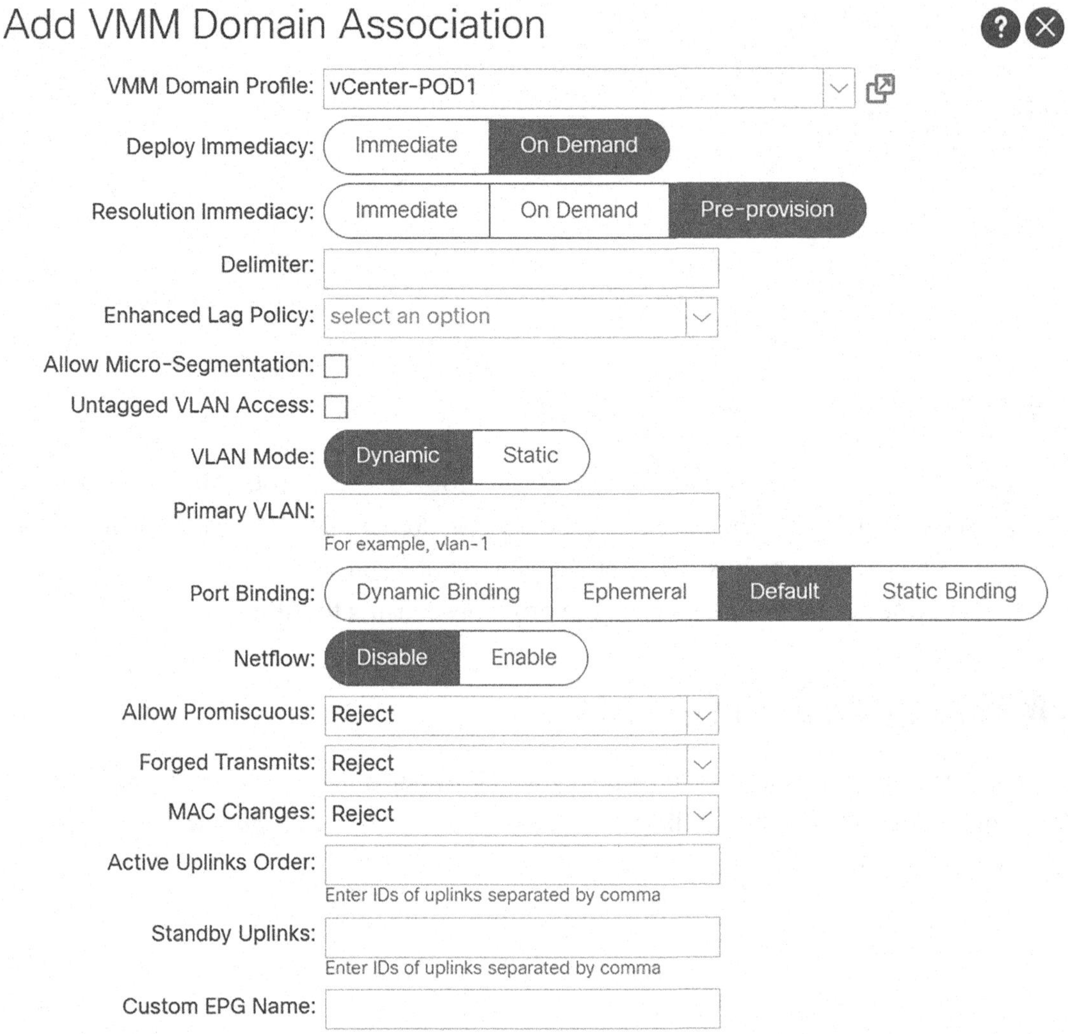

Add VMM Domain Association

VMM Domain Profile: vCenter-POD1

Deploy Immediacy: (Immediate | On Demand)

Resolution Immediacy: (Immediate | On Demand | Pre-provision)

Delimiter:

Enhanced Lag Policy: select an option

Allow Micro-Segmentation: ☐

Untagged VLAN Access: ☐

VLAN Mode: (Dynamic | Static)

Primary VLAN:

For example, vlan-1

Port Binding: (Dynamic Binding | Ephemeral | Default | Static Binding)

Netflow: (Disable | Enable)

Allow Promiscuous: Reject

Forged Transmits: Reject

MAC Changes: Reject

Active Uplinks Order:

Enter IDs of uplinks separated by comma

Standby Uplinks:

Enter IDs of uplinks separated by comma

Custom EPG Name:

Figure 9-10.   *VMM domain to EPG association*

Deploy Immediacy setting affect the moment when the ACI policies are pushed into the hardware TCAM tables of leaf switches. The *Immediate* option programs the TCAM instantly after the policy is downloaded from APIC. With *On Demand* mode, the leaf will wait to see the first packet received through a configured data path for a connected endpoint in this EPG. It helps to optimize the switch hardware resources.

Resolution Immediacy is then a very important setting related to the already mentioned discovery protocols LLDP and CDP. Here you choose whether to use them or not. The *Immediate* setting ensures that the policy is downloaded to all affected leaf switches as soon as the adjacency is detected with the ESXi server. However, LLDP or CDP has to be enabled and work correctly in order to dynamically deploy switch policies. Otherwise, you receive an EPG fault telling you there is a problem with a server discovery. The second option, *On Demand*, also looks for the ESXI adjacency before any policy is deployed on a leaf switch, but this time you have one additional condition: APIC waits for the first VM to be connected in the created port group in VMware corresponding to this EPG. The last option, the *Pre-Provision* setting, completely ignores the availability of the LLDP/CDP information and better configures EPG-related policies to all switches and interfaces described in interface policy groups mapped to AAEP object used by the VMM domain. This is the configuration option for indirectly connected ACI and ESXi servers described earlier.

The VLAN mode is by default set to dynamic, which implies dynamic VLAN assignment, from a dynamic VLAN pool to a port group created for this EPG in vCenter. In case you need a static VLAN assignment instead, make sure there is a static VLAN range in the VLAN pool in the VMM domain and by choosing this option, ACI will allow you to configure the VLAN ID manually.

All other settings from Port Binding further down are properties of the VMware port group itself and mostly you don't need to alter their default values.

After submitting this form, APIC creates a new port group in the managed virtual distributed switch with the default name <Tenant>_<Application_Profile>_<EPG> (or with other delimiters if specified) and you should see its presence in the vCenter interface. In Figure 9-11, you can see multiple such port groups created by APIC corresponding to ACI EPGs.

Figure 9-11. *VMware port groups corresponding to EGPs*

Table 9-2 summarizes all APIC managed port group properties. The same consideration about not manually changing any of them applies here as well as for vDS.

Table 9-2. *Port Group Parameters Managed by APIC*

VMware Port-Group Parameter	Default Value	Configurable from APIC?
Name	<Tenant>_<Application_Profile>_<EPG>	Yes (based on EPG or manually chosen)
Port Binding	Static Binding	Yes
VLAN	Dynamically chosen from VLAN pool	Yes
Load Balancing Algorithm	Based on a port-channel policy in VMM domain vSwitch and access policies	Yes
Promiscuous mode	Disabled	Yes
Forged transmit	Disabled	Yes
MAC Change	Disabled	Yes
Active/Standby Uplinks	Not specified	Yes

VM to Port Group Association

Now the last step is to get your VMs inside a proper port group. Right-click any VM in vCenter, choose Edit Settings, and map its network adapter(s) to the already existing port-group (see Figure 9-12).

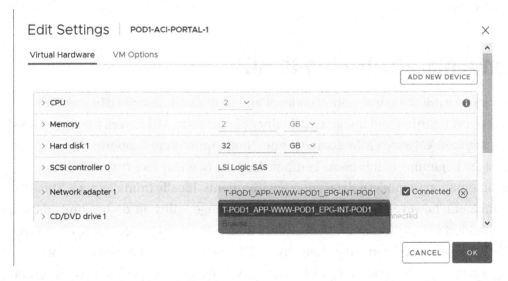

Figure 9-12. *VM Network adapter to EPG port group association*

If you successfully applied all the settings so far, VMs should appear in ACI as a learned endpoint from two different sources (refer to Figure 9-13):

- "vmm" meaning that APIC sees this virtual machine in a vCenter inventory thanks to their integration

- "learned" implies that the leaf switch sees in a data plane these endpoints communicating to the ACI fabric

Figure 9-13. *Endpoint visiblity after the VMM integration*

Thanks to the previous steps, now you can see how easy it is to get your virtual endpoints to any EPG, obtain detailed information about them and their location, with enhanced monitoring handled directly by APIC, and most importantly, without the need for any static path mapping anymore. This makes the VMM integration a very powerful ACI feature for significant resource and operation optimization in virtualized environments.

Container Integration to ACI

You can take the VMM integration concept and its benefits described in previous sections even further and integrate container platforms to ACI as well (deployed inside the integrated VMware VMM domain or not; both options are supported).

At the beginning of this book, I emphasized the need for security, visibility, and automation in modern datacenter environments, ideally from day zero. This requirement, however, goes a little bit against the huge agility, flexibility, and efficiency of containerized applications. Thousands of their microservices (containers) can spin up in a fraction of a second anywhere around the host cluster and usually without proper security enforcement or easily manageable networking policies. When running inside ACI, it would be highly desired for individual containers to achieve the same level of visibility and segmentability as any other bare metal server or virtual machine endpoints. Your goal is to include containers in ACI application policies (EPGs, contracts, etc.) like any other workload and as dynamically as with the previously described VMM integration. Additionally, ACI can provide L4-L7 services and especially distributed hardware-accelerated load balancing for containers with extremely simple and automated application service exposure to the external network.

Many of our customers consider Docker and Kubernetes to be industry standards for running containers. They usually deploy Kubernetes itself or some other enterprise variants, including Rancher, Cisco Container Platform, and Openshift. Regardless of your main platform, my goal in this chapter is to guide you through the deployment of a simple Kubernetes cluster that is fully integrated and cooperating with ACI APIC and publishing load-balanced services to the external network for user access. Since all Kubernetes variations follow a very similar integration approach (even Cisco itself recommends fully understanding basic Kubernetes integration first, before moving further), this should be the best starting point for you.

During my recent ACI projects, I realized there is a lot of information available directly from Cisco or other vendors regarding the Kubernetes topic, but they are commonly outdated, scattered, or lacking context. Many times, I found myself blindly following the offered steps without a proper understanding of the relationships between all the components. We need to change that. Hopefully, the next sections will help you to gain confidence and a strong understanding of all the aspects of running Kubernetes together with ACI and allow you to replicate the whole concept inside your own environment.

Kubernetes Platform Overview

If you are not familiar with Kubernetes, let me quickly summarize its basic principles and how it handles the networking inside the platform. I will only mention relevant components for us at the moment, but Kubernetes contains many more of them of course.

Kubernetes is an open-source orchestrator for running Docker (or containerd and CRI-O) containers in production-grade environment. Originally developed by Google, these days it is maintained by the Cloud Native Computing Foundation. It handles the whole lifecycle of managed containers, including their high availability, scalability, monitoring, and more. Kubernetes uses a highly modular, loosely coupled architecture, so all the components heavily rely on a centralized API server. The high-level overview of the Kubernetes platform is depicted in Figure 9-14.

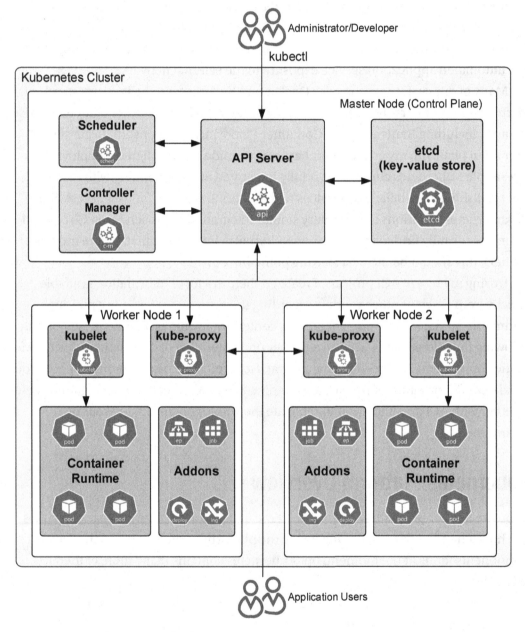

Figure 9-14. *Kubernetes platform overview*

Kubernetes uses dedicated master nodes (host servers) to run all the control plane processes, separating them completely from the main container workloads, which are scheduled on worker nodes.

Kubernetes Control Plane Components

All these components run exclusively on master nodes of Kubernetes:

etcd represents a lightweight and distributed key-value database to store all the configuration and state information needed for proper container scheduling at any point in time.

API Server provides JSON REST API for both internal and external Kubernetes management functions. It works with information and state objects saved in etcd, allowing administrators to configure container workloads on the platform. API Server further assists with the resolution of any state and configuration inconsistencies between actually deployed containers and their desired state described in the etcd database. API communications have a hub-and-spoke pattern, so all other components inside the master or worker nodes, if needed, communicate with these central API servers to interact with each other.

Scheduler is responsible for tracking the actual use of Kubernetes cluster nodes and tries to optimally schedule the PODs. It takes defined requirements for a containerized application that is being deployed and looks for the correct resources to match this definition.

Controller is the general name for multiple specific components (e.g.. Replication Controller, Job Controller, DaemonSet Controller), driving the current cluster state towards the desired state. It makes sure that all container resources are running according to the description in the initial manifest. If not, using API Server the Controller instructs the system to create, update, or delete managed resources (Pods, service endpoints, etc.).

Kubernetes Worker Node Components

The Worker Node is the main resource host where all containers are deployed. Each of them has to run a container runtime, most commonly Docker. Besides it, there are the following Kubernetes-specific components:

Kubelet is locally responsible for the state of a particular Kubernetes node. It takes care of starting, stopping, or monitoring container resources in a form of PODs according to the instructions from control-plane nodes. The Worker Node status announced every few seconds to master nodes.

Kube-proxy acts as load balancer and network proxy. Provides routing of incoming packets to the correct containers based on IP and TCP/UDP port information from a packet header.

Container is the smallest executable entity and it representing the microservice of an application with its libraries and dependencies. One or more containers are running inside a Pod in Kubernetes.

Addons represent a plethora of modular, installable components for each Kubernetes node. These include CNI plugins for networking and security functions, Service Discovery DNS server, Kubernetes Web Dashboard, or detailed issue reporting modules.

Kubernetes Networking Overview

Networking is actually not a Kubernetes thing. For the platform itself, it doesn't matter how it is being implemented. To ensure correct north-south and east-west communication inside the Kubernetes cluster, it uses the modular and standardized concepts of container network interface (CNI) plugins. They refer basically to virtual distributed networking layers among all Kubernetes servers with the following responsibilities:

- Pod-to-Pod communication (intra-node as well as inter-node)

- Service discovery

- Service exposure for external access

- Network security

- High availability

CNI brings a specification for connecting container runtimes to the network with all the software libraries required to do so and CLI tools to execute various CNI actions. It acts as an abstraction layer between container network interfaces and the host OS (external network). The CNI specification defines exactly how to configure container network interfaces and how to provide them with the expected connectivity.

We differentiate between several networking constructs and network segments in Kubernetes. First, we will look at the *Pod network*. A Pod is an elementary scheduling unit and can contain one or more containers inside. From a networking perspective, each Pod is automatically assigned with an IP address from the initially defined Pod subnet (usually /16). If multiple containers are part of the single Pod, they sharing a single IP address. In such a case, a developer has to make sure not to use overlapping TCP/UDP port numbers; otherwise, there would be a collision. Within a single Pod, all containers can communicate freely using localhost, reaching other containers by contacting their own IP, just specifying the different port. When trying to reach a remote Pod, the container has to use the remote Pod's IP over the Pod network.

Then we have the *node network*. As the name suggests, each Kubernetes host node has an interface in this segment and uses it primarily for API services. API servers of master nodes communicating with each Kubelet running inside Workers over the node network. You indicate the node network to the Kubernetes by configuring a default route via a particular network interface. When Kubernetes components start, they look for the default route and that interface is declared as the main Node interface.

To expose any containerized application to the external world, Kubernetes uses an abstraction concept of *services.* A service is constructed representing a VIP address (often called a cluster IP) or chosen port with a corresponding DNS entry dynamically assigned to the group of Pods. It serves for external access and load balancing between Pods that are part of the same service. For these functionalities it is by default responsible for the kube-proxy component of each Kubernetes server node. Sometimes (for example in your ACI case), the CNI plugin can take over with its own service management. There are the following types of services:

- **ClusterIP**: Default service type, exposing a set of Pods internally and making them reachable behind a single VIP from within the Kubernetes cluster. VIP is automatically assigned from a service-cidr range specified during the Kubernetes cluster initiation or manually by the administrator in the service definition.

- **NodePort**: Exposing the application service at the statically chosen port of Node IP. Behind the scenes, ClusterIP is automatically created as well and NodePort is routed to it. To contact the service, you just connect to <NodeIP>:<NodePort>

- **Loadbalancer**: The service used for external load balancer integration in the data path. For each Loadbalancer VIP, Kubernetes will create NodePort and ClusterIP to direct the traffic around all worker nodes. This approach represents two-stage load balancing:

first, an external load balancer chooses one of the Kubernetes worker nodes and routes the traffic to its <NodeIP>:<NodePort> and then traffic is internally load-balanced further based on ClusterIP. In the case of ACI, this is a common practice. During this chapter, you will learn that the first load balancer can actually be the ACI fabric itself.

- **ExternalName**: Associates a service's internal DNS name with the externalName property and returns a CNAME record with this value. No other forwarding or proxying is deployed.

Preparing ACI and Kubernetes Integration

In the following sections, I will describe the integration process and concepts behind it. All of you interested in practical labbing can follow me along in your own environment and use these lines as a kind of lab guide. I'm not aware at the time of writing this book about any other thorough and complete step-by-step cookbook. If the Kubernetes integration is not a topic for you currently, feel free to skip the deployment steps and focus just on the integration results with demo app deployment at the end of this chapter.

I've used the following components for the integration:

- Cisco ACI version 5.2(3e)

- Kubernetes version 1.23

- VMs OS - Centos Stream 8

- acc-provision tool/ACI CNI version 5.2(3.20211025)

These were the most up-to-date versions of each component at the time, but the whole concept is similar with others as well. There is a compatibility matrix available on the Cisco website, so make sure you use a supported combination at least of ACI version, ACI CNI version, and the container orchestration platform: `www.cisco.com/c/dam/en/us/td/docs/Website/datacenter/aci/virtualization/matrix/virtmatrix.html`.

In Figure 9-15, you can see the high-level networking overview of resources needed for running integrated Kubernetes in ACI.

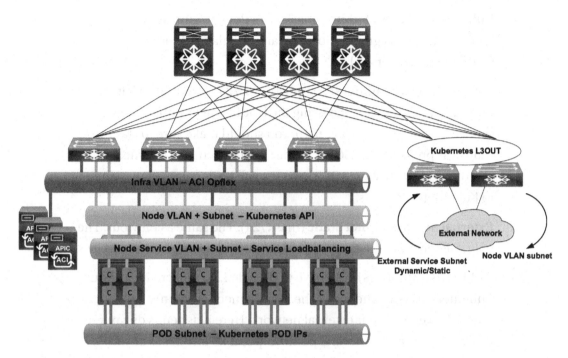

Figure 9-15. *ACI and Kubernetes network integration overview*

You will first prepare some information, which will be needed during further provisioning and working with the integrated solution. Create the following IP plan:

- **Node Subnet** (mask /16): Private subnet used for Kubernetes control plane traffic and API services. Despite its privateness, it should have network reachability with Cisco APIC and, for simplicity, it can be used for management access to the Kubernetes nodes as well. Each node server (master/worker) will have an interface with one IP from this subnet. The default route of node servers has to point to this subnet's gateway. As shown in Figure 9-15, ACI will automatically propagate this subnet using a predefined L3OUT later.

- **Pod Subnet** (mask /16): Private subnet for individual Pod IP allocation. This process is automated by Kubernetes.

- **Node Service Subnet** (mask /24): Private subnet, used in ACI service graphs for routing of hardware loadbalanced service traffic between ACI leaves and Kubernetes server nodes. You will get in touch with this subnet when deploying L4-L7 service graphs in ACI after the integration.

- **Kubernetes Cluster Subnet** (mask /16): Pool of addresses for dynamic IP assignment to internal loadbalanced services (Kubernetes cluster IPs).

- **External Service Subnet Dynamic** (mask /24): Externally routable pool of IP addresses for accessing the loadbalancer Kubernetes services. As shown in Figure 9-15, you should make sure to statically route this prefix to the L3OUT border leaves used for Kubernetes external connectivity in ACI. These IPs will be dynamically assigned to Kubernetes services.

- **External Service Subnet Static** (mask /24): The same as previous. The only difference is its usage for a static allocation to Kubernetes services.

- **ACI L3OUT Subnet(s)**: You have to provide L3 connectivity for your Kubernetes cluster and this is the interconnection subnet between border leaves and your external network. Here it depends on your decision: you can use several point-to-point L3 interfaces or sub-interfaces with /30 networks or one shared /29 segment, for example.

Note   Network masks shown in the IP plan are the default and recommended, but technically in Kubernetes can be any. I used smaller subnets for lab purposes.

Now prepare several VLANs for the integration. They match the ones from Figure 9-15 and will be used in ACI as well as Kubernetes:

- **Node VLAN**: This will be used as an encap-vlan on the wire between ACI and Kubernetes nodes to access their CLI and to ensure API-to-API communication. Each Kubernetes node needs to have an interface in the Node VLAN (individual or subinterface).

- **Service VLAN**: Used to deliver loadbalanced traffic to Kubernetes nodes. You will find it configured in the ACI L4-L7 device object, in policy-based redirect policies, and ACI will create a special internal EPG for this VLAN, deployed on all interfaces where Kubernetes nodes are connected. **DO NOT** configure the interface in this VLAN node on Kubernetes server nodes, ACI CNI will do it for you automatically inside the Open vSwitch and bridge the VLAN there.

- **Infra VLAN**: Already exists in the ACI infrastructure. You specify it
  during APIC initialization, and it is used for Opflex APIC <-> switch
  communications. The easiest way to find it is by using APIC CLI:
  `ifconfig | grep bond0`. The number behind "." is an Infra VLAN
  ID. Each Kubernetes node then has to have a *dot1Q tagged VLAN
  subinterface* in this VLAN with the DHCP client enabled. Over the
  infrastructure VLAN, the ACI CNI Opflex Agent will communicate
  with leaves/APIC.

The following information will be used in this lab. I write prefixes (except of cluster
subnet) directly in a form of default gateways for each subnet, because you will fill them
in later in this format in the initial configuration YAML document. See Listing 9-2.

Listing 9-2. Subnet and IP Plan for Kubernetes to ACI Integration

```
Node Subnet GW: 192.168.100.1/24
Pod Subnet GW: 192.168.101.1/24
Node Service Subnet: 192.168.102.1/24
Kubernetes Cluster Subnet: 192.168.103.0/24
External Service Subnet Dynamic: 192.168.200.1/24
External Service Subnet Static 192.168.201.1/24

Node VLAN: 100
Service VLAN: 102
Infra VLAN: 3967
```

Now deploy a simple server installation and connect four CentOS machines to
ACI-`OrchestratorVM`, `Kubernetes_Master`, `Kubernetes_Worker1` and `Kubernetes_`
`Worker2`. They can be as simple as bare-metal servers or VMs running inside the
VMware with ESXi host uplinks in ACI (the second is my case). They don't need to
have any superb properties either for lab purposes; 1-2 vCPU, 4-8GB RAM, 32GB HDD,
and 1 network interface will work just fine. Make sure each server has a unique Linux
Machine ID, otherwise Kubernetes cluster will have problems with clustering (if you
cloned them from a common VM template, change the machine id manually). If you use
virtualization in between your Kubernetes nodes and ACI, make sure the virtual switch is
correctly configured to support the required MTU and transparently forwards any used
VLAN tag to your VMs. For VMware, there are recommended security settings for each
port group:

- MTU of 9000 (Set this at the Virtual Switch level)

- Forged Transmit: Accept

- MAC Address change: Accept

- Promiscuous Mode: Reject

I ended up with the following lab topology for Kubernetes integration (as shown in Figure 9-16).

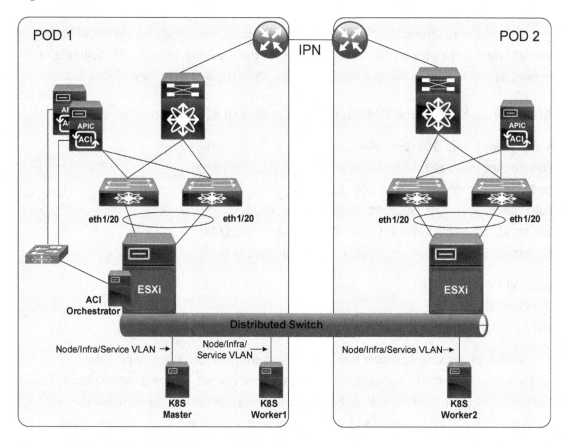

Figure 9-16. *ACI and Kubernetes lab setup*

Only the ACI Orchestration VM is connected to standard vSwitch with a dedicated physical server uplink to the OOB network. It generally needs L3 connectivity with an APIC and we will use it to deploy necessary ACI policies for integration. Kubernetes nodes then have connectivity through the distributed switch and their physical server uplinks are connected to leaf switches. Each VM has one network interface, on the VMware level configured to transparently trunk tagged traffic for Node, Infra, and

Service VLANs. Servers themselves have a VLAN tagged subinterface for Infra VLAN (dot1Q tag has to be added at OS level), and another tagged interface is part of the Node VLAN. The default route of servers has to be pointed towards the Node VLAN gateway via its subinterface. Kubernetes, based on the default route, identifies an interface to run its API on. Finally, ensure all machines have internet access (proxy is not a problem) for package installation (Kubernetes nodes will gain external connectivity over ACI L3OUT after the initial provisioning).

Next, you need to create several objects in ACI manually before we start orchestrating the integration. They include

Fabric Access Policies:

- **Leaf Switch Profile(s)**: Leaves where the Kubernetes nodes are connected

- **Leaf Interface Profile**: Interfaces on leaves for Kubernetes nodes

- **Interface Policy Group**: Set your interfaces according to the server configuration (individual access interfaces vs. vPC port channel, static vs. LACP)

- **Attachable Access Entity Profile (AAEP)**: Create an AAEP object and *Enable Infrastructure VLAN* by checking the option. We will specify this AAEP's name later in the provisioning script.

Tenant Policies:

- **Tenant**: Create your dedicated tenant for Kubernetes integration or alternatively use the system common tenant

- **VRF**: Separated IP space for Kubernetes containers

- **L3OUT**: Working external connectivity, ideally with some dynamic routing protocol to announce the Kubernetes prefixes. Create one default External EPG as well.

The next step is to provision ACI with already prepared information. To do this, you have to use the **acc-provision** tool from the Cisco software downloads website at https://software.cisco.com/download/home. Navigate to Application Policy Infrastructure Controller (APIC) downloads and APIC OpenStack and Container Plugins. There, find the *RPM package for ACI CNI Tools (acc-provision and acikubectl)* and download it to the ACI Orchestrator VM. There, unpack and install it as shown in Listing 9-3.

Listing 9-3. Acc-provision Installation

```
[root@OrchestratorVM ~]# tar -zxvf dist-rpms-5.2.3.1.tar.gz
acc-provision-5.2.3.1-66.el8.x86_64.rpm
[root@OrchestratorVM ~]# rpm -i acc-provision-5.2.3.1-66.el8.x86_64.rpm
error: Failed dependencies:
        python3-boto3 is needed by acc-provision-5.2.3.1-66.el8.x86_64
        python3-jinja2 >= 2.7 is needed by acc-provision-5.2.3.1-66.
        el8.x86_64
        python3-pyOpenSSL >= 0.13 is needed by acc-provision-5.2.3.1-66.
        el8.x86_64
        python3-requests >= 2.2 is needed by acc-provision-5.2.3.1-66.
        el8.x86_64
```

Sometimes the RHEL system has to install an additional repository called Extra Packages for Enterprise Linux (EPEL) to satisfy the required acc-provision tool dependencies. Compared with the main RHEL packages, the EPEL project is maintained by the community and there is no commercial support provided. Nevertheless, the project strives to provide packages of high quality and stability. See Listing 9-4.

Listing 9-4. Acc-provision Dependency Satisfying

```
[root@OrchestratorVM ~]# yum install -y epel-release
[root@OrchestratorVM ~]# yum install -y python3-boto3 python3-jinja2
python3-pyOpenSSL python3-requests
[root@OrchestratorVM ~]# rpm -i acc-provision-5.2.3.1-66.el8.x86_64.rpm
[root@OrchestratorVM ~]# acc-provision -v
5.2.3.1
```

Now create a sample configuration file with the acc-provision tool. You need to specify the "flavor" with the -f argument, matching your intended deployment. In our case, it will be Kubernetes 1.22 (if needed, you can use acc-provision --list-flavors to see available flavors). See Listing 9-5.

Listing 9-5. ACI Provisioning Configuration Template Creation

```
[root@OrchestratorVM ~]# acc-provision -f kubernetes-1.22 --sample > aci-
containers-config.yaml
```

Fill in all previously prepared information and ACI objects in the sample config file `aci-containers-config.yaml` (be aware, fields are case-sensitive). Important changed or added lines are marked as bold. I've added my own comments to some configuration objects as well. See Listing 9-6.

Listing 9-6. ACI Provisioning Configuration Template Filled with Prepared Information

```
#
# Configuration for ACI Fabric
#
aci_config:
system_id: K8S          # This has to be unique name of each cluster
                        and will be
  # included in ACI object names
  #apic-refreshtime: 1200        # Subscrption refresh-interval in seconds;
                                  Max=43200

  apic_hosts:                    # Fill all your APIC cluster nodes OOB
                                 addresses

  - 10.17.87.60
  - 10.17.87.61
  - 10.17.87.62
  vmm_domain:                    # Kubernetes container domain configuration
    encap_type: vxlan            # Encap mode: vxlan or vlan
    mcast_range:                 # Every opflex VMM must use a
                                   distinct range

      start: 225.20.1.1
      end: 225.20.255.255
    nested_inside:               # Include if nested inside a VMM
                                 #   supported for Kubernetes
    # type: vmware               # Specify the VMM vendor
                                   (supported: vmware)
    # name: myvmware             # Specify the name of the VMM domain

# The following resources must already exist on the APIC.
# They are used, but not created, by the provisioning tool.
```

```
tenant:                              # Add these lines if using your own
                                        ACI tenant

  name: K8S
aep: K8S_AAEP                        # The AEP for ports/VPCs used by
                                        this cluster

vrf:                                 # This VRF used to create all
                                        kubernetes EPs

  name: K8S
  tenant: K8S                        # Our own user defined or common tenant
l3out:
  name: K8S_L3OUT                    # Used to ensure external
                                        connectivity of K8S

  external_networks:
  - Default_ExtEPG                   # Used for external contracts
#custom_epgs:                        # List of additional endpoint-group names
#  - custom_group1                   # to configure for use with annotations
#  - custom_group2

#
# Networks used by ACI containers
#
net_config:
  node_subnet: 192.168.100.1/24        # Subnet to use for nodes
  pod_subnet: 192.168.101.1/24         # Subnet to use for Kubernetes Pods
  extern_dynamic: 192.168.200.1/24     # Subnet to use for dynamic
                                          external IPs

  extern_static: 192.168.201.1/24      # Subnet to use for static
                                          external IPs

  node_svc_subnet: 192.168.102.1/24    # Subnet to use for service graph
  kubeapi_vlan: 100                    # NodeVLAN for mgmt access and
                                          Kubernetes API
                                     #    (Kubernetes only)

  service_vlan: 102                    # Used by ACI L4-L7 Service graph
  infra_vlan: 3967                     # The VLAN used by ACI infra
  interface_mtu: 8900                  # !!! Default 1600 is incorrect. Use MTU
                                          between 1700
```

 # and 8900 or ACI CNI containers will crash !!!

```
#interface_mtu_headroom: 100   # MTU Headroom in bytes to be left
                                 for Header
                               # Must be >= 50
                               # Default value si set to 100
#service_monitor_interval: 5   # IPSLA interval probe time for PBR
                                 tracking
                               # default is 5, set to 0 to disable,
                                 max: 65535
#pbr_tracking_non_snat: true   # Default is false, set to true for
                                 IPSLA to
                               # be effective with non-snat services
#disable_wait_for_network: true  # Default is false, set to true
                                   if the ACI
                                 # CNI should not wait for datapath to be
                                 # ready before returning success for pod
                                 # interface creation
#duration_wait_for_network: 210  # Duration in seconds that ACI
                                   should wait
                                 # for datapath to be ready.
                                 # Default is 210 seconds.
                                 # Only enabled if disable_wait_
                                   for_network
                                 # is set to false.
...
```
rest of the config file omitted as no changes need to be done there

---

Note   It's possible and supported to combine both VMM and Kubernetes integration. You can run your server nodes inside the VMware VMM domain and connect them to the distributed vSwitch managed by APIC. To do so, specify VMM domain inside the configuration above. Look for section nested_inside: inside vmm_domain:.

With this initial configuration file, we can orchestrate the ACI configuration. The acc-provision script will create all the necessary objects for you and create Kubernetes deployment YAML. Download `aci-containers.yaml` ("-o" switch in the command) as you will need it later for the Kubernetes master node to spin up the ACI CNI containers, the control and data plane components of the ACI network inside Kubernetes. Notice instructions in the output on how to later deploy ACI CNI or alternatively clean the older deployment. See Listing 9-7.

Listing 9-7. ACI Automated Provisioning for Kubernetes Integration

```
[root@OrchestratorVM ~]# acc-provision -c aci-containers-config.yaml -o
aci-containers.yaml -f kubernetes-1.22 -a -u <username> -p <password>
INFO: Loading configuration from "aci-containers-config.yaml"
INFO: Using configuration flavor kubernetes-1.22
INFO: Generating certs for kubernetes controller
INFO:    Private key file: "user-K8S_POD1.key"
INFO:    Certificate file: "user-K8S_POD1.crt"
INFO: Writing kubernetes infrastructure YAML to aci-containers.yaml
INFO: Writing ACI CNI operator tar to aci-containers.yaml.tar.gz
INFO: Apply infrastructure YAML using:
INFO:    kubectl apply -f aci-containers.yaml
INFO: Delete stale objects from older deployments using:
INFO:    kubectl -n aci-containers-system delete configmap,secret,servic
eaccount,daemonset,deployment,clusterrolebinding,clusterrole -l 'aci-
containers-config-version,aci-containers-config-version notin (4d5f7779-
fe3e-4a1f-8a77-dec01aec4b59)'
INFO: Provisioning configuration in APIC
```

When you now check the ACI, you should see many new objects created (as shown in Figure 9-17). All have special graphical symbols meaning "created from orchestrator." These include

- VLAN pool with Node and Service VLAN included

- Physical domain attached to specified AAEP from configuration file

- New Kubernetes VMM domain attached to the same AAEP

- Kubernetes node and Pod bridge domains with unicast routing enabled and default GW set for communication. The Node BD is mapped to the specified L3OUT and its subnet is set as *Advertised Externally*. You should see the Node VLAN prefix on the external router at this point.

- Application profile inside the Kubernetes tenant

- Initial EPGs for the Kubernetes system mapped to a new VMM domain and with corresponding contracts applied. Later, if you don't specify a particular EPG for newly deployed Kubernetes Pods, they will end up here in the aci-containers-default EPG.

- Contracts with proper filters applied to specified L3OUT external EPG(s)

- User with a X.509 certificate for further automation tasks

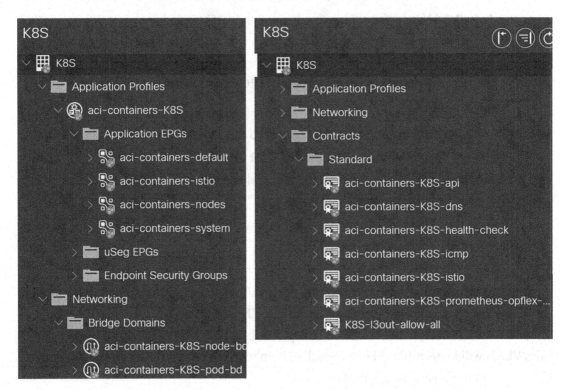

Figure 9-17. *Kubernetes ACI policies*

Before we move further, as the last step we need to configure routing to both *External Service Subnet* prefixes (static and dynamic). On your external router connected to ACI border leaves (and Kubernetes L3OUT), simply add static routes in your case for 192.168.200.0/24 and 192.168.201.0/24 with the next hop pointing to ACI.

Kubernetes Server Nodes Network configuration

After successful ACI provisioning, you need to focus on Kubernetes master and worker server nodes. All of the following steps should be done for each server unless otherwise stated. The first task is to configure networking for them. Each server has to have two network interfaces:

1. **Node VLAN interface**: Standard interface or subinterface with the statically configured IP address from a Node subnet. Set a server default route to the gateway of the Node VLAN.

2. **Infra VLAN interface**: This one has to be dot1Q tagged subinterface on the OS level. Containers will later look for a subinterface and, if it's not available, they end up in a crash loop. The IP address has to be assigned by DHCP from APIC.

Caution   Make sure both interfaces have MTU set at least to 1700, preferably to the maximal value of 9000. The default value of 1600 (even listed in documentation) is not enough to run the ACI CNI module. With 1600, I got the following error later in the container crash log: `"OpFlex link MTU must be >= 1700" mtu=1600 name=ens224.3967 vlan=3967 panic: Node configuration autodiscovery failed.`

Maybe you are thinking, what about the third VLAN interface we specified for the service node? This one will be created automatically and internally by the ACI CNI plugin. All additional potential VLANs except for the previously mentioned Node and Infra VLAN will be terminated inside ACI's Open vSwitch container for each host and bridged from the host's main interface.

Next, configure all servers according to the following example. This is a permanent interface setting in Centos Stream 8 (make sure to reflect your own interface id which can differ from mine; the default used to be ens192). See Listing 9-8.

Listing 9-8. Network Configuration of Kubernetes Node

```
[root@k8s-master ~]# nmcli connection add type vlan con-name ens224.3967
ifname ens224.3967 vlan.parent ens224 vlan.id 3967
Connection 'ens224.3967' (ee3776eb-4472-4eef-ab80-25b3eea72a04)
successfully added.

[root@k8s-master ~]# nmcli connection add type vlan con-name ens224.100
ifname ens224.100 vlan.parent ens224 vlan.id 100
Connection 'ens224.100' (61171ac4-4855-4ede-83ab-e87aaf367333)
successfully added.

[root@k8s-master ~]# vim /etc/sysconfig/network-scripts/ifcfg-ens224
BOOTPROTO=none
TYPE=Ethernet
NAME=ens224
DEVICE=ens224
ONBOOT=yes
MTU=9000

[root@k8s-master ~]# vim /etc/sysconfig/network-scripts/ifcfg-ens224.100
VLAN=yes
TYPE=Vlan
PHYSDEV=ens224
VLAN_ID=100
REORDER_HDR=yes
BOOTPROTO=none
DEFROUTE=yes
NAME=ens224.100
DEVICE=ens224.100
ONBOOT=yes
IPADDR=192.168.100.101
PREFIX=24
GATEWAY=192.168.100.1
DNS1=8.8.8.8
MTU=9000
```

```
[root@k8s-master ~]# vim /etc/sysconfig/network-scripts/ifcfg-ens224.3967
VLAN=yes
TYPE=Vlan
PHYSDEV=ens224
VLAN_ID=3967
REORDER_HDR=yes
BOOTPROTO=dhcp
DEFROUTE=no
NAME=ens224.3967
DEVICE=ens224.3967
ONBOOT=yes
MTU=9000

[root@k8s-master ~]# reboot
```

Immediately after the interfaces are up, you should gain connectivity through ACI via the Node VLAN to your servers from the external network thanks to L3OUT, and each Kubernetes node will receive its VTEP address from APIC over the Infrastructure VLAN. See Listing 9-9.

Listing 9-9. Kubernetes Node Network Verification

```
[root@k8s-master ~]# ifconfig

ens224: flags=4163<UP,BROADCAST,RUNNING,MULTICAST>  mtu 9000
        inet6 fe80::250:56ff:feb3:915f  prefixlen 64  scopeid 0x20<link>
        ether 00:50:56:b3:91:5f  txqueuelen 1000  (Ethernet)
        RX packets 7  bytes 1461 (1.4 KiB)
        RX errors 0  dropped 0  overruns 0  frame 0
        TX packets 21  bytes 2685 (2.6 KiB)
        TX errors 0  dropped 0 overruns 0  carrier 0  collisions 0

ens224.100: flags=4163<UP,BROADCAST,RUNNING,MULTICAST>  mtu 9000
        inet 192.168.100.101  netmask 255.255.255.0  broadcast
        192.168.100.255
        inet6 fe80::250:56ff:feb3:915f  prefixlen 64  scopeid 0x20<link>
        ether 00:50:56:b3:91:5f  txqueuelen 1000  (Ethernet)
        RX packets 439452  bytes 234217350 (223.3 MiB)
```

```
     RX errors 0   dropped 0   overruns 0   frame 0
     TX packets 309386   bytes 115762839 (110.4 MiB)
     TX errors 0   dropped 0 overruns 0   carrier 0   collisions 0
```

ens224.3967: flags=4163<UP,BROADCAST,RUNNING,MULTICAST> **mtu 9000**
        inet 10.11.40.64   netmask 255.255.0.0   broadcast 10.11.255.255
        inet6 fe80::250:56ff:feb3:915f prefixlen 64   scopeid 0x20<link>
        ether 00:50:56:b3:91:5f txqueuelen 1000 (Ethernet)
        RX packets 7 bytes 1363 (1.3 KiB)
        RX errors 0   dropped 0   overruns 0   frame 0
        TX packets 13   bytes 1989 (1.9 KiB)
        TX errors 0   dropped 0 overruns 0   carrier 0   collisions 0

Add a permanent static route for the whole multicast IP range with a next-hop interface of Infra VLAN subinterface. See Listing 9-10.

Listing 9-10. The Static Multicast Route via ACI infraVLAN Interface

```
[root@k8s-master ~]# vim /etc/sysconfig/network-scripts/route-ens224.3967
224.0.0.0/4 dev ens224.3967
```

Now you need to tune and override several requirements for the Linux DHCP client to receive special options from the APIC. For each Kubernetes server, fill in the proper Infra VLAN subinterface MAC address in the first line. See Listing 9-11.

Listing 9-11. Server DHCP Client Settings

```
[root@k8s-master ~]# vim /etc/dhcp/dhclient-ens224.3967.conf
send dhcp-client-identifier 01:<mac-address of infra VLAN interface>;
request subnet-mask, domain-name, domain-name-servers, host-name;
send host-name gethostname();

option rfc3442-classless-static-routes code 121 = array of unsigned
integer 8;
option ms-classless-static-routes code 249 = array of unsigned integer 8;
option wpad code 252 = string;

also request rfc3442-classless-static-routes;
also request ms-classless-static-routes;
```

```
also request static-routes;
also request wpad;
also request ntp-servers;
```

If you plan to deploy more than 20 EPGs inside the Kubernetes cluster, you should tune the IGMP membership kernel parameter. Current kernel versions allow by default joining only 20 multicast groups and this fact can be verified by the command in Listing 9-12.

Listing 9-12. Server IGMP Membership Support

```
[root@k8s-master ~]# sysctl net.ipv4.igmp_max_memberships
net.ipv4.igmp_max_memberships = 20
```

For each EPG count with one IGMP membership. To change the setting, edit file /etc/sysctl.d/99-sysctl.conf, add the following line, and load the setting, as shown in Listing 9-13.

Listing 9-13. Server IGMP Membership Setting

```
[root@k8s-master ~]# vim /etc/sysctl.d/99-sysctl.conf
net.ipv4.igmp_max_memberships = Max_Number_Of_EPGs (e.g. 100)
[root@k8s-master ~]# sysctl -p
net.ipv4.igmp_max_memberships = 100
```

Finally, use the DNS server or configure static DNS records for the individual Kubernetes nodes on each server. See Listing 9-14.

Listing 9-14. Static DNS Records in /etc/hosts

```
[root@k8s-master ~]# vim /etc/hosts
192.168.100.101 k8s-master.lab
192.168.100.102 k8s-worker1.lab
192.168.100.103 k8s-worker2.lab
```

Kubernetes Installation

Now as you have ACI and server nodes prepared from the configuration and networking point of view, you can move to the Kubernetes installation itself. There are multiple options for how to deploy the cluster, and none of them is recommended or preferred for the ACI integration itself. The decision is up to you in the end. Personally, I have a good experience with the **kubeadm** tool, so in this chapter, I will describe the process behind deploying Kubernetes this way.

Let's start with the Docker installation. To make sure DNS resolution inside Docker is working fine, you need to disable the Linux firewall on all servers. See Listing 9-15.

Listing 9-15. Disabling the System Firewall

```
[root@k8s-master ~]# systemctl stop firewalld
[root@k8s-master ~]# systemctl disable firewalld
Removed /etc/systemd/system/multi-user.target.wants/firewalld.service.
Removed /etc/systemd/system/dbus-org.fedoraproject.FirewallD1.service.
```

The latest Docker is available in an official repository, which you will add to the packaging system. Then you can install Docker and make sure the daemon will start and run after the reboot as well. See Listing 9-16.

Listing 9-16. Docker Installation and Verification

```
[root@k8s-master ~]# dnf config-manager --add-repo=https://download.docker.
com/linux/centos/docker-ce.repo

[root@k8s-master ~]# dnf install -y docker-ce

[root@k8s-master ~]# systemctl enable --now docker
[root@k8s-master ~]# systemctl status docker
docker.service - Docker Application Container Engine
   Loaded: loaded (/usr/lib/systemd/system/docker.service; enabled; vendor
   preset: disabled)
   Active: active (running) since Thu 2022-01-13 15:20:22 EST; 27s ago
```

Note   If you will run Docker with your own user instead of root, create a "docker" group and add your user there to avoid need for constant use of sudo with docker commands:

```
$ sudo groupadd docker$

sudo usermod -aG docker $USER
```

Docker uses a control group (cgroup) system to handle the resource management and to constrain resource allocation for individual container processes. There are multiple cgroup drivers available and Docker runs by default *cgroupfs*. However, from kubeadm version 1.22, if the user does not specify any cgroup driver, kubeadm will install *systemd* for Kubernetes nodes. You need to match both of them to run kubelet modules correctly by simply changing Docker's driver, as shown in Listing 9-17.

Listing 9-17. Docker cGroup Driver Setting

```
[root@k8s-master ~]# vim /etc/docker/daemon.json
{ "exec-opts": ["native.cgroupdriver=systemd"] }
[root@k8s-master ~]# systemctl restart docker
[root@k8s-master ~]# docker info
...
Server:
 Cgroup Driver: systemd
 Cgroup Version: 1
...
```

If Docker is running and with the correct cgroup driver, you can move forward to the kubeadm utility. First, a few system preparation steps. Set SELinux in permissive mode (disable it), as in Listing 9-18.

Listing 9-18. Disabling the SELinux

```
[root@k8s-master ~]# setenforce 0
[root@k8s-master ~]# sed -i 's/^SELINUX=enforcing$/SELINUX=permissive/'
/etc/selinux/config
```

Ensure the *br_netfilter* kernel module is loaded in the system by issuing lsmod | grep br_netfilter. Mostly it is already in place, but if not, load it manually using the modprobe br_netfilter command and ensure it is permanently available also after the restart. This will enable support of the bridging network functionalities needed on the Kubernetes host later for the ACI CNI plugin. See Listing 9-19.

Listing 9-19. br_netfilter Kernel Module

```
[root@k8s-master ~]# cat <<EOF > /etc/modules-load.d/k8s.conf
br_netfilter
EOF
modprobe br_netfilter
```

Now properly configure iptables to enable bridged traffic on the Kubernetes nodes by adding the lines in Listing 9-20 to sysctl.d (I will explain the need for a network bridge later):

Listing 9-20. Enabling the Network Bridging Feature

```
[root@k8s-master ~]# cat <<EOF | sudo tee /etc/sysctl.d/k8s.conf
net.bridge.bridge-nf-call-ip6tables = 1
net.bridge.bridge-nf-call-iptables = 1
EOF
[root@k8s-master ~]# sysctl --system
```

The Kubelet module won't work if the Linux swap is enabled, so you need to fix that in advance. Turn off the swap momentarily by the command swapoff -a and permanently disable it by commenting out the swap line in the */etc/fstab* file. See Listing 9-21.

Listing 9-21. Disabling Linux System Swap Partition

```
[root@k8s-master ~]# swapoff -a
[root@k8s_master ~]# vim /etc/fstab
...
/dev/mapper/cl_k8s-master-root
/                       xfs         defaults        0 0
UUID=afce698b-a44e-47bc-b1c1-f8cb5e827c5f /
boot                    xfs         defaults        0 0
#/dev/mapper/cl_ k8s-master-swap
none                    swap        defaults        0 0
...
```

Note   Generally, disabling a Linux swap can be risky in a situation when your server can run out of RAM memory. It can freeze with a hard reset as the only recovery option. Kubernetes is distributed, highly redundant system, so you are trading a swap partition for the higher performance needed for the platform.

Finally, let's install the kubeadm utility and Kubernetes itself. As before, add the official Kubernetes repository, install the necessary packages, and run the kubelet module. See Listing 9-22.

Listing 9-22. kubeadm and Kubernetes Installation

```
[root@k8s_master ~]# cat <<EOF | sudo tee /etc/yum.repos.d/kubernetes.repo
[kubernetes]
name=Kubernetes
baseurl=https://packages.cloud.google.com/yum/repos/kubernetes-el7-
\$basearch
enabled=1
gpgcheck=1
repo_gpgcheck=1
gpgkey=https://packages.cloud.google.com/yum/doc/yum-key.gpg https://
packages.cloud.google.com/yum/doc/rpm-package-key.gpg
exclude=kubelet kubeadm kubectl
EOF

[root@k8s-master ~]# yum install -y kubelet kubeadm kubectl
--disableexcludes=kubernetes

[root@k8s-master ~]# systemctl enable --now kubelet
```

At this moment, kubelet will stay in a crashloop on all nodes, but don't worry because as soon as you start the Kubernetes control plane and add workers to the cluster, everything will be fine. This time on a *master node only*, initialize Kubernetes control-plane by issuing the command in Listing 9-23,

Listing 9-23. Kubernetes Master Node Initialization

```
[root@k8s-master ~]# kubeadm init --pod-network-cidr=192.168.101.0/24
--service-cidr=192.168.103.0/24
...
Your Kubernetes control-plane has initialized successfully!
```

To start using your cluster, you need to run the following as a regular user:

```
mkdir -p $HOME/.kube
sudo cp -i /etc/kubernetes/admin.conf $HOME/.kube/config
sudo chown $(id -u):$(id -g) $HOME/.kube/config
```

Alternatively, if you are the root user, you can run

```
export KUBECONFIG=/etc/kubernetes/admin.conf
```

You should now deploy a Pod network to the cluster. Run `kubectl apply -f [podnetwork].yaml` with one of the options listed at `https://kubernetes.io/docs/concepts/cluster-administration/addons/`.

Then you can join any number of worker nodes by running the following on each as root:

```
kubeadm join 192.168.100.101:6443 --token otp7ka.81q96ha7tbyq66w4 \
        --discovery-token-ca-cert-hash sha256:63d7b71db0da7059405629226e
6e372d53cc7e5424606fe1c73072d2bd2a0d01
```

If you received the previous message at the end of the initialization, your Kubernetes control plane is running correctly, and you are ready to start adding worker nodes. As instructed, issue `kubeadm join` with the received token on your worker nodes. See Listing 9-24.

Listing 9-24. Kubernetes Worker Nodes Clustering

```
[root@k8s-worker1 ~]# kubeadm join 192.168.100.101:6443 --token
otp7ka.81q96ha7tbyq66w4 \
>         --discovery-token-ca-cert-hash sha256:63d7b71db0da7059405629226e
        6e372d53cc7e5424606fe1c73072d2bd2a0d01
...
This node has joined the cluster
```

You need to tweak the Kubelet DNS resolution. As you've changed the default Kubernetes Cluster subnet (default is 10.96.0.0/16 and your is 192.168.103.0/24), you have to let the module know about it; otherwise, it will tend to reach 10.96.0.10 for DNS resolution. In addition, add the --network-plugin=cni definition to KUBELET_ KUBECONFIG_ARGS= variable to instruct Kubelet to use the CNI plugin located inside default folder */etc/cni/net.d*. Add the lines in Listing 9-25 to the Kubelet configuration file on each node and restart the process.

Listing 9-25. Kubelet DNS Settings

```
[root@k8s-master ~]# vim /usr/lib/systemd/system/kubelet.service.d/10-
kubeadm.conf
Environment="KUBELET_KUBECONFIG_ARGS=--bootstrap-kubeconfig=/etc/
kubernetes/bootstrap-kubelet.conf --kubeconfig=/etc/kubernetes/kubelet.conf
--network-plugin=cni"
Environment="KUBELET_DNS_ARGS=--cluster-dns=192.168.103.10 --cluster-
domain=cluster.local"
[root@k8s-master ~]# systemctl daemon-reload
[root@k8s-master ~]# systemctl restart kubelet
```

Put this kubectl reference permanently into your environmental variables by adding the line in Listing 9-26 to the local user shell script.

Listing 9-26. Environmental Variable Setting for kubectl

```
[root@k8s-master ~]# vim .bashrc
export KUBECONFIG=/etc/kubernetes/admin.conf
```

Reconnect to the master node, where you can check the current cluster status and you should see all Kubernetes nodes there. After a few minutes since join, all workers should end up in the *Ready* state. See Listing 9-27.

Listing 9-27. Kubernetes Nodes Verification

```
[root@k8s-master ~]# kubectl get nodes
NAME               STATUS    ROLES                  AGE      VERSION
k8s-master.lab     Ready     control-plane,master   11m      v1.23.1
k8s-worker1.lab    Ready     <none>                 2m52s    v1.23.1
k8s-worker2.lab    Ready     <none>                 2m33s    v1.23.1
```

Now you have Kubernetes running but without any network CNI plugin. Remember that YAML file generated by the acc-provision script at the beginning? It's basically the Kubernetes deployment specification file for CNI and you will use it now to provision all ACI networking components into the running Kubernetes cluster. You need to upload the file to the master node and apply it this way, as shown in Listing 9-28.

Listing 9-28. ACI CNI Plugin Installation

[root@k8s-master ~]# **kubectl apply -f aci-containers.yaml**

After a while, when the whole ACI machinery is deployed, you should see the following containers running in your cluster (see Listing 9-29).

Listing 9-29. ACI CNI Verification

[root@k8s-master ~]# **kubectl get pod --all-namespaces**

NAMESPACE	NAME	READY	STATUS
aci-containers-system	**aci-containers-controller-64c454c9f4-76fc4**	**1/1**	**Running**
aci-containers-system	**aci-containers-host-m5r4t**	**3/3**	**Running**
aci-containers-system	**aci-containers-host-prf6h**	**3/3**	**Running**
aci-containers-system	**aci-containers-host-xzpm8**	**3/3**	**Running**
aci-containers-system	**aci-containers-openvswitch-bcfmw**	**1/1**	**Running**
aci-containers-system	**aci-containers-openvswitch-kfbpm**	**1/1**	**Running**
aci-containers-system	**aci-containers-openvswitch-m5prg**	**1/1**	**Running**
aci-containers-system	**aci-containers-operator-5d5c96856d-dth4w**	**2/2**	**Running**
kube-system	coredns-64897985d-69rdc	1/1	Running
kube-system	coredns-64897985d-rswn4	1/1	Running
kube-system	etcd-k8s-master.lab	1/1	Running
kube-system	kube-apiserver-k8s-master.lab	1/1	Running
kube-system	kube-controller-manager-k8s-master.lab	1/1	Running
kube-system	kube-proxy-4qfxr	1/1	Running
kube-system	kube-proxy-cj6vs	1/1	Running
kube-system	kube-proxy-n7fhf	1/1	Running
kube-system	kube-scheduler-k8s-master.lab	1/1	Running

Congratulations!! This is the goal you have been pursuing from the beginning and currently you've achieved a working Kubernetes cluster with an ACI CNI plugin and full

integration. As shown in Figure 9-18, when you navigate in ACI to **Virtual Networking ->**
Kubernetes and open the K8s domain, you should see all your Kubernetes nodes
(in the online state), their VTEP addresses (ACI considers them basically as remote
virtual leaves now), and discovered container endpoints.

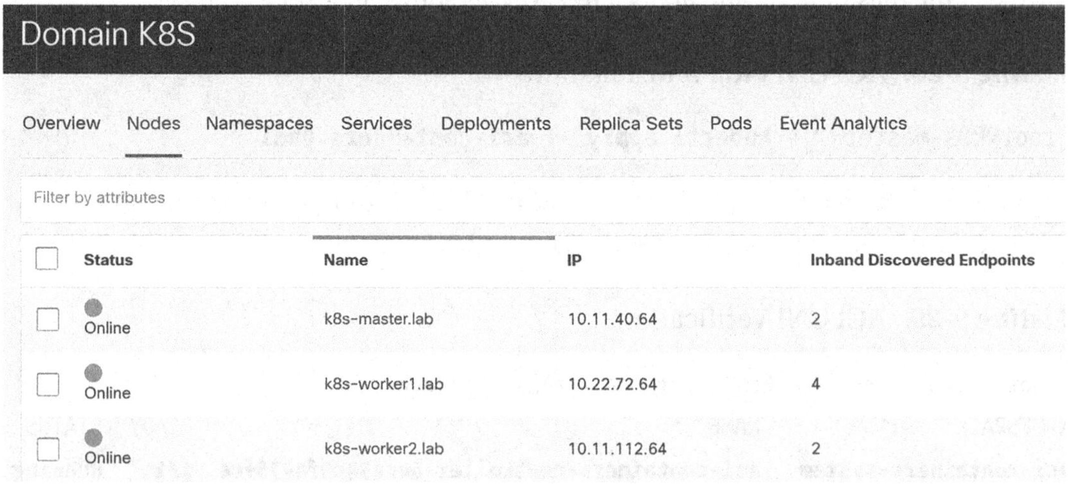

Domain K8S

| Overview | Nodes | Namespaces | Services | Deployments | Replica Sets | Pods | Event Analytics |

Filter by attributes

	Status	Name	IP	Inband Discovered Endpoints
☐	● Online	k8s-master.lab	10.11.40.64	2
☐	● Online	k8s-worker1.lab	10.22.72.64	4
☐	● Online	k8s-worker2.lab	10.11.112.64	2

Figure 9-18. *Kubernetes VMM domain overview after integration*

In this section, go through all menu options to see the acquired consolidated
visibility from the ACI point of view. If you open a particular container endpoint, you will
get its MAC address, IP address, network veth interface, VXLAN VNID segment, labels,
associated ACI EPG, potential issues, and much more. In the Pods sections, you can
see exactly on which Kubernetes node a particular Pod is running and which ACI leaf
interface is used for its communication (see Figure 9-19).

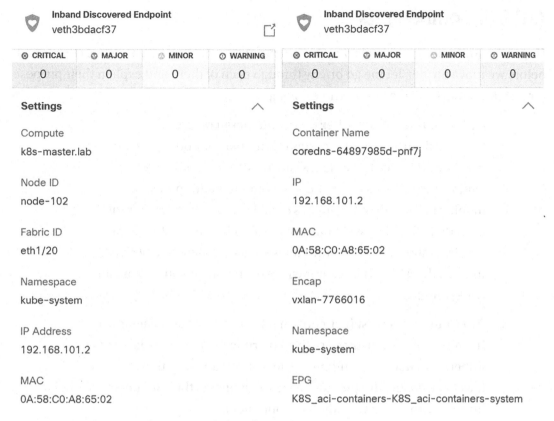

Figure 9-19. *ACI endpoint visibility for Kubernetes Pods*

You can easily get even detailed statistics about individual containers, as you can see in Figure 9-20. Go to the Pods section, click the number representing Inband Discovered Endpoints for a chosen Pod. In the newly opened form, choose the Pod's veth interface, click the symbol, and open the Statistics tab.

Now consider the fact that ACI's big advantage is an open API. Any object visible inside the Kubernetes VMM domain is accessible through it, which gives you powerful options to easily use this information inside your own management or monitoring systems.

ACI CNI Components

Hopefully you can see ACI CNI components running inside your Kubernetes cluster and before we move further, let me go briefly through each of them and explain their purpose for a better understanding of the whole concept.

1. **ACI Containers Controller** (aci-containers-controller): Communicates with Kubernetes cluster master nodes and the ACI APIC. The controller takes care of IP address management, loadbalancer VIP assignment, and container endpoint state monitoring and then automates configuration changes on APIC if needed. The high availability of this Pod is handled by the ACI CNI Operator Pod. The controller is stateless, so in case of any trouble, the ACI CNI Operator will restart it on any other available worker node.

2. **ACI Containers Host** (aci-containers-host): Runs as a daemonset (meaning that an instance of this Pod runs across all available Kubernetes nodes, including master). If you add additional nodes, it will automatically spin up there as well. Inside the containers host you can find three different containers:

   a. **aci-containers-host**: Configures interfaces with IP addresses for Pods running on this node and manages their metadata

   b. **opflex-agent**: Communicates with the OpFlex proxy agent running on leaves where the Kubernetes nodes are connected. For scalability reasons, to avoid constant querying of APIC directly, this two-tier OpFlex architecture is introduced. If the leaf doesn't know about policies for a new Kubernetes Pod, it sends a request to APIC and caches the result. Using the OpFlex protocol, ACI can install network policies into the Open vSwitch running on Kubernetes nodes.

   c. **mcast-daemon**: Broadcast, unknown unicast, and multicast (BUM) traffic handling

3. **ACI Containers Open vSwitch** (aci-containers-openvswitch): Again a daemonset running on all Kubernetes nodes, acting basically as a virtual ACI leaf switch inside the node. Manages

switching, routing, security policy enforcement (Kubernetes network policies or ACI contracts), and distributed loadbalancing for ClusterIP services. Open vSwitch policies are provisioned in a declarative manner using the OpFlex protocol.

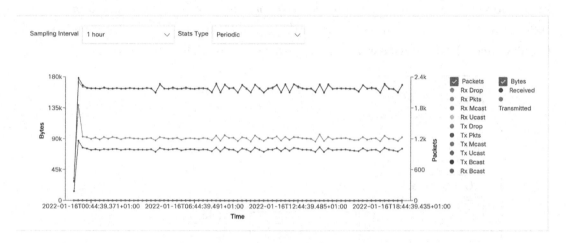

Figure 9-20. *Container statictics in ACI*

4. **ACI CNI Operator** (aci-containers-operator): Running in HA, this Pod was introduced in ACI version 5.0(1) and it is responsible for managing the whole lifecycle of other CNI components from their deployment to status monitoring.

Figure 9-21 graphically summarizes the architecture of ACI CNI plugin components.

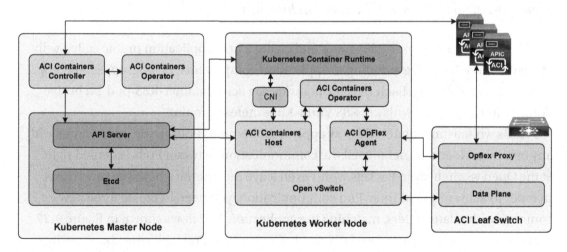

Figure 9-21. *ACI CNI architecture overview*

Demo YELB Application with ACI L4-L7 Service Graph and EPG segmentation

In the last part of this chapter, I will show you how to practically use the Kubernetes integration with ACI. You will deploy a sample four-tier microservice application called Yelb, whose architecture is shown in Figure 9-22, and expose its UI through ACI Loadbalancer (L4-L7 service graph) to the external network for user access.

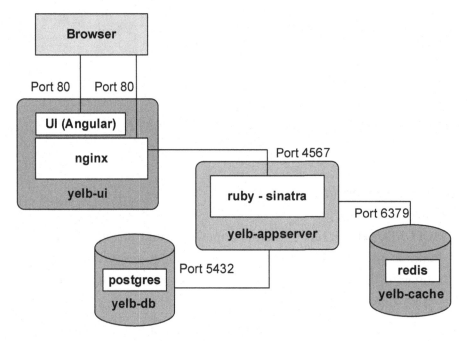

Figure 9-22. *Yelb demo application architecture*

In ACI, navigate to your K8S tenant and create a new application profile called yelb_app with four EPGs corresponding to application components: ui_epg, appserver_epg, cache_epg, and db_epg. Each EPG is put inside the aci-container-K8S-pod-bd bridge domain and associated with the K8S Vmm-Kubernetes domain.

ACI's whitelisting model will now apply to Kubernetes Pods in the same way as with any other workloads. By default, all the communication between Pods is denied right at the Open vSwitch layer. Packets won't even leave the interface of Kubernetes hosts. In order to allow required Inter-Pod communication, you need to create three new contracts with related filters, matching the application TCP flows shown in Figure 9-22. Additionally, you need to ensure DNS resolution for each Pod with core-dns containers, so you will consume an already existing DNS contract aci-containers-K8S-dns with each new application EPG. The contract is provided by aci-containers-system EPG, where CoreDNS Pods reside. The complete ACI application model for the Yelb application is depicted in Figure 9-23.

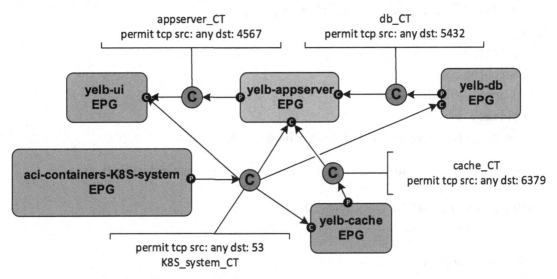

Figure 9-23. *ACI Application profile for Yelb*

Now download the Yelb Kubernetes deployment file on the master node and save it to the yelb-lb.yaml file. See Listing 9-30.

Listing 9-30. Yelb Demo application Download

```
[root@k8s-master ~]# curl https://raw.githubusercontent.com/lamw/vmware-
k8s-app-demo/master/yelb-lb.yaml > yelb-lb.yaml
```

You need to edit the individual deployment sections to specify their EPG affiliation by using annotations. Annotations are tools to simply associate any Kubernetes Pod to EPG of your choice. Listing 9-31 shows the Yelb-ui deployment section.

Listing 9-31. Yelb-ui Deployment

```
---
apiVersion: apps/v1
kind: Deployment
metadata:
  name: yelb-ui
```

```
  namespace: yelb
  annotations:
    opflex.cisco.com/endpoint-group: '{ "tenant":"K8S", "app-
    profile":"yelb_app", "name":"ui_epg"  }'
spec:
  selector:
    matchLabels:
      app: yelb-ui
  replicas: 3
... rest of the lines omitted - no changes there...
```

Similarly edit the Yelb-redis deployment section, as shown in Listing 9-32.

Listing 9-32. Yelb-redis Deployment

```
---
apiVersion: apps/v1
kind: Deployment
metadata:
  name: redis-server
  namespace: yelb
  annotations:
    opflex.cisco.com/endpoint-group: '{ "tenant":"K8S", "app-
    profile":"yelb_app", "name":"cache_epg"  }'
... rest of the lines omitted - no changes there...
```

For Yelb-db deployment as well, see Listing 9-33.

Listing 9-33. Yelb-db Deployment

```
---
apiVersion: apps/v1
kind: Deployment
metadata:
  name: yelb-db
  namespace: yelb
  annotations:
```

```
opflex.cisco.com/endpoint-group: '{ "tenant":"K8S", "app-
profile":"yelb_app", "name":"db_epg"  }'
... rest of the lines omitted - no changes there...
```

And finally, see Listing 9-34 for the Yelb-appserver deployment with increased container replicas to spread them across the Kubernetes cluster. You will later easily see loadbalancing between them in action.

Listing 9-34. Yelb-appserver Deployment

```
---
apiVersion: apps/v1
kind: Deployment
metadata:
  name: yelb-appserver
  namespace: yelb
  annotations:
    opflex.cisco.com/endpoint-group: '{ "tenant":"K8S", "app-
    profile":"yelb_app", "name":"appserver_epg"  }'
spec:
  selector:
    matchLabels:
      app: yelb-appserver
  replicas: 3
... rest of the lines omitted - no changes there...
```

Save the deployment file and apply Yelb application in your cluster. After a few moments, check that all PODs are ready and running as expected. See Listing 9-35.

Listing 9-35. Yelb Demo Deployment Verification

```
[root@k8s-master ~]# kubectl create ns yelb
[root@k8s-master ~]# kubectl apply -f yelb-lb.yaml
[root@k8s-master ~]# kubectl get pods -n yelb
NAME                              READY   STATUS    RESTARTS   AGE
redis-server-5c8c579489-fdp9l     1/1     Running   0          5m42s
yelb-appserver-5d9c79d959-2nw66   1/1     Running   0          5m42s
yelb-appserver-5d9c79d959-5jg4f   1/1     Running   0          5m42s
```

yelb-appserver-5d9c79d959-r9wxl	1/1	Running	0	5m42s
yelb-db-84748b97cb-d8npb	1/1	Running	0	5m42s
yelb-ui-798f4b69bf-gnwfv	1/1	Running	0	5m42s

Pods are already visible as learned endpoints inside the ACI fabric with detailed information about their MAC/IP addresses, location, physical interface, and VXLAN segment used for communication (as shown on Figure 9-24).

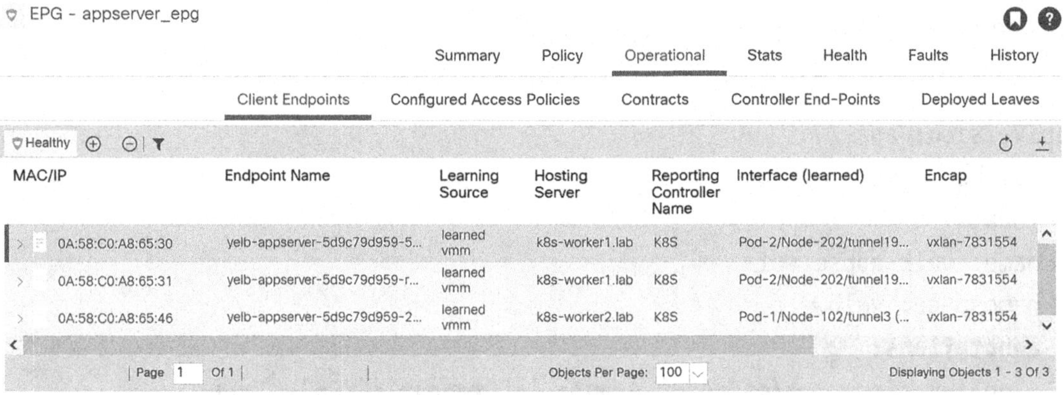

Figure 9-24. *Container endpoints learned in EPG*

You've just achieved the same level of segmentation, visibility, and network consistency for containers in ACI as for any other bare-metal or VM workloads. And this integration allows you to go even further in few moments.

But first, navigate to the Kubernetes VMM domain in ACI and go to the Services tab, or enter kubectl get services -A on the Kubernetes master node. You will find a LoadBalancer service listening on External IP 192.168.200.8 and tcp port 80 for yelb-ui PODs. This is an automatically assigned VIP for application access. See Listing 9-36.

Listing 9-36. Kubernetes Service IP and LB VIP Allocations

```
[root@k8s-master ~]# kubectl get services -A
NAME            TYPE          CLUSTER-IP        EXTERNAL-IP      PORT(S)
... ...
redis-server    ClusterIP     192.168.103.23    <none>          6379/TCP
yelb-appserver  ClusterIP     192.168.103.225   <none>          4567/TCP
yelb-db         ClusterIP     192.168.103.168   <none>          5432/TCP
yelb-ui         LoadBalancer  192.168.103.179   192.168.200.8   80:30839/TCP
```

If you have properly routed the external services subnet (192.168.200.0/24) to your L3OUT leaves and this prefix is accessible from your current IP, by entering http://192.168.200.8 in the browser, you should get the Yelb web interface (as shown in Figure 9-25).

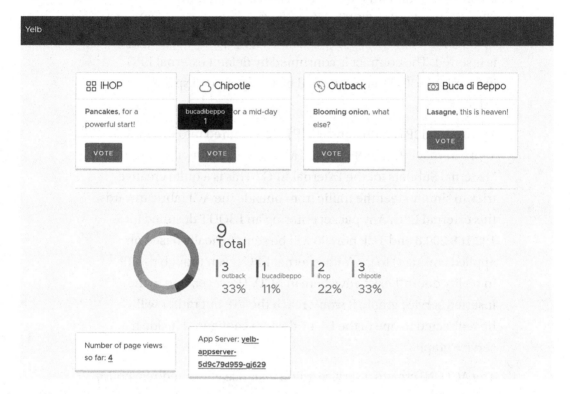

Figure 9-25. *Yelb container demo application*

It's that simple. Try to refresh this site multiple times to observe changes in the appserver container name listed at the bottom of the page. It's the verification that loadbalancing is working correctly and that it's actually happening internally. But how does ACI know how to route the traffic to this VIP?

During the Yelb app deployment, ACI automatically published yelb-ui Pods to the external network through L3OUT in the K8S tenant and for clients, ACI even serves as a hardware loadbalancer. To understand the magic behind this machinery, you need to explore several new objects created by the ACI CNI Controller in APIC.

The key initiator for all the automation is a loadbalancer service definition in your Kubernetes deployment file (for a service syntax, refer to `yelb-lb.yaml`). When integrated Kubernetes sees the loadbalancer definition, the following steps will happen:

1. The ACI CNI allocates an external IP, representing a loadbalancer VIP (from the dynamic external service subnet) and associates it with the specified Pod.

2. A contract named *K8S_svc_yelb_yelb-ui* is created with a filter allowing destination TCP service port (in your case port 80). The key part lies in its subject, where a new L4-L7 service graph is inserted. The contract is consumed by default external EPG in your K8S L3OUT and provided by newly created specific external EPG.

3. The external IP (loadbalancer VIP) is configured into this new Yelb external EPG in K8S L3OUT as a host /32 subnet with scope "External Subnets for the External EPG." This is a quite creative trick to simply steer the traffic from outside the ACI fabric towards this external EPG. Any packet entering an L3OUT destined for 192.168.200.8 and TCP port 80 will be sent (logically based on applied contract) to the Yelb external EPG (even though this IP in reality doesn't exist anywhere in ACI). However, due to the inserted service graph, it won't reach the VIP but rather will be redirected to one of the L4-L7 devices configured inside the service graph.

4. The ACI CNI creates a service graph instance with a redirect policy listing all your Kubernetes worker nodes with their IPs and MAC addresses from the service VLAN (102 in your example). This object is automatically updated every time you add or remove the Kubernetes cluster node where the related Pod is being scheduled, which is very useful from an operation perspective. Based on a hash, one of these nodes is chosen and the packet is redirected there via the service VLAN in in the service BD. Thanks to that, ACI provides HW accelerated loadbalancing capabilities.

5. The next-hop IP address (Node Service IP) in VLAN 102 for this policy-based redirect is configured inside an open vSwitch and all received packets are forwarded to the Kubernetes cluster IP, where the second tier of loadbalancing happens.

6. The ACI CNI in the open vSwitch creates an internal loadbalancer
    for each Kubernetes node to terminate the cluster IP. Its goal
    is to deliver traffic to pool of related Pods running on the same
    host. Additionally, it performs NAT to translate IPs and ports
    which can be for individual Pods different and non-related to the
    original VIP.

In the Figure 9-26, I tried to visualize all the components involved in traffic
forwarding from ACI L3OUT to a Kubernetes Pod. Hopefully, it will provide you a
complete picture and mental map of this interesting feature.

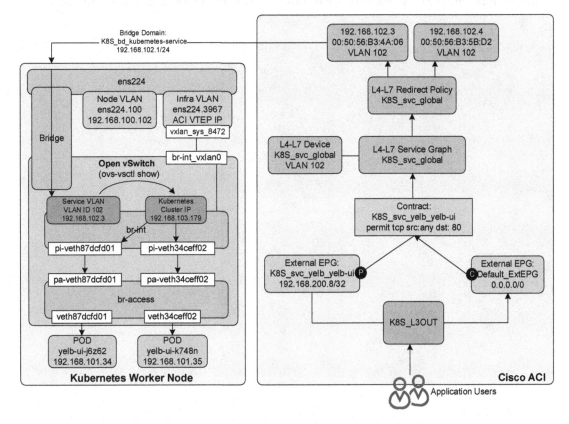

Figure 9-26. *ACI HW accelerated loadbalancing and traffic forwarding for
Kubernetes*

Summary

In this chapter, you had an opportunity to explore and gain practical experience with ACI integration capabilities, allowing you to achieve significant benefits for security, visibility, and maintainability of networking layers for your virtualized workloads and containers in a data center. This way, you can handle bare-metal servers, virtual machines, and containers as equal endpoints in the infrastructure and ensure that consistent policies are applied to them across all data centers.

The next chapter will discuss ACI remote leaf expansion capability, intended for smaller data centers and colocations without the need for a whole leaf-spine fabric.

CHAPTER 10

ACI Automation and Programmability

If you made your way to this last chapter through the whole book, congratulations and great job! I sincerely hope you learned a lot, and ACI is becoming (if not already) a strong part of your skill set. Maybe you incline a lot (like me) to network programmability, automation, software development, or the DevOps philosophy, and you have jumped here earlier, before finishing all the chapters, which is also perfect! If you are entirely new to ACI, though, I definitely recommend starting with building the solid basics first, as I expect at least a basic understanding of ACI structure, objects, and their usage for this chapter. In the upcoming pages, we will dive deeper together into a number of exciting and important topics related to ACI's programmability features, highly improving its provisioning speed, operation, change management, and troubleshooting.

This chapter will be different compared with the preceding ones primarily in the way you will interact with APIC. Instead of creating objects or verifying the configuration using the GUI and CLI, you will utilize a lower layer: the *application programming interface (API)* and tools consuming it. This involves a plethora of options, from OS utilities to the Python programming language, end-to-end orchestrator platforms, and more. You will explore how ACI can simplify the creation of hundreds (even thousands) of objects and policies in the blink of an eye, how you can write your own software to overcome limitations and unsatisfactory outputs (if any) of the GUI/CLI, and how to prepare troubleshooting workflow, gathering, and analyzing a quantum of information automatically on your behalf.

For the following sections, I also expect some experience with Python. You don't need to be a developer with years of experience at all, but at least minimal working proficiency will be very beneficial. Personally, I encourage all the network engineers out there more to learn Python basics. It can unbelievably simplify your life and increase your market value at the same time. Automation and programmability skills, in general, are in huge demand and almost mandatory for a wide variety of IT positions around the industry.

© Jan Janovic 2023
J. Janovic, *Cisco ACI: Zero to Hero*, https://doi.org/10.1007/978-1-4842-8838-2_10

ACI Programmability Introduction

ACI creators made a perfect decision step at the beginning of their journey, building the whole platform so-called "*API First*". Even though you maybe don't know about it yet, every time you opened the ACI GUI and did some operation there or issued some command on APIC's CLI, if fact APIC always communicated with a single northbound Representational State Transfer (REST) API.

This brings a considerable advantage when it comes to external tooling and their interaction with APIC. Any Cisco or third-party modules like software development kits (SDKs), Kubernetes CNI, Ansible, Terraform, and other end-to-end orchestrators get the same, completely open access to all ACI objects for Create, Read, Update, and Delete (CRUD) operations.

The REST API provides an interface to APIC's comprehensive object database based on the Management Information Model (MIM), as described in Figure 10-1.

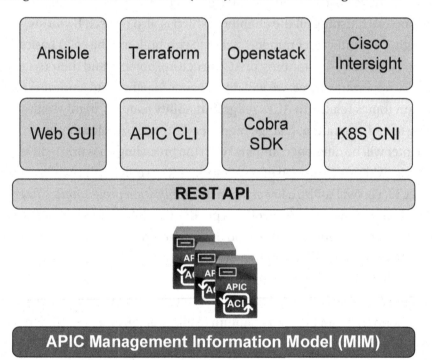

Figure 10-1. *APIC common REST API*

MIM carries a logical description of thousands of objects, defining the ACI solution with all their attributes and mutual relationships. Then, any HTTP/S client in general can be used to consume the REST API and access their actual instances in the APIC database.

REST APIs

The REST API implemented in ACI is a software technology providing a uniform communication interface between clients and servers (APIC) to transport information about ACI objects. It utilizes very similar concepts to the traditional World Wide Web operation (as shown in Figure 10-2). RESTful APIs come with these specifics:

- **Client-server architecture**: REST separates data stored on the server systems from the client manipulating them, improving portability and scalability of user interfaces. Consider, for example, how many various tools are available for ACI to reach the same information on APIC through the same API.

- **Stateless nature**: No session is retained by the server, significantly lowering the system overhead and resource consumption.

- **Resource identification**: The REST API describes accessed resources in each request using a Uniform Resource Identifier (URI).

- **Data format**: Server database implementation is decoupled from the data transport. REST uses primarily unified JSON and XML data formats.

- **HTTP methods**: Similar to the Web, the REST API supports standard HTTP methods of GET, POST, PUT, and DELETE.

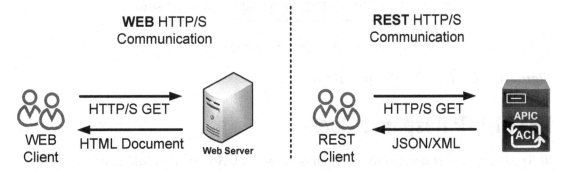

Figure 10-2. *WEB vs. REST communication*

REST clients, when communicating with API servers, must specify the object URI and intended operation with it using HTTP methods (as illustrated in Figure 10-3):

- **HTTP POST**: Creates a new object. In the case of ACI, it is also used for updating the existing one. The client has to send object attributes formatted as JSON/XML in the REST call payload.

- **HTTP GET**: The client requests the object identified in the URI. The server replies with the JSON/XML payload describing the object attributes.

- **HTTP PUT**: Updates any attribute of an existing object. Generally supported by REST APIs, but in the case of ACI, this method is not implemented and is substituted by POST.

- **HTTP DELETE**: Deletes existing objects from the server database.

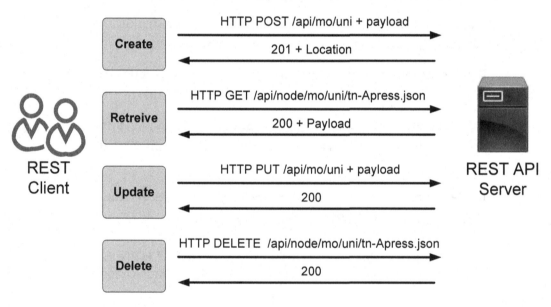

Figure 10-3. *REST CRUD operations*

REST HTTP Response Codes

REST APIs are not stateful, and each call is individual. However, we still need some mechanism for how servers can notify clients about a result of an execution of their calls. For these purposes, REST API servers reply with standardized status codes implemented in the HTTP protocol. The first digit divides the status codes into five categories:

- **1xx Informational**

- **2xx Success**

- **3xx Redirection**

- **4xx Client-side errors**

- **5xx Server-side errors**

In each category, there are many individual status messages implemented for HTTP, but we will cover just the most important ones for the REST API. The first informational category has just a single representative, show in Table 10-1.

Table 10-1. *Informational REST Status Codes*

Success (1xx)	Description
101 – Switching Protocols	ACI REST API sends it in response to an HTTP Upgrade message when switching from HTTP to the WebSocket protocol. More about this feature is in the "ACI Object Subscriptions" section of this chapter.

The success category confirms that your API operations were successfully done on the server side. In software development, checking for 2XX status codes can be tied to error identification and handling. See Table 10-2.

Table 10-2. *Success REST Status Codes*

Success (2xx)	Description
200 – OK	Any requested client action was carried out successfully. With 200 OK, the REST API should return a data object in the response body. Primarily used in ACI for any successful operation.
201 – Created	Notifies the client that the requested resource was successfully created. ACI actually doesn't implement 201 and sends 200 OK even when creating objects.
202 – Accepted	If the processing of a client's request takes a longer time, this status will notify the client that the request has been accepted and it's being processed. Not implemented in ACI.
204 – No Content	Used if the REST API declines to send any message in the response body. Usually, the resource exists in the system, but it has no attributes to send to the client. This one has not implemented in ACI.

The third category of status codes is, to the best of my knowledge, not implemented in ACI at all, but just for completeness, Table 10-3 shows their description in general for REST APIs.

Table 10-3. *Redirection REST Status Codes*

Success (3xx)	Description
301 – Moved Permanently	This response indicates that the underlying object model was significantly redesigned, and the client should use a different URI for this request.
302 – Found	Common way to perform a redirection to another URL, provided in the response's Location header field. The client is expected to generate another REST call with a new URL.
304 – Not Modified	Similar to status code 204, the response from a server doesn't contain any message in the body. 304 is sent only when the client asks if the resource was modified since the version specified in headers If-Modified-Since or If-None-Match and the resource is not changed.

The client-side error status codes in Table 10-4 are all implemented also for ACI, and they are an important tool to implement error handling in the client's automation software solution.

Table 10-4. *Client-Side Error REST Status Codes*

Success (4xx)	Description
400 – Bad Request	Generic error code returned when some mistake is made in the message body. It can be related to incorrect syntax or mandatory parameters missing.
401 – Unauthorized	Very common error returned when you are not authenticated to access the REST API. Usually caused by an expired, malformed, or missing authentication token.
403 – Forbidden	Even with the correct authentication token, if access to the requested object is prohibited by the server's role-based access control (RBAC), you will be provided with status 403.
404 – Not Found	Maybe the most "famous" status code, returned when you compose a request URI to the non-existing object.

And the last two server-side errors could be potentially seen when there is some problem with the execution of your call on the server, such as the web server running on the server threw an exception. See Table 10-5.

Table 10-5. *Server-Side Error REST Status Codes*

Success (5xx)	Description
500 – Internal Server Error	Failure on the server side, usually caused by an exception thrown by the web framework running there.
501 – Not Implemented	If the server cannot process your otherwise correct request due to missing implementation of the method used. Not implemented in ACI.

Data Encoding Formats

Before digging deeper into the ACI object model and its REST API, I find it very beneficial in this section to compare the three major data encoding formats we will use during ACI automation: XML, JSON, and YAML. YAML is not directly applicable to the APIC REST API, but is significantly utilized, for example, in the case of Ansible.

Why do we even need them? As already mentioned, the API alone wouldn't be enough to manage objects on the destination server system. There is a requirement for a standardized data format to transfer object attributes in and out. It's part of the decoupling philosophy between the actual implementation of an internal server database (often proprietary) and a common data transport format that is understandable by all REST clients.

All three data formats have multiple common characteristics:

- Pre-defined and mandatory syntax

- Concept of an object containing many attributes described as individual elements

- Key-value notation for object attributes

- Array or list concept with multiple nested hierarchy levels

- Case sensitivity

XML

Extensible Markup Language (XML) is one of the data formats used for the ACI REST API to describe structured object information. It's very similar to HTML documents but with strict syntax rules making it optimal for reliable processing by computer software. However, from a human-readability point of view, it's not preferred at all, and if possible, I personally always reach for other options.

XML elements must always be closed or defined as empty. Either you can use pair of tags, *<imdata></imdata>*, or a short form, *<fvTenant ... ... />*. Both options can be seen in the example from ACI in Listing 10-1.

Listing 10-1. XML Object Structure

```
<?xml version="1.0" encoding="UTF-8"?>
<imdata totalCount="2">
    <fvTenant annotation="" childAction="" descr="" dn="uni/tn-Apress"
    extMngdBy="" lcOwn="local" modTs="2022-08-02T15:06:57.000+02:00"
    monPolDn="uni/tn-common/monepg-default" name="Apress" nameAlias=""
    ownerKey="" ownerTag="" status="" uid="15374" userdom=":all:"/>

<fvTenant annotation="" childAction="" descr="" dn="uni/tn-common"
extMngdBy="" lcOwn="local" modTs="2022-04-22T15:24:33.830+02:00"
monPolDn="uni/tn-common/monepg-default" name="common" nameAlias=""
ownerKey="" ownerTag="" status="" uid="0" userdom="all"/>
</imdata>
```

All attributes included in XML objects must be always quoted: <fvTenant name=**"Apress"** uid=**"15374"** />. Regarding the whitespaces, XML differentiates between two types:

- **Significant whitespaces**: Within the elements (<name>**.....**</name>) and their attributes (<fvTenant name="**.....**" />)

- **Insignificant whitespaces**: Between element name and attribute names, so <fvTenant **.....** name="" />

Lists in XML are created just by putting multiple elements to the same hierarchical level.

JSON

JavaScript Object Notation (JSON) was derived from JavaScript to exchange the data between clients and server in human-readable format. Compared to XML, JSON is highly preferred whenever possible thanks to its readability. Another advantage is native JSON data mapping to dictionaries in multiple programming languages, especially in Python, commonly used also for ACI automation.

JSON objects use a key:value attribute format, which has to be delimited by curly braces, { }, as you can see in the ACI example in Listing 10-2.

Listing 10-2. JSON Object Structure

```
{
  "totalCount": "1",
  "imdata": [
    {
      "fvTenant": {
        "attributes": {
          "annotation": "",
          "descr": "",
          "dn": "uni/tn-Apress",
          "lcOwn": "local",
          "modTs": "2022-08-02T15:06:57.000+02:00",
          "monPolDn": "uni/tn-common/monepg-default",
          "name": "Apress",
          "uid": "15374",
          "userdom": ":all:"
        }
      }
    }
  ]
}
```

Both keys and values have to use quotes, and created attributes need comma separation between each other except for the last one. Whitespaces between JSON attributes and object are not significant.

To create an array, multiple JSON objects just need to be defined between square brackets, [ ] , and separated by comma (in the previous example, the value of a key imdata is array).

YAML

Often referred to as Yet Another Markup Language or by the recursive acronym YAML Ain't Markup Language, YAML is the third most used format to serialize and transport data in a standardized way. ACI directly doesn't support YAML for REST API operations, but based on its structure, Ansible configuration files (playbooks) are produced. Also, the ACI object structure can be easily described using YAML, as you will see later in this chapter.

YAML, similar to JSON, utilizes key:value attributes, this time without the obligatory quotes. Whitespaces are crucial as the indentation denotes hierarchical level and nested objects, while each new line represents a new object or attribute. No commas are used. See Listing 10-3.

Listing 10-3. YAML Object Structure

```
aci_config:
  aci_tenant_structure:
  - name: Apress_Prod
    state: present
    vrf:
    - name: PROD
    - name: TEST
    app_profile:
    - name: WebApp
    - name: JavaApp
```

Lists or arrays in YAML are created by lines starting with a dash, -. Each dash produces an individual list item, while by item can be considered all lines indented one level to the right from dash.

ACI Object Model

A significant common characteristic of these described data formats is that they carry object information and attributes for us when communicating with ACI's REST API. So far, we have worked with ACI objects from the user point of view. We have used their standard, well-known names: tenant, bridge domain, VRF, contract, and more. Then, the APIC GUI/CLI has handled any manipulations with them for us.

When it comes to ACI programmability, we will start looking at objects from a different perspective. The internal ACI database consists of *managed objects (MO),* organized into a tree hierarchy, where MOs of the same type belong to the particular *class.* In the following sections, we are going to explore together how to actually identify correct MOs names, their class names, and how to construct a REST URI, ultimately providing access to their attributes using an API.

Figure 10-4 shows a familiar ACI tenant object model, but this time with class names of all objects as defined in the internal MIM. Objects are further grouped into areas according to their usage, such as fabric virtualization (fv) for main tenant objects like VRFs, bridge domains and application profiles with EPGs, or virtual zones (vz) for all objects related with contracts. This grouping does not affect anything from a functional point of view, but the abbreviation enters the object class name: fvTenant, fvBD, vzSubj, vzFilter, and so on.

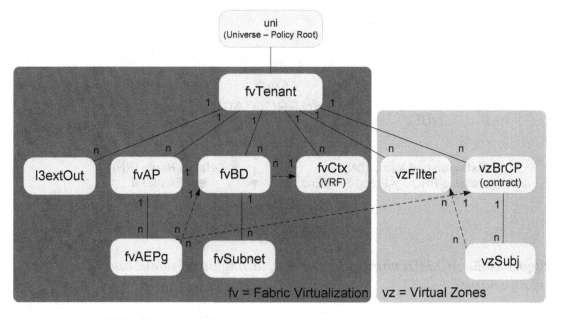

Figure 10-4. *ACI object model overview*

Each ACI object is situated in the precise place of the object tree hierarchy. This place can be uniquely described by a path through three branches needed to get there from a root, also called universe (or just "uni"). And that path produces a unique *distinguished name (DN)* for each object. The DN will become quite important soon as it directly enters object's REST URI when working with API. Besides the DN, each object can be also referred by a *relative name (RN)*, meaning just its own MO's name. The naming convention for both DN and RN can be found for each object in the information model documentation, which I will cover in the next section.

Figure 10-5 describes how to approach naming of well-known EPG objects:

- **Standard object name**: Endpoint Group (EPG)

- **Class Name**: fvAEPg

- **MO's relative name** – epg-FrontEnd

- **MO's distinguished name** - uni/tn-Apress/ap-PROD_AP/ epg-FrontEnd

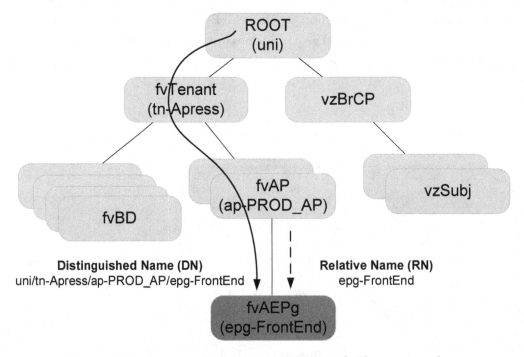

Figure 10-5. *ACI MOs names, class names, distinguished name, and relative name*

Managed Object Discovery Tools

A very common question and concern related to ACI programmability, when the discussion turns to MOs, is how to identify them. How to make sure you are really asking for correct class of objects through the API, how to create a switch profile and not an interface profile, and such. In this section, I will describe all the ways I'm aware of that you can use to obtain information about an object's class names, distinguished names, and attributes.

ACI Documentation

ACI is completely open platform from an API standpoint. Any object described in the internal object model can be accessed or modified using a REST call. However, this huge object database won't bring any advantage for this case without proper user documentation and the ability to search in it reasonably. Fortunately, the entire list of ACI objects with an extensive description and other useful data can be found at two places:

1. **Online**: https://developer.cisco.com/site/apic-mim-ref-api/

2. **Offline**: With each APIC version, complete offline documentation can be found directly on the server using the following URL: https://<APIC-IP>/model-doc/#/objects

Both variants provide exactly the same amount of information and the same user interface. The main page allows you perform a full-text search among all the policy objects or faults. Names of objects refer to their class names, but thanks to full-text search, usually it's enough to specify a standard well-known object name, and you will find its class easily in the search results. The specific object of your choice can be further examined when clicking in the upper right corner on the symbol shown in Figure 10-6. That will open object's detailed information.

Figure 10-6. *ACI's MIM documentation*

The object's main overview tab provides a lot of useful information including

- **Description**: Usually several sentences about the object/policy usage

- **Access rights**: Is the object configurable? Which ACI roles have write or read access to it?

- **Naming Rules**: Very important information on how to correctly assemble the object's relative name and distinguished name. For fvTenant, it's

  - RN: tn-{name}

  - DN: uni/tn-{name}

- **Additional Information**: Is the object associable with an ACI security domain? Does it have faults and events associated?

The second documentation tab informs you about all the object's attributes accessible through the REST API (as shown in Figure 10-7). By default, only configurable attributes are shown, so make sure to click the switch in the upper right side. This list is exactly the same set of key-value pairs with their variable types as configurable or as returned by the REST API.

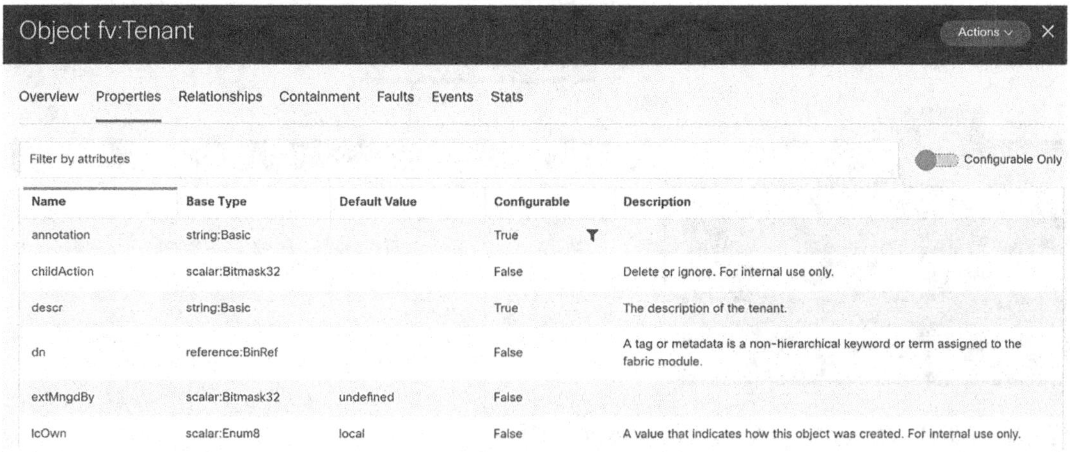

Name	Base Type	Default Value	Configurable	Description
annotation	string:Basic		True	
childAction	scalar:Bitmask32		False	Delete or ignore. For internal use only.
descr	string:Basic		True	The description of the tenant.
dn	reference:BinRef		False	A tag or metadata is a non-hierarchical keyword or term assigned to the fabric module.
extMngdBy	scalar:Bitmask32	undefined	False	
lcOwn	scalar:Enum8	local	False	A value that indicates how this object was created. For internal use only.

***Figure 10-7.** Documentation of all object attributes*

In all other tabs, you can check object's relationships, related faults, events, and statistics. statistics can be especially valuable from a monitoring point of view, if your monitoring solution is capable of utilizing API access.

Note All objects described in the documentation are just models, just their prescriptions or templates, if you will. Actual instances will be accessible differently, which we will explore in the following sections.

APIC URL/Debug Info

APIC's GUI or CLI offer another set of MO discovery and accessibility tools. The first is more like a web implementation characteristic than an official tool, but anyway when opening any particular object in APIC, have a look at the browser URL. After pipe symbol, |, there is always complete DN on the current object. This can be directly used to construct a REST call and get the object attributes via the API. See Figure 10-8.

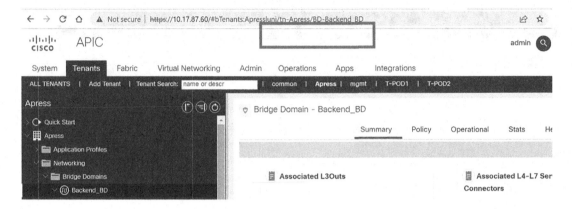

Figure 10-8. *Object's DN in a browser URL*

Next, APIC provides a feature to show so-called debug info. The user needs to enable it by clicking the settings icon (little cog wheel) and choosing *Show Debug Info* from the context menu. Then, in the bottom little status bar, APIC starts showing the current MO. The last word in the model path (before the left square bracket) is always the object's class name, and the string inside the brackets refers to the exact object's distinguished name (as shown in Figure 10-9).

Figure 10-9. *Show Debug Info tool*

Save-As Feature

Another way to get an object's DN, together with its entire JSON or XML representation, is by right-clicking the object's name in APIC GUI and choosing *Save As*. In the opened form, there are several options (as shown in Figure 10-10):

- Save all object's attributes or just the configurable ones.

- Get only the object itself, or all its children objects as well.

- JSON or XML output data format

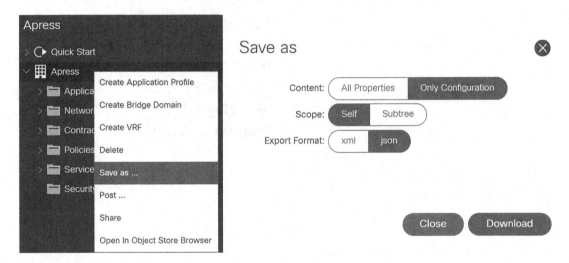

Figure 10-10. *Save As feature*

Some objects can be alternatively saved by clicking the little ⬇ symbol in the upper right part of their configuration form.

Listing 10-4 illustrates the resulting JSON file, which once again contains the two most useful pieces of information for object identification:

- Class name, preceding the attributes section

- DN, as part of attributes

Listing 10-4. Tenant Object Saved-As JSON Structure

```json
{
        "totalCount": "1",
        "imdata": [
                {
                        "fvTenant": {
                                "attributes": {
                                        "annotation": "",
                                        "descr": "",
                                        "dn": "uni/tn-Apress",
                                        "name": "Apress",
                                        "nameAlias": "",
                                        "ownerKey": "",
                                        "ownerTag": "",
                                        "userdom": ":all:"
                                }
                        }
                }
        ]
}
```

In fact, a downloaded object in JSON or XML format can be manually edited in case of need and returned back to APIC using the *Post* option from the context menu shown in Figure 10-10, without you even knowing anything about REST API calls.

Visore

In the documentation section, I've noted that it just describes object templates in the ACI's model database. However, there is another tool enabling you to actually browse the object instances graphically and see all their attributes in "raw" data format: *Visore* (also commonly referred to as object store).

Accessing Visore is simple; it's a native part of APIC with a URL: `https://<APIC-IP>/visore.html`.

This tool mostly expects that you already know either the class name, DN, or URL of the requested object. An alternate way to access Visore for a single object without knowing its API-related information is by right-clicking a given object in the APIC GUI and choosing *Open in Object Store Browser* (this option is visible in Figure 10-10).

Visore allows you to filter returned objects based on multiple logical operations related to the object's attribute value. Figure 10-11 illustrates requesting all bridge domains configured in ACI (based on the fvBD class name) that have "Apress" in their distinguished name, effectively filtering just those that are part of the Apress tenant.

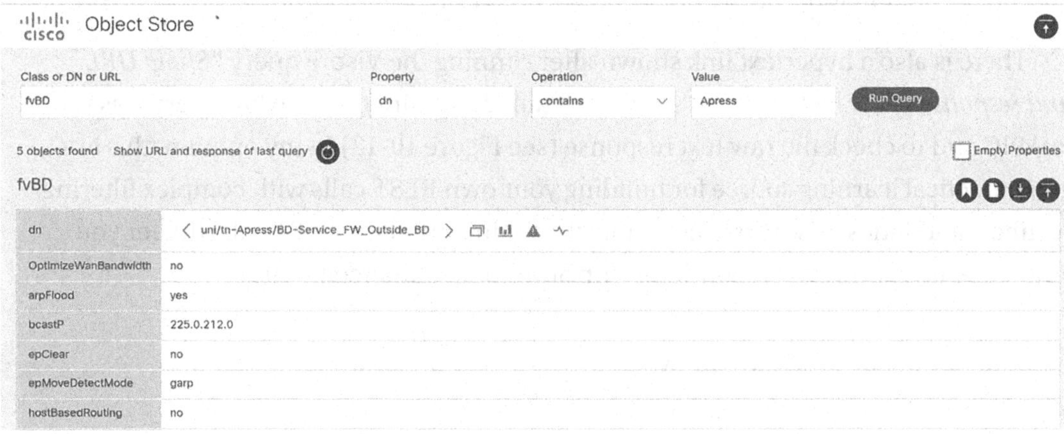

Figure 10-11. *Visore overview*

Even though it's not so apparent at first sight, Visore has considerably more useful features:

- The angle brackets, < >, bounding the DN of each object allow you to interactively browse the object model tree. Either you can show the parent object and move one level higher in the model hierarchy by doing so or request all child objects of the current one.

- The symbol ⧉ automatically copies the DN of an object to clipboard.

- The symbol ⏸ requests all statistics about the current object.

- The symbol ⚠ returns currently seen faults related to the object, if any.

- The symbol ⋏ shows related health score object.

- The symbols  near each returned object enables it to

  - Create favorite calls to be easily accessible from the left menu.

  - Open object class documentation.

  - Download the JSON or XML representation, same as the Save As function.

  - Upload edited JSON or XML to the APIC, same as the Post function.

There is also a hypertext link shown after running the Visore query *"Show URL and response of the last query."* It serves a detailed examination of what query was sent to APIC and to check the raw text response (see Figure 10-12) In my opinion, this is a great practical learning source for building your own REST calls with complex filtering/sorting capabilities. Visore will assemble the main part of the REST call URL for you automatically, and you can continue with additional enhancements.

URL and Response of last query   ✕

Response Type

JSON XML

URL   Copy URL

/api/node/class/fvBD.json?query-target-filter=and(wcard(fvBD.dn,"Apress"))&order-by=fvBD.modTs|desc

Response   Copy Response

```
{
    "totalCount": "5",
    "imdata": [
        {
            "fvBD": {
                "attributes": {
                    "OptimizeWanBandwidth": "no",
                    "annotation": "",
                    "arpFlood": "yes",
                    "bcastP": "225.0.212.0",
                    "childAction": "",
                    "configIssues": "",
```

Figure 10-12. *Visore examining the last query*

API Inspector

The last graphical tool and, in fact, a brilliant ACI automation assistant is available from the main settings context menu (the little cogwheel in the upper right GUI corner), when you click *Show API Inspector."*

You already know that all actions performed by the ACI administrator in the APIC's GUI are translated into a series of predefined REST calls. Wouldn't it be awesome to have an option to see in real time all the API calls flowing between your browser and APIC? That's exactly what API Inspector does (see Figure 10-13).

Figure 10-13. *API Inspector*

The API Inspector operation is simple. It will always open in the new browser window with a blank space in the middle, waiting for any REST call to happen. Then all you need to do is to click on something in the ACI or create an object--literally perform any supported GUI operation. The API Inspector will capture all the API communication needed to process your request, show all returned resources on the page, or create the defined object. The Inspector's output consists of individual REST calls, with four lines for each:

- **Timestamp**: To retain the correct call sequence and for logging purposes

- **Method:** HTTP method used: GET/POST/DELETE

- **URL**: Complete URL used for a particular call

- **Response**: JSON response from APIC for each call

Such a valuable insight about a GUI operation can be 1:1 replicated for your own REST calls. So, if you don't know how to get the required ACI information via the API, but you are aware of where to find it in the GUI, have a look through the API Inspector, note the call, and then reproduce it. The same applies to creating ACI objects. If you're unsure of the correct object name and its DN, create it in ACI while the API Inspector is open and then search for POST call in it.

APIC CLI

Besides various GUI tools, APIC offers one CLI tool worth mentioning for object querying: *MoQuery*. It has no browsing capabilities like Visore, but it still brings simple use options on how to view objects will all their attributes. Under the hood, this utility will generate REST calls on your behalf with extensive parametrization capabilities. You can ask for a single object, the whole class, filter the output, or choose the output format. MoQuery is able to return not only JSON and XML, but also data formatted into a table, or just plain, human-readable text blocks. The following MoQuery helps illustrate all the options. See Listing 10-5.

Listing 10-5. MoQuery Help

```
apic1# moquery -h
usage: Command line cousin to visore  [-h] [-i HOST] [-p PORT] [-d DN]
                                      [-c KLASS] [-f FILTER] [-a ATTRS]
                                      [-o OUTPUT] [-u USER]
                                      [-x [OPTIONS [OPTIONS ...]]]
optional arguments:
-h, --help              show this help message and exit
-i HOST, --host         HOST Hostname or ip of apic
-p PORT, --port         PORT REST server port
-d DN, --dn             DN dn of the mo
-c KLASS, --klass       KLASS comma seperated class names to query
-f FILTER, --filter     FILTER attribute filter to accept/reject mos
-o OUTPUT, --output OUTPUT Display format (block, table, xml, json)
-u USER, --user USER    User name
-x [OPTIONS [OPTIONS ...]], --options [OPTIONS[OPTIONS ...]]
                            Extra options to the query
```

Let's say you want to receive all distinguished names of EPG objects where the tenant parent is Apress. With MoQuery, simply ask for the fvAEPg class and grep the desired output, as shown in Listing 10-6.

Listing 10-6. MoQuery Quering for an Object's DN

```
apic1# moquery -c fvAEPg | grep dn | grep Apress
dn                      : uni/tn-Apress/ap-PROD_APP/epg-Frontend_EPG
dn                      : uni/tn-Apress/ap-PROD_APP/epg-Backend_EPG
dn                      : uni/tn-Apress/ap-PROD_APP/epg-Database_EPG
```

ACI REST API

Finally, after our discussions about the ACI's Management Information Model, naming conventions for objects and tools to identify them properly, let's look at what options we have when composing the REST URL and call body. Then, I will explain how to access the REST API using various HTTP clients directly.

URL and Body Format

First of all, to communicate with the REST API, you need to assemble a Uniform Resource Locator (URL). It will tell APIC about your intention to access particular objects directly via the API subsystem and perform CRUD operations (Create, Read, Update, Delete). The REST API URL has the following defined format that needs to be adhered to (shown in Figure 10-14).

				Mandatory			Optional
http(s)://	IP(DNS):port	/api	/node/{mo}|{class}	/{dn}|{class_name}	.{xml|json}	?[options]
HTTP or HTTPS protocol	APIC IP or DNS with optional port	API system	Keywords "mo" or "class". "/node"/ is optional	If MO: Distinquished Name If Class: Class Name	Input/Output Data Format	Filtering Sorting Other options

Figure 10-14. *ACI REST API URL format*

521

By appending /api to the standard APIC URL, you tell the web server to forward your request to the REST subsystem. Then followed by /node/mo or /node/class, you can choose if the returned output will consist of single managed object only, or all objects belonging to the same class. The keyword /node/ is optional. Based on a previous decision, the next part of the URL requires either DN or class name specification. As a file extension at the end of the URL, you have to define the expected input or output data format (.xml or .json). In fact, ACI's API ignores standard HTTP Content-Type or Accept headers, otherwise used for content specification, so only the URL suffix matters.

The whole section described up to now can be considered mandatory in a REST URL. However, you can optionally continue by expanding the definition with various options summarized in Table 10-6.

Table 10-6. *ACI REST URL Options*

Option	Syntax	Description
query-target=	{self I children I subtree}	Query returns single object, also children objects, or the whole subtree
target-subtree-class=	Class-name	Returns subtree objects only with defined class or classes separated by comma
query-target-filter=	[eqIgeIIe...] (attribute,value)	Returns only objects with attributes matching the defined expressions
rsp-subtree=	{no I children I full}	Another way to include children objects or the whole subtree in the response, with more additional options
rsp-subtree-class=	Class-name	Returns subtree objects only with defined class or classes separated by comma
rsp-subtree-filter=	Filter expression	Only objects with attributes matching the defined expressions are returned
rsp-subtree-include=	Category	Includes more related objects from the following categories: audit logs, event logs, faults, fault records, health, health records, relations, stats, tasks
order-by=	classname.property I {asc I desc}	Sorting based on a chosen object's attribute
time-range=	{ 24h I 1week I 1month I 3month I I range }	Applicable for all log objects: faults, events, audit logs. Range in yyyy-mm-ddIyyyy-mm-dd format

Listing 10-7 shows multiple query examples. Others can be constructed either on your own or using already described tools Visore and API Inspector.

Listing 10-7. REST Queries Examples

```
GET https://<APIC-IP>/api/mo/topology/pod-1/node-1/sys/ch/bslot/board/
sensor-3.json

GET https://<APIC-IP>/api/mo/uni/tn-Apress.json?query-
target=subtree&target-subtree-class=fvAEPg&rsp-subtree-include=faults

GET https://<APIC-IP>//api/class/fvBD.json?query-target=subtree&order-
by=fvBD.modTs|desc

GET https://<APIC-IP>/api/class/fvTenant.json?rsp-subtree-
include=health&rsp-subtree-filter=lt(healthInst.cur,"50")
```

For object creation in ACI you will use the POST method and there are two options to construct the URL:

- **Standard REST URL**: Referring to the exact DN of the object being created, for example POST `https://<APIC-IP>/api/mo/uni/tn-Apress.json`

- **Universal REST URL**: Common single URL adding any object described in the call body to the ACI "universe," such as POST `https://<APIC-IP>/api/mo/uni.json`

Regardless of the chosen option, the body of the POST call has to carry JSON or XML objects (based on URL suffix), describing at least the minimum required attributes for a particular object (in case of a universal URL it's the object's DN or name; with a standard URL you have to define the object class name but no other attribute is mandatory). Additionally, using the single POST call, you can also describe the whole object hierarchy to be created following the model tree. For such use cases, a "children" array of objects is required in the JSON/XML body.

Subsequent examples in Listing 10-8 show all of the approaches

Listing 10-8. Creating Objects with REST

```
POST https://<APIC-IP>/api/node/mo/uni.json
BODY:
{
        "fvTenant": {
                "attributes": {
                        "dn": "uni/tn-Apress"
                },
                "children": []
        }
}
```

```
POST https://<APIC-IP>/api/node/mo/uni/tn-Apress/ctx-PROD.json
BODY:
{
        "fvCtx": {
                "attributes": {
                        "name": "PROD"
                },
                "children": []
        }
}
```

```
POST https://<APIC-IP>/api/node/mo/uni.json
BODY:
{
        "fvBD": {
                "attributes": {
                        "dn": "uni/tn-Apress/BD-FrontEnd_BD",
                        "unkMacUcastAct": "flood",
                        "arpFlood": "true",
                        "unicastRoute": "false",
                        "status": "created"
                },
```

```
        "children": [{
                "fvRsCtx": {
                        "attributes": {
                                "tnFvCtxName": "PROD",
                                "status":"created,modified"
                        },
                        "children": []
                }
        }]
    }
}
```

- The first call creates a single tenant using a universal URL and the DN in the call body.

- The second call creates a VRF using a standard REST URL, without any attribute, just the VRF class name (fvCtx).

- Finally, the third call adds a bridge domain with VRF association in one step using a children array and a universal URL again.

REST API Authentication

From a security point of view, before sending any REST call to APIC, clients are required to authenticate themselves. This is done by sending a special authentication JSON or XML body to a predefined ACI object (URL). After a successful authentication call, APIC returns a token (text string) which is expected to be present as a cookie in all following calls. Tokens have configurable expiration (by default set to 600 seconds/10 minutes), in the **Admin -> Security -> Management Settings** tab and *Web Token Timeout(s)* field.

There are three authentication-related objects in ACI:

1. /api/aaaLogin: The POST call has to carry the body containing an aaaUser object with the name and password attributes. The token is returned after successful authentication.

2. /api/aaaRefresh: Either a GET call with no body or a POST call with the same body as for aaaLogin serves for refreshing the validity of previously received token

3. /api/aaaLogout: A POST call with an aaaLogin body, used to
    log out from the current session and invalidate the previously
    used token

Listing 10-9 describes authentication to the REST API using both JSON and XML
objects with a response containing a token.

Listing 10-9. APIC REST Authentication Using JSON or XML

```
POST https://<APIC-IP>/api/aaaLogin.json
BODY:
{
  "aaaUser" : {
    "attributes" : {
      "name" : "admin",
      "pwd" : "cisco123"
    }
  }
}

POST https://<APIC-IP>/api/aaaLogin.xml
BODY: <aaaUser name="admin" pwd="cisco123">

RESPONSE:
{
    "totalCount": "1",
    "imdata": [
        {
            "aaaLogin": {
                "attributes": {
                    "token": "eyJhbGci0iJSUzI1NiIsImtpZCI6ImljeW5xYXF
                    tcWxnMXN5dHJzcm5oZ3l2Y2ZhMXVxdmx6IiwidHlwIjoiand0In0.
                    eyJyYmFjIjpbeyJkb21haW4i0iJhbGwiLCJyb2xlc1Ii0jAsInJvb
                    GVzVyI6MX1dLCJpc3Mi0iJBQQkgQVBJQyIsInVzZXJuYW1lIjoi
                    YWRtaW4iLCJ1c2VyaWQi0jE1Mzc0LCJ1c2VyZmxhZ3Mi0jAsImlhd
                    CI6MTY2MDM5ODMyNiwiZXhwIjoxNjYwNDAxMzI2LCJzZXNzaW9u
                    WQi0iJKVU0dhdjd4NlJoaUhpTnRuSnJENnpnPT0ifQ.iQ1i3SP6J_
                    LWiPWx79CUuDT_VYM0JF_x99zjr7h64hFGPj7Dd2Y2F0m00s1-
```

vI33kRaNHQSJ2VyE8B5kd8dL5jNCv_UCOca0-wILzZrb9y8_
itzagaLss6dLOV8Z8VQEht5K-1ys0awWtSTtoORJQ-MvyZxc
XEr3cq-NO_OWRjTBDQcODYrRQEqYUZfX5hhEJF6izuVblm_
OlTAcVG133oti8uxepeRaNTgywyrDAgXZn6rg1tJuvKtS2Dh
HfkI3U5uXAY-qzNk-cC6oU4CzjCP50D1ZFyNKSDYpDmty1ebe7
fyGode7wYZYh-zVn3N5JBn3YIKDvh6mGNIfL10nQg",
        "siteFingerprint": "icynqaqmqlg1sytrsrnhgyvcfa1uqvlz",
        "refreshTimeoutSeconds": "600",
        "maximumLifetimeSeconds": "86400",
        "guiIdleTimeoutSeconds": "3600",
        "restTimeoutSeconds": "90",
        "creationTime": "1660398326",
        "firstLoginTime": "1660398326",
        "userName": "admin",
        "remoteUser": "false",
        "unixUserId": "15374",
        "sessionId": "JSGav7x6RhiHiNtnJrD6zg==",
        "lastName": "",
        "firstName": "",
        "changePassword": "no",
        "version": "5.2(3e)",
        "buildTime": "Sun Oct 17 03:10:47 UTC 2021",
        "node": "topology/pod-1/node-1"
      }
     }
    }
   ]
}

The token needs to be extracted (somehow, depends on the REST client implementation) and then appended to each next call in a cookie format: APIC-cookie=<token>.

ACI login domains for authentication against remote servers like Radius, TACACS+, or Active Directory LDAP are supported as well when communicating with REST API. Listing 10-10 shows the JSON body syntax to be used.

Listing 10-10. APIC REST Authentication Against Login Domain

```
POST https://<APIC>/api/aaaLogin.json
BODY:
{
  "aaaUser" : {
    "attributes" : {
      "name" : "apic:TacacsDomain\\userxxx",
      "pwd" : "password123"
    }
  }
}
```

Direct REST API Access

Thanks to REST API's client implementation-agnostic nature, there are many ways to consume its services. In general, for direct API access, you can utilize just any HTTP client capable of sending HTTP calls with raw text bodies and cookies. This gives you a plethora of options to choose from, and in the next sections, I will describe the most common tools, also used by many of our customers. Yet before, let's review the REST API request process and handle the responses.

Each API access sequence usually consists of

1. **Authentication**: Sending the authentication call and extracting the token

2. **GET/POST/DELETE calls**: Intended REST call themselves

3. **Status code verification**: Checking for the correct result of the REST call (2XX value)

4. **Response processing**: If any response body is returned, you may want to process the output.

Especially at the beginning of the automation and programmability journey, my students tend to struggle often with the fourth point, the response processing. If you look at the standard format of JSON object returned by APIC to your queries, it's important to realize how to access any attribute from it. Consider now a hypothetical GET call for the fvTenant class, which returns only the two following objects, shown in Listing 10-11.

Listing 10-11. JSON Response Processing

```json
{
    "totalCount": "2",
    "imdata": [
        {
            "fvTenant": {
                "attributes": {
                    "annotation": "",
                    "childAction": "",
                    "descr": "",
                    "dn": "uni/tn-common",
                    "name": "common",
                    <output omitted>
                }
            }
        },
        {
            "fvTenant": {
                "attributes": {
                    "annotation": "",
                    "childAction": "",
                    "descr": "",
                    "dn": "uni/tn-mgmt",
                    "name": "mgmt",
                    <output omitted>
                }
            }
        }
    ]
}
```

How would you extract, for example, their names? The actual implementation depends on the JSON processor, but most of tools and programming languages navigate through the JSON hierarchy using either square brackets as in `response["imdata"]` `[0]["fvTenant"]["attributes"]["name"]` or dotted notation as in `response.` `imdata[0].fvTenant.attributes.name`.

Note that in order to read the tenant name you need to first move into the imdata key. An often missed fact: it is an array (denoted by square brackets, []). Therefore, you need to address items from an array, starting at 0 for the first item and 1 for the second. Then, the object class name follows as a next key (fvTenant). Inside you will find the attributes key and finally the name attribute. Sometimes ACI objects can contain besides attributes also a "children" key, which is another array of extra objects. In the end, this philosophy is universally applicable to any object result returned by APIC.

Linux Command Line – cURL

One of the simplest-to-use implementations of an HTTP client suitable for REST operations is a Linux utility called *cURL*. You can start accessing ACI's REST API literally in seconds with it. If somebody is into bash scripting, cURL can be a pretty effective way to incorporate API access into your scripts.

The command in Listing 10-12 authenticates a client on APIC, automatically extracting the token and saving it into a text file named cookie.txt.

Listing 10-12. cURL Authentication

```
[root@localhost]# curl -X POST -k https://<APIC-IP>/api/aaaLogin.json -d '{
"aaaUser" : { "attributes" : { "name" : "admin", "pwd" : "cisco123" } } }'
-c cookie.txt
```

The next call will use the collected cookie and list all APIC tenants. Its output is piped to a simple JSON processor utility named *jq* and it will extract their names. This way, you can specifically read any object's attribute. See Listing 10-13.

Listing 10-13. cURL GET Tenants and Process JSON

```
[root@localhost]# curl -s -b cookie.txt -X GET -k https://<APIC-IP>/api/node/
class/fvTenant.json | jq --raw-output '.imdata[] .fvTenant .attributes .name'
```

To create a new object, specify its JSON/XML body directly in the command or put a file path containing the JSON/XML object as a -d (--data) argument. See Listing 10-14.

Listing 10-14. cURL Create Tenant

```
[root@localhost]# curl -s -b cookie.txt -X POST -k https://<APIC-IP>/api/
mo/uni.json -d '{"fvTenant":{"attributes":{"name":"cURL_Tenant"}}}'
```

Tip   If not already, install cURL or jq utilities on Linux using following commands:

Ubuntu/Debian

```
# apt-get install curl
# apt-get install jq
```

Centos/RHEL

```
# dnf install curl
# dnf install jq
```

Postman

Another very popular, this time graphical, tool for interacting with REST APIs is *Postman*. Besides being an HTTP client, it is a comprehensive platform to design, test, and document your own APIs. But for this use case, you will stay focused just on HTTP features. Postman's graphical interface is pretty intuitive. Figure 10-15 illustrates the main screen.

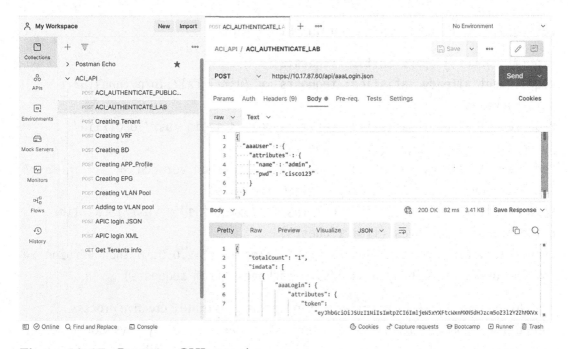

Figure 10-15. *Postman GUI overview*

Using separate tabs you are able to define individual REST calls. In the upper part of the screen, choose the HTTP method, enter the desired URL, and fill the body section below for POST calls. The bottom field show the response.

Each constructed REST call can be saved to Postman Collections (visible in the left panel). Their execution is then easily automated using the Postman Runner feature.

When authenticating against APIC from Postman, you don't need to manually extract the token and add it to all following calls. Postman is intelligent enough to create and use APIC-cookie automatically.

Python Requests Library

The most powerful, but at the same time the most complex, automation tool is without a doubt the Python programming language. It brings extensive, almost unlimited options to create your own end-to-end automation solution.

One of Python's libraries named requests brings complete HTTP client implementation perfectly suitable for direct REST access from the source code. If not already installed in your system, simply use the pip (pip3) utility to satisfy this requirement, as shown in Listing 10-15.

Listing 10-15. Python requests Library Installation

```
[root@localhost]# pip3 install requests
Requirement already satisfied: requests in /usr/local/lib/python3.6/
site-packages
Requirement already satisfied: certifi>=2017.4.17 in /usr/local/lib/
python3.6/site-packages (from requests)
Requirement already satisfied: idna<4,>=2.5; python_version >= "3" in /usr/
local/lib/python3.6/site-packages (from requests)
Requirement already satisfied: urllib3<1.27,>=1.21.1 in /usr/local/lib/
python3.6/site-packages (from requests)
Requirement already satisfied: charset-normalizer~=2.0.0; python_version >=
"3" in /usr/local/lib/python3.6/site-packages (from requests)
```

Writing source code in any programming language is quite a creative process, sometimes almost artistic. The same result can be achieved in many ways. Consider the example I will describe in the following paragraphs as a simple starting point, consisting of the main API operations: authentication, querying objects, and creating them.

Start by creating a new Python source file with initial imports and global variables used within the functions later. In addition to the `requests` library, you also import a JSON library, which is a native part of Python to process JSON objects. See Listing 10-16.

Listing 10-16. Python ACI Automation – Imports and Global Variables

```
#!/usr/bin/env python
import requests
import json

requests.packages.urllib3.disable_warnings()

# APIC Credentials:
APIC = <PUT YOUR IP HERE>
USER = "admin"
PASS = "cisco123"

AUTH_URL = "https://" + APIC + "/api/aaaLogin.json"
AUTH_BODY = {"aaaUser": {"attributes": {"name": USER, "pwd": PASS}}}
```

Next, you prepare an authentication function, sending an authentication POST call to APIC using `requests.post()`. With `json.loads()` you convert the returned raw JSON string from APIC to a Python dictionary and extract the token. As the last step, APIC-cookie is prepared and returned from the function. See Listing 10-17.

Listing 10-17. Python ACI Automation – Authentication Function

```
#Authentication to APIC
def apic_authenticate():
    login_response = requests.post(AUTH_URL, json=AUTH_BODY,
    verify=False).content
    response_body_dictionary = json.loads(login_response)
    token = response_body_dictionary["imdata"][0]["aaaLogin"]["attributes"]
    ["token"]
    cookie = {"APIC-cookie": token}
    return cookie
```

Listing 10-18 represents a function to query APIC for a list of tenants and return already preprocessed JSON object in the Python dictionary form.

Listing 10-18. Python ACI Automation – Get Tenants Function

```python
def get_tenants(cookie):
    url = "https://"+ APIC + "/api/node/class/fvTenant.json"
    headers = {
        "Cookie" : f"{cookie}",
    }
    response = requests.get(url, headers=headers, verify=False)
    return response.json()
```

The last function creates a new tenant object. As you are sending a POST call, the JSON payload needs to be prepared. See Listing 10-19.

Listing 10-19. Python ACI Automation – Create Tenant Function

```python
def create_tenant(cookie, tenant_name):
    url = "https://"+ APIC +"/api/node/mo/uni.json"
    headers = {
        "Cookie" : f"{cookie}",
    }

    payload = {
        "fvTenant": {
            "attributes": {
                "name": f"{tenant_name}",
                },
            "children": []
        }
    }
    response = requests.post(url, data=json.dumps(payload),
    headers=headers, verify=False)
    return response
```

Now, to execute all of the previous functions, you need to compose the Python main function, serving as an entry point to the application. Listing 10-20 also shows the way to iterate through an acquired Python dictionary with tenant objects.

Listing 10-20. Python ACI Automation – Create Tenant Function

```
if __name__ == "__main__":
    cookie = apic_authenticate()
    response = get_tenants(cookie)

    for tenants in response["imdata"]:
        print(f"Tenant name: {tenants['fvTenant']['attributes']['name']}")

    response = create_tenant(cookie, "Python_TENANT")
    print ("Status Code: " + str(response.status_code))
```

Note   The source code for this book is available on GitHub via the book's product page, located at www.apress.com/ISBN.

Cobra Software Development Kit

Directly accessing REST APIs in Python while utilizing the requests library objectively increases the complexity of the source code, mainly due to the need for manual operations related to authentication, token extractions, call bodies composition, and result processing. Software development kits (SDK) can significantly help with this disadvantage. SDKs are basically precreated libraries, offering ready-to-use functions, simplifying all common operations with the related destination system from a programming language. For ACI, the *Cobra SDK* is available specifically for Python (both versions 2.X and 3.X).

Cobra SDK Installation

Cobra's installation files are delivered as part of a physical APIC appliance, accessible through the following URL: https://<APIC-IP>/cobra/_downloads/. It comes in a form of two packages:

- acicobra: All the main functions and utilities are executable in Python.

- acimodel: Complete Python object set, exactly 1:1 modeling ACI's MIM. Each ACI object is mapped to a Python object for the particular ACI version.

The /cobra/_downloads directory contains the two platform-independent .whl files. Download them to your work station and install them using the following commands (the minimal supported Python version is 3.6). Make sure to install acicobra first and then acimodel. See Listing 10-21.

Listing 10-21. ACI Cobra SDK Installation

```
[root@localhost ~]# pip3 install ./acicobra-5.2.3.0.5-py2.py3-none-any.whl
[root@localhost ~]# pip3 install ./acimodel-5.2.3.0.5-py2.py3-none-any.whl
```

Note   Before using the previous commands, make sure to have the python3-pip package installed on some Linux machine. Python versions higher than 3.4 should include pip3 by default. For Python versions prior to 3.4, upgrade your installation in the following way:
```
#python -m pip3 install --upgrade pip
```

Using Cobra SDK for Querying and Creating ACI Objects

Previously defined functions for ACI REST operations can be considerably optimized from the source code point of view with Cobra SDK. Let's create a new Python file, import required objects from a Cobra library, define global variables, and create an authentication function. It will return the MO directory acting as a handle to access APIC REST API, handling the authentication token automatically. See Listing 10-22.

Listing 10-22. ACI Cobra Authentication Function

```
#!/usr/bin/env python
from cobra.mit.access import MoDirectory
from cobra.mit.session import LoginSession
from cobra.model.fv import Tenant
from cobra.model.pol import Uni
from cobra.mit.request import ConfigRequest
import requests.packages.urllib3
requests.packages.urllib3.disable_warnings()
```

```
USERNAME = "admin"
PASSWORD = "cisco123"
APIC_URL = "https://10.17.87.60"

def apic_authenticate():
    moDir = MoDirectory(LoginSession(APIC_URL, USERNAME, PASSWORD))
    moDir.login()
    return moDir
```

The next function will universally gather an array of ACI objects based on the specified class name. This time, it's not an array of JSON objects, but native Python objects 1:1 mapping ACI's model thanks to the acimodel library. See Listing 10-23.

Listing 10-23. ACI Cobra Object Class Query

```
def query_class(modir, object_class):
    object_set = modir.lookupByClass(object_class)
    return object_set
```

The third function creates a new tenant object and illustrates how to use a generic ConfigRequest to alter ACI's configuration. See Listing 10-24.

Listing 10-24. ACI Cobra Create Tenant

```
def create_tenant(modir, name):
    uniMo = Uni('')
    fvTenantMo = Tenant(uniMo, name)
    cfgRequest = ConfigRequest()
    cfgRequest.addMo(fvTenantMo)
    return modir.commit(cfgRequest)
```

Like in the previous case, you will finish with creating Python's main function, calling all others. The source code in Listing 10-25 first authenticates on APIC and queries for the class fvTenants. Then it iterates through the returned array of objects, but this time you can access all their attributes directly using dotted notation. Technically you are reading a Python object's variables. In the end, you call the function creating the tenant, check the status code of a reply, and log out from APIC.

Listing 10-25. ACI Cobra Main Function

```python
if __name__ == "__main__":
    mo = apic_authenticate()
    response = query_class(mo, "fvTenant")
    for tenants in response:
        print(tenants.name)
    response = create_tenant(mo, "Cobra_Tenant")
    print (response.status_code)
    mo.logout()
```

Note   The source code for this book is available on GitHub via the book's product page, located at `www.apress.com/ISBN`.

Automating ACI Using Ansible

Python is without a doubt a powerful programming language, finding its use in so many areas, and REST APIs are not an exception. However, not every network engineer is familiar with it yet and, when not using SDKs, the direct REST API approach can be pretty complicated at times. Thankfully, there are other options, which you will explore in the following paragraphs.

The first, and one of the most popular orchestrators on the market, is *Ansible*. Since 2012, Ansible represents a suite of software tools designed to easily automate provisioning or configuration management of a wide solutions ecosystem. It's delivered as an open-source project, significantly supported by the open-source community, but the core libraries are developed by the Ansible company, part of Red Hat. Ansible internally brings modular architecture, easily expandable by installing additional modules, which then manage a particular solution or a system (as shown in Figure 10-16).

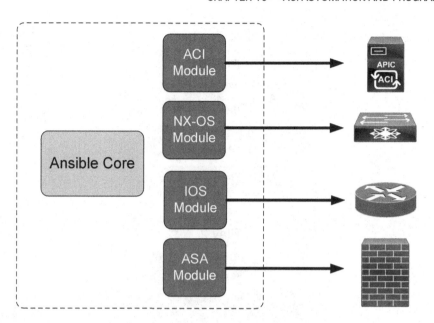

Figure 10-16. *Ansible system overview*

Ansible is able to use both APIs and CLIs, without the need for any agent installation, making it quite a universal tool not only to manage infrastructure devices but also operating systems and various applications. Core libraries as well as individual modules are written in Python, simplifying the expansion by the community and external contributors.

Although it's not my goal to explain every aspect of Ansible (in fact, that would be a topic for another book), in the following sections I will go through some basic components, structure, and operations. I will describe all the features needed to begin building interesting ACI automation scripts on your own.

Ansible Component Architecture

Ansible is a procedural tool, meaning that its operation is based on a predefined set of steps called *tasks*. Together they assemble the automation workflow. Individual tasks are organized into *plays* and multiple plays produce a *playbook*. In the end, the playbook completely describes the set of instructions and actions that should be taken on specific infrastructure. At the same time, the playbook is the main runnable entity in Ansible. Figure 10-17 describes this architectural hierarchy.

Figure 10-17. *Ansible components structure overview*

Playbooks are formatted exclusively in YAML, which is why we spent time talking about it at the beginning of this chapter. Remember to keep a close eye on your whitespaces in playbooks. Everything needs to be correctly indented, or you will receive an error when running such a playbook. Most mistakes and issues of my students during the training are related just to the text formatting. But don't worry. As with everything, it only requires some time to get familiar with YAML (and consequently Ansible).

Playbook Structure

Let's have a look at the structure of a simple playbook. Listing 10-26 gathers a list of ACI tenant objects and saves them to the defined variable.

Listing 10-26. Playbook Structure

```
- name: APIC Tenant Query
  hosts: aci
  connection: local
  gather_facts: false
```

```
tasks:
- name: Query all tenants
  aci_tenant:
    hostname: '{{ ansible_host }}'
    username: '{{ username }}'
    password: '{{ password }}'
    validate_certs: no
    state: query
  register: all_tenants
```

Each playbook carries list of plays. Therefore, it starts with a dash, -, which means a list in YAML. Ansible plays consists of several attributes:

- **name**: Description of a play according to your needs

- **hosts**: Reference to an individual host or group of hosts from the Ansible inventory file. This will tell Ansible which devices to connect to and where to perform specified tasks. The inventory file will be described in the next section.

- **connection**: Setting a "local" value here ensures that Ansible will perform the required automation tasks from localhost. In general, it has the ability to delegate tasks around the multiple hosts and then monitor their execution, wait for them to finish before moving to the next one, and so on. For simplicity, we will stick with local execution.

- **gather_facts**: Ansible is able to automatically gather information about remote systems, such as operating systems, IP addresses, attached filesystems, and more. They are inserted into the ansible_ facts variable before the tasks are executed, enabling you to potentially use some of these facts during the execution. The facts collection process takes a significant amount of time, so if you don't plan to use them, it's better to set this attribute to "false."

- **tasks**: This section represents a nested list of tasks to be executed on the remote destination machine(s) specified in the play's hosts attribute.

In the tasks section, similar to plays, each task inside a list has the following attributes:

- **name**: Description of a task. Not significant from a functional point of view.

- **module**: Name of installed Ansible module performing an action on the destination system. In the case of ACI, each object is created and managed with different modules.

- **module attributes**: Each module has its own set of required and optional attributes with their supported value. Refer to the documentation to find the proper module definition.

- **other task-related keywords**: Tasks can be further controlled by various Ansible functions associable with them. In the previous example, you can see the `register` keyword, creating a new Ansible variable and putting output of the task there. Other options could be iteration loops, conditionals, failure handling, and delegation. You will touch iteration features in upcoming practical examples in this chapter.

Inventory File

So, if the playbook defines what will be performed on the managed infrastructure, how does Ansible know which device(s) to use? That's what the inventory file is for. Written again in the YAML or INI format (which I find in this case much more readable), it describes a set of managed devices, usually organized into groups, to which we can refer from the playbook `hosts` attribute. The generic format of the INI inventory file is shown in Listing 10-27.

Listing 10-27. Ansible Basic Inventory File in INI Format

```
ipn-1.test.com

[APICs]
apic1.test.com
apic2.test.com
apic3.test.com
```

```
[NDOs]
ndo-node1 ansible_host=172.16.2.11
ndo-node2 ansible_host=172.16.2.12
ndo-node3 ansible_host=172.16.2.13
```

By default, Ansible uses an inventory file called /etc/ansible/hosts, but this is configurable for each working directory individually. [APICs] and [NDOs] in the previous example represent a group of hosts you can later refer to. If not specified otherwise, Ansible expects DNS resolvable names. For IP address-only definitions, you have to create aliases (e.g., ndo-node1) and specify the IP using an internal variable named ansible_host.

Ansible Variables

The next important function of an inventory file is its ability to define variables you can later call inside your playbooks instead of repetitive static values. Variables are either assignable to individual hosts or to the whole group. Listing 10-28 shows both options.

Listing 10-28. Ansible Variables in Inventory File

```
[APICs]
apic1 ansible_host=10.0.0.1 nodeID=1 serialNumber=FDOXXX1
apic2 ansible_host=10.0.0.2 nodeID=2 serialNumber=FDOXXX2
apic3 ansible_host=10.0.0.3 nodeID=3 serialNumber=FDOXXX3

[APICs:vars]
username = admin
password = cisco123
```

You can also put variables directly into the playbook itself, but they will become local and playbook significant, so it depends on a given use case.

Another common option to incorporate variables into Ansible operations (which I personally use quite a lot) is creating special directories named host_vars and group_vars. Ansible searches for them in a relative path to the inventory file (either in /etc/ansible/ or your own defined location). Inside these directories, you can construct individual variable files for device aliases or groups used in the inventory file. If I used in the previous example "apic1-3" in the "APICs" group, the resulting folder structure could look like the code in Listing 10-29.

Listing 10-29. Ansible Host and Group Variables

```
/etc/ansible/group_vars/APICs.yml
/etc/ansible/host_vars/apic1.yml
/etc/ansible/host_vars/apic2.yml
/etc/ansible/host_vars/apic3.yml
```

Later in playbooks variables are referenced by their names as shown in Listing 10-30 (quotes or apostrophes are mandatory).

Listing 10-30. Using Ansible Variables

```
tasks:
- name: Add a new tenant
  cisco.aci.aci_tenant:
    host: '{{ ansible_host }}'
    username: '{{ username }}'
    password: '{{ password }}'
```

Ansible Roles

In these practical examples you will be using roles as well. They group together multiple Ansible resources, including playbooks, tasks, additional plugins, variables, and more. The goal is to create easily reusable and shareable entities to be exchanged between Ansible users. Roles have a predefined and mandatory folder structure you have to adhere to. The structure has to be created in the working directory from which the role will be called (included) in a playbook. Multiple folders further require a main.yml file, serving as an initial entry point for the execution of the included files. Listing 10-31 shows the most important role components and the ones we have already talked about (but the list is even wider).

Listing 10-31. Ansible Roles Folder Structure

```
roles/
    aci/              # <-- Name of the Role
        tasks/        # <-- Set of tasks
            main.yml  #
```

```
files/              # <-- Additional files to be used
    source.txt      # <-- with Ansible scripts
vars/               # <-- Variables associated with Role
    main.yml        #
defaults/           # <-- Default variables
    main.yml        #
meta/               # <-- Role dependencies and metadata
    main.yml        #
library/            # <-- Custom modules related to Role
lookup_plugins/ # <-- Custom additional plugin
```

ACI Ansible Collection and Installation

The main distribution format for Ansible components including playbooks, roles, modules and plugins are *collections*. They are available for installation from an official Ansible repository called ansible-galaxy. You can easily install all the latest ACI modules to Ansible using the command in Listing 10-32.

Listing 10-32. ACI Collection Installation in Ansible

```
[root@localhost ansible]# ansible-galaxy collection install cisco.aci
Process install dependency map
Starting collection install process
Installing 'cisco.aci:2.2.0' to '/root/.ansible/collections/ansible_
collections/cisco/aci'
```

From now on, you can start using all ACI Ansible modules to create and modify ACI objects.

Tip   The complete Ansible module documentation for ACI collection can be found at https://docs.ansible.com/ansible/latest/collections/cisco/ aci/index.html and https://galaxy.ansible.com/cisco/aci.

Practical Example 1 – Create and Query ACI Objects

As you already know from the previous sections, I find it very beneficial to always get a hands-on experience with automation and programmability. And it won't be different with orchestrators here. I've prepared two practical examples for ACI automation using Ansible, the second building on top of the first one, so I recommend not skipping the following paragraphs if you want to lab this topic on your own.

For the first practical example, we will start with something relatively simple. Let's create a new tenant in ACI using Ansible, then query for the list of all tenants, and save their JSON representation to the disk. I expect that you have Ansible already installed together with the ACI collection from the Ansible galaxy.

In the working directory of your choice, create an inventory file named inventory, specifying the Ansible hosts group called "aci_group" and add single host with the alias "aci." See Listing 10-33.

Listing 10-33. Inventory File

```
[aci_group]
aci
```

Point Ansible to use this inventory file instead of the default one in /etc/ansible by creating the ansible.cfg file in the working directory. See Listing 10-34.

Listing 10-34. ansible.cfg File

```
[defaults]
# Use local inventory file
inventory = inventory
```

Now create a new directory host_vars and the aci.yml variable file there. Its name is a reference to the alias "aci" from inventory, so any variable present within will be associated with aci host. For now, you will put just a piece of login information to APIC. See Listing 10-35.

Listing 10-35. /host_vars/aci.yml File

```
ansible_host: YOUR_APIC_IP
username: admin
password: YOUR_PASSWORD
```

Tip   To avoid using plain text credentials Ansible offers a security feature called Ansible Vault. It's out of scope of this book, but if you are interested, here is the documentation: https://docs.ansible.com/ansible/latest/user_ guide/vault.html.

You are ready to prepare your first playbook, `create_tenant.yml`. In the host attribute, there is a reference to the "aci" alias from the inventory file. Thanks to the mapped variable file, instead of using a static IP, username, and password in each task, you can substitute them with variable names. Module `cisco.aci.aci_tenant,` used in the following example, will be based on its configured state (present, absent, query) to either create, remove or list ACI tenants. In your case, you will create a single tenant named Apress_Ansible thanks to the state set to "present." Note that even though Ansible is primarily a procedural tool, implementation of particular modules and the nature of a destination managed system can sometimes make it declarative as well. ACI modules will always ensure the desired state of the object defined in playbooks. See Listing 10-36.

Listing 10-36. create_tenant.yml Playbook

```
- name: APIC Provisioning
  hosts: aci
  connection: local
  gather_facts: false

  tasks:
  - name: Add a new tenant
    cisco.aci.aci_tenant:
      host: '{{ ansible_host }}'
      username: '{{ username }}'
      password: '{{ password }}'
      validate_certs: no
      tenant: Apress_Ansible
      description: Tenant created by Ansible
      state: present
    delegate_to: localhost
```

Try running this playbook from your working directory and, if all the files are correctly prepared, you should receive similar output to the tenant created in ACI. See Listing 10-37.

Listing 10-37. Running Playbook

```
[root@localhost ansible]# ansible-playbook create_tenant.yml

PLAY [APIC Provisioning] ********************************

TASK [Add a new tenant] ********************************
changed: [aci -> localhost]

<output omitted>

PLAY RECAP ********************************************
aci    : ok=1    changed=1    unreachable=0    failed=0    skipped=0
rescued=0    ignored=0
```

As a next step, you will create new playbook named query_tenant.yml, using the same ACI tenant module, but this time its state is set to query, requesting the list of tenants in JSON format. Ansible can save the output of the module (if any) to the specified variable with the register keyword, in your case creating the variable all_tenants. See Listing 10-38.

Listing 10-38. query_tenant.yml Playbook – Part 1

```
- name: Query APIC
  hosts: aci
  connection: local
  gather_facts: false

  tasks:
  - name: Query all tenants
    cisco.aci.aci_tenant:
      hostname: '{{ ansible_host }}'
      username: '{{ username }}'
      password: '{{ password }}'
```

```
    validate_certs: no
    state: query
  register: all_tenants
```

You will add another two tasks in playbook query_tenant.yml. The first debug module just prints the content of the variable all_tenants and the second task will perform a local copy action, creating a new file in the working directory per each returned tenant object. See Listing 10-39.

Listing 10-39. query_tenant.yml Playbook – Part 2

```
- debug:
    var: all_tenants

- local_action:
    module: copy
    content: "{{ item.fvTenant.attributes }}"
    dest: ./Tenant_{{ item.fvTenant.attributes.name }}_JSON
  with_items:
    - "{{ all_tenants.current }}"
```

In the previous local_action task you can observe one of the commonly used options to implement iterations: with_items. When provided with a list of objects (all_tenants.current), it will run the related task multiple times for each item in the list. By default, each item during an iteration is accessible from the task by referring to the local item variable (e. g., item.fvTenant.attributes). fvTenant and attributes are standard ACI JSON object keys. The item name is configurable, as you will see in the following example.

After running the finished playbook query_tenant.yml, in your working directory you should see individual text files named by your tenants, carrying the content of their JSON objects.

Note   The source code for this book is available on GitHub via the book's product page, located at www.apress.com/ISBN.

Practical Example 2 - CSV Based ACI Automation

Ansible iteration capabilities and parametrization using variables are made for creating hundreds of objects of the same type, just with different attributes. In ACI, there are many situations where this can be used: creating access policies for hundreds of physical interfaces, dozens of bridge domains, EPGs, static EPG to interface and VLAN mappings, and more. It wouldn't be feasible to create all legacy VLAN mapped objects manually, especially for network-centric migration to ACI.

I will now expand the previous example to show you how I approach ACI automation based on the initial comma-separated values (CSV) data set, easily manageable in Excel.

YAML Tenant Structure Definition

First, I usually create a static tenant, VRF, and application profile structure in the variable YAML file `aci.yml` in the `host_vars` directory. This will only serve for initial one-off provisioning of main needed objects, offering one data source for each use case, without touching actual playbooks. It is easily expandable according to your needs when other objects are needed in the future. See Listing 10-40.

Listing 10-40. Tenant Sample Structure in host_vars/aci.yml

```
#ACI Tenant structure
aci_config:
  aci_tenant_structure:
  - name: Apress_Prod
    state: present
    vrf:
    - name: PROD
    - name: TEST
    app_profile:
    - name: WebApp
    - name: JavaApp
  - name: Apress_Dev
    state: present
    vrf:
    - name: DEV
```

```
app_profile:
- name: WebApp
- name: JavaApp
```

Now let's compose a specialized Ansible role called `tenant_structure` to help with creating defined tenants, VRFs, and application profiles. A significant advantage of using roles here is the ability to actually implement nested loops in Ansible. What for? Consider the tenant structure defined in the variables file from Listing 10-39. You have a list of tenants, which is the first level of an iteration. You need to go through each tenant object and create it. Then, inside each tenant, you can have another two lists of multiple VRFs and application profiles; that is second nested level of iteration. To perform such a creation at once, Ansible roles are the solution.

In your working directory, create a new folder structure called `./roles/tenant_structure/tasks`. Inside the tasks folder, four YAML files will be created: `main.yml`, `tenant_create.yml`, `vrf_create.yml` and `app_create.yml`. `main.yml` is predefined by Ansible to serve as an initial point of execution when calling the role later. Therefore, it just consists of modular task includes. See Listing 10-41.

Listing 10-41.   ./roles/tenant_structure/main.yml File

```
# Every role hast to include a main.yml file.

- include: tenant_create.yml
- include: vrf_create.yml
- include: app_create.yml
```

All other role YAMLs will define just the tasks needed to create particular ACI objects. The `tenant_create.yml` file will use the already-known ACI module to create a new tenant. Note that the tenant's name isn't a static value, but rather a name attribute of a variable called `tenant_item`. The variable will be created in the main playbook later, with content of your tenant structure from `./host_vars/aci.yml` (`aci_config.aci_tenant_structure`) and passed to this role automatically. See Listing 10-42.

Listing 10-42.   ./roles/tenant_structure/tenant_create.yml File

```
- name: "Add a new tenant {{ tenant_item.name }}"
  cisco.aci.aci_tenant:
    host: '{{ ansible_host }}'
```

```
    username: '{{ username }}'
    password: '{{ password }}'
    validate_certs: no
    tenant: "{{ tenant_item.name }}"
    description: Tenant created by Ansible
    state: present
  delegate_to: localhost
```

The second file, vrf_create.yml, implements a nested loop over a list of VRFs from the tenant structure in the ./host_vars/aci.yml variable file. Another option to iterate over a list is shown in Listing 10-43 using the loop keyword.

Listing 10-43. ./roles/tenant_structure/vrf_create.yml File

```
- name: Add a new VRF to a tenant
  cisco.aci.aci_vrf:
    host: '{{ ansible_host }}'
    username: '{{ username }}'
    password: '{{ password }}'
    vrf: '{{ item.name }}'
    tenant: '{{ tenant_item.name }}'
    validate_certs: no
    state: present
  delegate_to: localhost
  loop: "{{tenant_item.vrf}}"
```

And the third role task YAML file, app_create.yml, is analogical to previous one, just the module used here creates application profile objects. See Listing 10-44.

Listing 10-44. ./roles/tenant_structure/app_create.yml File

```
- name: Add a new AP
  cisco.aci.aci_ap:
    host: '{{ ansible_host }}'
    username: '{{ username }}'
    password: '{{ password }}'
    tenant: '{{ tenant_item.name }}'
    ap: '{{ item.name }}'
```

```
    validate_certs: no
    state: present
  delegate_to: localhost
  loop: "{{tenant_item.app_profile}}"
```

The completed role now needs to be called from some standard playbook. In the main working directory, create deploy_tenant_structure.yml with the content in Listing 10-45.

Listing 10-45. deploy_tenant_structure.yml Playbook

```
- name: CREATE Tenants, VRFs and Application Profiles
  hosts: aci
  connection: local
  gather_facts: false

  tasks:
  - name: Create Tenant structures
    include_role:
      name: tenant_structure
    loop: "{{ aci_config.aci_tenant_structure }}"
    when: tenant_item.state == 'present'
    loop_control:
      loop_var: tenant_item
```

The previous task isn't using any particular Ansible module, but instead it is calling a precreated role named tenant_structure. Additionally, it loops through a list in your tenant variable structure in ./host_vars/aci.yml: aci_config.aci_tenant_structure. For each item in the tenant list, all tasks defined inside the role will be executed. Further, this is an example how conditionals can be implemented in Ansible; the when keyword checks if a defined condition is true and only then the loop action is performed. Finally, the loop_control and loop_var keywords enable you to change the default item name in the iteration from item to tenant_item in your case. That's the variable name you have already seen, which is automatically passed to role tasks to be used there.

Try running deploy_tenant_structure.yml and you should receive the output shown in Listing 10-46 together with main tenant objects created in ACI as described in the variable file.

Listing 10-46. Deploying Tenant Structure in Ansible

```
[root@localhost ansible]# ansible-playbook deploy_tenant_structure.yml

PLAY [CREATE Tenants, VRFs and Application Profiles] **************

TASK [Create Tenant structures] **********************************

TASK [tenant_structure : Add a new tenant Apress_Prod] ************
changed: [aci -> localhost]

TASK [tenant_structure : Add a new VRF to a tenant] **************
changed: [aci -> localhost] => (item={'name': 'PROD'})
changed: [aci -> localhost] => (item={'name': 'TEST'})

TASK [tenant_structure : Add a new AP] ***************************
changed: [aci -> localhost] => (item={'name': 'WebApp'})
changed: [aci -> localhost] => (item={'name': 'JavaApp'})

TASK [tenant_structure : Add a new tenant Apress_Dev] *************
changed: [aci -> localhost]

TASK [tenant_structure : Add a new VRF to a tenant] **************
changed: [aci -> localhost] => (item={'name': 'DEV'})

TASK [tenant_structure : Add a new AP] ***************************
changed: [aci -> localhost] => (item={'name': 'WebApp'})
changed: [aci -> localhost] => (item={'name': 'JavaApp'})

PLAY RECAP ******************************************************
aci: ok=6    changed=6    unreachable=0    failed=0    skipped=0
rescued=0    ignored=0
```

BD and EPG Automation from CVS Data

With the tenant structure in place, you need a source dataset for BDs and EPGs in the CSV format. I use either Excel to produce the file or a plugin in Visual Studio Code called Edit csv by author janisdd (as shown in Figure 10-18). Create the shown CSV in the Ansible working directory with the name ACI_VLAN_BD_EPG.csv.

	column	column 2	column 3	column	column 5	column 6	column 7	colum	column 9	column 1(	column 11	column 12	column 13
1	vlan_id	vlan_name	tenant	vrf	state	bdname	description	unicas	bdgw	bdmask	appname	epgname	PhysDom
2	100	FrontEnd	Apress_Prod	PROD	present	VL0100_BD	FrontEnd	yes	10.1.1.1	24	WebApp	VL0100_EPG	Apress_PhysDom
3	200	BackEnd	Apress_Prod	PROD	present	VL0200_BD	BackEnd	yes	10.2.2.1	24	WebApp	VL0200_EPG	Apress_PhysDom
4	300	Database	Apress_Prod	PROD	present	VL0300_BD	Database	yes	10.3.3.1	24	WebApp	VL0300_EPG	Apress_PhysDom
5	400	Backup	Apress_Prod	PROD	present	VL0400_BD	Backup	yes	10.4.41	24	WebApp	VL0400_EPG	Apress_PhysDom
6	150	FrontEnd	Apress_Dev	DEV	present	VL0150_BD	FrontEnd	yes	192.168.1.1	24	WebApp	VL0150_EPG	Apress_PhysDom
7	250	BackEnd	Apress_Dev	DEV	present	VL0250_BD	BackEnd	yes	192.168.2.1	24	WebApp	VL0250_EPG	Apress_PhysDom
8	350	Database	Apress_Dev	DEV	present	VL0350_BD	Database	yes	192.168.3.1	24	WebApp	VL0350_EPG	Apress_PhysDom
9	450	Backup	Apress_Dev	DEV	present	VL0450_BD	Backup	yes	192.168.4.1	24	WebApp	VL0450_EPG	Apress_PhysDom

Figure 10-18. *Source CSV data file editable in Visual Studio code*

The first row in the CSV is considered to be a set of column names, later referenced from Ansible modules as variable key names. The structure of CSV is completely up to you and your needs. Consider Figure 10-18 as an example to start with. I use several of such excel tables to create a different set of objects in ACI.

It's useful to put each CSV's file name to a variable file in `./host_vars/aci.yml`. If you later change the filename, only a single line in Ansible will be updated. See Listing 10-47.

Listing 10-47. CSV Filename in aci.yml Variable File

```
bd_epg_csv_filename: "ACI_VLAN_BD_EPG.csv"
```

The playbook `deploy_bds.yml` will read the data from the CSV file using `read_csv`, a native Ansible module, and save a list of its rows into the specified variable `bd_set`. With that, you can easily iterate over each row and access any column's value by the column name. With two iterations through all rows, you will create bridge domain objects and subnets. Note that all ACI object attributes are parametrized now. Just with a change in the CSV source file, you will alter the execution of the Ansible playbook. See Listing 10-48.

Listing 10-48. Playbook Creating ACI Bridge Domains from a CSV File

```
- name: CREATE BDs
  hosts: aci
  connection: local
  gather_facts: false
```

```yaml
tasks:
- name: Read data from CSV file {{ bd_epg_csv_filename }}
  read_csv:
    path: "{{ bd_epg_csv_filename }}"
    delimiter: ';'
  register: bd_set

- name: Add Bridge Domain
  cisco.aci.aci_bd:
    host: "{{ ansible_host }}"
    username: "{{ username }}"
    password: "{{ password }}"
    validate_certs: no
    tenant: "{{ item.tenant }}"
    bd: "{{ item.bdname }}"
    vrf: "{{ item.vrf }}"
    enable_routing: "{{ item.unicast_routing }}"
    state: "{{ item.state }}"
  delegate_to: localhost
  loop: "{{ bd_set.list }}"

- name: Create a subnet
  cisco.aci.aci_bd_subnet:
    host: "{{ ansible_host }}"
    username: "{{ username }}"
    password: "{{ password }}"
    validate_certs: no
    tenant: "{{ item.tenant }}"
    bd: "{{ item.bdname }}"
    gateway: "{{ item.bdgw }}"
    mask: "{{ item.bdmask }}"
    state: "{{ item.state }}"
  delegate_to: localhost
  loop: "{{ bd_set.list }}"
```

Similarly, you will create new EPGs from CSV data and associate them with bridge domains in playbook deploy_epgs.yml. See Listing 10-49.

Listing 10-49. Playbook Creating ACI EPGs from a CSV File

```
- name: CREATE EPGs
  hosts: aci
  connection: local
  gather_facts: false

  tasks:
  - name: read data from CSV file {{ bd_epg_csv_filename }}
    read_csv:
      path: "{{ bd_epg_csv_filename }}"
      delimiter: ';'
    register: epg_set

  - name: Add a new EPG
    cisco.aci.aci_epg:
      host: "{{ ansible_host }}"
      username: "{{ username }}"
      password: "{{ password }}"
      validate_certs: no
      tenant: "{{ item.tenant }}"
      ap: "{{ item.appname }}"
      epg: "{{ item.epgname }}"
      description: "{{ item.description }}"
      bd: "{{ item.bdname }}"
      state: "{{ item.state }}"
    delegate_to: localhost
    loop: "{{ epg_set.list }}"
```

It's completely fine to run previous playbooks individually whenever they are needed. However, the even better practice is to prepare a single main.yml and import them there in a modular fashion. See Listing 10-50.

Listing 10-50. Main ACI Ansible Playbook

```
################################################################
#####    Main playbook for ACI Configuration Management   #####
################################################################
```

```
- name: PROVISION main TENANT objects
  import_playbook: deploy_tenant_structure.yml

- name: PROVISION BDs from CSV
  import_playbook: deploy_bds.yml

- name: PROVISION EPGs from CSV
  import_playbook: deploy_epgs.yml
```

Note   The source code for this book is available on GitHub via the book's product page, located at www.apress.com/ISBN.

Automating ACI Using Terraform

Another significant player in the market of orchestration tools is *Terraform*. It's a younger sibling to Ansible (the first release was on July 28, 2014), but getting more and more attention and popularity due to its simplicity, human-readable source files, easy reusability, and wide solution support, enabling you to manage both on-prem and cloud infrastructures through their whole lifecycle. When you hear *Infrastructure as a Code*, Terraform is the main representative of this infrastructure configuration philosophy. Although developed by the Hashicorp organization, Terraform is offered also as a completely open-source tool, giving it another advantage and boost on the market.

The primary goal of Terraform is to use different provider APIs to perform CRUD operations on managed resources, getting them to the desired state described in Terraform configuration files. All in a stateful manner. Terraform compared to Ansible uses a declarative approach exclusively, meaning you have to define the final desired state, instead of the steps needed to get there.

Internally, Terraform system is also highly modular and expandable using *providers*. On top of common core libraries, providers serve as plugin connectors to various APIs, authenticating your actions and describing a set of manageable resources in the destination system (as shown in Figure 10-19).

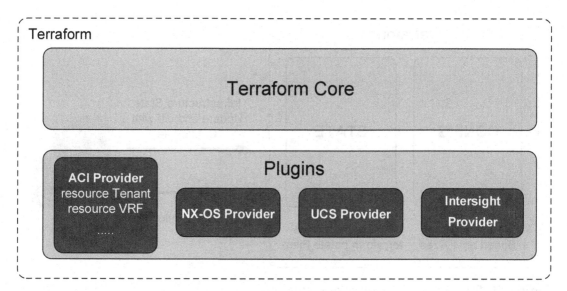

Figure 10-19. *Terraform system overview*

Terraform Config and State Files

Terraform configuration source files are written in HashiCorp Configuration Language (HCL) or optionally JSON. The definition of a managed system state can be split into multiple files, each with the .tf suffix. Terraform will then automatically merge all .tf files inside the current working directory during the automation job start. Before the deployment of any change to the actual infrastructure, Terraform checks and updates its local `terraform.tfstate` file with the current state of (already existing or to be) managed objects. State and config files are then compared, and the diff is presented to the user in order to confirm the required infrastructure changes (see Figure 10-20).

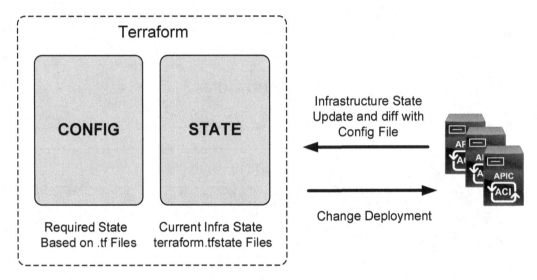

Figure 10-20. *Terraform source and state files*

Before proceeding with the definition of managed resources in the config file, you need to tell Terraform which providers you would like to use and usually configure their authentication to the managed system. The provider in Listing 10-51 is used for ACI.

Listing 10-51. ACI Terraform Provider

```
terraform {
  required_providers {
    aci = {
      source = "CiscoDevNet/aci"
    }
  }
}

provider "aci" {
    # cisco-aci user name
  username = "admin"
  # cisco-aci password
  password = "cisco123"
  # cisco-aci url
  url      = "https://10.17.87.60"
  insecure = true
}
```

Note   As soon as you first start an automation job later, Terraform will automatically install all additional plugins needed for its operation on your behalf thanks to the providers definition.

With providers in place, you can start creating managed resources. In Terraform, each resource is organized into code blocks with the consistent syntax shown in Listing 10-52.

Listing 10-52. HashiCorp Resource Configuration Syntax

```
<block type> "<resource type>" "<block name>" {
        <identifier> = <expression>
}
```

- **block type**: Always set to "resource"

- **resource type**: Name of resource in particular provider, such as "aci_tenant", or "aci_application_epg"

- **block name**: Unique name of resource block, differentiating it from others inside Terraform configuration

- **identifier = expression**: Key-value pairs for specifying managed object attributes. It's similar to setting some object attribute in JSON.

In the case of ACI, a sample resource block creating a new Tenant object could look like Listing 10-53.

Listing 10-53. Tenant Resource Block

```
resource "aci_tenant" "demo_tenant" {
  name        = "demo_tenant"
  description = "from terraform"
  annotation  = "tag"
  name_alias  = "tenant"
}
```

Individual resources can be easily linked between each other by referring to their names (it's the reason for the name uniqueness requirement). This function is handy in ACI as many objects have to be associated with their parent. In Listing 10-54, instead of using the static distinguished name of the tenant in the VRF resource block, all you need to do is refer to its resource name (more specifically, its ID). See Listing 10-54.

Listing 10-54. VRF Resource Block Referring to Tenant

```
resource "aci_vrf" "demo_vrf" {
    tenant_dn                = aci_tenant.demo_tenant.id
    name                     = "demo_vrf"
    description              = "from terraform"
    annotation               = "tag_vrf"
    bd_enforced_enable       = "no"
    ip_data_plane_learning   = "enabled"
    knw_mcast_act            = "permit"
    name_alias               = "alias_vrf"
    pc_enf_dir               = "egress"
    pc_enf_pref              = "unenforced"
}
```

A common question I get from students and customer is "If I start using Terraform for managing ACI, will it delete all other objects not specified in configuration files?" Of course not! Terraform will only take care of objects listed in resource blocks of configuration files; all others will stay intact. So, you can easily combine multiple configurations and automation approaches together and only selectively apply Terraform to some parts of the ACI configuration.

Terraform Commands

For its operation, Terraform uses several commands to initiate automation jobs or check the current state of the infrastructure.

terraform init

The first command to run inside the working directory with .tf files. Terraform will initialize the directory, search for required providers and their config blocks, and based on its findings; it will install all the necessary plugins. See Listing 10-55.

Listing 10-55. VRF Resource Block

```
[root@localhost terraform]# terraform init

Initializing the backend...

Initializing provider plugins...
- Finding latest version of ciscodevnet/aci...
- Installing ciscodevnet/aci v2.5.1...
- Installed ciscodevnet/aci v2.5.1 (signed by a HashiCorp partner, key ID
433649E2C56309DE)

Terraform has created a lock file .terraform.lock.hcl to record the
provider selections it made above. Include this file in your version
control repository so that Terraform can guarantee to make the same
selections by default when you run "terraform init" in the future.

Terraform has been successfully initialized!

You may now begin working with Terraform. Try running "terraform plan" to
see any changes that are required for your infrastructure. All Terraform
commands should now work.

If you ever set or change modules or backend configuration for Terraform,
rerun this command to reinitialize your working directory. If you forget,
other commands will detect it and remind you to do so if necessary.
```

Now you can start deploying the resource objects into ACI.

Note   The terraform init command needs to be rerun each time any change is made to the provider definition.

---

terraform plan

The plan command merges together all .tf files in the working directory, downloads the current state of defined resources from actual infrastructure, and just informs the user about found differences. It won't deploy any change yet (as illustrated in Figure 10-21).

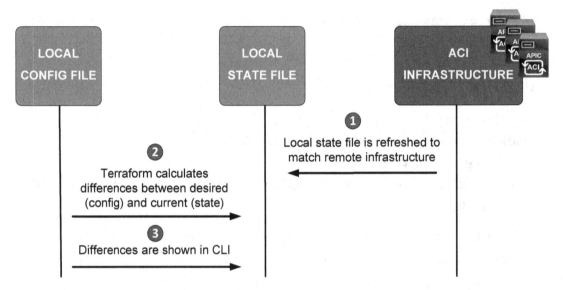

Figure 10-21. *Terraform plan command operation*

You will get the following output after running terraform plan if the config files specify a single new ACI Tenant. See Listing 10-56.

Listing 10-56. Terraform Plan Output

```
[root@localhost terraform]# terraform plan

Terraform used the selected providers to generate the following execution
plan. Resource actions are indicated with the following
symbols:
  + create

Terraform will perform the following actions:

  # aci_tenant.Apress_Terraform_Tenant will be created
  + resource "aci_tenant" "Apress_Terraform_Tenant" {
      + annotation                = "orchestrator:terraform"
```

```
    + description                      = "Terraform Managed Tenant"
    + id                               = (known after apply)
    + name                             = "Apress_Terraform"
    + name_alias                       = (known after apply)
    + relation_fv_rs_tenant_mon_pol = (known after apply)
  }

Plan: 1 to add, 0 to change, 0 to destroy.
```

terraform apply

The apply command will run terraform plan first, present you with identified changes, and then interactively ask for a deployment confirmation. There is a switch called -auto-approve to actually skip the plan confirmation, but in the default state, it's a useful measure to avoid deploying the configuration by mistake. Anyway, if you confirm the changes, Terraform apply will implement them right away to the infrastructure (as shown in Figure 10-22).

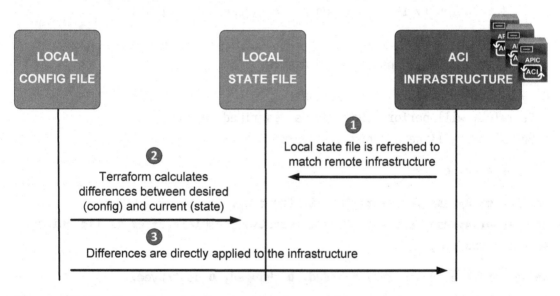

Figure 10-22. *Terraform apply command operation*

Sample output from running the apply command can be found in Listing 10-57.

Listing 10-57. Terraform Apply Output

```
[root@localhost terraform]# terraform apply
```

Terraform used the selected providers to generate the following execution
plan. Resource actions are indicated with the following
symbols:
  + create

Terraform will perform the following actions:

```
  # aci_tenant.Apress_Terraform_Tenant will be created
  + resource "aci_tenant" "Apress_Terraform_Tenant" {
      + annotation                   = "orchestrator:terraform"
      + description                  = "Terraform Managed Tenant"
      + id                           = (known after apply)
      + name                         = "Apress_Terraform"
      + name_alias                   = (known after apply)
      + relation_fv_rs_tenant_mon_pol = (known after apply)
    }
```

Plan: 1 to add, 0 to change, 0 to destroy.

Do you want to perform these actions?
  Terraform will perform the actions described above.
  Only 'yes' will be accepted to approve.

  Enter a value: yes

aci_tenant.Apress_Terraform_Tenant: Creating...
aci_tenant.Apress_Terraform_Tenant: Creation complete after 1s [id=uni/tn-
Apress_Terraform]

Apply complete! Resources: 1 added, 0 changed, 0 destroyed.

terraform destroy

The last main Terraform command worth mentioning is destroy. As you can probably
tell already, when initiated, Terraform performs the plan again, presents you with
expected changes, and after your approval, it will this time remove all managed
resources defined in configuration .tf files (as shown in Figure 10-23).

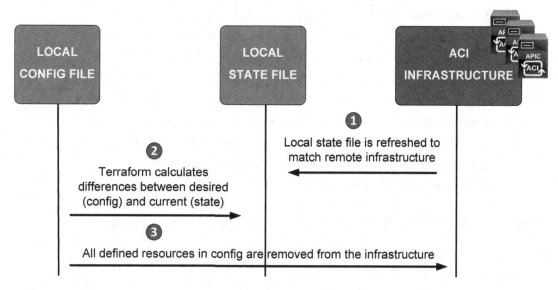

Figure 10-23. *Terraform destroy command operation*

ACI Terraform Provider Authentication Options

The ACI provider in Terraform defines three different options when it comes to authentication:

1. **Standard credentials**: You already saw this basic way to authenticate by sending the username and password to APIC. See Listing 10-58.

Listing 10-58. ACI Provider Authentication Using Credentials

```
provider "aci" {
  username = "Apress"
  password = "password"
  url      = "https://my-cisco-aci.com"
  insecure = true
}
```

2. **Signature base authentication**: Another, more secure option is to generate an X.509 certificate, save the private key locally, and upload its public key to the APIC user. This way, each API call generated by Terraform is uniquely signed without disclosing the access credentials anywhere. The ACI provider just needs to have a path to the private key and the name of the public key in ACI defined. If you are interested in how to generate and use such a certificate, refer to the next section, "Presigned REST API Calls." In the meantime, see Listing 10-59.

Listing 10-59. ACI Provider Authentication Using X.509 Certificate

```
provider "aci" {
  username = "Apress"
  private_key = "path to private key"
  cert_name = "user-cert-"
  url       = "https://my-cisco-aci.com"
  insecure = true
}
```

3. **Login domain specification**: If multiple login domains are used in ACI, it's not a problem to specify them in Terraform authentication as well. This way, you can authenticate against remote users present in a TACACS+, LDAP, or Radius database. See Listing 10-60.

Listing 10-60. ACI Provider Authentication with Login Domain Specification

```
provider "aci" {
  username = "apic:TACACS_domain\\\\Apress"
  # private_key = "path to private key"
  # cert_name = "user-cert"
  password = "password"
  url = "url"
  insecure = true
}
```

Terraform Config Drift

What happens if the ACI user manually changes any attribute of a resource Terraform is managing? This is another common question regarding ACI automation in general. The answer is simple: ACI users can implement any local changes in APIC or using other automation tools, but if an object or attribute managed by Terraform is changed, after the next `terraform plan` or `terraform apply` command is run, it will identify all the discrepancies and offer you a list of changes needed to return the infrastructure to the desired stated described in the configuration files.

Sample Terraform Configuration File for ACI

Putting it all together, here is a simple example of how to configure the ACI Terraform provider and deploy the Apress tenant with VRF PROD, L3-enabled bridge domain Frontend, and respective application profile with EPG in the BD. Use it as a basis for further automation of your own. See Listing 10-61.

Listing 10-61. Sample ACI Terraform Configuration File

```
terraform {
  required_providers {
    aci = {
      source = "ciscodevnet/aci"
    }
  }
}

#configure provider with your cisco aci credentials.
provider "aci" {
  # cisco-aci user name
  username = "admin"
  # cisco-aci password
  password = "password"
  # cisco-aci APIC url
  url      = "https://10.17.87.60"
  insecure = true
}
```

```
#Create Tenant Apress_Terraform
resource "aci_tenant" "Apress_Terraform_Tenant" {
  description = "Terraform Managed Tenant"
  name        = "Apress_Terraform"
  annotation  = "orchestrator:terraform"
}

resource "aci_vrf" "PROD" {
  tenant_dn               = aci_tenant.Apress_Terraform_Tenant.id
  name                    = "PROD"
  annotation              = "orchestrator:terraform"
}

resource "aci_bridge_domain" "Apress_FrontEnd_BD" {
  tenant_dn               = aci_tenant.Apress_Terraform_Tenant.id
  description             = "FrontEnd_BD"
  name                    = "FrontEnd_BD"
  optimize_wan_bandwidth  = "no"
  annotation              = "orchestrator:terraform"
  arp_flood               = "no"
  multi_dst_pkt_act       = "bd-flood"
  unicast_route           = "yes"
  unk_mac_ucast_act       = "flood"
  unk_mcast_act           = "flood"
}

resource "aci_subnet" "Apress_FrontEnd_BD_Subnet" {
  parent_dn      = aci_bridge_domain.Apress_FrontEnd_BD.id
  description    = "FrontEnd_BD_Subnet"
  ip             = "10.1.1.1/24"
  annotation     = "orchestrator:terraform"
  ctrl           = ["querier", "nd"]
  preferred      = "no"
  scope          = ["private", "shared"]
}
```

```
resource "aci_application_profile" "Apress_AP" {
  tenant_dn     = aci_tenant.Apress_Terraform_Tenant.id
  name          = "Apress_AP"
  annotation    = "orchestrator:terraform"
  description   = "from terraform"
  name_alias    = "Apress_AP"
}

resource "aci_application_epg" "Apress_Frontend_EPG" {
  application_profile_dn  = aci_application_profile.Apress_AP.id
  name                    = "Apress_Frontend_EPG"
  description             = "from terraform"
  annotation              = "orchestrator:terraform"
  shutdown                = "no"
  relation_fv_rs_bd       = aci_bridge_domain.Apress_FrontEnd_BD.id
}
```

Note   The source code for this book is available on GitHub via the book's product page, located at www.apress.com/ISBN.

When you apply the previous source file, the objects in Listing 10-62 will be created in ACI by Terraform (with information about their DNs).

Listing 10-62. Terraform Apply – Deployment to the ACI Infrastructure

```
[root@localhost terraform]# terraform apply

Terraform used the selected providers to generate the following execution
plan. Resource actions are indicated with the following symbols:
  + create

Terraform will perform the following actions:

<output omitted>

Plan: 6 to add, 0 to change, 0 to destroy.
```

```
Do you want to perform these actions?
  Terraform will perform the actions described above.
  Only 'yes' will be accepted to approve.

  Enter a value: yes
```

aci_tenant.Apress_Terraform_Tenant: Creating...
aci_tenant.Apress_Terraform_Tenant: Creation complete after 1s [id=**uni/tn-Apress_Terraform**]
aci_vrf.PROD: Creating...
aci_application_profile.Apress_AP: Creating...
aci_bridge_domain.Apress_FrontEnd_BD: Creating...
aci_application_profile.Apress_AP: Creation complete after 1s [id=**uni/tn-Apress_Terraform/ap-Apress_AP**]
aci_vrf.PROD: Creation complete after 2s [id=**uni/tn-Apress_Terraform/ctx-PROD**]
aci_bridge_domain.Apress_FrontEnd_BD: Creation complete after 2s [id=**uni/tn-Apress_Terraform/BD-FrontEnd_BD**]
aci_subnet.Apress_FrontEnd_BD_Subnet: Creating...
aci_application_epg.Apress_Frontend_EPG: Creating...
aci_subnet.Apress_FrontEnd_BD_Subnet: Creation complete after 4s [id=**uni/tn-Apress_Terraform/BD-FrontEnd_BD/subnet-[10.1.1.1/24]**]
aci_application_epg.Apress_Frontend_EPG: Creation complete after 4s [id=**uni/tn-Apress_Terraform/ap-Apress_AP/epg-Apress_Frontend_EPG**]

In the ACI GUI you can notice interesting behavior achieved by annotating all objects with the orchestrator:terraform label. First, the tenant is visibly differentiated from others, stating that it is managed by Terraform (as shown in Figure 10-24).

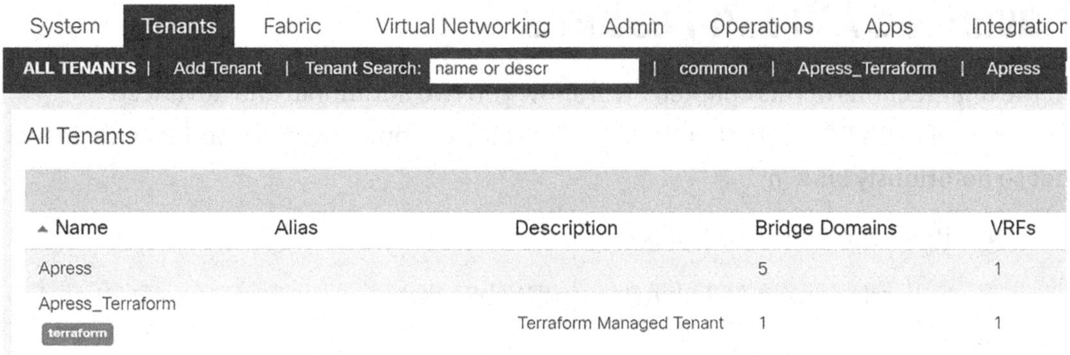

System	Tenants	Fabric	Virtual Networking	Admin	Operations	Apps	Integratior

ALL TENANTS | Add Tenant | Tenant Search: name or descr | common | Apress_Terraform | Apress

All Tenants

▲ Name	Alias	Description	Bridge Domains	VRFs
Apress			5	1
Apress_Terraform `terraform`		Terraform Managed Tenant	1	1

Figure 10-24. *Annotated tenant created by Terraform in the APIC GUI*

Secondly, when a user navigates inside the tenant, they will be warned about the fact that the tenant has been created by and managed from an orchestrator. All other annotated objects are also marked with a little symbol, meaning they are managed by an external automation solution (shown in Figure 10-25).

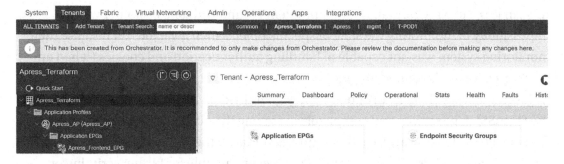

Figure 10-25. *Terraform managed ACI objects*

Tip   All documentation related to the usage of the ACI Terraform provider can be found at `https://registry.terraform.io/providers/CiscoDevNet/aci/latest/docs`.

Advanced ACI API Features

In the final sections of this chapter, I will show you two additional and advanced functions of ACI's REST API that I find quite useful for some use cases and that are in fact not so notoriously known:

- Pre-signed REST API calls

- Subscriptions to ACI objects using WebSockets

Presigned REST API Calls

So far, we have constantly assumed that before consuming ACI's API, the first step is authentication. This requires generating a REST POST call to a defined URL with an authentication data object, extracting the token (cookie) from its reply, and then attaching it to all subsequent calls. In situations where security is a big concern, the downside of using standard REST calls can be the need to send your credentials to APIC in JSON or XML format. Another problem I found with one customer was the impossibility of monitoring the state of specific objects in ACI via the API because their monitoring system was not capable of handling authentication and cookies (it had an HTTP/S client implemented, though).

Fortunately, ACI offers an option to presign individual REST calls beforehand using the OpenSSL Linux utility and completely overcome the need to authenticate when sending it to APIC. However, each new transaction with the API (with a different URL) has to be signed separately, so the signing process is suitable for further scripting or incorporating it into your own application.

During the following sections, I will guide you step-by-step through the whole process. First, a few preparational steps. Log into any Linux machine with the OpenSSL utility installed and generate an X.509 certificate. See Listing 10-63.

Listing 10-63. X.509 Certificate Generation

```
[root@localhost Apress]# openssl req -new -newkey rsa:1024 -days 36500
-nodes -x509 -keyout Apress.key -out Apress.crt -subj '/CN=User Apress/
O=Apress/C=US'
```

```
Generating a RSA private key
..................+++++
........+++++
writing new private key to 'Apress.key'
-----
```

This command should create two files: a private key called Apress.key and an X.509 certificate called Apress.crt. Make sure to safely store the private key; you will need it for every REST call sign later.

Now display the generated certificate in the Privacy Enhanced Mail (PEM) format. The most important part of the output is the Base64 encoded certificate block starting with *BEGIN CERTIFICATE* and ending with *END CERTIFICATE*. See Listing 10-64.

Listing 10-64. Displaying X.509 Certificate in PEM Format – Base64

```
[root@localhost Apress]# openssl x509 -text -in Apress.crt
<output ommited>
-----BEGIN CERTIFICATE-----
MIICRjCCAa+gAwIBAgIUWVnYjS2C+xZkrsIDt4tYlXMOuYOwDQYJKoZIhvcNAQEL
BQAwNDEUMBIGA1UEAwwLVXNlciBBcHJlc3MxDzANBgNVBAoMBkFwcmVzczELMAkG
A1UEBhMCVVMwIBcNMjIwNzMwMDY1ODUzWhgPMjEyMjA3MDYwNjU4NTNaMDQxFDAS
BgNVBAMMC1VzZXIgQXByZXNzMQ8wDQYDVQQKDAZBcHJlc3MxCzAJBgNVBAYTAlVT
MIGfMA0GCSqGSIb3DQEBAQUAA4GNADCBiQKBgQDbC4BYFiqRyBMD3Qp/hT23ecrv
oFO5FilFkXcgOR+rJUHWu2ikTBb+R+f4OX9OeagKrOt7b4be7RLVnOye2VYfAKfN
Kef+jLIt+VRhUyhn2QIDAQABo1MwUTAdBgNVHQ4EFgQUNQfU6ucQ6FJxsQpFbgU3
LUkrdWowHwYDVR0jBBgwFoAUNQfU6ucQ6FJxsQpFbgU3LUkrdWowDwYDVR0TAQH/
BAUwAwEB/zANBgkqhkiG9w0BAQsFAAOBgQCnDXG+E7LTnnWVvqV21ocHug14lbGn
Zp1q/C5T1Ua7DdQF/fC4/GiTJMcAFPBLZt4sQEvLW8vTcFEjJKjDSfGxSIJup/X5
w3ZBuiJabqnqpGDWTxQPjssBx/Lpwdzb8pKzoy6YfbFIoLKW6/j4FiHUiram9+EF
2Yh4++Rjp++bRg==
-----END CERTIFICATE-----
```

Copy the whole block including leading and trailing lines to the system clipboard and create a new local ACI user in **Admin -> AAA -> Users.** In the second step of the user creation form, add a User Certificate and paste the previous Base64 output there (as shown in Figure 10-26).

Figure 10-26. *Adding an X.509 certificate to the local ACI user*

When you double-click a created user, scroll down to its certificate and open it again by double-clicking. You will need to download the JSON representation of the certificate object in ACI using the Save-As function (see Figure 10-27).

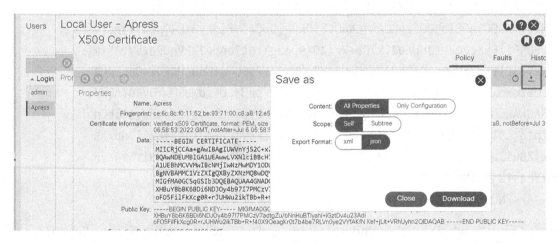

Figure 10-27. *Save-As ACI user certificate into JSON object*

In the JSON object, focus only on a single attribute: the DN of the ACI User Certificate (as shown in Figure 10-28). Note it and put it aside for now.

```
1    ⊟{
2    |        "totalCount": "1",
3    ⊟        "imdata": [
4    ⊟        {
5    ⊟            "aaaUserCert": {
6    ⊟                "attributes": {
7                        "annotation": "",
8                        "certValidUntil": "Jul  6 06:58:53 2122 GMT",
9                        "certdn": "/CN=User Apress/O=Apress/C=US",
10                       "certificateDecodeInformation": "Verified x509 Certificate, format: PEM,
                         ce:6c:8c:f0:11:52:be:93:71:00:c8:a8:12:e5:b2:ba:56:e0:2e:a8, notBefore=J
11                       "childAction": "",
12                       "data": "-----BEGIN
                         CERTIFICATE-----\nMIICRjCCAa+gAwIBAgIUWVnYjS2C+xZkrsIDt4tYlXMOuY0wDQYJKc
                         LMAkG\nA1UEBhMCVVMwIBcNMjIwNzMwMDY1ODUzWhgPMjEyMjA3MDYwNjU4NTNaMDQxFDAS\
                         MA0GCSqGSIb3DQEBAQUAA4GNADCBiQKBgQDbC4BYFiqRyBMD3Qp/hT23ecrv\nXHBuY8bBK6
                         rJUHWu2ikTBb+R+f40X9OeagKr0t7b4be7RLVn0ye2VYfAKfN\nKef+jLIt+VRhUyhn2QIDA
                         fU6ucQ6FJxsQpFbgU3LUkrdWowDwYDVR0TAQH/\nBAUwAwEB/zANBgkqhkiG9w0BAQsFAAOE
                         EvLW8vTcFEjJKjDSfGxSIJup/X5\nw3ZBuiJabqnqpGDWTxQPjssBx/Lpwdzb8pKzoy6YfbF
13                       "descr": "",
14                       "dn": "uni/userext/user-Apress/usercert-Apress",
```

Figure 10-28. *ACI User Certificate DN*

Finally, you are ready to start signing the REST API calls. Get the list ofTenants with the following class call:

- HTTPS Method: GET, URL: https://<APIC_IP>/api/node/class/fvTenant.json

In the Linux machine, create a simple text file called `payload.txt` (the filename doesn't matter). Its content needs to be in the format of an HTTP method (GET/POST), directly followed by a truncated REST call URL, just the section starting with /api/... so I recommend using the `echo` command in Listing 10-65 to make sure there are no hidden white characters that could potentially get there by plain copy-pasting.

Listing 10-65. Creating REST Call Payload File

```
[root@localhost Apress]# echo -n "GET/api/node/class/fvTenant.json" >
payload.txt
```

Based on the `payload.txt` file you will now generate a signature. With the OpenSSL commands in Listing 10-66, first create a binary signature (using a private key generated earlier), then extract the Base64 text representation and let "cat" write it to the terminal.

Listing 10-66. Signing Payload File

```
[root@localhost Apress]# openssl dgst -sha256 -sign Apress.key
payload.txt > payload_sig.bin
```

```
[root@localhost Apress]# openssl base64 -A -in payload_sig.bin -out
payload_sig.base64
```

```
[root@localhost Apress]# cat payload_sig.base64 RbjWLfSRO/K9NnWyO
9RRrY+BXSzOWkOcjA38skAK+Hz84X4r7mj3JIEEsuhXBcHk8ISOqt6impDM8BW/
m5PWYU++vG2Rbpx9ir1s50ZOZyfReDsOy9RsKUJ0dEAqnIcVQhYzpUuaBVhndfbVP
LBVb5yuEebKyjwTwGlrOnv2A5U=
```

Again, put aside the resulting key and make sure you don't copy any additional whitespace with it.

After the previous steps, you are ready to assemble the REST call. The specifics of a presigned REST calls are in the four cookies they have to carry, substituting the standard preceding authentication process. Each cookie has a key=value format with the following content (the order is not important; you just have to have all of them at the end):

- **APIC-Request-Signature**=<Base64 key generated from payload file>

- **APIC-Certificate-DN**=<Distinguished Name of ACI user certificate extracted>

- **APIC-Certificate-Algorithm**=v1.0 (Static permanent value)

- **APIC-Certificate-Fingerprint**=fingerprint (Static permanent value)

For your use case the resulting cookie set looks like this:

- **APIC-Request-Signature**= RbjWLfSRO/K9NnWyO9RRrY
  +BXSzOWkOcjA38skAK+Hz84X4r7mj3JIEEsuhXBcHk8ISO
  qt6impDM8BW/m5PWYU++vG2Rbpx9ir1s50ZOZyfRe
  DsOy9RsKUJ0dEAqnIcVQhYzpUuaBVhndfbVPLBVb
  5yuEebKyjwTwGlrOnv2A5U=

- **APIC-Certificate-DN**=uni/userext/user-Apress/usercert-Apress

- **APIC-Certificate-Algorithm**=v1.0

- **APIC-Certificate-Fingerprint**=fingerprint

In order to test the presigned call, use any HTTP client of your choice. The cookie attachment will be highly dependent on its implementation, so refer to the client's documentation. For Postman, click the Cookies hyperlink under the Send button (as shown in Figure 10-29).

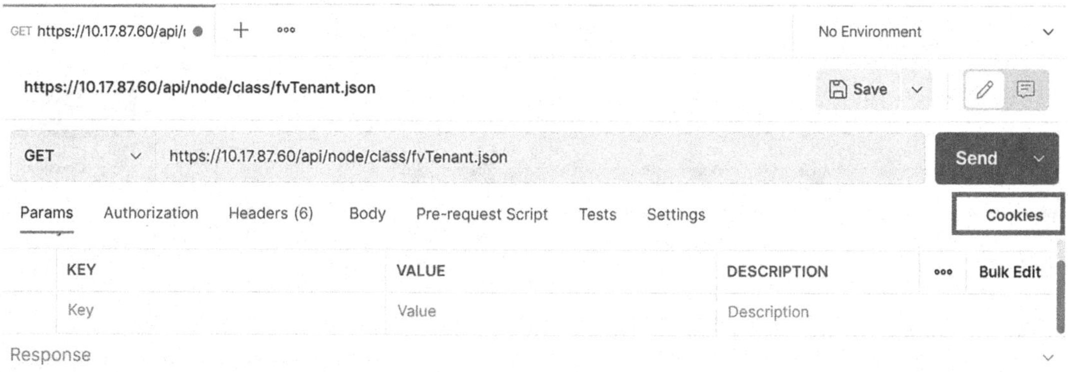

Figure 10-29. Postman cookies

Inside the cookie's configuration, fill in APIC's IP address or its domain name and click *Add Domain*. Subsequently, add the four prepared cookies. Always change just the first section CookieX=value; you don't need to touch the rest. In Figure 10-30 you can see the example of a signature cookie. Create the rest accordingly.

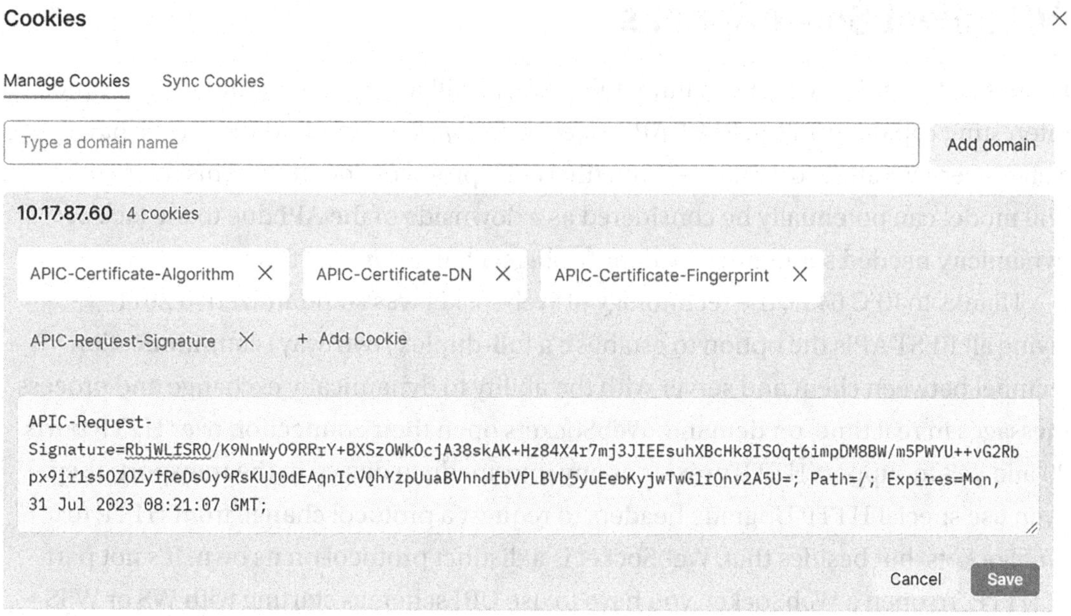

Figure 10-30. Postman

The finished REST call with the cookies in place now just needs to be sent to APIC and you should right away receive a reply, without previous authentication (see Figure 10-31).

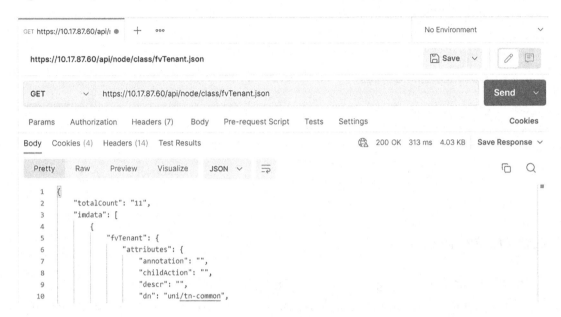

Figure 10-31. *Testing the presigned REST call in Postman*

ACI Object Subscriptions

For our last topic in ACI's programmability area, I will focus your attention on another interesting capability of the REST API: *object subscription*. Standard REST calls have a client-server nature, originating from the HTTP protocol operation. This query or pull model can potentially be considered as a downside of the API due to the lack of dynamicity needed sometimes to identify object changes in real time.

Thanks to RFC 6455, the technology of WebSocket was standardized in 2011, giving all REST APIs the option to establish a full-duplex (two-way) communication channel between client and server with the ability to dynamically exchange and process messages in real time, on demand. WebSockets open their connection over HTTP ports 80 and 443 to support HTTP proxies or any intermediate device in the transport; they even use special HTTP Upgrade headers to request a protocol change from HTTP to WebSockets, but besides that, WebSocket is a distinct protocol on its own. It's not part of HTTP. To open a WebSocket, you have to use URI schemas starting with WS or WSS (secured). A simplified WebSocket operation is illustrated in Figure 10-32.

WebSocket Client   **WebSocket Server**

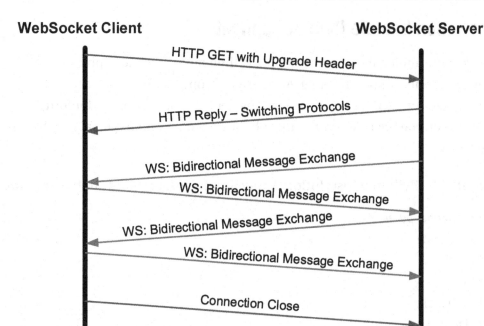

Figure 10-32. *WebSocket operation overview*

ACI has the WebSockets technology implemented and, actually, it natively uses it a lot in the GUI without you even knowing. I'm sure you have already noticed automatically refreshing graphs, tables, or lists of objects in the APIC GUI when configuring and automating the system. That's where WebSockets connections come into play and dynamically refresh the data after each object change.

In order to enable a subscription to the particular ACI object, you need to send a special ?subscription=yes option in the GET URL. Then with the refresh-timeout option, you can set the maximum amount of time for which the subscription will stay valid. After its expiration and without refreshing, APIC stops sending updates to the WebSocket. Let's suppose you want to subscribe to your Apress tenant. The resulting URL will look like Listing 10-67.

Listing 10-67. Subscription URL

https://<APIC_IP>/api/node/mo/uni/tn-Apress.json?**subscription=yes&refresh-timeout=60**

In a reply to such a call, APIC will return a Subscription ID with a standard ACI JSON object. This will uniquely identify all messages related to this object sent over WebSocket and will enable you to track subscriptions and their refreshments.

Subscription Sample Python Application

Let's look at the implementation of a simple Python multi-threaded application requesting the Subscription ID of the Apress tenant, opening WebSocket to APIC, and waiting for any update message to come. Consider it as a starting point for further experiments on your own. You will start with the necessary import global variables in Listing 10-68.

Listing 10-68. Python Subscription Application – Imports and Global Variables

```python
#!/usr/bin/env python
import requests
import json
import ssl
import websocket
import threading
import time
import sys

requests.packages.urllib3.disable_warnings()

# APIC Credentials:
APIC = "<APIC IP ADDRESS>"
USER = "<YOUR USERNAME>"
PASS = "<YOUR PASSWORD"

AUTH_URL = "https://" + APIC + "/api/aaaLogin.json"
AUTH_BODY = {"aaaUser": {"attributes": {"name": USER, "pwd": PASS}}}
```

Several Python functions will follow. The first one simply authenticates the application to APIC and returns a preformatted APIC-cookie. See Listing 10-69.

Listing 10-69. Python Subscription Application – Authentication

```python
#Authentication to APIC
def apic_authenticate():
    login_response = requests.post(AUTH_URL, json=AUTH_BODY,
    verify=False).content
    response_body_dictionary = json.loads(login_response)
```

```
token = response_body_dictionary["imdata"][0]["aaaLogin"]["attributes"]
["token"]
cookie = {"APIC-cookie": token}
return cookie
```

Next, you define a function to request a subscription to the Apress tenant and return the Subscription ID. Note the ?subcription=yes option in the REST call URL in Listing 10-70.

Listing 10-70. Python Subscription Application – Subscribing to ACI Object

```
# Subscribe to Apress Tenant
def subscribe(cookie):
    apress_tenant_url = "https://" + APIC + "/api/node/mo/uni/tn-Apress.
    json?subscription=yes&refresh-timeout=60"
    apress_tenant_subscription = requests.get(apress_tenant_url,
    verify=False, cookies=cookie)
    json_dict = json.loads(apress_tenant_subscription.text)
    apress_tenant_subscription_id = json_dict["subscriptionId"]
    print("Subscription ID: ", apress_tenant_subscription_id)
    return apress_tenant_subscription_id
```

Another function opens a WebSocket to a APIC's special web application endpoint /socket/, followed by an authentication token. See Listing 10-71.

Listing 10-71. Python Subscription Application – Opening Web Socket

```
# Create Web Socket to APIC
def ws_socket(token):
    websocket_url = "wss://" + APIC + "/socket{}".format(token)
    ws = websocket.create_connection(websocket_url, sslopt={"cert_reqs":
    ssl.CERT_NONE})
    print("WebSocket Subscription Status Code: ", ws.status)
    return ws
```

With subscriptions it's important to constantly keep looking for messages coming over WebSocket and refreshing the Subscription IDs, so the next function starts two threads responsible for these tasks. See Listing 10-72.

Listing 10-72. Python Subscription Application – Multi-Threading

```
#Thread definition and start
def thread_start(ws, subscription_id, cookie):
    thread1 = threading.Thread(target=print_ws, args=(ws,))
    thread2 = threading.Thread(target=refresh, args=(subscription_id,
    cookie, ))
    thread1.start()
    thread2.start()
```

Listing 10-73 shows the actual implementation of the associated target function in each thread.

Listing 10-73. Python Subscription Application – Subscription Refresh and WS Message Receive

```
#Print any new message in Subscription queue
def print_ws(ws):
    while True:
        print(ws.recv())

# Refresh subscription ID
def refresh(subscription_id, cookie):
    while True:
        time.sleep(30)
        refresh_id = "https://" + APIC + "/api/subscriptionRefresh.
        json?id={}".format(subscription_id)
        refresh_id = requests.get(refresh_id, verify=False, cookies=cookie)
```

And finally, you define the main function, serving as an entry point into the whole application. The main function primarily calls all previously defined ones. See Listing 10-74.

Listing 10-74. Python Subscription Application – Main Function

```
#Main Function
if __name__ == "__main__":
    cookie = apic_authenticate()
    token = (cookie["APIC-cookie"])
```

```
print ("*" * 10, "WebSocket Subscription Status & Messages", "*" * 10)
wbsocket = ws_socket(token)
subscription_id = subscribe(cookie)
thread_start(wbsocket, subscription_id, cookie)
```

When the described Python script is run, you should get the Subscription ID of specified tenant object from the source code. The application will run infinitely until you stop it using Ctrl+C and wait for any message incoming over WebSocket. See Listing 10-75.

Listing 10-75. Python Subscription Application – Running Script

```
[root@localhost Apress]# python3 subscriptions.py
********** WebSocket Subscription Status & Messages **********
WebSocket Subscription Status Code:  101
Subscription ID:  72058908314894337
```

While the script is running, try changing any attribute of the monitored tenant object in ACI, for example, its description. Instantly after submitting the change, you should get the following JSON data to object over WebSocket. It will provide the related Subscription ID, ACI object DN, changed attribute, modification timestamp, and status telling you about the object being "modified." See Listing 10-76.

Listing 10-76. Python Subscription Application – Received JSON Object Over Websocket

```
{"subscriptionId":["72058908314894337"],"imdata":[{"fvTenant":{"attributes"
:{"childAction":"","descr":"WebsocketTest","dn":"uni/tn-Apress","modTs":"2
022-07-31T20:33:33.166+02:00","rn":"","status":"modified"}}}]}
```

This way you can literally subscribe to any ACI object, ranging from a physical leaf interface, through its routing tables and endpoint database to ACI faults. The limit here is just your creativity. Subscriptions, when implemented properly, can become a powerful tool to construct a real-time monitoring system with automatic reactions to various events.

Summary

ACI automation and programmability is an extremely interesting and wide topic, as you saw during the chapter. APIC not only automates the deployment of various policies to the ACI fabric, but it also offers a completely open API to speed up the creation of these policies in the automation layer above. I hope in this chapter we have covered everything you need to do so, ranging from the REST API basic concepts through ACI's object model to the vast amount of practical automation aspects and tools.

Thanks to the single common API endpoint, at the end of the day, it's up to you and your preference as to which approach or tool you will use. They are mutually combinable, starting with simpler but less powerful options like the APIC GUI/CLI itself to completely unlimited possibilities with the Python programming language and Cobra SDK. Or, if writing Python source code is not your cup of tea, you can still reach for a popular orchestrator like Ansible or Terraform.

Useful Cisco ACI Resources

Although we have covered quite a lot of topics related to ACI in this book, there is always significantly more to explore. Here are additional useful study and technical resources directly published by Cisco. I often use them during ACI implementation projects.

Cisco Application Centric Infrastructure Design Guide

www.cisco.com/c/en/us/td/docs/dcn/whitepapers/cisco-application-centric-infrastructure-design-guide.html

ACI Fabric Endpoint Learning White Paper

www.cisco.com/c/en/us/solutions/collateral/data-center-virtualization/application-centric-infrastructure/white-paper-c11-739989.html

Cisco ACI Contract Guide

www.cisco.com/c/en/us/solutions/collateral/data-center-virtualization/application-centric-infrastructure/white-paper-c11-743951.html

ACI Fabric L3Out Guide

www.cisco.com/c/en/us/solutions/collateral/data-center-virtualization/application-centric-infrastructure/guide-c07-743150.html

ACI Multi-Pod White Paper

www.cisco.com/c/en/us/solutions/collateral/data-center-virtualization/application-centric-infrastructure/white-paper-c11-737855.html

Cisco Application Centric Infrastructure Multi-Pod Configuration White Paper

© Jan Janovic 2023
J. Janovic, *Cisco ACI: Zero to Hero*, https://doi.org/10.1007/978-1-4842-8838-2

www.cisco.com/c/en/us/solutions/collateral/data-center-virtualization/application-centric-infrastructure/white-paper-c11-739714.html

Cisco ACI Multi-Pod and Service Node Integration White Paper

www.cisco.com/c/en/us/solutions/collateral/data-center-virtualization/application-centric-infrastructure/white-paper-c11-739571.html

Cisco ACI Multi-Site Architecture White Paper

www.cisco.com/c/en/us/solutions/collateral/data-center-virtualization/application-centric-infrastructure/white-paper-c11-739609.html

Cisco ACI Multi-Site and Service Node Integration White Paper

www.cisco.com/c/en/us/solutions/collateral/data-center-virtualization/application-centric-infrastructure/white-paper-c11-743107.html

Cisco ACI Remote Leaf Architecture White Paper

www.cisco.com/c/en/us/solutions/collateral/data-center-virtualization/application-centric-infrastructure/white-paper-c11-740861.html

Service Graph Design with Cisco ACI (Updated to Cisco APIC Release 5.2) White Paper

www.cisco.com/c/en/us/solutions/collateral/data-center-virtualization/application-centric-infrastructure/white-paper-c11-2491213.html

Cisco ACI Policy-Based Redirect Service Graph Design White Paper

www.cisco.com/c/en/us/solutions/collateral/data-center-virtualization/application-centric-infrastructure/white-paper-c11-739971.html

APIC Software Upgrade/Downgrade Support Matrix

www.cisco.com/c/dam/en/us/td/docs/Website/datacenter/
apicmatrix/index.html

Cisco ACI Upgrade Checklist

www.cisco.com/c/en/us/td/docs/switches/datacenter/aci/
apic/sw/kb/Cisco-ACI-Upgrade-Checklist.html

Index

A

© Jan Janovic 2023
J. Janovic, *Cisco ACI: Zero to Hero*, https://doi.org/10.1007/978-1-4842-8838-2

I

Printed in the United States
by Baker & Taylor Publisher Services